James Barr is
Distinguished
Professor of Hebrew
Bible Emeritus at
Vanderbilt Divinity
School, Nashville,
where he taught for
ten years. His
illustrious teaching
career has also included professorships at
Edinburgh University, Princeton Theological
Seminary, Manchester University, and Oxford
University. He has held visiting professorships
and delivered major lecture series in Europe,
the United States, Africa, Israel, Australia, and
New Zealand, and was longtime editor of the
*Journal of Semitic Studies.* Among his numerous
influential books are *Biblical Faith and Natural
Theology* (1993), *The Garden of Eden and the Hope
of Immortality* (Fortress Press, 1993), *Escaping
from Fundamentalism* (1984), *Holy Scripture:
Canon, Authority, Criticism* (1983), and *Old and
New in Interpretation: A Study of the Two Testaments*
(1966).

*The Concept of*
*Biblical Theology*

*The Concept of*

# Biblical Theology

*An Old Testament Perspective*

James Barr

FORTRESS PRESS
Minneapolis

THE CONCEPT OF BIBLICAL THEOLOGY
An Old Testament Perspective

Cover design: Michael Mihelich

ISBN 0-8006-3191-9

Manufactured in Great Britain                    AF 1-3191

03   02   01   00   99   1   2   3   4   5   6   7   8   9   10

This book is dedicated
to the universities
of Oslo and Helsinki
in gratitude for the award
of honorary doctorates in theology
from each of them

# Contents

# Preface

This book is descended from the Cadbury Lectures, delivered in the University of Birmingham as long ago as 1968. Perhaps they should have been published at that time, but I felt the need, before publication, to read all through the classic works of Old Testament theology once again and verify my assessment of them, as it then was. This took time, and meanwhile important new studies were published; also my own ideas changed. And yet I still feel that my early volume *Old and New in Interpretation* (1966) remains the basis of the vision now presented. The delivery of the Firth Lectures at the University of Nottingham in 1978 provided a further stage in my thinking that is incorporated here. Basic earlier expressions of my thinking were those in the articles 'Biblical Theology' in the Supplementary Volume to *The Interpreter's Dictionary of the Bible*, 104–11, and later, in more developed form, in the article 'Biblische Theologie' in the *Evangelisches Kirchenlexikon*, I, cols. 488–94.

But the work in its present form is written as a sort of textbook: when I have given courses on Old Testament theology, especially in my periods of teaching in Edinburgh, in Princeton, in Oxford and at Vanderbilt, this is the sort of approach that I have adopted, though the book has been expanded to contain much more material than one could cover in a single course of the normal kind.

The work is not intended to be a biblical theology, still less to be 'my' biblical theology (an expression which I would find improper); rather, it is a discussion of the whole idea of biblical theology, its possibilities and its prospects. It is neither a survey nor a history, though it includes some elements of both of these. I have selected persons and themes which have seemed fruitful or significant for my own thinking but have made no attempt to survey all the Theologies that have been written or all the material that has been brought forward in the discussion. If there is any one theme that runs through this work, it is the *contested* character of biblical theology, as it has been in this century. Biblical theology has had its enthusiasts, who cannot understand why anyone would question its validity as a subject; it has also had its opponents, some of whom consider it to be impracticable as an area of research, or unacceptable as an academic subject, or useless to the religious community, or all three of these. It is my belief that these elements of opposition have to be faced and understood, and that the understanding of them may paradoxically assist in the continuance and future prosperity of biblical theology, or of something like it. Though I have been at times a severe critic of some tendencies within biblical theology, I have continued to be deeply involved in the subject throughout my academic life, and it has remained one of the two major elements in my professional interests, the other being language and text. I believe that at the end of the day something of the nature of biblical theology will remain necessary, and that not only biblical scholarship, but also theology as a whole, would be much the poorer without it.

As the title of the book indicates, I approach the subject from the Old Testament side and do not attempt to give an even representation of New Testament theology, although I do bring in some treatment of it in particular areas. Though very much interested in discussions in the New Testament field, I did not feel that I should venture into a more profound consideration of its currents and tendencies.

The book begins with the question why it has been so difficult to define biblical theology, and suggests that this is because 'biblical theology' is an essentially *contested* notion, which changes its character according to that with which it is contrasted. Six different contrasts are discussed, each of which causes 'biblical theology' to appear in a different light. We return to these contrasts later, in Chapters 5, 6, 8, 9, 10 and 12. But before doing this Chapter 2 gives a short historical survey of the origins of modern Old Testament theology, and Chapter 3 presents a typology of what seem to me to be the five main types, four of them emerging in the 'classic' period (about 1930 to 1965) plus one, the 'canonical' approach, more recently. The chapter gives a characterization of each of the types and then returns over each to describe some of the problems that have been seen in each. Chapter 4 is entitled 'A Wider Spectrum' and suggests that biblical theology takes many other forms than the writing of comprehensive 'Theologies' of Old or New Testament, or indeed of the entire Bible.

Chapter 5 discusses the contrast between biblical and doctrinal theology, Chapter 6 the difference seen between biblical theology and non-theological study of the Bible. Chapter 7 is a sort of interlude, and treats of the idea of evolution and the anti-evolutionism that has animated much biblical theology. It arose originally as an element in the next chapter but grew so much that it had to be separated off. Chapter 8 introduces the contrast with the approach through the history of religion and Chapter 9 considers the question of the *size* of the complexes taken as basic for theological study. Chapter 10 is concerned with the relations of biblical theology to biblical (and other) ways of thinking, and introduces relations with philosophy and, further, the question of natural theology. Chapter 11 asks about the degree to which Old Testament Theologies have established connections with the New. Chapter 12 tries to assess the opposition commonly seen between 'committed' and 'objective' approaches. Chapter 13 puts forward the suggestion that 'historical theology' offers a good analogy to biblical theology and helps to explain how it can be understood as having the character of 'theology' at all.

Chapter 14 tries to review the various ways in which scholars have stood in opposition to biblical theology. Chapter 15 introduces a difficulty that has often been neglected, namely the fact that doctrinal theologians are commonly sceptical of biblical theology and do not support the endeavours that lead into it. It includes also the associated question how far the contents of the Bible should count as 'theology' at all. Following this, Chapter 16 considers the effort to avoid 'Christianizing' of the Old Testament, Chapter 17 looks at the evaluation of post-biblical Judaism, and Chapter 18 at the possible prospects for Jewish biblical theology.

With Chapter 19 we look at some of the 'newer-style' Theologies that appeared in the 1970s, and Chapter 20 returns to attempt a general evaluation of the Theologies thus far discussed. Chapter 21 seeks to formulate some suggestions in the area of story and history in relation to theology. In Chapter 22 we consider the proposals of Professor Hartmut Gese, and Chapters 23, 24 and 25 are devoted to the 'canonical' methods as applied by Professor Childs and others, which are here examined in more breadth and detail. With Chapter 26 we come to some of the most recent Theologies, published in the 1990s. Chapter 27 considers the impact which the revival of natural theology is likely to have on any sort of biblical theology.

Chapter 28 seeks to expound the ideas of Professor Manfred Oeming, who has both provided a keen critical analysis of the work of Gerhard von Rad and made important proposals of his own. In Chapters 29 and 30 I discuss two sharply contrasting sets of ideas, the 'Biblical Dogmatics' of Friedrich Mildenberger on the one hand and the proposals of the Finnish New Testament scholar Heikki Räisänen on the other. In Chapter 31 I was able, only at the last moment, to include a discussion of the latest Old Testament Theology to appear in the United States, that of Walter Brueggemann.

There follows in Chapter 32 a discussion of the Apocrypha and their place in biblical theology, and Chapter 33 is devoted to the relation between Old Testament theology and the later contexts of Judaism on the one hand and the New Testament and later Christianity on the other. This includes a brief assessment of the idea of a 'pan-biblical' theology of the entire (Christian) Bible.

The final Chapters 34 and 35 will be mentioned in a moment.

One additional feature may be mentioned here. Those who think critically about biblical theology are likely to evoke the objection that they have no interest in Christian theology in the proper and traditional sense. In whatever way we consider the work of biblical theology to relate to the varied forms of Christian (or of Jewish) belief and theology, it is proper that we furnish some sort of indication of relations and parallels that may exist. In order to give some evidence of how my thinking may be related to current theological opinion, therefore, I have at certain points inserted quotations or footnotes which indicate parallels, similarities or divergences. For the convenience of readers and students I have chosen one particular book, the *Christian Faith* of Professor Hendrikus Berkhof (Dutch original 1973). Berkhof, doubtless the greatest theologian of his generation in his country, had the admirable Dutch gift of combining strongly held convictions with tolerance. I had the pleasure and honour of working with him on various international study groups. He belonged to the Calvinist tradition but was appreciative of the entire width of Christian possibilities. His particular interest in the Old Testament, and his creative ideas about it, made him the ideal source for the comparisons I have interjected. These references are not made either to prove or to disprove my own arguments, nor to confirm or to dispute Berkhof's theological positions. They are there simply in order to show a location, within modern Christian systematic theology, for some judgments that are relevant to my own discussions, whether agreeing or disagreeing. My own arguments were worked out entirely on a basis within biblical theology, and the references to Berkhof's thinking were all added subsequently, after my own position was complete.

Something similar applies to Chapter 34, with the difference that this entire chapter is devoted to the thought of one Christian theologian, Professor David Brown. Even for those who hold that biblical theology is an independent discipline and separate from the considerations of doctrinal theology, the appeal and the acceptability of any proposal within biblical theology is likely to be dependent on the kind of Christian (or, likewise, Jewish) theology with which it might be expected to fit. Professor Brown's thinking is for me an ideal example of a type of theology with which I would be very happy for my own work to be associated. Here again the work of his which I have used became known to me only at the very last stages of preparation of the present book: I did not derive my thoughts, in the other chapters, from him, but find his work to represent a direction in which biblical theology, as practised in a Christian context, might well develop.

A short Conclusion is presented in Chapter 35.

As I indicate at the beginning of the first chapter, the subject of biblical theology remains both productive and controversial, and new works are known to be in preparation which may well have been published by the time this book appears in print. For my writing, it was necessary to make a 'cut-off' date, more or less in the middle of the year 1997, and this meant that some important works had to be left without any proper discussion. At most, a few footnotes referring to recent books and articles have been added here and there. In some exceptional cases, through the kindness of friends or through other contacts, I was able to include substantial reference to other works, then still unpublished, which will appear in 1998 or later. Since the book has the nature of a textbook, and if it finds a sizeable readership, then it may be possible to bring it up to date in these respects in a future edition.

Thanks are due to many who have helped me. Laura Newsome Pittman, a graduate student at Vanderbilt University, was my research assistant in this field for a time and greatly assisted me with discussion and with the obtaining of material. I owe much to my many long-suffering students, especially at Vanderbilt, who have heard various versions of this material in the course of its development. Colleagues have helped me with many kindnesses in providing advice, criticism and information, and these are generally acknowledged at the relevant points. The staff of the Divinity Library at Vanderbilt University and of the School of Theology at Claremont made wonderful and untiring efforts in locating material. Particular thanks are due to Dr John Bowden of SCM Press, who himself undertook, very swiftly, the much-needed editorial work on my long and unwieldy typescript.

Most of all I have to thank my beloved wife Jane for her thoughts, her learning, her counsel and her unceasing work.

James Barr
Claremont, California 1998

# I

# Definitions: The Many Faces of
# Biblical Theology

First a word about terminology. In this book, in general, I understand 'Old Testament theology' and 'New Testament theology' to be particular species within the genus 'biblical theology'. I mean therefore *biblical* theology as contrasted with other kinds of theology, such as *doctrinal* theology or *philosophical* theology. This I believe to be in accord with most modern usage in English.[1]

At certain points, however, and especially in recent years and in German usage, 'biblical theology' has been used for a particular operation, namely the construction of one single theology of the entire Christian Bible, i.e. of both Old and New Testaments, as distinct from individual theologies of Old or New Testament.[2] When this is the theme, I have generally used the term 'pan-biblical theology'.[3] If this is not done, the difference between the two usages remains confusing.[4]

Again, I make a distinction by using a capital letter when a particular book is meant, and a lower-case letter when the subject is meant: thus 'he wrote an Old Testament Theology' means that he wrote a book on this subject, but 'she is interested in Old Testament theology' means that she is interested in the subject.

'Biblical theology is a subject in decline,' wrote J. J. Collins in a volume published in 1990.[5] He went on to say: 'The cutting edges of contemporary biblical scholarship are in literary criticism on the one hand and sociological criticism on the other.' Perhaps so. The nature and causes of dislike for biblical theology, opposition to it, and indifference to the pursuit of it will be considered later.

Nevertheless it must be counted as doubtful whether Collins' judgment is right, especially if European scholarship is taken into account (he himself expressly qualifies his statement by adding the phrase 'at least in the United States'). In fact scholarly activity in the area of biblical theology, or what appears to be close to it, continues to flourish.[6] The years 1991–92 saw the publication of the two volumes of H. D. Preuss's *Theologie des Alten Testaments*, and 1992 of Brevard Childs' massive *Biblical Theology of the Old and New Testaments*. In

1993 there appeared a Theology by the late Professor A. H. J. Gunneweg and the first volume of one by Otto Kaiser. In the United States 1991 saw a volume of essays edited by John Reumann, 1992 a volume of essays by Walter Brueggemann, 1994 a substantial study by Leo Perdue, and 1995 a volume of essays by R. P. Knierim and another dedicated to the honour of J. Christiaan Beker. In 1992 Ollenburger, Martens and Hasel jointly produced a large and valuable reader, *The Flowering of Old Testament Theology*, which contained many of the basic documents of the subject, some of them in English translation for the first time. In 1997 there appeared another large Theology from the pen of Walter Brueggemann and Francis Watson's *Text and Truth: Redefining Biblical Theology*, as well as a volume of essays in honour of Knierim entitled *Problems in Biblical Theology*, and some other works. In addition there has been a series of important books which, without being actual Theologies of the Bible, were certainly devoted to the subject of biblical theology – a number of these will be specially reviewed at a later point. This is as high a rate of production as there ever was in the field. In the last fifteen years at least two journals or serials specifically devoted to biblical theology were founded: *Horizons in Biblical Theology* (Pittsburgh, from 1979) and *Jahrbuch für biblische Theologie* (Neukirchen, from 1986).[7] Volume 4 (1989) of the latter contains a valuable classified bibliography of the subject covering the period 1985–88, and the listing covers some 44 pages, with hundreds of items. If biblical theology is in decline, it seems not to be because of under-nourishment. Obviously vast amounts of scholarly energy are being devoted to it. Moreover, on the level of the consumer rather than the producer, I have personally found that, where I have offered courses on Old Testament theology or the like, student demand and interest has been intense – particularly in the United States. My own experience and thinking agrees with the judgment of Leo Perdue: 'biblical theology today is a vibrant, living organism of interest to both the academy and the church'.[8] In fact biblical theology is likely to survive and to outlive some of its more fashionable, possibly more sensational, but also more ephemeral, competitors.

One of its weaknesses, however, has been the difficulty of defining exactly what it is. The very idea of 'biblical theology' seems to hang uncertainly in the middle air, somewhere between actual exegesis and systematic theology.[9] Perhaps three aspects may be usefully named at this point, aspects that are not often mentioned but that seem to be generally accepted or implied and may therefore help to clarify the situation:

1. Biblical theology is something that is done by biblical scholars,[10] whether of Old or New Testament. Although doctrinal or dogmatic theologians may at times have tried to use methods and levels belonging to biblical theology, such attempts have been very partial and on the whole have received rather little

serious attention. All the major work in biblical theology has been done by biblical scholars.[11] There is little controversy about this and no sign that this will change. This is not a matter of mere designation, but has considerable significance, as we shall see.

Such statements as those by B. S. Childs to the effect that Calvin was 'doing biblical theology' (e.g. *Biblical Theology*, 47ff.), or that Karl Barth was doing the same (*Biblical Theology of the Old and New Testaments*, 588ff., cf. below, 412ff.) are incorrect, depending as they do on *ad hoc* redefinitions of the terminology. This was rightly pointed out by K. Stendahl in his 'Method in the Study of Biblical Theology' (esp. 208). Although Karl Barth greatly stimulated modern biblical theology, the widely disseminated idea that he actually supported, and gave a place in his main theological scheme to, a discipline of 'biblical theology' is quite mistaken, as will be shown below, cf. Chapter 15.

2. Biblical theology is something new, in the sense that it is searching for something that is not already known. Biblical theology is not, at least according to its implicit assumptions, something already laid down in a past or ancient tradition: in this sense it belongs to a different category from (say) Calvinist theology or Anglican theology. The theology of the Bible, as most modern biblical scholarship has envisaged it, is something that *has still to be discovered*. One is looking for it, rather than simply restating something that has been handed down from the past. Naturally, practitioners may well hope, according to their starting preferences, that it will turn out to be rather like (say) Lutheran theology or Methodist theology or whatever their own theological background may be; but what they are looking for is something of a different intrinsic nature. Its base and its mode of scholarly identification are of a quite different kind from the base or the mode of scholarly identification of any one of the traditional theological positions.

3. It follows that biblical theology has commonly been seen as possessing an *ecumenical* potential. All traditions of Christianity – and Judaism in a different way – have claimed to have the Bible as a source and base; but the actual theologies that have emerged have been very different, and not only have they differed in style and substance but they have led to severe denominational and sectional conflict. But what if the theology of the Bible itself could be identified and described? Perhaps the various traditional theologies fell into conflict because on the one hand they failed to absorb all the range of biblical material, or on the other hand allowed non-biblical sources, ideas and methods to influence their argumentation? If so, then might not a really biblical theology lead to results that would transcend these differences? And which among the traditions could really resist the requirement that it would recognize the superior weight of a *biblical* theology? How then could a biblical theology fail to be a uniting force in relation to the variety of the multiple theological traditions?

4. On the other hand there remains the insistent question whether biblical theology is really *theology* in the proper sense at all. Even if it is *called* 'theology', this designation may be partial or misleading. And the question as expressed just above, whether biblical theology is really 'theology in the proper sense', is useful only if we already know what is the 'proper sense' for the term 'theology' in the first place. Perhaps the situation is as follows: biblical theology, though not being theology in the proper sense, has features and aspects that are *analogous* to the working of theology in the proper sense, and these analogies, though partial and imperfect as all analogies are, are sufficient to make it reasonable that the term 'biblical theology' should be used. We shall not attempt to settle such questions at this point: they are mentioned only in order to orientate the reader to some of the questions that will underlie the following chapters.

5. The term 'biblical theology' has clarity only when it is understood to mean theology as it existed or was thought or believed within the time, languages and cultures of the Bible itself. Only so can its difference from doctrinal theology, from later interpretation, and from later views about the Bible be maintained. What was thought about the Bible by Irenaeus or by Calvin is thus something quite other than biblical theology as here understood.[12] What we are looking for is a 'theology' that existed back there and then. If it is asked how closely we define 'then', e.g. whether we refer to the time of the events referred to, or to the time of original writing of the texts, or to the time of their finalization, the answer is that any or all of these are included or may be so. All of these count, for my purpose, as 'biblical times and cultures'. If we specify Old or New Testament, then I would prefer to treat these as two sets of times and cultures – which is, incidentally, one reason for doubts about the possibility of one 'pan-biblical theology'. Those who do think of a pan-biblical theology would have to think of a continuum including both Old and New Testament as one 'time' and culture, or else to think of this as a two-part theology which somehow comprised two separate times and cultures.

It is true that some may object to the idea that biblical theology concerns, or ought to concern, the theology that existed in the minds of biblical persons. It ought rather to be the theology which we, or other persons of modern times, create upon the basis of the biblical texts. Taken in this way, it would not matter what the biblical people thought: everything depends solely on the relation between the text and the modern theologian. Such an approach would perhaps commend itself in the light of recent intellectual fashions. And it might work for certain parts of the Bible, at least in some degree – in the book of Job, perhaps. But for other parts it would produce grotesque consequences. Who, for example, would read with respect an account of Paul's theology which made it clear from the start that for this depiction of the theology it was of no importance whatever what Paul actually thought or

intended, and that it made no difference to the theology if it entirely contradicted Paul's thinking?

Or, to put it in another way, the more we insist that the Bible is 'theological'
in character, the more that same affirmation leads us to look for the theology that
motivated it and lived within it in ancient times.

The fact that biblical theology has its identity within the Bible's own times,
languages and cultures provides, of course, an explanation for the point already
made above, namely that biblical theology is something that has to be done, and
is done, by biblical scholars – doubtless with some exceptions.

These then are some aspects which have marked much of the thinking of
modern biblical theology, and taken together they go some distance towards
characterizing the profile of its tradition. Yet the recognition of these aspects
is not sufficient to overcome the difficulties that lie in defining its nature.
Uncertainty about the nature of the subject, and even about whether such a
subject exists at all, has certainly contributed to the sense of decline mentioned
above. And it is not surprising that the term presents difficulty, because various
uses of it appear to point in quite contradictory directions. The remainder of
this chapter will seek to explain why this is so and to explain the terminology
that will be used in this volume.

'Biblical theology' is essentially a *contrastive* notion.[13] It never derived
directly from the Bible, as if, given the Bible, it was obvious that the study of it
was biblical theology. Rather, it came to be used in contrast with various *other*
modes of studying the Bible that already existed. Thus it does not have clear
independent contours of its own: it depends for its existence upon that with
which it is contrasted. When contrasted with one operation or mode of argument, biblical theology becomes something other than what it would be when
contrasted with another operation or mode of argument. It will be suggested
here that there are at least five or six such contrasts, each of which casts 'biblical
theology' in a somewhat different light; hence it is not surprising that the concept has been difficult to define. The Roman god Janus had two faces, looking
in opposite directions; but biblical theology is more like those Hindu deities
with multiple limbs, and it tends to be pointing or looking at any time in five
directions or more.[14] Biblical theology, I suggest, takes on a different shape
according as it is contrasted with each of the following:

1. Doctrinal (systematic, dogmatic or constructive) theology.[15]
2. Non-theological study of the Bible.
3. History of religion and corresponding approaches.
4. Philosophical theology and natural theology.
5. The interpretation of *parts* of the Bible as distinct from the larger complexes taken as *wholes*.

Along with these five we shall take another aspect, which is not so much a contrast between biblical theology and some other approach, but is rather a conflict lying within biblical theology itself and one that is rather characteristic of the shape that it has taken.

6. The uncertainty as between two concepts of biblical theology: on the one hand, the concept of it as a descriptive discipline, describing the theology that was there in biblical times, and on the other hand the concept of it as a discipline involving normative authority, personal commitment, and interpretation for the present day and the modern religious community.

We shall look at each of these briefly in turn and then return to examine them in greater detail.

*1. Biblical theology as seen in contrast with doctrinal theology.* This is, in many ways, the mode in which the idea of biblical theology was first conceived: Gabler's oration of 1787, often referred to, was entitled *de iusto discrimine theologiae biblicae et dogmaticae regundisque recte utriusque finibus* – 'On the right differentiation between biblical and dogmatic theology and on the correct drawing of the boundaries of each'.[16] In many ways this differentiation, as I shall argue, remains the most important today. I shall not, however, attempt a detailed interpretation of the learned Gabler himself. As the distinction which he made has effectively worked out in modern times, it functions somewhat as follows.

Doctrinal theology states, clarifies and illuminates the faith of the church today; biblical theology concerns itself with the theology of the Bible itself. Doctrinal theology is, perhaps, authoritative and prescriptive: it lays down what is to be believed. Biblical theology by contrast is descriptive rather than normative: it seeks to state what the theology of the biblical books, or the theology implied by them, was. The implication may be that doctrinal theology takes into consideration situations, factors or sources other than the Bible alone. As Gabler put it, while religion is 'every-day, transparent knowledge', theology is 'subtle, learned knowledge, surrounded by a retinue of many disciplines, and by the same token derived not only from the sacred Scripture but also from elsewhere, especially from the domain of philosophy and history'.

Or, as Eichrodt put it in a more modern form in his preparatory essay of 1928 on Old Testament theology,[17] Old Testament theology lay entirely within *die alttestamentliche Wissenschaft*, within the recognized academic discipline of the subject: it did not belong to the 'normative disciplines' such as dogmatic theology or philosophy. It did not involve dependence on church authority; and it did not involve any appeal to faith, to special modes of cognition or to special kinds of authority.

Whether these distinctions are satisfactory or not I shall not discuss here; all we have to note is the character and effect of the distinction itself. The distinction explains how biblical theology is *not* doctrinal theology. The emphasis is on *this* difference. The character of doctrinal theology, for this purpose, is taken as known: it is, after all, the real, the original, 'theology', properly so called, and biblical theology is the newcomer. If the former is subtle, philosophical and didactic, the latter is descriptive; if the former seeks to explain in relation to many disciplines, the latter works only on the plane of biblical scholarship; if the former has scope, material and sources in many areas, the latter has scope, material and source only in the Bible. Biblical theology is thus very *different* from doctrinal theology.

2. *Biblical theology as contrasted with non-theological study of the Bible.* Older definitions of 'biblical theology', like those of Gabler, had emphasized such matters as philology, distinguishing between poetry and prose, distinguishing the meanings that terms had had in biblical times from the meanings that might suggest themselves to modern readers, and making sure that we did not attribute to the biblical writers thoughts that they had never had. All these operations were generally agreed upon: what was at first not so easily perceived was that they could, at least apparently, be carried out without any substantial interest in 'theology' at all. By the late nineteenth century it seemed obvious that quite a lot of biblical scholarship was not really 'theological', however much it concentrated upon the Bible and its text and language. Textual criticism, though significant for theological results, was not in any way governed by theology: theology could not legitimately decree in matters of the Masoretic text and the Septuagint, in questions of meaning of Greek words as between explanation on the basis of the *koine* and explanation on the basis of 'biblical Greek'. Scholars often worked on these questions in a way that suggested that theology was of no importance for their operations. Not only so, but these apparently 'non-theological' operations seemed to be regarded by some as the central area for 'real' scholarship, the area in which it was essential for the scholar to prove his distinction (or hers: but female scholars were few at the time!).

'Biblical theology' came early to be used as a term to combat these tendencies. If under 1. the stress has been on *biblical* theology as contrasted with other modes of theology, in this case the stress is on biblical *theology* as contrasted with other modes of biblical study. Seen in this way, there is an area, a very important area, in biblical scholarship which is not interested primarily in textual criticism, in matters of philology, or in historical background, but is concerned with the vital central 'message' of the biblical texts, with the interrelations of ideas that link one text with another, and with the deep underlying convictions that inspired the texts and united them as a composite and yet unitary 'witness' to ultimate theological truth. 'Biblical theology' in this sense of the term has claimed to be a fully 'theological' undertaking, and yet it has been anxious to claim the same fully academic or 'scientific' character that attached to 'non-theological' operations like textual criticism or philology.

Such claims make good sense, but they carry with them one obvious problem: namely, that they point in exactly the opposite direction from the idea of 'biblical theology' that I have delineated under 1. above. The conception of 1. above tends, as far as possible, to distinguish biblical from doctrinal theology; the conception discussed under 2., distinguishing biblical theology from non-theological work on the Bible, tends to pull biblical theology back closer to doctrinal theology.

The contrary pressures of these two conceptions have remained a central problem of biblical theology to the present day – perhaps indeed ultimately its most serious problem. Is biblical theology sharply distinct from doctrinal theology, and if so in what sense is it truly 'theology' at all? Or is it, as 'theology', sharply distinct from the non-theological elements involved in biblical study, and if so how does it escape from becoming absorbed within some kind of doctrinal theology?

A preliminary word should be said here about the place of 'historical criticism'. By this is commonly meant the sort of study that from the end of the eighteenth century and on to the present day, though now decreasing in prominence, went into historical operations on the biblical books: questions of authorship and date of books, separation of different strata or 'sources', description of the different religious conceptions attaching to each stage, correlation of the literary sources with the stages in the history of the religion, and eventually the production of a widely agreed picture of these matters which was regarded by some as the 'agreed results' of a period of very intensive research.

Many have regarded historical criticism of this kind as an important example of the non-theological study of the Bible against which biblical theology may define itself, or indeed as the primary such example. And indeed, as we shall see, a certain weariness with historical criticism has been an important part of the reaction which produced biblical theology in its twentieth-century form. Thus self-definition as against historical criticism has been perhaps the most powerful expression of biblical theology, and also the one which has caused most trouble to all concerned.[18]

This will be further discussed at a later point. Here, however, I only mention it and refrain from according it centrality for two reasons. It is not clear that traditional historical criticism is in fact non-theological. Most of those who have practised it have both used theological criteria in doing it and have valued it for the theological results that it brings. It did indeed become the fashion in some quarters to label it as 'non-theological' and to consider it irrelevant for theology, but this depends on a narrow and particularistic definition of what theology is and contains. I do not therefore accept without further analysis the common opinion that 'historical criticism' is the prime example of non-theological study against which biblical theology arose. 'Historical criticism' seems to me to belong much more to pure theology than does, say, textual criticism, the value and necessity of which is generally accepted and agreed. Moreover, as we shall see throughout, almost all the main currents of biblical theology have accepted in some degree the substantial validity of the critical approach, even when they wanted to go beyond it in some way or other.

Nevertheless the impression that much biblical study was in some sense 'non-theological', even if the identification of historical criticism as that element is inexact, has been an important ingredient in the mind-set of modern biblical theology.

To repeat, then, the main point: the opposition felt to exist between biblical theology and 'non-theological' study of the Bible had the effect of bringing biblical theology closer to doctrinal theology – exactly the opposite effect from that exercised by the first distinction mentioned above.

*3. Contrast with the history-of-religion approach.* 'History of religion' (I shall later define and analyse this term more closely) has some common elements with the historical criticism of the Bible but has nevertheless been a somewhat different factor. For one thing, the history of religion has operated *comparatively*. While historical criticism touches upon the internal material of the Bible, one major aspect of the history of religion touches upon its external relations with other, environing, religious traditions. The two have often had a common impact; but there are important differences between them.

The older theology and biblical study had little material to work on other than the Bible itself, classical (Greek and Latin) literature, and Jewish and Christian traditions of religious interpretation. The nineteenth century produced volumes of new evidence which impinged upon biblical study: knowledge of Egyptian culture and language, similarly of Mesopotamian, later of Hittite; in the twentieth century Ugaritic, even closer to the biblical home, was discovered. Studies in worldwide folklore, made famous by Sir James Frazer,[19] offered countless 'parallels' which, it was thought, could explain features of the Old Testament. Similarly relevant to the New Testament might be material from the Greek mystery religions; and later on Coptic texts gave much greater first-hand knowledge of Gnostic religion.

All these, taken together, raised several problems. First, elements in the Bible which had hitherto been taken as direct and special divine revelation might have been adopted – 'borrowed' was the usual word, rather incongruously, since such borrowings were never paid back – from an earlier Oriental religion. Secondly, it became possible to project a development or evolution in world religion, of

which some stages were known from other cultures, while certain biblical
elements might be a 'survival' from these more ancient stages and others might
be interpreted as products of a developmental or evolutionary process, which
might run through the Bible and reach a culmination – perhaps in prophets like
Isaiah, in the New Testament, or in Christ, or in some more modern realization?
Thirdly, whether or not jointly with these 'external' relations, within the
'internal' development of biblical religion it was perhaps possible to trace
changes and developments. Perhaps later stages were 'higher' than the earlier?
Or perhaps things got worse, and the religion deteriorated at some stage?
Perhaps the prophets gradually 'purified' the religion? Or did 'legalism'
eventually damage it? Obviously this sort of intra-biblical history-of-religion
approach, while possible in part even without historical criticism of the sources,
was greatly facilitated by such a historical view, and in fact historical criticism of
the sources on the one hand, and an emphasis on the history of religion on the
other, have commonly been seen as belonging together or indeed as being the
same thing.

Moreover, the Bible did not tell us everything we might want to know about
the religion of its own times. It condemns the worship of Baal but does not
explain very clearly what the beliefs of Baal-worshippers were. The New Testament letters contain much polemic against (often unnamed) opponents, but
scarcely give an adequate explanation of the viewpoint and theology of these
persons or groups. Our understanding of these negatively portrayed groups
depends in large measure on sources outside the Bible itself, on historical data
about ancient religions which may fill in gaps left by the Bible itself. The Bible,
according to this view, presents some kind of dominant viewpoint, a regnant
theology or group of theologies; but it does not fairly or properly depict the
general or popular religion. Indeed, some will urge that the Bible presents
the viewpoint of the groups that survived and succeeded. It does not speak for
the religion as it was. For this we have to turn to the history of religion.

As against these approaches biblical theology, for the most part, again has not
defined itself absolutely negatively. It has not generally denied that some of the
relevant parallels and similarities existed. Nor has it disputed the existence of
diachronic change within Hebrew religion itself. But it has sought, on the whole,
to subordinate all these to a central theological structure, which it is the task of
biblical theology to disengage. When religious elements were adapted into Israel
from other religions and cultures, according to this approach, they came to be
controlled or governed by their new setting within Israel: for example, mythological elements found in surrounding, polytheistic cultures were 'historicized'
through subjection to the Hebrew theology of history, or were otherwise
neutralized by their new setting within a dominant monotheism. Where changes
took place in Hebrew religion, they could be seen as diachronic sub-variations

within the larger theological structure. It was this deeper and larger structure that in face of religious similarities outside provided distinctiveness and in face of religious change within provided continuity and stability.

Moreover, the biblical theology of the twentieth century has for the most part followed that change of terminological values, associated with dialectical theology, whereby 'theology' came to be thought of as something substantially different from 'religion'. Where an earlier generation of scholars had thought it central and profound to write about 'the religion of Amos' or 'the religion of the prophets', modern biblical theology for the most part turned away from this emphasis. 'Religion' has come to be seen somewhat negatively, and the positive emphasis has come to fall on 'theology'. 'Religion,' wrote Karl Barth, 'is the concentrated expression of human unbelief,' while 'theology' comes exclusively from the Word of God.[20] 'Religion', according to this approach, is no more than a complex of human religious styles and dispositions, while 'theology' is thought above all to be concentrated on a reference to the divine, a 'witness', as people said. Even within Israel, therefore, and quite apart from the question of any adoptions from other religions, an investigation of the religion and how it developed has come to be widely thought of as quite different from a theology of the Old Testament, and possibly as of marginal importance to it or even totally irrelevant to it. Whether this very strong distinction can be upheld will be discussed later.

To sum up, in face of the apparent challenge of the history-of-religion approach, biblical theology has generally sought factors of constancy which supported the distinctive identity of the Bible and its religion or theology, while accommodating rather than denying the facts of religious change within and religious similarities without. Generally speaking, biblical theology has given the impression that this position is reasonably compatible with the needs and forces of doctrinal theology, while a strong and express history-of-religion approach would not be so.

*4. Biblical theology seen as in contrast with philosophy and natural theology.* Biblical theology has also defined itself as in essence an entry into an ancient mode of thinking which differs from traditional philosophy and logic, particularly from the Greek tradition of thought, and sometimes indeed, vaguely and rather grandiosely, from all 'modern ways of thinking'.

Here lies a major difference from an older exegetical tradition which had often sought to show that biblical materials were 'in accord with reason'. For at least the last century biblical scholars have ceased to work in that way. They are interested in the minds of the biblical people and no longer care whether these minds conform to the ideas of modern reason, logic or psychology.[21] 'On the whole they chose the opposite path: if the thoughts of biblical people were entirely *different* from what modern rationality might demand, so much the better for biblical people. The discovery of the mentality of ancient people might uncover a mode of thinking that, while different from modern modes, was valuable and constructive when taken in its own right.'[22] Stendahl wrote: 'It became a scholarly ideal to creep out of one's Western and twentieth-century skin and identify oneself with the feelings and thought-patterns of the past.'[23]

Much or most biblical theology has followed this line. Seen in this way, biblical theology is a theology that works with biblical concepts and biblical logic, as against any theology that works with philosophical concepts, with Hellenic presuppositions, or with modern schemes of thought.

Working in this way, biblical theology has seemed to offer a powerful apologetic for many ideas of doctrinal theology, traditional and modern. Ideas that had been challenged on grounds of philosophical incoherence, internal contradiction, or failure to fit with facts as known from other sources, could now be defended on the ground that in terms of biblical thought they were quite coherent. It was only through a mistaken or even dogmatic (!) prejudice in favour of Greek, philosophical or modern ways of thinking that any criticism had been directed against these theological views.

It would be difficult to exaggerate the degree of alienation that the average biblical scholar has felt in relation to the work of disciplines like philosophical theology or the philosophy of religion. Their modes of discussion and decision seem to him or her remote and unreal. The questions they discuss and the criteria which they apply seem to be contrived and artificial, and the world of discourse in which they move seems to be a quite different world from the world of the Bible, to which the biblical scholar feels he has a sort of direct and empirical access. And in this respect the biblical scholar, at least in the English-speaking world, has felt himself to be closer to the atmosphere of the church and the practical work of the average clergyman, who (it is supposed) is more anxious to get to grips with the Bible and its message than to discuss such apparently theoretical matters as being and becoming, the nature of knowledge, or the subject-object relationship. Relief from the felt unrealities of philosophical theology has been an unquestionable part of the motivation of those attracted to biblical theology.

In no respect, however, has this kind of argument been more conspicuous or more potent than in respect of natural theology. Natural theology implies that human persons, just because they are human, or because of the environment of God's creation around them, know something of the true God. Extended somewhat further, it may imply that something valid about God can be worked out on the basis of human reason, and that philosophical enquiry can guide us to some aspects of the truth about God. Much of the Western tradition of natural theology built upon the Greek philosophers and their thoughts about God, the soul, immortality and so on, and much of this tradition was incorporated into later Christian theology, as also into philosophical traditions of Judaism. This incorporation has been notably explicit and evident in Roman Catholic theology, but something similar, if less conspicuous, has obtained also in wide strata of Anglican and Protestant theology.

In the twentieth century, however, natural theology was strongly attacked, especially by Karl Barth and his followers. In Barth's view humans had no access to knowledge of the true God except by special divine revelation. Whether right or wrong, this view fitted very well with what was actually happening, namely the fact that many modern people were becoming indifferent to the arguments of natural theology and were even becoming unaware that they had ever existed. Moreover, the attack on natural theology appeared to give renewed emphasis to the place of the Bible, for the Bible had been regarded as an obvious channel of divine revelation, while the channels of natural theology had been thought of as largely independent of the Bible. Biblical theologians saw this as a way in which their own area of interest, the Bible, would achieve a new centrality. On the one hand the Bible was supremely a document of revelation, and on the other hand the denial of natural theology would eliminate the sort of thoughts and arguments which, it was supposed, had tended to damage the perception of biblical thinking and to mitigate its influence. Much biblical theology, therefore, even if its practitioners did not themselves particularly agree with Barth or understand him, allowed itself to become a slave to the twentieth-century rejection of natural theology which he had led. It set itself to provide what appeared to be not just theological opinion but hard cultural counter-evidence, built upon detailed empirical studies in biblical expressions, concepts and words and upon wide-ranging researches in the general trends of the Bible, that would support and confirm a purely revelatory mode of theology from which natural theology would be completely absent.

And in this respect biblical theology has been, it seems, remarkably success-ful – at least in the short term. This has been one of its most popular and influential modes. But the question remains: what if, after all, it turns out that natural theology is a significant constituent of the theology of the Bible itself? We shall return to this later.

As against philosophy and natural theology, then, biblical theology has generally defined itself not as just for or against doctrinal theology, but above all as an enterprise that sought to work out a basis in biblical thought for the particular revelatory trends, hostile to natural theology, which have been domi-nant throughout the central part of the twentieth century.

*5. The interpretation of the Bible as a whole, or of at least one Testament, as distinct from the interpretation of parts of it.* Biblical theology has, in general, been interested in the whole rather than in the part. Its motto has been: the bigger the chunk of the Bible the better. A little part taken alone tells us nothing significant: only when 'seen in the light of' a much larger context does it become meaningful. Here there is a connection with that hostility to historical-critical analysis which has already been mentioned: historical criticism has been disliked because, it is said, it splits up the material into different sources of different times. Most biblical theology has wanted to put the pieces together again. The important thing therefore is not to grasp the theology even of complete strata or books of the Bible, like the theology of the Priestly Document or the theology of the prophets, the theology of St Paul and that of the Johannine literature – which, it seems to be implied, can be done with no great difficulty – but to grasp the theology of the entirety, the theology of the great collections taken as wholes. Thus, as compared with (say) the theology of Ezekiel or the theology of St John, the theology of the Old Testament or of the New tries to deal with the entirety. And in some ways this has been the general impression in modern times: the major comprehensive task lies in the construction of Theologies of the Old Testament or of the New. And such Theologies have been among the greatest monuments of biblical theology: on the whole, also, they have escaped from some of the criticisms which have so badly damaged some of the other aspects of biblical theology.

When so much stress is placed upon entirety, however, it is also possible to look farther and say that biblical theology must be above all a theology of *the entire Bible*. Seen from this point of view, it may seem that separate theologies of the Old and New Testaments do not achieve much towards the task of a truly *biblical* theology. Such a work, it may be thought, has to take the totality of the entire Bible as its theme. To avoid confusion, as already stated, in this book the enterprise of writing a Theology of the entire Bible will be called *pan-biblical theology*. Some works of pan-biblical theology have indeed been published: for instance, Millar Burrows' *Outline of Biblical Theology*,[24] or W. Harrington's *The Path of Biblical Theology*.[25] Neither of these works, however, were deemed, for one reason or another, to come up to the highest standards as seen in the major Theologies of Old or of New Testament. The work that most fully seeks to realize the pan-biblical ideal thus far is Brevard Childs' *Biblical Theology of the Old and New Testaments*. But the whole idea of 'writing a biblical theology' (i.e. a pan-biblical theology) in this sense has had a lively discussion in the last twenty years, especially within German scholarship.

To sum up, then: seen from this point of view, biblical theology defines itself as an operation concentrating on expressing theological evaluations of the larger units: more than individual passages or sources, more than the individual books, usually one Testament as a whole. This approach sometimes gives the impression, incidentally, that the study of the smaller units is less than theological.

6. *Biblical theology as evaluative and as actualizing?* This sixth contrast is somewhat different from the five that have preceded, for it is less an aspect by which biblical theology is distinguished from other approaches and more an area of conflict within biblical theology itself. It will nevertheless be useful to give it some preliminary discussion at this point, for the existence of this disagreement has been one of the marks that have characterized biblical theology and indicated its interests and its nature.

Biblical theology has often defined itself as a discipline that would perceive and state the theology contained in, or implied by, the biblical texts themselves. Its proudest boast has been that it gave an account of the total underlying theology of one Testament or of the other, or of the entire Bible, all within the mental framework and presuppositions of the Bible itself. To claim this might seem to be to claim quite a lot. But there has equally been a tendency to say that this in itself is not enough. It is not enough simply to say what the theology of the Bible was, to *describe* it: one has to go on to evaluate it, to make value judgments, to show the excellence of this theology and give reasons, not only why we should recognize its existence, but also why we should be moved and influenced by it. Evaluation in this sense has been an aim, overt or hidden, in much biblical theology.

Related to this, or (some would say) another way to express the same thing, is the question of relevance for the present day, or *actualization* as one might call it. Does biblical theology have a role that can be called hermeneutical in this sense? That is, does it not only tell us what the theology of biblical times was and explain to us its inner relations and connections as the people of the Bible understood them, but also explain how that theology is to be interpreted and realized in the actual life and thought of the religious community today?

Within modern biblical theology different currents have answered these questions in very different ways, and some, one may suspect, have sought to evade any definite answer and tried to sit on the fence. At this point I offer only a limited survey of some of the characteristic arguments.

Arguments for an evaluative aim commonly begin with an attack on 'objectivity': one cannot examine the Bible with cold objectivity and describe its deepest thoughts and interconnections as if it did not in the slightest matter to us what these thoughts and interconnections were. Equally, these arguments attack a strictly historical perception on the ground that, being by its nature confined to what was there in the past, it makes biblical theology into a sort of antiquarian study; in the phrase of James Sanders, it 'locks the Bible into the past'.[26] Moreover, theology itself, it is said, is by its nature a matter of evaluation and affirmation, of conviction and 'proclamation', and a discipline that does not include these elements does not really deserve the name of biblical 'theology'.

Similar arguments are used to urge that biblical theology provides interpretation for the present day and its problems. The scholar of primarily historical interests, it is alleged, may have explained the material within its context of long ago but done nothing to show how it can be relevant for the problems and issues of today. On the contrary, the reading of the Bible, even when done historically, should and must at once provide perspectives which change our perception of the world and affect our deepest interests and purposes.

In addition, an ecclesial and pastoral, homiletic aspect has often been introduced. Just as 'theology' in the general sense guides the judgments and attitudes of the community of faith, so biblical theology should guide and inspire them. Biblical theology has thus often been thought of as a means by which 'biblical preaching' would be restored to influence and effectiveness: it would be able to disengage and formulate from the Bible the message that would be 'good for' the hearers of today. This homiletic aspect, this interest in what might be 'good for them', has often drawn the notice of critics of biblical theology and has been admitted even by its friends.[27]

This is one side. On the other side, powerful arguments against the evaluative and the actualizing conceptions of biblical theology can be advanced. If there is a theology concealed within the Bible or implied by it, surely the essential thing is to discover what that theology is; to know what that theology in itself is must surely take precedence over any decisions about how far that theology is a good one or not, or about what effects it may have or should have on decisions about modern problems. Where this has not been so, unquestionably preferences within modern theology or proposals for religious answers to modern problems have been allowed to influence perceptions of what is 'there' in the Bible: even enthusiasts for biblical theology have generally admitted that this has been so. Like some other trends in theology, 'biblical theology' has been guilty of distorting biblical material in order to provide proposals and answers that seem agreeable to later or modern theological trends or to perceptions of religious and social needs. That this is so is generally admitted. The obvious answer then is to say that biblical theology can have no criterion or principle other than what is there in the Bible as understood in its own times.

It remains a question how this apparent dilemma can be resolved. At a later stage we will return to the problem, provide some further discussion of the formulations of it, and seek to offer a possible solution. For the present it is sufficient to note that disagreement about the problem has been a characteristic of modern biblical theology, especially in its Anglo-Saxon – and most of all in its American – currents.

This particular 'face' of biblical theology, then, displays very well the contradictory forces that have plagued the subject. The logical strength of any approach through biblical theology must necessarily be that it states and displays correctly the theology that is there, that is at least implicit, in the Bible. Yet the motivation and the purpose has often been to get away from 'mere' statements of the biblical situation, to give an evaluative estimate of the biblical material, to show how it 'works' for the present day, how it provides right answers and attitudes for the religious community, how it can answer the difficulties and uncertainties of the Christian (or indeed the Jewish) preacher. But, when one goes a step farther, the claims that it 'works' for the present day, the assurances of the modern preacher, depend on the assumption that biblical theology has actually described the situation correctly: for otherwise the evaluations are mistaken, and the assurances given by the preacher are deceptive. The problems associated with these questions will remain with us as we proceed.

This chapter has indicated, then, something of the many-sided character that attaches to the idea of biblical theology, as of Old or New Testament theology. I have shown why no simple definition of these activities can be given. It is highly likely that the multiple set of motivations and choices described has led to confusion within the work of biblical theology. As their opposition to the role of philosophy indicates, biblical theologians have not generally been strong in logic or in philosophical reasoning. This in itself, however, does not necessarily diminish the value of much of the content that the discipline has produced. It is quite possible for work of richness and value to be produced even where there is some confusion about the methodological principles involved. Nevertheless the existence of these various contradictory pressures makes it more difficult to understand the problems.

All that I have done here is to indicate something of the complexity of motives, issues and contrasts which have affected the various strands of biblical theology in modern times. The discussion of these is thus far only preliminary, and I shall return to some of these questions and discuss them at greater length.

The next chapter will proceed with a historical sketch of the origins of modern Old Testament theology.

# 2

# The Origins of Modern Old
# Testament Theology

The origins of modern Old Testament theology have been retold often enough, and one cannot expect to say anything sensationally new about them; but they provide a good introduction into the essential problems of the subject, and for this reason can be recounted with profit here.

Throughout the nineteenth century and into the first decades of the twentieth a characteristic scholarly activity had been the critical source analysis of the Old Testament books. This analysis was a literary operation, but it was also a religious and theological operation. In distinguishing different strata within the literature it took into consideration differences of religious or theological viewpoint within them or between them: thus it not only *arrived at* a distinction between different religious conceptions animating the authors of different strata, it used such a distinction as an essential instrument from the beginning. It thereby disintegrated – and rightly so – the older mode of understanding, under which the biblical books had, with certain limited qualifications, been understood as representing a unitary theological truth, with at the most some differences of emphasis – ultimately, one might say, God's own theology, directly expressed by the Bible.

Granted, however, that it was right to separate into differing strands the hitherto seamless fabric of biblical truth, analysis of this kind, it was felt, could not be a final goal. It was understandable that among those generations of scholars who pioneered source analysis some would find it all-absorbing and see no reason why their energies should be taken up with anything else. But by the earlier years of this century the main structure of a critical analysis, as it has continued in a broad sense to be accepted even to the present day, was already complete, and the question could now be put: assuming the critical analysis, and eschewing all desire to return to a unitary Bible in a fundamentalist sense, was there not something that could be said about the Old Testament as a whole? Was it right that the religious elements and utterances of each passage or document should be studied primarily as indicators of a stage in a development from one level to another, or should it be asked what they were in themselves, or what they were when they were taken together? In particular, were the religious conceptions to be studied as part of a religious development the beginning and ending of which lay outside the Old Testament itself, or could their essence be brought together as a *theology* which belonged particularly to the Old Testament and expressed its central concern? Thus anti-evolutionism and reaction against developmental approaches were characteristic of the early moves towards modern Old Testament theology. The impulse was one for *synthesis*.

Secondly, there was a concern for *distinctiveness*. The later nineteenth century and the earlier twentieth had not only concentrated on the *internal* analysis of the documents and worked out from it a historical sequence of their origin; it had also been interested by the growing mass of *external* parallels which seemed to throw new light on practices and ideas of the Old Testament and to suggest new ways of understanding them. Previously the material for this kind of comparison had been slender – some Greek sources, some hints from Arab tradition – but now scholars were ready to bring forward a large mass of parallels or possible parallels made available from Egyptian evidence, from the young discipline of Assyriology (made luridly evident by the 'Babel-Bibel' lectures of Friedrich Delitzsch in 1902),[1] and from the frequently ill-digested results of comparative folk-lore. Some at least of these parallels seemed to be valid, and it became clear that the Old Testament was not only fallible as a historical source and diverse in origin as a literary entity, but also as a religious and theological document might be less unique than had been supposed. Moreover, conservative opinion, which had been suspicious of all the source-critical operations carried out within the biblical text, has often looked with greater sympathy on these materials from the environing cultures, thinking that they might provide information that would confirm the historicity of biblical narratives after all. During the twentieth century discoveries of possible parallels continued to multiply, and especially the Ugaritic sources seemed to show many close similarities. Moreover, a similar problem existed in the New Testament, for voices were to be heard declaring that large elements of it were derived from, or at least were very close to, the mystery religions or other cultural phenomena of Hellenistic times. Indeed, it may be suspected that the challenge of such ideas about the mystery religions was a more important impulse than any other in causing scholars to seek a different approach.[2] Naturally, the validity of comparisons could be, and was, challenged; not all of the comparisons suggested stood the test of time. Few, for example, now take seriously Robertson Smith's wide-ranging detection of totemism within the Old Testament. But at least room had to be made for some element of truth in these comparisons. It was no longer possible to hope that they would all in due course turn out to be ill-founded.

Scholars therefore began to ask themselves: granted that these things are true, and that all sorts of parallels exist between Old Testament texts and other religions or popular practices, is there not a central framework which belongs distinctively to the Old Testament and which in its outlines is distinctive, even if many details are not? Do we not have to distinguish between a centre and a periphery? If so, we may realize that the characteristics of the periphery should be understood through their subjection to the centre; and if so, though peripheral details can be read also in relation to a different centre, let us say another religion or another culture, in so far as they are to be interpreted as part of the Old Testament, do we not have to understand them *as they are related to the centre of the Old Testament itself*? Thus, even if the sacrificial system of Leviticus, or the general institution of the Jerusalem temple, have close analogies in environing cultures, is it not possible that this system and this institution, when taken within the complex of specifically Old Testament thinking, came to have a different, and a distinctive, meaning?

The third need which motivated the Old Testament theology movement was a need for depth in meaning. The pioneers in that movement, if I read their minds correctly, were dissatisfied by a type of thinking which seemed to them reductionistic towards the levels of meaning discernible in texts. I think, for instance, of the 'aetiological' interpretation of the story of the Garden of Eden: the story, according to this approach, originated in order to explain why snakes had no legs, why women had pain in childbirth, why man had to work on the land to make it fruitful – a trivialization, perhaps, of the story, and one which makes it explain difficulties which for the ancient Israelite possibly needed no explanation in the first place. Granted that an aetiological motive was an important factor in many ancient stories, was it not a pity to reduce the many levels of meaning to this one alone? In the prophetic books, the mystery of verbal prediction seemed to have gone, and it was not necessary to bring it back; however, one wanted more than an indication of the contemporary situation: one asked for something that seemed as theologically powerful as the older understanding had provided. Of too many of the critical commentaries of the turn of the century it was felt that they made no attempt to state the *meaning* of a passage in any profound way at all: they dealt with the textual questions, provided a complex analysis of sources, discussed the problem of authorship, authenticity and date, touched on the historicity or otherwise of the content, and – on to the next passage!

In this respect the movement towards Old Testament theology came at a point of a shift of sensibility among scholars. Just as at an earlier date scholars had reacted against the older traditional theological interpretations, often falsely spiritualizing and Christianizing in character, and had found it meaningful and liberating to see a meaning lower in key and more earthly in character, so now once again they reacted against what seemed to be the pettiness of interpretation, against its refusal to accept the wider dimensions of the texts, against its failure to discern and to map out the deeper spiritual currents and problems at issue behind the historical facts. Old Testament theology was an attempt to recognize this dimension of depth.

The fourth concern was that of establishing adequate contact with the New Testament. Old traditional modes of establishing this contact, principally through predictive prophecy, through typologies, and through reading Christian concepts directly into the Old Testament texts, had been severely weakened if not destroyed by modern scholarship. Yet the scholars were mostly Christians, and mostly of a rather traditional kind, and they had – with very few exceptions, if any at all – no doubt about the continuing authority of the Old Testament within Christianity. But how was this authority now to operate? There was one Bible, but how was the gap between the two great parts of it to be bridged? The Old Testament was in Hebrew, the New in Greek, and some centuries of time separated the one from the main part of the other. The New Testament was verbally and literally Christian on every page; even the most critical scholarship hardly questioned that. But the Old Testament belonged to the religion of ancient Israel. That religion certainly was the historical ancestor of Christianity, and the New Testament could not be understood without the Old: this was true, and was said often enough, but it did not seem to be enough. The fact remained that the pages of the Old Testament contained no verbal or literal account of its mode of connection with Jesus. Critical commentaries, correspondingly, failed to say much about that aspect. And perhaps this was right: but, if so, then should there not exist some other kind of comment which would supplement them by making explicit what this connection was and how it worked?

These four elements, then, existed within Old Testament scholarship and joined to stimulate the movement which produced modern Old Testament theology. A synthetic approach rather than an analytic; distinctiveness as against environing religions and cultures; depth of meaning as against superficial explanation; and some kind of integral connection with the New Testament – a connection not merely in occasional word resemblances or accidental typologies or in the reading back of Christian ideas into pre-Christian texts, but 'integral' in the sense of having a base in some major principle or contextual basis – these were the needs which scholars reached out to fulfil. Synthesis, distinctiveness, depth of meaning and connection with the New Testament, these were the values that Old Testament theology, in its classic modern form, professed to furnish.

To these should be added another factor, which came rather from a general theological change. I spoke above of a 'shift in sensibility', and this belonged to theology more generally, in particular to the rise of the powerful movement of dialectical theology. This provided the basis for the adoption of the term 'theology' for the new movement in Old Testament studies.[3]

Older scholarship had tended to favour the term 'religion': the religion of Israel, the religion of Amos. 'Theology' was thought to be academic, scholastic and derivative; 'religion', like 'faith', was direct, personal and living. These sentiments were shared by Old Testament scholars with the doctrinal theology of their time. But around the end of the First World War this position was abruptly reversed by dialectical theology, in which the term 'religion' was suddenly moved in status from being the positive pole to being the negative pole in the contrast. Whether we take the pair 'revelation/religion' or the pair 'theology/religion', in either case religion became the bad thing of the two, at best not much more than a necessary evil. According to this new trend, the serious theologically-conscious scholar must now ask not after the religion of the Old Testament, for that is in the end only human religiosity, but after the revelation, for that is what comes from God. The subject-matter of theology is not people's religion, not even the religion of Amos or of Paul, but God and what he has to say to man. If the older type of Old Testament scholarship, with its interest in religious development and religious experience, had been well in line with the thought of contemporary doctrinal theologians, the question now was whether the newer theological current would produce its image in Old Testament scholarship also. The return to favour of the term 'theology' was a sign that this was happening. Earlier there had indeed been books with titles like 'Old Testament Theology', but it was now felt that the actual content of these had very much been the historical development of religion. From now on books with the same title would turn in a different direction. Of course the Old Testament was not a traditional theological textbook, nor was it a systematic treatise; no one supposed it was. Nor could 'theology' be distilled from its verses in the older orthodox manner. But nevertheless its total synthetic structure, properly analysed and investigated, could testify to an underlying 'theology', and equally one could properly speak of the 'theology' of Deuteronomy, the 'theology' of the stories of the Judges, of Ezekiel's plan for a new temple, of Deutero-Isaiah and so on. And this way of speaking has to a large extent come to be accepted, even among scholars who are far from being supporters of biblical theology in other respects.

The rise of dialectical theology, especially in its Barthian and Brunnerian form, had a further effect. This theology was, in conscious return to the Reformation, deeply interested in the Bible – indeed 'interested' is an understatement; one should say rather that it professed to be wholly and emphatically biblical. Moreover, it emphasized the Bible as a complete whole, and in this respect abandoned the fashion which had been common under liberal theology, namely of working with certain approved strata and looking upon others as at best only imperfect or transitory strivings towards something what was to develop elsewhere or later. Again, its christocentric emphasis, when combined with this pan-biblical scope, immediately raised once more the question how the Old Testament could be supposed to have testified to Christ. It was not enough to have a more lofty or elevated view of the deity. The true God was known only through Christ: but how did this work for the Old Testament? Finally, dialectical theology produced a view of biblical authority which was able to accept historical criticism of scripture in principle[4] and yet to insist on biblical control over the thinking of doctrinal theology: to see the Bible as the Word of God and yet, by denying that the Word of God was simply identical with the Bible, to avoid a regression into merely conservative and fundamentalist positions.

It is by no means the case that these newer theological currents were immediately embraced with fervour by the fraternity of Old Testament scholars: they may well have occasioned some distaste and some fear of the effects they would have if they ever got loose among scholars, and indeed there are many scholars who to the present day remain largely untouched by them. But in the minds of scholars who did have some sympathy for the newer theological current, the first question was surely: is it possible, in accepting the rightness of this current, also to discipline it in such a way as to avoid the excesses which are likely to spring from it? Or can these excesses be avoided solely by an absolute rejection of the newer current and a strict confinement of Old Testament scholarship to historical and critical studies?

What were in fact the 'excesses' in question? During the 1920s and the early 1930s, a time of considerable ferment within dialectical theology and one of much uncertainty about the direction in which it would eventually go, there were certain experiments in 'spiritual', 'pneumatic' and 'christological' exegesis.

For English-speaking readers, the most definitive expression of these directions lay in the work of Wilhelm Vischer, whose general position can be summarized in a phrase of Luther's which Vischer later made the title of an essay of his own: 'Everywhere the Scripture is about Christ alone'.[5] Vischer was widely understood to have reintroduced a kind of allegorical exegesis. However, this misrepresents his ideas: he himself was consistently opposed to allegory. As I have suggested, his position was more one of 'universal Christ-history'. The life and history of Israel had a christomorphic pattern, and the evidences of this came to literal and verbal expression at occasional, unpredictable, but repeated points.

Anyway, the existence of this sort of interpretation, which both had the support of, and conversely influenced, the major doctrinal theologian Karl Barth, a close friend of Vischer's, caused scholars to look more eagerly for a mode of understanding which would both do justice to the newer theological trends and also have a more solid base in the modern traditions of Old Testament scholarship.

One interesting and influential attempt to cope with this problem came from

Otto Eissfeldt, a distinguished scholar in Old Testament and in Near Eastern religious history, and one known more for his excellent work in that area than for theological originality.[6] This being so, it was all the more striking that he put forward a proposal which was still being quoted and supported many years later. In his essay of 1926 he argued that two entirely different approaches to the Old Testament are possible, the first a scientific, historical-critical one, and the second a theological one, and that they operate through entirely different modes of cognition. If the one looks for history, the other looks for revelation; and if the former works by reason, the latter works by faith. The only danger would come about if the two modes of operation were allowed to become confused. This was, in effect, the giving of permission to the practitioners of the new theological exegesis to carry on with their own kind of work, provided that they did not attempt to bring it inside the doors of the club of academic Old Testament exegesis. The proposal was historically significant. Though Eissfeldt himself did not write an Old Testament Theology, and indeed seems to have done little to follow up this early essay, his article had later influence, both through those who explicitly rejected his proposal and through those who accepted it.

The rejection of it was a feature of the Old Testament Theology of Eichrodt which, though not exactly the earliest, was the clearest and best realization of the approach to the subject in that early stage, and which – contrary to some expectations – has perhaps remained the most satisfactory and the one most followed by later writers in the field.[7]

The task of Old Testament theology, according to Eichrodt, was to detect and describe the fundamental underlying structure of the 'Old Testament world of faith'. Accepting the fact of historical development, and the reality of elements held in common with other religions, it will nevertheless work out a comprehensive statement, 'a cross-section through the historical process, thus laying bare the inner structure of the religion and the relationship of its various contents to each other. It will then become manifest what are the constants in Old Testament religion.'[8] And, according to Eichrodt, this operation lay entirely within *die alttestamentliche Wissenschaft*, within recognized scholarly study. It did not belong to the 'normative disciplines', as he called them, such as dogmatic theology or philosophy, and it did not involve appeals to special modes of cognition, to faith, or to special kinds of authority.

Eichrodt's scheme had a 'double aspect' and looked towards two opposed problem areas. On the one side there was the comparative study of religions. It was obvious that there were manifold contacts and similarities between the Old Testament and the 'whole world of Near Eastern religion'. But – and this is implied rather than expressly stated at this point – these contacts and similarities have to be seen in relation to the total context within Israel, a context which would be very different from the total context for the same phenomenon within another religion, e.g. that of Mesopotamia or of Egypt or of Ugarit. The cross-section plan therefore did something to cope positively with the influence of comparative religion.

On the other side Eichrodt maintained that there was an essential relationship between the two Testaments and that Old Testament theology must do justice to this; the essential uniqueness of the Old Testament could be grasped only when it was completed in Christ. Nevertheless he envisaged the work of Old Testament theology basically as a descriptive and synthetic one, and thought that the neglect of precisely this approach had greatly impoverished Old Testament study. There is a 'movement' in Old Testament religion which, though occasionally obstructed, always 'breaks through once more, reaching out to a higher form of life'. This movement 'does not come to rest until the manifestation of Christ, in whom the noblest powers of the Old Testament find their fulfilment'. That which binds the two Testaments together is 'the irruption of the Kingdom of God into this world and its establishment here'. This is the unitive fact 'because it rests on the action of one and the same God in each case'. The central message of the New Testament leads us back to the testimony of God in the old covenant. And there is not only a historical movement from the Old towards the New, there is also 'a current of life flowing in the reverse direction from the New Testament to the Old'. The synthetic, comprehensive picture now being built up must do justice to this essential relationship with the New Testament.

From this question of relations with the New Testament Eichrodt goes on to a survey of the rise of historical method, which he sees, interestingly, as having at first brought about an important advance as against older rationalism with its 'meaningless confusion of *disiecta membra*'. Dismissing the intellectualist view, which looked only for doctrine, the historical approach made it possible 'to grasp the totality of religious life in all its richness of expression'. This reaches its high-water mark with Wellhausen. But meanwhile it becomes obvious that the systematic approach was being severely neglected. This had had a fatal influence on Old Testament theology, because 'it fostered the idea that once the historical problems were clarified everything had been done'. Thus the essential inner coherence of the Old and New Testaments was reduced 'to a thin thread of historical connection and causal sequence' instead of a 'homogeneity that was real because it rested on the similar content of their experience of life'. As a result the Old Testament had 'completely lost any effective place in the structure of Christian doctrine'. In face of this 'full flood of historicism' there was no longer any unity to be found in the Old Testament. Old Testament theology had nothing much left to do and, not surprisingly, such products as it did bring forth were more aptly named histories of Israelite religion.

It is high time, therefore, that the 'tyranny of historicism in Old Testament studies' should be broken. We must understand the Old Testament world of faith in its structural unity. There are indeed difficulties. The religion of Israel has a quality which obstinately resists all efforts to subject it to systematic treatment. This is partly because it is acutely personal and historical, the very factor which has tempted scholars to stick to the tracing of a historical development. Thus the historical cannot be neglected or pushed aside. The right policy is 'to have the historical principle operating side by side with the systematic in a complementary role'.

Eichrodt's solution thus answered, or at least offered to answer, all the needs sketched above. By contrast with analytic study, it was synthetic; by contrast with comparativism, it promised to disengage what was distinctive; by penetrating to underlying structures rather than superficial details, it offered a more profound level of meaning; in principle, it hoped to do all this through its comprehensive and synthetic approach. It also suggested, rather more vaguely, that a comprehensive and synthetic appreciation of the Old Testament would also provide the essential connections with the New; and, of course, by calling itself a 'theology' and not a history of religion, it aligned itself with the rising tendencies in doctrinal theology. While highly critical of anything like a 'domination' of historical study, it avoided any suggestion of a pure anti-critical fundamentalism by accepting the historical as a complementary aspect along with the systematic – this again in parallel with similar trends in doctrinal theology. With Eichrodt, many of the essentials for the re-establishment of Old Testament theology as a recognized discipline were realized. Not all of these aspects, as we shall see, were equally attended to or realized in the resultant product. But the combination of them provided the shape of the aspirations which were to motivate much Old Testament theology.

His was nevertheless only one among a variety of types of Old Testament theology which were proposed in the seminal period of about 1930–1960, and the next chapter will seek to identify their various features and emphases and to analyse some of the differences between them.

# 3

# A Typology of Old Testament Theologies

As it turned out, then, Eichrodt's was only one – though certainly one of the finest representatives – of the volumes entitled 'Old Testament Theology' or the like that were to appear. I shall suggest that there were four or five different manifestations of this general movement. The first four types could be called the 'classic' types, and they culminated in the work of von Rad about 1960. To these I add a fifth type, the 'canonical approach' as developed by Professor Childs, which began to be adumbrated around 1970 but did not appear in the form of full Theologies until the 1980s and 1990s. There are numerous other forms of Old Testament theology, some of which will be discussed, and many of these have individual forms and patterns which do not necessarily fit into the typology set up here; indeed their importance lies in the fact that they mostly do not do so. Nevertheless for the sake of clarity it is useful to start with a fairly simple classification of the types which have been most discussed. They are designated and classified as follows:

| *Principle* | *Best example* |
|---|---|
| 1. Collection of ideas and doctrines, on a pattern said to follow that of traditional systematic theology | Köhler |
| 2. Synthetic, comprehensive view of the Old Testament world of faith | Eichrodt |
| 3. Explicit Christian approach working with Christian view of revelation | Vriezen |
| 4. Following out of development of various traditions, with their own inner reinterpretations and actualizations | von Rad |
| 5. 'Canonical' approaches | Childs |

In this chapter I shall provide a brief introduction to each of these five types, and after that I shall go back again over all five in order to discuss more deeply some of the characteristics and problems of each.

*1. Köhler's type*

Although the previous chapter concentrated on the development which led up
to Eichrodt, there were other works entitled 'Old Testament Theology' which
were contemporary or indeed had appeared slightly earlier. Among these was
the work of his Swiss contemporary Ludwig Köhler,[1] well known as a lexi-
cographer of Hebrew and, theologically, identified with 'liberal' thought and
thus remote from the demands of dialectical theology.[2] Köhler defines his work
rather simply: the task of Old Testament theology is to 'contain a systematic
representation of the religious views, thoughts and conceptions which are contained in the Old Testament taken as a whole'. He organized his presentation
under the three heads of 'God', 'Man', and 'Judgment and Salvation'. Though
many were to object to this on the grounds that it repeated the traditional
Christian dogmatic categorization of material under the heads of theology,
anthropology and soteriology, Köhler himself was not worried and followed this
pattern unconcernedly. 'The Old Testament itself does not offer any scheme for
that compilation we call its theology,' he wrote. He was quite aware, indeed, that
it was difficult to fit everything in. He found no quite natural place for a treatment of the ritual and sacrificial cult, since it has to do, he thought, with man's
mistaken effort to save himself by his own works. He therefore included this
aspect as an appendix to the section on the doctrine of man, which to some
readers seemed shocking. To Köhler this was no grave issue. He was easy-going
about it. Köhler was much less a serious theologian than most of the others who
wrote such books. Since the biblical material did not offer its own classification
of itself, the ordering of it in a modern Theology was a matter of convenience,
or one of usefulness or ease of intelligibility to the reader. Such at least was the
impression given by his approach.

Though Köhler himself might not have worried about his principle of
organization or about his adoption of (allegedly) a traditional Christian
doctrinal scheme, others after him were to worry a great deal about these same
questions. The opinion of Eichrodt that the Old Testament *did* provide its own
organizing principle carried greater favour on the whole. Nevertheless there
were plenty of others, as well as Köhler, who thought that one could work
reasonably well with some given scheme of organization, even if it could not be
validated on the basis of the Old Testament texts themselves. Thus the
American Episcopal scholar R. C. Dentan, who wrote one of the early Old
Testament Theologies (1950), also followed a traditional pattern of the same
kind (theology, anthropology, soteriology); and the same was the case with
several Theologies of Roman Catholic origin.

Against this approach there were essentially two different lines of opposition.
The first was to say that the Old Testament *did* provide its own centre and

scheme of organization. Eichrodt himself so argued. The covenant, coupled with the relational scheme of 'God and [people, world, man?]', furnished the centre. Equally, however, it generated a very substantial debate: if the 'centre' was not, as Eichrodt maintained, the covenant, what then was the centre? The second was to say that the Old Testament was not interested in ideas anyway, so that the collection and classification of ideas, however organized, could not properly represent its interests at all. 'There is a real question as to whether biblical faith can be compressed into a "system" at all,' wrote George Ernest Wright in his influential *God Who Acts* (1952, 31). Criticizing the work of Dentan, he pointed out 'the fact that the biblical writers were uninterested in ideas in the sense that we are. They were not primarily systematic teachers of religious ideas' (ibid., 37).

Nevertheless, ideas were likely to remain important for any work that called itself a Theology. What, after all, was Wright's *God Who Acts* but a plea for the *idea* that the God of Israel acted in history and that this idea was a different one from anything that could be found in the environing polytheism? Why should not the ideas implied by the biblical text be organized and presented, even if not very systematically? Köhler is thus perhaps the best representative of a group of Old Testament theologians who organized their work on the basis of a scheme that seemed, wherever it was derived from, to be *familiar to the reader* and there-fore useful and intelligible, rather than on the basis of a scheme that was rigorously derived from the textual material itself. Though the material was derived from the text, the organization and presentation were based on what could make sense to the reader.


## 2. Eichrodt's type

Eichrodt's starting-point and first arguments have already been adequately out-lined in the last chapter. But we have to say something about his organizing principle. Eichrodt himself, though insistent on the synthetic aims of the discipline and its systematic affinities, emphasized that the organization must not be dictated by any 'dogmatic scheme'.[3] The Old Testament contained very little actual *doctrine*. The Israelite knew about God through the standards and usages of law and cult. Through these he gained 'daily experience of the rule of God', and 'by this means he comprehends the divine essence much more accurately than he would by any number of abstract concepts'. Eichrodt was critical of those other writers who adopted a traditional outline from doctrinal theology, such as that of 'God-man-sin'. The arrangement, he thought, must spring from the Old Testament material itself. Otherwise alien ideas would be introduced. His own organization, which he regarded as given by the Old

Testament's own dialectic, was a double one. On the one hand he worked with a triple division. The Old Testament's own dialectic, he asserted, 'speaks of a revelation of the God of the People, who in his rule proves himself to be the God of the World and the God of the Individual'. From this followed his scheme: 1. God and People; 2. God and World; 3. God and Man. In this he followed the organization used by Otto Procksch (the latter had been Eichrodt's teacher, but his own Old Testament Theology was published only later and posthumously).[4] These three formed the substance of Eichrodt's three volumes (which were actually published as two).

But he combined with this a unitary principle, and it would be more true to say that the controlling concept in Eichrodt's work is that of the covenant, the dominant influence of which is to be seen especially in the first volume on 'God and People'.

The centrality of the covenant – and Eichrodt means essentially the covenant *with Moses* on Sinai, or at least this is the covenant that he uses in his main initial arguments – brings together several different things that are all dear to Eichrodt's heart. The covenant is there in all the sources including the earliest; even if the word *b<sup>e</sup>rit* is absent, the meaning is still there; ever afterwards, all thoughts of a gracious God go back to it; it is a bilateral relational term; and all these, taken together, lead on to an exposition of the theological values deriving from it.[5]

And 'covenant' was not a bad choice.[6] Many disputed it, and made other suggestions for the 'centre', as we shall see; but in doing so they at least followed Eichrodt's general principle, that some organizing centre from within the Old Testament material should be found. And, though many other suggestions for the centre were made, probably no one of them received a higher degree of acceptance than Eichrodt's covenant. Yet there was, as usual, a paradoxical side to this. Eichrodt's argument in favour of a new scheme of Old Testament theology had laid great weight on the importance of connection with the New Testament; yet in precisely this connection he had made a rather poor choice, for it was fairly easy to show that, whatever the New Testament had taken as basic concept from the Old, 'covenant' it was not.[7] His contention that the covenant of the Old Testament was really the same thing as the Kingdom of God in the New – an argument not explicit in his *Theology* itself but made express in his French article of 1955 and therefore probably present in his mind all along – is really too strange to be taken seriously. In one way this might look like a weakness. On the other side it was possibly a strength, for it meant that his arguments for the centrality of the covenant were in fact entirely based within the Old Testament itself, which is what his own principles required, and not on the putative connections with the New. Such, anyway, was the basis of the structure that he set up.

It is probable that, of the Old Testament Theologies written during the central period 1930–1980, the majority followed something roughly like Eichrodt's general approach.[8] An indication of this is the widespread discussion of the question of a 'centre' of the Old Testament. This arose indeed from dissatisfaction with Eichrodt's identification of the covenant as the centre; but the attempt to identify and define the centre in another way shows that the general plan of Eichrodt, a synthetic and structural account with a definable centre, still prevailed.

## 3. Vriezen's type

A marked contrast can be seen in the work of the Dutch scholar T. C. Vriezen, or at least in the principles which he set out (for, as will be seen, his actual product may not have differed so much). The idea of a synthetic and comprehensive description, which we have seen argued by Eichrodt, is in Vriezen's opinion not enough to make the work into a *theology*. It is no more than 'the phenomenological branch of theological study' and it 'indicates the historical and phenomenological position of the religion of the Old Testament amid the religious life of the nations and of Christianity'.[9] Though Eichrodt's work made great advances and overcame the domination of 'developmental historicism and positivism', it still does not go far enough to establish the subject as a *theological science*. And here, somewhat surprisingly,[10] Vriezen returns with strong approval to the earlier position advocated by Eissfeldt: theology is a matter of faith and revelation 'and is concerned with the reality of God and with the faith of the Christian church; for that reason Old Testament theology has its own place alongside the history of the religion of Israel as a separate branch of scholarship' (ibid.). The only objection made by him (following Porteous)[11] against Eissfeldt's position is that the latter, in the fashion of the earlier days of dialectical theology, made theology concerned 'not with the past but with the timeless present; and Old Testament theology must deal with history'. But, granted this point, it remained for Vriezen that: 'Only when Eissfeldt's line of thought is followed out consistently can we arrive at a definition of Old Testament theology which guarantees a science independent in name and content' (122).

The object then is not the religion of Israel but *the Old Testament*, i.e. 'the Old Testament *as* the Holy Scriptures of the Jews, and more especially of the Christians' – this seems to imply, with some degree of justice, that Eichrodt's Theology had its base ultimately in the religion of Israel rather than in the books of the Hebrew Bible – and, since it is a kind of theology, and since theology is about revelation (120), it 'seeks particularly the element of revelation in the message of the Old Testament' (122). The connection with the New Testament is not occasional or accidental but must be integral to the whole operation: the study is 'a part of Christian theology' and 'gives an insight into the Old Testament message and a judgment of this message from the point of view of the Christian faith'. Again, there was perhaps some justice in implying that Eichrodt, although he had emphasized the linkage between Old and New Testament, had worked in effect from the Old and thought that, if properly understood, it would provide a sort of bridge to the New. Anyway, Vriezen emphasized the New Testament as the viewing point from which the whole question could be seen.

How this principle was worked out by Vriezen remains to be discussed. But one point should be made here. As with many works of biblical theology, there was a difference between the principles as set forth and the actuality of the work that resulted; indeed, differences between principle and performance have been a sign of the poor theoretical coherence of biblical theology from the beginning. In Vriezen's case, this weakness is manifested in one particular way: his work exists in two parts, the first on the principles, the second on the actual content of Old Testament theology. What has been said above depends very largely on the first part. In the second part, however, when Vriezen turns to the actual content, it is not clear that he is really following the methodological principles for which he himself has argued, or that he has really turned away from Eichrodt's method which he criticized. For the most part, the second portion of his work seems to be another essentially structural production, not greatly influenced by the Christian view of revelation or by relations with the New Testament.[12] Thus, in spite of his vigorous opposition to Eichrodt's conception in the regard mentioned above, it is not clear that he departed so very much from Eichrodt's type in respect of method. He still had to propose a 'centre' around which the Old Testament material, seen mainly on its own terms, had to be organized. But for the present I simply note his enunciation of his principles. Among other theologies which accept something of the same approach I may mention those of G. A. F. Knight and of B. S. Childs (part).[13]

### 4. Von Rad's type

It is difficult to find a simple label for the many-sided and influential theology of Gerhard von Rad. From one point of view it might be called a 'consistently *heilsgeschichtlich*' approach:[14] for, while many Old Testament theologies have emphasized the historical, narrative character of Hebrew theological think-ing, this particular work goes much the farthest towards making this its basic architectonic principle of design. For a simpler term, I am tempted to say that it is an 'imitative' or 'mimetic' approach to Old Testament theology. Von Rad clearly argues (against Eichrodt) that the purpose is not to produce a systematic organization or comprehensive cross-section of the world of faith; here he comes somewhat close to Vriezen's argument that such a work would be a phenomenology rather than a theology.[15] Going beyond this, he seems to say not only that Old Testament theology has to restate the content of the Old Testament but that it can restate it validly only if it follows the form and style in which the Old Testament itself presents it. As I wrote in a full review article in 1962:[16]

> Since the basis of the theological witness of the Old Testament is the *Heilsgeschichte* or history of salvation, the main task and method of a work called 'Old Testament Theology' must be to re-tell this history. In other words, the dominance of *Heilsgeschichte* means that an Old Testament theology must assume a historical form. 'The most legitimate form of theological speech about the Old Testament is always the retelling of narrative (*die Nacherzählung*)' (1, 126). Israel stated its confession in historical statements, and we cannot state it in any other way; we cannot rearrange its order or set it within another framework.

Von Rad thus rejects the idea that Old Testament theology is concerned with the elaboration of a *structure* of the Old Testament 'world of faith'. The subject is emphatically not the Israelite mental or theological world, but 'only what Israel itself has directly enunciated about Yahweh'. Israel did not witness to its own world of faith, but to what Yahweh had done – a comment that seems analogical to the contrast between religion and revelation, which we have seen to be characteristic of dialectical theology. All this implies an almost complete rejection – at least in theory – of the approach I have exemplified from Eichrodt. And, just as that structural approach had been in part at least a reaction away from a historical presentation, so von Rad returns with a flourish to a historical type of organization.

But the 'historical' mode to which von Rad turns is not the same as the 'historical' mode from which the structural approach had turned away. Apart from the special section which he explicitly devoted to the 'History of the Faith in Yahweh', von Rad was not presenting a 'history of Israelite religion' in the older sense. It was more a sequential account of the theological witnesses on the one hand, and an account built upon Yahweh's action in history on the other.

The main body of the book is in two sections. In one he presents the theology of the Hexateuch, and this is worked out as the kerygma of each successive layer of tradition; in the other he presents the theology of the prophetic traditions, and these again follow the sequence of the various prophets and the traditions attached to them. The whole is preceded by a brief historical sketch of Yahwism and followed by a discussion of relations with the New Testament, in which a very considerable emphasis is laid upon typology.

One of the main themes in von Rad's work is the idea of the fresh presentation, 'updating' or 'actualization' (*Vergegenwärtigung*) of older traditions, and this has its background in the particular critical school to which von Rad belonged.[17] In the Hexateuch there were ancient themes, for instance the theme 'Exodus from Egypt' or the theme 'Promise to the Fathers', and these themes attracted to themselves traditional material from a variety of places (local sanctuaries were much emphasized as the seat of traditions). Tradition criticism does not seek to pare off accretions in the hope that it will thus reach exact historical data; rather, by assigning the passages to the basic themes and institutions to which they belonged, it discovers the 'kerygmatic' intention with which they have been used. In this way traditional material is used for continually fresh presentations of the basic *heilsgeschichtlich* creed. Thus the idea of a fresh presentation of an ancient theme of tradition ran throughout the Old Testament; it is also used for von Rad's account of the relationship between the Old Testament and the New, where it controls his use and understanding of typology; and in a sense his own Theology is trying to do just the same thing yet again, to reactualize it all for today.

Almost all work in Old Testament theology, we may say, emphasized *history* as a central category in Israelite faith. But von Rad took it as a methodological principle in a very special way, which both accentuated its importance and also created a certain ambivalence. As has been said, his theological thinking had close analogies to the mode of critical analysis which he followed, and the order in which the various traditions are expounded is more or less an historical order: in Vol. 1 from the Primeval History down through the Patriarchs, the Exodus, Sinai (where much of the Priestly Document is slotted in), the Wilderness, Moses and the entry into Canaan, then under the title 'Israel's Anointed' we have David, the office of the Anointed in the Royal Psalms, Saul, the Judges, the Deuteronomic Theology of History (which more or less equals the Books of Kings), and the Work of the Chronicler.

Volume 2 carries us down from the traces of early prophecy, along with general features of the prophetic movement, through Amos and Hosea, Isaiah and Micah, to Jeremiah, Ezekiel, Deutero-Isaiah, later prophets such as Trito-Isaiah, Haggai, Zechariah and on to Daniel and apocalyptic. So in this aspect the presentation is, as von Rad himself claimed, distant from Eichrodt's cross-section method and close to a picture of historical development.[18]

On the other hand history in the sense of the history related, which is the bearer of the theological message and the milieu in which God distinctively revealed himself, is something rather different: it is not history as the historian sees and relates it; it is rather the history as Israel 'confessed' it or 'witnessed to' it. This cleft between history as it really happened (if we may be permitted that phrase!) and the history as it is told in the Old Testament is probably a matter of importance for any Old Testament theology; but for one which insists on history as a central guiding category, and which at the same time insists on the re-telling of the history as Israel itself told it, the problem becomes extremely severe. And it is this point more than any other that has suffered criticism from von Rad's critics, from such different viewpoints as those of Hesse, of Eichrodt, of Conzelmann, and, to include a doctrinal theologian, of Pannenberg. This question is one to which we shall have to return.

Von Rad does not spend much time in arguing with his predecessors in Old Testament theology: he mentions Köhler and Eichrodt only occasionally. The first page of his Preface indicates a strong sense of deep difference between the various works calling themselves 'Theology of the Old Testament'. He found it amazing that 'under one and the same title such different works could be offered as the "Theology of the Old Testament" by E. Jacob or T. C. Vriezen on the one hand, and on the other, the one offered in this book'. This could be explained only on the ground that 'no agreement has been reached up to now as to what really is the proper subject of . . . a Theology of the Old Testament'.[19] There was, then, in his mind a wide gap between what others had done and what he was doing.

It is not surprising therefore that he shows a distinct coolness towards his German-language predecessors, Köhler and Eichrodt. In the Postscript added to his second volume he looks back at the hopes raised by the prospect of a 'systematic' approach to the subject, and he writes:

> In many respects new territory was then opened up by the important works of Köhler and Eichrodt. The question today is, of course, whether there was then firmly established a system which allows the contents of the Old Testament to be developed in a really pertinent and organic way. And, in spite of the great stimulus which all Old Testament scholars have received from Köhler and Eichrodt, we have to give the answer 'No'.[20]

Again, speaking of the theological revival which began in the 1920s and which 'became again conscious of its special theological task' as exemplified by Eichrodt's work, and acknowledging his own great debt to it, he passes the judgment that 'even here Old Testament theology has still not yet completely envisaged its proper subject'.[21]

This seems to have been von Rad's main criticism of his predecessors: they had done excellent work, but they had not succeeded in getting a grasp of what was the real subject-matter of Old Testament theology. They had worked hard on the 'concepts' – here he linked their work with the *Theologisches Wörterbuch zum Neuen Testament* of Kittel and Friedrich – and this had provided excellent material. But, in a key sentence, von Rad goes on: 'Whether their results – knowledge of the concepts of "faith", "righteousness", "the covenant", "the sacrifices", "zeal", "the glory of God", etc. – play a part as constitutive elements in a theology of the Old Testament is another question.'[22] One might laboriously put together these concepts and arrive at a complex of ideas, but the effect could only be a generalized and abstract depiction. Thus 'a theology which attempts to grasp the content of the Old Testament under the heading of various doctrines (the doctrine of God, the doctrine of man, etc.) cannot do justice to these credal statements which are completely tied up with history'.[23] Again, at 1, 356 he refers to recent attempts to describe the biblical picture of 'man', a 'neutral method of taking a cross-section', and it is likely that he is referring to Köhler's *Hebrew Man* and/or Eichrodt's *Man in the Old Testament*. These works have produced 'general concepts of man which theologically do not amount to much': they amount to no more than 'a variant of the understanding of man generally common in the ancient East'.

Thus the new starting-point lies in the way in which traditions were built upon ancient credal affirmations. Von Rad greatly emphasized these short, ancient, historical credal statements, of which the central example was Deuteronomy 26.5–11:

> A wandering Aramaean was my father and he went down into Egypt . . . and the Lord brought us out of Egypt with a mighty hand . . . and behold now I bring the first of the fruit . . . (RSV).

'If there is any truth in the recognition that the whole of the Hexateuch is built upon a very few ancient credal statements which became constitutive for the Israel of all ages, then this is so important that a theology of the Old Testament would practically have to start out from this fact.'[24] Probably the most important part of Israel's theological activity lies in 'those ever new attempts to make the divine acts of salvation relevant for every new age and day – this ever new reaching out to and avowal of God's acts which in the end made the old credal statements grow into such enormous masses of traditions'. The credal statements are 'completely tied up with history' and 'this grounding of Israel's faith upon a few divine acts of salvation and the effort to gain an ever new understanding of them'[25] forms the basis for von Rad's new departure in Old Testament theology.

With this we have gained an insight into some of the basic characteristics of von Rad's approach:

(*a*) The linkage of his theology with the tradition criticism practised especially by Noth and himself. That critical method dovetails into the theological method and provides some of the essential insights into the theological directions believed to be implied by the texts.

(*b*) As against a theology based upon concepts, upon a 'world of faith', upon generalizations, a theology that seemed to be static and unhistorical, von Rad works through a variety of theologies which are historically linked.

(*c*) From the beginning we see, in the effort to 'gain an ever new understanding of' ancient credal statements, the path which, according to von Rad, will provide a typological scheme and thus lead to integration with the New Testament.

(*d*) The idea of 'witness' or 'testimony' follows and re-enacts the distinction between religion and revelation characteristic of dialectical theology (see above, Ch. 2). Israel does not 'witness to' its own concepts or its own world of faith: it witnesses to what Yahweh has done. This principle on the one hand provides a linkage with the stress on revelation through historical deeds, and on the other hand is supposed to undermine the kind of approach represented by Köhler and Eichrodt.

This is sufficient to furnish a first introduction to von Rad's thinking. We shall return later to consider some of the problems in it.

Although many of those working in the field have considered von Rad's Theology to be the best single product of the kind, few of those who came after his time have in fact followed his pattern. As mentioned above, it is Eichrodt's general pattern that has been more commonly followed. The numerous attempts to define the 'centre' of the Old Testament, though much differing from one another, make it clear that von Rad's denial that there was *any* centre at all had not given satisfaction. The one main Theology written after von Rad which belonged very much to his own style and pattern was that of Westermann (German 1978).

## 5. Childs' type

Here we introduce the best-known of the 'canonical' approaches. In a series of well-known works, much discussed, Brevard Childs has developed an approach to Old Testament theology in which the *canon* is the basic principle. In his *Biblical Theology in Crisis* (1970) he sketched the rise of the 'Biblical Theology Movement' and, as he saw it, its decline.[26] In spite of its apparent lack of success, it represented values that were indispensable. He experimented with ideas centred upon the canon, which he thought might lead to a new and more successful revival of biblical theology. The failure of the movement, he thought, could be explained on the grounds that it had not sufficiently taken the canon into consideration. His commentary on *Exodus* (1974) developed some of these ideas further in a direct exegetical situation. His *Introduction to the Old Testament as Scripture* (1979) worked through each book in turn, arguing that traditional historical criticism had led to inadequacies, antinomies, and failures in appreciation, all of which would be resolved if sufficient attention was given to the canon. His *The New Testament as Canon. An Introduction* (1984) sought to cover roughly the same ground for the New Testament. In 1985 his *Old Testament Theology in a Canonical Context* appeared (= *OTTCC*), a rather slight treatment of what was, after all, supposed to be his own major theme. In 1993 there came his *Biblical Theology of the Old and New Testaments* (= *Biblical Theology*), a large and sprawling work which, we may presume, represents the culmination of the canonical approach. Along with these I must mention numerous articles in which aspects of the canonical approach are explained or defended.[27]

'Canon' is meant by Childs in all of several senses: first, canon as the collection of sacred books which must be seen as all belonging together; secondly, canon as the final, canonical shape of each book; and thirdly, canon as a holistic mode of appreciation ('construal', one of his favourite words).

A full discussion of the impact of this work upon Old Testament and biblical theology must be left until later. But certain outlines must be mentioned here. First, Old Testament theology is considered to be expressly a Christian activity, corresponding to the canonical place of the Old Testament (as the term 'Old' indicates). Interaction with the New Testament is a normal and essential part in its activity. Secondly, there is much stress on the irrelevance of historical and critical work: such work is not in itself totally illegitimate, but it belongs outside the proper theological enterprise. The 'final text' is what matters, and 'reconstruction' of historically earlier forms and stages is speculative and theologically valueless. Theological evaluation reaches its highest point in 'canonical' perceptions. Thirdly, not only does *critical* history lose its importance, but the *theological history*, *Heilsgeschichte* and the like, which had been so stressed by other writers, also fades into the background: in *OTTCC*, 36ff., 'Revelation through history' is only the third in a series of sections on revelation, coming after revelation through (*a*) creation and (*b*) wisdom, but before (*d*) revelation through the name [of God]. The emphasis is much more on theology established through the total text than on history, even the history of revelation. Fourthly, some of the problems that have concerned earlier Old Testament theologies seem also to fade away. Thus the question of the history of religion and influences from other religions magically disappears: since everything depends on the books as we have them, they are authoritative as Israel's 'confession', independently of where their content may have come from. Scholarship which seeks to answer theological questions through the history of religion is treated with extreme negativity throughout.

Some of these points are not so very novel: that Old Testament theology is a distinctly Christian enterprise had been affirmed by several, notably Vriezen, as we saw above. That Old Testament theology set out to provide something *different* from historical-critical interpretation had been widely acknowledged from Eichrodt's time onwards. And in a sense, as I shall elaborate later, most Old Testament Theologies were 'canonical' in character, though they did not make the point as vigorously as Childs has done. Nevertheless the combination of the features of 'canon', as set forth by Childs, has produced a quite new over-all departure in the subject.

Other examples of 'canonical' approach may be seen in Sanders (though thus far only in the form of a brief sketch, and not as yet in the form of anything like a full Theology), perhaps in Clements, and in Rendtorff (cf. Preuss, 20f.)

At this point I insert a preliminary discussion of some of the points of difference between the main types I have thus disengaged.

## 6. *Köhler again*

The first type, represented by Köhler, Dentan and several Roman Catholic Theologies like that of van Imschoot, was criticized, as I have said, for working with a simple organizational scheme such as 'God-man-sin', or in longer words 'theology-anthropology-soteriology'. These, it was often said, were Christian dogmatic schemes and therefore imported an alien categorization into the Old Testament.

It is doubtful, however, whether this criticism is an accurate one. There is nothing particularly Christian about a scheme like 'God-man-sin'. A distinctively Christian scheme might be something like 'Father-Son-Holy Spirit' or 'Trinity-Incarnation-Resurrection', but no one seems to have approached Old Testament theology with such a proposal. 'God-man-sin' seems to be rather a simple common-sense approach. Suppose that one is parachuted among some formerly unknown people and wants to give a survey of their religion, or suppose that one has to write a short encyclopaedia article on some theology, one might take it as an obvious set of starting-points: does this religion have a god or gods, what are they like, what sort of view of humanity does it entail, does it have anything to say about evil or does it profess to do any good for man or for the world? One would end up with the scheme of God-man-sin/salvation or something like it. It may not be perfect, but it is a rather obvious starting classification. There is nothing either Christian or dogmatic about it. If Christian dogmatics has used it, which may be very likely, the reason is that dogmatics also accepted it as a useful common-sense approach. It is not clear therefore that it is necessarily so very distorting in its effect. Moreover, even if distortions can be found in the work of those who have used this style of presentation, it may be that they are the consequence of inefficiency in use of this method, rather than in the method itself.

Thus, in discussing some examples, and in particular the work of Roman Catholic writers like García Cordero, and the criticisms directed from within Old Testament theology against the use of this approach, Hayes and Prussner quote Terrien's opinion:

> It is now recognized that such attempts, inherited in part from Platonic conceptual thinking and Aristotelian logic, were bound to translate the *sui generis* thrust of biblical faith into the alien idiom of didactic exposition.[28]

They go on to say: 'Such a verdict seems overly harsh.' I think that they are right in this. They continue:

> The organization of the material along such lines can contribute to the integration of biblical perspectives into both the confessional life of religious communities and the more academic pursuit of theology proper and it does so in categories and structures that are certainly at home in both of these areas.

Again this seems to be both right and suggestive. The customary criticism has surely been unfair to scholars like Köhler, Dentan, van Imschoot and Cordero. Moreover, it leads on to a more profound question, which Hayes and Prussner do not raise and which, so far as I know, has not been basically faced anywhere in the literature of biblical theology: what if the theological structure *ought to be and must be* one brought from without and inserted into the material? What if the ideal of a theological structure derived purely from *within* the material is a will-of-the-wisp, perhaps a fundamentally biblicistic dream that the Bible will supply, generate and control its own theology? After all, it has been a common judgment of those Old Testament scholars who stand outside Old Testament theology that any theology it 'finds' has in fact been read into the text or imposed upon it. What if this is the truth, and if so, would it not be better to accept that the theology is a scheme, a model, *applied to* the text, rather than one derived from it by some explicit authority?

It may well be true that there are weaknesses in the 'collection of ideas' type of Old Testament Theology. But it seems mistaken to identify it as the result of a pattern taken from dogmatics. We saw that some, objecting to this approach, rejected the notion of a 'system' of 'ideas'. But those who worked in this way thought so too. Köhler himself, for instance, expressly said that he chose his scheme precisely in order to avoid that result: 'no scheme could be borrowed either from the New Testament or from systematic theology if it were going to obtrude itself. A very simple scheme has therefore been chosen . . .'[29] Köhler was no lover of dogmatic theology, and he stressed the non-systematic character of Hebrew thought in just the same way as most others did: thus he wrote: 'It is typical of the unsystematic nature of the Old Testament revelation that its spirit terminology is extensive' (139).

The real defect in the 'collection of ideas' approach seems to be its tendency to overlook the strongly *narrative* character of much of the material. Even when ample biblical material is presented, as is often the case in these works, it tends to end up with a collection of rather obvious attributes. Look for instance at Köhler's section 30 on 'God upholds the world' (90f.). Numerous passages are cited and strung together, but they all seem so obvious, the impression given is rather superficial, and in the end what do we learn from it?

Another possible criticism would be to say that the questions were ill adapted, not because they were too simple, but because they were too much directed towards the collection of *ideas*. They are the *topoi* of traditional theology. Clements makes just such a criticism.[30] The 'growing interest in a phenomenological approach to the study of religion' not only shifted the emphasis 'away from simple evaluations of religions in terms of their fundamental ideas, but it challenged the very basis of what had become an essentially "ideological" approach to the study of religions in which rites and institutions were treated as secondary to, and sometimes claimed to be derivative from, a number of basic religious concepts. For example the study of rites of sacrifice had tended to be treated as an expression of ideas of atonement, with little real interest in the rites themselves.' Thus according to Clements the impact of this kind of phenomenology of religion, plus increased knowledge of the ancient religions of Mesopotamia, Egypt and Canaan themselves, brought about this shift.[31]

This is a better explanation of the turn against 'collections of ideas' than others that we have considered. Seen in this way, rather than looking for the ideas under rubrics like 'God-man-sin', we might do better to look for narratives, practices and institutions under a set of headings such as 'stories-practices-institutions'. This might well be suggestive, but major theologies built on such a pattern have not as yet appeared.

## 7. Eichrodt again

When we turn to the structural or cross-section type, we find ambiguities once again, both in the claims that were made and the criticisms that were directed against them. Eichrodt, as we saw, was one of those who rejected the collection-of-ideas approach on the grounds that it was of dogmatic origin, and put forward his own scheme: 1. God and People; 2. God and World; 3. God and Man – which, he claimed, emerged from the material itself.

This claim, however, is misleading. It would be more correct to say that Eichrodt's scheme itself was also of dogmatic origin. Perhaps its origin did not lie in the *older* dogmatic tradition: all the more obvious is its close kinship with the *recent* dogmatics of dialectical theology. For nothing is more clear in this modern dogmatic approach than its *relational* emphasis: it speaks not of God alone, but of *God and*. This was elementary. 'The biblical revelation in the Old and New Testament deals with the relation of God to men and of men to God. It contains no doctrine of God as he is in himself, none of man as he is in himself,' wrote Emil Brunner.[32] That the same applied to the relation between God and the world was likewise elementary. That God dealt primarily with a people and only secondarily with the individual human person was again a standard opinion. All along the line the very scheme which was advocated because of its non-dogmatic character and its basis in the material itself was in fact an assimilation to a normal current dogmatic approach. This is not said to discredit it: one may say that it was indeed dogmatic, but it did also fit the material very well. Quite so. But it is mistaken to suppose that it excels over any other simply through being more removed from the dogmatic. The approval which this part of Eichrodt's scheme certainly received came largely, though often unconsciously, from its *closeness* to the dogmatic tendencies then dominant.

Thus when George Coats writes that 'Eichrodt's theology was epoch-making because he broke decisively with the pattern of exegesis current at the time, which sought structural unity from the categories of systematic theology',[33] I fully understand what he means but would rephrase this as: 'Eichrodt's theology was epoch-making because he identified himself decisively with the new pattern of exegesis becoming current at the time and found structural unity through assimilation to the categories of the newer systematic theology.'

As for the other part, namely the use of the covenant as organizer, this too could easily be explained as closely related to dogmatic traditions, and especially those of Calvinism. The insistence on the key role of covenants as a theological organizer is manifest in Calvinist tradition; among Old Testament theologians, compare its place in Zimmerli and Childs.[34] Scholars of Lutheran tradition, on the other hand, seem to find it easier to see this concept as late in origin, limited in textual evidence, or otherwise ill fitted to have any controlling function.[35] It is particularly in the Calvinist tradition, if I am not mistaken, that there is the custom of referring to 'the' covenant as a basic theological datum, and also the idea of a number of contrasting covenants (e.g. a 'covenant of works' and a 'covenant of grace').[36] The relationship to Eichrodt's theology is rather strong.

## 8. Vriezen again

In the third type, for which I have taken Vriezen as the primary example, we have noted the problem created by the disparity between his prolegomena section, which makes it clear that Old Testament theology is in his opinion a distinctively Christian operation, and his content section, which appears scarcely to fulfil this methodological plan. Another problem is this: when Old Testament theology is a distinctively Christian operation, then the lines of its distinction from Christian dogmatics must become faint or uncertain. To 'seek particularly the element of revelation in the message of the Old Testament' and to produce 'a judgment of this message from the point of view of the Christian faith' – if this is to be done, how is it to be done, except by dogmatic theology? How can a theology do this and still call itself 'biblical theology'? Or, to put it in another way, if biblical theology can do this, then what is left for dogmatic theology to do?

Moreover, if the task is to 'seek particularly the element of revelation in the message of the Old Testament', this would seem to imply that the material of the text can be divided as between what are elements of revelation and what are not. But Vriezen's carrying out of his programme appears not to perform this. Does it anywhere say of any element that it is not revelation? Does it separate out the revelatory elements at all? I do not find in the book *any* substantial elements of the Old Testament material that are designated as not being revelation. There are indeed points at which he indicates a *deficiency* in the Old Testament, an aspect where it has, in his judgment, failed to realize some concept known from the New Testament. Thus he judges that:

> In the Old Testament we find no unequivocal pronouncement on the sinful nature of man which is brought out so severely and emphatically in the New Testament . . . [In the Old Testament] the consciousness of sin is still too fragmentary . . . There is no awareness of belonging to the *massa perditionis* because of sin which creates a gulf between God and man (285).[37]

Even this, however, falls short of declaring an element in the Old Testament not to be revelation: it suggests, rather, a judgment that the Old Testament *is* revelation but still defective or imperfect revelation.

Perhaps the only way to understand it is to suppose that everything actually *mentioned* in Vriezen's Theology is considered by him to be an element of revelation, while if things are left out and nothing is said about them then they are not. Such elements might include, for example, the detail of some of the stories (the 'saving history' is discussed in principle, 192–7, but the narrative detail is mostly left aside) or the connection of the religion with the *land* of Israel. But, if this is meant, it is strange to regard elements as non-revelatory without actual discussion and without an explanation of the reasons why this decision is made.

Deeper consideration suggests a different explanation of what Vriezen meant in his criticism of Eichrodt. As indicated above, there seems to be unfairness in his categorization of the latter's work as purely 'phenomenological', as not concerned with revelation or as not involved with the New Testament or with Christian theology.

In fact, I suggest, Eichrodt believed his work to be all these things in its results. Perhaps Vriezen was disturbed by Eichrodt's clear principle that Old Testament theology, as carried out by him, did not belong to 'the normative sciences' such as dogmatics or philosophy (whether philosophy is really a 'normative' discipline may be left aside for the present purpose; that is how he classified it). Vriezen, arguing that Old Testament theology must be a part of Christian theology, may have thought that it must be normative, against Eichrodt's view. But if so, this is probably a misunderstanding of Eichrodt.[38] Eichrodt meant that the content of Old Testament theology was not dictated by, or received from, normative sources such as dogmatics or philosophy; it came from the same processes as produced normal academic exegesis and biblical scholarship. Its working was not normatively controlled. And Vriezen probably agreed with this. But the *results* of Old Testament theology were surely, in Eichrodt's mind, normative for Christian theology and in that sense were a part of Christian theology. (There remains a question, in just what way such results could be 'normative'.)

The real difference, which Vriezen indicated but did not bring out very clearly, was something else. Eichrodt implied, if he did not clearly state, an opinion of Calvinist type according to which *everything* in the Old Testament, provided that it was related to, or seen in the light of, the comprehensive 'world of faith', was fully and equally revelatory for Christianity.[39] The New Testament connection was essential for him, as he made clear, but this did not alter the fact that the theology of the Old was in itself fully revelatory for Christianity. It was the Hebrew text in its entirety, as comprehended in a theology which formed a cross-section of the entirety, that fitted with the New Testament. It was here that Vriezen differed. He thought that the connection with the New Testament was essential but that the New Testament took up a *selective* and *critical* stance in relation to the Old. Thus not everything in the Old was fully revelatory in the long run, and so the place of Old Testament theology 'as a part of Christian theology' involved the distinction between what in the Old Testament was revelatory and what was not.

Basic therefore to Vriezen's approach was his conviction that Jesus, and the New Testament generally, was critical towards the Old Testament even while accepting that it was the Word of God and authoritative. This is included in a full exposition in the opening pages of his book, and a long footnote expands upon it:

> In spite of the fact that the Holy Scriptures are admitted to be the Word of God there is a strong sense of freedom . . . Jesus, and later St Paul, expressed ideas in which the critical element is unmistakable (12).

Jesus speaks as one greater than Moses; he sometimes rises above the Holy Scriptures even while never suggesting that these Scriptures have lost their value for him. Vriezen returns to these relationships in an important section on pp. 92ff.:

> The Law has been superseded by Jesus Christ as the central point of revelation . . . the Mosaic Law came to be regarded as intermediate in character, while Abraham's faith became the expression of true revelation. This meant a disintegration of the Law, at any rate a certain reversal of the order . . . The characteristic element of this view is essentially the ambivalence in its appreciation of the Law, and therefore of the Old Testament, which consists in retaining its revelatory character and at the same time abolishing its authority in favour of the Word of God revealed in Christ (94f.).

Vriezen's principles that Old Testament theology is part of Christian theology, should work by Christian faith and seek the element of revelation, should be understood in this way. All these factors require and impose a theologically *critical* and evaluative stance toward the Old Testament. Revelatory value attaches to materials not because they are simply there in the Old Testament but because they somehow fit with these standards. Where they do not, or where they are simply not relevant for these Christian revelatory standards, they are for the most part disregarded. What Vriezen means by his principles that Old Testament theology is part of Christian theology, works by faith and seeks the element of revelation is thus quite different from what some others derive from the same principles. Thus Childs, who approves these same principles of method, would probably disagree with the consequences drawn by Vriezen, if I have interpreted them correctly.

## 9. Von Rad again

The differences between Eichrodt and von Rad were also by no means identical with what these two scholars themselves thought them to be. The modes of presentation were very different. It would be just to categorize Eichrodt's thought as much more rational in character, but with a strong pietistic attitude. Von Rad was much more romantic and poetic. His formulations were at times cloudy and the implications obscurely stated. Though influence from Barth is obvious, a thought-pattern common with that of Bultmann can also be easily observed.[40]

One of the points of difficulty in von Rad's work lay in the place of the *Wisdom literature*. The principle that the re-telling of historical-type narrative is the basic mode of theological statement must, at least at first sight, leave the Wisdom material in a precarious position. The two great presentations, corresponding to the design of his two volumes, were built upon the historical traditions and the prophetic traditions respectively. Where then is the Wisdom tradition to come in? In his Theology, von Rad brings it in towards the end of the first volume, in section D, entitled 'Israel Before YAHWEH (Israel's Answer)'. This includes not only the Wisdom books but also the Psalms and some other materials. Subsection headings include: 1. Methodological Pre-considerations, 2. The Praises of Israel, 3. The Righteousness of Yahweh and of Israel, 4. Israel's Trials and the Consolation of the Individual, 5. Israel's Wisdom deriving from Experience, 6. Israel's Theological Wisdom, 7. Scepticism. The Psalms are the main subject in 2; Job is dealt with in 4 (408–18); Proverbs in 5–6; Qoheleth and some other materials in 7. (It will be remembered that von Rad considered that the story of Joseph belonged to the Wisdom genre and laid considerable emphasis upon this.)[41]

This whole section of the Theology is introduced, as already indicated, under the rubric 'Israel before Yahweh'. These materials are a response to the saving acts of God. Yet it must remain uncertain whether the placing of all this material in *this* context forms, in relation to von Rad's own general plan, an adequate way of incorporating the Wisdom literature into his scheme. For – to voice only the most obvious objection – one of the facts about the Wisdom literature is that much of it does *not* express itself as a response to the saving acts which von Rad has so much emphasized. Does it not suggest that, if the Wisdom literature is really to be incorporated into the total theological structure, that structure would have to be fashioned in a different way from the beginning? In fact von Rad later returned to the Wisdom texts in a fuller and separate book, *The Wisdom of Israel* (1970, ET 1972). This later work, however, though rich in thought and observation, somewhat surprisingly seemed not to go back to the author's own Theology and reconsider the placing of Wisdom in the light of this fuller consideration. One has to assume, if this is right, that von Rad still did not intend any alteration in his theological siting of Wisdom and remained satisfied with the way in which he had described it in his Theology.

One other potential weakness in von Rad's work will be mentioned at this point. As has been seen, his mind turned sharply away from a theology of ideas or concepts, from one based upon the cross-section of a 'world of faith'. Theology should, on the contrary, be based on 'what Israel herself directly enunciated about Yahweh'. Only this latter was 'witness'. This is a clear enough idea, but it is not clear that von Rad himself succeeded in following his own precept at this point. In 2, 99–112 we have a whole section dedicated to 'Israel's Ideas about Time and History', but how is this other than a concept or a part of a cross-section of the world of faith? We have seen above that von Rad strongly criticized the attempts of predecessors to produce – from the totality of the evidence – a picture of 'man in the Old Testament'; but how is what he himself produces, immediately afterwards, in his section on 'The Righteousness of Yahweh and of Israel' and the following one on 'Israel's Trials and the Consolation of the Individual' (370–418), different from an account of the biblical concept of 'righteousness'? What von Rad seems to argue about the idea of man (1, 356) is that previous writers have made a *general* concept, 'summoning up all the material that is in any way relevant' and thus producing a general concept, largely common to the ancient Near East, while his own portrayal will be based only on 'such striking statements . . . over and above those general concepts of man'. This then would seem to mean that these other writers were wrong not in basing themselves upon a concept, but in basing themselves on a *general* concept, while his own work will be based on a limited selection of statements which go beyond that general concept. However, the result will then still be a concept, but one of a more limited, specialized and distinctive kind.

Moreover it is difficult to see how 'history', a key term in von Rad's theology, is other than a *concept* of a complicated and many-sided kind, one which he cannot state succinctly but has to work out in lengthy expositions and exemplifications. But it is still in its own way a concept, just as much as (say) Eichrodt's 'covenant' was. And this argument leads us on to ask whether, in the long run, a theology based on 'history' and the revivification of historical memories is so very different in kind from one based on the cross-section through a 'world of faith'. For 'history', once it is so emphasized and made so central as it is by von Rad, seems to become a sort of 'world of faith' in itself. Similarly, although von Rad thought that there were many different theologies in the Old Testament and therefore rejected the attempts to formulate a 'centre', one must ask whether 'history' or, better, 'the reactivation of past traditions', in his own work does not also become a 'centre' and carry out the same functions. But the fuller discussion of this question must wait until later.[42]

## 10. *Childs again*

Most of the Old Testament theologians I have discussed in this chapter provided some review and discussion of what previous workers in the same field had achieved. It is noticeable by contrast that Childs, in spite of his very wide reading and numerous citations of scholarly work, discusses other Old Testament theologians less in proportion. Thus the short introductory chapter in *OTTCC* (1–19) mentions a few names, but gives very little idea of how these earlier scholars worked or what the real differences were. It is quite justified to say, as he does (2), that the survey can be brief because the history has been frequently rehearsed by others; but the same is not true of such statements as that 'the volumes of Eichrodt and von Rad marked major methodological advances' (4) and that both of these two 'introduced normative categories without adequate acknowledgment or methodological clarity' (5), without saying how and why. Statements about major methodological advances, accompanied by inadequate methodological clarity, require to be explained and justified at some length. The brief and passing mention of earlier Old Testament theology contrasts markedly with the endless and wearisome polemics against every sort of historical, critical, history-of-religion or sociological scholarship which – with a few welcome but incongruous moments of relief – take up so much space in Childs' two theological treatises.

The reason for this can easily be conjectured. Childs is strongly in favour of biblical theology and Old Testament theology, and this, one would have supposed, would make him look with warm approval on such other workers as have affirmed the value and importance of these fields. But he is even more convinced that there is no sound basis for biblical theology except in his own canonical approach. Although, as we shall see, there had been some earlier tendencies which *anticipated* the canonical approach as Childs develops it, no earlier Old Testament theologian knew or used it in its complete and integral form; and so he cannot afford to be too warm towards his predecessors without ruining his own argument. Hence the imbalance in his degree of attention to predecessors. Thus the phrase in the Preface 'my unforgettable teachers, W. Eichrodt, G. von Rad and W. Zimmerli' makes an odd contrast with the actual content of the two books. In the pages of these books there are indeed references to these scholars and often quite justified disagreements, but there is seldom if ever an attempt to state their total achievement and furnish an estimate of its value.

For the reader who has not worked in this area before, Childs' antagonism to the historical is the aspect which differentiates his work from that of most other biblical theologians. Earlier in the history of the subject a scholar like Eichrodt had attacked the 'domination' of historical viewpoints and sought to bring in the systematic as a corrective; but provided this was done he was happy to allow the main body of historical-critical results to remain intact and indeed to be incorporated into his work. Most Old Testament theologies had in fact assumed these critical approaches and had not bothered to say much about them as if they were a question for theology. However, Childs' canonical approach *began* – apart from earlier exploratory soundings – on the level of traditional 'introduction'. Here, where traditional criticism had gone through book by book discussing authorship, origins, sources, dates, influences from the environment and so on, Childs went methodically through, depicting historical criticism as in a state of disarray or breakdown, damaged by hopeless antinomies and disagreements, wildly speculative in its reconstructions of what had happened, and disabled by its wrong appreciation of the appropriate hermeneutical techniques. The arguments *for* the canonical approach were overwhelmingly concentrated on the weaknesses and antinomies of historical criticism on the one hand and the virtues of the canonical reading on the other.

It is true that Childs does not consider historical criticism to be totally illegitimate. His position is rather that, though legitimate for certain purposes, it is mainly irrelevant for *theology* and indeed confusing and damaging for theological purposes. Thus the legitimacy of historical-critical study in principle does not alter for Childs the fact that his arguments are overwhelmingly directed against its truth, its relevance and its usefulness.

In fact, in a recent article, published some years after the appearance of his *Biblical Theology*,[43] Childs argues that the acceptance of the historical-critical method as a base is *the one basic fault* running through the entire series of modern Old Testament theologies before his own. It can safely be understood that this is his true position on the matter.

Added to this is the emphasis and relish with which Childs uses the term 'Scripture'. In this usage 'Scripture' means more than 'the Bible' does: it is a distinctively religious usage that evokes holiness, authority, the Word of God. We note therefore the implication of the title of the first volume of the series: *Introduction to the Old Testament as Scripture*. It implies: this approach will explain the Old Testament 'as Scripture' in a way that other approaches do not.[44] The canonical approach's arrogation to itself of the connotations of 'Scripture' is obvious.

Equally central to Childs' form of canonical approach is the centrality of the concept 'church'. He speaks (*OTTCC*, 5) of 'the issue whether the discipline strives in some sense for theologically normative appraisals of the biblical literature *for the life of the church*, or whether the discipline entails primarily an objectively historical description of an aspect of ancient culture whose method of research is shared with the study of any ancient Near Eastern religion' (my italics). There is no doubt that the first of these alternatives represents Childs' own view. There remains the vagueness of 'in some sense': is he really satisfied if this condition is fulfilled 'in some sense', or does he think it is fulfilled only in the sense which he himself requires? In any case, 'the church' brings together the points I am making here. The Bible is the Holy Scripture of the church, and the church 'confesses' the canon of scripture; the church is the context for theology; biblical theology, as part of Christian theology, seeks a 'normative appraisal' for the life of the church; historical and religio-historical description, even if valid and true in some other context, is not valid or relevant for the needs of the church. The canonical approach in Childs' form is thus very strongly related to the church and its needs, and it is likely that this aspect has been a major reason for the appeal of the canonical approach. How far this is justified will be discussed later.[45]

The other primary aspect of Childs' approach which needs to be noted at this point is his idealization of 'theology'.[46] All works of biblical and Old Testament theology have been interested in 'theology' and have promoted its claim to be a serious academic operation and one necessary for the full appreciation of the Bible. But Childs goes far beyond this. He writes as if 'theology' is for him a pure and entirely independent subject, quite separate from historical criticism, sociology, history of religion and other such subjects, existing on a different level and able to provide final and authoritative exegesis through processes controlled by the 'canon' and untouched by any factors existing, or supposed to exist, on these other levels.

This might be acceptable, just as an idea, if he really meant this favour to extend to theology in general, to anything that was truly 'theology'. Unfortunately this is not so. It applies, as we shall see, only to one theology, his own. Where another scholar argues a case as support to a different 'theology', he uses the theological adherence of the scholar as a ground for rejecting his or her position. His position is therefore not an argument for theology, but an argument for one personally favoured theology. In some earlier work of Old Testament theology there was often something of this, but never was it raised to the magnitude that we find in Childs. Here, however, I anticipate, and we shall return to these aspects in a later chapter. Thus far I have given only preliminary orientation to the canonical approach.

To sum up, these various classic types within the Old Testament theology of this century show considerable difference and conflict of point of view. However, this should not be exaggerated, as has been done by some commentators, to the point of suggesting that the area was a scene of violent conflict, or that the degree of conflict was so great as to cast doubt on the viability of the subject altogether. There are in fact considerable elements of overlap between the types, and various compromises remain possible. In fact the overlap has been greater than was understood by the biblical theologians themselves, for the reason already mentioned, namely that their actual performance often failed to fit exactly with the rigorous (or not so rigorous!) methodological standards that they themselves set up. Although all of them indulged in criticism of the other theologians, none of them thought that the work of the others was so totally disastrous that it would have been better if it had never been done. All of them had common ground in a belief that there should be books on Old Testament theology, and all were pleased by the fact that there was a common enterprise, a common impulse, working in this direction.

Before we go farther in the discussion of Old Testament Theologies, however, I propose to enlarge the picture with the inclusion of other sorts of literature which do not bear that title but which are, I suggest, equally relevant to the subject.

# 4

# A Wider Spectrum

All the scholars surveyed in the previous chapter had written largish volumes entitled *Theology of the Old Testament* or something similar, and they seemed to be agreed that the production of volumes of this style and content was a good thing. Nevertheless the field of Old Testament theology, or of biblical theology, is a much wider one than is encompassed by the existence of written 'Theologies' in this sense. Indeed, it should not be taken as axiomatic that the production of such works is the only way, or the best way, in which biblical theology can be pursued. The production of large and comprehensive volumes of this kind is not necessarily the highest goal within the discipline. There are other forms of scholarly activity which are equally relevant. Thus Childs' description of the 'Biblical Theology Movement' rightly includes the major Theologies written, such as those of Eichrodt and von Rad, but also mentions all sorts of special studies, such as O. Cullmann's *Christ and Time*, the importance of which is rightly emphasized, along with activities such as 'word studies' which were less distinguished but were engaged in by a large variety of people. It also refers to ideas of biblical authority and of general hermeneutics, and to the impact of work in ancient Near Eastern religions. All this, as Childs rightly depicts it, belongs to the general realm of 'biblical theology'.

It may therefore be mistaken to take the large and comprehensive Theologies of the Old Testament (or of the New, or of the Bible) as being the prime example of biblical theology or as the ideal to which all work in biblical theology should strive. It is quite possible that the most important work in the discipline is done in other ways. We certainly do not gain a proper picture of the discipline if we look only, or even primarily, at the major works of this type. The question sometimes posed, 'How would you write "your" Theology of the Old Testament?', is not necessarily a proper, or a very important, one.

In fact only a small proportion of the work that has counted as 'biblical theology' has taken the form of a comprehensive Theology of the Hebrew Bible, of the New Testament, or of the Bible. Much of it has taken the form of a monograph or article investigating some *aspect* of the Bible, and investigating it with a theological interest, with a desire to perceive the theological concepts involved and their relevance for theological thought as a whole. Many such studies have had an interest that overran the separation between the Testaments: for example, they might investigate the Old Testament background for a New Testament expression, or they might investigate an Old Testament practice or tradition with a view to letting it have some fresh influence on Christian thinking. But others have effectively confined themselves to the Hebrew Bible, or to the New Testament, or to certain sectors within either. Works of this kind would have certain common characteristics with the work done in the full-size Theologies: they might be synthetic, in that they would take into consideration all the passages and examples of the relevant expressions, but they would not be synthetic in the sense of producing a total Theology of everything. They would take into account the differences made visible through historical and critical considerations but they would also seek to come to some sort of general conclusion. They would have to face the possibility of parallels in other religions and cultures and of influences from these; but they would also seek to disengage what the material had meant for and within Israel herself. In some cases they would be interested in establishing the relations, in respect of the expressions or passages studied, between the two Testaments. They may thus have accomplished something like the concept of an Old Testament Theology, but over a limited area only, without essaying the grandiose task of verbalizing the total theology of the whole. We shall have to consider the possibility that the real work of Old Testament and biblical theology lies along these lines rather than along the lines of the major volumes which attempt a comprehensive synthesis.

Indeed, it is possible that many of the problems of the discipline arise from this very cause, i.e. from the idea that, if we are to do the thing rightly, we have to get a comprehensive statement of everything within the bounds of one or two volumes. After all, if we want to be 'theologians', comparatively few doctrinal theologians plan to produce a comprehensive statement about God, humanity, the world, sin and redemption within one volume or two. Mostly they write about one aspect or another, no more, or they suggest or discuss a limited structure rather than a comprehensive synthesis. Even 'systematic' theologians do not necessarily, or even commonly, seek to comprehend *everything* in their work.

Another possibility is that separate 'theologies' of individual biblical books, or groups of books, should be produced. Such studies ought, one would have thought, to escape from some of the difficulties of design and method which attach so easily to attempts at a 'comprehensive' Theology of Old or New Testament or of the Bible. After all, in a minor way, a number of traditional commentaries on biblical books contained, usually in their introductions, a few pages on the theology of the book. In recent years Cambridge University Press has produced a series of such volumes on New Testament books; the five I have consulted are all on epistles or groups of epistles. It seems that a Theology written for a single book or source is much closer to the traditional historical and critical style than one written for the entire Old or New Testament could be. This may avoid some tensions; yet, on the other hand, it may lose something of interest and excitement in comparison with the more comprehensive work. For, readers may always be asking themselves: I know the theology of one single book, how am I to know how this relates to the theology of any or all of the others? But certainly the idea of Theologies written on one book is creative and promising, and possibly it indicates a way in which the subject should move forward in the future. If a Theology were to be written for every single book (or conceivably for strata like J or P of the Pentateuch, or Q in the Gospels), would the sum of these be a Theology of the entire Bible? I have a feeling that it would not: for the most serious problems lie in the *interrelations* between books and sources, not in the content of each one. But certainly Theologies of the single book present a useful possibility.

In any case, the numerous particular studies of biblical concepts and traditions have to be counted and given positive value in our thinking. There are literally dozens or hundreds of such works. The series called Studies in Biblical Theology, initiated by SCM Press in the 1950s, gives a good sample of the sort of thing that is meant. Looking more widely and listing only a small representative group, we have works like monographs on 'Man in the Old Testament' by Köhler and Eichrodt; on covenant by McCarthy, by Perlitt,[1] by Nicholson and many others; on 'oppression' by Jacques Pons, *L'Oppression dans l'Ancien Testament*; on psycho-somatic expressions (R. Lauha, *Psychophysischer Sprachgebrauch im Alten Testament*);[2] on myth and reality and on memory (Childs);[3] studies on particular concepts like Westermann's on 'blessing';[4] or particular themes like G. W. Coats, *Rebellion in the Wilderness;* S. E. Balentine, *The Hidden God;* or John Gammie, *Holiness in Israel;* or works on immortality and resurrection like those by Cullmann. Among works by Jewish scholars, Jon Levenson's *Creation and the Persistence of Evil* is an outstanding example, widely appreciated. To these must naturally be added the work of the whole genre of 'Theological Dictionaries' and of the 'word studies' which were so prominent a feature of the 'Biblical Theology Movement'. That some of these operations have contained many faults, as I in particular have pointed out,[5] does not alter the fact that they may *in principle* be serious and positive contributions to the theological appreciation of Old and/or New Testament and to the relations between them. Some of the later theological dictionaries, like Botterweck-Ringgren-Fabry's *TDOT* and Jenni-Westermann's *THAT*, have made serious attempts to take these criticisms into account and have produced many researches that are linguistically powerful as well as being theologically significant.[6]

But if we think that these individual studies of terms, concepts and expressions can count as biblical theology, then it is difficult to think otherwise of works which make more comprehensive studies of the same, even where such works did not think of themselves at all as theology. An obvious example is Pedersen's *Israel*, one of the great and seminal works of the century and one that, in spite of numerous criticisms that can perhaps be made, was both epoch-making in itself and also close to many of the tendencies of the contemporary impulses toward Old Testament theology.[7] Thus, for instance, Pedersen's study is entirely synthetic and pays little attention to source analysis, dates of authorship, and the like. Theology is (or should be) interested in the soul, which is the centre of much of Pedersen's great book. Any biblical study which goes deeply into the questions that concern theology, even if its own intent is not theological, must be positively significant for biblical theology.

Similar ground is covered by H. W. Wolff's *Anthropology of the Old Testament*, and it is distinctly closer to the mood of biblical theology and imbued with its spirit. The same is true of Norman Snaith's *The Distinctive Ideas of the Old Testament*, one of the central works of the Biblical Theology Movement in its classic form.

Again, a study such as George Ernest Wright's highly influential *God Who Acts* could hardly be called an 'Old Testament Theology' in the comprehensive sense. It is an essay (Hayes and Prussner call it 'a programmatic essay') setting forth a limited but powerful thesis. It does not attempt to cover all the ground or even a small proportion of all the ground: but it claims to supply one or two basic structures which are all-important. It certainly belongs to the world of Old Testament theology.[8] Though not seeking comprehensiveness, it puts forward structures – and especially so when taken together with the companion volume *The Old Testament against its Environment* – which are intended to be fairly pervasive and are understood to provide a near-absolute distinctiveness from the environing mythological and polytheistic religions, Greek thought, and more or less all philosophical and 'propositional' reasoning. They are also supposed to provide some connection with the New Testament and a programme for modern theology and church. All these features class it very definitely as a form of Old Testament theology.

Similarly works on the *ethics* of the Old or New Testament would certainly count as part of the field. This is particularly relevant in view of the recent (1994) publication of Eckart Otto's *Theologische Ethik des Alten Testaments*, but along with this one would also have to add numerous other, shorter, contributions, such as those of Barton, McKeating, Knight. I have to apologize for not having included as much on the ethical side as I consider ought to be included in this volume.

Works discussing *biblical authority* and related topics may also count as belonging to the area of Old Testament (or biblical) theology. To give an example, John Bright did not write 'a Theology', but his book *The Authority of the Old Testament* contains the assertion that the 'underlying theology' is the element in the Old Testament that establishes its authority.[9] 'It becomes, therefore, our task to examine its ancient answers and to discern the theology that expresses itself through them, so that we, praying at every step for the Holy Spirit's guidance, may give that theology a new expression in the answers we seek to give.'[10] Remarks like these, though not written within an explicit 'Old Testament Theology', are just as much expressions of an Old Testament theology as any work so entitled could be.

Yet another rich expression of biblical theology is to be found in *commentaries*. Within this genre we are probably, most of us, conscious of a distinction between commentaries that are 'less theological' (being primarily textual, philological, historical) and commentaries that are 'somewhat' or 'highly' or 'extremely' theological. The difference is not usually given formal marking, but the user has the sense of it. Commentaries like the classic and time-honoured ICC series tend to be textual and philological, and have often seemed to be not very theological. Some of those in the Old Testament Library series are distinctly more theological: obviously so von Rad's commentaries, such as those on Genesis and Deuteronomy, which are closely related to his work in Old Testament theology. On the Book of Job, Dhorme's much-esteemed commentary is mainly textual-philological, Tur-Sinai's is philological, but that of Terrien is distinctly more theological. Commentaries that seek to express the effects or consequences of the book on the modern world, like the Interpretation series with its sub-title 'A Bible Commentary for Teaching and Preaching', are obviously theological in that aspect.

Indeed, we may say that the category 'theological' is too wide, and that we need to make more distinctions. There are degrees of religious concern. Probably the term 'theological' should be confined to commentaries that speak to the world of *academic* theology. Some others should be classified more as 'religious', 'spiritual', 'devotional' or 'homiletic' in character. Thus in the New Testament no one would question that Hoskyns' commentary *The Fourth Gospel* is a highly theological commentary, working on the plane of academic theology,[11] while some other commentaries may seem by contrast to be mainly textual or historical. Others again, like Archbishop Temple's *Readings in St John's Gospel,* would count as basically devotional, in spite of the high standing of the author in academic theology.[12] It is often complained that most commentaries are 'not theological' or not theological enough. But the complaint may be an unreasonable one, for there may be reasons why it is difficult for a commentary really to 'be theological'. For one thing, it depends on the book commented on. Hoskyns' method may have worked well because it was a commentary on *John*, and the content of John is all about Jesus, who is the central theme of Christian religion and theology. Could a Christian commentator have done the same for, say, Joshua? How can Joshua, for Christians, be so close and so directly related to fundamental beliefs as John is? Probably commentaries on New Testament books are (for Christians) more naturally inclined to 'be theological' than Old Testament commentaries (except for those on the Psalms) are. Among Old Testament commentaries in modern times perhaps Ulrich Simon's *A Theology of Salvation* (basically a commentary on Isa. 40–55) might be the best example of a 'theological' commentary on a book of the Hebrew Bible. This was a case, incidentally, of a book which was theologically profound but which made little mark on scholarship for a quite other reason, namely that it espoused a historical–critical theory that was little favoured.[13]

One important endeavour to plan a series that would be fully 'critical' but at the same time theological produced the Biblischer Kommentar in Germany. Commentaries in this series have at the end of each major section a concluding portion entitled *Ziel:* 'Aim' or 'Goal' (in some English translations rendered as 'Purpose and Thrust', so in Scullion's version of Westermann's *Genesis*). Concerning the effectiveness of this method, opinion is divided.

Though commentaries may be, or may contain, material that is part of biblical theology, there is a certain feeling that this does not happen very much, a feeling that is voiced by Childs in the note above. Can we explain this?

Roughly we may say, perhaps: the boundary comes at this point. A commentary may ask: What did the author (or redactors, or readers) think? What part of their belief system was this? Or it may go farther and ask: What if their thoughts were true? What if God is as they thought him to be, or depicted him to be? What are the consequences for the total religious picture of the world? A commentary becomes fully 'theological' when it enters into this second set of questions. This would seem, at least at first sight, to be a possible distinction.

In effect, however, it is more difficult to differentiate. Perhaps Hoskyns' *The Fourth Gospel* fits most obviously as a 'theological' commentary. Barth's *Romans* goes so far in that direction that it almost ceases to be a commentary: the earlier stage, the asking what Paul actually thought, often drops out of sight, and what remains is a theological essay planted upon the Pauline text.

The fundamental point is, as we saw with Theologies of one single book, that one verse, one passage, even one book cannot in itself be determinative for ultimate theological decisions. In older times it may have been thought that this was so, because it was supposed that the Bible was homogeneous and any one portion of it said the same as all the rest. But this is no longer widely accepted. Thus the modern commentator often seems 'non-theological', not because he or she is not theologically involved or interested, but because, in the commentary format, it is obvious that theological decisions cannot be made on the basis of one text or of one book.

To this must be added another consideration. The more commentaries venture into ultimate religious decisions, the more they are likely to find themselves forced into a partisan position. Commentaries written to give support to a Lutheran view will be answered by commentaries that affirm a Calvinist or a Catholic standpoint. Still more is this the case with modern social, ethical and political matters. If commentaries commend the mixture of mild (or sometimes rabid) liberalism and political correctness that the mainstream churches commonly promote, one loses the right to complain if conservative commentaries are written to promote the opposite social views. If we write commentaries that make biblical texts call for the abolition of nuclear weapons, we cannot complain if someone else writes a commentary that makes the same text call for the preservation of the same weapons.

It seems to me that commentaries provide the best material for biblical theology when they concentrate on *what the writers/redactors/readers/audience* thought: what was their idea-world, their background, their sense of an opposition? For them to go farther and seek to make regulative theological judgments in the sense of what the reality is, of what should be believed and done, can be done only by the importation of dogmatic arguments. Thus commentaries are, though often not in an obvious way, and certainly in varying degree, a form of expression that may belong to biblical theology.

It remains, however, unclear that the commentary is a good vehicle for the work of biblical theology. If the aim is still that of a comprehensive view of the theology/theologies of the Bible, then something other than a commentary is needed, and this may be exactly the justification for the rise of the Old/New Testament Theology format. For it is arguable that the task of the commentary is to provide an account of the linguistic, textual, literary and historical *constraints* which limit theological reflection, while the theological reflection is something that the reader, or the religious community, can do for himself, herself or itself. If this is so, it provides something that has often been lacking, namely, a *theological* justification for the *non-theological* character of many commentaries. The ICC may not be a 'theological' commentary series, but it may be the type that *serves* theology best. With this, however, we leave the matter of commentaries.

To sum up, then: it is mistaken to suppose that the field of Old Testament theology is identical with the enterprise of writing (or reading) largish volumes with the title of *Theology of the Old Testament* (or a similar title). It is by no means certain that the production of such volumes is essential to the discipline. Old Testament theology might be sustained and carried forward on the basis of essays on particular aspects, studies of terms and concepts, and also of major studies which have an overlap with Old Testament theology but are not concentrated upon it. Indeed, there are some reasons for thinking that the discipline would go forward better if it was seen in this way. It is likely that Old Testament theology, far from being definitively located in the production of large volumes dedicated purely to this theme, is rather an aspect which is likely to be present, in varying proportions, in almost all activity of study of the Bible and comment upon it.

The matter is of central importance. Biblical theology or Old Testament theology is in essence not a book but a *level* of scholarship. Whether it is possible to represent this entire level in one book, i.e. whether one can encapsulate in a single definitive statement this variety of subjects and approaches, is an interesting practical question, but not one that affects the total status of biblical theology as an undertaking.

It may thus have been a misfortune for the subject that Eichrodt, and many others after him, in setting before us the ideal of a *synthetic* or *comprehensive* study as opposed to an analytic one, which in itself might be quite a justifiable principle, allowed it (perhaps inadvertently) to seem that the production of a single-book statement was the real task and goal of the subject. On the contrary, such books may have the character more of *suggestions, hypotheses, possible alignments of evidence*, and in this sense be actually *subsidiary* to the main course of thought in biblical theology, of which main course these books are only one manifestation among others.

For this there is an important theoretical reason: in order to be comprehensive, a book must also be, paradoxically, *selective*. On such a subject, any single book that aspires to be comprehensive must also by the same token be *selective*. No book, however long, can contain all the material or even give references to all of it. Equally, there are many different ways in which the materials may be *grouped, ordered and classified*, and many differing degrees in which each element can be either emphasized or treated as marginal. The books that appear, therefore, even accepting their high quality and even leaving aside the various criticisms which may be directed against each, are statements of individual approaches and hypotheses rather than definitive expressions of what biblical theology is. It is not necessarily a fault, but part of the nature of the undertaking, that the unsympathetic reader will be able to perceive gaps in the evidence cited: naturally, the writer will have to *know* all the evidence, in so far as that is humanly possible, but to *present* it all is more than can be demanded.

The question, often posed, of 'methodology' in writing a work on biblical theology is thus a relatively unimportant one. There is no such thing as a 'right' methodology for carrying out such a task.[14] The differences of ordering and approach in the various works surveyed in the last chapter are not a matter of fault or defect; rather, they are what is to be expected. Certainly there are questions of principle, of 'methodology' if one wants to call it so, in such matters as perceiving the theology implied by a text, or relating it to the theology of some other text: these are of real importance, and the question of ordering and organizing the individual book about it is of much lesser importance.

A realization of this might do much to obviate some of the criticism and opposition with which biblical theology has sometimes had to contend.[15] The idea of someone writing a book which aspires to be 'the' theology of the Old Testament has something grandiose about it which tends to invite mockery. Can anyone really put together the essentials, perhaps even the totality, of such a theology within a few hundred pages? Does not the very title suggest a claim to definitiveness, to ultimate authority? Does it not suggest that the author, however he or she may differentiate their work from that of doctrinal theology, is implying a claim to ultimate authority similar to that which (some) doctrinal theology claims? Studies of a particular theme, or aspect, or text, may be able to avoid that sort of criticism. Thus, for instance, many Christian theologies of the Old Testament have aspired to establish some sort of connection with the New. This fact, however understandable, has in turn provoked some scepticism toward such theologies, for by their own comprehensive nature and design they have given the impression of stating 'the' one true relation between the Testaments. A study of some particular theme, on the other hand, can pass more easily from the Hebrew Bible into the post-biblical era and thence into the New Testament, without suggesting that the relations thus traced constitute 'the' essential connection between Old and New. No one doubts that *some* themes or aspects are enunciated in the Old and reactualized or recontextualized in the New. Such a limited and partial study can therefore – at least in principle – successfully perform a function which, when attempted by the full-scale one- or two-volume Theology of the Old Testament, is likely to meet with questioning or opposition. Moreover, as has been said above, the comprehensiveness of the full Theologies also implies a selectivity within the material, and this possible weakness can at least in part be overcome by a more partial and limited study, which can seek to handle *all* the material relevant to that particular theme and consider it in a variety of aspects – say, textual, historical, sociological and so on – for which the comprehensive Theology does not have space.

This has great importance, for it shows that the detailed work of biblical theology is closer to the normal activity of exegesis than is commonly realized: it is, I suggest, a 'level' within the latter rather than a special and separate activity. There is nothing wrong with the special activity of writing a book called 'a Theology' of the Old Testament or the New, but it is not the paradigm for the activity of biblical theology in essence; rather it is a special case, which in fact is dependent on a large number of limited and particular studies that may not be mentioned but are presupposed.

If I am right, it means that Old Testament (or biblical) theology is not a matter of the production of large and comprehensive volumes. Nor is it an activity sharply separated from other kinds of study that concern the Bible. It does not have strict rules to demarcate it from other kinds and levels of biblical study. On the contrary, biblical (or Old or New Testament) theology is a level of study that is present in varying degree in all sorts of teaching, courses, texts, dictionaries, encyclopedias, articles and books. Information and scholarship of any kind – historical, linguistic, textual, cultural, comparative – can at any point move into the position of significance for biblical theology. Anyone who wishes can, of course, refrain from making that transition, and can decide simply to keep out of the area of biblical theology. Many scholars do this. There is no harm in it: they simply refrain from entering into certain questions, as they are entitled to do. But their work remains as work that may potentially be significant in the field of biblical theology.

The variety of forms that the total enterprise of biblical theology can take has a further important consequence. It means that there can be no such thing as the one appropriate method for biblical theology. Even if a regulative method could be worked out for writing a complete 'Old Testament Theology', that method would not be regulative for other formats. For instance, a complete Theology, seeking to cover the entire Old Testament, would be forced to use an approach both synthetic and selective, there being no other way to cover the ground required. On the other hand someone writing a monograph on some particular theological aspect, let us say the theology of war and peace or the theology of the restoration period with Haggai and Zechariah, would almost necessarily have to provide completeness of coverage along with historical location of the materials to be used. For some sorts of enquiry, such as the Hebrew idea of humanity or of body and soul, the question of historical difference might prove to be unimportant (at least until the Hellenistic period), while for others, such as the idea of monotheism, a historical framework with dating of different sources would very likely prove necessary. In general, one cannot predict what sort of method will be needed until the outlines of the particular question have been examined for each case.

# 5

# Difference from Doctrinal Theology

Central to all discussion of Old Testament theology (or of New Testament theology, or of biblical theology) is the question: how does it differ from doctrinal (dogmatic, systematic) theology?

It is customary to begin with the distinction as defined by Gabler in the late eighteenth century. Doctrinal (in his words dogmatic) theology was didactic and philosophical: it taught what was to be believed. While doctrinal theology used the Bible and depended on it, it had to be influenced also by other factors, such as philosophy and church tradition. Biblical theology was historical; it concerned what the biblical authors in their own time had believed.

This might seem clear enough, but further distinctions made the difference more obscure. 'True' biblical theology was 'thus conceived as a purely descriptive task: a true and accurate description of the religion (= religious ideas) of the Bible in its various periods and contexts and in a systematic and historical presentation' (Hayes and Prussner, 63). There was also a 'pure' biblical theology, 'a systematic presentation of God's eternal truths or the unchanging ideas found in the Bible which were valid for all times' (ibid.).[1] Here 'the descriptive task moves to the level of the normative task'. Within biblical theology there was something that appeared to attain to supreme and authoritative status.

Here then, in this early attempt to define biblical theology, we find present one of the antinomies which has continued to bedevil the subject down to the present day – not least, as we shall see, because the problem has not been properly faced by biblical theologians themselves. On the one hand it is recognized that normative status and prescriptive function belong to doctrinal theology, while the scope of biblical theology lies within the historical thinking of the biblical writers in their own time; on the other hand there is an expectation that the work of biblical theology will somehow produce insights of maximal theological status and authority.

In the beginnings of the modern development of Old Testament theology, with Eichrodt, we find a position similar in some ways but significantly altered in others. In comparison with Gabler's statement, Eichrodt was unhappy with the authority of *history*. It was 'high time that the tyranny of history in Old Testament studies was broken and the proper approach to our task rediscovered' (Hayes and Prussner, 180). Typical of the turn against historical domination of scholarship in his time, he was critical – and quite reasonably – of 'the idea that once the historical problems were clarified everything had been done'. But scholarship should not therefore go over to a procedure dictated by faith, as Eissfeldt had suggested, or return to being a province of dogmatics. Old Testament theology was to remain an academic or 'scientific' subject. It was not normative and prescriptive as doctrinal theology was. As we have seen, the centre of his own proposal was the synthetic, comprehensive approach. Beneath the historical changes there lay a unitary 'world of faith', a cross-section through the historical process, and the disengagement of this cross-section would lay bare 'the inner structure of the religion and the relationship of its various contents to one another' (Porteous, 'Old Testament Theology', 323). This was what his great *Theology of the Old Testament* undertook to do. In a sense, therefore, the principle of the whole work still lay on a historical plane: the difference was that its interest lay not primarily in diachronic *changes* on that plane, but in pervasive structures or patterns which ran all across that plane. Eichrodt looked for 'constants'.

Eichrodt was sure that his structural pattern differed from diachronic study of historical change, and that what it generated was theology. Yet he did not want to bring it close to doctrinal theology: its procedures lay just as much within the reach and scope of ordinary Old Testament scholarship as historical study did.

And yet into this very argument he built in another feature which once again was to bring Old Testament theology, as he conceived it, rather closer to doctrinal theology. Against the emphasis of the historian (as he perceived it) on purely empirical work or a purely empirical approach, he appealed to *the philosophy of* history.[2] Even historical study, he argued, cannot be purely positivistic: it involves 'congeniality', 'a certain affinity or relationship between the historical researcher and the subject of his research' (Porteous, 'Old Testament Theology', 323); it involves goals, selection, and decision. Similarly, he accepted that there was a similar need for selection and decision in a work like his Old Testament Theology.

> In every science there is a subjective element. The fact that the theologian makes an existential judgment which, in part at least, determines the subjective element to be found in his account of Old Testament religion does not imply that he uses any distinctive historical method. It is clear that at this point Eichrodt, while admitting the necessity of an existential judgment on the part of the Old Testament theologian, wishes to ensure that, by making this admission, he will not lend any countenance to the charge that Old Testament theology is unscientific in character . . . At the same time Eichrodt

allows for the possibility that the Old Testament theologian may at times feel unable to keep strictly within the limits of his science and find himself obliged to make pronouncements regarding the Old Testament which properly belong to the sphere of the dogmatic theologian. What Eichrodt wishes to avoid is the claim that such value judgments should be a normal part of Old Testament theology (Porteous, 'Old Testament Theology', 323f.).

In this position of Eichrodt's there are several elements that will occupy us. But here again we can see an element of inconsistency. His essential position followed Gabler in considering that Old Testament theology was not a dogmatic subject. But he had to qualify this, and then the only thing left was to qualify the qualifications by saying that they would be exceptional. Eichrodt did not try, it seems, to clarify when or how they might occur. He had to leave it that, even if the scholar had at times to take decisions that came close to doctrinal ones, this was exceptional, and his or her basic work remained clearly distinct from doctrinal theology.

The essential point at which he thought he could be firm and clear in this respect was in the matter of organization of an Old Testament Theology. As we shall discuss in another connection, it was clearly wrong, in Eichrodt's eyes, as in those of many other Old Testament theologians, to accept any kind of dogmatic scheme, traditional or non-traditional, as the principle of organization of the Theology being written. To Eichrodt this seemed a very central matter. He was departing, as he saw it, from the idea of a narrative history of Hebrew religion, and he wanted to make a more systematic statement. But on what principle could such a statement be ordered? To him it was of extreme importance to say that the choice of organizing principle arose from the Old Testament material itself and was not dictated by any external dogmatic force. In this, as we shall later see, he may have been mistaken; but his reason for making the argument is clear. The basic structure as seen by him was securely anchored in normal biblical scholarship and had just as strong a basis within it as any historical presentation had. Doctrinal theology, a normative and prescriptive discipline, was another matter, and it had other factors to concern itself with in addition to the Bible, such as philosophy and church tradition.

Here there were several difficulties. One is that there was really no discussion of how *doctrinal* theology should handle the Bible, or the Old Testament in particular. One might have expected that Old Testament theologians, as well as working out a mode in which their discipline should be practised by themselves, would give some thought to what should be done with the same material by doctrinal theologians, who, by the same argument, were the people with the normative and prescriptive task to perform and were therefore, one might have supposed, the more important and the more likely to cause trouble if they went wrong. Yet not only Eichrodt, but Old Testament theologians as a whole, with only limited exceptions, have seemed more concerned to insist on the distinctness of their subject from doctrinal theology than to enter into the world of the latter and offer some advice. For, if Old Testament theology is so very important, and promises so much, how will it be possible for doctrinal theologians to continue on their own peculiar (and undefined) way, if that way seriously differs from what is being done within Old Testament scholarship itself?

Among the 'limited exceptions' mentioned above we may cite the case of Childs. Here the emphasis is the opposite of what has been said above, and yet the problem remains the same. For Childs the emphasis is on the *nearness* of biblical and doctrinal theology to one another. Biblical theology is to serve as a 'bridge' to doctrinal theology. 'The major function of biblical theology is to provide a bridge for two-way traffic between biblical exegesis and systematic theology's reflections on the subject matter' (*Biblical Theology*, 481, 595, cf. 592, 629). This is somewhat similar to Jacob's notion of a biblical theology that 'processes' the biblical material and passes it on.[3] But Childs more emphasizes the need for *interpenetration* of the two. And this is what appears in his own actual discussions, in which it is frequently impossible to tell on which of the two levels he is speaking.[4] He resists the idea that doctrinal theologians should think of working apart from the Bible. But, if they are working with the Bible, how does their work differ from that of the biblical theologian? He tells us that biblical scholars, because of their initial training and interest, will make a contribution 'concentrated largely on describing and interpreting biblical texts' (89), which is a dazzling glimpse of the obvious. Systematic theologians conversely bring to bear 'a variety of philosophical, theological and analytical tools' which are 'usually informed by the history of theology' and are 'invaluable in relating the study of the Bible to the subject matter of the Christian life in the modern world', again just a platitude. There is in this no real definition of any difference between biblical and doctrinal theology. All the 'precision in theory' he offers (again 89) is 'to urge biblical scholars to be more systematic, and systematic theologians to be more biblical, and to get on with the task', again a platitude. Neither biblical nor doctrinal theology, he then tells us – much to my surprise – is an end in itself. They remain 'useful tools' by which to enable a fresh access to the living voice of God in sacred scripture.

To sum up, although Childs puts greater emphasis on the nearness of biblical and doctrinal theology to one another, he no more makes clear what the character of doctrinal theology is and how its operations work than do those who emphasize the difference between them. He leaves the general impression that it is just the same as biblical theology except for a greater use of the intellectual 'tools' mentioned.

The second difficulty has been that the argument from these 'other factors' which were taken into account in doctrinal theology might *in the past* have made a clear contrast with biblical theology. But by the mid-twentieth century it no longer worked so well. In this respect Eichrodt's solution, similar as it was to Gabler's of a century and a half earlier, was anachronistic. For with the rise of dialectical theology and its efforts to return to a Reformation position, the differentia which had previously distinguished doctrinal theology from work in the Bible seemed to have largely disappeared. Natural theology had been expelled. Philosophy scarcely counted: no serious doctrinal theology, at least in many major currents of Protestantism, would now accept *it* as a factor of authority. Church tradition might be something, but in any case it would be Reformation tradition which would appeal solely and entirely to the Bible and to every part and detail of the Bible. The Bible was now to be the overwhelmingly dominant factor in doctrinal theology: only Christ himself stood higher. And the Old Testament, and all of it, was emphatically authoritative for doctrinal theology.

This being so, there no longer seemed to be 'other factors' that differentiated doctrinal theology from biblical theology. If biblical theology could therefore produce an important construction of the total world of faith of the Old Testament, how could that be other than a powerful entity that would immediately, in the nature of the case, have status directly within doctrinal theology? If the Old Testament itself, or the Bible as a whole, had a theology which could be identified, how could such a theology fail to have primacy in the doctrinal field?

This therefore produced one of the many possible contradictions that have troubled biblical theology. Granted its distinction from doctrinal theology, which most practitioners agreed on, one option was to understand it in an ancillary sense. Old Testament theology would thus, as it were, process the biblical material. Expert scholars would disentangle the developments, disengage the essential structures, package the resultant synthesis in a large but readable volume or two, and pass this on to the doctrinal theologian who would then do – what? No one made this clear.

In fact the 'ancillary' conception of biblical theology tended very easily to slide over into a conception of it as dominating. Edmond Jacob, who continued to use the 'other factors' argument, accepting (unusually) the place of natural theology, and who did more than most biblical theologians to express a view of the working of doctrinal theology, showed this change of emphasis very well:

Dogmatics does not confine itself solely to the Bible; it takes much account of the contributions of philosophy and natural theology, as well as that of church tradition; but if it wishes to remain 'Christian' it will always have to make fresh assessments of its declarations by comparing them with the essential biblical data, the elucidation of which is precisely the task of biblical theology, itself based on well-founded exegesis. By supplying the basic material, biblical theology will remind dogmatics of its limits and will preserve it from falling into a subjectivism where the essential might be sacrificed to the accessory.[5]

Thus, given the circumstances of the time, the question of relations with doctrinal theology has tended, in the minds of enthusiasts for biblical theology, to reverse the roles of the two. According to Eichrodt and others, biblical theology was not normative and doctrinal theology was. But, since biblical theology expressed the central essentials of the Bible, it could hardly fail to become *more* normative than doctrinal theology. It could tell doctrinal theology what it should be doing. Edmond Jacob again well expressed this inevitable logic:

> However, since in accordance with the scriptural principle a biblical theology has to be the inspiration and the norm for all theology, today I would like to show, in an attempt which will necessarily remain fragmentary and inadequate, how the Old Testament can inspire the whole of theological reflection . . .[6]

Since the Bible, by the 'scriptural principle', was the norm of theology, it was obvious that a biblical theology would have not an ancillary function but one of leadership; it would be a source of inspiration to any other kind of theology that there might be, and would more or less be able to tell all such theology what it ought to be doing.

This feeling is to be found again and again. George Ernest Wright, for example, was not concerned only to express merely the correct evaluation of the Old Testament in itself. From the beginning he sought to rescue *doctrinal* theology from its bad state. If the word 'theology' is to be used for 'the characteristic nature of the biblical presentation of faith', he argues in the first paragraph of *God Who Acts*, 'the term must be rescued from the exclusive and private use of the systematic theologians'. He goes on: 'To most of them, as to most others, it has meant propositional dogmatics, stated as abstractly and universally as possible and arranged in accordance with a pre-conceived and coherent system.'[7] Wright is not saying that this abstract, propositional presentation is unsuitable for the Old Testament itself, but may of course afterwards be applied by doctrinal theologians if they see fit; he is saying, as the sequel in his book makes clear, that doctrinal theologians had better mend their ways in their own area and do so quickly. Their traditions must be abandoned in favour of the biblical theological approach. Abstract propositional dogmatics must be eschewed if the biblical faith is to be expressed in appropriate terms. Biblical theology, as he sees it, can teach them what they ought to be doing.

Biblical theology, therefore, has found it difficult to avoid claiming a position of leadership and normative status. In an older theological environment it might have been easier to accept an ancillary position, but the renewed insistence on total and holistic biblical authority made it difficult for biblical theology to avoid assumptions of normativity. For what sort of knowledge could doctrinal theology have that would entitle it to override not just the Bible but the carefully constructed picture of the essential deep structures of the Bible?

To repeat: it was dialectical theology that furnished the assumptions and impulses under which modern biblical theology arose. But it equally provided paradoxes and contradictions from which biblical theology continues to suffer. Some further words about dialectical theology and its influence should be added here.

First of all, dialectical theology expressed itself to a large extent in the form of *exegesis*. Bultmann, one of its leading figures, was one of the greatest New Testament exegetes of the century, and also wrote the leading Theology of the New Testament. Barth, as I shall shortly indicate more fully, though a dogmatic theologian and not a biblical scholar in the usual sense, incorporated into his *Church Dogmatics* a very large amount of detailed exegesis, sometimes of extended passages. Dialectical theology appeared, then, to favour a climate in which biblical exegesis of a theological character and interest would be fostered and cherished and would have profound influence and authority. It is not surprising that such a theology attracted the sympathetic interest of many biblical scholars.

For Old Testament matters, secondly, the influence of Barth was much larger and more positive than that of Bultmann. Though Bultmann did have a view under which the Old Testament, through a series of 'failures', contributed positively to Christianity,[8] this was a narrow basis, and it left unsatisfied many of those who were more deeply committed to a high and direct theological value for the Old Testament. Barth on the other hand had a more Calvinistic view, in which it was axiomatic that the Old Testament had a full and positive role in all matters of Christian theology. The Barthian side of dialectical theology therefore appeared to promise and to favour a thorough revival of authority and influence for the Old Testament in the church. To the great majority of Old Testament scholars this was highly attractive.

Two significant parentheses may be included at this point. First, another note relevant to the position of Bultmann, which has just been mentioned. Berkhof, *Christian Faith*, 247, notes Bultmann's position and appears to reject it: 'Characteristic is his [Bultmann's] statement: "For man nothing can be promise, except as the failure of his way, as the realization of the impossibility of getting a direct hold of God in his own history within this world and of directly identifying his history in this world with the acts of God." His

[Bultmann's] vision is almost generally rejected because with him this *Scheitern* [failure] is based on the idea – one totally at variance with the Old Testament – that authentic existence is nonhistorical, not part of this world, and a purely individual happening.'

Berkhof thus rejects Bultmann's *reasoning*; but his account of the reality is not so very different. He too writes: 'The certainty of the failure of the covenant is implied in the earlier narratives as well [as in the later] . . . the historical and prophetic books of the Old Testament depict the way of Israel as an irreversible way from the establishment of the covenant to the failure of the human covenant partner' (238). Again, 'in and after the exile there was a much deeper awareness of the wonder of God's covenant faithfulness toward a guilty people than in previous centuries, yet the way in which this faithfulness could also make the human partner faithful had not become convincingly clear. Out of a mixture of fear and expectation all sorts of solutions were proclaimed which were no real solutions or did not touch reality' (244f.). This is not so completely different from Bultmann's *Scheitern* concept. In order to avoid 'a negative evaluation of the entire way of Israel in the Old Testament', which might arise from this, Berkhof turns to a concept of Israel's *vicarious* action for all humanity. It is a fundamental presupposition 'that Israel in going this way acted vicariously for all mankind . . . Israel, in her refusal to follow God on his redemptive way, bears vicariously the guilt of all men and the condemnation upon all and is vicariously driven into this impasse' (245). What Berkhof does not explain is what hard evidence there is for the existence of the 'crisis', 'failure' and 'impasse' to which he refers.

Secondly, dialectical theology has often been seen, rightly or wrongly, as a reaction against 'liberal' theology. This opinion was connected with the place of the Old Testament. For it was widely supposed that persons of 'liberal' opinions had been estranged from the Old Testament or negative towards its authority. 'All the liberals rejected the Old Testament', wrote James Sanders.[9] This is indeed an impression that was sometimes created in the time of the rise and power of dialectical theology. And it might have been true in some areas, for example at the level of some of the 'liberal' churches in North America.[10] In scholarship, however, the realities were quite otherwise. The 'liberal' period in theology was a time of very high achievement in Old Testament scholarship, and of the many major names within it there is hardly one, if any, who could be said to have 'rejected the Old Testament'.[11] In fact, as I hope to show elsewhere, there was a very significant continuity between the biblical scholarship of the 'liberal' period and the rise of modern biblical theology. For many biblical scholars dialectical theology offered not a violent turn away from their previous thinking but a confirmation and a stronger mode of expression of what had already been their central concern. I therefore return to the point made above:

dialectical theology, as represented by Brunner and Barth, attracted scholars because of its clear affirmation of the authority of the Old Testament, their own professional area and their own object of existential commitment.

Just here, however, there lies another paradox. Early modern biblical theology, running as it so often did in parallel with the impulses of dialectical theology, often drew from that source ideas and directions that were unintended or were intended in a quite other way. In particular, we may say, biblical theologians tended to interpret these impulses in a much more biblicistic mode than the leading dialectical theologians had intended. By 'biblicistic' I mean any conception that suggests that the Bible alone is the final decisive authority in theology.[12] We shall see that the impulses of dialectical theology were often interpreted by biblical theologians in a biblicistic way. Their biblicism was not the literal-historical or infallibilist biblicism of conservative and fundamentalist people; it was more a professionally-orientated biblicism, coming from an expertise focussed dominantly upon the Bible and a confidence in the decisiveness of scholarly exegesis. It was nourished by a knowledge, distinctly more limited, of ancient and mediaeval theology, by a low degree of involvement in philosophy, and by remanent effects of popular, mainly Protestant, biblicism. Anyway, the effect of it within the rising modern biblical theology was to suggest the ideal of a biblically-dominated theology of a kind which the leading dialectical theologians themselves would have moderated or indeed rejected.

When the clear distinction between doctrinal and biblical theology was obscured and there emerged a sort of mixture of the two, this was often a sign of a sort of amateurism pretending to be professionalism. Biblical theologians sometimes gave the impression that, though the more purely historical efforts of scholars might be more or less theologically irrelevant, the newer 'holistic' approaches of biblical theology could settle major theological questions;[13] conversely, dogmatic theologians, while usually accepting – though often with some inward doubt – that biblical scholars were well ahead of them in matters of history and background, developed techniques by which they thought they could outflank the certainties of critical exegesis. Some of the principles of biblical theology lent themselves very well to this.

There have been, then, many elements of paradox or contradiction in the matter of the distinction between doctrinal and biblical theology. These can be suitably illustrated from a further consideration of the influence of the dominant figure of Karl Barth.

No influence had been stronger than that of Karl Barth in re-establishing the idea of the total authority of the Bible, and in particular that of the Old Testament, and in supporting and inspiring the move towards a more 'theological' orientation of biblical scholarship. Biblical theology, as I have suggested elsewhere, made itself in a sense a slave to the Barthian aspect of dialectical theology, providing culturally-based arguments (from the character of the Bible, of Hebrew thought in contrast with Greek, from revelation as against autonomous reason, and so on) for the great Barthian dogmatic claims: above all, for the rejection of natural theology.

One way in which Barth may have encouraged a confusion of the boundaries between biblical and dogmatic theology was through the massive incorporation of exegesis into his *Church Dogmatics*. Granted that he was a dogmatic theologian, the fact remained that the many pages of his doctrinal work were made all the more numerous because they contained long stretches of what might be called 'theological exegesis'. In this sense Barth harked back to the Reformation. He sought to emulate Luther and Calvin and to base his doctrinal decisions on detailed and specific biblical exegesis. Thus in his section on the doctrine of election (CD II/2) he devoted about thirty pages of small print (366–93) to an exegesis of the story of Saul and David, following this up with about nineteen (392–409) on the enigmatic story of the 'man of God from Judah' in 1 Kings 13 and his relations with the prophet of Bethel.[14] Again, in *Church Dogmatics* III/1, the start of Barth's doctrine of creation not only contains but is built around a lengthy and detailed exegesis of the texts of Genesis 1–2. Numerous other examples can be quoted. The extreme lengthiness of his *Dogmatics* can indeed be explained in large measure by their absorption within themselves of large masses of biblical exegesis – plus, equally, large masses of historical theology. The point of this is that, in so far as anyone might take this sort of theological work as a pattern or an ideal, the effect would seem to be that doctrinal theology came very close to being biblical theology, or at least looked that way. This, then, is one of the inheritances of the Barthian side of dialectical theology: the impression that it left on some biblical theologians that a proper doctrinal theology should in principle be, or at least include, a sort of compendium of biblical exegesis in which all and any materials, however remote-looking, should be explained as deeply and closely connected with central Christian doctrines. In other words, just as biblical theology seemed to come closer to doctrinal theology, doctrinal theology seen in this way was more like what some practitioners of biblical theology aspired to. This, as we shall later see, was in considerable measure a misunderstanding of Barth; but it is not surprising that such a misunderstanding took place.

Barth's exegesis, moreover, was not only exegesis: it was exegesis conducted in a peculiarly contemptuous and superior way in relation to the main currents of Old Testament scholarship. Not that Barth ignored scholarly opinion. He wrote some of his exegeses in fairly constant conversation with it – in Genesis 1–2, for instance, with Gunkel and with Franz Delitzsch, also – more marginally for modern scholarship – with Benno Jacob. He took into account materials like the Mesopotamian myths (CD III/1,87f.). He did not deny the propriety of 'historical' exegesis in some degree. Nevertheless the total impression given by his work is, as I have said, a contemptuous and superior one. It is summed up in the chilling statement of the preface to *CD* III/2 (published in 1948; ET, ix): 'The time has not yet come when the dogmatician will be able to relate himself with good conscience and confidence to the results of his colleagues in Old and New Testament' – this at a time when Hoskyns' *The Fourth Gospel,* Eichrodt's Old Testament Theology, and the earlier parts of the Kittel Theological Dictionary had been available for at least fifteen years, and when von Rad's *Genesis* was to appear in the very next year, 1949.[15] Fundamentally and in essence, in spite of the degree of respect that Barth showed towards his exegetical colleagues and contemporaries, he thought that they had little or no idea of what exegesis was really about. They asked the wrong questions, and the answers they produced were at best of marginal importance and at worst quite insignificant. He could do better himself. Thus, having presented at length his explanations of the story of Saul and David in the Books of Samuel, and of that of the man of God and the prophet in I Kings 13, he leaves them with a challenge to any possible rival: if anyone has an objection to what I say, then he has to do better! (so, in effect, *CD* II/2, 393, 409).

Now the actual grounds and merits, if any, of Barth's alienation from biblical scholarship can be left aside for the moment. The important point for the present is that this particular line of doctrinal theology professed an ability to carry out its own comprehensive exegesis of long stretches of the Bible, both Old and New Testament, and claimed that this was theologically meaningful in a way that was not true of current biblical scholarship. Obviously, where this line of doctrinal theology was accepted or admired, it seemed that doctrinal theology itself had come very close to providing that to which biblical theology aspired. Barth's dogmatics, or at least their exegetical sections, were more or less an ideal exemplar of what biblical theology might be and of how it should work. Certainly Barth thought biblical scholarship should be 'more theological', and he was so unwise as to pronounce the production of Kittel's *Theologisches Wörterbuch* – certainly a resource which led some doctrinal theologians to suppose that they could with ease outflank biblical scholarship – to be a sign of hope in this respect.[16] At times it could be claimed – perhaps mistakenly (see below) but at least understandably – that what Barth was doing, in his exegetical work, could count as 'biblical theology' or come close to it. Thus in Childs' use of this expression the two terms confirm one another: 'Barth is doing biblical theology' seems to mean (*a*) Barth is right because what he does is biblical theology, and (*b*) biblical theology is right because Barth does it.[17] There is no doubt, then, that Barth's thinking and procedures encouraged many to see, and to look with favour upon, something like a coalescence of biblical and doctrinal theology rather than a clear distinction between the two.

On a more serious level, however, this was a superficial and biblicistic understanding of Barth. In fact his thinking had no significant place for any such thing as 'biblical theology'.[18]The situation and the set of problems which among biblical scholars had led towards biblical theology did not exist for him. For him there were two things only: text along with exegesis, and dogmatic theology. So far as I can see, he had no theory of biblical theology,[19] no idea of a separate level on which biblical theology could or should be done. For him there was no 'theology' that was not dogmatic in level and category. Thus although, as has been said, Barth's influence stimulated biblical theology, although much biblical theology acted as if it was an ancillary to the Barthian impulses in theology, and although many followers of Barth were warm supporters of the idea of biblical theology, a more profound understanding of Barth would suggest the contrary. In his view, no judgments that claim to be truly theological can be made unless they are truly dogmatic. For him 'biblical theology', if there were such a thing, would therefore be mistakenly aping something that by its own nature it can never be.[20]

The following is a restatement of a paragraph which I wrote some years ago:[21]

'Biblical theology' is a mode of organizing and interlinking the biblical material that differs indeed from the historical mode; but that in itself does not make it into theology. Theology can never be simply an organization of the biblical material, in whatever mode or on whatever level, but must be the construction, criticism and refining of *our* concepts of God in Christ and in the church. For such a theological task the biblical material is of extreme importance, but no amount of consideration of the biblical material, in whatever mode, will in itself perform that task. In relation to making actual theological decisions, biblical theology thus takes us no farther forward than purely historical exegesis does. In fact, it makes the position worse, because its own self-designation as 'theology' and its own clearly expressed theological values only make it look all the more like theology when in fact it is not theology at all. The most advanced biblical theologies do not reach as far as the point at which actual theological thinking begins. The whole strenuous effort to establish that biblical theology is distinct from historical exegesis has been unimportant. In relation to real theology, if one of them is merely preparatory, then so is the other.

The above, when written (in slightly different terms), was intended as an argument derivative from Barth's own position – as well as from that of others.

Another mode in which dialectical theology, especially in its Barthian form, reduced the distance between biblical and doctrinal theologies was in its 'kerygmatic' character. Faith was 'proclaimed', and therefore was not either proved (which would have been 'apologetics') or made subject to criticism.

Exactly these two aspects, reasoned support and criticism, which are the opposite ends of the same axis, would have helped to make a meaningful distance between biblical and doctrinal theology. The former would explicate the connections within the biblical material, its coherence and its basis in the theological thinking of biblical times. Doctrinal theology on the other hand would make clear how far the biblical material is believed to correspond to the external, extra-biblical, reality that is the real object of faith. Doctrinal theology might offer reasons in favour of such correspondence (thus the 'apologetic' end of the axis), or might offer reasons why the correspondence is limited (the 'critical' end of the same axis). Not everyone will agree that these operations are desirable, but it is beyond question that they provide a good ground for a distinction between biblical and doctrinal theology. In my own opinion dialectical theology, in so far as it ruled out these operations, was leaving aside operations that are essential to 'theology' in the proper sense of the word. It was thus insisting on its own character as 'theology' while adopting a practice that was, in certain respects, essentially 'non-theology'. Hence some of the difficulties we have been discussing.

## Conclusion

1. Biblical theology has the Bible as its horizon: its source material is the biblical text, its subject is the theology which lies behind or is implied by the Bible, and its scope is determined by the meanings as known and implied within the time and culture of the Bible. In this sense Gabler was right in saying that biblical theology was historical in character. This does not mean, however, that it consists of nothing more than historical research.

2. Doctrinal theology, however much it works with the Bible and acknowledges the Bible as authoritative, is not primarily *about* the Bible: it is primarily about God and its horizon is God. Its task is to elucidate, explain, and make intelligible and consistent the regulative principles which influence or control the action and the speech of the religious community. Even given the maximum authority of the Bible, the Bible is not the sole or even the sole controlling factor in its work. Its work is related to later traditions, to philosophy (as Gabler said) and to natural theology (as Jacob said), and to the modern situation. The ultimate reason for this is that the source of doctrinal theology is not the Bible. It would be more correct to say that the source of doctrinal theology is the tradition of regulative decisions which had a part in the formation of the biblical texts. Or, in other words, the prime and ancient paradigm for doctrinal theology is not the Bible but the Creed. The extant creeds are, of course, historically later than the completion of the Bible; logically, however, they have precedence, because they represent something that, in earlier forms, antedated the Bible.

I am here disagreeing, therefore, with Emil Brunner when he began the second chapter of his *The Divine-Human Encounter* with the sentence 'The source and norm of all Christian theology is the Bible.' [22] This, he goes on, 'is the presupposition . . . for my attempt to work out the opposition between the biblical understanding of truth and the general, rational understanding of truth as determined by the Object-Subject antithesis'. The Bible may in a certain sense be the norm, or rather one of the norms; but it cannot, strictly speaking, be the source. The source is a theological tradition which *preceded* the Bible and accompanied it, guiding and influencing its utterances, as well as following it. Precisely its ability to identify and describe this tradition, or at least its aspiration to do so, is the justification and meaning of biblical theology.

Robert Morgan is thus right in writing:

> The dependence of both the Bible and theology upon a prior revelation of God, and the denial that theology consists simply in deductions from the Bible, can be confirmed by recalling that Christian theology antedated the Christian Bible. The beginnings of Christian theology can be traced within the New Testament to a period before it was described as either 'Christian' or 'theology'.[23]

The same thing, we must add, would be true, *mutatis mutandis*, for the Hebrew Bible. This insight is of vital importance for the conception of biblical theology.

Doctrinal theology does indeed have a scriptural test which affects its status. But the test is not whether a doctrinal theology is full of biblical exegesis or not, or whether it is derived from the Bible or can be proved by the Bible – on the contrary, many of the great doctrines could never be 'proved' from the Bible. The test is rather whether the theology can provide matrices suitable for the interpretation of the Bible. The suitability of these matrices is not any better proved by massive exegesis of the Bible than by the explication of other modes in which the Bible may be integrated into theology.

3. The effect of dialectical theology in some of its forms was to diminish the distance between biblical and doctrinal theology; this coincided with a biblicistic view of theology on the part of many biblical scholars. It was, however, a misunderstanding of dialectical theology: in many respects the major dialectical theologians took the opposite view.

4. Precisely because biblical theologians have not seriously faced the fact of a doctrinal theology that is quite different in type and operational mode from their own work, they have given little thought to the nature of doctrinal theology and have not tried to converse meaningfully with it. The tendency to think that it would be good to merge biblical and doctrinal theology as far as possible is a symptom and a result of this failure.

5. I mention here another aspect which will be discussed later, but must be

mentioned here because it concerns the relation between doctrinal and biblical theology: it remains a serious question how far any sort of 'biblical theology' is really and authentically *theology*. Biblical theologians cannot rightly justify this title by simply *asserting* that their work is, as they see it, 'theological'. For the question how far it is really theology depends not on their assertions but on the judgment of the doctrinal theologians, whose province 'theology' in the proper sense of the word it is. We will return to this below, Chapter 15.

The distinction between doctrinal theology and biblical theology is therefore very important. That is not to say that the two may not be mixed up. They may very well be mixed up, in the sense that considerations on both levels may occur together. But even if thus mixed up, they have to be clearly distinguished. Ideas that may be creative in biblical theology may often come out of the older theological tradition, which is primarily doctrinal. Ideas formed within biblical theology may require to be considered in doctrinal theology. Biblical theologians may well wish to point out ways in which doctrinal theology could better orientate itself in relation to the Bible. Doctrinal theologians may wish to point out to biblical theologians consequences in their concepts – say of 'history', or of 'tradition', or of 'parable' – which have not been taken into account. All this is the more the case because 'biblical theologians' and 'doctrinal theologians' are not, in essence, two different sets of people: rather the terms signify, not always but at least sometimes, two different sets of operations, which may go on in the same mind. But the maintenance of the distinction remains very important.

Some such position as this, I submit, will provide adequate differentiation between biblical theology and doctrinal theology. Further justification and elaboration of it will be added in later chapters.

# 6

# Difference from Non-Theological Study

1. From early times biblical studies had included operations that were not themselves in the strict sense 'theological' – the comparison of different textual readings, the registration of geographical and cultural *realia*, the learning of Hebrew and Greek, the awareness of relevant contemporary history, things of that kind. In the larger sense these matters did belong to 'theology' – as they still do, for the student of theology has to learn something of them. And in a time like Gabler's, at the end of the eighteenth century, it could still be largely taken for granted that such things were part of 'theology' and that the persons who occupied themselves with them were 'theologians' – as is still the speech convention in some countries.

But by the earlier twentieth century the independence of these areas from theology in the stricter sense of the word had become more evident. They were relevant for theological study as a whole, but they seemed to operate without truly theological criteria or standards. Theology, it seemed, could no longer decide, could no longer even offer authoritative guidance, about questions of Semitic languages, the meanings of words, their origins, the dates and authorship of documents, the significance of archaeological remains at Jericho or elsewhere. Scholars worked with such matters in a way that suggested that theology had no vital part in their operations. It was not uncommon to meet scholars who were experts in these areas but who said with some pride and satisfaction that they were 'not theologians' and knew nothing about theology. By the 1960s or so this was a common situation in many countries. 'Biblical studies' could be carried on, it seemed, in an environment completely unrelated to theology.

In view of this apparent disappearance of theology from large areas of biblical study, one began to ask whether there still remained any function for theology within biblical studies. The rise of biblical theology was thus a reaction against the existence of this apparently non-theological component in the biblical disciplines, and still more against its rise in importance to a point where it threatened to expel theology altogether from the area. Against these tendencies some currents of biblical theology have maintained that, in order to understand the texts, it is necessary to use *theological* insights and criteria. The Old or New Testament scholar, some biblical theology has insisted, must also be a theologian; otherwise his or her work will be at best marginal or preparatory, and does not begin to engage with the real questions. This tendency is already present with Eichrodt, though it appears to conflict with some of his other principles: among Old Testament theologians it is most marked in Childs.

As I have already remarked, the effect of this opposition to the non-theological components is the contrary of the contrast with dogmatic theology which we have already discussed. In contrast with dogmatics, biblical theology had argued, we are not dogmaticians – that is another affair, though somehow connected; in contrast with the non-theological components, it argued, Yes, we have to do theology. The Old – or New – Testament scholar must be something of a theologian, must think theologically – and that must mean be a theologian in a mode that comes somewhere near to the doctrinal. Indeed it has sometimes been thought – notably by Childs – that biblical theology would come markedly closer to doctrinal theology in its recent, strongly biblical form, as seen in Barth, than to other types such as philosophical theology, so that there would be a sort of alliance or convergence between these two.

It is a serious mistake, however, to suppose that the presence of these various 'non-theological' factors makes exegetical work as a whole 'non-theological'. Fundamentally, exegesis can never be a purely theological activity. It is by its nature a reaction between (*a*) material some of which is of itself not specifically theological and (*b*) theological conceptions and interpretations. There is thus no possibility of a purely theological exegesis: such an exegesis would be no more than a reiteration of the theological views one already held. In a text the potential theological implications are indicated through the effect of manifold factors. All these manifold factors are *always and in principle* theologically relevant. But theology alone, understood as operating separately from all these other factors, cannot interpret them. In other words, the longing for a 'theological' exegesis which would be something other than an exegesis involved with non-theological factors is the consequence of a wrong conception both of theology and of exegesis.

Particularly to be avoided is the instrumentalist concept, according to which the 'non-theological' elements in exegesis are viewed as 'tools' to be 'used' or 'employed', means towards the 'end' of theological decision.[1] Note that Childs uses the same instrumental conception in relation to the rational and philosophical language used by systematic theology: this also is only a 'tool'. The 'tool' conception betrays a serious misunderstanding of texts and interpretation. Knowledge of Hebrew grammar is no more a 'tool' in the understanding of Hebrew texts than prayer is a 'tool' in communication with the deity.

The language of the Bible is not in itself a theological reality. The Hebrew language is not a theological phenomenon and is not symmorphous with the theology of the Hebrew Bible; nevertheless through the Hebrew language statements with theological implications can be made and are made. The Greek language is no different in this respect. Language, however, is not a 'tool' which can be 'used'. It is the field in which meanings exist, the means of communication. If the words are different, then the meaning is different. Language is not a tool but is essentially an entity in which the biblical material is built and within which it exists. Theology therefore has rightly emphasized the need for a command of the biblical languages if the Bible is to be rightly interpreted.

But the other 'non-theological' components are not tools either. The difference of texts is part of the character of the Bible: to put it grossly, a different text means a different Bible. The references to cultural and geographical realia are part of the meaning: without them the text becomes, at relevant points, empty words.

Thus a theology that does not accord positive value, value for theology itself, to the 'non-theological' elements in exegesis is a mistaken theology. It is interaction with these 'non-theological' elements that provides the decisive selection between theological possibilities. There is no 'pure' theology, at least not in the realm of exegesis.[2] The only 'pure' theology, if such could exist, would be a speculative philosophical theology. A theology related to biblical exegesis must speak positively of its own 'non-theological' elements and factors.

2. It has been common in the modern discussion to use a model which thought of theology as a 'goal' which had to be 'reached'. Exegesis, according to this model, 'starts' with so-called 'introduction', including questions of language, text, date, authorship, sources and so on. The question thus posed is how from this somewhat 'non-theological' beginning one 'goes on' to the further stage of theological assessment. It is often complained that that further stage is never reached: the goal remains remote, indeed the further stage is not even commenced. Hence come the many vocal demands for theological exegesis.

This model is a mistaken one. It may indeed have some sort of pedagogical basis: students commonly hear courses on 'introduction' before they hear any on biblical theology or on theological exegesis. As a teaching procedure this may be quite justified. But it does not correspond to the way in which exegesis and theology are intrinsically related. It is obvious that in the mind of the typical hearer theology comes first; it is there before the 'introduction' is studied. Theological interpretation is already there in the mind of the student before any exegetical courses are undertaken. Theology has priority. It comes from the religious tradition and is inculcated *as the essential meaning of scripture* before any academic exegesis is done. Exegesis therefore does not work by *initiating*, in the absence of theology, a move which should eventually lead to some sort of theological interpretation. On the contrary, it operates as a *critical* force, questioning the theology that is already there, asking whether it really has a biblical basis, enriching it with new information and perspectives. Most commonly of course it ends up by confirming and re-establishing the theological evaluations and perspectives with which one began; at the most optimistic, it may modify them and commence the slow process of change, of theological re-thinking. Only very exceptionally, and with exegetes of great distinction, does an exegesis in itself lead to a new and fresh theological result quite unconnected with the pre-existing tradition.

Theological ideas, then, come normally out of the tradition, not out of the Bible; and this is not accidental but fits with the reality of the whole matter, as we have seen.[3] Exegesis presents data, material, connections which may support or may challenge the theological overview of the student. Whether the material presented is of 'theological' or of 'non-theological' character makes no difference.

3. The reader may have noticed that this chapter has not begun with any extensive reference to 'historical criticism'. The absence of such a reference was deliberate. It has indeed been a common idea that historical criticism is a 'non-theological factor', indeed the most obviously non-theological of all, and in addition the most pervasive and therefore the most damaging and dangerous of all. It has been castigated on the grounds that its methods and procedures are 'secular'. Why then have I said so little about it thus far?

For one thing, I wanted to show that historical criticism, as usually under-stood, is not the only reality involved at this point in the discussion. To me it is not even the most important. To me the base for modern critical scholarship does not lie in historical criticism, but in language. Language is built into the essence of the Bible whether we have any critical concepts or not. But in deal-ing with grammar and language structure we are necessarily entering a 'secular' field, one from which theology can learn but one where theology as such has little or nothing to tell us. Moreover, the centrality of language was emphasized in the theological tradition itself, even though it was recognized that language was a humanistic theme and not an indigenously theological one.

Secondly, it seems to me quite false in any case to suppose that traditional historical criticism is non-theological. In the Bible, where one often has rather little external information about the surrounding circumstances, historical criticism is often, perhaps mainly, directed through religious perceptions, especially through the perception of religious differences between parts of the Bible itself. In this respect 'historical' criticism developed out of the many theological disputes especially of post-Reformation times. The perception of theological differences, rather than the imitation of 'secular' history, generated biblical criticism. Thus the discovery of the sources and differences within the biblical books is largely a sequel to the doctrinal controversies within Christianity, between Catholic and Protestant, and still more within Protestantism.

Historical criticism, therefore, far from being a 'non-theological' aspect of biblical study, seems to me to be much more a theological aspect than some others are. The generating force within it was the large amount of apparently historical narrative within the Bible, both Old and New Testament, and the very large extent to which Christian doctrine was developed on the basis of these narratives, traditionally treated as historically accurate.

It is true that it became a modern theological fashion, largely in response to the quest of the historical Jesus, to say that theologically important truth could not be established on historical grounds. Any historical approach came to be castigated as 'liberal' and it came to be thought that historical study was inappropriate for theological realities. The idea that historical study was 'not theological' was reinforced through the association of it with liberal theology, for it was suggested that liberal theology, being historical in character (actually this is only partially true), was therefore not true theology at all. This opinion, however, being aimed at discrediting liberal theology, should not be taken seriously: the fact remains that the historicity of biblical narratives has been a central theme of all classical Christianity, and it is the odd opinion of dialectical theology that is in conflict with the main tradition. That odd opinion ought not to be dismissed as if it had no significance, but it should certainly not be accepted as obviously regulative. In the main tradition of Christian theology, history, or at least some history, has a theological character. Historical criticism, that is, the criticism of the apparent historical assertions of the biblical documents, shares in that same character.

It is not my intention here to enter into a full discussion of history, historical criticism and theology; at this point I am thinking only of the way in which these questions affect the matter of the 'non-theological' elements in exegesis. As has been said, a good theology ought to welcome the 'non-theological' elements and make clear their positive value, while the historical interest should not be counted a 'non-theological' element at all. Two other aspects in this connection may be mentioned briefly.

An aspect of historical criticism which has often been mentioned with disfavour is its *analytic* character: precisely in reaction against this, much modern biblical theology set out deliberately to be *synthetic*. The merits of this, one way or the other, will be discussed later. All that needs to be mentioned here is that there is nothing untheological in being analytic. An analytic approach – say, one distinguishing different strata in the Pentateuch – is actually of high theological relevance. On the one hand it depends among other things on differences and similarities of theological significance; on the other hand it establishes new continuities of the same which had not hitherto been evident. These differences and similarities are among exactly the relations with which Old Testament theology has to deal. Far from it being the case that analytic study was non-theological or even anti-theological, it was a perspective that almost all biblical theologians built into their work. By contrast, the sort of conservative, anti-critical scholarship that rejected analytic study never produced any serious contribution to biblical theology.[4]

Moreover – and this is a very serious point – just as analytic study was not truly non-theological, so equally synthetic procedures were not, and are not, automatically theological. It is one of the clear fallacies in Eichrodt's introductory chapter that he seems to suppose that, if an approach is synthetic, that in itself makes it theological. This simply does not follow – and it is this fact that led to the later objections, such as that by Vriezen, to the effect that Eichrodt's plan produced a phenomenology rather than a theology.[5] This criticism is not necessarily fully valid, but Eichrodt had not guarded properly against it: he wrote as if, through being done with a synthetic and comprehensive method, his work was therefore obviously theological in character. Further effects of this will be discussed below.

A related point is this. Eichrodt in his introductory chapter made it a central aim to escape from the 'tyranny of historicism' (I, 31). By 'historicism' he probably meant more than the mere practice of historical writing or analysis: he probably meant, or at least hinted at, the entire philosophy/theology of history associated with the name of Troeltsch.[6] Even if he himself did not intend this, it was an argument typical of the rising tide of biblical theology. Troeltsch is thought of as the theoretician of historical criticism, but this was not the experience of critical scholars themselves: most of them, certainly in the English-speaking lands, regarded his views as extreme and incompatible with their own Christianity. He was regarded as a total relativist and one who thought that no sort of explanation other than historical explanation was possible for anything. As a theologian, even in the liberal period, though certainly a big name he was far from popular. But this is just the point. The objection against 'historicism' was a theological conflict: if opposition to it satisfied the claims of biblical theology to be really theology, then the same was true of the 'historicism' which it opposed. In this sense biblical theology, as thus explained and defined, was not standing for theology as against historical study, but for one theology as against another. And this has certainly been the case whenever the case for biblical theology has been linked with affirmations of dialectical theology as the true and only genuine representative of 'real' theology.

Another aspect is the sense of some voices in biblical theology that historical study by its own nature failed to provide relevance for the present day. It 'locked' the Bible 'into the past' (Sanders). Relevance for the modern world and church was of high importance, and could not be provided by an historical approach. In some quarters it was thought that biblical theology would help by providing material for preachers, thus reviving biblical preaching and making the Bible more alive for the present day. At the worst some biblical theology can look like a mishmash of homiletic material or a rewriting of old sermons. This interest in relevance attracted support to biblical theology and in some quarters drew it farther away from historical study, closer to theology. On the other hand it did great damage to the subject, for biblical material that was of theological importance could easily come to be ignored because no present-day relevance in it was seen, or could be distorted by the attempt to make it seem relevant. Examples of this can be seen, for instance, in the neglect or deliberate denial of the chronological interests of the Old Testament[7] or in the covering up of the biblical material which pointed towards the immortality of the soul.[8] Generally it may be said that the pressure for relevance impaired such methodological rigour as biblical theology might be said to have possessed and tended to reduce it to a vague groping after insights that seemed to be homiletically or practically useful.

To sum up on this point, difference from non-theological study has been a false and deceptive principle where biblical theology has been led by it. On the one hand, there is no such thing as 'pure' theology, or if it exists it exists only in the doctrinal realm; it certainly is a will-of-the-wisp for any idea of biblical theology. Theology, seen as a total enterprise, is a collection of different disciplines of which theology, in the strict sense, is only one. All these disciplines such as linguistics, archaeology, sociology and history, both biblical and later, though not 'theological' in their methods and criteria, have to be taken into, and are in fact taken into, the total enterprise of theological thinking. Biblical theology may thus have a sort of mediating function between critical biblical study and theology in the stricter sense. Thus a relation to critical study is proper to biblical theology, and, as stated above, no serious biblical theology has arisen where the truly conservative anti-critical principles have prevailed. On the other hand it seems to me to go too far when J. J. Collins asserts that biblical theology must be *founded upon* historical criticism.[9] This seems to me to misjudge the mood of the main movement of biblical theology, and also to invite a contrary reaction. Biblical theology has been more a *combination* of historical-critical perceptions with perceptions of a different kind.

Contrary to opinions now popular, the association between critical scholarship and biblical theology in this century has been a striking success, as later chapters in this book will show. Attempts to carry on biblical theology while breaking its links with critical scholarship have equally proved to fail. Critical study has of course produced mistakes, false starts and the proliferation of misleading theories, but this is true of all other currents of study, and especially of theological approaches themselves. It should be recognized by now that there is absolutely no sound theological reason why critical study should be deemed damaging to religious perceptions. The fact that such study is in a certain sense 'non-theological' is precisely the reason why it has a vital positive part to play within theology as a whole. Theologies which deny this are simply theologically wrong, and wrong not because they are against biblical criticism, but for many other and intrinsically theological reasons.

# 7

# Evolution and Anti-Evolutionism

This chapter was originally written as one of several components in the follow-ing chapter on relations between biblical theology and the history of religion. In the course of writing, however, it expanded to such a degree that it seemed better to separate it off and make it into a chapter on its own. In part it antici-pates elements that have to be considered later, but in part it provides a power-ful illustration of an aspect of modern biblical theology, and a possible hint of a direction in which it may go in the future. It may, however, be omitted by readers, who can go on to the next chapter if they wish.

No one who knows the literature will question my assertion that opposition to evolutionary ideas has been a major characteristic of biblical theology during most of the twentieth century. A very definite turn against developmental and evolutionary depictions of religion was a feature of it from the beginning.[1] This was particularly evident in English-language scholarship; I have not noticed it as so prominent in the continental literature. The evolutionary approach had been a very influential one. Goldingay tellingly quotes the great Old Testament scholar and Hebraist S.R. Driver, who did more than any other single person to make modern biblical criticism accepted in England, as writing:

> Progress, gradual advance from lower to higher, from the less perfect to the more perfect, is the law which is stamped upon the entire range of organic nature, as well as upon the history of the civilization and education of the human race.[2]

A more typical representative, writing on a more popular level and more widely read, was the liberal clergyman Harry Emerson Fosdick with his *A Guide to Understanding the Bible* (1938), characteristically subtitled *The Development of Ideas within the Old and New Testaments*. This work, presented as 'an objective, factual picture of unfolding biblical thought', was called by the author 'not primarily a book on biblical theology but a genetic survey of developing biblical thought'. 'Not expository but genetic,' he continued, 'it tries to trace the high-roads traversed by biblical ideas from their origin to their culmination; when they have reached their culmination it makes no endeavour to give a systematic and adequate exposition of them.' The unity Fosdick found within the Bible 'was to be measured not in terms of coherence of thought but "on the factually demonstrable basis of a coherent development"'. Nothing could more aptly describe his [Fosdick's] historical outlook than the assertion that 'the story of developing scriptural ideas . . . makes of the Bible a coherent whole, understood, as everything has to be understood, in terms of its origins and growth'.[3]

On a more scholarly level again, Oesterley and Robinson's *Hebrew Religion: Its Origin and Development* was one late flowering of this style, still in use as a textbook when I was a student – not that it was necessarily so highly thought of even then: it should be remembered that not one of the Old Testament Theologies now regarded as standard then existed in English.[4] A scheme of gradual progress through stages was used: it might go back to animism, then polydaemonism, then to polytheism, to henotheism or monolatry, to mono-theism and to the culmination, ethical monotheism.[5] Various elements in the Bible might be survivals from earlier stages in this evolution. I remember hear-ing it said (not too seriously, no doubt) that, when Israel was forbidden to use hewn stones in building the altar (Exod. 20.25), this was because there was a spirit alive in the stone: they might chop his ears off![6]

In the newer theological climate after the 1930s, still more after 1945, many people found this kind of thing abhorrent. The older traditional religious resis-tance against any kind of evolution remained in existence and if anything revived in force. The emphasis on the Bible as the Word of God seemed to defy evolutionary explanations. Particular religious interests felt the concept threatening: Jews, for instance, might feel that Christians used it in order to portray Christianity as a 'higher' stage in evolution – though such an argument, properly thought through, would have worked to the advantage rather of Islam than of Christianity![7]

Anyway, returning to biblical theology, Goldingay is right in saying that biblical theologians were quick to describe evolution, when applied as an interpretative possibility to the Bible, 'as a theory which is now quite passé, a mere "historical curiosity"' (this last phrase, characteristically, from James D. Smart).[8] George Ernest Wright in his early works, so influential in the first stages of the Biblical Theology Movement, is almost speechless with indignation against evolutionary ideas.[9] There was no evolution, he maintained, for Israelite faith could not have evolved out of previous or contemporary pagan religions: it was 'an utterly unique and radical departure from all contemporary pagan religions' (*God who Acts*, 19). 'It is impossible on any empirical grounds to understand how the God of Israel could have evolved out of polytheism. He is unique, *sui generis*, utterly different' (ibid., 21). (The frequency of the word 'utterly' escalated enormously in the rhetoric of this period.)

In taking this line Wright was doubtless following in the footsteps of his teacher W. F. Albright. The highly evolutionary study of Fosdick has been mentioned just above. The *Journal of Biblical Literature* invited Eichrodt to review it, and he did so at considerable length: ten pages of German! Because of the war, the journal did not receive the review until the autumn of 1945, and Albright very sensibly prepared an abstract of three and a half pages in English to aid the reader. One may assume that his doing of this was a sign of deep sympathy with the tone of the original review. Fosdick's approach, he said, paraphrasing Eichrodt, was based 'almost wholly on an evolutionary histori-cism' and reflected 'a period of biblical scholarship which is now drawing to an end'. One could not deny 'that there were early survivals from still earlier stages of religious culture'; the great mistake was 'to construct a system out of such survivals, arbitrarily disregarding or rejecting all contrary evidence for a higher level of ethical and spiritual life and thought'. Fosdick had adopted 'certain general religious ideas derived from the individualistic spirit of Hellenism as his guide through the essentially different conceptual world of the Bible', and thus the author's choice of data was 'determined by his subjective premises rather than by any scientific method'. 'Mere description of evolutionary stages' was being 'treated as equivalent to real understanding of what is essential in any phenomenon belonging to the history of the human spirit'. Thus Albright was aligning himself with the spirit of early biblical theology, as personified by Eichrodt, and strongly condemning the evolutionary perspectives of Fosdick.

The turning away from evolutionary perspectives, especially in the religiously-conscious public, was very marked. The scholarship of men like Robertson Smith (who had identified a considerable element of totemism in ancient Semitic society) or of Sir James Frazer with his world-wide collections of folk-lore, which had had very substantial esteem, now came to decrease abruptly in influence. The new Old Testament theology, for example in Eich-rodt's approach with its effort to state a transhistorical cross-section, was a very conscious turning away from a developmental approach.[10] Albright's very deliberate alignment with this anti-evolutionary piece was one of the reasons for the high reputation and popularity he was to gain among the more conserva-tively-minded sections of the religious public.

As in so many matters in biblical theology, however, even this anti-evolution-ist trend was shot through with contradictions. More recently Walter Bruegge-mann, writing in 1985, claimed: 'It has long been clear that a hypothesis of religious developmentalism or evolution is no longer a viable model for biblical interpretation, even though that notion continues to exercise enormous popular power.'[11] He adds in a footnote that 'William F. Albright, in *From the Stone Age to Christianity*, delivered the telling blow against such evolutionism'. And historically this is partly right: Albright's influence was widely so seen at the time.

In fact, however, things were far otherwise, and Brueggemann, partly realizing this, adds to his note the further sentence: 'In retrospect, it appears that Albright's "organismic" articulation was not as remote from developmentalism as appeared at the time.'[12] This is a great understatement. Not only in retrospect, but at the time itself it should have been clear to any perspicacious observer that Albright's position was entirely an evolutionistic one.

The very title of his book – *From the Stone Age to Christianity. Monotheism and the Historical Process* – smacks of evolution. And its final paragraphs are a resounding and eloquent evolutionist statement:

> A double strand runs through our treatment: first, the ascending curve of human evolution, a curve which now rises, now falls, now moves in cycles and now oscillates, but which has always *hitherto* recovered itself and continued to ascend; second, the development of individual historical patterns or configurations, each with its own organismic life, which rises, reaches a climax, and declines. The picture as a whole warrants the most sanguine faith in God and in His purpose for man. In detail it does not justify either fatuous optimism or humanistic meliorism . . . It is only when the historian compares successive configurations of society that the fact of real progress makes itself apparent.[13]

To the thoughtful reader there can be no doubt that Albright's major work *From the Stone Age to Christianity* was a capable and fairly consistent evolutionary approach. Why then had Fosdick been so severely condemned? Where was the difference? 'We are today acutely conscious,' Albright wrote, paraphrasing Eichrodt, 'of the danger of assuming *unilinear* evolution of institutions or ideas' (205). This was thought to be the key point. Since the evolution was not unilinear, Albright and others following him could claim as 'historical' reports and traditions which by unilinear evolution must be unhistorical but by this more random evolution could perfectly well fit in anywhere. Thus by producing a 'conservative' picture of ancient Israel, by maintaining that the essentials were there more or less from the beginning, by placing the origins and fundamentals right back there with Moses, Albright, and Wright after him, seemed to overcome one of the aspects of evolutionism that most troubled many religious people.

Wright likewise, following Albright, at times combined evolutionary terms and values with his anti-evolutionary emphasis. In those same works in which he so freely castigated evolution, Wright can be found to say things that appear to treat it as a good thing. 'What is the Israelite *mutation*,' he asks, 'which made the particular and peculiar *evolution* of biblical faith a possibility?'[14] Polytheism, which he treated very negatively, was 'a religion of the *status quo*'; never has it been 'a dynamic force for social change'. Even when, as sometimes happens, a philosophical idealism may have been evolved out of it, 'the religion has not been a power for social *evolution*' (my italics). Evolution, therefore, would have been a good thing, but polytheism was incapable of fostering it. In *God Who Acts*, polemicizing as he so often did against the Greek view of history, in which, according to him, history was cyclical and meaningless, he wrote that 'such a view excludes completely any *progress or movement* (my italics) toward an earthly millennium, whether the latter is to be achieved through the gradual evolution envisaged by modern liberal idealism, or through the revolution conceived by Marxist communism. History is in movement, but it is going nowhere' (41). Contrasting this with the situation in early Christianity, he says of the latter: 'Human history, on the contrary, far from consisting of a series of repetitive patterns, is in sure movement, even though unsteady, to an ultimate goal.' This looks awfully like a positive (and Christian) kind of evolution.[15]

Moreover, in later years, in his *The Old Testament and Theology* (1969), 84–95, Wright incorporated a quite substantial evolutionary viewpoint into his treatment of creation. He sought to combine with this his older conviction that the highest or decisive stages might be at the beginning: 'many phenomena are at their finest degree of development when first encountered' (84). He now claimed (wrongly, as we shall see) that: 'The theory of evolution as originally expounded in the last century involved the assumption that the movement was always in one direction, toward future emergents and higher ideals' (84). Since evolution can move in different directions, one cannot apply any simple pattern: history may be 'chaos', and, 'if there is a creative providence of God in history, it can only be observed in faith' (85). But the entire chapter continues with firm confidence in an evolutionary perspective. 'The examination of the story of human evolution furnishes concrete illustration of how the creative works in time, and sees the necessity for change and adaptation as sources of continuous conflict in human life,' it concludes. 'In some such manner one can today see the importance of the doctrine of God the creator.'

This was a late work by Wright, but the same tendencies can be found to go back to the beginnings of modern biblical theology. Thus Eichrodt also often made statements that moderated his more anti-evolutionary remarks. Attacking (and deservedly) the highly evolutionistic approach of Fosdick, Eichrodt nevertheless writes such sentences as these: 'It is certainly uncontroversial that an evolution is to be perceived in the history of which the biblical writings give testimony. And it is equally beyond doubt, that the knowledge of this evolution makes comprehensible many peculiarities of the biblical writings that at first seem to be enigmatic.'[16] Only if we over-extend this principle, and make it into the governing principle of mental history, do we go too far. And Eichrodt goes on to admit that Fosdick himself has shown some praiseworthy self-criticism in his application of evolutionary principles. All this fits in well, for, after all, Eichrodt himself appealed to the inner-biblical development as an evidence for ultimate theological meaning: 'Anyone who studies the historical development of the Old Testament finds that throughout there is a powerful and purposive movement which forces itself on his attention. It is true that there are also times when the religion seems to become static, to harden into a rigid system; but every time this occurs the forward drive breaks through once more, reaching out to a higher form of life and making everything that has gone before seem inadequate and incomplete.'[17]

Opposition to evolutionism, then, failed to recognize the survival of that same phenomenon, in a more intelligent and sophisticated form. Nevertheless hostility to evolutionism of any kind was to remain the dominant note in most currents of biblical theology. It was the crasser forms of it that came most to people's notice. Reaction against evolutionary ideas, in their impact upon biblical study, was a very powerful force. 'In the faith of Israel, even in the earliest preserved literature, there is a radical and complete difference [from other religions] at every significant point.'[18] The essentials were there from the very beginning. For G. E. Wright, though Israel's faith was built entirely upon *history*, historical change within *religion* had no very positive place. The important thing, distinctiveness, was there from the earliest knowable beginning and constituted a quantal leap quite unlike the product of an evolution. Such views, as against evolutionary views, tend to a conservative position about Hebrew religion; and, by contrast with all evolution, they tend to favour a *static* presentation of the theology. Thus Eichrodt wrote: 'developmental analysis must be replaced by systematic synthesis, if we are to make more progress toward an interpretation of the outstanding religious phenomena of the Old Testament in their deepest significance' (I, 28).

Reaction against evolutionism, then, was undoubtedly a major element in the new determination to produce an Old Testament theology which would have some sort of unity or homogeneity. What are we to say of the significance of this anti-evolutionist emphasis for the nature of Old Testament theology in general?

Undoubtedly we must grant, I submit, that there was a sort of primitivism in this, an urge to get away from modernity with its scientific hypotheses and to return to an older world where the Bible was whole and complete, with no serious internal development in substance and no overlap into or from other religions. Very likely this came from the popular impact of dialectical theology, even if the dialectical theologians themselves had more sophisticated accounts of these relations.

And yet in the last resort some of the phenomena which had been cited as evidence of evolution remained there and still had to be explained. Robertson Smith's totemism can perhaps be forgotten, but the evidences upon which he based his views remain in existence; his genius lighted on many features within the Old Testament which, if we seek an explanation, are still likely to carry us back to some sort of 'earlier stage' or to conceptions and practices anterior to the biblical sources, contexts and explanations. The later fashion of Old Testament theology was to point to the way in which these ancient materials were re-sited, used and interpreted within the biblical period itself – and quite justifiably. But such emphasis on the intra-biblical contexts, uses and interpretations often leaves unaccounted for the very individualities and particularities of the stories or laws as they stand, and makes them into vehicles of a somewhat homogenized general biblical theology which applies to everything. Leviathan, the great sea monster, for instance, was scarcely a creation of the Yahwistic context: on the contrary, he was an inheritance from some more ancient context. But it is Leviathan, and not the way in which he is reinterpreted, that gives the real colour and life to the passages in which he appears. Jephthah's vow which led him to kill his daughter[19] is scarcely typical Israelite behaviour, and yet clever exegetes may be able to show how this ancient story was taken up into the general theology of the book of Judges. However, it is not that general theology and interpretative framework, but Jephthah's vow, his daughter and her actual death, which lend the real character and importance to the story. Similarly with numerous laws. Take instances like the lists of unclean birds (Lev. 11.13–19; Deut. 14.11–20). Of course this material has been taken up within the thought of the Levitical purity system, and sophisticated explanations of its motivation have been suggested, e.g. by Gese and Milgrom.[20] It had meaning therefore in Israelite times, in the time of Leviticus and Deuteronomy and after. But did the thinkers of that time actually *make up* for themselves the list of birds? No one has explained how they did so. Was it not an inheritance from a past stage: not necessarily a past stage of *evolution*, but nevertheless a past stage? The material from these 'past stages' provides much of the life and variety of the Bible.

Anti-evolutionism also produced contradictions in its interpretation of modern scholars. Wellhausen is a central example. Opponents often branded him as an evolutionist: Albright on the first page of a major lecture series as late as 1968 spoke of Wellhausen's 'unilinear system of religious evolution' and attributed to him a 'Hegelian view of religious history as a development from "fetishism", through henotheism, to monotheism'.[21] This was but a repetition of what countless anti-Wellhausenian anti-evolutionists had said. But it was somewhat anachronistic. By this time the main wave of anti-Wellhausen criticism had started to go in the opposite direction: Wellhausen was in the wrong, not because he saw religious progress taking place through time, but because he thought that the best had been there at the beginning and that the late period was a degeneration![22] Seen this way, Wellhausen must have been an anti-evolutionist himself! What is shown by exchanges of this kind is the degree to which populistic slogans and homiletic condemnations took the place of serious penetration into the realities of evolution and the history of past scholarship. Practically no one in biblical scholarship since Eichrodt has wasted a page on serious investigation of evolutionists like Fosdick: he is written off as a person to be forgotten. And, indeed, not surprisingly, for he was no kind of serious scholar in the field he wrote about. Yet anyone who achieves the dignity of a ten-page review from Eichrodt, backed up by a three-page resumé from Albright, could hardly be said to have been unworthy of notice. The incident is symptomatic of the fact that in this matter biblical theology was following the currents of a widespread cultural mood, to which we shall return shortly.

To sum up this point, then, hostility to evolution has been a major force in the Old Testament theology of this century. When Brueggemann writes that 'it has long been clear that a hypothesis of religious development or evolution is no longer a viable model for biblical interpretation', he is certainly expressing what has been widely thought among biblical theologians. But substantial elements in the scholarly tradition point in the opposite direction. It is hardly possible to say that the influential Albrightian tradition is 'clearly' not 'viable'. After all, all those thousands who by their reading of Albright and Wright (and now indeed of Brueggemann) were persuaded that evolutionism was out-of-date and wrong will now, through the reading of these pages and the rethinking of these same arguments, become evolutionists – a powerful force indeed. The notion of evolution does not only 'exercise enormous popular power' but has behind it support from Albright and, more clearly within the area of biblical theology, from Wright, and indeed from Eichrodt himself in his carefully limited admissions.

Nevertheless the general atmosphere of the subject has been understood as Brueggemann depicts it. The common assumption is that evolution, as a working scheme, is no longer an option. Anyone who uses the word 'evolution' in a scholarly paper has to be ready to be laughed at as behind the times, indeed as a dinosaur which has itself miraculously escaped the forces of evolution. Only late in the century, with Gerd Theissen's *Biblischer Glaube in evolutionärer Sicht* (1984: ET *Biblical Faith. An Evolutionary Approach*, 1984), has someone had the temerity to say, once again, that evolution had some sort of positive role in the whole matter, and this argument has as yet hardly begun to have an impact on the subject.

Something more should be said here about Theissen's work, which has not as yet become well known. It contains four parts. The first is entitled 'Evolution and Faith: An Outline of the Theory of Evolution'. It discusses the relations between scientific thought and faith, and – very importantly for our purpose – describes the analogies and the differences between biological and cultural evolution. The second part treats of 'Biblical Monotheism in an Evolutionary Perspective', and the third of 'New Testament Christology in an Evolutionary Perspective'. Finally, the fourth is entitled 'Faith in the Holy Spirit: The Experience of the Spirit in an Evolutionary Perspective'.

What is important in Theissen's work, at this stage in our argument, is that it shows that an evolutionary approach need not be subject to the familiar objections which have been raised against it. Here are some examples:

1. It has commonly been argued that biblical phenomena are so completely distinctive that they cannot be derived by a sort of gradual development from other religious phenomena. Theissen, however, not only admits this fact but affirms it as outstandingly good evidence in favour of evolution. Evolution works not by gradual development but by quantal mutations. Thus the sort of argument used *against* evolution by Albright, Wright and others actually fits particularly well with an evolutionary approach.

2. It has commonly been argued that, granted the fact of biological evolution, human cultural products, and religion in particular, work in a completely different way. This, it has been thought, makes it impossible to bring religion within an evolutionary framework. For Theissen, however, the difference between biological and cultural manifestations is entirely to be granted, and in fact forms a main element in his conception. 'Human tradition and genetic "transmission" are fundamentally quite different . . . The forms of the process of cultural evolution transcend those of biology. This transmission is brought about by the intervention of human consciousness to give direction to the process. Therefore the step from the biological to the cultural phase is an "evolution of evolution"' (16–17).

3. Another objection against the idea of evolution is that it is 'not theological', i.e. that it leads to a diachronic description of religious phenomena coloured by a presupposed favouritism for certain stages which are supposed to be culminations or high points in the process. But what Theissen produces is certainly a *theology* and nothing else. Naturally he uses the history of religion, but his product is a framework of philosophical and theological conceptions within which biblical material, and other religious material, can be seen.

4. Again, it has commonly been objected against evolutionary approaches that they are excessively optimistic, emphasizing progress and failing to give place for regressions and disasters, in particular for sin and evil. Not so with Theissen: his evolutionary approach includes something close to the traditional idea of 'original sin'. 'I shall be protesting as clearly against the modern dismissal of what the Bible calls "sin" as against the illusionary assumption that world history could not end in catastrophe' (xii). Again, 'the truth could be what liberal theologians love to deny, that we have a "natural" inclination to sin, in other words that we have pre-programmed tendencies of behaviour which are held in check by strong cultural control in the opposite direction and that when the cultural systems of restraint collapse they unleash a terrifying "proneness to degeneration among human beings" . . . "Original sin" is certainly not a good term, but the repression [does he mean 'denial'?]

of the inner disposition of human beings towards degeneration is a dangerous illusion' (146–7).

In these and other respects Theissen stands on their heads the various arguments which were typically used earlier this century against evolutionary approaches. These arguments, intended to oppose evolution, actually supported it when evolution was rightly understood. This is confirmed by the obvious sympathies with evolution which the anti-evolutionists themselves occasionally betrayed, as seen above. Whether evolutionary ideas help us positively or not will be left aside for the present; and equally we shall leave aside questions of the acceptability of Theissen's own approach. I quote him at this point only in order to show the non-viability of many of the arguments that were directed against evolution.

To sum up, the anti-evolutionary strain which was characteristic of much mid-century biblical theology was ill-thought out and confused. One of its effects was to accentuate people's disapproval of the history of religion and to make them think that some kind of unchanging theological unity ought to be sought. The impression that the history of religion would be infused with evolutionary perspectives made people turn against it.[23]

Here again they were ill-informed: in the burgeoning discipline of twentieth-century history of religion, evolutionary ideas have played only a small part. I recently consulted a friend who works in the history of religion and asked him if he could name any of his colleagues who took an evolutionary approach, and he was unable to name any such person. In a paper at a conference on the general science of religion, Svein Bjerke wrote in 1979: 'It is a central fact in the history of our discipline that evolutionary points of view have been sneered at and that evolutionism has been considered an utterly outmoded strategy of research for almost two generations. The turning away from evolutionary viewpoints also in large measure accounts for the loss of interest in all kinds of general theories of religion'.[24] Thus, as I have suggested, when in the earlier part of this century Old Testament scholars turned away from evolutionary approaches, this was far from being a bold and decisive return to a Christian theological perspective: on the contrary, it was a conformity with a general cultural tendency of the time. The reverse is probably the case: evolution had appealed to the older Christian scholars because it seemed to fit in very well with the historical layering of the Bible and the place of Jesus as culmination, in rather traditional Christian terms. More advanced historical study, far from confirming evolutionary ideas, had tended to be perceived as discrediting them.

As we have seen, when biblical scholars turned against evolution, they often argued in such a way as to imply that evolution was 'unilinear', i.e. that the evolutionary stages were 'fixed and necessary sequences which every single culture had to pass through' (words of Bjerke, 'Ecology of Religion', 244). In this they were simply accepting the common conservative anti-evolutionary misconception. In fact the classical evolutionists had no such idea: they were 'clearly aware of the fact that not all cultures had to pass through an unvarying sequence'. When Bjerke writes that 'the view that the classical evolutionists were unilinear evolutionists is, I believe, still prevalent among historians of religion', exactly the same could be said of biblical theologians, at least up to very recent times.

We thus see that newer evolutionary approaches are being discussed within the history of religion: see for instance M. Sahlins and E. Service, *Evolution and Culture*, and within the volume edited by Honko cf. the essay of James L. Peacock entitled 'Notes on a Theory of the Social Evolution of Ritual' (390–401 with following discussion). Thus anyone who supposes that an evolutionary theology like that of Theissen must be an out-of-date phenomenon, based on assumptions long since disproved, will be deeply mistaken.

That evolutionary concepts are still alive and significant in the study of Hebrew religion is shown by a passage near the end of Mark Smith's *The Early History of God*. He writes:

> Though the reasons for Israelite 'convergence' are not clear, the complex paths from convergence to monolatry and monotheism can be followed. The development of Israelite monolatry and monotheism involved both an 'evolution' and a 'revolution' in religious conceptualization, to use D. L. Petersen's categories (56).

Smith's detailed arguments cannot be followed out here. Nor do I express an opinion on whether he is right or not. But Smith is a first-rate scholar, who is fully aware of the intellectual issues about 'evolution' and 'revolution', and whose work on the evidence is of central importance for Old Testament scholarship. It would be folly to dismiss his thinking as a mere throw-back to the ignorant nineteenth century. The existence of the argument which I quote, in its modern and sophisticated form, is enough to show that the category of evolution, far from being passé and a survival from outdated concepts, is a very active and progressive force again today. The ignorant older theological pretence that it could be laughed off as an out-of-date, nineteenth-century concept must now be abandoned. What Mark Smith says is modern and sophisticated and requires attention.

And one at least among the Old Testament theologians has turned his attention to the same matter. Claus Westermann – whose work in general will be surveyed below – produced in 1988 an article on 'Creation and Evolution', in a book of essays devoted to the relations between evolution and faith in God.[25] Because of the anti-religious position with which evolutionary ideas had earlier been connected, a certain armistice between the two sides had been achieved, Westermann argued, and one result of this was that people in church and theology believed in the *creator*, but no longer bothered about the *mode* of creation. The *doctrine* of creation was handed on, but the story of creation was no longer listened to. However, as most theologians and most church members who know anything about science accept the doctrine of evolution, a gap between theology and natural science has developed which has still not been overcome.

On the contrary, Westermann goes on, a thorough study of the biblical material shows that 'in the Bible creation and *development* belong necessarily together'.[26] Traditional dogmatics asserted both creation and *preservation*, but the idea of preservation, as then maintained, left no room for development.

Westermann goes on to argue that the 'primitive history' of Genesis 1–11 is evolutionistic in character. Creation is not instantaneous but is spread over time. The development of living things in different 'kinds' is emphasized, and is connected with the medical wisdom of the priests. Length of time is shown in the early genealogy of Genesis 5. Nature is not fundamentally contrasted with man: rather, nature and humanity stand together before God. The earth has beginning and end: according to L. Oeing-Hanhoff, as quoted, 'According to dialectical materialism the world is eternal. Modern physics in this respect speaks clearly in favour of the Jewish-Christian belief in creation.'[27] Man experiments: Noah tried three times to get the bird's eye to see for him. Man is in a process of *becoming*: cultivation leads on to the building of a town, elsewhere to music and metallurgy. Societal forms develop from family to people and to the multiplicity of peoples, later in Israel to tribes and to the political form of the kingdom. 'God's history with Israel takes place in the form of a historical evolution' (245). Man can *speak; names are given*. Human life is *limited* by birth and death; death is not just a time of ending, it is a force that enters into life as sickness, weakness, loneliness, frustration. Death also is important because it is the basis for *tradition*: 'Tradition exists because man is mortal. The earliest form of tradition is the blessing with which the dying father blesses his child.'[28] Man is also fallible: he can go wrong. The sinner is also the *inventor*. As the serpent rightly said, they came to *know* as a result of their disobedience. The tower of Babel was destroyed, but the invention of sun-dried bricks which had made it possible remained. In the whole story, God punishes and also is merciful, and it is this greater weight of mercy that makes possible the development of the world and of humanity. But, in the final sentence, 'The goal at the end is not reached through the summit of development, but through the greater weight of the mercy of God.'

We cannot discuss this here at greater length. There may be problems in Westermann's view. It may be felt that the six-day creation of Genesis still falls rather far short of evolution in the modern sense, and so similarly for the rest of his argument. Nevertheless this summary is enough to make it clear that evolution has been a major positive interest for one of the most significant Old Testament theologians of the latter part of the twentieth century. Writing later in the Knierim Festschrift (1997), Westermann returns to the subject, deploring the one-sidedness with which Western theology has orientated itself to the side of intellectual history and 'entirely lost contact with the natural sciences' (Sun and Eades, *Problems in Biblical Theology*, 392). And other theologians contributed to the same volume in which Westermann's original article was published, including one no less than Karl Rahner. I have done enough, therefore, to show that the whole realm of evolutionary thought has been seen as relevant to some biblical theology in the last decades.[29]

Moreover, this is not all, and there are other ways in which the matter of evolution may reflect upon the nature and texture of biblical theology as it has been and as it may be in the future. Two illustrations follow.

In 1986 the 1983–84 Gifford Lectures by the Oxford philosopher of religion Richard Swinburne were published in a book entitled *The Evolution of the Soul*. As connoisseurs of biblical theology will know, one of the achievements of that discipline in the mid-twentieth century was to eliminate the human soul and still more the immortal soul from religion, arguing that it was a Greek and non-biblical idea. In my 1992 book *The Garden of Eden and the Hope of Immortality* I sought to show that there was more basis in the Hebrew Bible for both soul and immortality than had usually been believed. At that time, unfortunately, I had not read Swinburne's book, which would have greatly enriched my knowledge of my theme, and I will not try to summarize its arguments here. But in essence it provides a philosophical account of the human soul and links it with the reality of evolution. 'Four thousand million years of evolution produced man, a body and soul in continuing interaction' (298). Now Swinburne argues entirely philosophically and does not use biblical material, but at the very end of his book (311f.) he adds a note in which he indicates that he believes the position elaborated by him to be in agreement with the biblical view of the soul. 'The theory of the evolved human soul which I have been advocating in this book is, I believe, that of the Bible'. And, incidentally, 'substance dualism', i.e. 'the view that those persons which are human beings (or men) living on Earth, have two parts linked together, body and soul' (145), is correct – though this aspect is incidental to the present argument, which merely wants to point out that all this includes an affirmation of *evolution* as the way in which these conditions came to obtain.

Such an argument, whether we agree with it or not, immediately opens the way to quite new explorations in biblical theology. For it was exactly through its work on the nature of humanity – 'anthropology' as it is rather quaintly called in the theological lingo – that the biblical theology of this century made much of its main impact upon contemporary religion. If in fact there is a philosophical position about soul which is directly related to biological evolution, this must have effects upon biblical theology.

The effects go beyond biblical interpretation in the narrower sense. As we have seen, one of the major emphases of dialectical theology was its rejection of apologetics, of attempts to prove theological beliefs right through arguments from science, from philosophy, from history, from any source outside the strictly defined channels of divine revelation. If, however, some element in the biblical view of human mentality is to be substantially illuminated through evolutionary insights, then that prohibition of apologetics becomes frustrating and negative. I leave this instance here, without following it out further, as it deserves.

A second example: the hostility to ideas of religious evolution, or of cultural evolution, also has repercussions on ideas of biological evolution. Naturally it can be claimed that religious and cultural evolution is a quite different matter from biological evolution. But it is not accidental that religious and cultural evolution came to be banned from biblical theology at the same time as biological evolution largely disappeared from consideration in doctrinal theology. Biblical theologians believe that God created the world. On the other hand they are not fundamentalists or creationists, and as such they presumably believe that our world came into existence through an evolutionary process, i.e. that evolution was involved in God's creating of the world. However, apart from the works of Theissen and Westermann quoted above (and I would say that they are rather isolated in this respect), one will have to look far through the works of biblical theology to find any mention of evolution in their accounts of creation. Naturally, it can be said that there is no mention of evolution in the Old Testament and that the concept is entirely lacking. But to leave it at that means that biblical theology is ultimately merely rewording the biblical narratives and remaining remote from the reality of the world as it is believed to be.

In this, once again, it is obvious that biblical theology has followed the lead of dialectical theology. Karl Barth in his *Church Dogmatics* III/1 built the doctrine of creation upon the biblical texts and, in a fatal sentence of his preface, stated that all the data and interests of science lie *beyond, outside*, what theology has to do in describing the work of the creator.[30] The exclusion of apologetics and of the corresponding theological criticism led to this and continues to support it.[31] The Barthian 'realistic' approach to the creation story necessarily makes the text into a myth or, more precisely, makes the mythical aspects of the text into the base for theologically regulative doctrinal statement. The example is an illustration relevant for numerous problems which we shall have to consider later. But, to give a first adumbration of the consequences, it provides a good example of the distinction between biblical theology and doctrinal theology. A biblical theology must attach serious value to all those elements like the seven-day scheme, the chronology, the order of events, which in Genesis are clearly of first importance for the story, its creators and its readers. But such a theology cannot be transferred directly into the realm of doctrinal speech. If this is done, it produces a doctrine which is unconnected with the real world in which we live. A doctrinal theology – unless it is fundamentalist or creationist – has to include reference to the category of evolution, just as it has to make it clear that the chronological scheme of Genesis is legendary and that the text is, in this respect (and perhaps others), of a mythological character. Certainly the biblical theology of creation should have an influence upon the doctrinal theology of the same, but its categories cannot be simply and directly transferred to the doctrinal realm. Doctrinal theology must therefore be both apologetic and critical in a way that was discouraged or rejected by dialectical theology, at least on the Barthian side. It must make reference to reality as known from outside the Bible, and it must act in a theologically critical sense towards the Bible.

In conclusion, it is worth while reminding ourselves that, if not so much the idea of evolution, at least the idea of *development* of doctrine has a respectable and significant place in Christian theology. Moreover, it was worked out and established as a theme before the time when modern biblical scholarship became widely established and before modern biblical theology came on the scene at all. John Henry Newman's *Essay on the Development of Christian Doctrine* was published in 1845. Certainly his ideas have remained controversial, and there are those who, for various reasons, feel it necessary to rule out all ideas of development or evolution.[32] One main reason for this is the suspicion that philosophies of evolution and progress have been imported into theology. Against this, however, it should be noted that Owen Chadwick wrote:[33]

> In a way Newman was a prodigy. He was a prodigy because he came to believe in historical development without also believing in liberal philosophies of development.

Returning to modern biblical theology, it is fitting to note that important moves in the direction suggested here were already advocated by John Barton in an article published in 1989.[34] He must have been one of the very first biblical scholars to notice the thoughts of Theissen and to incorporate them into a brief but very suggestive account of God's working in history, one that makes sense of evolution, that combines it with the history of Near Eastern religion, that gives positive meaning to the 'digging beneath the surface' or reconstruction of persons like the prophets of Israel, and that offers a very significant set of possibilities for modern theology. His highly imaginative article deserves to be much more widely known.[35]

# 8

# Difference from History of Religion

If biblical theology has been ready to differentiate itself from doctrinal theology, though not without hesitations and vacillations, it is even more clear that it aspires, in at least some of its forms, to be something different from the history of religion. As the previous chapter has shown, the widespread reaction against evolutionism spilled over into a hostility against historical approaches to religion in general. (In fact, this was ill-advised: a truly historical approach would have been the most obvious and effective way to overcome evolutionary ideas.) Anyway, when modern Old Testament theology began in the later 1920s, it was customary to look back with disdain on works that, in the previous decades, had had titles like *Old Testament Theology* but, as it was now said, had actually been no more than histories of religion. By contrast, the turn away from the history of religion was an essential element in what Hayes entitles the 'rebirth' of Old Testament theology. In spite of the many uncertainties in the newly reborn theological trend, most of its practitioners in the early years were clear that, whatever they were doing, it was not history of religion.

## 1. Terminology

'History of religion' is not always a clear designation of the subject that concerns us. It was commonly called *Religionsgeschichte* in German and the term has stuck, but actually a variety of approaches to religion may be meant. The study of religion itself is often embarrassed by uncertainty about what its own name should be. 'Comparative religion' has been a strong candidate, 'history of religion' another, and people have tried 'the scientific study of religion' or 'the science of religion' (in German *Religionswissenschaft* is well established) and often ended up with something vague like 'religious studies'. In other words, the subject is not always, and not necessarily, a strictly historical one. The use of the term 'history' in its title should therefore not be taken too literally. 'History of religion' can very well include the same synchronic and holistic descriptions that are sought for in some Old Testament theologies. The difference, therefore, is not purely or necessarily one between 'history' and 'theology'. A more adequate differentiation might be like this: 'history of religion' is concerned with all the forms and aspects of all human religions, while theology tends to be concerned with the truth-claims of one religion and especially with its authoritative texts and traditions and their interpretation.

For biblical theology, however, the central feature was the availability of *new information*: exploration of remoter parts of the world, discoveries of civilizations hitherto unknown, the beginnings of anthropology, the decipherment of ancient languages, the reading of inscriptions which – unlike the Bible – had not been handed down through long ages of interpretation but still existed as they had lain for thousands of years, the discovery of papyri and scrolls.

The older Christian theological tradition had had, for really ancient times, little to work on other than the Bible itself plus the sources in Greek and Latin. And the Bible, though authoritative, left many areas inadequately covered, even within the periods to which it referred. Biblical scholars of the patristic and Reformation periods were polymathic, and worked over their sources in great detail. But religion and theology were ill prepared to cope with the flood of new information that arrived in the nineteenth and twentieth centuries. In a very rough way we may say that the history of religion was ready to embrace and assimilate all this new information, while many currents of theology, though aware of the new material, sought to fit it in with, to accommodate it in, the older theological traditions, among which the Bible was enormously preponderant.

The first and obvious case is constituted by the existence of some marked similarities between Hebrew religion and the religions of environing peoples.

## 2. *Religious similarities with neighbouring peoples*

The question of the influence of environing religions upon Israelite faith and life arose not so much from evolutionistic theory as from actual discovery in the Near Eastern domain, taken in conjunction with various materials within the Hebrew Bible itself. Some elements in the Mosaic Law had close parallels in Mesopotamian laws. Several chapters in Proverbs had something approaching a verbal identity with an ancient Egyptian document of the same kind. Institutions like kingship were thought to belong to a general Near Eastern pattern, which had effects on ritual and poetry very similar to those found in Israel. The Jerusalem temple belonged to a Phoenician/Canaanite pattern and the Bible itself makes clear the debt to Phoenicia in the building of it. More recently discovered, the Ugaritic myths or legends contained many close verbal similarities to biblical poems, especially in the Psalms. Something very like the story of Solomon's judgment in the case of the two women is said to have circulated widely, especially in India. In the New Testament, as has been mentioned, some found substantial evidence that the Greek mystery religions had been the source of terms and perhaps of conceptions in the New Testament. All these are at first sight more a matter of *comparison* than of *history*, but a historical process is envisaged: laws which exist in Mesopotamia at a very early time suggest that similar Hebrew laws descended historically, whether by adoption from Mesopotamia or by temporal descent from some prehistoric and pre-biblical stage among ancestors of the Israelites. In any case, such phenomena would commonly be spoken of as being in the domain of 'history of religion'.

Old Testament theology has reacted to these questions in two or more different ways. One way has been to dispute the reality of the similarities and parallels. At first sight, one argument goes, there appear to be very close parallels and indications of borrowing, but on closer examination these become fainter. Basically, this approach uses the history of religion itself to diminish the similarities between Israelite and environing religions. A clear instance is the influence exercised upon G. E. Wright's early books by Frankfort and others, *The Intellectual Adventure of Early Man* (1946),[1] a volume which tended to indicate a high degree of difference between the polytheistic religions of Egypt and Mesopotamia and thus to leave open a gap within which an equal distinctiveness for Israel's religion might emerge. A similar function was later served by Frankfort's major book, *Kingship and the Gods*.[2] In essence the argument has been: far from there being a mass of common religion, to which Israel must in all probability have belonged and which it must have shared, there was a variety of highly different religious types, which fact leaves room for Israel's religion to be highly distinctive also. Argumentation of this kind has been familiar.

And indeed it might serve to distinguish Old Testament theology from assimilation to other religions. But the weakness is obvious: the argument itself depends on argument on the level of the history of religions. Biblical theology in itself has no means to rule on the question how far Egyptian, Mesopotamian and other world religions share common elements: all it can do, at best, is to make what it can of results promulgated by experts in these various fields. This line of argument may make biblical theology free from assimilation to environing religions; but it can do so only by appealing to the history of religion itself to help it.

The other argument is a more general and philosophical one, built upon a 'holistic' approach akin to the 'Gestalt' approach in psychology. Biblical theology might accept the reality of many of the phenomena that suggested parallels, borrowings and influences from other religions, but might handle them in a different way. The core of Hebrew religion, it might argue, is comprehended by Old Testament theology, and although these influences, borrowings and adoptions from other religions certainly existed, they came to be subsidiary to this core. Once accepted within the Bible and its traditions, they came to be expressions of that central Hebrew faith and ceased to have the associations which they had had in their earlier and foreign context. Myths, it is said, were 'historicized' or made into metaphors or jokes; polytheistic deities were reduced to *dramatis personae* in some cosmic drama in which only Yahweh came out as a real deity. Local deities were reduced to the level of demons. It is easy to see how the comprehensive, synthetic, approach of many Old Testament theologies was adopted precisely with this problem in mind. Individual elements in Israel might be very similar to an Egyptian, a Ugaritic or a Mesopotamian element, but the total picture of Israelite religion, seen with a holistic view, is something quite different. In this sense the construction of an Old Testament theology, which has been definitely holistic in this sense, has appeared to answer the problem of similarities with other environing religions.

And yet here again there are limitations to the argument. A holistic view may have the advantage that it shows a distinctive shape for Israel's religion, taken as one totality, as against any other religion, even if there are common elements. But the same argument depreciates its own value. For, if every religious system, holistically seen, is highly distinctive as compared with every other, in spite of the numerous common elements, then the distinctiveness of Israel's religion does not amount to much, since every religion, holistically seen, is distinctive! In other words, nothing is easily achieved by this argument that shows a special or absolute distinctiveness of Israel's religion in relation to the general history of religion.

In all this realm of discussion, then, we see that the conflict of theology with the history of religion involves entering into the domain of the history of religion itself; and even results which appear to vindicate the special status of Hebrew religion remain in the last resort what they were all along: arguments from the history of religion!

There is, indeed, a way in which this consequence may be avoided, or apparently so at first sight: to maintain that theology has really nothing to do with religion, and that the history of religion is therefore totally irrelevant for theology and thus is entirely negative and distorting when taken into account by biblical theology. We shall see that this approach does indeed come to the surface in some of the arguments about biblical theology.

## 3. *An historical account of Israelite religion itself*

Within the Hebrew Bible itself there was such a thing as a history of religion.[3] Most people have accepted this, even highly conservative scholars where there was obvious evidence of it. Religion in the time of Abraham is depicted as quite different from that of Moses' time, and that again as different from the period of the Judges. Things changed when the monarchy was established; they changed again with the exile and the return. The books of Kings describe reform attempts and actual reforms of the religion. A difference in piety, ethos and style as between late sources like Chronicles, Qoheleth and Esther and earlier comparable materials is sufficiently obvious.

Nevertheless most scholars do not believe that a history of religion in all its details can be read off directly from the pages of the Bible. For instance, in the texts attributed to the time of Moses there are differences about the priesthood, the laws about homicide, and other important elements. When the source analysis attached to the name of Wellhausen was achieved, one of the main features in it was its correlation of the various text strata, J and P for instance, with aspects of the history of religion.[4] Thus the 'historical-critical' view, as it is called, of the Old Testament is closely linked with a 'critical' arrangement of texts relating to the history of religion. A pivotal example was the correlation of the demand of Deuteronomy for a single sanctuary with the religious reform ascribed to Josiah in II Kings. The linkage with the history of religion was thus fundamental to the success of the critical analysis of literary sources.

The analysis of the biblical sources, however, was only one among several things. Alongside it there lay another factor, the discovery of information from within Israel which could supplement the biblical data. Inscriptions, though not many, could be found; archaeology could yield new information about cities, temples, the pattern of houses, styles of living and ecology. Thus the history of religion could not be written from the evidence of the Bible alone. In fact the history of Israelite religion developed into an immensely complicated network of connections involving archaeology and inscriptions, indications from comparative religion, evidences from Mesopotamian and Egyptian texts, societal parallels and sociological hypotheses, as well as biblical texts themselves. And the history of religion, of course, was not bounded by the temporal boundaries of the biblical canon: it ran back towards prehistory, and forwards into the time after the Bible was already complete.

Two or three points in the history of the subject should be mentioned here. The most important book to express the historical approach in this sense in the late nineteenth century was R. Smend (Senior)'s *Lehrbuch der alttestamentlichen Religionsgeschichte* (1983). He avoided the word 'theology' in the title and stated the principle that 'the representation of the religion of the Old Testament must not be a systematic one'.[5]

In this connection also we often hear of 'the *Religionsgeschichtliche Schule*'.[6] When this phrase is used it usually refers to a particular group who sought to exploit the material from ancient oriental cultures for the illumination of biblical religion, including the New Testament as well as ancient Israel. The persons in this group who are best remembered today are H. Gunkel, still venerated as a major Old Testament scholar,[7] perhaps the greatest in the generation after

Wellhausen, and W. Bousset, whose work impinged more on the New Testament. I do not think that they, or their impact, should necessarily be taken as the paradigm of what the history of religion might be as it would work today.

Thirdly, works with titles like 'Old Testament Theology' continued to appear; but later, after the rise of modern Old Testament theology from the 1930s on, it was often said that these older works, in spite of their titles, had really been histories of religion. Whether this is a right understanding may be left aside for the present: I question it a little bit, because, for those who wrote these works within the theological atmosphere of the time, the history of religion *was* itself a sort of theology.

In any case, the profound swing in the direction of theology from the 1930s on, with the rise of dialectical theology, meant a sharp turn away from the history of religions, most notably in German-speaking Protestantism, and especially in the Old Testament sphere; on the New Testament side, on the other hand, Bultmann among the dialectical theologians continued to include elements of history-of-religion lines within his work. Within theological faculties much interest turned towards Old Testament theology.

In the English-speaking world the change was slow to be felt. Few textbooks reflecting it existed in English and translations of continental works hardly began to flow before the 1950s. Class instruction tended to include some history of religion because of its linkage with historical-critical analysis of the texts, as mentioned above, but history of religion as a distinct approach was little pursued. In Great Britain and Scandinavia a tradition of comparative religion was well established, at least in some centres: I well remember the lively interest with which the question was discussed whether the *intichiuma* ceremonies of the Arunta tribe in Australia could solve some problems in the Hebrew Bible.[8] In general, in the English-speaking world the reception of Old Testament theology was mixed: some centres were deeply interested in it, while others rejected it, and influences from comparative religion and the history of religion continued. By the time the main continental Theologies had been translated, and by the time the culminating figure of von Rad had been published and translated, there was hardly any time left before the 'crisis' of biblical theology, in Childs' terms, arrived.

## 4. Relations to the New Testament

Christian biblical theology, as has been said, was interested from the start in relations between the Old Testament and the New. Now it has been commonly understood that there is no doubt that Christianity, historically speaking, was a descendant from the Old Testament and from post-biblical Judaism. But not all have been satisfied with this formulation. The New Testament, it is suggested, implied, or even expressly claimed, more: it seemed to claim not only a historical derivation, but a deep and special theological relation, and not one primarily with the Judaism of the intervening period, but one primarily with the thought and experience of the Hebrew Bible itself. It is agreed that this special relation could no longer be expressed in the simple terms of prediction which had once been used, nor in crude typologies: but these predictions and typologies, which had appeared on the surface of the New Testament text, might be taken as signs, as surface manifestations of a deeper theological community which held the two Testaments together. Somehow a truly 'theological' account of this relationship had to be found. People wanted a statement such as that the God who spoke through the Old Testament was the same God who spoke through the New. And of course this is what all Christian Old Testament theologians, more or less, have thought. Here again the history-of-religion approach has been thought to be inadequate.

It is not clear, however, that a more 'theological' approach is really so different in the long run from a *religionsgeschichtlich* one or so dissociable from it. For the assertion that the same God spoke to Abraham or to Moses as spoke to, let us say, a Greek-speaking Christian of AD 350 or a Latin-speaking one of AD 400 is meaningful only on the assumption that there is a religious continuity over two millennia or so in which these various, very different, persons had some sort of identifiable place. Much of the relevant history of religion may be unknown to us, but the theological assertion itself assumes that there is a continuity within which beliefs, practices, attitudes and interpretations of groups and individuals moved from one point and another, involving changes, conversions, repentances, regroupings, reformulations and so on, all of which are in principle material intelligible through the history of religion. Or, to put it negatively, it is doubtful whether even biblical theology has the means to judge whether 'the same God has spoken' in two sets of theological affirmations which have no *religionsgeschichtlich* linkage of any kind between them.

In this connection, moreover, there is one other point that has often passed unnoticed. The argument, as set out at the beginning of this section, was that there was an obvious history-of-religion connection between the Hebrew Bible and early Christianity; but, given that this was so, some theologians wanted more than this. They wanted a kind of theological community which was more important for them. It is possible, however, that things might be seen the other way. Some Jewish opinion, and possibly some Christian opinion too, considers the history-of-religion connection to be very slim: seen from this point of view, Christianity is not a genuine descendant from roots in Israelite religion. Christians have traditionally said that it is so, and have quoted the Hebrew Bible abundantly, but in fact the two religions are entirely different and discontinuous.[9] Theologically Christians may *claim* continuity or even identity, but that is just their claim: in fact the Hebraic ancestry of Christianity has very limited reality behind it. I do not say that this argument is *correct*: for present purposes all that matters is that *at this point* the question on the level of history of religion is the *more important* one.

## 5. Religion and dialectical theology

I have mentioned above that the swing in much theological thought from the 1920s on was most clearly marked in dialectical theology. It means, as I said, a sharp turning away from the history of religion. How did this work out in relation to our present subject?

Central to dialectical theology was revelation rather than religion: the former was viewed positively, the latter negatively. This parallels the very positive view of *theology*, contrasted with the negative placing of religion in comparison with it.

To repeat Barth's assertion: 'Religion is the concentrated expression of human unbelief.'[10] Religion was a human phenomenon, part of human culture like art or literature; more negatively, it was part of the human defences against God, part of man's self-assertion against the true God, a form therefore of idolatry.[11] Religion was the worst of human cultural endeavours, because more than any other it pretended to the status that rightly belonged only to the one God's revelation through his Word. It became fairly common to say that Christianity was 'not a religion'; it was a response to divine revelation, which by-passed all religion and made it irrelevant.

Obviously this position would have great effects on the study of the Bible. The Bible may in fact contain what may, from a certain point of view, be seen as 'religion' and may belong within the world of religions. But the Bible is not about religion: it is about God and his action, his revelation, and so on. A biblical writer is not speaking about his religion, he is speaking about God. It is the latter relation that is relevant for theology and thus also for biblical theology. Talk about his religion or where it came from is thus in principle misleading for biblical theology; it is talk about a different thing altogether. If this viewpoint is pressed hard, it means that the study of religion may have some meaning some-where, but it is quite unrelated to theology. *Religionsgeschichtlich* explanations of anything in the Bible are therefore automatically wrong if they are allowed to impinge upon biblical theology. We shall see that this type of argument recurs from time to time within discussions of modern biblical theology: there is some-thing of it in von Rad, and a lot in Childs. Here is an example from the latter, on the subject of creation (*Biblical Theology*, 384f.):

The attempt to replace Israel's own witness to creation with a history-of-religions reconstruction akin to early Canaanite religion from which Israel is alleged to have emerged (e.g. H.H. Schmid) is a retreat to an earlier *religions-geschichtlich* dogma of the nineteenth century which had crippled the theological enterprise through these very assumptions.

Schmid might of course be right or wrong; the allegation that he really tries to 'replace' Israel's witness is probably quite unjustified: he is trying to interpret it. The central point is the absoluteness of Childs' rejection, apparently of *anything* done by history of religion. Along with this goes his argument from the history of scholarship: history of religion is 'earlier', belongs to the nineteenth century, and is therefore wrong: it is 'dogma' (here a bad thing, though Christian dogma is a good thing); it 'crippled' the theological enterprise.[12]

Again, Childs in his major work, at the point where he turns from the Old Testament to the New, says in his first sentence that 'our major concern will be to describe briefly the main lines of the growth of the New Testament's witness to Jesus Christ within the context of the early Christian church'.[13] Having said this, he immediately goes on to make it clear that he wants to keep away from the history-of-religion approach. 'The approach is that of tracing traditio-historical trajectories from within the tradition, rather than approaching the material from a history-of-religions perspective which strives for an allegedly objective description of religious phenomena.'

Religion seems to be to him, in a sense familiar from dialectical theology, a bad thing. 'The chief theological point to be made is that the canon has contained within itself a major critique, not just of cultic religion, but of religion in general. The attack is grounded in a vision of God which renders totally inoperative all human response seeking to merit God's favour.'[14] We hear in his *Biblical Theology* that 'the threat of falsely compartmentalizing the material, whether by means of traditio-historical, history of religions, or literary categories, is acute and must be continually tested critically' (486).

These are typical arguments that seek to dissociate a 'theological' approach from one involving the history of religion. However, they contain many weaknesses and unclarities. How does a 'traditio-historical trajectory' really differ from a proposal within the history of religion? Why should we suppose that the history of religion 'falsely compartmentalizes the material', and if this is true then why is it not also true of the traditio-historical categories which Childs himself embraces on the same page? How does Childs know that 'religion in general', i.e. all religion, is a 'human response seeking to merit God's favour'? Unless he has studied all religions, which would be a history-of-religion undertaking, he cannot know whether this is the case or not. Is not the idea that religions seek to 'merit God's favour' a mere reflection from one current of

Christianity, based on no real study of other religions? Above all, are the 'trajectories' really 'historical', in the sense that they can be established, verified and falsified through historical methods, or are they really purely theological connections expressed as if they were historical 'trajectories'?[15] The weakness in these arguments is not untypical of many attempts to dissociate biblical theology from the history of religion.

The advantage of the argument of dialectical theology, if advantage it is, is that it certainly makes a sharp and decisive distinction between biblical theology and the history of religion. But this clarity is outweighed by the fact that the argument itself is no more than a trick with words. For talking about God, witnessing to one's God, telling of his mighty acts, expounding christology and the like, are not something *other than* religion: they are precisely what we mean by 'religion', or at least a part of it. Isaiah's 'witness' to his God *is* his religion or part of it, and the shape of his religion is part of the mode through which we can discover something of what sort of God his thoughts and words were directed towards. The argument implied here should therefore be rejected unreservedly and from the beginning. However, we shall meet with it and its effects from time to time.

But biblical theologians did not succeed in abolishing religion entirely from their purview. After all, Calvin had written his Institutes of the Christian *Religion* and Barth had a chapter in his Dogmatics on 'The True Religion' (I/2, §17.3, 325–6). Given the analogy that there can be a true religion, as there can be a justified sinner, then it is true that 'the Christian religion is the true religion' (326). As I have argued elsewhere, Barthianism in the end proved to be very much on the side of religion and dependent on it.[16] Eichrodt in his introductory chapter speaks of the 'power' of the Hebrew religion, which bursts out from time to time and causes it to move forward. And even Childs occasionally allows himself to emphasize the importance of the *religious* content of the texts (cf. the examples below, e.g. 435). In fact the tendency, as we come towards the end of the century, has probably been to become tired of the striving to make a sharp distinction between theology and religion and, if anything, to reinstate 'religion' as a fully positive term. Thus the Oxford New Testament scholar John Ashton delivered his Wilde Lectures in 1998 under the title 'The Religion of the Apostle Paul', the choice of the term 'religion' rather than 'theology' being undoubtedly deliberate and significant.

There is another reason why some biblical theologians retain some positivity towards religion and yet combine this with a suspicion of history of religion. Though often intellectually negative towards 'religion' (as explained above), they are actually committed to religion, however much they prefer the term 'theology'. What worries them about the history of religion is that it is used – as they see it – to explain religion away. They feel that historians of religion, or some of them, use every opportunity to explain religious changes and religious history as motivated by social factors, economic forces, power struggles or the like. Theologians do not want to deny or to minimize these forces, but they do not think that religious changes are *always* or *merely* the product of them. The historian of religion is thus seen as one who himself does not believe in religion, who sees it as no real force or factor in itself but as a disguise for non-religious factors. This is what is meant by 'reductionism', a not uncommon term in the modern discussion.[17] Biblical theologians, however higher they place theology in status above religion, are thus really anxious for the recognition of religion. And in this I think they are right. For, even once we have allowed for all the social, economic and political factors that affect religion and theology (both alike), I believe we have to allow that people do things and think things for religion itself and that religion in this sense is an immensely important force in history and in human life. Good historians of religion should recognize this and, I believe, do recognize it. But some biblical theologians are not sure that it is recognized, hence their negativity towards the history of religion in general. Here, then, they are distinctly arguing for religion and not against it. In any case, this consideration is not a valid ground for distrust of the history of religion as such, but only ground for a distrust of an improper use of it.

## 6. *A mixture of elements?*

In fact many Theologies – somewhat surprisingly, in view of their wish to differentiate themselves from histories of religion – contain some rather good *religionsgeschichtlich* material. To take an obvious example, Eichrodt's Chapter 2 on the key concept of the covenant includes a (somewhat vague) passage affirming the Mosaic origin of the concept, and then goes on to trace how it was jeopardized by the Canaanite culture, later adjusted to the same and reformulated, and how it continued in six successive historical periods, namely in the early Pentateuch strata J and E, in the classical prophets, in the Deuteronomic writings, in the P stratum, the later prophets Jeremiah, Ezekiel and Deutero-Isaiah, and the post-exilic period running down to the LXX (49–66), each of these being traced in relation to particular passages and linguistic usages. Though one can challenge various particular ideas, it is unquestionable that this is a solid historical analysis of the use of a term and the place of the corresponding concept in the history of the religion – or the history of theology, for in a case like this the two seem to come to the same thing. Similar material can be found elsewhere in Eichrodt and, *mutatis mutandis*, in other comparable modern Theologies (and of course, Theological Dictionaries). Thus the various names of deity are a traditional subject, briefly investigated in many Theologies, but this can hardly be done without some discussion of the process, for example the processes by which the name El came to be applied to the God of Israel. Many Theologies discuss this.[18] For some purposes and in some areas, indeed, some Old Testament Theologies, paradoxically, serve as good textbooks for the introduction of students precisely into the *historical* aspects of the religion. Why therefore has it seemed so important to differentiate Old Testament theology from the history of religion? Where does the essential difference lie?

It cannot be said that the two types of work are written by different types of people, because in several cases the same scholar has written both: so, among the names prominent in this book, Eichrodt, Vriezen, Fohrer;[19] if we count those who have written not a full-length History of Religion but a survey of history of religion in article form, we would add Zimmerli,[20] and there are doubtless others. Von Rad incorporated within his Theology a *Geschichte des Jahweglaubens* (von Rad, 1, 3–102). In this he followed the example of older scholars like Schultz, who in the fourth edition of his Theology (1896) began with a history of the religion and then went on to the main, systematic part.[21] By using the term 'history of Yahweh-faith', however, von Rad appears to be dissociating himself somewhat from the history of *religion*, faith not being coextensive with religion, though he appears not to explain this. Von Rad also said at one point that if he did not establish good connections with the New Testament, all that he had done would have been 'only' a history of religion: this was certainly wrong, but it shows how near he thought his work had come to the history of religion, and indeed some readers said, mistakenly in my view, that this is what he did achieve. Various compromises were possible.

If one looks at those who have written both types of work, the chief impressions are two. First, a number of them, though writing works in both genres, do not bother to give any substantial discussion of the difference. Neither of Fohrer's two books, for instance, appears to offer any explicit statement of how and why it differs from the other. Secondly, in a number of cases, when works in both genres are written, one has more sense of their similarity than of their basic difference. Thus in Fohrer's Religion his chapter §13, *Die Glaubensströmungen* ['Currents of Faith' – of Yahwism during the monarchy] appears to recount exactly the same *Daseinshaltungen* (attitudes to existence) as are basic to his Theology. Works on the religion tend to include more purely comparative material; thus Vriezen's Religion includes sections on the religions of Egypt, Babylon, Canaan, the Edomites and others. This makes a natural difference from his Theology; and his Theology, as we have noted, includes a long section covering the Christian principles involved in his conception of the subject. But when it comes down to the discussion of actual texts, events, persons and ideas or concepts within the Old Testament, which is surely the key question, we find the Religion running along very much the same tracks as the Theology. Thus, commencing a paragraph on 'the character of Israel's religion', Vriezen assures us: 'Despite the many tokens of an affinity with the religions all around, it is amply clear that Israel's religion is something altogether different from them.'[22] F. F. Bruce, rightly noting the problem, discussed Vriezen's two books and, saying that his Religion was more 'objective' and descriptive than his Theology, nevertheless went on to add:[23] 'Descriptive as the treatment is, however, there is no lack of value judgments: Israel's religion is seen as reaching its finest flowering in the great prophets, from Amos to Second Isaiah . . . Even this work, moreover, reveals a Christian perspective' [and he quotes]:

> Through its fidelity to the Law Judaism maintained itself, spiritually; but at the same time, because of this bondage to tradition it created, to begin with, no new forms of living. The renewal that came with Christianity was repulsed. After the destruction of the second temple Pharisaism was for centuries the undisputed guide and leader of Judaism.[24]

In other words, there has tended to be an overlap of values and interests between the history of Israelite religion and the theology of the Old Testament. It thus becomes less surprising if, at the end of the nineteenth and the beginning of the twentieth centuries, works calling themselves *Biblical Theology of the Old Testament* or the like were in content very much histories of the religion. Conversely, even if these works were really histories of the religion, as later observers often remarked, their authors thought that even as such they were really Theologies of the Old Testament. If it is thought that the term 'theology' implies personal religious commitment, then there can be no doubt that the same commitment was implied by and expressed in these older histories of Hebrew religion, or almost all of them – and this still often continues often to be the case, as we shall see.

No more acute case of the difficulties people had in making a clear distinction here can be found than in A. B. Davidson, honoured as a teacher of Hebrew and author of one of the few Old Testament Theologies published in English toward the end of the nineteenth century. Although his work was entitled a Theology – and was indeed one – it contained quite a strong argument to the effect that a history of religion was the only possible and feasible approach:

> Though we speak of Old Testament *Theology*, all that we can attempt is to present the religion or religious ideas of the Old Testament. As held in the minds of the Hebrew people, and as exhibited in their Scriptures, these ideas form as yet no Theology. There is no system in them of any kind. They are all practical religious beliefs, and are considered of importance only as they influence conduct. We do not find a *theology* in the Old Testament; we find a *religion* – religious conceptions and religious hopes and aspirations. It is we

ourselves that create the theology when we give to these religious ideas and convictions a systematic or orderly form. Hence our subject really is the History of the Religion of Israel as represented in the Old Testament (revised edition, 11).

This is a perfectly persuasive argument but for one fact: the book that contains it is itself quite obviously a Theology and *not* a history of religion, though it does contain some aspects of the latter.[25]

Where writers have sought to make a clear definition of the difference, they have commonly had some difficulty. As a good example we may take an well-known work like H. Ringgren's *Israelite Religion* (German original 1963; ET 1966). Ringgren is from Sweden, where there has always been a strong tradition of comparative religion and history of religion.[26] There can be no doubt that Ringgren stands on the side of the history of religion and intends his book to be understood in that way; and in his Foreword he uses the phrase 'the comparative approach'. He clearly states that the book is not a Theology of the Old Testament, and mentions as an example that it will avoid 'points of view based upon *Heilsgeschichte*', which, he says, 'have their place, but only within a theological presentation'. His Introduction comes back to the question briefly (1–3). He distinguishes between two possible approaches to Old Testament theology. The first sees the Old Testament 'specifically as a preparation and prototype for the definitive revelation in Christ'. The second would be simply a 'systematic presentation' of religious ideas, just as one might do historically for Augustine or Luther, and 'without taking into account how these ideas are related to the teaching of the New Testament'. Seen in this latter way, 'Old Testament theology is purely descriptive'. After some discussion of von Rad's special perspective, Ringgren points out that the Old Testament does not have one unitary theology but 'a multiplicity of theologies' (which, as we have seen, was von Rad's own view, as a theologian, anyway). This is 'a difficulty in the theological approach'. Historical changes and differences must be taken into account, and a theology that took the religion of Israel 'as a constant' would clearly misinterpret it.

This variety of religious phenomena within Israel, Ringgren continues, 'must be the decisive factor in a religio-historical study'. Given the deficiency of the sources, a historical treatment requires 'a critical evaluation of the documents'. From this point of view the Old Testament texts are not 'basically different from other religious documents. They must be taken primarily as human, historical documents, which can and must be examined with the methods of historical criticism. The question of divine inspiration or revelation does not fall within the scope of the history of religions. If the religio-historical method can neither presuppose nor prove the revelational nature of the Old Testament writings, neither does it exclude such an interpretation on the part of faith. The history of religions simply cannot deal with this question as long as it seeks to retain the character of a strict scientific discipline.' And then Ringgren adds the very striking final sentence, which much modifies the effect of his previous remarks: 'It should be added that a purely descriptive theology of the Old Testament also comes very near this goal if it does not overlook the variations within Israelite religion.'

Ringgren has thus mentioned a number of different factors which might differentiate an Old Testament Theology from a History of Israelite Religion. They include: 1. historical criticism; 2. preparation for final revelation in Christ; 3. possible relation to the New Testament; 4. multiplicity of theologies; 5. fact of historical change in religion; 6. documents to be taken as human documents; 7. question of inspiration or revelation. And these, as stated by him, do provide a rational foundation for a history-of-religion approach. But in effect many or most Old Testament Theologies fit in, to greater or lesser degree, with the requirements that Ringgren sets out. Though sometimes unhappy about the divisive effects of historical criticism, they mostly accept it and use it to some extent as an organizing principle; though interested in the final revelation in Christ, they do not in fact say so very much about this. Though professing interest in connections with the New Testament, many of them in fact pursue these only half-heartedly. The multiplicity of theologies is expressly accepted by von Rad and made into part of the core of his programme, and could be said to be at least implied by some other Old Testament Theologies. Historical change in religion, within the biblical period, is generally openly accepted, and information about such historical change is in many cases clearly furnished. That the documents are human, historical documents is also probably generally accepted, and is sometimes cordially agreed even by such scholars, far removed from the history-of-religion approach, as W. Vischer.[27] And though some Old Testament Theologies hover uncertainly around questions of divine inspiration or revelation (e.g. Vriezen, cf. above, 31f., 43f.), and are certainly in the long term directed toward such questions, it could not be said that most of them are really dominated by these questions in their direct methodological approach. In other words, as it turns out, many or most Old Testament Theologies, by Ringgren's criteria, 'come very near the goal' of a history-of-religion description.

Thus we find, approaching it in the other way, that Ringgren's own determinedly history-of-religion approach contains quite a lot that sounds very like what one would find in an Old Testament Theology. Take the example of election and covenant, key concepts to so many theologies. Ringgren has a considerable discussion of these (115–20), plus other remarks elsewhere in his book. The passage mentioned begins: 'For the Old Testament writers, Yahweh's action in history is concentrated in what he has done for Israel. Two concepts are of pre-eminent importance in this regard: election and covenant' (115). Later we hear that 'it would be difficult to separate the idea of election from the concept of the covenant' (117), and, a little further on, 'the covenant concept clearly was extremely important for Israel's religious consciousness, and therefore demands our special attention'. After discussion of the features involved in a covenant, we hear that Israel was understood to have broken its covenant with Yahweh, and the idea of a 'new covenant' emerges. So, we hear, 'the covenant idea, then, was so basic to Israel that even the restoration of the broken relationship with God was conceived as a covenant. The covenant became the normal form for Israel's association with God' (119). There then follows a page-length discussion of the covenant with David. All these thoughts are very similar to what one would expect to find in an Old Testament Theology. Is there then no difference after all?[28]

However, this does not mean that there is no real difference between approaches here: it only means that Ringgren's statement has described it only partly. I shall try to suggest a sharper distinction shortly.


## 7. Triumph for theology?

In spite of the mixture of elements, and a certain fuzziness of the boundaries, in at least some countries Old Testament theology became a subject of great interest, and positive interest in the history of Israelite religion faded away. Publications in biblical theology and theological hermeneutics flourished, and much work went into the production of theologically-orientated commentaries. A charismatic teacher like Gerhard von Rad had an audience of hundreds of students over many years. Commenting on the German scene in 1963, Rendtorff remarked that 'Old Testament studies in Germany have to a large extent ceased in practice to work along the lines of history of religion'.[29] This may, indeed, have been exaggerated: does it accommodate such distinguished work as that of Gese (1970)?[30] It is not to be thought that work in history of religion in Germany ceased to exist: consider such central figures as C. Colpe or Kurt Rudolph. But the question is not whether such work went on, but whether it had recognition in theological faculties. R. Albertz begins his two-volume work (German original 1992) with the complaint that the history of Israelite religion has only a marginal place in most theological faculties.[31]

In the English-speaking world, the situation may have been somewhat different. Much biblical study was carried on in faculties and institutions that were not explicitly or entirely theological: there were departments of biblical studies in arts faculties and liberal arts colleges, departments of Semitic languages and – increasingly – departments of religious studies which stood rather aloof from theology. A good example is provided by the great American scholar W. F. Albright, who created what can fairly be called his 'school', and an influential school it was. Central to his approach was archaeological method and the reconstruction of past historical development. Albright's own work certainly came closer to history of religion than to theology; yet he had an interest in biblical theology and had some work published in that area,[32] often associating himself with Eichrodt's approach, though he changed his opinions quite a lot from time to time. Among the earlier members of this school, G. E. Wright was notably active in both archaeology and Old Testament theology, and John Bright, while most remembered for his *History of Israel*, also wrote works distinctly belonging to theology.[33] Somewhat later, F. M. Cross's *Canaanite Myth and Hebrew Epic. Essays in the History of the Religion of Israel* (1973) was the obvious dominant work of this current, but numerous detailed studies of similar character were published, for example studies by Patrick D. Miller, Jr. As far as I can see, it could not be said that the history of Israelite religion was neglected or ignored in Old Testament studies in this period. What could be said, perhaps, is that it was not pursued consistently and for itself: rather, it was mixed in with historical criticism, with exegesis, with theology. Perhaps, of course, this is how it should be. But an emphasis on the history of religion as an independent discipline with claims to override or displace other approaches was absent or muted. The situation in the United States and in Britain was thus more mixed in character. Continental trends were mediated, however, by scholars who had studied in Germany and Switzerland: a leading person among these was my own teacher, and later colleague, Norman W. Porteous, who never wrote a full Theology but interpreted the newer movements in his article 'Old Testament Theology' in the widely-read volume *The Old Testament and Modern Study* (1951), edited by H. H. Rowley.

Nevertheless, in a general way Rendtorff's remark seems justified: much Old Testament work that had a theological character stayed rather far away from the history of religion and looked upon it rather negatively (the inheritance of this attitude persists in the United States with Childs, whose negativism towards history of religion seems to be absolute). And, apart from specialized scholars, the awareness of history of religion within the general theologically-educated public had greatly decreased.[34] The twentieth-century religious consciousness had become markedly revelational.

In any case the situation has changed once again. True as Rendtorff's remark just quoted may have been for its time, there is every sign that German Old Testament studies in the history of religion have now been blossoming for some time. With the assistance of several co-workers, Walter Beyerlin produced his *Religionsgeschichtliches Textbuch zum Alten Testament* in 1975 (ET *Near Eastern Religious Texts Relating to the Old Testament*). Consider also such important contributions as those of H. Gese, already mentioned, or H. Donner; those of B. Janowski and H. Weippert; and in Switzerland the distinguished work of Othmar Keel on religious iconography. The work of Albertz himself will be separately discussed below.

Thus from about that same time the situation began to change, and history of religion began to have increased influence within the theological realm itself once again. Interest in Assyriology and the Ugaritic texts at one end of the spectrum, and in the Qumran scrolls at the other, provided new data on which many Old Testament scholars worked and which necessarily drew them farther into the area of history of religion.

In fact, as we have seen, most of the Old Testament Theologies found it impossible to work without some entry into history-of-religion material and information. Thus, as time went on, some of the later writers of Old Testament theologies found it less and less important to lay emphasis on the contrast between biblical theology and history of religion. This trend was not confined to biblical scholars, but was confirmed by the agreement of some central doctrinal theologians. Thus Hendrikus Berkhof wrote in his *Christian Faith* (1973; ET 1979):

> In the nineteenth century a contrast developed between those who dealt with the way of Israel as 'the history of Israel's religion' and those who treated it as 'biblical theology of the Old Testament'. Slowly the insight has gained ground that this contrast, also in terms of the criterion of scientific description, is untenable . . . It is becoming increasingly clear that relative to results it makes little difference whether one starts from the religious development of Israel or from the content and purport of the books of the Old Testament (228).[35]

Returning to Old Testament specialists, W. H. Schmidt in his *The Faith of the Old Testament* (1968, ET 1983) characterizes his own book as 'standing midway between a "history of Israelite religion" and a "theology of the Old Testament"'.[36] On this work, indeed, R. Albertz comments that it 'shows that a mere mixing of the two disciplines is problematical, because too many uncontrolled prior decisions and evaluations go into such an account'.[37] But this criticism is not necessarily final, for it does not enter into specifics; again, even if a mixing of the two disciplines is 'problematic', this does not prove that it is impossible, provided that adequate controls and distinctions are included. In fact it is not impossible that Schmidt's work has inaugurated a kind of approach which many other scholars have followed or will follow.

The difference made by Albertz's work is that he calls for a *strictly* history-of-religion approach, avoiding the mixtures and compromises of past work, and for the more or less complete abandonment of Old Testament theology. He follows the widespread criticism of Old Testament theology on the ground that it reduces the material to concepts and intellectual history.

> It is therefore no wonder that in many Theologies little comes over of the lively religious life or of the exciting theological disputes, and that they often have an effect that is remarkably static, lifeless and at times also boring.[38]

## 8. Albertz

I wrote earlier that the wide area often called 'history of religion' is not always strictly historical, but may be comparative, synchronically descriptive and so on. But Albertz's approach is intended to be emphatically *historical* in the full sense of the word.

An indication of the direction of his thinking was already given in his earlier work on 'Personal Piety and Official Religion', published in 1978.[39] It begins with a general discussion of *Religionsinterner Pluralismus*, pluralism *within* a religion, and goes on to distinguish between personal religiosity and official religion, distinguishing also between 'popular piety' and 'Yahweh religion', and between 'personal God' and 'national God' (*Volksgott*). Clearly, differences between these different settings of religion – individual, familial, small-group, large-group, organized state – are going to be important for his concept. He goes on to discuss these distinctions as they work within the religions of Israel and of Mesopotamia. One of the fields he uses in his research – much to my pleasure, since I have emphasized the same area – is the religious content of the *personal names* of Israelites. Here, incidentally, one should remark that it is a shame that no adequate full-length book on the names has been written in English since G. Buchanan Gray's (in 1896), while the still standard work of M. Noth, *Die israelitischen Personennamen im Rahmen der gemeinsemitischen Namengebung* (1928), has never been translated into English, and it is probably too late to do so now.[40]

Anyway, through personal names and other evidence, such as the expressions of lamentation psalms, he tells us:

> It was for me one of the most exciting discoveries to see how closely the utterances of personal piety in Israel and in Babylon corresponded with one another, although the two religions on the official plane are deeply distinct from one another.[41]

I personally had had the same feeling when working on South-Arabian inscriptions and other materials in Semitic languages.

Albertz gives an account of the theological changes of the century which fits well with what has been said above:

The loss of interest in history of religion, and the blooming of Old Testament theology, was a direct result of the swing in theological opinion which followed the First World War in Germany and meant a break with the 'liberal theology' of the nineteenth century and the victorious march of 'dialectical theology'. If today the 'history of Israelite religion' is once again seen as meaningful and theologically necessary, this is connected with the general theological situation of the present, in that the great systematic approaches of Bultmann and Barth and their followers have lost all their all-dominating fascination.

So, he continues:

We find ourselves – even if on a different plane – thrown back upon the problems as presented by the theology of the nineteenth century.

This has much in common with the viewpoint of this present book.

The actual merits of his major work, taken purely as a history of religion, lie beyond what can be treated here; but one or two short remarks may be useful. Chapters distinguish different elements such as 'Religious Elements of Early Small Family Groups', as distinct from 'The Religion of the Large Liberated Group' and later 'The Religion of the Pre-State Large-group Federation', 'The Major State Cult in the South', 'The Major State Cult in the North', 'The Conflict over Official Syncretism in the Ninth Century', 'Theological Disagreements of the Eighth Century', 'Family Piety in the Late Period of the Kings', ending up with 'The Deuteronomic Reform Movement'. This covers the first volume only. Similar distinctions apply in the second volume, covering the post-exilic period. There is an emphasis on the *later* history as against the earlier, previous historians having been blamed for emphasizing the early period too much and ignoring the post-exilic time, in which, it is held, many of the great developments took place.

It would be impossible within this volume to offer any proper description, evaluation or assessment of Albertz's work as a whole, but a few characteristics of it, taking it just as the history of religion that it is, may be helpful.

The reader might expect, from the title 'history of religion', to find the detached scholar isolated from the modern world. With Albertz the opposite is the case. His earlier book on personal piety and official religion began by evoking the scene of German mobilization in 1914, when the Kaiser called out 'Forwards with God!' and goes on to ask how modern Germans may understand 'God with us'. History of religion for him is deeply involved with questions for *today* – exactly, of course, what much Old Testament theology also has promised to face. Again, the infinitely repeated call by theologians that others should 'reveal their presuppositions' is here stood on its head: Albertz is entirely happy to reveal them.[42] Moreover, as we shall see below, if he were to accept that some new kind of 'Old Testament theology' was possible, for him it would be 'one that would start from the burning problems of the present'.

If there used to be a gap in scholarship between the two sides of the Atlantic, I felt the reverse on reading Albertz: some of it is very like what we are hearing in North America. The sociological emphasis is there, and with it the ethos stemming from liberation theology. There really was a 'liberated major group' stemming from the Exodus. 'The Yahweh religion of Israel originates in the liberation process of an oppressed outsider-group in Egyptian society, and their religious symbolism is therefore directly related to the process of historical political liberation' (47). The emphasis on listening to Jewish positions and Jewish criticisms is marked; Levenson's arguments (on which more below, Chapter 18) are taken as more or less beyond criticism (but Albertz later accepts correction from the Jewish participant Isaac Kalimi, *JBTh* 10, 1995). There is a distinct similarity to the picture, drawn by Gottwald and others, of an early Israel that was an egalitarian society, while the Canaanites, who in older days used to be guilty of orgies and religious abominations, here tend to become monarchical organizers and oppressors, if not capitalistic exploiters. El and Yahweh were symbols of opposition to domination (76). The tendency is to paint popular, family and folk religion in warm colours, but to look more critically at the religion of the elite. 'Those involved will have seen the incorporation of a female element into Yahweh religion [in the period of the Judges] and thus also its religious embedding in the sexual sphere as represented by the worship on the cultic high places and elsewhere as an enrichment' (87). Seen from a modern point of view, there is a certain tragic element in the fact that this whole realm of sexuality was opposed by the prophets, beginning with Hosea. The emphasis on the late period, often said to have been neglected, is indicated by the presence of a full second volume devoted to the time after the end of the kingdom.

As I remarked above, the older historical criticism was closely linked with the history of Israelite religion. With Albertz the opposite seems to have happened. He is of course a fully critical scholar and accepts the disappearance of the J source, formerly supposed to be antique, so that 'the main mass of the text [about the exodus] is of exilic or early post-exilic origin, i.e. separated from the events by between seven and eight hundred years' (1, 43). This might suggest that very little is known in detail about the events described. Nevertheless there is a certain conservatism in his operation (cf. Preface, viii) – with which I entirely agree, but it creates a certain incongruity. For at the present time, when so much modern criticism is moving the texts down to a late period and when even the time of David and Solomon is darkened with the shadow of uncertainty, Albertz for his presentation of the religious history requires that all sorts of details from the story of early times should be fairly accurate. The 'empire of David and Solomon' is still part of the data (1, 129). How do we know that the Israelites in Egypt were really oppressed, and that this is not what the elites of a later age (for reasons of their own) wanted to be believed? Is it a certain historical fact that 'Gideon overcame the Midianite camp in the middle of the night with loud shouting and noise' (1, 82)? I do not suggest that Albertz is in any way wrong in this. His acceptance of so much of the detail as historical provides much of the richness in material in his book. But a certain incongruity remains.

We cannot discuss the details of his depiction of Israelite religion here, but some features should be mentioned. The book provides a sort of exegetical commentary on a rich variety of biblical texts, so that it can be read as a sort of companion to the Old Testament, following, however, an historical order rather than the sequence of the texts. The suggestions are often bold and fascinating. The patriarchal narratives belong very largely to family religion. Liberation, equality and opposition to domination characterize the exodus story and other early materials. The special features of Yahweh religion 'can be explained only from the extraordinary social conditions in which it came into being'. It is curious that Moses is depicted as really a political leader; nothing seems to be said about his possible contacts with monotheistic trends within Egyptian religion.

Contrary to the frequent attempts to emphasize that Israel 'knew no god-king; rather, the king was regarded as only the adopted son of Yahweh', the relevant texts come very close to Near Eastern notions and there is no clear boundary: 'In Israel too the divine sonship had a clear physical component (Ps. 2.7; 110.3) and a mythical dimension'; this 'should be interpreted as the divine rebirth of the king at his enthronement, in analogy to Egyptian notions' (1, 117). The theology of the state temple in Jerusalem is 'stamped with an official syncretism' (1, 132). Some of these thoughts would have been felt to be difficult for older biblical theology to accept. At other points, however, Albertz comes closer to biblical theology: 'it is not the individual elements but the structure as a whole that makes the religion of Israel distinctive' (1,20) – but it can hardly be said that Albertz's actual work produces a picture of a 'structure as a whole'. Contrary to some of the earlier histories of Israelite religion, his presentation seems to have no evolutionistic aspect in it.

Here, however, we shall concentrate on his views of the relations between history of Israelite religion and Old Testament theology.

In his introductory chapter Albertz provides a careful discussion of this (especially 1–21). Though his discussion is brief and provides no complete reasoning to demonstrate his views, he comes to the conclusion that the history of religion is 'the more meaningful comprehensive Old Testament discipline' (16). For this he gives several reasons:

1. because it corresponds better to the historical structure of large parts of the Old Testament;

2. because it takes seriously the insight that religious statements cannot be separated from the historical background from which they derive or against which they are interpreted;

3. because it is not compelled to bring down its varying and sometimes contradictory religious statements to the level of intellectual abstraction;

4. because it describes a dialogical process of struggle for theological clarification, demarcation and consensus-forming which clearly corresponds to the present-day synodical or conciliar ecumenical learning process of the churches and Christian-Jewish dialogue;

5. because it sees its continuity not in any religious ideas which have to be appropriated by Christians but in the people of Israel itself, to which the Christian churches stand in a brotherly and sisterly relationship through Jesus Christ;

6. because in a consistently historical approach it openly dispenses with any claim – even a concealed one – to absoluteness and deliberately does theology under 'the eschatological proviso', which befits a minority church in a multi-religious and partially secularized world community;

7. because its approach from a comparison of religions facilitates dialogue with the other religions.

To this Albertz adds that 'alongside such an overall view from the history of religions, an important place could come to be occupied' by another theological view: one that would start from the burning problems of the present and the controversies in church and theology about how a Christian solution can be achieved, and would take on the task 'of making thematic cross-sections through the history of the religion of Israel and early Christianity in order to describe what insights or patterns of behaviour found there in connection with analogous problems and controversies can be important, helpful and normative for the church today'. Such an approach, he adds, would be 'a different kind of "Old Testament theology" from what has been customary so far'. There is still room in his mind, therefore, for some sort of Old Testament theology, though something different from what we have had hitherto.

It is not quite clear how all these remarks are to be understood, but one thing is clear about them. Again and again in this century it has been urged that historical approaches tie interpretation to the past and damage relevance for the present; they serve the antiquarian interests of the technical specialist and have no concern for present-day religion. In particular, the history-of-religion approach has no interest or value for the church, which wants to work, and should work, exclusively from the Bible and its theology. Here now we find Albertz arguing *on theological and religious grounds*, and for the church, that in exactly these regards an approach through the history of religion has *more to offer* than the dubious, uncertain and badly divided enterprise of biblical theology! His arguments take over, in favour of the history-of-religion approach, one of the main sets of arguments which have hitherto been used in order to justify biblical theology *in contrast to* that approach. It is for the church in particular that the approach through history of religion is needed! Has not the older biblical theology, or its more recent 'canonical' forms, been a programme for the ghettoization of the church within very restrictive walls?

Should Albertz's enthusiastic commendations be accepted in full? They are certainly highly stimulating, and form a good corrective to the thought of those biblical theologians who have sought to see history of religion in a purely negative light. And his positive principles as stated may seem convincing. But it may be suggested that in his enthusiasm he underestimates the importance and potential which biblical theology, even of a somewhat traditional kind, continues to have.

## 9. Discussion following Albertz

Albertz's ideas have not passed unnoticed. The serial *Jahrbuch für biblische Theologie* devoted most of its tenth volume, 1995, to a discussion of them. It would be impossible here to go through the wide-ranging discussion by numerous scholars within it. Among the contributions a number (e.g. Lemche) are totally negative towards Old Testament theology, and a number consider that the argument presents us with a false alternative (e.g. Crüsemann), but rather few among them seem to rest content with the tradition of Old Testament theology as it has been and to defend it; rather, they tend as a whole to suggest that the subject has to move at least in some degree in the direction demanded by Albertz. Thus the general impression gained from a study of the volume is that Albertz's arguments have been felt to be serious and weighty, and that the pendulum of scholarly opinion, even among those devoted to biblical theology, is swinging towards a much greater recognition of the history of religion. Albertz himself contributes to the volume a concluding response to the discussion, giving it the intriguing title 'Is There Still a Chance for Old Testament theology?' (177–87).

I pick out three of the articles for special mention.

Professor John Barton clearly sympathizes with some part of the arguments of Albertz against Old Testament theology, but he thinks that there is still a place for such a discipline. He follows the tradition of Gabler and Eichrodt in believing that it is essentially a descriptive undertaking, *e genere historico* as Gabler put it, but considers that description is not a purely factual assembling of data. 'It has an interpretative aspect too.' When we talk about it we have to compare the religious categories of the Hebrews with ours.[43]

There are themes of Jewish and Christian theology in which there is an interesting ambiguity between the biblical material and the theological utterances of later times, and most of the current types of hermeneutics fail to deal with this adequately. There are conceptions which, being preserved in the Hebrew Bible, unambiguously derive from ancient Israel, but which nevertheless represent a further development of these convictions, a further development in directions which the ancient Israelites themselves could not have imagined. In their mature form these theological conceptions could even become the interpretative framework within which later generations of Jews and Christians read these same texts from which the conceptions derive (30).

The concept of omnipotence provides an example. The Old Testament, by its own categories of thought, does not fit very well with what later counted for monotheism, omnipotence and omniscience in both Jewish and Christian theologies. Thus it is clearly stated that God does not change his mind (I Sam. 15.29). But he also rejects Saul, whom he had previously elected. This is not seen as a weakness in God; rather, it demonstrates his unerring obligation to justice and proper handling of people. Later philosophical reflections, suggesting that since God was omniscient he must have already known that Saul would sin, miss the point of the biblical author.

Barton further illustrates his argument from the book of Ezekiel, 'which has often been taken to exemplify what might be called "biblical monotheism" but which on a modern critical analysis is much nearer to the polytheism from which Judaeo-Christian monotheism emerged than a practitioner of Old Testament theology might want to think'. Thus in Ezekiel, when Yahweh acts 'for the sake of his holy name', that originally meant not 'out of his own sovereign freedom' but something more like 'in order to protect his (fragile) reputation'; and this concern looks like the opposite of what, in the more philosophical stream of later Judaism and Christianity, is meant by divine omnipotence. And yet that later notion of omnipotence would not have come into being without texts such as Ezekiel, which laid the foundation for thinking about divine transcendence in such a way that something emerged that is not unreasonable to call 'biblical' monotheism. Again: 'We partly misread Ezekiel if we think it is about monotheism or divine omnipotence in our sense; yet the distorting lens through which we read the book is itself partly a result of the book's existence and contents.'

Barton sums up his position thus:

> Biblical theology as I am defining it is a critical analysis of the reception history of biblical texts, but one which compares that history carefully both

with the original meaning of the texts and with the theological doctrine that has both resulted from and been read back into the text in question.[44]

These ideas of Barton's are both important in themselves, and also because Albertz, looking back over the discussion in his concluding response, opines that, of all the ideas put forward in the discussion, Barton's is the one that comes nearest to what he himself would find acceptable.[45]

Secondly, I would cite parts of the response of Frank Crüsemann. His position is that the choice posed by the question 'History of Religion or Theology?' is a false alternative. 'Neither history of religion alone nor theology alone can really do justice to the religious and theological content of scripture' (70). His first argument is an interesting one. The historical narration of the Hebrew Bible is mainly devoted to the 'early' period – Abraham, Moses, the Judges, David – a period about which we know rather little from either a historical-critical or a history-of-religion viewpoint. Yet that is where the great events are placed: the revelation of the Torah on Mount Sinai, the conquest of the land. But it is actually from the *late* period that the literary emphasis on these events comes. The time narrated, the *erzählte Zeit*, is at the other end of the scale from the time of narration, the *Erzählzeit*. From the viewpoint of history of religion, therefore, these narratives should really be treated in the history of the late, post-exilic period, the time when the narratives were told, a period which has to be reconstructed critically, since we have little information about it.

But we can go another way and work from the final text, as it stands, and that would lead to a historical interpretation in the time of finalization and canonization. Thus we would take the book of Amos as it stands, including the later additions, which make the conclusion of the book so positive. But on the other hand it belongs precisely to the canonical forms of Amos and other such books that they are explicitly anchored to a stated point in the period of the Kings. Thus the 'canonical' sense cannot be grasped purely by relating it to the time of the canonical final form. He concludes this section: 'Form and content of the canon do not permit either a purely diachronic or a purely synchronic interpretation' (72). 'Whether the narrated time or the time of narration dominates, something important is lost; neither can bring the entirety to expression' (72).

This is only the first of a series of arguments by which Crüsemann criticizes Albertz's plan and the execution of it in his book, and leads the reader back towards a complementarity of the history of religion and the theology of the Old Testament. 'The basic problems of historical understanding of the religious and theological content of the texts in the context of the constellations and conflicts of their time are equally real for both a history of religion and a theology of the Old Testament' (74). Space forbids me to go into further detail.

Thirdly, I would cite the article by Sundermeier. His contribution is important because he is a comparative and general religionist, but one whose thinking
is also closely related to theology and willing to express itself in theological
terms. He is able to point out that there are various schools within the science of
religion (I use this for the term he uses, *die Religionswissenschaft*), which imply
different evaluations of theology. Albertz, he argues (200), belongs to a group in
which the strict separation of theology and science of religion is represented.

Here we come to the matter of the phenomenology of religion (202), which
has been touched on earlier. Phenomenology has been vehemently opposed, and
by the current to which Albertz belongs. It is thus noticeably absent from
his book: questions about the meaning of rites and forms of the temple cult,
questions that go beyond the mere performance of prophetic and cultic acts, are
found only in traces. Against this Sundermeier claims that phenomenology in
the science of religion has always been the bridge over to understanding and to
theology. If one breaks it off, then the next step, the quest for the *Summe*, for the
theology of a religion, cannot take place (203).

On the other side there is a theological decision in Albertz: he belongs to the
'division model' as represented by dialectical theology. But just as a historian of
religion he has to leave himself open to the institutions, the elite, the reformers,
the founders. Where he blames Old Testament theology for the levelling out of
differences, the same can be said of himself. The theologies of the prophets, for
example, are subordinated to their *function*. The anti-elitism produces a distortion. There must, even in the history of Israelite religion, be a place for theology
and developments in the history of theology. Once again, the alternative is a
false one. In the history of ideas and in theology Israel has had greater effects
through its theology than through its religious history. A theology of the Old
Testament cannot be produced independently of the latter, and must build
upon the knowledge gained by the history of religion; but the two are the two
sides of the same coin, two ellipses which overlap.

The importance of this is that many biblical theologians, puzzled by the
problems of understanding religions that lie outside the Jewish-Christian
biblical orbit, need a formula in traditional theological language to help them.
This is what Sundermeier supplies: the religions [of the world] 'belong to the
first article [of the Creed]' (204). There is a common ground for the co-existence
of theology and the science of religion.

It is the 'primal experience of religion, common to all religions', which is still
to be grasped in the 'tribal religions'. On the basis of them it can be shown
how religion serves the well-being of man and holds him fast in his
Humanum. In them the action of God in creation and his preservative force
is comprehensible in a special way. The religions have something to do with

God. To follow the terms of Claus Westermann, through them he blessed the nations. They belong to the 'world action' of God and dogmatically should be thought of in the framework of the first article of the Creed (204).

That is: there is a place within Christian orthodoxy which makes reference to the human religions, just as it includes creation and the image of God.[46]

Returning to Albertz, I should add that he himself is not the only one to advance arguments of the kind we have followed above. The well-known scholar Erhard Gerstenberger argues in very much the same way. Concluding an article on the social institutions of ancient Israel and their religious connections, he claims that this sort of research is very central to 'contextual theology'.[47] He writes:

> Analysis of the growth and change of Israelite religious institutions should not be understood as an anti-theological task. On the contrary, this kind of evaluation of Scripture and society should set contemporary theologians free to take over full responsibility for their concepts and systems of doing theology in the present. To recognize the historical, social, and institutional conditioning of every assertion about and communication on behalf of God means that we must abandon claims of absolute, timeless truth, valid for all people and through the ages. God must be different in varying historical and social situations, even if the deity's name should remain the same . . . There is no way of finding pure, unchangeable truths like gold nuggets in the biblical past. What we do find are conglomerates of religious faith and social dynamics – a faith that is born anew at each juncture of social and historical turmoil.

The history of religion, then, when combined with the study of social institutions, far from being anti-theological, is the true basis for the 'contextual theology' needed for the community of each modern age. Though Gerstenberger does not make this quite explicit, his implication seems to be: a biblical theology which keeps apart from the study of religion in society belongs to that same category of 'claims of absolute, timeless truth' which the same biblical theology has so often condemned. It would be, we might perhaps say, as if one studied in the modern world only the thoughts and works of professional theologians, and never looked inside the synagogues, churches, workplaces and homes of the religious or asked about the economic and political systems under which they lived.

A very different judgment on Albertz is expressed by Philip Davies, who, while if anything more negative towards biblical theology and himself probably more favourable towards the history of religion, feels that Albertz's new initiative in favour of history of religion remains too close to the nature, and to the faults, of biblical theology. The fact that Albertz argues for history of religion on the grounds that it will be even better for the church than biblical theology does not impress Professor Davies; for he thinks that what is good for the church is no concern for academic biblical studies in any case.[48]

In conclusion it is relevant to consider another argument which is not directly about Albertz's work but may in part be connected with his thinking, as suggested above, and which needs to be mentioned since it has been heard more often in recent years: according to it the biblical texts do not, as has so often been said about them, represent what 'Israel thought' or what 'Israel believed' or 'Israel confessed'. They represent, not what Israel thought, but what was thought by the (smallish?) group who composed and edited the texts.[49] The Bible, therefore, is the product of an elite, and tells us only what that elite wanted people to think.[50] It follows that, even if a Theology of the Old Testament can be written, its contents would be only the theology of that elite. 'Elitism', it will be unnecessary to remind the reader, is one of the deadly sins in the postmodernist canon. If we want to know the true theological views of 'Israel', we have to turn to the actual history of the people's religion.

It is not easy to see how this argument can be met. Perhaps one might say: even if this argument is right for the Israel of biblical times, the Hebrew Bible became for Jews of later times the popularly accepted and thus democratically authoritative expression of what ancient Israel had thought and believed and done. This is a little like one of the arguments used by the 'canonical' approaches, later to be reviewed. And perhaps Albertz would say: his kind of study of popular and state religion would show that the biblical texts did *not* emerge from any such 'elite' but from a process of diversity and conflict over many centuries, in which many different dimensions of society, and not only an 'elite', were involved. Seen this way, the 'elite' is a general and non-historical idea, taken from modern life and applied to a history where, as the historical facts show, 'elites' were by no means the sole controllers of the traditions.

Moreover, perhaps we should accept that in theology we *are inevitably* dealing with *leadership*, and we should not be deceived by the egalitarian and apparently democratic hostility to the 'elite'. We do not consider that the thoughts of Plato or Aristotle are no better than those of the average man in the ancient Greek street. Of course the thoughts of the average person should be known and taken into account; but it is a mistaken populism to suppose that they should be privileged (the true postmodern word!) simply because they are no more than average. Nevertheless it must be admitted that the argument about elitism presents a new face to biblical studies, one that has not as yet been fully taken into account, and one that may mean a new set of difficulties for biblical theology.

To sum up thus far, following Albertz's work it seems likely that the tension between the history of Israelite religion and the theology of the Old Testament – and this tension may be very strong – may well be the most important problem for our subject in the coming half-century. At least on the surface this will be so, because it shows itself so obviously in the practical organization of departments and the procedure of courses and dissertations. As stated earlier, the relations between Old Testament theology and doctrinal theology may well be more profound; but the history-of-religion question looks like being more immediate.

## *10. Where does the difference lie?*

Where then does the essential difference between history of Israelite religion and Old Testament theology lie? First we can answer negatively, by ruling out certain defective answers.

As I have indicated, the difference does not lie in the conception that one approach is historical and the other is not. 'History of religions' may well include methods and operations that are not strictly historical.

This applies in both directions. The reaction of much biblical theology against *history* has been mentioned above. Some biblical theologians have argued for a kind of transhistorical or synchronic description, rather than a diachronic one: Eichrodt's design for his Old Testament Theology may be seen, from some points of view, as an obvious example. But the approach we call 'history of religion' is not necessarily historical in this sense: on the contrary, it may be directed towards transhistorical or synchronic description in exactly the same way in which Eichrodt's plan was. Conversely, some biblical theologians have taken an approach that was very much historical in design: von Rad, the most central in our century, is the obvious example. Some went so far as to say (unkindly, I think) that he had written a History of Hebrew Religion and called it a Theology. He himself wrote, with injustice towards himself in my opinion, that if he did not succeed in establishing the relations of the Old Testament with the New all he had written would be no more than such a history.[51] Thus, in general, the difference between historical and other (synchronic, transhistorical, 'phenomenological') approaches exists on both sides.

Secondly, it seems mistaken to define the difference in terms of objectivity. Objectivity has indeed often been claimed as a characteristic of the history of religions, but then it has also been claimed by some biblical theologians, including some who are themselves highly critical of claims of objectivity.[52] The difference does not seem to be that between the history of religion, a completely objective and scientific subject, and Old Testament theology, a confessionally-directed discipline meaningful only within religion. In these regards the two operations seem to be on a rather equal footing. For while the history of religion may quite reasonably set out to be a scientific and objective study, it remains a question whether particular works written under that rubric have in fact attained the qualities pursued. In my experience historians of religion are not noticeably less opinionated or prejudiced than (say) theologians are.[53] They have their likes and their dislikes within the multifarious material, they favour one source and neglect another. Their criticisms of one another make it clear that they are conscious of this. Just as some theologians are ideologically opposed to the history of religions, so it must be confessed that some historians of religion have been severely prejudiced against theology. Many of them have had past involvement with theology or are casualties from the internecine wars of theology, which leaves them anxious to avoid all future contact with it. They then tend to deny the existence of any sort of theology within the religions that they study. But, in religions which have theology within them, the historian of religion is bound to include that theology in his or her work: and this is properly done, for example, by Albertz. He talks, for instance, of a 'kingship theology', very close to that of the ancient Near East (e.g. 1,116). Of the Deuteronomists, whom he often calls 'theologians', he writes (1, 24) that they created:

> The very first thoroughly, conceptually and intellectually structured, total theological account of Yahweh religion . . . Deuteronomic theology can be described as a large-scale mediating theology.

In connection with the convergence [of official religion and personal piety in the post-exilic period] 'there was a theologizing and a splintering of personal piety . . . There developed a regular personal wisdom theology, so-called "theological wisdom"' (2, 441). 'Theologized wisdom' is described as 'a personal theology of the upper class' (2, 511–23). Again:

> In the early Hellenistic period, in which pressure was felt to achieve a comprehensive theological synthesis at the level of official religion in order to meet the challenge posed by the Samaritan separation and the first contacts with the Greek world-culture, a new type of personal theology came into being, probably at the level of personal piety (2, 556–63).

Thus Albertz's approach to the history of religion freely recognizes theology, its existence and its importance. But theology is *part* of the religious history and is not universally present.

Again, even if one fully accepts the history-of-religion approach, along with historical criticism, the comparative method and so on, the fact remains that the history of Hebrew religion, like Old Testament theology, even if taken on a strictly objective basis, does not write itself automatically. The same data which are uncertain, confusing and ambiguous to the theological approach are still uncertain, confusing and ambiguous to this other. There are many different ways in which elements can be weighted, associated with one another, and formed into what seems to be a satisfactory historical picture. The writer has to think out a mode of organization, to select which facts belong in which context, to make some kind of a plan. He or she may even find it necessary to think of a 'centre' or 'theme' or a classification around which a presentation can be built. Thus the rubrics which Albertz uses to design the structure of his chapters – 'Family Religion', 'State Cult', 'Personal Piety' – do not present themselves automatically but have to be worked out, or 'constructed' (in the [post]modern phrase), as the 'centres' or themes of each section. Even where the history of religion is intended to be free from commitments and biases in respect of any particular religion, it is likely that other general ideological schemes, sometimes or often of a non-religious kind, have the same kind of effect.[54] In respect of their problems of design and approach the history of religion and the theology of the Old Testament have much in common. In both cases our assessment of the success and value of any given presentation depends on its handling of the material, the convincingness of the weighting of different elements, the fullness of its coverage of the realities treated, and other such criteria.

Nor is it to be supposed that the difference can lie in the religious allegiance of the scholar. Undoubtedly the normal position of the biblical theologian is one of religious commitment to the Bible as religious source and criterion. The historian of religion describing the rites of a distant culture may well feel no such commitment. But this again does not form a real point of discrimination between the biblical theologian's work and that of the historian of religion. For the latter may have a religious commitment also, and often does have: a Muslim scholar may be a historian of Islam, a Hindu one of Hinduism. One cannot escape this unless one turns to the totally secularist and ultimately destructive principle that no one who belongs to a religion can speak about his own religion. Historians of religion mostly do not wish to go that way. Undoubtedly religious allegiance can be, and often is, a serious distorting factor, but the way out of this is by informed criticism and debate, and not by prohibition.

One important difference, which might perhaps be agreed on both sides, is that biblical theology emphasized particularly (some would say, unduly) the *intellectual* aspects of the religion: ideas, formulas, arguments, mental concepts, disagreements, theological developments, all as they can be derived from *written texts*. History of religion gives much more place to other factors: customs, rituals, magic, sacred objects, iconography, architecture, relation to groups and classes, social, economic and political setting, psychology and so on. Biblical theology probably has to admit this; its defence is, probably, to point to the high degree to which written texts, given an intellectual exegesis, are central in the mode in which ancient religion has passed on its heritage to later times.

Theologians hostile to the history-of-religion approach often say that it *describes* but does not *evaluate*, that it withholds all value judgments. This, however, though often said by historians of religion, is not necessarily true. There are different schools in the history of religions as in other subjects. C. J. Bleeker is a good example for the rejection of value-judgments:

> The theologian ultimately assumes a personal attitude towards religious values. The historian of religions acknowledges the existence of religious values and tries to understand their significance. But his method should be completely free from any value judgment.[55]

Importantly for our concerns, this is explicitly denied by Albertz:

> Even if a 'history of Israelite religion' can prove neither the truth-claims of the Bible nor the superiority of 'the faith of Israel' (as Eissfeldt sees quite clearly), the historian of religion, too, cannot get by without criteria for assessment . . . But he will seek to reach these judgments not out of present-day church dogmas or problems, but out of the religious discourse which he has to represent . . . he will not want to share and excuse everything. Manifestly wrong decisions and wrong developments must be identified as such . . . Only in this way can the drama and the seriousness of the religious struggle of Israelite people of the time again be brought to life.[56]

Value judgments about salutary and unwholesome turns in Israelite religion, then, are entirely proper within the history of religion. Thus Albertz writes of the 'positive' effect on the history of Israelite religion of all the social and theological problems into which the social crisis of the fifth century hurled the community of Judah (2, 507): 'positive' is a value judgment. Again, he speaks of the 'dangers' of the imperial syncretism under the monarchy which 'became clear only later' when, under the influence of Assyrian religion, the sole worship of Yahweh was threatened through the astral cult (1, 132). And value judgments are particularly evident when we read:

> It was certainly a great defect that Chronicles had nothing to say about the social problems which were such a heavy burden on the community of Judah in the Hellenistic period . . . The scribal theologians masked the notorious social problems from their superiors with pious zeal. This lack of courage in the face of the upper class and lack of sensitivity to the suffering of the lower class was to have devastating consequences for subsequent history (2, 556).

History of religion, then, at least in this form, cannot be blamed for abstaining from value judgments. I think, indeed, that the reverse could be true, and that biblical theology might be more blamed for the same fault. As we shall see (below, Chapter 12), those within biblical theology who have most demanded value judgments have often been the same people who resisted them when they were made.

The fact is, it seems, that there is a considerable overlap between biblical theology and the history of biblical religion. And the ultimate reason for this is that the *stuff* of which biblical theology is built is really biblical religion, or, as I indicated above, those elements of biblical religion which are commended, supported and advanced by the main currents of the Bible. Realities like the personal names of Israelites, the nature of altars, the idea of the tribal system, the chronology of the earliest times, belong to religion, but a theology could not ignore them; rather, it would have to build them into its picture of Israel's theological world. That same material which is historically ordered and described by the historian of religion may be, perhaps, more topically and thematically organized by the biblical theologian. This may not be enough for some, but it seems to me to be the consensus implied in most of what has actually been done. On the contrary, no one has succeeded in showing a valid way in which the two aspects can be set in opposition in principle. On the other hand, where there is theology within a religion, or implied by a religion, the history of religion has to accept that fact and explain what that theology is. There may of course be religions which have no theology; but, if there is a reasonable case for the perception of a theology, then the history of religions betrays its own purpose if it does not acknowledge that fact.

It seems to me that the real difference is one of *scope* and *field*. The one, Old Testament theology, is related to *certain texts* and to the theology *implied* by them; the other, the history of religion, is related to a large social and intellectual field, for which these texts are part of the evidence, and often indirectly so, through hints they give of the contemporary world rather than through the values that they directly affirm. Thus the history of Israel's religion must give equal weight to all aspects and manifestations of that religion, as the Hebrew Bible and other sources reveal them. A theology of the Old Testament, at least as it has been generally conceived, takes its stand alongside the dominant viewpoint or viewpoints which the Old Testament, or its major currents or elements, represents: those are the viewpoints in which it is primarily interested; it wants to know in whiat respects they are (generally, not necessarily universally) 'good' and 'right'.[57] It is interested in the theology that lies behind Abraham, Moses, Isaiah, the Deuteronomist and so on.

No one has proposed to write a 'theology' based upon the views of Ahab and Jezebel, or upon those of Aaron when he made the Golden Calf. No one has written a 'theology' of Israelite Baalism, though the Old Testament itself makes it clear that it was a very substantial religious phenomenon. In principle it would not be impossible to write such a 'theology', if we had sufficient material. It would then be a sort of parallel companion volume to an Old Testament Theology. But Old Testament theology, as generally understood, aligns itself with the 'main line' of the biblical books. The same is true in the New Testament field: a New Testament theology labours to inform us what was the theology of Paul or John; it does not give the same place to the theology of Judas Iscariot or that of Judaizers (if that is what they were) in Galatia or groups disobedient to Paul in Corinth or Colossae. This seems to be the real underlying difference. Naturally, preferences of this kind could be subject to question, and some day someone might argue that Baalism was the real basic message of the Bible. When this happens, we will have to discuss it. But the basic orientation of the subject will remain as I have said.

Yet this argument should not be pressed too far. Hayes and Prussner wrote: 'A history of religion would be as interested in the prophets which the biblical traditions now condemn as in those whom the traditions now canonize', and Räisänen mentions this and carries it farther.[58] I do not think I agree with this. It seems to me to go too far to suggest – if these writers do suggest it – that biblical theology is 'not interested' in the 'false' prophets, in the opponents of Paul, in the theology of polytheism in ancient times or of Gnosticism later. It is very interested, or would be very interested if it had the necessary information. Indeed, it tends to need a picture of exactly these factors: precisely because they are the 'opposition' against which the approved biblical figures struggle, and precisely because they are condemned in the Bible, biblical theology very much wants a good description of them, and the longer the description it can obtain, the more it will say about them. For, obviously, the more one knows about the 'opposition', the more sense one can make of the theology of the biblical sources. And for this one has to turn to the history of religion. Thus many biblical theologies, at least in parts, depend very heavily upon information about the 'opposition' religions. As we have seen, G.E. Wright's two seminal books *God Who Acts* and *The Old Testament against its Environment* both showed an extreme dependence on a particular picture of ancient Near Eastern polytheism, one drawn by a particular group of scholars in the history of the relevant religions.[59] Efforts to identify the 'opponents' against whom Paul was writing have been manifold and have shown how essential a picture of these opponents has been for any formulation of Paul's theology, and how serious the damage to Christianity has been when they have been wrongly depicted. The trouble with biblical theology has not been that it excluded an *interest* in the 'opposition'; it is rather that, where information about the opposition was meagre or lacking, it tended to *imagine* what that opposition must have been like. This is nothing new: depictions of what Canaanite religion must have been like have had a lively existence in the popular imagination for centuries.[60] It is not biblical theology, but the original biblical sources themselves that are at fault here: it is they that failed to give any proper description of the religious position of the opposition, tending rather to characterize it as 'rebellion', 'wickedness', 'abominations' and the like. In this regard the history of religions seems to me to be in the same position as biblical theology. Where it works from the biblical sources it has no more to say than biblical theology has. The history of religion cannot tell us what was in the mind of Aaron when he made the golden calf or of Judas Iscariot when he turned against Jesus. If it has other sources, then biblical theologians will also use that same extra information, for exactly the realities of the 'opposition' are what they want and need. This remains so even if they do not give to the 'opposition' the same kind of place within a Theology of the Old or New Testament.

Some may argue that the history of religion is no concern of the synagogue or church: preachers have to speak on the basis of the Bible or the Jewish-Christian tradition. But the time is past when this could work. The old-time answers that preachers gave to questions like 'What did the Canaanites do that was so wrong?' or 'Why was it wrong to boil a kid in its mother's milk?' will not satisfy. People know that preachers and church authorities know nothing about Canaanite religion. The Bible, religious tradition and preachers are no longer the only, or the main, source for information about such things. People know about them, much more, from television and the press, from archaeology and the museum. These media educate people mainly, or overwhelmingly, from the aspect of history of religion. Preaching and the ecclesial setting no longer give anyone a hiding-place from the history of religion.

In fact, then, the relation between biblical theology and the history of religion is and should be one of overlap and mutual enrichment. And the ultimate reason for this is that the *stuff* of which biblical theology is built is really biblical religion, or, as I indicated above, those elements of biblical religion which are commended, supported and advanced by the main currents of the Bible. If it is true as history of religion that

> the historically based relation to God of the Exodus group is much more strongly coloured in its substance by human decision and human participation than is the ancient trust-relationship to God in the small-group family unit. The Yahweh religion is from the ground up more strongly based on a relation of *correspondence* between divine and human behaviour (Albertz, 1, 49),

this cannot fail to have a serious effect on any theology of the Old Testament. Exactly this sort of thing is where Old Testament theology is blamed for harmonizing two attitudes that were in fact different, and doing it, in this case, in favour of the small-group attitude, which appeals more to most currents of Christianity.

Moreover, the history of religion may provide material that throws new light on aspects that Old Testament theology has already been emphasizing. Thus Albertz tells us that:

> The other Near Eastern religions know of such a personal relation to God only with reference to small groups and individual persons ('personal God', 'protective deity'). The personal bond of a God with a large group is a peculiarity of the Israelite religion (1, 62f.).

Thus history of religion by no means necessarily seeks to 'merge' Hebrew religion into a uniform mass of environing religion: in certain cases it provides evidence of distinctiveness (we remember the use made by G. E. Wright of this type of demonstration much earlier).

Anyway, the point is that the same material which is historically ordered and described by the historian of religion may perhaps be more topically and thematically organized by the biblical theologian. This may not be enough for some, but it seems to me to be the consensus implied in most of what has been actually done. On the contrary, no one has succeeded in showing a valid way in which the two aspects can be set in opposition in principle. Thus it is not surprising to me that what were really histories of biblical religion were widely regarded by their writers as 'biblical theologies' a century ago. Indeed it is quite likely that we are coming back to something of the same kind.

It remains to indicate another reason which may justify or explicate the continuance of biblical theology as a discipline distinct from, though overlapping with, the history of religion. The important feature seems to me to be this: that the history of religion, taken in itself, does not organize the material into a form suitable for the asking of the question of *truth*. Indeed, many formulations of history of religion expressly exclude the asking of that question. But, even if the history of religion could have a formulation of such a kind as to permit the asking of questions of truth and value, its organization of the material does not easily allow this to be done. A limited body of text or texts makes that question more intelligible. In this sense the existence of a *canon* proves itself to be convenient, whether this was the reason for its existence or not. It is easier to ask 'Was Plato right?' than to ask 'Was Greek philosophy right?' and it is easier to ask 'Is the Old Testament view of God true?' than to ask 'Were all views of God held by any ancient Hebrews true?'. And that a body of ancient texts should be interrogated for their 'theology' seems to me a perfectly proper and reasonable academic undertaking. Even accepting the maximum possible place for history of religion, I do not see that it can perform this task for us. One can, of course, in principle work from some other 'canon': for instance, 'Was the theology of the Jews of Elephantine true?'. In principle the question could be asked, but in practice it would not easily work.

## 11. Conclusion

In conclusion we may briefly review a few areas in the Old Testament which well exemplify the problems we have been discussing. Each of these is a matter which is involved in the history of religion and which, in my opinion, is also an essential for any serious Old Testament theology; however, on some views – especially some 'canonical' views – of the nature of Old Testament Theology these might be eliminated from consideration as lying outside the interest of the subject altogether.

The first of these would be the process – I do not know if it really has a name – which we might call 'coalescence' of deities. The God of Israel is of course Yahweh, but in early stories of Genesis, for instance, we hear of the centrality of one named El, or, as some would have it, of various Elim like El Shaddai, El Olam, El Roi and so on. El is also well known from Ugaritic texts and the like. We also have the well-known phenomenon of the 'god of the fathers', a god who is designated not by a personal divine name but as the god of a family (from the past). Now one can of course read all these as just different designations of the one God. But scholars who specialize in this material perceive here a coalescence in which features of El come to be combined with the features of Yahweh.[61] It is very plausible that something of this kind should have taken place, and some of the evidence of it is there before us in the Bible. Thus Albertz tells us (1, 79) that Yahweh may have inherited from El the idea that Yahweh is the real owner of the land. If this is right, and if it is to be evaluated theologically, it must mean that there was something akin to 'divine revelation' in the El religion. To me it seems that the understanding of such a process is just as much a theological necessity as is the explication of the thoughts of Isaiah or Jeremiah, and it might provide us with some very valuable clues for biblical theology. A more narrowly canonical approach might, by contrast, simply rule this out, either because it is history of religion, which would automatically exclude it from theological consideration, or because it lies back in prehistory and outside the boundaries of the canonical process and is therefore irrelevant.

A second case of the same kind, and connected, is that of 'monotheism'. While the monotheism of Israel has been much celebrated in ancient and modern culture, some recent biblical theology has looked with disdain on the subject, thinking that the term was an 'abstract' or 'philosophical' one, or otherwise lacking in the 'kerygmatic' flavour supposed to attach to biblical concepts. But what difference is there between 'monotheism' and the 'kerygmatic' demand 'Hear, O

Israel, the Lord thy God, the Lord is One'? Grammatically they are different, but historically they are deeply related.[62] And in fact 'monotheism', even if pronounced by Childs to be 'theologically inert',[63] may well have been – along with the opposition to idols – perceived as one of the most important elements of Judaism in the years of the Greek and Roman empires and in the time of Christian origins. For the junction between Old and New Testaments it may have been just as important as, indeed perhaps more important than, all the ideas of 'events', of salvation history and 'kerygmatic' proclamation. A 'theology' that leaves it out, on the ground that it is a matter for history of religion, is ignoring one of the major themes of the entire subject.

The third case of the same kind is the matter of sexuality in the deity. That the God of Israel was a markedly male figure has long been noted by various observers. But, unlike familiar deities of the Greek and Near Eastern worlds, he seemed to be without a female consort of any kind. Modern inscriptional discoveries, however, have suggested that this may not have been always or universally the case. There may have been a period, or a stratum, in which the God of Israel was understood to have a female consort.[64] If so, there may well have been a very considerable reorientation of the religion in which this bipartite relation within deity was attacked and eliminated. Such a process would fit within the numerous biblical reports of idolatrous and polytheistic tendencies in Israel, although this particular form, i.e. that of a male and female deity together, is hardly explicit anywhere in the Bible. But it could be that a struggle against sexuality of this kind within deity was the core of the establishment of monotheism, in other words, at some important stage, it was thought more important and more immediate to have no female goddess than it was to have one single deity. If so, this struggle could well have been one of the most important stages in the development of what became the biblical tradition. Some forms of biblical theology, however, ignore these possibilities totally and on principle: in part because they are not expressly described in the biblical texts, and in part simply because they are classed as belonging to history of religion. In my submission, such phenomena are central to any task of Old Testament theology, and are far more important than are the adjustments made by the canonizers in the final stages of the literary development.

To sum up, it seems to me that the history of religion must be accorded full recognition and importance by biblical theology. The two cannot be separated and works on the latter must recognize not only the material of the former but also the positive theological importance of its researches and results. George Brooke writes well:

> There should be nothing controversial about stating that if Old Testament theology is to claim any historical validity, then the texts which form its basis

cannot be studied apart from particular sociopolitical and religious contexts. Sound exegesis, the basis of sound theological extrapolation, will always try to take account of such contexts. The theological bases of the worldviews of the individuals and groups belonging to those contexts cannot be definitively derived solely from the canonical texts; even the theological principles of those who determined the final extent of the canon cannot be derived solely from those texts. More obviously, the validity of any community's theological worldview cannot be verified from the texts alone.[65]

On the other hand, however, there are differences of scope and interest which justify the recognition of the two as separate but overlapping disciplines.

# 9

# Difference in the Size of Complexes

Much Old Testament theology has been concerned from the beginning with the *size* of the areas to be discussed and evaluated. Here again there was a reaction against the procedures of traditional criticism. Criticism, by identifying author-ships and dates of various elements, had separated out numerous different layers in many individual texts, e.g. in books such as Amos or Jeremiah or Genesis. Moreover, the analysis which led to these results had to a large extent depended on theological factors: since one piece of text differed theologically from another piece of the same text, but agreed with another text from else-where, one could infer historical layering of the texts. Later, it came to be felt that this had been 'atomistic', dividing the material into many strata, each of which had its own theological positions and concerns. Old Testament theology, by contrast, has often sought to be 'holistic': it has wanted to interpret not only the books as wholes (though that, as we shall see, was thought of by some as the basic goal) but, so far as possible, the entire Old Testament as a whole. A 'mean-ingless confusion of *disiecta membra*'[1] was to be replaced by an approach which would show forth the structural unity of the Old Testament and thereby its 'profoundest meaning' (ibid., 31). The important thing is not to grasp the theology of particular strata of the Bible, like the theology of St Paul or of the Johannine literature or of the prophets or of the Priestly Document – which, it seems to be implied, can be done with no great difficulty – but to grasp the theology of the entirety, the theology of the great collections, Old and New Testaments, taken as wholes. In particular, with typical historical criticism, scholarship might manage to explain the meaning of the smaller units, but it could not penetrate to the meaning of the larger. It was Old Testament and New Testament theology that promised to do this. This was, at least on one formu-lation, the central promise of these disciplines. Thus, if critical study has been analytic, and has divided the biblical books into different strata and sources, the theological task is to bring all this together again.

A little thought, however, soon makes it clear that this conception is mistaken. The problem of theological understanding existed in full at the level of the indi-vidual text even, indeed especially, at places where there was no critical splitting of the text, no separation of sources, no critical problems of the customary kind. To think of biblical theology as essentially a task of synthesis at the level of the great complexes is to talk is if there is just no problem in the theological under-standing of a paragraph in Ezekiel or in Romans, but a problem only in the bringing together of these disparate materials into one. The reverse is the case: the difficulty of giving a theological explanation of a chapter, or indeed a verse, in Romans may in fact actually be *greater* than that of giving a synthetic account of New Testament theology. The task of theological understanding lies just as much on the analytic level as it does on the synthetic. Of course any individual text has to be compared and correlated with others in any discussion of its meaning, but this is done in analytic approaches anyway, just as much as in synthetic ones.

It is in fact an illusion to suppose that the move from smaller units to larger constitutes a move from non-theological to more theological modes of under-standing. The size of the complexes has nothing particular to do with the estab-lishment of a study as 'theological'.

I add here a thought suggested to me by Professor Ben C. Ollenburger, who is certainly no opponent of Old Testament theology.[2] The matter I have in mind is not that of *opposition* to Old Testament theology, but that of its *rank* or *dignity* within the hierarchy of the various departments of Old Testament study. Ollenburger points to 'the traditional notion that Old Testament theology is the crowning achievement of historical-critical Old Testament scholarship; theo-logians, or people very much like them, should take note and consider the benefits, just because this *is* its crowning achievement'.[3] He cites Preuss's claim that it is 'the noblest and most important task of Old Testament scholarship'.[4] He goes on: 'I do not want to contest the notion here, but I do want to insist that it requires justification.' I agree entirely with his judgment. It is by no means clear that Old Testament theology, even if it is entirely necessary, also has the massive preponderance of importance that some have attached to it. The ulti-mate justification for it may, as Ollenburger suggests (94), be a *pragmatic* one. It is not necessarily the summit of all achievement.

There is, however, perhaps a more theoretical reason why biblical theology should have a sort of 'summit' status accorded to it. It depends on other things, which can be done without entering, or entering fully, into the realm of biblical theology. Things like textual criticism, Semitic linguistics, form criticism, historical criticism, history of Israel, history of religion and indeed exegesis, even in some degree theological exegesis, can be done without entering into biblical theology, but biblical theology cannot be done without the anterior presence of these approaches. In this sense there is a sort of pyramid in which biblical theology is the top. This is not a matter of superiority. Indeed it may seem more like an inferiority, in that it makes manifest the *dependence* of biblical theology on other factors and other levels of work. The top of the building is upheld, obviously, by what is 'underneath' it. This figure, needless to say, does not include the relations between biblical theology and doctrinal theology; for that we would need another pyramid, or some other type of figure.

Returning to what I was saying before we came to Ollenburger's wise question, two or three illustrations may confirm my observations. First, several lines of thought in biblical theology came to the conclusion that there was no one theology of the Old Testament or of the New. Indeed, this may be said to be the position of the *most imposing* works in each Testament, that of von Rad in the Old and that of Bultmann in the New. Von Rad thought that there were different theologies within the Old Testament: various theologies of the Pentateuchal traditions, various of the prophetic, and he built his total Theology on this basis. He did indeed bring them together, in that all of them come within the compass of his one book; but the differences are more conspicuous. Bultmann similarly found it necessary to give separate accounts to the Pauline and the Johannine traditions within the New Testament, while the message of Jesus, the kerygma of the earliest church and the kerygma of the Hellenistic church apart from Paul are all handled separately as 'Presuppositions and Motifs of New Testament Theology'.

The position that seems to result is this: one can build up a fairly 'holistic' theology for complexes that specially belong together (on literary, historical grounds and grounds of common terminology and modes of thinking), but the larger these complexes become, the *more difficult* it is to bring them into a unity. Unities can be established where there is literary, historical, cultural and 'philosophical' commonage – in other words, on the same grounds which are basic to critical analysis – but not where the latter does not exist.

A special case of this kind will be discussed later, namely, the difficulty of passing from a theology of one Testament or the other to a theology of the entire (Christian) Bible.

The point made here has been of importance in the history of the subject. Even where theologies of Old or New Testament have been in existence, it is likely that the writers of commentaries on individual books – and even of commentaries that aspired to be, and were, 'theological' – never felt that they gained a great deal of help from them. Struggling with a difficult verse in Isaiah or in Romans, they might look up a Theology of the Old or New Testament to see what it would say about the general theme, but, having done so, they might well have to return to the refractory verse with no more explicit guidance about what it meant. The Theologies seemed to give some general guidance, but no specific answer on the individual question. And, if this is true of the writers of commentaries, the same is true of their readers and, naturally, of clergy and others who have to work on the meaning of the texts. Not least is this the case with those occupied in the task of preaching: for while the preacher may well be glad to know the 'meaning of the Bible as a whole' – if there is such a unitary meaning – and while the knowledge of that meaning as a whole may be of some help in handling the individual passage, it remains that the individual passage is commonly the material that the preacher has to cope with, and if he or she is to express the individuality of that passage the need is for a theological penetration into that passage in particular, and not a general overview of everything else in the Bible. 'We do not read the Bible,' wrote Dietrich Ritschl, 'we read *in* the Bible.'

Thus, as already indicated above, some of the books which have most fulfilled the ideals of biblical theology have not been comprehensive Theologies of Old or New Testament but have been commentaries or studies on *one particular* text or group of texts. I have already cited Hoskyns' commentary on John as a case. Karl Barth's *Romans* would be a distinguished example in the minds of many. Von Rad's *Genesis*, though on a more popular level, would be another. On a much more advanced level, but similar in orientation, would be Westermann's great Genesis commentary. All these were studies of a particular book or text. It may be said that they saw that text within the context of the whole Bible, and of course they did, but that is not their distinguishing mark: for the most part they concentrated on *that particular book or text*. The traditional, more 'critical', commentaries, often described as arid and untheological, also interpreted the text within the context of the other relevant texts. The distinguishing characteristic of the 'more theological' commentaries was not that they interpreted the whole Old or New Testament, or the whole Bible, but that they interpreted the *individual* passages, and all of them, in their own sequence but on what was felt to be, and intended to be, a 'deeper' or perhaps a 'higher' level. This 'deeper' or 'higher' level would come when one asked about the ultimate axioms and assumptions that were implicit in the text and that were, potentially, significant for regulative statements within theology. This is what the comprehensive volume on Old or New Testament theology or on pan-biblical theology could hardly do: such volumes had to be selective and could not bring in everything. They could not take every passage in its sequence.

In other words, it was a mistake, though an understandable one, to suppose that the move to a 'holistic', comprehensive statement in the form of one or two volumes was also a move from the non-theological to the theological. Actually, it had nothing to do with that difference. The theological was and is in principle as much concerned with the individual text as it was and is concerned with a vision of the Bible as a whole. The mistake took place because historical and critical explanation was (wrongly) diagnosed as being 'non-theological' and the shift to a holistic, comprehensive account was therefore thought of as a uniquely effective mode of passage to theology.

This is not to say that the holistic, comprehensive statements of the type initiated by Eichrodt and others are not valuable and necessary. They are both of these. For it is not possible to work on the detailed text without having some picture of the entirety within which it is set. The essays at comprehensive description provide an articulate and critical basis upon which such pictures can be thought over and refined. But it has been erroneous to suppose that in themselves they are in some sense the culmination of the task of biblical theology.[5]

Another possibility (cf. above, 53) would lie in the production of 'Theologies' of individual books or groups of books. After all, in traditional commentaries it has not been uncommon for the writer to include, commonly within the Introduction, a section on the theology of the book. Some have gone farther and done something similar after each chapter or section. The German commentary series Biblischer Kommentar had at the end of each section or chapter a short piece entitled 'Ziel' or 'aim, purpose'. These have often been felt to be rather 'thin' or 'slight'. Childs likewise in his Exodus commentary has at the end of many (not all) of his chapters a section usually entitled 'Theological Reflection' – sometimes longer, e.g. four and a half pages on the manna and quails (299–304), sometimes remarkably short and thin again, e.g. less than two pages on the exodus from Egypt (237–9), two on the Passover (212–14), one on the plagues (169f.), one and a half on the call of Moses (87f.), only two on the Ten Commandments (437–9)! A number of chapters (there are twenty-four in all) have no 'Theological Reflection' attached at all, so that the average for this section remains thin and slight. This may well be because much theological reflection is already included within the other sections of the article. In any case it shows that the inclusion of a 'theological conclusion' of some sort within chapters of a commentary has not as yet been shown to be very successful.

Another possibility is to produce *individual* Theologies for individual books or groups of books. For a number of books of the New Testament this has recently been done by Cambridge University Press, and these are of good scholarly quality. Yet the feeling remains that a Theology of one book does not have the significance that is raised or the excitement about it that is felt when one turns to a Theology of the Old or of the New Testament. For, whatever one learns about the theology of one book, say of I Peter, is distracted by the question: what then about II Peter or about Paul or about Hebrews? One may perhaps argue thus: since no one book can be authoritative on its own, therefore the theology of any one book can never probe the more profound questions. This is perhaps one way of expressing the effect of the canon.

This chapter has not exhausted the questions which have been raised: for example, it has not touched on the question of a pan-biblical theology as distinct from the theology of either Old or New Testament. This and other related questions will be taken up later.

From this point of view it is clear that the search for a *pan-biblical* statement, as if this was the essence of theology or the culmination of all biblical study, was a mistake. The search for generalization over large areas – over entire books, over all the Psalms, or the Gospels as a whole, or the New Testament as a whole, may be very valuable and very necessary. But it is misleading to suppose that the move to larger and larger areas is a move away from non-theological consideration and towards theological depth. Theological depth is something that must be applicable over individual passages – certainly not over elements too short to be semantically meaningful, like single words, and certainly not without consideration of context – but still over individual passages when seen properly in context.

This in turn helps to explain why historical-critical operations were never so damaging to theological perception as modern fashions would have us believe. If one feels that one cannot theologically understand a passage, just because it comes from a different source from the passage just before, or from a different author or redactor, or from a later historical period, it seems that one is saying that no passage can be understood in itself. In fact that sort of critical differentiation was never a serious difficulty to theological understanding, except for those for whom it was in principle impossible to understand a text if there were critical differentiations within it.

# 10

# Difference in the Way of Thinking:
# Philosophy and Natural Theology

## *1. Philosophy and biblical scholarship*

Biblical scholarship is in general rather remote from philosophy.[1] Naturally, biblical scholars are not ignorant persons, and in the course of their education they may doubtless have read some Plato and Kant, some Descartes or Locke. But as they advance in biblical scholarship these interests seem to fade into the background. Philosophy does not seem to solve biblical questions. So much in biblical scholarship depends on knowledge of a different kind: it is concerned with linguistic phenomena, with features of different kinds of texts, with *realia* of the ancient world, with all sorts of detailed empirical knowledge and experience which fails to classify itself under philosophical categories. A knowledge of Kant will not enable the scholar to distinguish between the *piel* and the *hiphil* of a Hebrew verb, and a reading of Hume will not explain why the Greek texts of Jeremiah and Job were considerably shorter than the present Hebrew text. For the major daily-life questions of biblical scholarship one needs not the general ideas of philosophy but quite specific knowledge and experience, specific to particular languages, regions, places and texts. It is a technical knowledge. Biblical scholarship is like a combination of slices from linguistics, literary appreciation, geography, history and various other disciplines.

Being thus something of a technical operator, the biblical scholar, like any other technician, tends to take a slightly sceptical common-sense view of matters that are more metaphysical in nature. At its lowest level this reveals itself in those scholars for whom the replacement of a Hebrew or Greek word by its corresponding English or German word is the final statement of meaning and the highest level of human thought – and there are great scholars who appear to have lived on exactly that principle. But, more generally, it means that the questions and answers of philosophers are felt to be rather unreal, remote, artificial: they neither meet with the needs of biblical scholarship nor can they be answered by its resources. For ordinary purposes a naive realism will suffice. Biblical scholars think of themselves as hard-headed, down-to-earth persons, hostile to the abstract, accustomed to dealing with realities and events. Where they are more theological in their attitudes the situation remains the same: they have tended to be more interested in the truth and authority of the Bible, more affected by the imperatives of 'positive' biblical preaching than influenced by processes of reasoning which seemed to be 'abstract'. There is little patience for the philosophical theologian with his 'It depends what you mean by God': to the biblical scholar 'God' means the God of the Bible, as recognizable by this designation as is Jack Jones or Joe Smith by his. In general, therefore, not to extend this theme unduly, modern biblical scholarship by its own functional character has been substantially isolated from philosophy.

## 2. The influence of dialectical theology

This was already so before the rise of dialectical theology. That movement, however, both altered and intensified the attitude of theologically conscious biblical scholars towards philosophy. Dialectical theology worked in several contrary directions. On the one hand it encouraged a strong personalism and existentialism; on the other hand it encouraged scholars to ignore philosophy, to regard it as an enemy of theology. In yet a third development, it encouraged some of them to suppose that the Bible itself provided something, hardly a philosophy, but a way of thought, a mental pattern, which could be derived from the Bible and then reapplied to the Bible with the assurance that the result would be the right interpretation of the Bible.

First of all, existentialism. Existentialism, along with associated personalisms, was a key concept of many currents of dialectical theology. Kierkegaard was often quoted; Buber's *I and Thou* with its drastic contrast between the 'I-Thou' relationship and the 'I-It' relationship was a household word. In Scotland John Macmurray was similarly cited. Heidegger was also quoted and cautiously respected, though not so well known by the majority. In New Testament theology, and New Testament scholarship generally, the central figure of Bultmann showed the high degree of relevance that existentialism could have. But for Old Testament scholarship the situation is best described on the basis of Emil Brunner. Thus Childs describes the impact of Richard and Reinhold Niebuhr, and the introduction of names like Buber, Kierkegaard and others in the origins of the biblical theology movement. Then he goes on:

> Perhaps more influential than all of these . . . was the impact of Emil Brunner. The impact of his *Divine-Human Encounter* (1943), followed by *Revelation and Reason* (1946) – both in unusually lucid English prose – can hardly be overestimated. Here was a theology that was equally adamant in placing the Bible at the centre of its work. Moreover, Brunner's sharp attack on the

Fundamentalists to the right and on the Liberals to the left was highly compatible with the mood of the biblical scholars.[2]

Quite right. But – and this aspect goes beyond Childs' remarks – Brunner affected the relation to philosophy in two mutually contradictory ways. On the one hand he introduced certain philosophical trends and supported their relevance to biblical studies; on the other hand, by denying that they were really philosophical, he supported the anti-philosophical ethos of biblical theology and encouraged its practitioners to go on thinking that their work was contrary to philosophy.

Thus, addressing 'the Object-Subject Antithesis in Thinking', he tells us that:

The antithesis or the correlation of object and subject has dominated all western philosophy since its very beginning. Being and thinking, truth and knowledge – this is the problem around which philosophical thought has turned at least since the Sophists and Socrates – a problem that emerges again in Kant's question about the relation between the 'thing-in-itself' and experience. The ultimate validity of this way of stating the problem has not been questioned until very recently. One did not ask if the truth could be found by means of these methods of reasoning, but merely which of the two great categories, the Objective or the Subjective, should be considered primary and what sort of relation obtained between the two. On this issue the great systematic trends of thought separated, Realism with its primary emphasis upon the object, Idealism with its primary emphasis upon the subject, Pantheism or the Doctrine of Identity with its tendency to make the antithesis a matter of indifference. It was left to the newest form of philosophy, the existential, to question the validity of the antithesis itself. It is no accident that the source of this new thinking is to be found in the greatest Christian thinker of modern times, Søren Kierkegaard. It is therefore particularly suggestive for us theologians to attach ourselves to this philosophy, the entire bent of which seems to correspond with ours (56).

Note how fulsome the praise for existentialism is. Western philosophy has been stifled since the beginning, its three conflicting schools unable to cope with the basic problem. Existentialism has suddenly showed that the underlying antithesis is mistaken. The achievement of existentialism, it seems, is enormous. On the other hand, at this point Brunner seems to realize that he is sailing close to some dangerous rocks, and that he may be accused of making his theology depend on a particular philosophy. So he continues:

Our considerations are purely theological, hence they are not dependent upon the correctness or incorrectness of that philosophical undertaking which seems to run parallel – apparently or really – with our own. There are no preliminary philosophical judgments which we carry over to be added to theology.

Theology is *sui generis*. The nature of the relation between the Word of God and faith cannot be derived from any philosophical propositions, not even from those of existentialist philosophy. Brunner's argument therefore, he continues, is essentially a defensive one: if the relation of the Word of God to faith is *falsely* subordinated to the Object-Subject antithesis and the associated concept of truth, then that misunderstanding has to be combated, and for this a use of the philosophical argument is necessary.

Bultmann argued somewhat similarly. He was not borrowing Heidegger's categories, he wrote, and forcing them on the New Testament. 'The philosophers are saying the same thing as the New Testament and saying it quite independently.'[3]

The case of Barth was only slightly different. His earlier works were strongly marked by existentialism, and similarly his *Christliche Dogmatik*, his first adumbration of a doctrinal statement. Afterwards it was always said that these had been his 'eggshells' and that he had extracted himself entirely from any dependence on existentialism. But it is scarcely to be believed that the existentialist element ceased to exist. In any case, many followers of Barth continued in this respect to use many of the arguments and standpoints of other representatives of dialectical theology, certainly including Brunner and Bultmann. Although Old Testament theologians who favoured Barth tended to turn away from thinkers like Bultmann in their attitudes to the Old Testament, they tended to retain that general existentialism and personalism which had characterized the entire movement.

Thus G. Ernest Wright, trying to cope with 'the biblical teaching regarding man', quoted almost a complete page from Brunner:[4]

> The Bible says nothing of a God as he is in himself and nothing of a man as he is in himself, but only of a God who from the first is related to man and of a man who from the first is related to God, and, indeed, in such a way that in this relation God is inconvertibly the first, man inconvertibly the second . . .

And continuing:

> This two-sided relation between God and man is not developed as doctrine, but rather is set forth as happening in a story. The relation between God and man and between man and God is not of such a kind that doctrine can adequately express it in abstract formulas . . . It is not a timeless or static relation, arising from the world of ideas – and only for such is doctrine an

adequate form: rather the relation is an event, and hence narration is the proper form to describe it.

It is obvious to any reader of *God Who Acts* how much of that book is drawn from principles of this sort, as set forth by Brunner. And quite possibly we should admit that, at the time and in that situation, these thoughts were helpful: they did in some measure engage with some of the realities of the Bible and enabled these realities to be valorized in a salutary way.

In the end, however, some of these ideas in the hands of biblical theologians became dogmas which it was heresy to question, or slogans which were endlessly repeated as a substitute for thought. Certainly they still appear plentifully in the literature: personal involvement, existential decision; events rather than static entities; God in relation, not God in himself;[5] holism but not analysis; declaration rather than discussion; hostility to any idea of objectivity.

That these thoughts form a sort of philosophy is beyond question. Nevertheless their existence and popularity has not meant that the importance of philosophy is granted; on the contrary, their presence has tended to be combined with a continuing hostility towards philosophical seriousness. Brunner's own argument as quoted makes it clear why. On the one hand he claimed that existentialist philosophy was the right one and saw things in a way that fully agreed with the Bible and Christian theology; on the other hand he insisted that the theology did not at all depend on this philosophy and had adopted nothing from it. And, this being so, there was no reason for anyone in theology to continue serious study of philosophy, since theological truth was known independently of the one true philosophy, while little would be gained from study of the many wrong ones.

From this it has been a short step to regarding philosophy as an enemy of theology altogether. There is of course a long tradition of this sentiment: 'philosophy and empty deceit, according to human tradition' are coupled together in Col. 2.8. The emphasis on revelation in dialectical theology revived this tradition. What God reveals about himself is something quite different from what man has worked out about God: there is a complete discontinuity between divine truth and human wisdom. Philosophy, as that part of human wisdom which has been most inclined to work out ideas about God, is particularly dangerous. And the more it has said about God, the worse it has been. This is why biblical theologians, when they have said anything about the matter at all, have tended to be most severe against idealist philosophies: for they are the ones which may invoke a deity, which thus look more like a theology, and which may therefore seep into theology and distort it. Biblical theologians have thus tended to be particularly anti-idealist: anti-Platonic, anti-Hegelian[6] – except for certain qualifications which will be mentioned later.

These tendencies were greatly accentuated by the Barthian rejection of all natural theology, which will be discussed more fully later. Barth himself, it should be noted, did not share the rather absolute rejection of philosophy which in the minds of many accompanied his position in this regard. It is, he wrote, a 'grotesque piece of theatre' when someone points the finger at another and 'accuses him or her of being a victim of this or that philosophy' (*CD* II/1, 728). It is not a meaningful criticism to say of a theological utterance *only* that it betrays the speaker's philosophical education or that it makes use of some or other philosophical conceptuality (ibid., 729). But this was not enough to stop it: what Barth blamed here was in fact going on, as he doubtless knew very well, and still is; and though he did not like it, he was somewhat responsible for it, for what else was one to expect?

Generally speaking, serious involvement with philosophy is alien to the atmosphere of dialectical theology. For philosophy means not just 'having' a philosophy but conducting continual philosophical enquiry on an open basis. Biblical theologians have generally known something about philosophy, but they have seldom engaged in any such enquiry. In Barthianism, whatever Barth himself may have thought, philosophy has been cultivated, if at all, not as a way towards truth but as an instrument, indeed as a weapon. Knowing some philosophy sharpens the mind and improves its power in controversy. But philosophy gives no positive information about God, no guidance that leads towards him. Rather, the detection of philosophical affinities proves to be a powerful means of discrediting opponents. It suggests that they are preferring the deceptive wiles of human wisdom over the Word of God.

In fact much biblical theology has been much more dependent on a particular philosophy than was recognized. Brunner's statement already quoted was naive. In it he is not really, as he professes, using philosophy only negatively and defensively: he is teaching people, telling them how to recognize the true character of truth, knowledge, events, love and other such central concepts within the Bible. He is pointing to 'the abyss that lies between the biblical and the general, rational understanding of truth' (63). Biblical theologians might be happy to forget about the subject-object relationship – many of them might not understand what he was talking about at this point – but they were certainly happy to learn about the nature of truth, knowledge, love and the rest within the Bible. And what Brunner had to say about these august matters *did* to a large extent derive from exactly the sort of philosophical position that he expounded. I do not say that the views of truth, knowledge, etc. expounded by biblical theologians have been totally dependent on that philosophical orientation; in part, they doubtless did derive from biblical material examined for itself. But almost certainly these philosophical principles have had a significant *heuristic* role in guiding biblical theologians towards these particular perceptions of meanings, and in doing so they may well have caused these theologians to ignore evidences which pointed in other directions. On the other hand the insistence of Brunner (and doubtless many others) that theological perceptions were actually totally independent of philosophical considerations, and that biblical truth stood worlds apart from rational truth, made it easier for biblical theology to see itself as in general opposed to philosophical thinking and immune from any serious criticism that might arise from it.

This is not, after all, surprising: the idea of 'biblical theology' suggests a theology based upon the Bible, while any theology taking full account of philosophy would have to go far beyond the Bible. It is clearly disturbing to any idea of biblical theology if it is found that in its work on the material of the Bible it has actually followed the guidance of philosophical assumptions, where alternative assumptions would have produced different results within the Bible itself. We shall see in due course that exactly this is very likely. What it means is that biblical theology has chosen to rely eclectically on philosophical assumptions that seemed helpful for its own aims, while ignoring others that would seem to lead in another direction.

One of the ways in which these questions come to the surface has been through the hoary question of presuppositions in biblical scholarship. Biblical scholars who are theologically conscious have been sensitive to the criticism, especially from the more historically inclined,[7] that their theological presuppositions damage the validity of their scholarly research. The standard reply to this has been the obvious counter-attack: history is just as stuffed with presuppositions as theology is, and the philosophical assumptions of historians are just as damaging to *their* work. And this argument is not without strength so far as it goes. But those who used it have often failed to carry through with it. They left it at the point where it appeared to enunciate:

(*a*) Biblical theologians have theological presuppositions

(*b*) Historians have philosophical presuppositions.

But if the argument was to be valid, it would have the further extension:

(*c*) Biblical theologians have theological presuppositions, but they (like historians) have philosophical presuppositions as well.

Practically no one within biblical theology noticed this further stage. The effect of the (incomplete) argument therefore has been to suggest that biblical theologians have as their *sole* presupposition a theological belief, and that that belief is not itself dependent on philosophical assumptions. And this in turn is the reason for one obvious fact, namely, that those who most loudly called on others to reveal their presuppositions have been the same ones who neglected to do so themselves.

I wrote above that biblical theology, in so far as it has had a philosophical orientation, has been anti-idealist, in common with the (at least apparent) argumentation of dialectical theology. I remarked that there was a qualification to this. The qualification lay in the question of *history*. In the matter of history most biblical theology has taken an idealist line. While biblical scholars in their practical work have emphasized history and historical criticism quite a lot, teaching dates, tracing simple sequences, aligning sources, when they became biblical theologians they have tended to a markedly idealist point of view concerning history. Any concern to establish 'facts', to want to know 'what really happened', has been sternly condemned as 'historicism' and 'positivism'. Thus von Rad regarded it as an intolerable 'positivism' to wish to distinguish between more accurate accounts of a historical event and legendary ones. Childs writes as if the mere concept of 'what really happened' was too childishly absurd to be even considered.[8] Particularly noticeable in the writing of works on biblical theology is the sympathetic attention given to the more idealist philosophies of history of Collingwood and others.

This is not difficult to explain. Most biblical theologies have emphasized 'history' as a category of Old Testament revelation and literature; but they have equally felt a need to go beyond a merely historical presentation of the material. To move towards an idealistic philosophy of history has seemed an obvious solution. Yet the contradiction with the general anti-idealism of the tradition of biblical theology is glaring.

The whole thing shows clearly the weaknesses of the use of philosophy within biblical theology. Biblical theologians may cite philosophers of history, they may list them and provide surveys of them, but what they do not do, generally speaking, is to engage in philosophy of history itself. Still less do they engage in general philosophy. This means that their comments on philosophic aspects are powered and motivated by their theology. They use eclectic selections from philosophy in order to support their own theological drives or, even more commonly, to discredit contrary theological positions.[9] This in turn reveals a serious inadequacy in the handling of philosophical problems. Would it not be better, and more in line with the implications of dialectical theology, to say that philosophy had nothing at all to do with the matter and that no gain was to be had from any sort of philosophical alignment at all? Unfortunately, this will not work, because many positions taken within biblical theology *require* intellectual support from outside and cannot stand without it.[10]

The inadequacy of much biblical theology in handling philosophical questions appears most clearly in the *incoherence* of its language, even when the subject under discussion is not philosophy itself but biblical and theological in character. Take this sentence from Childs' *Biblical Theology*:

Biblical theology serves critically to check types of exegesis which so deconstruct the Old and New Testaments by various approaches of historical, literary and sociological criticism as to render inoperative the theological use of the Bible as the authoritative scriptures of the church (481).

What is meant here? How do we know when a type of exegesis 'deconstructs' the Old and New Testaments? Does the sentence mean that *all* exegesis that deconstructs is to be checked, or only those types of exegesis which deconstruct 'by various approaches'? Does 'various approaches' mean 'certain approaches of historical, literary and sociological criticism which render inoperative the theological use (and not others)', or does it mean 'any or all approaches of historical, literary and sociological criticism, all of which approaches render it inoperative'? In other words, is Childs trying to make a criteriological statement which should serve as a guide to the *method* of biblical theology, or is he only assembling terms of disparagement which can be loosely applied to various disapproved approaches? Perhaps he intends the former, but the latter is what emerges. This aspect well illustrates the 'homiletic' air of much biblical theology, to which Childs himself calls attention.

Another example, again from Childs. In *Biblical Theology*, 592f., he is discussing a 'hard-hitting, provocative thesis' of Kelsey about the nature of humanity. In a negative concluding assessment he includes the sentence:

In my judgment, it is fortunate that there remain important dogmatic theologians who continue rigorously to resist the acceptance of modern philosophical and cultural positions as axiomatic for Christian theology.

What is it that these theologians are resisting? Do they resist the acceptance of *any or every* such position? Or do they resist the acceptance of *some* such positions? Or do they resist them only if they are accepted *as axiomatic*? If this last alternative is intended, then is it true that Kelsey *says* it is axiomatic that they must be accepted? If it is not, then this is not a relevant criticism of Kelsey but an unjustified slur on his thinking.

Again:

The approach is that of tracing traditio-historical trajectories from within the tradition, rather than approaching the material from a history-of-religions perspective which strives for an allegedly objective description of religious phenomena (211).

What is the criterion here? Is the approach that is rejected rejected because it is history of religion? Or is it rejected because it strives for an objective description? If it was history of religion, but did not strive for objective description, would that be all right? Or, again, if it was not only 'allegedly' objective but was in fact objective, would that make a difference? If it was objectively true, would Childs still reject it? What he means, of course, can easily be surmised. He is against the rejected approach because it is one through history of religion, *and* because (he thinks) all history of religion claims objectivity, *and* because (he thinks) this objectivity is always illusory. Why this last? He does not tell us: probably because it is a fashionable opinion and one likely to be favoured by readers.

In general, then, this type of loose thinking, with avoidance of precise criteria and with the piling up of negative associations, has been common in the tradition of biblical theology and especially so in the English-language tradition.

As I have said, the use of philosophy tends to be subordinated to theological needs. This can be illustrated from another aspect. In traditional theology it has been customary to use the category of heresy as an argumentative technique. You say that an opinion is 'Marcionite' or 'Pelagian' and the reader is supposed to know that the opinion is thereby discredited: argument or justification is usually considered unnecessary. Theologians carry a mental list of bad opinions listed under these names; if an opinion is listed, you know that it is a bad one, whether you can remember anything about the reasons for and against or not.

This applies in biblical theology as in other areas of theology. Everyone in theology is familiar with this technique, and no more needs to be said about it here. The point to be added is that philosophical affinity is commonly treated in the same way. 'Positivism' is certainly on the heresy list, so is 'historicism' and 'rationalism'. 'Objective' is also on it. 'Idealism' is probably on it too, even among those who espouse an idealist view of history, since they are often not fully aware that it is idealist. Sometimes the identifications are remote from reality: Alan Richardson for instance appears to have regarded Bultmann as a positivist, although by any normal understanding Bultmann was a determined foe of positivism.[11] Von Rad's idea that it is 'positivism' even to distinguish between a legendary narrative and a historically probable one is surely preposterous. Leo Perdue also betrays the idea – probably a common one – that historical criticism is 'positivist' in principle.[12]

To sum up: most work in biblical theology has tended to ignore philosophy and to depict philosophical work as a rival or enemy. Where it has been cited and used, it has commonly been used not in itself and for its own sake, but as an instrument to validate theological positions that have already been determined in principle. Actual levels of competence in the handling of philosophical issues have been low. The identification of ideas under the labels of 'idealism', 'historicism', 'positivism' and other such terms has often been vague and inaccurate, suggesting that no deep philosophical ability underlay it. The perception that some positions in biblical theology very much depend on a particular philosophy will mostly be regarded as damaging to these positions and damaging to the possibilities of any independent biblical theology.

It is equally possible that there are particular areas in biblical theology which have suffered neglect or distortion because scholars were shy of the philosophical aspects that seemed to attach to them. Thus John Barton writes:

> The study of Hebrew Bible ethics has sometimes suffered from an unwillingness on the part of scholars to contemplate 'philosophical' questions at all, on the grounds that the people of ancient Israel simply were not interested in, or could not have understood, questions of such a kind. A case could undoubtedly be made in favour of such a belief, but it *needs* to be made: it should not be asserted as though it were obvious.[13]

Childs (*OTTCC*, 206) gives us an example. Reporting on the discussion of Eichrodt's ethical views, he points out that the area of ethics has been particularly 'vulnerable to the criticism of imposing unsuitable philosophical categories on the biblical material'. In the eyes of many critics, he goes on, Eichrodt's categories have seemed 'unusually dependent on a post-Kantian perspective'. Quite right: this is the sort of thing people will have said. But then we ask: is 'post-Kantian' a bad thing? Probably, in the atmosphere of biblical theology, readers would feel it so. But then can we be told of any philosophical categories which would be 'suitable'? Or does the phrase mean 'philosophical categories, all of which are unsuitable'? It is typical of some biblical theology to give no answer. Now Childs is merely reporting on other people's opinions; but the way in which he does it well exemplifies the customary handling of such questions. Could the average biblical theologian expound Neo-Kantianism to us, or explain to us what is good or bad about it? Probably not. Could Childs himself do so? We cannot tell, because his use of the term leaves us with no idea. Biblical theologians do not generally know that sort of thing. Actual understanding or explanation of the philosophical identifications made has not been felt necessary: to give the name is enough.

If it should come to be accepted, therefore, that some or all biblical theologies have deep philosophical dependence, and that they have to have full and proper philosophical justification, the recognition of this will probably lead to drastic changes in the whole concept of biblical theology.

In the long run much biblical theology has been a response to philosophical critiques of traditional Christianity or, even more, to those philosophical influences which tended to soften the edges of 'orthodox' Christianity and moderate its confessional and biblical character. In this respect it ran parallel to the 'neo-orthodox' positions which were rising to dominance at the same time.

## 3. *The character of biblical thought*

Another response to the same set of problems is the idea that the Bible itself contains or implies a scheme of thought which, while hardly a philosophy in the usual sense, is a fully valid and independent mode of thinking. This biblical mentality, it is supposed, copes just as well with the basic problems of life as any philosophy or any other mode of thinking does. The emphasis here, then, is not so much on the truth of the things said in the Bible, but on the validity and distinctiveness of *the way in which* these things are thought out and the way in which they cohere.[14] Biblical thought in this sense has been a major theme for biblical theology, and it is easy to see the reasons why:

1. Biblical thought has been seen as distinctive from most or all philosophies and perhaps from other informal ways of thinking.

2. Biblical thought has therefore been seen as a sort of informal logic, which thus grants coherence to the biblical material, easily seen as internally contradictory by other logics.

3. With the rejection of natural theology, biblical thought carries out the function of an underlying logic and metaphysics for the Bible, a function which had in the past been carried out to some extent by natural theology.

4. Biblical thought is seen as common to Old and New Testaments and thus provides a basis for belief in the unity of the Bible.

5. Biblical thought, it is supposed, is not just an idea thought up by someone, but can be validated and elaborated on the basis of hard linguistic, cultural evidence through the expertise of biblical scholars.

The movement that led to the emphasis on biblical thought (or Hebrew thought, Hebrew mentality, which for the most part is taken to be the same thing) went back to before the rise of modern biblical theology. In this respect biblical theology was deeply indebted to the historical-philological scholarship that went on through the nineteenth century and into the early twentieth. If some older scholarship had been happy to analyse the texts on the basis of thought-forms then current, in the hope of showing that the Bible conformed to the standards of modern rationality and morality, the more recent scholarly tradition turned in another direction, and especially so after the work of the *religionsgeschichtliche Schule*. I quote a striking passage from Krister Stendahl:

What emerged out of the studies of the *religionsgeschichtliche Schule* was a new picture of the men, the ideas, and the institutions of biblical history. Those elements and traits, which did strike modern man as crude, primitive, cultic and even magical, were now given equal and often greater emphasis than those which happened to appeal to enlightened Western man . . . J. Pedersen applied V. Grønbech's studies of human self-understanding in old Nordic religion to an extensive study of OT anthropology, where cherished distinctions between soul and body, magic and religion, cult and ethics, individual and collective, were thoroughly intermingled and lost much of their meaning. It became a scholarly ideal to creep out of one's Western and twentieth-century skin and identify oneself with the feelings and thought-patterns of the past.[15]

There was a current of ancient humanity, it now seemed, which had a quite consistent body of thought. However, it was quite different from that of rational, propositional, philosophical modern man. If that ancient thinking differed from modern conceptions, so much the better: this showed that it was an internally logically consistent system which ought to be valued and appreciated for itself and not devalued by comparison with 'modern' rationality. The Bible was a major source through which this special way of thinking could be seen and enjoyed; conversely, appreciation of this mode of thinking was an essential for the proper appreciation of the Bible, and anyone who approached the Bible with the categories of logical, rational or analytic thinking, ancient (which meant Greek) or modern, would certainly misinterpret it.

It was therefore the historical–cultural scholarship of an earlier era, not necessarily very theological in its interests, that laid the groundwork for the emphasis on Hebrew thought within biblical theology. But it was obvious that, if there was a peculiar or special way of thinking characteristic of the Bible, such an insight might hope to advance many of the objectives of biblical theology. It formed a reason for differentiation from the older doctrinal theology (which, it could be argued, had been too much influenced by Western rational thought); it might also help to show a difference from environing religions; if it extended over both Testaments, it would form a link between them; and, if this mode of thought could be seen as specially linked with revelation, it would support a revelatory kind of theology and one remote from the influences of philosophy and natural theology. Moreover, it would defend the Bible against critical questioning, which could now be turned aside on the ground that that questioning derived from Western or modern categories and was therefore necessarily inappropriate.

Some probably sensed another advantage in the scheme of Hebrew thought. As we have seen, much biblical theology has been anxious about the supposed dominance of historical criticism, in the sense of dating of sources, distinctions between various authors, and that sort of thing. Now, the delineation of Hebrew thought to a large extent ignored critical niceties of this kind. I have said that the identification was the fruit of historical-cultural study, and indeed it was historical, but in a broad rather than a narrow sense. It was historical in that it sought to know how the Hebrews thought in ancient times or, let us say, in biblical times. But it was not very interested in distinguishing J and P or in working out how many different prophets had worked on the Book of Isaiah. Detailed source criticism of that kind did not seem to matter. Hebrew thought, as commonly portrayed, was the same in P as in J or E, and the same in the various parts of books like Isaiah; only in the later, 'apocryphal', books, possibly influenced by Greek thought, was there some doubt about it. And indeed Hebrew thought, seen thus as substantially unitary, was thought to be dominant right through into the New Testament also. This was, for many, the whole point of the exercise.

Thus the most eminent single monument of this investigation, Pedersen's *Israel*, handled the Old Testament more or less as one block and paid little attention to such criticism: his work was one example of that Scandinavian trend which moved away from analysis and division of sources.[16] Investigation into Hebrew thought thus appeared to be a 'holistic' approach and to do something to overcome the analytic emphasis so blamed upon historical criticism.

Once again it was the dialectical theologians who exploited the contours of biblical thought, which, as it turned out, was remarkably similar to the existentialism we have already seen them to support. In essence, most of the time it has been a sort of existentialist personalism. The I-Thou relationship is paramount, the I-It relationship is suspect. Self-involvement is central and the idea of objectivity is to be deplored. Analytic questions, dividing up a problem between distinguishable meanings and elements, are to be ignored; synthetic claims about wholes are to be made. One is not concerned with being and becoming, with causes and results; one is interested in confrontations, in events, in demands.

Something like this, though seldom made explicit, is evident in the values with which questions in biblical theology are argued. And it is not surprising, as a result, that this sort of informal philosophy is not only used as a criterion in theological exegesis but is read back into the texts themselves, and especially the Hebrew texts, as being 'Hebrew thought', the Hebrew point of view, or at least a good modern representation of it. The result is that this philosophy, if we call it that, becomes unchallengeable as a key to interpretation: for, being the inherent Hebrew point of view, it will naturally produce interpretations which entirely fulfil the meanings of the text.

In this we have something similar to the use of existentialism in dialectical theology, especially by both Brunner and Bultmann: it was, according to them, a philosophy which was independent of Holy Scripture and yet, rather marvellously, ran parallel to it. It was thus not a natural theology, i.e. not a completely alien system attached to the scripture from without, but one which expressed the same understanding of existence and could thus be used of it without the danger of distortion.

Thus Brunner in the work already quoted made some statements that were to become typical, and he went on to the decisive step of proving these from the linguistic structure of Hebrew:

> The decisive word-form in the language of the Bible is not the substantive, as in Greek, but the verb, the word of action. The thought of the Bible is not substantival, neuter and abstract, but verbal, historical and personal.[17]

And again:

> The New Testament differs from the Old in a manner which is seductive and dangerous for our generation. The New Testament is written in Greek. It makes use of Greek concepts to express the message of salvation in Christ . . . The Greeks are our scientific tutors. Owing to the unprecedented esteem and practical significance which science enjoys today, the Greeks are more than ever the tutors of our time. Even the thinking of the ordinary man, who knows nothing of the Greeks, is infused with Greek thought from the school, the newspaper and daily associations.
>
> Now it is a strange paradox of reality that the Gospel is presented to us in the language and concepts of the people whose thought constitutes today the greatest opposition to the content of the Gospel. To mention only one example, the Greek conception of spirit, and therefore of the true and the good, is a kind which equates spirit with the abstract and represents the physically concrete as its opposite, as that which ought not to be . . . The identification of the spiritual with the abstract is one of the most fateful facts of our intellectual history . . . for us the Greek conceptual world of the New Testament is above all a hindrance because it presents the temptation to Hellenize the content of the New Testament . . . In the Old Testament we come upon a world completely unaffected by the whole Hellenic spirit . . . That which is peculiarly biblical, veiled in the New Testament under Greek form, appears to us in Old Testament form unveiled – yes, perhaps even enhanced, in a certain sense exaggerated. But this is what we need especially today; and this is why for us the Old Testament is necessary in a special way for understanding the New.[18]

Here we have the group of ideas that was basic to many studies in biblical theology: the idea that the Hellenic spirit was *the great potential enemy* to the Christian message; its idea of spirit, its *abstraction* and its opposition to the concrete; the biblical thought, basically in Hebrew but 'veiled' in Greek; the 'verbal' character of Hebrew, correlating with ideas of the historical and personal, not with those of the neuter and abstract.

The implication of this must be that the Hebrew language is the product of special divine revelation, or that it has an affinity with such revelation or is specially attuned to it. Von Rad wrote:

> The religious language of Israel corresponds to a reality which was open on all sides to God. Therefore one can say: with the reality, which God has opened to himself through his historical self-revelation, he has also opened to himself the language of ancient Israel. This language is appropriate (*sachgemäss*) because it knows how to name appropriately the realities created by God's speaking.[19]

As pure theory this might seem quite good, but acute difficulty is caused by the next stage, namely the idea that language is also a major common element and link between the Old Testament and the New. For obviously, if a language like Hebrew is moulded by divine revelation and bears the stamp of a distinct reality, then a quite different language like Greek will display a quite different and non-revelatory reality. Brunner, perhaps conscious of this difficulty, called it 'a strange paradox of reality' that the Gospel was in Greek. Von Rad, recognizing the same fact, asserts that 'in a higher sense' the language of the two Testaments was a unitary one.

This was no isolated opinion of a few. The influential exegete Oscar Cullmann, for a time a leading figure in biblical theology, was more extreme, and came close to asserting a total incompatibility between Greek and biblical thinking, so that *difference* from Greek thought became a valuable criterion for discovering the central elements in Christianity:

> We must recognize loyally (sic!) that precisely those things which distinguish the Christian teaching from the Greek belief are at the heart of primitive Christianity.[20]

Interestingly, Karl Barth himself expressed a certain moderation and reserve towards the theological use of hostility to Greek thought:

> The witch-hunt against Greek thought, which has made itself noticeable in the theology of the last decade, has not been a good thing, and its continuance could only mean that in the course of some time we would be sure to succumb to the Greek danger afresh, and this time in reality.[21]

It remains obscure, however, what Barth had in mind in talking of 'succumbing to the Greek danger afresh, and this time in reality'. In fact, in spite of these words of moderation from Barth, he more than anyone else was responsible for the hostility to Greek thought. For Greek thought was disliked, not just because it was Greek thought, but because Greek thought was understood to be the main source of natural theology, and it was Barth, and no other, who had made opposition to natural theology the cornerstone of his theology and indeed, as he claimed, of Protestant theology altogether. It was natural theology, and nothing else, that was the cause of distortion of the biblical message, and Old Testament theology, following to a large extent the Barthian wing of dialectical theology, saw its task as the recovery of the basically revelational message of the Bible, a message which had been obscured more than anything else by the invasion of natural theology, a phenomenon of which Greek language and Greek philosophy were the prime and standard representatives.

Ideas about biblical thought were also, one may believe, the product of a great deal of apologetic argument on behalf of the Old Testament within the churches and homiletic support for it. Was it not a thrilling book, full of action and events, the sense of time and history, the clashing of personalities, deep passions, fervent promises? How remote it was from the airy metaphysics of Plato or the logical precision of Aristotle, from the cold detachment of mathematics and the neutral, hypothetical research of the scientist, or from the detached theorizing of almost any philosopher ever since! Its thinking was all in flesh and blood, etched into living history and social reality.

Such being the case, whether we dignify it with the name of a philosophy or not, these attitudes have been deeply-held values in much biblical theology throughout the century and have scarcely ever been challenged from within the discipline. Moreover, in the nature of things, these values were not present only in the interpretative process but tended to be read back by biblical theologians into the Old Testament itself. These values were valid as guides to interpretation because they were the values inherent within the text itself and fundamental to its thinking.

Nevertheless the emphasis on Hebrew mentality produced serious difficulties for biblical theology. For one thing, here as in many places of the older biblical theology there is a lack of perception of what Jews might think. For, on the basis of the philosophy of language followed by both Brunner and von Rad, the obvious conclusion would be that the Old Testament, being in Hebrew, represented one sort of reality, while the New, being in Greek, represented another and quite different sort of reality – which should be a very natural Jewish perception, but very uncomfortable for Christian biblical theology. Moreover, if biblical Hebrew, just as a language, bears the stamp of special divine revelation, is it not probable that the same applies to the post-biblical Hebrew of the rabbis? By contrast, in order to make it apply to the Greek of the New Testament, does one not have to resort to Brunner's 'paradox' or von Rad's 'higher sense', or indeed to some kind of miracle, in order to rescue what is really a simply mistaken theory?

There was another difficulty which the emphasis on Hebrew thought raised for Christian biblical theology: what about the patristic period? Biblical theology moved in parallel with the neo-orthodox trends of doctrinal theology. But if

Hebrew thought, seen as opposition to Greek, restored a sort of orthodoxy for the biblical period itself, what happened in later Christianity, when influences of Hebrew language became very thin, when Greek thought became highly influential, and when natural theology was received but also transformed?[22] How does this affect such important matters as the doctrines of the Trinity, and later christology? The question has not been very fully discussed, but where something has been said about it two opposite directions have emerged.

One is to say that, Greek thought being an enemy from the beginning, the great doctrinal theologies of the patristic period are thoroughly distorted and have to be rethought on a fresh, biblical and Hebraic, basis. The doctrine of the Trinity might be reconstructed, let us say, by removing the Greek philosophical basis built into it and replacing it with Hebrew thought. Some few biblical theologians have taken this line, G. A. F. Knight for example, and it seems to be the logical line to take if one starts from this basis.[23]

Others, on the other hand, have given the fullest commendation to documents like the Chalcedonian formula, which seem to be totally dependent on Greek philosophy for their meaning. This, if less logical, is at least more orthodox. Thus Childs, saying that 'no one would defend the terminology of *homoousios* as biblical', goes on to approve the judgment of T. F. Torrance that: 'Far from imposing an alien Hellenism on the Gospels, the terms *ousia* and *homoousios* were adapted to allow the evangelical witness . . . without distortion through an alien framework of thought.'[24] Orthodoxy is here victorious over biblical thought. In general, the fact remains for Christian theology: the sort of emphasis on Hebrew thought that has been widespread in biblical theology is likely to create difficulties in understanding the patristic period or in accepting its theological decisions as authoritative. Biblical thought does not easily lead towards traditional orthodoxy.

Similar questions arise over other connections with later theology, especially with the Reformation. Generally speaking, some biblical theology has pointed in a roughly 'conservative' direction, and for Protestants this has meant that it pointed away from recent 'liberal' notions and towards something closer to Reformation doctrines and methods: 'election', for example, once again became a favourite concept. But at certain points the reverse happened, and this has notably been the case in the ideas of human nature. Hebrew mentality came to be understood to imply a psychosomatic unity, quite unlike the 'Greek' idea of an immortal soul encased in a mortal body. This could be quite right in itself, but there is no doubt that it is a modernist idea, and a notable departure from what traditional Christianity had maintained.[25] The existence of an immortal soul, and its separability from the body, had been essential doctrine over centuries. Calvin, for one, devotes some pages of the *Institutes* to it (*Institutes*, I. xv. 2), including the key expression about souls surviving 'when freed from the prison houses of their bodies'.[26] Quite contrary to the anti–Platonic sense of modern writing, Plato's depiction of the immortality of the soul was one main reason why he was highly esteemed in older Christianity.[27] Thus when Childs writes (*Biblical Theology*, 590) that 'the issue of man's nature is not that of his having a spiritual core which is tragically locked into a mortal body, but a human being is a whole self. The Old Testament knew it long before Freud!', this may be quite true (though I doubt whether the Old Testament has anything much in common with Freud) but is an apologetic for a modern position far removed from that of the Reformation or other traditional religion.[28]

Moreover, there is always the possibility that some of the attitudes and concepts attributed to the ancient Hebrews were not peculiar to them but were attitudes and concepts common to ancient peoples who were in a roughly similar stage.[29] It was always noticeable how similar the Hebrews of Pedersen's *Israel* were to the Vikings of Grønbech's parallel study on which he modelled his own.[30] One notices how often statements about 'Hebrew man' flow over into statements about 'ancient man' or 'primitive man' or 'Semitic man' or even 'Mediterranean man'. If 'Hebrew man' is just the same as 'ancient non–Greek man', then his thinking can no longer be aligned with special divine revelation, nor indeed specifically with the Hebrew Bible.

In the last resort much of the appeal to Hebrew thought was ethnocentric: it supposed that all persons of a particular people spoke the same language and thought in the same way.[31] It is quite possible that some parts of the Old Testament had a quite different underlying mentality from others, and the same seems to me even more likely for the New Testament. In that case we have to prove our identification of the mental pattern individually and in detail for each relevant passage. This has not always been done.

The emphasis on Hebrew thought or biblical thought along these lines increased throughout the period up to 1960 or so. 'Word studies', widely pursued in this time, were one of the main channels of endeavour.[32] The genre of 'theological dictionaries' prospered. Particularly prominent were studies which took a Greek term of the New Testament and sought to prove that, though the word was Greek, its 'content' was Hebraic. This enterprise lost its impetus after my *The Semantics of Biblical Language* was published in 1961.[33] A certain amount of the faulty procedures then criticized does persist,[34] but the strength has gone out of that particular movement. What, however, is the contrary position? Is there a more helpful concept that arises out of this set of problems? Surely it remains true that there is a difference between Hebrew thought and Greek thought?

Of course there is, and the difference is highly important for biblical theology; not, however, for the traditional reason that all the Bible is Hebrew thought and opposed to Greek, but for the opposite reason, that the entry of Greek thought into the biblical tradition is of high positive importance for the development of *theology* within the Bible.

I do not argue that Hebrew thought and Greek thought are identical or necessarily that they are very similar, though striking similarities at certain points can well be seen. Nor do I deny that the admixture of Greek thought may sometimes have caused much distortion or damage to Jewish or Christian traditions. Nevertheless, in fact we shall see that the difference made by contact with Greek thought is highly significant for biblical theology.[35] If we take Deuteronomy or Amos as examples of Hebrew thought, and Plato or Euripides as examples of Greek thought, of course they are very different. But the difference lies in the *content*, in the literary style, in the type of argument, in the things that they say: it cannot be tied to the language as such, as if no Hebrew speaker could think other than Amos and no Greek speaker other than Plato. The difference or similarity does not correlate exactly with the difference or similarity of their linguistic structures. It was quite possible to convey much of Hebrew thought adequately – though with some stylistic loss – in Greek, as the Septuagint shows, and to convey some Greek thought adequately in Hebrew, as Maimonides later showed.

Moreover, it is wrong to suppose that all users of the same language thought in the same way. There is no reason to believe that the Hebrew thought of the Old Testament was a monolithic block, and the same applies to the thought of the New. The traditional position about biblical thought implied such a monolithic block for each Testament, and indeed for the entire Christian Bible. Even when we can show, as we easily can, that some New Testament terms, concepts and passages are closely modelled on Hebrew originals, it is quite unjustified to suppose that this can be extended to apply to every term, concept and passage in the New Testament. No matter how many terms can be shown to have Hebraic 'content', there are likely to remain others that do not. In respect of underlying logic, there is no reason to doubt that the New Testament may well be a mixture in these respects – as is the case with Jewish books probably composed in Greek, like the Wisdom of Solomon.

Thus I argue that, however we define the terms and parameters, it is highly probable that the New Testament does contain serious and substantial elements which, by the criteria used in biblical theology, must be counted as Greek thought rather than Hebrew, or as Greek thought as thought by Jews. Transmission in Greek, through the Septuagint, is an essential element in the linkage between Old and New Testaments. The New Testament may well contain plenty of Hebrew thought, expressed in Greek; but it is highly likely that its Greek language also contains elements of thought which are of real Greek cultural origin. If this is so, the older argument from biblical thought, tied to Hebrew language, falls to pieces.

There remains the further question: even if we ignore for the moment the problems of the relations between Hebrew and Greek, and by-pass the other difficulties that have been mentioned, has Hebrew thought or biblical thought been correctly described in the first place? 'Much of the modern search for the recovery of only internal biblical categories has been extremely naive,' writes Childs.[36] What has been the cause of this naivety?

Probably one of the sources of it was that same existentialism which, as we have seen, has been a popular and powerful force in much modern biblical theology. Doubtless the Bible contributed something to that philosophical trend, but it is at least equally likely that that philosophical trend read into the Bible some of its own values and ideas. Not all the existentialists, after all, were lovers of the Hebrew Bible. Existentialist attitudes existed and were favoured; and biblical theologians who shared these attitudes saw confirmation of them in the Bible. The Hebrew Bible, as already said, was vivid and full of life, uninterested in the abstract and the objective, deeply based in personal contact and confrontation.

Unfortunately this picture is a selective one, which leaves out the many contrary aspects of the material. The Hebrew Bible contains a great deal that does not fit with this point of view. It contains a lot that is *not* thrilling to the average reader, who begins to skip passages as early as the fifth chapter of Genesis, when the first of the genealogical lists appears. Even less appetizing, from this point of view, are the first nine chapters of Chronicles, containing practically nothing but genealogies, or the latter part of Joshua, with its extensive lists of places and boundaries. These can be highly interesting for the meticulous scholar but they cannot be said to be, from the average reader's point of view, full of action, life and personal involvement. (Jewish reading, of course, works on different principles, and I am speaking here of the situation within Christianity.) Indeed, one of the main reasons why active apologetics on behalf of the Old Testament was necessary within Christianity was not that people tended to Marcionite heresy, as has so often been argued, and wanted to reject it on positive religious grounds, but that in spite of innate positive religious favour towards it, they found large stretches of it boring and unreadable. The apologetics which were produced by some biblical theologians dealt with this by ignoring these passages and dwelling entirely on those that were full of life and involvement. But the material that did not obviously fit with this category remained considerable. How many readers find their pulse quickening when they read Ezekiel's nine chapters on his planned reconstruction of the temple, or the lists of the figures for the different tribal camps in Numbers? Are the lists of unclean birds and animals vitally filled with existential involvement?

The fact is that the personalist, mildly existentialist values which much biblical theology has used for its Old Testament interpretation and commended for others were untrue to a lot of the material and gave an incorrect picture of

Hebrew thought. Actually a considerable portion of the Hebrew Bible is of a different kind altogether: this other portion consists of lists, maps, numbers, boundaries and regulations. It organizes the world in a particular way. It may work geographically, chronologically, ethnically, ritually and legally. It is often schematic and theoretical. For the understanding of these materials the contrast between personal involvement and detached objectivity is irrelevant. A line is drawn, and you are either on one side of it or on the other. A time is marked, and events are before it or after it. A rule is laid down, and you either obey it or you do not. In practice there may be many compromises, but the lines and boundaries remain. A rule may be theoretical, even abstract, and projected as a plan for the future, but it remains on paper as a rule. A chronological statement may be schematic and created (or modified into a new form) for a particular purpose, but it remains as an essential marker in the text. The legal material is the area in which this is most obvious and traditionally most meticulously discussed. Much of the legal material *is* interested in 'objective' fact. The question it raises is: did this in fact happen, was this or that done by this person, yes or no? – but the same applies in all these forms of mapping.

The case of chronology is a good example. Biblical theology included several attempts to explain the biblical notion of time as an existential one and not a chronological one. Not only was this the basis of lengthy speculations by John Marsh and J. A. T. Robinson,[37] but von Rad himself included in his Theology an entire chapter on 'Israel's Ideas about Time and History', which tells us that 'Israel was not capable of thinking of time in the abstract, time divorced from specific events. She found the idea of a time without a particular event quite inconceivable; all that she knew was time as containing events' (2, 100). The value of this, supposedly, is that it helps to integrate various Hebrew linguistic terms with the idea of time as comprised in the calendar, with the festivals, and with the view of history. More important still, it helps to build up the idea, basic to typology, that past events were not only in the past; they give 'its tone to the constant "today" which the paraeneses in Deuteronomy drum into their hearers' ears' (109). As I have shown, the effect of these arguments is to depreciate the importance of the chronological material of the Bible and its intended 'objective' character. Quite contrary to the existential interpretation, this material is of the greatest importance for an understanding of the working of the biblical mind.[38] The anti-objectivist obsession of much biblical theology is a deep misunderstanding of many biblical passages.

The legal material was mentioned a moment ago. That the legal material may have a schematic, analytic and theoretical aspect is significant not only for our thought about the Hebrew Bible in itself, but also or even more as a basis for our understanding of the way in which the rabbinic tradition of interpretation arose and flourished. It is not to be ignored that the anti-objectivist, existentialist line of approach has been a factor that increased the Christian bias of Old Testament theology as against the reality of many legal passages of the Bible.

In general, then, much biblical theology has worked with a semi-existentialist picture of reality which was read into the Hebrew Bible. Even if this is valid for some materials, there are other major sectors in the Old Testament which do not fit into such a picture. It is true, as I have said above, that the argument from Hebrew mentality has been much less emphasized in more recent years. The trouble is that it is not easy to see how aspects of traditional biblical theology, and especially those interested in the connection between Old and New Testaments, can continue to function without such an argument. In particular, if it is admitted in even the smallest way that terms of the New Testament come out of Greek thought rather than out of biblical, and that these terms have some importance in the New Testament argumentation, then how is it possible to resist the suggestion that some kind of natural theology is present in the New Testament? But if it is in fact present, then the strategy of much traditional biblical theology in its use of biblical thought is at fault. Our next section will begin the consideration of this question.

## 4. Natural theology: first stage

As we saw, Edmond Jacob considered that doctrinal theology had to deal not only with the Bible but also with philosophy and natural theology; this, along with other factors, provided a logical difference between biblical and doctrinal theology. But by the time Jacob wrote these words, they had already become something of an anachronism. The consequence of dialectical theology had been that philosophy and natural theology had been in effect largely expelled even from doctrinal theology. The result of this was twofold: first, that doctrinal theology itself became much more purely concentrated upon the Bible; secondly, that biblical theology came to act as a servant of that same trend in doctrinal theology. Throughout the modern movement in biblical theology, with only limited exceptions, one finds almost complete negativity towards natural theology; or, to be more exact, not so much negativity, which might suggest strong polemics against natural theology, but rather indifference and unawareness, an absence of any sign that natural theology might be a subject for discussion. As I say elsewhere, 'dictionaries and encyclopaedias of biblical studies produced in modern times contain no article entitled "Natural Theology". Works in biblical theology, for the most part, proceed as if they had never heard of any such thing.'[39] The first time I have noticed even the mention of it as a theme within any major work of biblical theology is in H. H. Schmid's interesting and stimulating theology of creation, order and peace.[40] He soon found that anyone who talked in this way fell under suspicion of 'intending a natural theology'. This was enough, it seems, to prevent people from listening to him.[41] He at least was aware of the question: most works of biblical theology say nothing about it.

This is remarkable, when the subject of natural theology had been the focus of one of the most famous doctrinal disputes of modern times. It looks as if Barth was the winner, at least for biblical scholars.[42] Yet some further explanation is necessary, for we have seen how deeply biblical theology was influenced by Brunner in other respects. And certainly many biblical scholars, though under influence from Barth, did not follow him very far.

One reason may be that the epic contest between the two great theologians did not concern itself very much with the Bible.[43] Thus Barth seems to have simply assumed that there was no evidence for natural theology in the Bible, and Brunner for his part did not seriously try to valorize the biblical evidence as a weapon against Barth. It seemed that the contest took place on the dogmatic/philosophical level, and that is indeed where it was then decided, for most of those who knew of it. It was known that there were biblical passages that had traditionally been quoted as evidence for natural theology, but this kind of evidence was regarded as outmoded and unimportant for a modern debate.

There was certainly also a denominational aspect. Barth seems to have been successful in convincing many Protestants – quite wrongly in my opinion – that natural theology is a Catholic thing and that it is disloyal to Protestantism to give it any consideration. Roman Catholic thinkers, for their part, seem not to have pressed the positive case for natural theology with great energy against Barth. Catholic scholars who were interested in biblical theology seem often to have felt it good to get away from natural theology, and found themselves happier in the biblical themes of covenant, reconciliation and people of God. Historically, moreover, much influence was exerted by the common Barthian propaganda which associated natural theology with German National Socialism: especially so after the war, when people (notably in the United States) became afraid to resist such an association.

Like many other things, the disregard for natural theology among biblical scholars has a basis in their occupational concerns. Natural theology involves arguments that lead outside normal biblical scholarship. The mere existence of it suggests that theological questions cannot be answered from the Bible alone. The decisiveness of biblical scholarship is challenged.

Moreover, there were features in the current state of historical scholarship that made it easier for the Barthian position. In particular, it has been common to judge that the 'Paul' of the Areopagus speech in Acts 17 is not the historical Paul, the person who wrote Romans and Galatians. Since this speech is one of the central evidences for natural theology, and since for many Protestants 'Paul' is virtually the central pillar and foundation of faith, the belief that this vital evidence is not really Pauline makes it much easier for them to reject natural theology. If Paul really had made the speech, things would have been different: it would then have been essential to take its theology seriously. '*Das ist nicht Paulus*' is the most common objection I have heard in Germany whenever I have quoted the passage. Historical criticism thus favoured the Barthian position.

It was also, perhaps, thought that natural theology was a 'liberal' phenomenon in Christianity. Much Barthian theology in the English-speaking world – perhaps to the surprise of German-speaking theologians – has been distinctly 'conservative', and those influenced by this trend have been naturally reluctant to favour a position which could be 'liberal' in its effect. Such people are suspicious that natural theology, the slightest drop of it, might undermine biblical and confessional authority. And it is quite true that some natural theology has been associated with highly liberal directions. But this suspicion, however well or ill founded, should be seen to be irrelevant; for my argument is that the Bible itself did utilize, imply and express judgments that belong to natural theology, so that it is the *denial* of natural theology, if anything, that detracts from the authority of scripture and is in that sense 'liberal'. Moreover, historical experience should make it clear that the effect of natural theology in the history of doctrine has commonly been highly conservative, as its influence in the Roman Catholic church makes clear. Indeed, it was a common argument within Protestantism that the conservative and anti-libertarian social effects of natural theology in the Roman Catholic church were a self-evident reason for rejecting its validity.

Anyway, whatever the causes, most modern biblical scholarship and practically all biblical theology lost the question of natural theology from sight. Though there were theologians who continued to show interest in the question,[44] and though even Barth himself is said, amazingly, to have moved back closer to it,[45] the possible biblical foundations for it continued to be neglected. My 1991 Gifford Lectures, *Biblical Faith and Natural Theology*, formed the first substantial re-examination of the question, at least in English.

The effects of a reconsideration of natural theology as a significant element within the Bible will be examined at length in a later chapter.

## 5. *The place of psychology*

Only a final note on psychology will be added here. Generally speaking, the classic tradition of biblical theology has held aloof from psychological considerations – here again in parallel with the tendencies of dialectical theology. There was, indeed, the interest in Hebrew mentality or biblical mentality, which could also be expressed as 'Hebraic psychology'.[46] But the effect of this interest was largely to eliminate any interest in the psychological realities of biblical life and biblical persons. Just as revelation put religion into the background, so biblical theology put psychological considerations into the background. Those older traditions of scholarship which had attempted such consideration were now thought to be discredited. Childs, commenting on the call of Moses in Exodus 3, expresses well the modern ethos:

> The subtle dialectic of the chapter is certainly missed by commentators who would subsume the divine element within the category of the psychological. Moses' call then becomes the internal brooding of a man over the problems of his people and the mounting religious conviction that God wanted him to aid.[47]

Actual psychological dimensions of the biblical texts tended to be neglected.

As against this we may quote the thought of Dietrich Ritschl: 'a heavy price will at some time have to be paid for the neglect of the psychological'. Beyond this we shall not follow out this question at the present time.

# 11

# Connections with the New Testament

Many Old Testament Theologies,[1] especially in the earlier part of the modern period, have professed to establish connections with the New Testament, and some indeed have claimed that the establishment of such connections is a central aim of Old Testament theology or even its *most* essential purpose. Sometimes they also suggest that these connections were both present and obvious at older stages within Christian exegesis, and go on to allege that they were lost during the period of historical-critical investigation. Just as critical analysis divided the books into sources of different periods, so it also created a serious division between Old and New Testaments. The return to a holistic, comprehensive presentation of the theology of the Old Testament would therefore also lead to a restoration of the essential links with the New. A properly theological view of the Old Testament would also make clear its organic relation with the New.

Many of the classic works make clear their devotion to these purposes. Eichrodt in his first few pages expounded these connections in eloquent language and concluded: 'Hence to our general aim of obtaining a comprehensive picture of the realm of Old Testament belief we must add a second and closely related purpose – *to see that this comprehensive picture does justice to the essential relationship with the New Testament* and does not merely ignore it' (I, 27). Vriezen in his chapter on 'Basis, Task and Method of Old Testament theology' writes that 'the method of Old Testament theology is not purely phenomenological . . . but it also gives the connection with the New Testament message and a judgment from the point of view of that message' (149). Von Rad concluded his two-volume work with a section of over 100 pages on 'The Old Testament and the New'. A number of other Old Testament Theologies made similar professions.

Thus the bringing together of Old Testament and New, in some fashion or other, has been a commonly accepted purpose of the movement. Nevertheless there are two contrary circumstances which cut across this motivation and make its presence less dominant. First, some of the scholars who most emphasized the importance of connections with the New Testament seem not to have done very much to realize this purpose; and secondly, some other Old Testament theologians seem to have decided to work with the Old Testament alone and have found it unnecessary or undesirable to introduce the question of connections with the New.

To take the first of these: in view of the strong statements made by Eichrodt, Vriezen, von Rad and others, it is surprising how little seems to have been achieved along these lines. We have to distinguish between general statements about the relation of the two Testaments and actual engagement by Old Testament scholars with texts and details of the New. The former can be found in adequate number, but what we are looking for at the moment is the latter. While the principle of engagement with the New Testament is clear, the matter of close engagement in exegesis is often more obscure.

This is particularly clear in Eichrodt's approach. The index to his first volume includes only nine references to New Testament passages. I refer to the English; there are only two in my German edition, the fifth (1957)!; that to his second lists about seventy-five. These indexes may, of course, be defective; but it is not a matter of numbers only. Spriggs says that the only chapters in Eichrodt without links to the New Testament are 5 and 14 C (73). But one needs also to differentiate between chapters with substantial discussion of the links and those which have only rather bare mentions. In fact it seems to me that long stretches of his writing on important matters appear to proceed without any reference to the New Testament. Thus his Chapter 2 (I, 36–69), which covers the meaning and the history of the covenant concept, gets to the LXX's expression of the concept with διαθήκη (65), but there is no more than the most marginal mention of any New Testament aspect and there seems to be, remarkably, no mention of the obvious supreme problem of any approach through covenant: namely, the rather small number of cases where the term covenant is actually used in the New Testament.[2]

Of the occurrences of the Greek διαθήκη in the New Testament, a number definitely mean 'testament, will', and another considerable proportion are references back to the Old Testament situation. Actual evidence of covenant as a central and powerful concept within New Testament Christianity is thin.[3] Again, Eichrodt's Chapter 13 (II, 46–68), a chapter on the Spirit of God, appears to contain no mention of the New Testament and no reference to it, though actual references to the Spirit of God are certainly plentiful there. In the following section, Chapter 14 (II, 69–92), which covers the Word of God and the Wisdom of God, there again seems to be no mention of the New Testament until suddenly we find a section on 'Spirit and Word' (79–80), much of which is devoted to 'the thought of the New Testament'. But even there, there is little attempt to deal with actual New Testament passages: rather, we have a fairly general exposé of general Christian doctrines about Spirit and Word.[4] Following this the chapter goes on to 'C. The Wisdom of God', and this covers such central aspects as '2. Wisdom as the Principle of Cosmic Order, and as

Hypostasis', '3. Wisdom as a Principle of Revelation' and '4. The Importance of the Concept for the Problem of Truth'. On all of these one would have expected the New Testament to provide some insights, but it seems nowhere to be mentioned or even cited.

In Chapter 21, on 'The Fundamental Forms of Man's Personal Relationship with God' (II, 268–315) we have a brief mention of the New Testament (281 n.4), and an assertion that 'faith' in Isaiah 'clearly points the way to the justification belief of the New Testament' (283), and under the theme of 'love' we hear, in a passage against antinomianism, that 'the Deuteronomic association of love and obedience is best rendered by the word of Jesus in John's Gospel, "If you love me you will keep my commandments"' (298). In the final section on post-exilic piety, there is a brief mention of Heb. 11 (313), and the section comes to an end with an assertion about how Jesus and the apostles had overcome 'the inner schizophrenia of Jewish piety', but no detailed citation from the New Testament is given here.

One cannot help fearing that the New Testament is brought in on an occasional basis, to help with some particular problem, rather than systematically integrated with the discussion, or else that it is introduced as an expression of Eichrodt's general theological position rather than as a detailed exegesis of interrelations between texts. By a curious paradox, although Eichrodt argues (I, 35) that the apocryphal or 'extra-canonical scriptures of Judaism' are not very relevant and are only marginal to Old Testament theology, his references to passages from 'apocryphal' books are actually much more frequent than his references to the New Testament, as a glance at the index of Vol. II will make clear.

A similar weakness is found with Vriezen. As we have seen, he is even more emphatic about the role of the New Testament in Old Testament theology: Old Testament theology '*is a study of the message of the Old Testament both in itself and in its relation to the New Testament*' (148). But, as we have seen, Vriezen's Theology falls into two parts, the Introduction and the part devoted to Content. And it quickly emerges that most of the New Testament material in the volume is to be found in the former. Moreover, the actual discussion of New Testament passages is very thin: the index both in the Dutch and the English forms refers to only thirteen New Testament passages that are cited, and of the nineteen places where they are cited only eight are in the Content section, while eleven are in the Introduction section. This suggests that Vriezen has not at all found it possible to integrate the New Testament into his discussion of Content.

He does admit that his programme in this respect is an 'ideal objective, which could only be realized by the close cooperation of theologians in the fields of both the Old and the New Testaments' (149 n.2). An Old Testament scholar working on his own can achieve 'no more than patch-work' (so the English translation; the Dutch is *stukwerk* – I think this means something more like 'partial work'). But the close cooperation mentioned, which would not have been so difficult to achieve, seems not to have come about very much. The passage may indicate an awareness on the writer's part that, in spite of his own principles, the representation of the New Testament in his great work remains rather slight. And it seems difficult to accept the implied reason that Old Testament theologians lacked the necessary specialized knowledge of the New Testament. They were not then, and are not now, so ignorant of the basic documents of Christianity. Certainly they have not, generally speaking, kept pace with the most advanced researches in the New Testament, but it is highly doubtful to me whether they have lacked the kind of knowledge that would be necessary and adequate for the application of it within the context of an Old Testament Theology. More probably, in my opinion, Vriezen's argument covers a different fact: namely a semi-awareness that the New Testament material really did not fit with the sort of plan he had announced, nor with the sort of thing that Old Testament theologians in general were doing.

In von Rad's Theology also, within the main body of his work, citations of the New Testament and discussions of its content are quite limited.[5] The index of the first volume shows only sixteen references to New Testament passages, and a glance at these reveals that most of them refer to minor verbal similarities and the like. The second volume has many more, but a very large majority of these are confined to the concluding section of the book, Part 3, on 'The Old Testament and the New'. In the main part of the second volume, the treatment of the prophetic traditions of Israel, there is only a small handful of references to the New Testament. This seems to be in accord with his policy of letting the Old Testament 'speak for itself'. His programme of typological relation of the New Testament to the Old may thus in part be intended to present the New as an actualization of the Old (or of elements within it), without implying that New Testament elements and standards were necessary for the theological understanding and evaluation of the Old itself.

Thus at least some of the classic works which have insisted on the importance of connections with the New Testament have been somewhat weak in the realization of this within an Old Testament Theology.

On the other side, as indicated above, there have been other Old Testament theologians who either thought that their subject could (or should) be pursued without mention of the New Testament, or else provided only a cursory mention of the New Testament while in reality devoting themselves entirely to the Old alone.

An example of the latter may be found in the classic Theology of Edmond Jacob. Of it, Laurin writes: 'Apart from an occasional sentence (e.g. pp 61–2, 112), Jacob limits discussion of the relationship betweeen the Testaments to only a few statements in the Introduction.' He does indeed have general statements which lead in another direction: 'A theology of the Old Testament which is founded not on certain isolated verses, but on the Old Testament as a whole, can only be a Christology, for what was revealed under the old covenant . . . is in Christ gathered together and brought to perfection.'[6] Again Jacob maintains: 'A line not always straight, but nonetheless continuous, leads from the anthropomorphisms of the earliest pages of the Bible, to the incarnation of God in Jesus Christ'.[7] The New Testament, he argues, according to Laurin, is itself a theology of the Old Testament. But all this does not mean that he is actually doing much work with New Testament texts in elucidating how all this works out. The actual content of his Theology as it stands is very substantially confined to Old Testament material.

I have said that some scholars went farther and expressly stated that they found no need to take account of the New Testament in their work.

The most explicit, engaging and unworried statement to this effect comes from the Roman Catholic scholar John L. McKenzie in his *Old Testament Theology* (1974). He says explicitly: 'I wrote it as if the New Testament did not exist,'[8] though he fully expects that reviewers will be displeased at this. He does not think, he writes, 'that it is the concern of the Christian Old Testament theologian to explain or to justify the use of the Old Testament in the New Testament; this is the task of the New Testament theologian, for the problems arise in the New Testament. Still less is it the concern of the Old Testament theologian to explain the use of the Old Testament in the post-apostolic church . . . The Old Testament theologian will do well if he states the theology of the Old Testament clearly and accurately. Quite simply, I have not found the Old Testament so alien to the Christian faith which I profess that the relations of the two are a serious problem' (27f.).

Later he discusses the role of the theologian's personal faith: 'Theology seeks an understanding of faith; it is the Christian faith, not the Israelite faith, which he seeks to understand. The scholar cannot prevent his faith from giving form to the questions he asks: what he can prevent is allowing his faith, instead of the Old Testament, to determine the answers to the questions of the Old Testament theology.' And so with the place of Jesus himself: 'The total reality of Jesus Messiah is found nowhere in the Old Testament, not even in its totality. Jesus could have emerged from nothing except Israel and the Old Testament; but the study of the Old Testament does not demand that Jesus Messiah emerge from it' (29).

McKenzie's viewpoint is interesting and powerful, both in itself and because of the principle that it illustrates: namely, that Christian commitment can, in respect of the relation between the two Testaments, work in either of two opposite ways. It can lead to the position that the Old Testament can be theologically interpreted only in relation to the New (and so an Old Testament theology on its own cannot be Christian), and it can equally well lead to the opposite position, namely that the Old Testament in itself is so thoroughly Christian that there is no need at all to interpret it through the New (and so an Old Testament theology on its own is fully and positively Christian). For McKenzie's view is one of outspokenly Christian commitment. His choice of the second of these alternatives is clear. Some other writers may be suspected of shifting back and forward between both of the two positions. Or is there some third possibility?

I began this chapter with a mention of some of the 'classic' Old Testament Theologies, more or less those up to von Rad's two volumes of about the 1960s. As I have shown, a good proportion of these works emphasized the relation to the New Testament as an essential element in Old Testament theology, whether they carried this out successfully or not. In the later period, say from 1970 on, there seems to be a change in this respect. On the one hand we observe a marked tendency to play down the importance of the New Testament for any Old Testament Theology; on the other we see some works that pursue these connections with greater vigour, and to this we add the rising current of fresh interest in pan-biblical theology. I shall shortly return to give illustrations of these differing tendencies.

On the one hand, many works in the later development of Old Testament theology came to say less about the New Testament. Zimmerli, for instance (German 1972), is very muted in this regard.[9] Even his final section §23 (pp. 238ff.), entitled 'The Openness of the Old Testament Message', speaks of future expectation but scarcely goes on to affirm that this is fulfilled in the New Testament. When he does quote the latter, it is often only to confirm something that is already clear in the Old Testament, as with his citation of Heb. 1.1 (240)[10] or his assertion (165) that the New Testament's speech about 'divine and human wisdom in the encounter with Jesus Christ' follows the line taken in the Old Testament. So also his mention of the expectation of the 'son of David' in New Testament times: Zimmerli is not saying that Christianity fulfils this expectation, but that the mention of it in the New Testament indicates the continued strength of it (thus 212, 153, 105, 128, 154, 74). Sometimes he refers to a New Testament passage only in order to correct it on the basis of the Old, e.g. 105 on Acts 3 and 7. It seems clear that interaction with New Testament passages is not essential to Zimmerli's plan of Old Testament theology.[11] Yet no one who knew him would doubt the devout and theologically committed Christian character of Zimmerli's life and thought.[12]

The same is true of W. H. Schmidt's *The Faith of the Old Testament* (German 1968, ET 1983), in which there seems to be no mention of the New Testament at all. Clements (1978) cites a handful of New Testament passages and touches

on some of the problems of connection between the two Testaments but makes
no effort to show that the establishment of this connection is a main task of
Old Testament theology. Preuss's recent Theology has few New Testament references within the first volume and their character is mainly confirmatory, of
much the same kind as we saw with Zimmerli. His key section §1, 'Standort-
bestimmung', the definition of his standpoint, mentions the New Testament a
little, but these mentions are really part of his comments on what other people
have said, and there seems to be no sign that it is part of his own essential
approach to his undertaking. On the 'Tun-Ergehen-Zusammenhang', for
instance, the relationship between actions and their consequences, a subject that
has interested Preuss considerably (184–94), he mentions two New Testament
passages (187–8) in contrast to the late Jewish development in Wisdom and
Sirach, but there is no other New Testament citation in this quite long and
involved discussion and no sign that the New Testament is anywhere invoked
as a necessary part of the strategy. On the contrary, he writes that 'this is not the
place to discuss the New Testament' (191). Here and there he concludes a
chapter with some reference to Christ, the New Testament or Christianity: thus
on p.38 his final paragraph addresses Christian readers who look for biblical
texts which Jesus later 'fulfilled', and he tells them that they should rather be
looking for the 'fundamental structures' which were later taken up into the New
Testament witness to Christ. At II, 66 he ends the chapter with an expression of
'a tension between the God who has come and the God who is to come', which
might have a hint of a Christian nuance, but if so, is not a very clear one. II, 283
ends with a purple passage which brings Judaism and Christianity together:

> The Old Testament awaits the sovereignty of God, and Judaism awaits it.
> Christianity awaits this sovereignty together along with both of these and
> offers the prayer, 'Thy kingdom come'. The one who taught her this prayer
> knew that in his speech and actions the kingdom of God was dawning.[13] This
> tension is to last until YHWH will be entirely accepted as king and will be
> revealed 'on that day' (Isa. 2.17; Zech. 14.9; cf. Obadiah 21).

But remarks of this kind are actually very sparse within the dense structure of
Preuss's two volumes.

Thus, within at least one current of recent Old Testament theology, it seems
to be accepted that active engagement with the New Testament is no essential
part of the undertaking. What are the reasons for the increasing visibility of this
position? Several may be mentioned. One is the force of the argument from a
history-of-religion viewpoint, to the effect that it is unscientific to work with
New Testament materials as if they offered authoritative clues of some kind to
text or theology of the Old; cf. the arguments of Ringgren as mentioned above.[14]
Another is the increasing interaction of Christian and Jewish scholars from the

1960s on, which naturally brought with it objections against any arguments that sought to adduce the New Testament as a guide to meanings of the Old. A third is the observation, made explicit in this present chapter but probably felt more vaguely by many, that many of the earlier classics of Old Testament theology, though insisting on engagement with the New, had actually made rather little out of it. A fourth may well have been a consciousness of the sheer methodological difficulty of establishing valid connections with the New, unless one was to fall into purely history-of-religion evidence on the one side or into some traditional dogmatic scheme on the other. A fifth has already been mentioned: the heritage within some currents of Christianity itself of a conviction that the Old Testament in itself was a fully Christian book and therefore did not require to be integrated with the New in order to be theologically interpreted. Any or all of these factors are significant, when seen in the context of the fact that all the Old Testament theologians mentioned are or were active Christian believers and completely convinced of the essential place of the Old Testament within Christian faith, life and theology. They believed this as a matter of faith and life, but they saw it, perhaps, as a doctrinal matter, as something that existed on a different level from that on which the theology of the Old Testament could be expressed.

This is not to say that the quest for engagement with the New Testament did not continue to be pursued by some other Old Testament theologians. Among the Theologies published after von Rad, perhaps the most positive in this respect has been the work of Claus Westermann (German 1978, ET 1982). Westermann's Theology is notable as one that gives particularly large space and particularly strong attention to the relations with the New Testament. Of the six parts in which the book is organized, the sixth is entitled 'the Old Testament and Jesus Christ', and in the German text is 14 pages long, out of a total of 200 for the entire work, leaving aside contents page and index. But in fact more is said about the New Testament than this might suggest, for in sections about particular themes of the Old Testament comparisons with the New are commonly introduced. Thus the section on Sin and Punishment is introduced with two paragraphs which compare 'Sin in the Old and New Testaments' (German 102). On p. 100, seeking to explain the existence of materials such as the creation and flood stories, which contain elements shared with other cultures all over the world, he suggests that this can be illustrated for the Old Testament through the parallel of the Gospels, each of which has a different prologue: that in John connects with creation and the story of the beginnings, that in Matthew with the history of Israel through the genealogy of Jesus, that in Luke with the Old Testament as a whole. Similarly Genesis has a prologue, which connects with that which is known about the beginnings in humanity as a whole. Westermann's Old Testament Theology seems to be one that incorporates more comment on the New Testament within the basic discussion of the Old, even apart from his sixth chapter which is specifically on 'The Old Testament and Christ'.

Moreover, Westermann's use of New Testament materials is often original and, in particular, avoids simple identifications between Old and New. He looks critically, for example, at certain aspects of Paul's teaching. Thus on p. 202 he tells us that there was no basis in the Old Testament itself for the idea that there might be two different ways of salvation, one through the works of the law and the other through deliverance through Christ. Paul's spiritual home was not in the Old Testament itself, but in the 'Jewish theology of the preceding centuries'. Again, according to him Paul takes 'commandment' and 'law' together under the concept 'law'. This he had taken over from his Jewish teachers, and it corresponds to the *latest* stage in the use of *torah* in the Hebrew Bible. But earlier usage had distinguished very clearly between commandments and laws. Thus – I omit some stages of the argument – 'important as the contrast between law and gospel was for Paul's theological situation, it cannot be definitive for the determination of the relation of the Old Testament to Christ'.

With Westermann's impressive work, therefore, and with some others, the tradition of Old Testament Theologies written with the purpose of engagement with the New is continued, and possibly indeed reaches its culmination.

From about the same time, however, a fresh current of thought emerges, the current which we have called that of pan-biblical theology (in German, usually *biblische Theologie*). In this current of thinking the basic aim is a theology of the entire (Christian) Bible. It is not enough to have an Old Testament theology which makes some contact with the New, or a New Testament theology which registers its inheritance from the Old: the basic purpose is a theology of the two, taken as a totality. One work which might be classified in this way is Terrien's *The Elusive Presence* (1978), which follows a particular theme through both Testaments but does not aspire to providing a total and comprehensive theology of either. More obviously central is the work of Hartmut Gese (various essays from the 1970s on): Gese argues that the entire body of material throughout Old and New Testaments is one *continuum* and that a theology can be built only upon the basis of this entire continuum. A similar scheme is adopted by the New Testament scholar Peter Stuhlmacher in his *Biblische Theologie des Neuen Testaments* (Vol. 1, 1992) and in other writings. Finally, there are various possible 'canonical approaches', of which the best-known thus far is the work of Brevard Childs, in several volumes culminating in his *Biblical Theology of the Old and New Testaments* (1992). This large work includes, among other lesser portions, major sections on 'the Discrete Witness' of the Old Testament and that of the New, and a lengthy section entitled 'Theological Reflection on the Christian Bible'. Each of these will be further discussed in later chapters. All of them may in a general way be regarded as attempts at 'pan-biblical' approaches, for which the interrelation between Old and New Testament is thought to be not one part among others of the undertaking but the centre of the entire enterprise. However, they differ from each other in many ways, and some of them will be discussed separately at a later point.

Moreover, among the many Old Testament Theologies which do attach major importance to connections with the New, there remains some considerable difference concerning the *way* in which they seek to do this. Some Old Testament Theologies seem to adduce references and themes of the New in a haphazard way, so that it does not become clear why *these particular* connections are made and why others are not made. Some other Theologies, as already stated, assert that their comprehensive and structural character provides the required connections with the New Testament, but do not make clear quite *how* this takes place. Perhaps the implication is that the comprehensive structure, once detected in the Old Testament, will be found to be the same as that of the New. But this would be a very grandiose claim which would require to be demonstrated from the New Testament side with a very full discussion and justification. Others again identify a particular principle or aspect which is thought to bind the two Testaments together: in von Rad typology is an obvious example, as is salvation history in him and in a number of others. Childs, as we shall see, works in a quite different way. Although stressing the importance of seeing Old and New Testaments as one, in his major *Biblical Theology* he handles the 'Discrete Witness' of each in large separate sections, then bringing them together in an even larger final section under the title of 'Theological Reflection on the Christian Bible'. In this approach the section on 'the Discrete Witness of the Old Testament' actually contains extremely little reference to the New. Thus the concluding Excursus on 'The Theological Problem of Old Testament History' (196–207) contains ample reference to modern thinkers (Collingwood, Dilthey, Kuhn, etc.) but none to the New Testament at all. His corresponding New Testament section naturally has many references to the Old; but it is in his long concluding section that the interrelations between the two are most thoroughly worked over. It remains slightly odd that one so convinced of the need for the Testaments to be considered together remains able to handle the 'discrete witness' of the Old with hardly any reference to the New.

Central to the problems involved here is the difference of chronology and direction between Old Testament and New. The Old Testament came first; there was no New Testament for it to refer to. The Old Testament may have many echoes in the New, may enunciate many concepts that are later used in the New, may (according to traditional Christian beliefs) point forward to the New and be fulfilled in it: but it does not actually say anything about the New. The

New, on the other hand, contains a very large number of references to the Old and quotations from it. From this fact there come the many suggestions that, if there is to be a connection between the two, it must start from the side of the New. Or, as others have put it, 'theology' as a real category does not exist in the Old Testament, but comes on to the scene only in the New.

The New Testament might then seem from this point of view to have a certain priority. But any use of it for these purposes raises a further question: within the New Testament itself, to what sort of evidence are we to appeal? What are the pointers and indicators within its text that should be taken as decisive?

One obvious approach is to start from the references to the Old Testament actually made within the New, whether the express quotations or (more vaguely) the references to content and ideas. This has the attraction that it provides some sort of hard evidence, definable and countable within certain limits. The quotations, at least the express ones, can be identified and counted. They are hard evidence of the ways and degrees in which appeal to the Old Testament is made. And in fact some important works have sought to draw from them the outlines of a basic theology. Thus C. H. Dodd's little book *According to the Scriptures* (1952) argued that the use of the Old Testament formed the sub-structure of New Testament theology: indeed, this phrase formed the sub-title of the book, *The Sub-Structure of New Testament Theology*. In the same tradition, though with differences of emphasis, Barnabas Lindars wrote his lengthier *New Testament Apologetic*, with the sub-title *The Doctrinal Significance of the Old Testament Quotations*.[15]

Another work that does not claim in itself to be a theological study but is surely relevant is the composite volume edited by D. A. Carson and H. G. M. Williamson, *It is Written: Scripture citing Scripture*; this devotes separate chapters to the Old Testament quotations of the different books or groups of books within the New Testament.

From more recent years, mention must be made of the New Testament Theology of Hans Hübner which, of those that I have seen, is the one that shows by far the deepest involvement in the Old Testament. Hübner takes the *Vetus Testamentum in Novo receptum*, the Old Testament as it is received in the New, as the basic guide to all New Testament theology. Such a study involves not only the identifiable quotations but also the more indirect references, as the author recognizes. But here, in spite of numerous differences, we have another case of a Theology built largely upon the New Testament's own uses of the Old and references to it. Hübner's work follows the modern tendency, after Gese, of pan-biblical theology, and will be discussed later.

Much, then, has been attempted and achieved through work upon the New Testament's own use of the Old, quotations from it and references to it.

Nevertheless studies built upon this basis, if adopted as a way to identify or assess a common theology of Old and New, may seem to have defects. A primary reason is the fact that all the quotations taken together cover only a limited fraction of the Old Testament text. Moreover, some of them are clearly used in the New Testament in senses remote from that which they bore in the Old. It must be remembered also that the New Testament passages are in Greek, and the translation may differ substantially from the original Hebrew; in addition, there are often textual problems that affect the Greek form of the quotations, both in the New Testament itself and also in the LXX.[16] Sometimes there may be doubt whether a phrase is a quotation from the Old Testament or one from a Greek writer who said something similar.[17] Again, however great the importance of the quotations, there still remains the task of assessing all the passages in the New Testament which do *not* appeal to Old Testament quotations or which use arguments quite foreign to the Old.[18] Books built upon the quotations can easily pass by and ignore all the material within the New Testament which reasons on 'non-biblical' grounds.

If we turn away from express quotations, then we may think of common concepts: terms like 'love', 'body', 'good news', 'law', and a hundred others, of which it can be argued that the Old Testament use of these terms forms the basis for the use of them in the New. But then again there remains the question of terms which may be used in the New but in senses different from their sense in the Old, and of terms used in the New which have no substantial basis in the Old. At the moment I shall not seek to choose between these various methods: my point is only that, when we seek to establish the relation between Old and New Testaments, there is no one way of doing this in concrete detail that is obviously the perfect and correct one.

Partly because of these uncertainties, some have turned to a quite different approach: in essence, it does not matter how much the Old Testament may be quoted or referred to in the New. The two Testaments as totalities belong together. This appears to be the approach taken by Childs, or part of it.[19]

Before we go farther we should give some thought to the converse question, how far the classic works of New Testament theology took the Old within their purview.

When we turn to New Testament theologians, we find in many cases even less eagerness to establish connections with the Old Testament. For instance, of Bultmann's classic two volumes the first contains many references to the Old Testament – one would have thought that it would hardly be possible to write about the New Testament without making such references – but only rather limited discussion of the Old Testament as such, as a particular problem requiring a full treatment in itself. The section 'The Church's Relation to Judaism and the Problem of the Old Testament', in Chapter 3 on 'The Kerygma of the Hellenistic Church aside from Paul' (1,108–20), divides into two portions: first a discussion of particular tendencies or documents (Radical Gnosticism, Barnabas, Hebrews, Clement, Justin etc.), and secondly certain particular themes about the incorporation of the Old Testament in the New (1, 114–21). This does not seem to constitute a full-face approach to the question of how the Old Testament fits with the New. The second volume seems to have even less: even references to the Old Testament are very sparse, and actual discussion of it almost non-existent. The portion of its Epilogue entitled 'The Task and the Problems of New Testament Theology (The Relation between Theology and Proclamation)' (2, 237–41) does not mention the Old Testament at all, and the following section on 'the history of New Testament Theology as a science' (2, 241–51), which goes into some of the principal questions, hardly so.

It is of interest that Bultmann's most complete and worked-out discussion of the relation between the Testaments does not come in his New Testament Theology at all, but in his article 'The Significance of the Old Testament for the Christian Faith'.[20] On the central idea of this article above, 68, and below, 328, 460.

Again, the fine work of Conzelmann seems in its preface and introduction to say nothing about the Old Testament at all. A section called 'Paul's Use of the Old Testament' appears at pp. 166ff., as part of 'The Method of Working'. It is mentioned again on p. 296. But on the whole it seems not to be a major integral part of the study.[21]

The New Testament Theology of L. Goppelt has more of a kinship with lines of Old Testament theology in that he feels an affinity with von Rad's approach to the latter.[22] The two scholars had in common a strong interest in a *typological* relation between the two Testaments, and Goppelt had written a monograph on the subject;[23] for him also salvation history was central, as it was for von Rad. Thus see Goppelt's I, 280f., where he says that 'the more theology as a whole focuses upon the questions of God and history, the more the relationship of the New Testament to the Old Testament is going to become a key issue for theology as a whole'. His section §30, 'The Christ Event and the Old Testament according to Paul' (II, 51–62), enters into some of the central questions, and we have again a reference to von Rad; yet the two volumes as a whole remain rather unsatisfactory in their relating of the two Testaments.[24] Goppelt's *heilsgeschichtlich* principle does seem to lead towards an interest in the interrelation of the Testaments, and he certainly seems to go into the Old Testament background of various New Testament themes. And yet one still does not feel that the question of integral linkage with the Old Testament occupies him as much as does opposition to Bultmann or reassertion of *Heilsgeschichte*.

In summing up, we return to the essential point: some of the earlier Old Testament Theologies of modern times laid great stress on the goal of achieving adequate contact with the New Testament. Eichrodt in his introduction says that 'once more to make practicable the long obstructed path from the Old Testament to the New' is the goal which all the the exposition in his book strives to reach,[25] and this purpose is restated emphatically in his first chapter (I, 26ff.). Von Rad in the last paragraph of his great work tells us:

> One final word: only when Old Testament theology takes this final step to the threshold of the New Testament, only when it makes the link with the witness of the Gospels and the Apostles perfectly openly, and when it is able to make men believe that the two Testaments belong together, will it have the right to term itself a theological undertaking, and therefore 'biblical theology'. If instead it analyses the Old Testament in isolation, then, no matter how devotedly the work is done, the more appropriate term is 'history of the religion of the Old Testament'.

Both these statements make very absolute assertions about the essential character of the task of establishing contact with the New Testament. The weakness of the actual results in this respect only makes the gap between profession and realization all the greater.

Readers will evaluate these observations in different ways.

1. Some will think that scholars like Eichrodt and von Rad had the right intention but did not sufficiently carry it out. All that is needed is to try harder.

2. Others may feel the opposite, that they were trying the impossible; the best is to admit that Old Testament theology works perfectly well without reference to the New.

3. Others again may hold that the connection is essential, but has to be established from the side of the New Testament, not from that of the Old – perhaps for the reason, as McKenzie puts it, 'that the books of the Old Testament were written when the New Testament did not exist' (319). Of these, some may want to put the blame on the New Testament theologians for not caring enough about the Old.

4. Some may think, with McKenzie, that the Old Testament, taken in itself, is so fully in accord with Christian faith that there is no need to make an effort to establish its connection with the New.

Picking my way between these possibilities, I would suggest:

1. The connections of the Old Testament with the New are a matter of the greatest importance, but it was a fundamental mistake of (say) Eichrodt to suppose that the kind of structural Old Testament theology which he projected and carried out would also in itself bring with it the fulfilment of this task. A synthetic theological account, expressly formulated as one of the Old Testament for itself, cannot necessarily cope with, or be improved by, or establish, connections with the New Testament.

2. Eichrodt and some other Old Testament theologians were misled in this by their own antipathy to the historical approach to the Bible. The effect of the historical approach, they thought or implied, had been to separate the Old Testament from the New. If one could work out a new structural, holistic, comprehensive or otherwise not historical approach, the result would be to bring these two great elements together again. This entire reasoning was faulty, as would have been swiftly evident if it had been properly set out. For the Old Testament had long been, in all currents of Christian theology, markedly different from the New, even where historical methods of study had not yet been applied. The difference between the two was by far the deepest of the cracks which ran across the apparently smooth surface of holy scripture. The organization of the Christian canon, with its two different 'Testaments', and with late ideas of two different covenants or the like – and especially where the 'apocryphal' books were discounted – was a reason for the separation before any historical criticism came into the picture. The existence of innumerable possible typologies, cross-references, hints, clues and similarities did not alter this fact: here one was in the Old Testament, there one was in the New. Theologies which built upon 'the whole' did so by using this distinction as a basic guide and marker. When historical methods came to be received, they fitted into a recognition of difference that already existed and was acknowledged and presupposed. If therefore there was a difficulty in explaining the connections between Old and New Testaments for Christianity, it was vain to suppose that the removal of the *historical* perspective was the specific remedy.

3. The ultimate reason for this – and this may be a more original contribution – is that the theology of the Old Testament is not the same as the theology of the New. When taken as wholes – which is the stated purpose of most biblical theologies in general – they are not congruent, nor even closely analogical. There are a multitude of connections, similarities and relationships, which many scholars have been engaged in tracking down. But the synthetic, holistic shape of the one is very different from that of the other.

Since this is likely to be misunderstood, I have to say more about it. I am not suggesting that Old and New Testaments do not belong together theologically: as a Christian I believe that it is essential that they do. But the mode in which they belong together, in so far as this is to be expressed as holistic theologies, is a mode of two very different theologies in which the later nevertheless adopts and recontextualizes innumerable themes, figures and terms from the earlier. A theology which, like that of the New Testament, is centred in a person sent from God as mediator with humanity, who is crucified and risen, is something of a quite different character from a theology that can be built upon any holistic reading of the Old Testament.

And this is not so novel or outlandish an idea. For many who have worked in this area have come to think that the ultimate establishment of relation between Old and New Testament is a matter of faith; or, in other terms, it lies beyond the abilities of biblical theology and belongs to doctrinal theology.

4. Connections and relationships between the Old and New Testament are a very important area for Christian theology and life. And some forms of 'biblical theology' in tracking themes and concepts have done something to illuminate these. But the attempt to associate this with a synthetic or systematic 'theology' of one Testament or the other produces obvious difficulties.

5. A central problem, inadequately discussed in most of the literature, is this: the 'theology of the Old Testament' that was known and was reacted to by Jews and nascent Christians of the first century or so can hardly have been the theology of the Old Testament that existed in 'Old Testament times'. Even if we could state a theology of central Old Testament times, say a theology based on sources like Deuteronomy, the framework of the Deuteronomistic history, and Jeremiah – and such a statement should not be impossible – that theology would have been at best imperfectly known to either Jews or Christians of the first century, even granted that they possessed these texts and took them to be authoritative. For them the received 'theology of the Old Testament' would have been the theology – including, of course, later interpretations of the texts – which had prevailed in the second and first centuries BCE. They would not have known the theology of five or six centuries back, still less that of earlier times. An Old Testament Theology which would incorporate and handle these questions would not be impossible, but only to a limited extent has this challenge been met, or even perceived, in the main works produced so far. Perhaps the proposals of Gese, to be discussed later, come the closest to answering this need; or else it requires an approach through the history of religion. This is relevant for the questions of later Judaism and the 'apocryphal' books, which will be discussed later.

In support of these views, I would urge:

1. The number of Old Testament Theologies, or similar works, which have managed to handle their subject-matter without any reference to the New Testament at all points towards the intrinsic separateness of the two fields. I suggest that this should be accepted, rather than that vast amounts of further energy be poured into a task that has proved to be neither necessary nor salutary.

2. It has been disturbing to note the very slight extent to which Old Testament theologians who insisted on the vital role of the New Testament in their total perspective have actually engaged with New Testament texts in any extensive and serious way. On the whole, they have made occasional passing references to particular texts, or else they have expressed generalities about the New Testament, often customary platitudes or traditional pulpit formulations,

or else they have held back from any serious engagement with the New Testament at all. Since it is impossible to believe that they were so devoid of knowledge of the New Testament as to be unable to do serious exegesis of its texts, we have to reason in the other direction and perceive that serious exegesis of the latter would have led in a quite other direction, in fact into a wider separation between Old and New Testament theologies than the theoretical theological positions of these scholars would have found congenial.

On this aspect, on the whole, one must enter a negative verdict about the performance of Old Testament theology, so far as it has gone. On one side, it has accepted that its task was to work purely on the Old Testament and on its own terms, and where this has been accepted it has worked quite well and produced reasonably satisfactory results. On the other side, it has sought to demonstrate connections with the New Testament and even, perhaps, to show that only these connections could supply the necessary linkages within the Old and thus permit the construction of a theology of the entire Bible. But, since the actual detailed work on New Testament texts has been limited, or even at worst negligible, the result has been rather to prove the converse, and to suggest that the real Old Testament theology can be, and probably should be, reached and expressed on the terms of the Old Testament itself and that the New Testament neither assists in this process nor can be adequately connected with the Old as a result of this process.

In this section we have considered the proposals for involvement of the New Testament within Old Testament theology, and the citations of New Testament passages within that undertaking. Another question, that of the possible 'Christianizing' of the Old Testament, I shall handle as a separate matter, and it will be discussed shortly.

# 12

# Evaluation, Commitment, Objectivity

The sixth 'face' of biblical theology has been the conflict between those who think of it as an 'objective' discipline which describes what historically was the theology of biblical people, and those who think of it as a faith-committed discipline. This latter view insists on personal religious involvement. In addition, it tends to assert that biblical theology should not only state what was there in biblical times but should provide interpretations for the present day. Interpretations for the present day require, however, personal identification with the life and needs of the present-day community of faith. An introductory survey of possible arguments has been given in Chapter 1, Section 6 above. We now return to look at them more fully.

We may begin by noting that this particular question is one of the most hotly disputed in all biblical theology, and especially so in the modern American discussion. The 'cool, descriptive' historical and objective position was classically stated by Krister Stendahl in a famous article in the *Interpreter's Dictionary of the Bible*.[1] Central representatives of the contrary view have been, at an earlier stage, James D. Smart, and, more recently, Brevard Childs.[2] Very strong opinions, often approaching personal insults, have been expressed. Smart not only said that Stendahl was wrong about this but went on to suggest that his teaching had gone far towards destroying his students' ability to interpret the Bible. 'Why,' he asked, 'do the preachers of today, trained by the Stendahls in biblical exegesis, find a veritable abyss between the Then and the Now, between the original meaning and the contemporary meaning, an abyss which they did not even discover until they were faced with the task of preaching?'[3] Childs for his part asserts outright that Stendahl's approach 'destroys from the outset the possibility of genuine theological exegesis'[4] – a drastic judgment on one of the greatest exegetical thinkers of twentieth-century America.[5] Given this atmosphere, it will not be easy to achieve sweet reasonableness or compromise.

There seem to be the following different elements involved in the argument for faith-commitment:

1. Biblical theology dealing with revelation, its data and contours is not perceptible except to committed faith. An 'objective' approach makes this sort of insight unattainable.

2. Biblical theology should not simply 'describe objectively' what was there

in the Bible but should evaluate it, explain why it is good and show how it is a positive theological resource.

3. Biblical theology should not only state what was there in biblical times but should provide an interpretation for modern times or at least the key to, or the method for, such an interpretation.

4. The biblical theologian is the servant of the modern community of faith and cannot fulfil this task except through sharing in the faith of that community.

In favour of the faith–commitment approach one must say that it is the one that fits in better with modern ideas, at least in much of the world of religion. In it the person who claims to speak 'with objectivity' is likely to be laughed at: objectivity is an old idea, a outmoded fallacy long ago exploded.[6] Everyone, it is thought, has some kind of personal 'agenda' that he or she is pursuing. Not only is this so, but this is how it ought to be. It is fashionable to emphasize existential involvement and political activism and to look with scepticism at all thoughts of 'objectivity'. The argument for faith–commitment thus has the wide support of current popular ideology.

This opinion may surprise some and may indeed be disputed. Nevertheless I think it is right. I was surprised therefore to find that Ollenburger in his valuable article referred to above (ibid., 61) thinks that Stendahl's opinions have been generally accepted. He writes that 'they have profoundly affected the way biblical theologians, particularly in this country, think about their work and reflect on certain central, methodological questions. In fact, the distinctions for which Stendahl pleaded have come to be seen as virtually axiomatic, and self-evidently so, particularly for distinguishing biblical from systematic theology and the other theological disciplines. It is in locating biblical theology within the theological curriculum, and in providing a rationale for this location, that Stendahl's proposal has proved most persuasive.'[7]

This may be right, but my impression is the opposite. I have heard far more dissent from Stendahl's position than acceptance of it; and, as he himself saw it, his proposal was deliberately made as *in opposition* to what was normal among biblical theologians. I certainly do not agree that his ideas have been seen as 'virtually axiomatic': this seems to me remote from reality. I am more inclined to agree with Walter Brueggemann's opinion[8] that Stendahl's distinction between 'what it meant' and 'what it means' is 'increasingly disregarded, over-looked, or denied' – whether such a judgment is right or wrong.

It is certainly possible that the 'curricular location of biblical theology', as referred to by Ollenburger, has had a certain resemblance to Stendahl's ideas. Biblical theology is indeed commonly taught for the most part – rightly in my opinion – as a study of the theology implied in the context of biblical times and cultures. This, however, is not necessarily the result of persuasion by Stendahl's arguments. It could be the effect rather of classroom practicalities. For faith-commitment cannot easily be introduced as an essential into the classroom situation unless all participants are of the same faith, and indeed the same form of the same faith, in which case biblical theology would have to become an explicitly denominational activity. It is not easy to insist on faith-commitments as an essential in biblical theology when one is instructing a class that includes some Lutherans, some Anglicans of different currents, some Barthians, some progressive/liberationist/feminist Presbyterians, some Roman Catholics, some conservative Baptists, some liberal Methodists, some Mennonites and Disciples of Christ, perhaps two or three Jews and a few enquirers who are searching for a faith rather than possessing one. If pedagogical practice has seemed to agree with Stendahl's ideas, this may be a result of such educational practicalities rather than the influence of his arguments. Indeed these same practicalities may well have been an important factor in the formation of Stendahl's own mind, for he has been an experienced educational administrator as well as a theologian.

Even where scholars have found that educational practice made it easier or necessary to teach along something like part of Stendahl's lines, I think that many of these scholars remained personally unwilling to adopt his principles as their own. In spite, therefore, of respect for Ollenburger's opinion cited above, I continue to think that the common ideology is more on the side of faith-commitment.

Moreover, it can be argued that faith-commitment has the support of present and recent practice on its side in another way. In general, one must say, the whole operation of biblical theology, like that of biblical exegesis as a whole (including critical and historical exegesis), has been massively driven and motivated by faith. There have been exceptions here and there, but as a whole the enterprise has been the work of persons who understood themselves to be standing behind the Bible, identifying with its essentials, and advancing its potentialities for the nourishment of faith and true religion. And – to start at the lowest level of argument – how many people, if they were without lively religious faith and uninterested in the life of synagogue or church, would be likely to want to become involved in biblical theology at all? Biblical theology is likely to continue as a field of faith and commitment through sheer lack of interest from any other quarter. The vision, sometimes conjured up, of numerous sceptics and agnostics entering biblical theology and seeking to write Theologies of the Old or New Testament, is not a serious cause for worry.[9] People interested in biblical theology are likely to continue to be religious believers, as they always have been.

This, however, does not prove that faith-commitments are logically or methodologically necessary for the operations which biblical theology in fact undertakes. We may begin by illustrating this again from the case of Vriezen. As we have seen, in his extensive introductory section he emphasizes the essential place of faith and the task of evaluating the Old Testament by theological standards and seeking the element of revelation in it. But when we turn to the content section, which occupies the main part of his volume, it is not clear what parts of that discussion actually depend upon faith or commitment. So far as I can see, though occasional final evaluations and comments may be so dependent, the general exposé of material and the main argument do not so depend at all. In principle, anyone could do it. If you take typical sentences like

> The holiness of God does not only imply a consciousness of his unapproachableness, his being completely different, his glory and majesty, but also his *self-assertion* (302),

or

> This idea of the jealousy of Yahweh is closely connected with the religious exclusiveness of the religion of Israel and must be recognized as inherent in Yahwism; it is the main cause of the development of theoretical monotheism, which does not only forbid the worship of other gods but also denies their existence (303),

these observations, whether right or not, seem not to have any logical dependence on the faith of the writer or reader: they are comments that any intelligent and interested person who had read the Old Testament might make.

Later, in the 'canonical approach' of Childs, something of the same kind happens. As we have seen, he strongly rejects the 'cool, descriptive, historical' approach supported by Stendahl (which will be discussed in more detail below). According to Childs, it 'destroys from the outset the possibility of genuine theological exegesis'.[10] The arguments which he puts forward at this point are three. First, that 'the text must be seen as a witness beyond itself to the divine purpose of God'; secondly, that 'the analogy between the two [Testaments] is to be sought on the ontological [as over against a historical] level'; and thirdly, that 'there must be movement from the level of the witness to the reality itself'. These arguments may be quite reasonable in themselves, though I shall later question their relevance to this point in the dispute. Stendahl answers reasonably and moderately,[11] saying that these points made by Childs are 'useful formulations of the step from the descriptive to the normative and theological', but do nothing to substantiate Childs' main point, i.e. 'the fallacy in isolating the descriptive task'. Childs' own canonical approach is said to belong within faith-committed Christian theology. This would suggest that it contained insights that would be invisible or untenable for anyone without this commitment.

But what happens in fact is otherwise. The actual procedures of the canonical approach are methods that can be adopted by anyone, whether they have theological commitment or not. In effect, many of them were accepted by literary critics who thought it right to move in this direction, but who were by no means believers in the theological sense. Believing in the virtues of a literary canon, being interested in the final form of the text and not in its historical location, and seeking a holistic 'construal' of the whole, they could follow out or produce exactly the same kinds of exegesis. It must have been an embarrassment to Childs to find his proposals supported from this quarter.[12] Like Vriezen before him, Childs was not able, or did not try, to point to interpretative decisions made under his method which could not have been made by intelligent unbelievers interested in canonical and holistic method. Moreover, Childs' argument, if valid, must count not only against Stendahl's view but against that of Eichrodt and, indeed, against those of many leading representatives of biblical theology.

Incidentally, the reader should bear in mind that Childs may have either changed his mind about some of this, or contradicted himself. In the later *OTTCC*, 12, he tells us that 'the canonical approach envisions the discipline of Old Testament theology as combining both descriptive and constructive features. It recognizes the descriptive task of correctly interpreting an ancient text which bears testimony to historic Israel's faith. Yet it also understands that the theological enterprise involves a construal by the modern interpreter, whose stance to the text affects its meaning.' But this (with some question perhaps about the final phrase) is just what Stendahl maintained. Exactly both these steps were the centre of his proposal. The only difference might be over how much of one or the other is to be included under the term 'biblical theology'. Certainly they are so close here that, if Stendahl's proposal destroys the possibility of theological exegesis, the same is true of Childs' own, and Childs owes him an apology for the very drastic judgment he expressed. In view of many other passages, it might seem more likely that the opinion expressed in *OTTCC*, 12 was a slip and that Childs' original statement represents his continuing position. But in the still later *Biblical Theology*, Childs discusses the need 'to *describe* carefully both the continuity and discontinuity between these two different witnesses of the Christian Bible' (93f.). He points out the variety of modes in which Old Testament and New Testament materials may be related to one another. Then he continues: '*Only after this descriptive task has been done* will it be possible to turn to the larger task of trying to engage in theological reflection of [sic! – is 'on' meant?] the whole Christian Bible in the light of its subject matter of which it is a witness' (my italics). He goes on to refer to the following sections of his massive work 'as part of this descriptive task'. How does this differ from Stendahl's programme?

In this respect the position of Eichrodt seems to be more accurate in defining what has actually happened in biblical theology. The subject, according to him, is not dependent on faith or on any special mode of cognition, but lies within the field of traditional Old Testament studies: it differs from historical studies not through moving to a different plane altogether but only in that it is structural or systematic rather than diachronic (and, of course, as I have argued, structural study of this sort was always inherent in historical study in any case, so that there is at the most only a difference of emphasis). The operation works in the same way and on the same logical basis as any other of the normal scholarly operations practised by Old Testament scholars. In other words, though Eichrodt himself did not express it in exactly this way, it no more depends on faith-commitment than does historical criticism or any other operation of biblical scholarship.[13]

To put it in another way: it may be argued that theology by its nature depends on faith and revelation. Of course. But this applies only to theology proper, 'authentic' or 'real theology';[14] it is for the moment uncertain, however, whether biblical theology can necessarily claim to be theology in the authentic sense at all, and therefore the argument cannot yet be legitimately extended to it.

Put it again in these terms: it can be said that biblical theology is part of Christian theology, and several have argued in this way. But the argument is indecisive. For there is both a wider and a narrower definition of what is comprised in 'Christian theology'. In a narrower sense it may be that 'Christian theology' means 'Christian doctrinal theology' or 'Christian practical theology', and in that case one might argue that one cannot work in that area without personal faith and commitment (though even then it would be a stiflingly narrow and exclusivist view, which many active theologians would repudiate). But in the wider sense 'Christian theology' would include all the subjects studied in a course of Christian theological study. These would include such disciplines as church history or Hebrew grammar, and it is doubtful whether personal faith and commitment is a necessity for serious work in these areas. Biblical theology might be like church history, or it might be like history of doctrine. Thus just to claim that it is 'part of Christian theology', even if true, does not prove anything. Christian theology in the wider sense includes many subjects which can be studied, and indeed must be studied, independently of personal faith. In order to justify the claim that one cannot work in biblical theology without personal faith-commitments, it has to be shown that there are observations, insights and conclusions that could not be made by persons who did not have these commitments. Thus far this has not been shown, or indeed been attempted. The material thus far written under the heading of biblical theology – including the material written by those who insist on a faith-commitment – suggests the reverse: that it requires an *interest* in theology and an *empathy* with it, but not a personal faith-commitment.

What might with more justice be said in favour of faith-commitment is something else: namely, that a biblical theology worked out with a faith-commitment will be a somewhat different biblical theology from that written with the cool, objective, descriptive approach. The argument is not for or against a biblical theology but for or against a particular *kind* of biblical theology. Thus, to cite again Childs' sentence written against Stendahl, 'that the text must be seen as a witness beyond itself to the divine purpose of God' simply does not touch the intended target: for Stendahl's proposal stands whether Childs' objection is true or not. The point raised by Stendahl's position is: even if the text is seen as a witness beyond itself, how do we know what it is witnessing to? We have to know what the theology of the text is before we can tell what aspect of 'the divine purpose of God' it is saying something about. Childs' objection therefore stands only if it is already known what 'the divine purpose of God' is. It is therefore an argument not for theological exegesis as such, but for his own personal theological position, or, more precisely, a call for all biblical theologians to presuppose that by their own personal faith they know exactly what the divine purpose of God is.

There is another way in which the difference between accurate 'description' and faith-related 'commitment' to the 'normative' tends to dissolve in practice. Obviously, for those who hold a strong enough view of the authority of the Bible, if something is a good 'description' of biblical beliefs and attitudes, then it is *ipso facto* 'normative' and they are committed to it. In terms of method of discovery, there is no difference. Sermons, for instance, which by their own nature are appeals for commitment, contain constant claims that they are giving an accurate description of persons, entities, situations and doctrines of the Bible. Those who assume 'committed' faith-attitudes are continually uttering what they claim to be accurate descriptions of situations within the Bible. Because they are accurate descriptions, they are normative. The difference is not one of method in the knowledge of the biblical situation, but one of the view of biblical authority. This is why those who deplore the idea of description continually return to using it themselves.

The same applies in another aspect, namely the special position of *Old Testament* theology. For how can a theology of *part* of the Old Testament, or even of the whole of it, be 'normative' *in itself* for Christianity? How can it be normative for Christianity except as it is considered in relation to the New Testament and the basic patristic sources of Christian theology? It would obviously be reasonable to think of it as normative for the Jewish reader, but for the Christian it could hardly be normative in itself, unless one takes the view that all theological positions of the Old Testament are *identical* with those of the New and with those of mature Christian theology. Unless this is so, one would have to have a view of the 'normative' which is itself relative: that is, it is normative *in so far as* any Old Testament information, taken in itself, can be normative for Christianity. Here again the question of normativity is not an indication of a *method* or attitude with which to approach the theology, but is rather a function of the view of biblical authority with which one works. And even within the most orthodox currents of theological tradition such views are numerous and variable.

Another way in which our problems can be formulated is by use of the *temporal* distinction of past and present, the distinction between 'what it meant' and 'what it means'. This distinction is best known from the famous and clear – or perhaps one should say 'at first sight fairly clear' – formulation of it by Krister Stendahl. Stendahl thought that biblical theology in itself should not be primarily evaluative. According to his view,[15] biblical theology is a descriptive undertaking which, historically, and as objectively as possible, tells us what sort of 'theology' existed in ancient times. 'Objectively' here means: independently of whether one advocates this theology or disapproves of it, or thinks it is the ultimate divine revelation, or thinks it does not matter. These issues do not matter: we are concerned only with knowing what was there at the appropriate stage in biblical times. What the corresponding biblical texts mean for our time is a different affair.

Take, let us say, the New Testament picture of a world of demons: it would be very wrong if we allowed our description of that time to be affected by the question whether or not we ourselves think it is good to believe in demons or a personal devil for today. We have to say, as honestly as we can, what *they* thought at the time.

Or, to take the example which actually, I believe, was very seminal in forming Stendahl's mind on this matter: the role of women in the church. When the ordination of women was discussed, a commission of the Church of Sweden discussed the matter and came to the conclusion that, on the basis of the New Testament, there was no case for women's ordination.[16] Stendahl agreed that, as descriptive biblical theology of the New Testament regarding this matter, this was quite correct. But, he thought, this was not decisive for the present day. A multitude of factors had altered the social setting since New Testament times: simply to repeat the New Testament judgment in modern times would be to falsify it. Thus it would be wrong, just because one thought the ordination of women to be right for the present day, to read back this opinion into the New Testament and to obscure the theology of the matter which they had actually held. It would be equally wrong, just because one knew (correctly) that the New Testament opinion was against this sort of thing, to suppose that this in itself settled the interpretative issue for modern times. Biblical theology is in principle historical and descriptive; the move to interpretation for the present day is a separate matter and involves other factors. Biblical theology concerns 'what it meant'; a further and different hermeneutical step is involved in deciding 'what it means'. Such is the position taken by Stendahl.

Stendahl's own work illustrates the problems very well. His study on the place of women in the church has been a major example; to this we may add two others of his most important areas of impact on biblical interpretation: first, his support for an emphasis on bodily resurrection and his opposition to the idea of immortality of the soul, and secondly his essay on 'St Paul and the Introspective Conscience of the West'.

1. In the matter of resurrection and immortality,[17] Stendahl maintains that the biblical books show little, or practically no, interest in the immortality of the soul, and says that this result is the product of 'cool, descriptive biblical theology' – exactly the correct terms of his own programme as described above. But in fact his thoughts on the matter are very deeply and passionately intermingled with what, as he sees it, 'it means'. He thinks – or then thought, for he might have adjusted his opinion later – that people nowadays have factually lost interest in the immortality of the soul, that they *were right to lose interest in* it, and that it is *good for them* that they have done so or will do so. I believe I have shown that these strongly held sentiments about the modern relevance of the theme have distorted his treatment of the biblical material itself.[18]

In the second case Stendahl basically argues that St Paul in his thoughts about 'justification by faith' was talking about something very different from the introspective problems of individual sin and guilt which became the dominant Western inheritance from Paul especially after Augustine and Luther.[19] A shift to an understanding of what Paul was 'really' talking about – the status of communities in relation to the church – would clearly, in Stendahl's mind, be very salutary for modern theology and religion. Here, without claiming to be an expert, I think that Stendahl is very likely right, and I do not see that his convictions about the present have distorted the biblical evidence. On the other hand, it cannot be doubted that, on this occasion, 'what it means' is very much mixed up with 'what it meant', and it is the importance of the modern message perceived that has in part prompted and fired this particular presentation of 'what it meant'.

Stendahl's principle is thus somewhat compromised in its actual working out. Nevertheless in general he is emphatically in the right in this whole matter, although certain modifications will be suggested below. It would be quite wrong to suppose that, even if he had not universally succeeded in maintaining the distinction for which he pleads, this shows that the distinction is wrong. On the contrary, the fact that we are able to criticize his exegesis on these grounds shows that his principle is right. It would be fatal to biblical theology if every worker in the field felt at liberty to 'discover' in the biblical material whatever message or implication he or she thought to be 'good for' modern humanity to hear. Individual failures on Stendahl's part to observe his own principle do not at all prove that the principle is wrong: indeed, the possibility of detecting that they are failures is dependent on the rightness of the principle itself.

Particularly important is the principle in those cases where there is some element in the Bible which is distasteful to the biblical theologian. 'I don't much like this, why shouldn't I leave it out?' is a temptation that many of us have felt from time to time. That it can be successfully resisted is shown by Stendahl's own work on the place of women in the church. He was himself convinced that women should be ordained, that this was theologically right. But he made it clear that he agreed with the view of the Swedish theological commission, to the effect that the biblical evidence, taken for itself, pointed in the opposite direction.

This recognition of a difference between what one oneself believes and what one perceives to have been the case in the Bible can be illustrated from other instances. Thus Albert Schweitzer is often credited with having discredited the 'liberal' picture of the historical Jesus, and justifiably so. But it would be wrong to suppose that Schweitzer's own theology was opposed to liberalism. On the contrary, he was very much a liberal. But he was able to paint the picture of the 'eschatological fanatic' Jesus, one quite dissimilar to his own belief. We can conjoin with him the name of Johannes Weiss. Räisänen rightly takes them as an example of how relative (not absolute) objectivity works: 'they dared to paint a Jesus who held a faith different from their own'.[20]

To put it in another way, a hermeneutic that will tell us 'what it means' for today must be prepared to include an element of *critique*. This aspect has been missed by many biblical theologians, because they thought that, the more deeply the biblical theology was probed, the more obviously, directly and profoundly it will supply the correct and relevant meaning for today. Again Stendahl grasped this point well. Characteristic biblical theology of the 1940s and 1950s, he thought, worked out the biblical or Hebraic thought-forms of biblical times, indicated the complicated network of concepts and ideas that they implied, and then dumped the whole thing on the lap of twentieth-century theology, declaring that it was all authoritative as it stood and had to be accepted as such. And, in spite of the alleged 'decline' of biblical theology, some people are still doing the same. As I have just said, Stendahl himself to some extent did it with the immortal soul.

This view of Stendahl's, indeed, has been much resisted by others. The opposition has argued, perhaps, from two angles, different but perhaps complementary. On the one hand, the ideal of objective description has been contested: the Bible could not be studied with cold objectivity, one could not enter into it without personal involvement and decision. According to this point of view, objective historical examination is illusory. James D. Smart went so far as to suggest that the ideal of objectivity is an actual *obstacle* to the discovery of truth about the Bible, and that passionate commitment was the sure way to true knowledge – a notion that flies in the face of all experience of the workings of religious enthusiasm.

On the other hand, biblical theology, it has been argued, is above all a mode in which the Bible is made more alive and relevant for today. Much of the discussion of the subject has shown the influence of homiletic needs and the pressure of rhetorical techniques: if one can come to perceive certain aspects as central to the Bible, how can one possibly rest content with observing that fact and not at once go out to proclaim that essential message to modern humanity? And, if biblical theology cannot show us how to preach the Christian message for today, what use is it?[21] Note the emphasis on *utility* implied by this part of the argument.

Actually, of course, it may well be that biblical theology will have a great deal of utility for questions of today. Nevertheless the approach to it must not be governed by expectations of utility, otherwise these considerations will inevitably corrupt its accuracy in representing the biblical material itself.

In any case, even continuing with the matter of utility, arguments depending on faith-commitment are bound to lose their own utility if they are honestly presented as such. For those, whether scholars or preachers or laypersons, who build an argument on the basis of biblical material and add, 'of course, this is the biblical view *only because* I approach it as a faith-committed liberal or evangelical, or Lutheran or Presbyterian', have in effect destroyed their own argument and its utility. For the faith-commitment arguments to have force and utility, they have to be presented *as if* they were built upon the descriptive model which the faith-commitment supporter denies.

Stendahl's argument has sometimes been so read as if to suggest that, in his opinion, biblical scholarship should do nothing to provide interpretation for today.[22] It should have been obvious that this was not so. His whole scheme was intended precisely to provide interpretation for today, and clearly did so in all the three cases I have cited above. Arguments against his thinking on the ground that it is 'purely historical' or 'antiquarian' or the like are complete misrepresentations. The centre of his scheme is that there are two distinct stages: we have to know correctly what the theology of the Bible was before we go on to state its meaning for the present day. This first stage he calls 'biblical theology', but the naming of it does not seem to be so essential. It would not much alter Stendahl's scheme if we were to use 'biblical theology' for the two stages combined, so long as the distinction between them were clearly observed. But in using 'biblical theology' strictly for the first stage only Stendahl was, I suggest, following the main line of what has been understood by this term in the twentieth century. In interpreting for the present day we have to be clear and honest in indicating those points at which the modern interpretation is distinct from the theology of ancient times.

Stendahl's position has often been misunderstood, and a discussion of some of these misunderstandings may be helpful. It seems to be misunderstood by Tsevat, a Jewish scholar whose important contributions to our subject will be discussed below. He takes the investigation of 'what it meant' to be, for Stendahl, purely history of religion, while 'what it means' is real and normative Christian theology.[23] The reverse is the case: for him the biblical theology was the objective description of the theology as it existed in biblical times. The move to 'what it means' for today is the task of a hermeneutic procedure which can lead to results that are, at least on the surface, very different from 'what it meant' in biblical times. The hermeneutic procedure very definitely takes into account the changed situation of people in medieval and modern times.

For another possible misunderstanding see F. Mildenberger's article 'Biblische Theologie versus Dogmatik?', 273f.[24] He works mainly from Stendahl's early paper in Hyatt, *The Bible in Modern Scholarship*. He appears to think that Stendahl is attacking the possibility of dogmatic thinking and insisting that his own historical-descriptive method is final. Actually Stendahl is seeking to *limit* the claims of biblical theology, which he describes as (at least potentially) 'imperialistic', in order to increase the freedom of dogmatics to take decisions which lie beyond the proper scope of biblical theology. This is an important positive emphasis, in view of the tendency of biblical theology, as already seen above in Chapters 5 and 6, to raise itself from the position of an ancillary discipline to one of superior authority over all other forms of theology.

A grosser and more serious misrepresentation of Stendahl's thought appears in Francis Watson's *Text, Church and World*, 30–3.[25] He follows an early reaction of Childs in describing Stendahl's position as 'a naive empiricism' (33). Stendahl's argument 'is important not because it is original but as a clear statement of the self-understanding of most practitioners of historical-critical exegesis' (31). Watson emphasizes the contrast between the descriptive task, which is relatively simply and straightforward ('we can all join in and check each other's results against the original', 30), and the task of interpretation for the present day, 'an arduous road towards a goal that we glimpse only from afar'. The emphasis is 'on the autonomy of the historical task and on the need for great circumspection in undertaking the theological one' (31).

All of this is wrong. First of all, 'naive empiricism' is mere abuse, for I do not see anything empirical in Stendahl's approach. It presupposes, if anything, the categories of biblical theology and of hermeneutics as then understood, and if it has a fault it lies on that side and not in 'empiricism'. Nowhere, so far as I can see, does Stendahl speak of, or advocate, an empirical procedure. Nor does Stendahl state the self-understanding of practitioners of historical-critical exegesis. Historical criticism, as a matter of fact, scarcely enters into his presentation. His position is predicated upon the concept of biblical theology. Admittedly, he does not make it very clear how one reaches that biblical theology in the first place. But his main point is that if there is a biblical theology, then it is a theology that existed in the past. This would be the same for a biblical theology built upon a quite anti-critical basis, denying historical criticism entirely: it would still, as purporting to be a biblical theology, be a theology intended as the theology of the people of biblical times.

Again, if Stendahl's position was 'a clear statement of the self-understanding of most practitioners of historical-critical exegesis', it is surprising that most such practitioners found it highly controversial and were unable to agree on whether they supported it or not.

Moreover, Watson's criticism on the grounds that for Stendahl theological assessment and construction were extremely remote and difficult of access is obviously untrue. As has been shown by all the examples I have put forward, the matter of ordination of women, the matter of soul and immortality, and the matter of justification by faith, Stendahl was swift to perceive and express present-day theological decisions arising from biblical exegesis. On one of these matters, that of justification by faith, the importance of his initiative for contemporary theology has been widely recognized by a variety of exegetes, including Watson himself, as indicated above.

Historical critics, Watson alleges, 'find that theology subjects the text to alien norms' (32). The reality, however, is quite the reverse: it is the tradition of biblical theology itself, as we have seen, that has repeatedly emphasized the danger that (traditional) theology subjects the text to alien norms.

Watson asserts that historical-critical description 'is dependent on a prior interpretation of these texts as historical artefacts – chance remnants of a previous stage of human history – whose meaning is wholly determined by their historical circumstances of origin' (33). Of course they are historical artefacts – even Watson probably does not deny this – but his argument is really that they are understood as *only* historical artefacts and nothing more at all, having *no meaning* at all beyond their historical circumstances of origin. This is rubbish and only shows how far the force of his argument has made him remote from the actualities of the people he is talking about.

Finally, Watson instructs us:

To appeal for an autonomous 'description' is to ignore the fact that there is no such thing as a pure description of a neutral object; description always presupposes a prior construction of the object in terms of a given interpretative paradigm (33).

How amazingly original a thought! Who in the hermeneutical discussion has not heard it proclaimed a hundred times? To suppose that Stendahl, who had his finger uniquely on the pulse of exegetical discussions, was unaware of this elementary argument is only one part of the contemptuous superiority with which Watson approaches his subject.

In spite of my support for Stendahl's position, however, there are important modifications and corrections which ought to be suggested. In particular, I shall argue that his definition of biblical theology was excessively hermeneutical in character. It was dependent on a hermeneutical model based on *meanings* – 'what it meant' against 'what it means' – and on a hermeneutical model that is faulty.

On the one hand it is somewhat misleading to define the object of biblical theology as 'what it meant'. Probably Stendahl did not intend his distinction to be taken too exactly: for him the point was the distinction between 'meant' and 'means', and the temporal distinction is very clearly conveyed by his formula. But the word 'meant' suggests the meaning of the text, or of the Bible, in ancient times, what it then meant to people. What it meant to people could be a variety of things, but in any case it does not seem to coincide with the *theology* of the Bible (or of its various texts). Biblical theology is not looking for what it *meant*, but for *what it was*: what the theology of the Bible, or underlying the Bible, was (or perhaps *is*? – for it could be argued that, if a biblical theology can be discovered and stated, then that theology not only *was* but *is* and *remains* the theology of the Bible). The question is therefore about the 'it' rather than about the tense of 'means' or 'meant'. If Stendahl's formula had been expressed in this way, it might have received wider acceptance.

A more serious and far-reaching observation is this: what 'it' means (for the present) is never in fact what the Bible alone means. Theological interpretation of the Bible for today, which is what Stendahl had in mind, is never interpretation of one thing only, namely the Bible. In this assertion there are two elements. First, interpretation for today is interpretation in which the Bible is related to other relevant elements: the theological traditions, philosophy, modern religious and social situations and – very likely – natural theology. Or, to put it more vividly, it is not we who interpret the Bible but the Bible which interprets us and our world: cf. the title of Perlitt's article 'Auslegung der Bibel – Auslegung der Welt'. What is normally intended when we talk about interpretation for today is not interpretation of the Bible alone.

This means – still more important – that the model of an interpretation which takes the ancient biblical message or material and transfers or translates this into the modern world is a mistaken one – not only from the historical but also from the religious/theological point of view. This is not a new idea, for it has been explored by Dietrich Ritschl and others, but its potential is as yet insufficiently realized.

We cannot take an ancient passage or an ancient work like the Bible and say that its meaning has to be up-dated, brought into the modern world. 'What it meant' in Stendahl's terms is its *only* meaning. The process of religious appropriation of the Bible is not that we produce a new meaning, 'what it means' for today. It is, on the contrary, that we, the modern religious community, sink ourselves increasingly into its *past* meaning. In the doing of this, that past meaning, which is the only meaning, interprets and criticizes our modern life as it comes into contact with our modern thoughts, traditions, experiences and histories. This process can inaccurately be called the finding of 'the meaning of the Bible for today' but it is not really that, for the Bible has this 'new' meaning only because it is brought into contact with a mass of non-biblical knowledge (or pseudo-knowledge). In other words, we are saying that the traditional idea of hermeneutics, as applied in much modern theology, has worked in a biblicistic manner, as if the thing being interpreted was (uniquely) the Bible and the process involved was (uniquely or primarily) one of overcoming the temporal distance and producing from the one source, the Bible, a meaning *of that source* for today.

These thoughts, if valid, are of great importance for our general subject. For they mean that the religious appropriation of the Bible is much closer, much more analogous, to the historical study of it than has generally been perceived. It is not at all that the religious use of the Bible is identical with the research of the historian or the historical critic, but the historian's penetration into biblical times is a more technical and methodically controlled process which operates in a mode analogical to the basic religious use of 'what it meant'. In this respect Stendahl was mistaken in expressing his distinction, in itself a right one, in terms related to the 'actualizing' hermeneutics then current. And, to forestall an obvious objection, the analogy with *theology* is also valid. The tendency to place *theology* in serious contrast with *history* – a tendency very visible in much biblical theology and particularly so in Childs' canonical approach – is certainly a deep contradiction. This is shown not so much by abstract arguments about history and theology but above all by the fact that the very approach which so sets theology apart from history is one whose theology is overwhelmingly *historical* in character. Childs' own argumentation, as is obvious, is not really theological argumentation, but is above all historical argumentation, which uses the history of theology as a grid upon which value judgments are fixed.[26]

There remains one other criticism of Stendahl's formulation which is also

relevant for other wide areas of biblical theology. The question is: can the term
'descriptive' be accepted for use without further qualification? Let us agree with
the term 'descriptive' as against the opposing faith-commitment position. And
let us accept that the description of the (implied) theology of the Bible is the aim
of biblical theology. Stendahl is therefore basically in the right. But his term
'descriptive' does not well describe the process by which the work has to be
done. The reality with which biblical theology is concerned is not an accessible
entity, the contours of which are readily available for description. The process
is essentially an *imaginative* one, which involves imaginative *construction*. It is
indeed historical, as Stendahl rightly puts it, in the sense that it works within a
historical framework and is subject to historical questioning and verification; but
historical description, without the additional specification of imaginative construction, will not suffice to provide an answer. If Stendahl had modified his
formula in this sense, some of the objections voiced against it might have been
avoided.

Again, it may be questioned whether 'description' is the right term for some
of the relations that biblical theology seeks to express. Given an entity with an
apparent unity, one may speak of 'describing' aspects of that entity: thus, let us
say, we may try to describe the tendencies of the book of Deuteronomy or the
thought of the prophet Amos, or to describe how terms for 'soul' and 'spirit' are
used throughout the Bible, if there is in fact some unity in this group of terms.
But the relations between the Old and New Testaments are not an entity of that
kind. To use 'describe' as the term for the way in which one may seek to relate
the Old Testament to the New is a strange use of language. Thus it is not surprising that Preuss in the concluding sentences of his recent Old Testament
Theology looks back on his main work as one of 'pure description' but goes on
to add: 'the discovery and unfolding of these basic structures of Old Testament
faith can . . . not remain only a historically orientated and purely descriptive
[undertaking]'. For then he goes on to speak of a 'biblical theology' (in my terms
a pan-biblical theology) which would open out into the basic structures or structural analogies of the complete (Christian) Bible. The perception and expression
of these larger structures and wider analogies seems to go beyond what can be
properly counted as 'description'.

Moreover, description requires the use of terms and categories belonging to
*our modern* speech. Only in the most extreme formalistic approaches can we
describe biblical texts and realities without some reference to our own categories. Formalism can be valuable because it gives us some important data, but
for most purposes we have to go beyond that. If we set out to 'describe' the
meaning of Hebrew *nephesh,* we can do much of value with sheer statistics, with
syntactical matrices, with parallelisms and so on, but we soon come to a point
where we use English words of today, and then we have to start explaining that

it does not mean exactly 'soul' (and there is a question what that word means in English today, if it means anything) and yet in certain contexts it really *is* rather like 'soul' after all – a familiar exercise to everyone who tries to talk about such things. There is an unavoidable element of *comparison* with the way we think about things today, whether religiously or unreligiously.[27] And so 'description' of ancient things involves a certain critical examination of modern things, and 'what it meant' comes to be somewhat mixed up with what something or other means today.

We have to discuss more fully the matter of objectivity.[28] Those who insist on faith-commitment are commonly very hostile to the idea of objectivity, and argue that perfect objectivity is an unrealistic notion which cannot be realized in this world. Everyone who says anything has some purpose or agenda which influences and possibly distorts the subject spoken about. Quite so. But this argument is irrelevant, for we are not speaking about perfect objectivity. We are speaking about the willingness to seek *some limited but adequate measure of* objectivity. We are asking for the admission that some limited degree of objectivity is better than a complete abandonment of objectivity. The faith-commitment argument is commonly so extremely hostile to objectivity that it is unwilling to set any limits at all to prejudice, special pleading and propaganda. Thus fairness and open-mindedness are seldom mentioned in works on biblical theology. Stendahl's argument does not ask for perfect objectivity or for the objectivity of natural science. But it does ask, and rightly, that the person of faith-commitment should, in the face of the biblical material, to some extent hold his or her faith-commitment in suspense, place it, as it were, in a state of questioning, in which one asks oneself: does the biblical material really fit in with my existing faith-commitment, or may it be that my faith-commitment has to be adjusted in view of my new insights into the biblical material?

There is another way in which the anti-objectivist arguments should be discounted. They are, as we have seen, part of the set of existentialist ideas which have been so influential in the entire base of biblical theology (and in many quarters are now being superseded by 'postmodern' ideas, which are slightly different). It should not be believed, however, that these ideas are employed consistently. A consistent anti-objectivism might well be found in Bultmann; but just at this point many Old Testament theologians will turn away from him and look in another direction. Barthianism, which, as we have seen, was more influential in Old Testament theology, has also often had an anti-objectivist air and has opposed the supposed objectivist aims of historians. But Barthians who follow this line are not against objectivity all the way. They deny it to historians for a quite different reason: it is not that they are against objectivity – on the contrary they are in favour of it – but that they want it for themselves. That the Barthian theological vision has objectivity has been a basic conviction, and the same is true of the canonical approach as developed by Childs. Unquestionably much of the attraction of the canonical approach lies in the impression that here, in the canon, at last, in contrast with the varieties and speculative theories of critical interpretation, we have something *objective* as a foundation. The tirades of biblical theologians against objectivity are therefore by no means always to be taken too seriously.

That these have inner contradictions can easily be seen. In his *Introduction*, Childs announces that it 'seeks to describe as objectively as possible the canonical literature' (16). But his Exodus commentary began with a solemn declaration that he 'does not share the hermeneutical position of those who suggest that biblical exegesis is an objective, descriptive enterprise'.[29] In his later *Biblical Theology* he tells us that he attempts in this volume 'to focus in more detail on the descriptive task of relating the Old Testament witness to the history of Israel, of course, according to its canonical form' (101). He wants to 'describe' a trajectory of psalmic tradition (92). He refers to 'a careful descriptive reading of the two Testaments in reference to the law' (551). However, he refers disparagingly to a 'purely descriptive, sociological explanation' as the 'least satisfactory approach' to questions about the historical Jesus (604). Referring to Hermisson's study of faith, he tells us that 'the appeal within the Old Testament to a reality called faith is a feature constitutive of Christian theology and is hardly a neutral descriptive reading of the literature' (617). These contradictions are a surface symptom of a contradiction about objectivity in deep structure. Those who despise and attack the value of objectivity are desperately in need of it for themselves.

Another matter that may be mentioned in this connection is the question of the 'time-conditioned quality' of interpretation. It has often been argued that attempts at 'objective' work involved the illusion of standing outside the stream of time and producing a result wholly independent of one's own modern position. This argument is often used in order to discredit historical-critical studies. It is one of the many myths thought up by the fertile imaginations of anti-historical writers. For, of course, it is entirely untrue that the great historical critics like Harnack, or the great theorists of critical history like Troeltsch, had any such idea of themselves. And as applied in justification of more modern exegetical proposals, the notion is a hypocritical one. Thus to take one example, Childs uses this argument repeatedly ('the canonical approach . . . rejects a method which is unaware of its own time-conditioned quality', *OTTCC*, 12, cf. again on 14).[30] But nowhere in the literature of the canonical approach are we told that this novel approach is conditioned by the background of the writer and by the social, economic and political situations of the period 1960–1990. Still less are we told that the value of the canonical approach will be merely one phase which will last for one generation at most, and that by the end of that time people will all have become historicists again or return to some other non-canonical stance. In fact the 'time-conditioned' argument is an important element in the present-day trend towards complete relativism, which rightly distresses Childs. But if it distresses him, he should not use the arguments that sustain it. Arguments like this were used because they seemed to be a good stick with which to beat the historical emphasis; those who used them often did not consider how they would rebound upon themselves.

A conclusion to this difficult controversy may now be attempted. First, as I have said, few are likely to embark on biblical theology without a faith-commitment. If any do, well, that is fine. They may surely be welcomed, for they may well come upon insights which the religious believer might not think of. Biblical theology should certainly not seek to be a religiously or denominationally closed and exclusive preserve. But, if most workers certainly work from a faith position, their faith-commitment in this case can properly be only a commitment to discover what is really there in the Bible, even if what is found disagrees with our present faith-commitments, extends them in a quite unexpected way, or goes in a quite different direction from them. Otherwise commitment tends very easily to mean that we see in the Bible what we already consider to be right, or useful, or in agreement with a particular church tradition, or relevant, or 'good for' other people or useful for preaching. Examples of this are richly demonstrable in the literature of biblical theology. In this sense Stendahl's position, though in part wrongly expressed, seems to be right. It is particularly important in the sort of cases on which he himself worked, cases where the biblical evidence reveals something that seriously clashes with current faith-commitments. On the other hand, those who have opposed Stendahl have often spoken as if faith-commitments meant that everything in the Bible must be directly right, acceptable, relevant and authoritative just as it stood. The value of his ideas appears best when we consider cases where this is not so.

A good example is the case of natural theology. For many twentieth-century Christians – if they are theologically trained, since otherwise they will probably never have heard of the question – it is a faith-commitment that natural theology is totally wrong. But what if there are passages in the Bible which use natural theology and depend upon it? Those who oppose Stendahl's position will also tend to ignore these passages, or to explain them away, or to deny their obvious meaning. This may then be an indirect denial of an important element of scripture. Now it may still be a right faith-commitment to say that natural theology is wrong. But if so, Stendahl's approach provides a way of working. One can state and describe historically a body of ideas that are there in the Bible, while at a separate (doctrinal or hermeneutic) stage one will have to explain how or why these elements are of limited value, or limited to their own time, or in some other way not finally authoritative. [I myself would not do this, but this is just an explanation of a possible example.]

Thus it is far from the case that the task of biblical theology is to explain what the text 'means for the present day' or how it fits with the various more recent theological traditions or how it determines what should be done about modern socio–ethical questions. It is far from the duty of the biblical scholar to judge on these matters, though of course he or she may incidentally do so. This is, or should be, the judgment of the church or religious community itself. The church has plenty of people who are competent and ready to tell whether an interpretation of a part of the Bible is meaningful for the present day, or whether it fits in with Lutheran, Calvinist, Methodist or Catholic traditions, or what it means for modern social questions. All these people are ready and willing to be heard. What the church requires from biblical scholars is not that they should join them in this vociferous pleading, but that they should make clear how far these various resultant interpretations, whether apparently 'relevant' or not, whether in accord with church tradition or not, whether socially meaningful for today or not, are firmly based in the Bible itself. Biblical scholars, therefore, whatever their allegiance in these matters, work usefully in so far as they ask the question: granted that I believe this or that to be in accord with my theological tradition, to be relevant for today, to be socially and ethically desirable, my duty to the church or community is to put into brackets, into parenthesis, these my own convictions and to ask whether or not the Bible itself supports them. If it does, then one can continue as one has been; if not, then a process of theological change may have to begin.

The apparent conflict between personal commitment and objective description is therefore a poor model,[31] which can lead only to severe and irreconcilable conflicts between opposed and partially valid positions. In essence, faith-commitment requires and supports a search for adequately objective description.

# 13

# Historical Theology – A Possible Analogy?

As we have seen, there has continued to be uncertainty and debate about the question to what extent 'biblical theology' is really theology, and this question has remained central to some of the questions discussed in the previous chapter. This chapter will consider one possible way of understanding this matter, namely that biblical theology is akin to that sector of theology which is often called 'historical theology'.

I do not know if historical theology has ever received a comprehensive definition or explanation, but the term is not infrequently used and the reality must be familiar to most of those who do any study in theology at all.[1] The majority of works in theology do not take as their subject-matter simply God, or creation, or faith, but the understanding of these themes, or others, in the work *of past theologians*. Even of those theologians whose thought is most worthily described as 'dogmatic' it is true that their work is largely historical theology in this sense. Only perhaps in the area of philosophical theology, or else in acutely innovative theologies, is it possible to escape from this, and even there only with some difficulty. Much or most theology – and here I mean 'theology' in the 'proper' or 'authentic' sense – operates through the exposition and evaluation of past theological traditions.

Thus theologians study God as God was understood in the patristic period, or creation as understood by Augustine, or analogy in Aquinas, or the devil in the thought of Luther, or Schleiermacher's understanding of culture, or Barth's eschatological views, or whatever it may be. They may well go beyond the simple historical presentation of these complexes of ideas, and may well use them as *authority* for their own theological proposals and suggestions. They may also, equally though perhaps less commonly, point to deficiencies in the views of Augustine or Luther or whoever it may be. Upon such evaluative judgments they may build important elements of their own theological positions. Either way, their theologies go beyond exact historical description.

Nevertheless, the historical element remains very largely in control. If it can be shown that elements in Augustine's ideas of creation derived from his Manichaean experiences or from other sources more dubiously related to traditional Christianity, then it is very likely that the authority of these ideas for theology will be affected. If research can show that Luther did not have quite the ideas about the devil that are generally supposed to have been his, then these ideas must cease to enjoy the validation that comes from association with Luther.

Thus historical research can work both positively and negatively in relation to theological traditions. The average person who identifies with a theological tradition may have only a vague idea of its original sources and their historical context, and may well have read none of its classic sources. Thus, for example, a person may declare himself 'a Calvinist' without having read Calvin or knowing anything about the world in which Calvin lived. What such a person is doing is in effect to declare his own identification with what *he* in the twentieth century, or some group with which he is associated, *understands* to be Calvinism. Historical research may show the reality to have been very different.

The (doctrinal, dogmatic or systematic, if we must use these terms) theologian is thus characteristically involved in historical theology, and the element of historical theology has a very considerable authority over his thinking. Ideas that are incorrectly attributed to authors, or that are understood without a knowledge of the cultural environment of the time, or that are anachronistically read back into the wrong epoch, are all likely to suffer some diminution in force and effect. Thus the correct historical reading of older theological sources is of great power and influence for theology itself. In this sense historical theology is a very important element in most forms of theology.

Historical theology, however, cannot work in isolation from other forms of historical knowledge: political, social and economic. Theology was seldom, if ever, 'pure'. Important decisions in the patristic period and in the Reformation were heavily influenced by the interests of nations and their rulers. And, most obviously, historical theology is deeply related to the history of religion – in the case of Christianity, the entire history of Christian people, their churches and their organization, their modes of worship, their rituals and practices, their social setting. No one, perhaps, doubts this. But it provides an immediate parallel to the relation between biblical theology and the history of Israelite religion. Luther's doctrine of justification may count as 'theology', but it cannot be properly understood without a knowledge of late medieval penitential practice, which comes closer to religion. Practice in the churches has often diverged from theology, and the difference has eventually brought about a redirection for theology itself. In the Bible it was the same. Thus the embedding of historical theology within general historical knowledge should have a parallel in the embedding of biblical theology within the relevant history of Israel and especially the religious history.

This does not mean, however, that historical theology is no more than history. Historical theology lies fully under the constraints of history and historical method, but it continues to be also a form of theology. It is the re-creation of the theology which lies behind the texts, which existed in the mind of Augustine or whomever else. The person who seeks to know, even just historically, the theology has to enter into the workings of theology: not necessarily to agree with it, but to know how it works, to empathize with it. Historical knowledge is regulative for historical theology, but historical knowledge does not of itself provide historical theology. Historical theology requires not only the questions of times and influences and environment, but those of what God this is like, how he relates with human beings, what ethical consequences his nature entails. In this sense historical theology is part of, belongs to, and is commonly an essential contributor to, true theology.

Yet this does not mean that historical theology is controlled by, or subservient to, 'true' theology. One who does historical theology on Calvin is not 'committed' to ending up with a Calvinist solution as the basis for his own theology, and one who does his historical theology on Augustine remains free to conclude that the influence of this great thinker on later Christianity was seriously damaging. It cannot be doubted, indeed, that in practice the personal theological predilections of the scholar affect his or her assessment of the historical questions; but in principle these are two different matters, and it is simply a fault in scholarship when they are allowed to confuse each other. Historical theology is related to 'true' theology but in principle retains an independence in relation to it.

This position is not dissimilar from that which obtains in a subject like ancient philosophy. For ancient philosophy one must obviously be informed about the culture and language of the time; it can be important to know the order in which Plato's Dialogues were written, the sequences in which Aristotle changed his mind. As with biblical criticism, stylistic analysis may be able to tell us which works of the Platonic or Aristotelian corpus are not works of the master himself but are later or spurious imitations, and decisions of this kind can be of importance in determining the total outlines of thought within the corpus. All historical decisions of this kind are regulative. And yet historical research in itself does not tell us what Plato or Aristotle thought. To know that we turn not to a historian but to a philosopher, to one who is willing to follow out the lines of Plato or Aristotle's thinking, to consider seriously the possibility that their thoughts are true, to reconstruct the cosmos which they indicate. Yet philosophers who do this are not 'committed' to being Platonists or Aristotelians: they remain free to see these positions as ultimately seriously defective. But they enter into them before making this negative judgment. The parallel with historical theology is considerable.

Why should biblical theology not be seen in the same way? The similarities are great. As with past theological traditions, historical differences have to be taken into account. One cannot read Calvin as though Luther did not come earlier; one cannot (probably) read Chronicles as though Samuel-Kings did not come earlier. Critical observations about authorship of texts have substantial importance. No scholarly worker in historical theology supposes that the Dionysius the Areopagite who appears in Acts 17 actually wrote the body of mystical theology that was later attributed to him, and while it may be possible to connect the writing of the Fourth Gospel in some way with the original disciple John, every biblical theologian knows that the theology of the New Testament has to be founded on other sorts of supposition than that. Again, no matter how much the continuity and consistency of the tradition is emphasized, no one who works in historical theology disputes that there are theological differences between the different theologians, even when closely associated in time, area or interest: between Augustine, Ambrose and Jerome, for instance, or between the Cappadocian Fathers, or between Luther and Melanchthon. Similarly, the biblical theologian commonly perceives and works from the differences between Pentateuchal strata, or between Isaiah and Jeremiah, or between the different Gospels or their sources.

And, finally and perhaps most important, just as historical theologians read their sources in an evaluative and critical way, so biblical theologians may do. It is quite proper for biblical theologians to judge that a particular passage or a particular theme represents a more central, or higher, or more positive contribution than others do, and conversely to judge that another passage, or theme, or writer, represents an unfortunate turning, a declension or deterioration. As historical theologians may take an emphasis from their sources and develop it into a theme that will be positive and important for modern theology and religious life, so too may biblical theologians. Yet in both cases alike this development of a theme for its modern use must be done in such a way as to retain the accurate description of the ancient reality and not to conceal any differences and departures involved in the modern development of them.

The only objection that I can see to the understanding of biblical theology as continuous with historical theology, and akin to it in insights, methods and aims, is if one says that historical theology is perfectly suitable for the rest of the theological tradition, but the Bible is a special case and does not come under the same rules of approach and method. But is the Bible really a special case? I do not think that it is. There are, however, two or three different arguments which might be advanced to show that the Bible is a special case, and these have to be looked at separately.

1. It may be argued that the contents of the Bible are not theology in the sense that works by Augustine or Schleiermacher are theology. In this, as we shall see, there is some truth. If it is true, it may count in some degree against there being any idea of a biblical theology at all. But *if* we consider favourably the possibility of biblical theology, even only as a hypothesis, then the argument does not

really count against the view that the analogy with historical theology is valid and helpful. For the approach of historical theology is not essentially different from what is done in other branches of the humanities, e.g. in investigating folk-lore, mythology, philosophy or political ideologies. In any case we shall discuss later on how far the contents of the Bible themselves are or are not theology in the proper sense of the word.

2. It may be argued that the function of the Bible within Christianity (let us leave Judaism out of the argument for the moment) is such that the theological tradition is not a parallel. The Bible is said to be supreme norm, *norma normans*; theology is therefore an interpretation of the Bible and the Bible is the criterion for the validity of theological ideas; it is read liturgically in church, while the works of theologians are generally not so read (though exceptions do occur). It provides, or is supposed to provide, the texts for preaching; it is also the centre of personal prayer and devotion. For all these reasons the Bible is a special case. The canon is a symbol of this fact.

And of course the Bible has a different range of functions from the theological traditions. But we are not talking about the functions of the Bible as such. We are talking about the mode by which we may discover and express *the theology* of the Bible. By setting ourselves the task of knowing not just how the Bible functions and is used, but knowing *the theology* of the Bible, we commit ourselves to the same types of investigation and expression that are found in understanding *theology* of the past anywhere else. And historical theology is the dominant mode in which this is done.

In any case it seems to me that though it is conventional to think of the Bible as supremely normative, in a way that sets it on a different level from other instances such as theology, things do not work in this way in the churches as a matter of fact. Though the Bible as a whole is demarcated by the canon, churches do not work liturgically with the Bible as a whole, but with selections. Preaching commonly tells us little about the Bible, and more about the theology of the preacher. And, above all, it often seems that the theology which guides the interpretation of the Bible is thus the operative norm rather than the Bible itself. And this, if we may return to the consideration of Judaism, may be not so dissimilar to the situation in Orthodox Judaism where, it is sometimes said, the Bible itself (or rather the Torah itself) is so elevated as supreme norm that it seems to fade out of sight, the real and effective concern being with the interpretation of it.

3. It may be argued that the post-biblical theological tradition, being largely an interpretation of the Bible, is not continuous with the Bible but is a different sort of thing. The theological tradition may be traced by historical theology, but the same approach cannot be extended into the Bible. This may fit with certain doctrines of scripture which set the Bible in contrast with the theological

tradition. But the modern emphasis on the degree to which the interpretative process goes on within the biblical text, and in the gaps between various portions of it, makes this objection unrealistic today. At one time, at least in some traditions of Christianity, the Bible was seen as a totally unique block of divine revelation, and tradition as a purely human exposition of completely different quality and nature. Today it is almost universally agreed that the Bible itself is a product of tradition. This makes it difficult to suppose that theological tradition within the Bible is wholly different in nature from theological tradition after (and, indeed, before, and in the midst of) the Bible.

I do not insist that the analogy with historical theology must be accepted. I place it here only as a suggestion that may be helpful and that seems to offer a position answering some of the questions that have been raised so far. Some of the suggestions made here will come in for further discussion below. This short chapter is an interlude, providing a possible working position before we go any farther.

This will be a suitable point at which to say something about historical criticism, which has been mentioned briefly several times above. The model which I have presented implies the acceptance of historical criticism, in the sense that one must have some knowledge, or at least some hypothesis, of order, of times, of circumstances and of persons in order to practise historical theology. Theology exists only in the minds of persons, who live by the memories and effects of past persons and past traditions. Consider the emphasis now commonly placed upon the 'presuppositions' of thinkers: but nothing can be done to fulfil this emphasis unless we know what was 'supposed before' they formulated their reactions. Thus, whether or not historical criticism fits well with ecclesial use, or with devotional practice, or with literary appreciation, for the purpose of understanding *the theology* of the Bible historical-critical perceptions seem to be necessary. This is, indeed, the opposite of what has been thought by those who have argued that *for the sake of biblical theology* the role of historical criticism ought to be minimized: on the contrary, whatever the values of historical criticism from other points of view, for the enterprise of biblical theology it is particularly necessary.[2]

It is true that this would seem to imply that, if historical-critical judgments are to change, a change in the biblical theology will have to follow. And I think this is in some degree true. If, for example, it should be thought, with some historians,[3] that the figure of Abraham and his story are phenomena of late post-exilic times, then these would no longer count as an older memory reacted to, as a presupposition for further thought, in a central period like the eighth century. In fact, however, almost all the tradition of modern biblical theology has worked with a moderate historical-critical view: this is true even of those who have included continual disparagement of historical criticism in their work. No substantial work in biblical theology has as yet been produced by scholars who really oppose the historical-critical approach. And, equally, the differences between the Old Testament theologies surveyed in this volume are seldom, if ever, the result of difference on historical-critical questions.

It is quite possible, of course, that attempts will be made to produce a biblical theology on the basis of a 'synchronic' reading, totally ignoring historical questions. In what sense such a work could really be a 'theology' remains a question.

It should be noted that historical criticism, in the sense used here, is not a private professional interest of biblical scholars but enjoys full support from major currents among doctrinal theologians. Central theologians take the value and necessity of historical criticism for granted and – in my opinion rightly – do not consider it any more to be an area of major controversy. As we shall see in a later chapter, so central a scholar as Emil Brunner judged that historical-critical study does no damage to the theological unity of the Bible.[4] To move to more recent times and to quote again my example of H. Berkhof, he quite frequently refers to historical criticism and clearly takes it for granted, nowhere so far as I see treating it as a matter of controversy. He accepts the changes that it has made in theological procedure. 'After the rise of the historical criticism of the Bible, Protestant theologians could no longer start from its demonstrable infallibility' (43). 'The critical study of the Bible has rid us of an exclusivistic and authoritarian use of Gen. 1 in the doctrine of creation' (159, cf. 156). 'The historical-critical investigation of the biblical traditions of creation has made us aware how much these traditions look upon creation as the first of the series of God's redemptive deeds and how they describe it as analogous to it' (166, cf. 167). 'The historical-critical study of the Bible and the hermeneutics based on it has, quantitatively, taken away much information, but qualitatively given back much more' (173). Note the inclusion of 'and the hermeneutics based on it', for there are probably some who might accept historical criticism as a factual entity but would regard with suspicion any hermeneutics based on it.

Again, according to Berkhof, it was the historical-critical study of the Bible that led men like Barth and von Rad to their insight into the convergence of creation and redemption (174). 'We point again to the historical-critical way of reading the Bible and the hermeneutics based on it . . . In the Bible, people in diverse situations and using different concepts articulate what they think of man in the light of the encounter with God. The Yahwist in Gen. 2 has a more "Aristotelian", the Priestly Codex in Gen. 1 a more "Platonic" approach' (181). (I wish he had said more about these Aristotelian and Platonic approaches, which puzzle me somewhat!). In the prophets from Amos to Ezekiel it is a difficult question how far 'the words about a blessed future to come are really from the great prophets of doom' (241). In Amos 'they are likely a later addition'; a paragraph of discussion follows. Coming to the still more controversial matter of the quest of the historical Jesus, Berkhof writes:

> This supposed 'purely historical-scientific' approach was often motivated by the desire to prove that Jesus had not been the Son of God, but only a uniquely gifted and inspiring man. Yet that does not as such justify the church's opposition. If in Christ the Word has become flesh, it should be able to stand the test of historical-critical investigation. Precisely from the standpoint of faith, historical investigation is to be left free (267f.).

On the same theme, 'For reliable information about Jesus we have only the three synoptic gospels to go by, since it is clear that John is far less interested in providing coherent historical information' (269, cf. 279). The results of form criticism in the New Testament are taken for granted (e.g. 272, 275). Or, to go back to an earlier stage and perhaps a more fundamental point:

> All this [here following a section on authority of scripture, 86ff.] does not mean that concepts such as inspiration and the authority of scripture have become meaningless. What has happened is that they have been removed from the sphere of things that are rationally and empirically verifiable. The so-called 'higher criticism' of the Bible was a salutary judgment on the attempt to make God's authority humanly transparent and accessible. The confession of the inspiration of the Bible and the authority that is based on it express the experience of faith that the words of Scripture give genuine guidance, that they mediate an encounter with God. This irreducible experience is based on certain words and passages in the Bible, and it evokes the expectation that eventually it will be enriched and deepened by further words from Scripture. The term 'inspiration' expresses this union of experience and expectation. Unfortunately, it is so closely linked to the inspiration theory of the seventeenth century that its usefulness has become dubious (88).

Thus this comprehensive work of central and traditional theology seems to be quite at home with historical criticism; it accepts it, uses it, and nowhere suggests that it is problematic or dangerous to church or religion.

Naturally, there are further possibilities which have to be borne in mind. There will certainly be doctrinal theologians who are doubtful about historical criticism or hostile towards it. And, on the other hand, it is possible that there are dangers in it that Berkhof did not perceive. Again, it is possible that historical criticism may in recent years have produced more troubling results than were perceptible through the moderate criticism to which Berkhof mainly referred. An example related to the concept 'covenant' will be mentioned shortly. Going farther, some recent studies in the history of Israel have suggested that a large proportion of what appears in the Bible as 'history' is in fact ideological writing from a late time, so that we have no evidence, for example, that the unified kingdom or 'empire' of David or Solomon ever existed. Ideas of this kind, right or wrong, might be likely to make some difference to the discussion of Israel within doctrinal theology. Many such possibilities may have to be considered. It remains the fact that central currents of doctrinal theology in the 1970s, as represented by Berkhof, were happy to take historical criticism for granted as a salutary force in the history and in the present of theology, and did not feel the necessity even to discuss it as a potentially problematic or negative force.

It can also be objected that recent biblical scholarship in itself, quite apart from trends in doctrinal theology, has been moving away from historical criticism and developing other modes in which to work. John Barton, editing *The Cambridge Companion to Biblical Interpretation*, tells us that, when the book was being planned, 'some advisers suggested that there should be no chapter on historical criticism at all, since it was now entirely *passé* (2). Now the question of approaches to biblical study quite other than the historical-critical cannot be discussed here, in detail or in general. The only question for us here is how it is related to biblical theology. The matter of historical criticism was raised as part of the parallel I suggested with historical theology; and since historical theology requires historical criticism of the source, I went on to show how historical criticism, far from being rejected or felt as an obstacle by leading theologians, is warmly welcomed, at least by many. Thus Robert Morgan writes:

> Most Western theologians today continue to insist that since the Bible is a collection (or two) of ancient texts, historical exegesis based on linguistic competence and some understanding of their original contexts remains an indispensable guide to their meanings and provides some control against arbitrary readings.[5]

Such controls are necessary if the texts are ever to guide the life of communities.

As for the numerous new methods and approaches being sought and adopted in biblical scholarship, an obvious feature of many of them is their disinterest in theology. It is, in fact, biblical scholars rather than doctrinal theologians who, coming from various directions, have been anxious to question both the principles and the practice of historical criticism. But from the viewpoint of central theological tradition, one cannot do better than re-echo the words of John Muddiman:

> Unhindered biblical criticism and the continuous tradition of Christian faith need each other, if the truth of scripture is to become available to the church today.[6]

Biblical criticism, in the wide general sense, has become part of the total world-vision, at least of Christianity.

It is not so certain, however, when biblical theologians assert that historical criticism, or 'the historical-critical method', is, or should be, 'the basis' for the theology of Old or New Testament.[7] This seems to me to be questionable from several points of view.

It is, indeed, *a* basis, or has been so, in the sense of a network of relations between parts and strata of the Bible that has been generally assumed as correct. Not that one could not agree with it: of course one could disagree, or challenge it. But if one challenged it, one would have to give some reasons and mount an argument why one would differ from it. Yet in this, very weak, sense of 'basis', quite a number of other things were also bases. The history and geography of Israel are also a basis. So is some knowledge, however slight, of what Egypt and Mesopotamia were like. So is some idea of what constitutes the unity and genre of a text. More important, however, Hebrew grammar is a basis, and so is the Hebrew vocabulary. But vocabulary is theologically useful, not as a mere list of words, but through an understanding of meanings. However, once we talk of 'meanings' of words like the words for God, for 'create', for 'right' or 'justice', we are already moving into something close to theology. Word meanings are not a basis for theology: they already involve us in theology. Historical criticism, understood in the usual sense, cannot therefore be regarded as *the* one essential basis for biblical theology. There would be more sense in taking *semantics* as the one essential basis.

In fact, I do not see how historical criticism, taken in the most customary sense, i.e the identification of sources like J and P, or like Q in the Gospels, or the discussion of dates and of the degree of historical accuracy of documents, can be thought to *lead us to* a biblical theology. It can certainly do something to dismantle an erroneous, non-biblical, theology attached to the same documents. But the actual *construction* of a theology, even of a single stratum like P in the Pentateuch or Q in the Gospels, and much more of a larger block like the Pentateuch of the Old Testament, requires something more, or something other, than this. As we have seen to be the case with historical theology, it requires an ability to enter into the theological process as it took place in the minds of persons of biblical times.

And in this sense – another reason why we should not take historical criticism to be the basis – theology is not something that can or will emerge from historical criticism. On the contrary, historical criticism emerges from theological perception, and not only from that, since purely historical matters come into it as well, though nevertheless primarily so. If we can see a difference between J and P, it is primarily because we can see a common theological insight that runs through a group of texts that we call J, and a different insight that runs through those that we call **P**. No doubt many of the theological perceptions that produced these decisions were crude and primitive; but they had this in common with the older theological views which they overthrew.

Two points remain: one about exegesis, one about exegesis and its relation to historical assertions.

As in historical theology, so in biblical theology, generalizations depend on detailed exegesis of texts. Or perhaps we should state it negatively: the detailed exegesis of texts does not in itself, even cumulatively over many texts, provide the needed generalizations; however, it does operate to test and in some cases to negate generalizations that have been made.

Theology and history cannot be separated. At least in Christian theology, historical affirmations have to be made at many strategic points. It can often be difficult to perceive on which level of history an assertion is intended to apply. Here is a good illustration, which I take again from my honoured exemplar H. Berkhof, at a point where we seem to disagree. He writes (*Christian Faith*, 233):

> The term 'covenant' and what it stands for are rooted in Israel's early history and have, with interruptions, remained characteristic for Israel's faith through the centuries (this contra J. Barr , 'Some Old Testament Aspects', in *Weerwoord*, 1974, 13–19).

The book *Weerwoord*, literally 'A Word Back', was a volume of essays in appreciation and evaluation of the original Dutch edition *Christelijk Geloof* (1973). In that essay I was particularly interested by the place taken by the covenant and the theology of covenant in Berkhof's thinking. The pervasiveness of the covenant concept in his book was strongly marked: something that, I think, no reader would doubt. I went on to say: 'He shows no sign of awareness, unless I am mistaken, that this position might be exegetically contested' (13). I outlined positions – now well known – taken by Kutsch, Fohrer, E. W. Nicholson, and above all by L. Perlitt.

Now when Berkhof writes that 'the term "covenant" and what it stands for are rooted in Israel's early history', he may be meaning one or other of two things. He may mean that the biblical texts *depict* the covenant as rooted in Israel's early history. In that case his assertion is not about that early history, but about the way in which the biblical writers imagined it. Taken in this sense, very likely there would be no question from the side of exegesis. On the other hand, he may mean that the covenant was actually there in the early history of Israel: back in ancient times, let us say in the fourteenth century BCE, and maybe before that, it was an actual, living symbol for the people who lived then. Persons of later times, like the Deuteronomists or Jeremiah, were simply continuing a tradition that had been historically there for most of a millennium. Possibly Berkhof did not distinguish between these things. But recent exegesis forces one to consider them as separate. Perlitt had argued in great detail that covenant theology 'is a late fruit of the Old Testament; it arose with the Deuteronomic movement, and if the earlier prophets said nothing about covenant this was because no such theology then existed'.[8] In the first case, if Berkhof referred only to the *depiction* of early times, probably most exegetes would agree with him. In the second case, if he meant that this covenant emphasis obtained historically from earliest times, then he should have faced the fact that important exegetes denied this, and that he was making a historical assertion which could not be proved from the Old Testament text itself. Of course Perlitt could be opposed, but in fact he was ignored. After this exchange, for years I asked myself: how would Berkhof have answered Perlitt?

The matter makes much difference to our picture of Old Testament theology. On the one hand we have a depiction of ancient Israel as a community guided by the covenant concept, over perhaps fifteen hundred years; on the other hand we have a history in which the covenant concept was developed only at a late stage. The difference is not a learned theological one, but appears in such situations as that of preaching: if one says that Israel lived fifteen centuries on the basis of the covenant, people will generally believe that this is a historical assertion. The covenant was what kept people going. If Perlitt is right, this assertion is false and deceptive. If one wants to argue that Perlitt is wrong, then one has to enter into the exegetical detail with which he worked.

There is an important difference between assertions about the way in which things are depicted and assertions about what is true or is to be believed. Both may be theologically significant, but the difference between them has to be observed.

Detailed exegesis, then, makes a difference to biblical theology, as it ultimately does to doctrinal theology also. But the relation of exegesis to biblical theology also works in another way. The ultimate reason why biblical theology is justified, and indeed unavoidable, is that it is a part of exegesis itself. All exegesis of a limited piece of text ultimately implies some view of the totality of that text, whether that view is expressed or tacit. Biblical theology is a provisional attempt to express that view, taking as the 'totality to be expressed' the Old Testament, or the New, or both together, or a major segment of either (like the Prophets, the Wisdom Literature, the Gospels, etc.). But the totalities demarcated by the biblical canon are not exclusively authoritative, for it is equally necessary to extend the field of view into the environing cultural and religious world (which is itself an object of reference within the canonical books in any case). Beyond this lies a still wider totality of one's world-view and/or general theology.

Not all scholars wish to enter into the fullness of these wider perspectives. They wish to stay within a narrower field of vision, concentrated on a limited text, a limited period of time. A common form of this is the decision to have 'nothing to do with Old Testament theology'. This just means that certain wider perspectives are deliberately not surveyed. If one leaves these aside, then a restriction of exegesis results. If one surveys them, one finds oneself entering into biblical theology.

One should not think, however, as many enthusiasts for biblical theology appear to think, that the more restricted kind of scholarship is invalid, or useless, or ruined through its self-limitation. The 'higher' levels of exegesis are often tempted to disregard, or even to try to stifle, the lower, simply because the latter are, in this sense, 'lower'. This is mistaken. For, as I have argued, quite small decisions of exegesis – for example, of textual criticism – can have their repercussions throughout the structure of biblical and indeed of doctrinal theology.

Finally, then, I would argue that, if one is to speak of a 'basis' upon which biblical theology is built, it would be more correct to think of the basis as a semantic, rather than a historical-critical, one. When we say that *'amar* means 'say' or that *'elohim* means 'God', we are giving only a rough indication, a pointer towards a profound area of texts, words and meanings, involving the comparing and relating of numerous texts, sources and periods that lie beyond the ones that concern us at the moment. The making conscious of these relations is the beginning of biblical theology. But the semantic perception of texts and usages that arose over a wide period of time leads us to a historical approach. The idea of a 'synchronic' approach, now increasingly fashionable, does not weigh against a historical approach but positively requires it. In the case of the Bible we have a historical sequence of levels which, at the time, were synchronic.

# 14

# Opposition to Biblical Theology

From the beginning biblical theology, whether of the Old Testament or of the New or of both, faced several kinds of opposition. We have already discussed the matter of conflict with the history-of-religion approach. Apart from it, we may perhaps classify six types:

(*a*) Opposition from those who think that biblical studies are purely historical and have nothing intrinsically to do with theology;

(*b*) Opposition from those who think that biblical studies do have a theological aspect and are important for theology, but that there is still no basis for a discipline of Old or New Testament theology, no way of achieving results in it, and no value in it for theology anyway;

(*c*) Opposition from those who consider *all* theology to be inadmissible in academic life;

(*d*) Linguistic criticism for its use of biblical language;

(*e*) Opposition from the side of sociological and literary studies;

(*f*) Opposition from theologians who think that all ideas of 'biblical theology' involve a misunderstanding of what theology really is. This case will be discussed separately in the next chapter.

Biblical theologians likewise may be classified according to the various kinds of response they make to this opposition. There seem to be three classes:

(*a*) Those who cannot see *any* sense in *any* sort of criticism of biblical theology and look on it as an outbreak of ignorance or evil intention or both. To them the idea of 'biblical theology' seems to be beyond criticism. This, which we may call the 'sacred cow' school, is well represented by James D. Smart and Brevard Childs, perhaps by others.[1]

(*b*) Those who probably take to heart some of the criticisms and reflect on them in their work but say nothing specific about them. These are doubtless the majority.

(*c*) Those who think that the criticisms are not only important, in the sense that they show what people, competent biblical scholars, are thinking about the subject, but also positively creative, in that a study of them may reveal important clues for the furtherance of the subject and for the avoidance of existing impasses. I hope that I am not the only member of this school, but so far as I know I am the first to approach the subject on paper in this way. I hope to show that important positive leads for future biblical theology have come from voices which have seriously questioned the viability of the subject or have opposed its existence altogether.

We shall look at the various forms of opposition in turn.

(a) *Opposition from those who think that biblical studies are purely historical.* The modern movement in Old Testament theology faced a good deal of opposition from the beginning. The more obvious opposition, and the one that was expected by the biblical theologians, came from those for whom biblical scholarship was necessarily historical and nothing else. James D. Smart, remembering the early days of the American Biblical Theology Movement, burned with resentment at the way in which scholars at the Society of Biblical Literature clapped and cheered the assertion that 'We are all historians'. An excellent expression of this position came from W. A. Irwin:

> We are not theologians, in the narrow sense of that word. Some of our number, it is true, are of such energy and ability that they may span areas impossible for us lesser men; interest and endowment may lead them far in theology. But that is personal choice, it is not the function of the Old Testament scholar, *qua* Old Testament scholar . . . We are first of all historians – a special sort of historian, it is true, but nonetheless historians. The unique feature of our historicizing inheres in the special character of our subject matter that will not long leave us content with mere facts, but impels us to the difficult and dangerous search of meaning in history . . . Yet all this, it is apparent, is only our special extension of the historian's normal responsibility.[2]

Irwin was aware that in all this he represented an ideal that was now considered old-fashioned. 'I stand here closer to the men of fifty years ago,' he wrote. And, he continued,

> They held that the responsibility of the biblical scholar was to find the facts of Israel's life and of the making, interpretation and significance of the Bible; these he should pass on to the professional theologian to be worked up by him into assimilable results for the thought of modern times.

Irwin was not contemptuous of the achievement of Old Testament theologians such as Eichrodt. Their work was excellent in many ways, and a great achievement. However, in all its excellence, to him it simply was not theology: it was 'systematic exegesis'.[3] Thus he referred to 'Bultmann's and van Imschoot's "theologies"', using quotation marks to indicate that he did not consider them to be theologies at all.[4]

Irwin made very clear his view that he himself, *qua* biblical scholar, was a historian. He thought that this was true for all biblical scholars. But his arguments did not depend on this role as a historian alone. He noted other relevant factors. One of these was the denominational aspect: how could Old Testament theology, if it was defined as such, fail to exclude Jewish scholars, who were in fact every bit as competent as Christian ones? He also perceived, though less clearly, the degree to which 'Old Testament theology', at any rate as it was in his time, stood closer to homiletics than to actual theology.

Irwin, then, well represents one of the fairly strong and clear positions in the matter. Biblical scholars are by profession historians. Theology is done by other people. They may meet and discuss occasionally, but this is accidental. It would be good if theologians paid attention to the historical results of biblical scholars, but that is entirely their business: if they do not do so, then so be it. If biblical scholars try to do Old (or New) Testament theology they are deceiving themselves: either they are doing a mixed-up kind of historical exegesis, or they are indulging in dogmatics and/or homiletics.

Here and there, everywhere, there were some few scholars who took this line: everyone knew of some Old Testament specialist whose total judgment of the subject was contained in the six simple words 'There is no Old Testament theology'. Few, or more assuredly none, of those who said this knew that they were repeating the exact words of Emil Brunner (on which see below). Anyway, by the 1950s and before that they were falling out of fashion, and those like Irwin knew it. People might cheer at the SBL meetings when it was said that all biblical scholars were historians and nothing else, but of course most of them were nothing of the sort. The *persona* of the historian might be what they donned for the occasion of such meetings, but inwardly a very large proportion of the Christian scholars lived and thought under strong dogmatic and theological influence. They were uneasy about the fate of religion if the Bible did not seriously enter into theology and if professional exegesis could offer nothing but historical assessment. They were ready to slide in large numbers into the Biblical Theology Movement, then rising to near the peak of its influence. Old Testament and New Testament theology were a growing subject, deeply interesting to many, and seemed to be a main growing edge in the whole field of Bible and theology taken together. At the time, arguments like those of Irwin actually tended to stimulate people in the opposite direction and made them more favourable to biblical theology.

In fact, Irwin's arguments, and those of others like him, had an important effect on the subject – not an effect which they themselves had considered. These arguments only strengthened the belief of many biblical theologians that it was *history*, the historical component in biblical study, that was their real enemy. If people disagreed with Old Testament theology, it seemed, it was because they insisted on a purely historical interpretation of the texts. By giving this kind of impression, people like Irwin made easier the task of biblical theologians in promoting their own perspective. On the one hand it provided them with what seemed to them an easy and successful argument: historians have their presuppositions, and are biased too![5] – an argument which may well be true about historians, but does not in the slightest provide a justification for biblical theology. On the other hand it encouraged the kind of strong anti-historical sentiment that sometimes came to expression within biblical theology. Most of all, it deceived biblical theologians into a quite false sense of security about their enterprise. Having, as they rightly or wrongly thought, arguments that would easily overcome those of Irwin, they went on to act as if there were no other, or more powerful, arguments that would undermine their enterprise. This false sense of security is easy to demonstrate: in all the vast literature of biblical theology in this century, one finds little attempt, among the enthusiasts, for that movement to take seriously the body of arguments that could be marshalled against it.

(*b*) *Opposition from those who think that biblical studies did have a theological aspect and are important for theology, but that there is still no basis for a discipline of Old or New Testament theology.* In fact, as time went on, it became clear that dissatisfaction with Old Testament theology had other causes than a purely historical or historical-critical orientation. There were many people who were deeply concerned for the theological role of the Bible and who might have sympathized with the general aims and ideals of biblical theology, but who came to be doubtful of its prospects.

Some were affected by my own demonstration of the linguistic and logico-linguistic defects which were found in the movement (though I never maintained that these defects were necessarily intrinsic to the movement or that their existence invalidated its entire programme). The wild assertions and bizarre interpretations of words found in a work like G. A. F. Knight's *A Christian Theology of the Old Testament* seemed to damage the credibility of the entire movement. Others were perplexed by the variety of different manifestations of Old Testament theology and its apparent failure to get anywhere near a consensus or even an agreed method or starting-point – the quadrilateral mutual criticisms of Köhler, Eichrodt, von Rad and Vriezen hardly strengthened the status of the subject! There seemed to be too many contradictions in the plan. In particular, the idea of a systematic or comprehensive presentation seemed to conflict with the corresponding and equally necessary requirement that the presentation must be selective – since obviously no one could get *everything* into any presentation, under any scheme at all.

Moreover, even granted that a comprehensive theology of the entire Old (or New) Testament could be constructed, there remained the question to what degree this could be helpful for the exegesis of the individual passage. The teacher and his student, let us suppose, are struggling with an obscure verse in Habakkuk or Nahum. They cannot work out what it means. Suppose they decide to turn to the current Theologies of the Old Testament: how can these large volumes, however well composed, deal with the problems? They may, perhaps, not mention the verse in question at all. They will certainly have sections about prophets, about eschatology, and so on. They may well have a section that explains what was usually thought or said by late prophets, of roughly the exilic period, about a variety of subjects. But how can the student be sure that the content of this particular verse conforms with what the Theology declares to be usual for prophets of the time? Perhaps it is an aberrant verse, which says exactly what, according to the Theology, prophets of this time should not have said! How can a complicated exposition of the general theology of the whole provide detailed guidance for dealing with the individual part? To this, it seems, no biblical theology has been able to give an answer unless it appealed to what were declared to be universal tendencies of human thought, which therefore *must* have been definitive in every individual passage. The consequent *aporia* is difficult to escape.

Thus the most common objection to Old Testament theology, which I have not seen much in print but have certainly heard from many, was that the thing just could not be done: the production of anything like a final or truly valid Old Testament Theology was not possible.

So we find a scholar like Whybray, a scholar of theological sensitivity and far from a 'pure historian',[6] totally unable to believe that there is, can be or should be any such discipline as Old Testament theology. By no means does he think that the Old Testament is irrelevant to Christian theology. But the Old Testament 'can only be properly understood if it is studied independently. Only in this way can it be used in the service of Christian theology'.[7]

This means, in his opinion, that the connection with the New Testament should be left aside as irrelevant and distorting. It is quite right, however, Whybray continues, to consider the ways in which the Old Testament *as a whole* should be understood and evaluated. But in what sense is the Old Testament 'a whole' in any case? Because it comprises 'the only extant literary products of a particular stage in the development of a particular national religion'. These products are 'the primary evidence for a single phenomenon: the religion of Israel in its earliest stage'. This can be investigated either historically or structurally. The historical approach actually provides *more comprehensive* information about the religion than Old Testament theologies have done[8] – these latter, for instance, have tended to fail to deal with the Wisdom literature, although this literature, in Whybray's opinion, includes books like Job and Qoheleth, that come closer than any other to being really 'theological', 'on the very rational grounds that they are entirely devoted to serious discussion about God and man and the relationship between them'. The books commonly taken as particularly 'theological', like Deuteronomy and Deutero-Isaiah, may not be a good key to the characteristic beliefs of a people, for which it is misleading to turn to the theologians anyway. The structural approach, on the other hand, is unable to provide an answer to the problem of the 'centre' of the religion, because the religion was in fact a mixture: a mixture between earlier and later stages, but also a mixture between contrasting elements at any one stage. There was in fact no one 'centre', as Morenz had shown for Egyptian religion[9] and – a rather surprising example – Rowley in his *The Faith of Israel* had shown for Israel. These two, dealing with very different materials, 'demonstrate how a religion can constitute a real unity and yet comprise a number of quite distinct and not necessarily logically connected dominant features'.[10]

It is a minor point, however, whether Whybray has been right in citing Rowley as an example of what he thinks ought to be done. What he seems to mean is that Hebrew religion can be described either historically or structurally, but either way the distinctness of features and their lack of logical coherence is supreme. Therefore, the implication seems to be, an Old Testament theology is impossible and, even if apparently achieved, would be valueless. The argument has some idiosyncratic features, but it gives expression to a group of feelings that are much more widespread. Published in 1987, it is clear evidence that Old Testament theology has continued to have difficulty in proving its viability and its usefulness, even for theology itself.

It is clear, then, that a current of seriously argued opposition to the entire idea of Old Testament theology continued to exist in biblical scholarship. A person like Whybray had certainly heard all the arguments in favour of Old Testament theology and was familiar with them, but they had failed to carry conviction. Looking back on it late in a distinguished career, his only feeling was that the whole thing was useless: 'a non-existent beast'. And Whybray, though certainly a critical scholar, could not really be classified as motivated primarily by 'historical-critical' impulses. On the contrary, his *Introduction to the Pentateuch* is a rather thorough repudiation of traditional source criticism, and in this respect comes closer to the synchronic approach favoured in canonical theology. His familiar work, say on the Davidic succession narrative or on the book of Proverbs, has a distinctly theological flavour. He is not against theology as such. It may be useful, he concedes, to speak of particular 'theologies' within the Old Testament, such as the theology of the Deuteronomists or of Deutero-Isaiah. 'But taken as a whole the Old Testament has no central figure, nor is it given coherence by an identifiable creed.'[11]

Whybray, then, we may well believe, spoke for many others. He was, after all, willing to devote a full academic lecture, indeed his Presidential Address to the

Society for Old Testament Study, to the subject. Most of those who thought the same way probably kept quiet about it, or might talk about it conversationally, but would not bother to put together a serious academic argument on the matter. Among serious Old Testament scholars, then, significant doubts and negative feelings about the entire enterprise of Old Testament theology have continued to exist.

Another example of the same kind is furnished by the thoughts of a friend and colleague of mine over a year or two. In his inaugural lecture as Professor of *Biblical Theology* at Princeton Theological Seminary, J. Christiaan Beker expressed doubts about the 'imperialism' and other defects of biblical theology, thoughts which were published in *Theology Today* and in a somewhat different form in *Interpretation*.[12] He also joined with colleagues in writing a composite volume, *Commitment without Ideology*, which followed up the same themes and contained some of the same material.[13] The venture aroused a wrathful comment from James D. Smart,[14] not surprisingly, for, according to Smart, Beker announced his 'complete disillusionment with biblical theology' and 'advocated its abandonment'. Whether these expressions are accurate or not, the main argument seems to be that biblical theology really depends on doctrinal theology (Beker, in Batson et al., 23f.), and that it formulates the biblical material into the concepts and categories of theology (Beker cites as examples 'kerygma', 'eschatology', 'the Word' and so on).[15] These concepts are abstract and remote from experience. Biblical theology, therefore, according to Beker, tends to *remove* the student from any live contact with the Bible and make him or her into a manipulator of concepts. Beker thus supports 'a return to biblical religion' (so the title on p. 31) and the centrality of experience. Or, to sum it up in the terms of the book's title, the Bible should call us to 'commitment', which is based on, or leads to, experience, but biblical theology is rather *ideology*:

> One inescapably develops a conceptual system which is unresponsive to new experiences . . . Ideology becomes the standard of truth to which experience must conform. One's ideology, his most deeply held truth and concern, thus becomes his greatest oppressor.

'Commitment without ideology' means a commitment that is not a commitment to any *thing*. It is not defined by its object – whether a doctrine, a person (either God or Jesus), or an ethical principle. 'Instead of being committed to some *thing*, the Christian is challenged by Jesus to be committed to growth in a particular direction, outward toward others; and, moreover, to expression of this growth in responsible action' (12f.).

Smart, who objects to this proposal, as he does to most others, does not produce any clear ground against it. The proposal is certainly not very clear, and it is not very clear how it would work out in practice. There may well be a weakness in the appeal made by Beker and his colleagues to the phenomenology of Merleau-Ponty, but it is not clear whether Smart objected to this philosopher in particular or to any philosophical approach whatever. He cannot understand how theology can work without 'concepts'. Smart's comment that the New Testament tells us little about the 'experiences' of the first Christians with Jesus is no more than a common neo-orthodox sneer and should be ignored. The fact is, as already mentioned, that Smart was indignant at *any* sort of doubt or question raised against biblical theology.

It seems to me that the sort of opposition raised by Beker is quite serious and probably has much wider support within the religious use of the Bible than is generally perceived. That biblical theology should turn out to be a rather technical and scholastic operation, busy with its array of concepts and categories, is a real possibility and a real danger. That it has already at times fallen victim to such dangers seems to me to be obvious. Only the sort of critical surveillance of its work that Beker represents can obviate such defects. That a theology, even a true theology, and this including a biblical theology, can become an oppressive ideology to those who hold it seems to me also an evident fact of experience.

Actually, and contrary to the hostile forebodings of Smart, Beker's rather doubting and critical starting point proved to be the basis for a very substantial advance in biblical theology. Thus P. D. Miller, Jr, certainly a theologically sensitive judge, writing in 1995, speaks of Beker's *Paul the Apostle. The Triumph of God in Life and Thought* (1980) as 'the major treatment of Paul in this generation'.[16] A series of colleagues and former pupils joined in celebrating his powerful influence, precisely as a biblical theologian and nothing else.[17] A volume dedicated as a Festschrift to him in 1995, though uneven in quality, as such volumes normally are, is one of the best collections of essays on aspects of biblical theology ever to be published in the United States.[18]

Miller correctly writes: [One thing that stands out in Beker's inaugural address of 1968] 'is his intensely critical stance toward a discipline that is essentially constructive and to which he has contributed substantively . . . he was highly conscious of the precarious position in which, as a biblical theologian, he found himself'.[19] This is in exact agreement with my own position. I had already adopted the word 'precarious' as a key expression for this book before I read Miller's article. The possibility of biblical theology remains, even for its own practitioners, a very precarious thing – even if we do not quite agree with Beker in the form of his critical expressions. Nothing is achieved by expressions of undying commitment to biblical theology or enthusiasm for it. It is those who look critically at it who can hope to make some progress in it.

For another position which opposed Old Testament theology, and from an earlier time, we may go back to a short but powerfully-argued essay by the Swedish scholar Rafael Gyllenberg, published in 1938 and thus in the earlier days of this century's work on the subject. Gyllenberg's essay is in a rather inaccessible source and is not well known, but he made his meaning clear in the lapidary title 'The Impossibility of a Theology of the Old Testament' (*Die Unmöglichkeit einer Theologie des Alten Testaments*).

Gyllenberg recognized the excellent values in the then recent Old Testament Theologies of Sellin, Eichrodt and Köhler: they were systematic treatments of the material, meaningful and indispensable, but 'biblical theology of the Old Testament' they were not! If one is to talk of biblical theology, one must take the New Testament as a starting point. There cannot be an Old Testament *theology*, because the isolated Old Testament, without the New, is not a Word of God for us or to us. Old Testament study does indeed have to occupy itself with this 'isolated' Old Testament. It is and remains linguistics, archaeology, history, literary history, history of religion. But it is not theology. Precisely within this limitation, i.e. in *not* being theology, it is the basis *for* theology. Paradoxically, it is in the theological exegesis of the *New* Testament that the theological interpretation of the Old has its assured place – but only there. If there is a 'message about Christ' in the Old Testament, it is only in the New that it is to be found, never in the Old taken for itself, and this connection of the Old Testament with Christ belongs entirely to New Testament theology. 'There is an Old Testament theology only as an integrating part of New Testament theology' (67).[20] Christ cannot be dragged into the Old Testament, nor can he be read out of it, for he was never there within it. Nor can there be a biblical theology to which the Old Testament belongs as a part, for the 'biblical' theology is the theology of the New Testament. Thus, far from depending on the separation of the two disciplines of Old and New Testament studies, Gyllenberg regards their separation as a misfortune. The problem of the Old Testament arises, he says, in large measure from the parallelism of the relevant professorial chairs and from the mistaken assumption that the material of the two possessed similarity and parallelism. The two forms of exegesis should be seen as one, and then it would be seen how their respective objects interrelate, both historically and in subject-matter. As I understand this, the final statement of his article, he means that to see the two fields as one would demonstrate the deep differences existing between them and the fact that the Old Testament had a 'theology' only when it was taken as part of New Testament theology.[21]

Gyllenberg's conception is subtle and interesting, but we do not have to decide at this point whether it is right or wrong. For our purpose at this moment, the interesting thing is that it is an entirely theological conception: it is purely on theological grounds that he argues against any idea of an Old Testament theology. The idea that Old Testament theology is to be rejected on grounds of history, or because of the history of religion, or because of the variety of conceptions within the Old Testament, or because historical criticism makes it impossible – none of these arguments are even considered in his article. His general theological conception, his emphasis on Christ as the centre of theological integration, his mode of perceiving the unity of scripture, all these, and no other factors, lead him to deny the possibility and the value of any Old Testament theology.

(*c*) *A more 'secularist' criticism.* A strong criticism of biblical theology from a somewhat different direction is expressed by Philip R. Davies in his book *Whose Bible is it Anyway?*. His argument includes criticism both from the historical side and from the history of religion, but its particular emphasis lies in its opposition to *theology* itself, and theology of any kind, as part of an academic subject. Theology is a 'confessional' activity, and work done in Old Testament theology, as he sees it, is ultimately work directed towards the support of Christianity and the church. Such work may have some significance within the church community, but should be done there, and has no place within 'the academy'. If done within the academic world, it means the 'privileging' of Christian religion and interpretation. True academic study should be done within 'Biblical Studies', which has no religious affiliation or commitment.

Davies' argument at this point is not directed in the first place against biblical theology or Old Testament theology; rather, it is directed against the (possibly closely-related) claim that biblical studies as such ought to be primarily 'theological'. Thus it takes as starting examples the thinking of Francis Watson, whose book *Text, Church and World* carries on its dust-jacket the challenging words 'Should biblical studies continue to exclude theological concerns from its agenda?', and the Introduction of Childs. But these, at least the latter, are closely related, for Childs' *Introduction* is intended to lead on into a biblical theology, and the concept of biblical theology implied requires that it should be a church-related and purely Christian activity.[22]

Davies does address the question 'What is Biblical Theology?' in a brief Appendix (76–80). In a few paragraphs he makes the points:

1. He cannot see how the necessary blend of 'historical and systematic ingredients' can be attained. Mere description does not yield a theology; any attempt at a systematic approach must lead to evaluation, which can only serve the Christian religion.

2. 'How does one judge which is a better and which a worse Old Testament theology?' There follows a cheaply contemptuous account of the ways in which theologies have been organized 'by dividing the drawer into compartments'. 'One fits in everything possible. What doesn't fit has to be ignored or glossed. The winner is the one with the least left over and the neatest drawer.' And, in the end, 'What has been shown? What learnt?'

3. 'Old Testament theology' is not a history of Israelite religion, nor is it 'the

theology of any religion that ever existed historically'. It is 'not a theology that any modern Christian is expected to adopt'. It is 'a totally *academic* exercise (in the idiomatic as well as the literal sense) yet paradoxically one which, unlike biblical studies, or Christian theology, offers little or no scope for a non-confessional discourse'.

4. Finally, he suggests that 'what might correspond to "biblical theology"' within biblical studies [as this term is understood by him] is 'what is contained in the succeeding pages of this book' (80). They are studies of 'the characterization of the deity', of the way in which 'the power of the deity was invoked to explain and control economic inequality' and of the way in which 'what is seen as a history run wild is mythically presented as the death of an old god and the birth of a new generation'. These studies are not 'systematic', nor were the authors of the literature themselves 'systematic'. 'They are simply instances of the way in which texts that deal with metaphysics, society, ethics and history in terms of myth, that is, in terms of stories about gods, can engage a reader whose own social world finds no place for these myths (he has others).' There follow four essays on Adam and Eve, on Abraham, on the Psalms, and on Daniel. From these one can gain some impression of what the 'biblical theology' of 'biblical studies' as envisaged by Davies would be like.

Davies' remarks about biblical theology are brief, and have little contact with many aspects of the past discussion. It is not clear how he would react to some of the other conceptions of biblical theology which have been discussed. His thinking will be cited in one or two other connections at a later point.

*(d) Linguistic criticism for its use of biblical language.* Here I must restate something of the effects which my own work on the semantics of biblical language were intended to have. As is clear, the faults in the use of linguistic evidence which I detected and criticized were for the most part located in 'biblical theology' as it was practised at that time, and I said so. And the effects of these criticisms on the Biblical Theology Movement of the time were seriously damaging. Thus Brevard Childs in his survey of the movement kindly wrote:

> Suddenly an attack was launched which struck with such incisive and devastating criticism that the defences appeared like a Maginot Line facing a new form of blitzkrieg . . . Barr's major point was that biblical theology had been guilty of a fundamentally erroneous approach to the semantics of language . . . In reflecting on the effect of Barr's book, one cannot help being impressed with the success of his attack. Seldom has one book brought down so much superstructure with such effectiveness. Barr's argument seemed to most English scholars and a majority of Americans to be fully convincing . . . Even among those biblical theologians who remained unconvinced, there was

agreement that the emphasis of the Biblical Theology Movement on a distinctive mentality could never be carried on without a major revision.[23]

Biblical theology was the area in which these misuses had developed and flourished, and it was the fault of biblical theology that its pressures and ambitions had allowed this to happen. Certain aspects of traditional biblical theology as then practised – such as the Hebrew-Greek contrast when applied with the parallelism of language and mentality – required to be severely rethought, if not totally discarded.

It should be added that, though these misuses of linguistic evidence were welcomed and developed within biblical theology, they did not necessarily originate there. Thus in my *Semantics* I called attention at several places to faulty arguments from Hebrew usage made by Pedersen in his *Israel*; and, as pointed out above, Pedersen, though he shared much of its 'holistic' values and its coolness towards historical criticism, was himself, so far as I know, remote from biblical theology and gave no thought to it. For the same reason, however, I doubt whether Pedersen's work was a very large influence on the rise of biblical theology – partly because, 'holistic' as it might be, its orientation was much more towards the history of religion. Incidentally, in spite of the examples from his work that I criticized, I thought then, and still think now, that his *Israel* was one of the great and seminal works of biblical scholarship in the twentieth century. I used to tell my students that, if they could read only one book on the Old Testament, this was the one they should choose. (Few, probably, took the advice: the book was for a long time expensive, and difficult to obtain.)

Similarly, there were large areas within biblical theology, as defined in this present book, which were not necessarily affected by my arguments of that time. Thus I did not level any substantial criticisms against the main arguments of the major Old Testament Theologies such as those of Eichrodt or Vriezen (von Rad's Theology had scarcely appeared at the time of my writing – German 1957 and 1960, ET 1962 and 1965 – and I did not take it into consideration).[24] Some examples were drawn from the Theology of E. Jacob, but these were occasional slips and I had no idea of suggesting that they were such as to invalidate his entire general approach.[25] On the contrary, I honoured Jacob and highly appreciated his work, and was delighted to have the honour of being his colleague as Visiting Professor in Strasbourg in 1975–76.[26] Certainly there were some examples of the same problems in other major products of Old Testament theology, for example in the magisterial work of von Rad, but I never said or thought that these problems were of such magnitude that they alone could damage or discredit the general achievement of such a work.[27]

Thus when Joseph Bourke in a fine discussion in 1963 wrote,

It is, in fact, strikingly apparent that Old Testament theology, with its far greater emphasis on the event, the reality and the unit of tradition as distinct from the individual 'key word', has remained relatively immune to the exaggerations and distortions which Professor Barr so trenchantly attacks. This is particularly evident in the case of W. Eichrodt's *Theologie des Alten Testaments*,[28]

what he expresses is exactly what I myself thought at the time.

The major aims of the then Old Testament Theologies, namely those of stating a comprehensive theology of the Old Testament and indicating its connection with the New, seemed to me to be valid and proper, and not to depend upon the linguistic errors which had unfortunately accompanied other manifestations of biblical theology. Perhaps this was an over-optimistic assessment; but anyway it is what was in my mind at the time.[29]

I did, however, see the linguistic mistakes as an indication of the importance of the distinction between dogmatic theology and biblical scholarship. On the one hand the biblical languages had been used (or misused) as an instrument by which dogmaticians – whose actual knowledge of the biblical languages and of linguistics was slight – could nevertheless enter into the realm of exegesis and pretend to a 'proof' of novel dogmatic ideas through word studies, etymologies, and other tricks with words. T. F. Torrance was the outstanding example.[30] On the other hand biblical theology of the same kind seemed to me to be a mode in which biblical scholars – whose actual ability in systematic theology might be limited – could appear to be 'proving' doctrinal positions through manoeuvres with words rather than exegesis of texts. The moral of this seemed to be that biblical theology, as a sort of intermediate zone, was a danger zone, likely to produce confusion, and that it would be better to accept that a greater separation between the two would be more salutary.

Well-meaning people often argue that the work of theology and the work of exegesis should be made to overlap or to coalesce, as much as possible. I am not sure that this is right, and I can offer definitive proof with a quotation from Karl Barth:

> It is to be feared that in a dogmatics which itself tries to master the task of exegesis, or in an exegesis which itself tries to assume the functions of dogmatics, both theological tasks will in their own way necessarily suffer.[31]

At that time, 1961, to a very large extent I still accepted the framework of Barthian theology – which, as we have seen, was one of the stimuli leading to the rise of the modern Biblical Theology Movement. But it seemed to me that the essential Barthian positions, which were entirely on the dogmatic level, could be safeguarded only if they were kept apart from the dubious or even rubbishy pseudo-exegetical, linguistic or historical arguments which had been used to prop them up. Thus the semantic argument led me to feel more doubtful about any hope that a level of biblical theology could or should exist as a support for dogmatic theology. This view, it may be added, was probably in agreement with the major theologians like Barth and Brunner themselves, as will be seen below. Believing as I then did that the main thrust of dialectical theology was right and valid, I had come to think that its rightness and validity were better maintained *without* the apparent but deceptive support of biblical theology. Believing that biblical theology was an important area of study and investigation, I became sure that it was corrupted and made dishonest when it was used as a tool for the sustenance of a particular dogmatic position. And, sharing the hostility of dialectical theology towards apologetics, I came to think that much of the exegetical activity within biblical theology was an essentially apologetic activity and deserved the same criticisms as a rational, historical or scientific apologetic. Another aspect was this: it was the linguistic argumentation of biblical theology – say in the classic Biblical Theology Movement period as described by Childs – that gave it the air of being a sophisticated, scientific endeavour built upon irrefutable evidence. It was not a matter, it seemed, of mere opinion or personal theological preference: it was founded on deeply-laid strata of evidence, and thus depended on scholarly sophistication not only equal to that of traditional critical scholarship but far superior to it in subtlety and pro-fundity.[32] The revelation that all this was false, and that the linguistic/semantic arguments had been ignorant and deeply misconceived, could not but damage the entire credibility of biblical theology. Once its linguistic methods were exposed as dubious or worse, it looked as if it might once again be a matter of mere opinion or personal theological preference.

There were also other aspects in which I expressed doubt or negativity towards biblical theology; these will be mentioned elsewhere. But I have never in fact thought or uttered some of the negative expressions I have found ascribed to me: e.g. when John McKenzie thought that I would be displeased with him because he had written a Theology;[33] or when my late friend Moshe Goshen-Gottstein wrote that I felt 'that one should stop writing textbooks on theology';[34] nor did I ever think most of the things that are ascribed to me by another late friend, Gerhard Hasel, in his widely-used survey *Old Testament Theology: Basic Issues in the Current Debate*, 94–8: almost everything he says in these pages is wrong.[35] In contrast to such judgments I might point to the article 'Biblical Theology', written in my mid-career for the Supplementary Volume of *IDB* and published in 1976, which I consider to be a moderate, balanced and sympathetic account of the subject, and one obviously written by one who lived within the world of biblical theology. Nor, I think, would I have been asked to write the article 'Biblische Theologie' for the authoritative encyclopaedic work *Evangelisches Kirchenlexikon* (it appeared in Vol. 1, 1985, cols. 488–94) if I had been a fanatical opponent of the subject as portrayed by Francis Watson in his *Text and Truth*, 18–26 and *passim*. Nor would I have ended that article with the sentence:

> The field of operation of biblical theology remains lively, and promises many interesting advances in the coming years.

One further point in retrospect may be useful. In *The Semantics of Biblical Language* I *assumed* normal exegetical procedure. I was sometimes asked why I did not outline a 'new method' that would emerge from my work. What was necessary, as I saw it, was not a new method, but a correction of *aberrations* which had crept unnoticed into existing method. I had confidence in exegetical scholarship, and this was right, as was made clear by the almost universal acceptance of my arguments after a short time of hesitation. People *knew*, for example, that etymologies did not tell you what words meant in their present usage: all they required was that this should be pointed out to them in relation to examples of what was currently being done. I thought, and still think, the same not only about linguistics but about biblical theology in general. The whole thing has been a vastly creative undertaking, without which biblical scholarship would have been very incomplete; but it has had its aberrations too.

*(e) Opposition from sociological and literary approaches.* A more recent opposition to biblical theology has come from Norman Gottwald, a deeply committed representative of the sociological approach to the Bible. Sociological approaches have become very influential since the 1970s and, as we have seen, John J. Collins thought them to be prospering in recent times to a much higher degree than the discipline of biblical theology. Nor is it to be supposed that the sociological approach is necessarily hostile to the latter: on the contrary, we may note approaches such as those of Theissen in Germany or of Meeks in the United States which link sociology creatively with interests of biblical theology.[36] There do exist, on the other hand, sociological approaches which stand very consciously in contrast with the ideals of biblical theology. The most obvious representative of this position is Norman Gottwald.

Gottwald, favouring a Marxist type of analysis, considers the 'reality' of ancient Israel, as of any society, to have the form of relations of social power and economic production. Theologies are ideal constructions, thrown up by the underlying social realities, and are epiphenomena which disguise these realities. To get at the real truth of the Bible, therefore, one has to discover the social realities. The modern attempt to emphasize a 'biblical theology' is an idealistic structure of thoughts with no social reality and only joins in obscuring what was really going on in biblical times.

Gottwald's approach is associated particularly with the familiar problem of the origin of Israel and the mode of its 'conquest' or possession of its land. As against the biblical picture of a unitary military invasion under Joshua, Gottwald, like many other scholars, supports a view of events more like an internal revolution, where a class of dispossessed persons succeeds in taking over control from a 'privileged but dysfunctional' upper class. His approach to understanding the Old Testament claims to be a sociological one throughout. Biblical theology is thus to be condemned as an obfuscation of the reality of ancient Israel. The connections that it sees are fictional, illusory and unreal. Only a penetration into socio-economic realities is meaningful. 'The good intentions of biblical theology were thwarted at every turn by its failure to treat the religion of Israel as a social phenomenon.'[37] 'Only a sociological approach to the notion of the chosen people can give it credibility and rescue it from absurdity. Other approaches, however ingenious, lose their way in mystifications, invoking idealist and supernatural notions of divine favouritism toward one people for no discoverable reason or else appealing to ethical or metaphysical attributes possessed by a superior gifted people. The end result of such non-sociological interpretations of "chosen people" is either irrelevant supernaturalism or exclusivist racism, or both together . . . Israel was an egalitarian social system in the midst of stratified societies, a system which congealed diverse peoples and functioned viably in the Canaanite highlands for at least two centuries.'[38] To conclude, 'it is this persistent mutant social base to Israelite religious praxis and ideology, deeply rooted in a movement for equality, that preserves the instincts biblical theology was groping to express while simultaneously freeing us from the mystifying idealist and supernatural dregs of "Biblical Theology"'.[39]

As has been said, it is not to be thought that all sociological work on the Old Testament is as opposed to biblical-theological work as that of Gottwald is. Gottwald, however, has directed his arguments particularly against the biblical-theological interests of Childs, and conversely Childs has been highly critical of sociological approaches.[40] It is not clear that he necessarily rejects *every* conceivable sociological approach, but he probably comes near to this, for in his *Biblical Theology* he sternly rejects almost every sociological approach that he mentions.[41] And it is likely that, even where sociological approaches are not as hostile to biblical theology as those of Gottwald, the general tendency of sociological interest has been to direct many minds into an avenue of thought very different from that of the typical biblical theology.

The only aspect of this that I would mention here is the following. If biblical theology can be criticized for being remote from social reality, one cannot but believe that the same is true of the sociological theories and explanations put forward by Gottwald. His idea of Israel as a primitive economic democracy, struggling against a sort of feudalist-capitalist Canaanite society, seems to be a wish-fulfilment dream generated by his own unmistakeable egalitarian and liberationist values. Equally unreal is the position of Childs, who in his stern rejection of every sociological consideration only succeeds in providing some partial but substantial justification for Gottwald's opposition. I shall say no more about this for the present, but may return to it later.[42] For the present I simply register the fact that sociological approaches may sometimes, in the minds of some, be a factor discouraging interest in biblical theology. It is equally likely, on the other hand, that sociological approaches may be of major positive value to biblical theology. As has been noted above, the attempt to make an absolute distinction between biblical theology and the history of Israelite religion should be abandoned, and the two should be seen as overlapping and complementing one another; the history of religion – and indeed general exegesis of texts – cannot operate without a sociological dimension, as Albertz particularly has indicated.

Similar difficulties may arise as a result of the growing interest in 'literary' approaches to the Bible. The modern movement of biblical theology seemed at times to have something in common with literary approaches such as the 'New Criticism' and to derive some support from such modes of understanding.[43] This fitted particularly with the reaction of much biblical theology against the historical approach to the Bible. Texts should be studied as they are, not through an historical investigation into the mode in which they came into existence. They should be studied as a whole and not as a composite made out of earlier sources, even if such sources can be identified, which is usually hypothetical and uncertain. Thus David Ford, commending the mode of Barth's exegesis, compares it with the modes of literary understanding displayed by Auerbach, by Helen Gardner and by Hans Frei.[44] Wimsatt's 'The Intentional Fallacy' was eagerly seized upon because it was supposed to undermine the emphasis on authorial meaning believed to be basic to traditional biblical criticism.[45] Fashions of literary appreciation seemed to support the holistic and canonical tendencies of biblical theology. But only to a degree. These literary tendencies were not founded on a desire to support biblical theology. On the contrary, their tendency, it soon emerged, was in the opposite direction. Literary scholars, far from supporting the theological use of the Bible, were interested in taking the Bible over as a basically literary body of material. It could be and should be read and understood 'as literature', and the doing of this, it often appeared, was something quite independent of what synagogues, churches or theologians might think or desire. If Frank Kermode enjoys thinking of the Bible as a 'Canon', his motives and interests are quite different from those with which Brevard Childs thinks of it as a canon.[46] Thus Childs notes in his *Biblical Theology*, I think rightly from his point of view, that at an earlier stage, e.g. when he wrote his introduction to the Old Testament, he had looked with favour on the literary taste for 'narrative theology' as a holistic and non-historical mode but had later changed his mind:

> The major antagonist to serious theological reflection on the Bible [then] appeared to be from the diachronic legacy of nineteenth-century historical criticism. Consequently I greeted largely as an ally the growing twentieth-century appeal to narrative theology as at least a move toward recovering a holistic reading of the Bible. After all, was not Karl Barth considered a great narrative theologian by some? More recently, it has become increasingly evident that narrative theology, as often practised, can also propagate a fully secular, non-theological reading of the Bible. The threat lies in divorcing the Bible when seen as literature from its theological reality to which scripture bears witness . . . The effect is to render the biblical text mute for theology (722–3).

Quite so. A pity, however, that this awareness had not dawned somewhat earlier, for then it might have mitigated the anti-historical sentiment that, even in the *Biblical Theology*, still remains by far the dominant note of his view of biblical scholarship.

(*f*) *Conclusion.* All the above are various ways, doubtless unequal in their importance, in which opposition to the idea of biblical theology has been expressed. There remains, however, one other aspect, which may be more important than any of these, namely the doubts of doctrinal theologians themselves about biblical theology. This falls into two parts: first, general scepticism about the validity, the usefulness, and the truly theological character of biblical theology, and second, questions about whether the contents of the Bible themselves constitute theology. These are of such importance as to deserve separate treatment, and will be handled in the next chapter.

# 15

# 'Real' Theology and Biblical Theology

*'There is no "theology of the Old Testament"'.*

The person from whom I quote these words was not a rabid zealot for historical criticism, but the influential dogmatic theologian Emil Brunner; they were published in German in 1941, in English in 1946.[1]

That so strong a statement to this effect came from *Brunner* – surely then still the best-known and most accepted voice of dialectical theology in the English-speaking world – is surprising.[2] Did anyone pay attention to it? Most biblical theologians, I imagine, remained quite unaware of it until much later, or are still unaware of it. The phrase and its impact had widely escaped notice, at least until scholars were reminded of it by Smend's article of 1982. Nor do I remember it being quoted or discussed in all the many discussions of biblical theology in which I took part in the intervening years. Such a remark falls like a shower of icy water upon the head of those enthusiastic for biblical theology. For surely, in pressing for the development of their rapidly growing discipline, they were confident that Brunner and his theological emphasis supported them. In this, it seems, they were wrong. And if they were wrong about Brunner, then very likely this implied Barth also: for, though these two disagreed in many things, it is quite likely that in this particular point Brunner was expressing common ground, as will be shown shortly.[3]

Although the great theologians of dialectical theology, Brunner and Barth, did very much to inspire the rise of modern biblical theology, they themselves were distinctly cool towards any idea of such a discipline. Their thinking did not depend on it and they did not build it into the structure of their thinking.

A lack of enthusiasm for biblical theology on the part of doctrinal theologians has been noticed before. Thus Childs in his *Biblical Theology in Crisis* properly notes (64f.) the critical article of Langdon Gilkey, 'Cosmology, Ontology, and the Travail of Biblical Language'. And, more generally, Childs correctly writes that with the dissolution of 'the amorphous category of "neo-orthodoxy"',

> The effect of the breakdown of one dominant theological position was increasingly to isolate the biblical theologians from the active support of the systematic theologians (78).[4]

But Childs' presentation does not make clear that this was no new development: something like this had been the feeling of most doctrinal theologians over a long time, and still is today. Gilkey's sharply-focussed article was specially relevant because it addressed a particular weakness specific to biblical theology. But it, and Childs' presentation of it, did not make clear that this was only one aspect of a more general scepticism on the part of doctrinal theologians, which had prevailed throughout the rise and apogee of modern biblical theology. Only a small minority of them were enthusiastic for biblical theology or had confidence in its products. Taking together all currents of Christian doctrinal theology, neo-orthodoxy was never so very dominant, and for many the dependence of biblical theology upon it was a good reason for scepticism towards the latter. As I will show, even within neo-orthodoxy, scepticism towards biblical theology goes back to the foundational thinkers like Barth and Brunner themselves. Certainly, my own contacts and conversations with doctrinal theologians were an important source of confidence in the criticisms of biblical theology that I advanced.

Theologians proper, doctrinal or dogmatic theologians, never really gave full support to what biblical theologians have been trying to do. They did not much want what Old Testament and New Testament theologians were seeking to provide, and when they saw what had been provided they did not much like it. To quote from an earlier article of my own:

> The fall from grace of biblical theology was welcomed with warm acclamation by a very large number of leading theologians; its demise, if it was a demise, was greeted with cordial accents of joy.[5]

At the very least it can be stated: biblical theology, whether of the Old or New Testament or of both, can no longer be assured of the acceptance and support of doctrinal (dogmatic, systematic) theology. Indeed, as a matter of fact, it never had such support. If it is to succeed, it has to show why it should gain that support.

I must say that I have had difficulty in convincing people of this. None of my writings relevant to biblical theology has been more misunderstood than the article which I have just quoted.[6] Let me put it again in simple words. In that article I am not saying that *I* have theological arguments against biblical theology. I am reporting the fact that *doctrinal theologians* have arguments against it. I knew, after all, though I refrained from saying so, that I had Barth and Brunner on my side. It was from them, after all, that I got the freedom to be critical of biblical theology without thinking that I was thereby ruining the biblical basis of faith. We biblical scholars are often urged to work with doctrinal theologians and I think I have done so more than most people. When I have done so, this is what I have found. With few exceptions, they are sceptical of the idea of biblical theology. They do not think that they stand in need of any such thing and they do not think highly of what has been produced by it thus far.[7] They do not believe that biblical theology has a secure standing *as a form of theology*, or as an ancillary support necessary for theology. In this I am not expressing my own opinion: I am stating what I have heard from doctrinal theologians. If this is not the case, and if doctrinal theologians are longing for biblical theology to proceed and to assist them in their endeavours, I shall be delighted to retract what I have said. All I can say is that my own experience has been otherwise. Thus Hans Frei, much quoted in recent biblical theology as a source of inspiration, himself personally told me how pleased he was by the 'destruction of biblical theology' (or similar terms) in the 1960s. The whole point of this, therefore, is not an 'attack' on biblical theology by me but an indication to biblical theologians that their arguments for their discipline have to be directed towards meeting the distrust and scepticism of many doctrinal theologians. Far from agreeing with these sceptical positions, I have planned the arguments of this book precisely with the hope and intention of going some small distance towards meeting them. My own opinion is that the scepticism of doctrinal theologians towards biblical theology is short-sighted, and that biblical theology will have to be recognized in the long run as an important and indeed an essential component in the total structure of theology.

I should also point out that the question at issue is not whether doctrinal theologians can or should interpret the Bible or not. In my opinion they both can and should and normally do, though a theology that is more abstracted from biblical detail is also perfectly possible.[8] But *of course* theologians may and should interpret the Bible. That is not the question. The question is whether there is, or should be, a 'biblical theology' which seeks to bring together the entire biblical witness, or large portions of it, as a sort of intermediate activity between normal exegesis of individual texts and the regulative decision-making of doctrinal theology. That is a quite different question.

Why then does an uncertainty of this kind exist? We return to Brunner's emphatic statement: 'There is no "theology of the Old Testament".'

What was Brunner's argument? He had been arguing for several pages that one must recognize the *differences* of doctrine (*Lehre*) in the various parts of the Bible. The most important of these is the difference between the teaching of Jesus and that of the apostles. Similarly, it is impossible to reconcile the teachings of Paul and James, of John's Gospel and the Johannine Apocalypse, if one takes them just as teachings or doctrines. They complement each other, but they do so just because they disagree, not because they say the same thing. Faith benefits from them all because faith is not directed to a uniform doctrine or teaching but to a *person*.

Similarly, Brunner goes on, there is no 'theology of the Old Testament'. It is often difficult to know what the doctrinal content of Old Testament passages is at all. Even if one does know, there is such a difference of levels and ideas that one would be much embarrassed if one tried to reach a unitary picture. The most primitive lies alongside the most sublime; there are irreconcilable differences between rival tendencies; there is material that is more or less ossified (*erstarrtes*) and material that is living. Who can bring the priestly and the prophetic, the archaic and the post-exilic, under one title? Thus 'the contrasts seem to mock at every view of a unity' (319) and so 'anyone who attempts a scientific unitary view of this differentiated and contradictory material will have to suffer shipwreck'.

And here, obviously, he comes to Eichrodt, who of course has been trying this very thing. In a footnote he first recognizes the values of Eichrodt's work, especially in its 'connecting of the salvation-*historical* viewpoint with the theological' (his italics) and its contrast with the views of those who want to repristinate Hengstenberg's 'Christ in the Old Testament'. But then he goes on to write: 'One would only wish that Eichrodt would recognize still more clearly the different stages in their distinctiveness as childlike and complete and would thus destroy the last remaining shreds of the opinion that by doing so one would destroy something of the "revelatory impressiveness" of the Old Testament.'[9]

Brunner was not the only one to have this feeling: that Eichrodt's presentation of Old Testament theology had in it something of a rational-apologetic aspect, that it tried to make deep connections and sensible explanations for materials which were in themselves more crude and lacking in rational interrelation, was a not uncommon reaction.

In the following sentence Brunner makes clear what this means. The 'unity view' of the Old Testament, as of the New, can be grasped only in that faith which goes back behind the doctrine. In other words, though he does not put it in just this way, it is a matter for dogmatic, and not for biblical, theology; for faith and not for scholarly demonstration. The most important point then is that what biblical theology cannot and must not do is just what many biblical theologians were trying to do: to provide a picture of the theological unity of the Bible. Brunner then goes on (p. 320 of the later German edition) to point out that, exactly for this reason, historical-critical study does no damage to the theological unity of the Bible. The fragmented, somewhat disparate, sometimes deeply contradictory character of the Old (and New) Testament material was something to be prized, something that could only be obscured by Old Testament theology and similar endeavours.

Not only was this Brunner's opinion, but Karl Barth seems to have taken a similar line. Although the theology of Barth, like that of Brunner, did a great deal to stimulate the rise of modern biblical theology, it is not clear that the course taken by the latter has been in accordance with Barth's own theological

judgment. Although Barth occasionally referred to biblical theology as something that could be done, he had no developed theory[10] of it and produced no
arguments that made it integral to the structure of his own theology.[11] On the
contrary, the thrust of his references is such as to minimize its positive value.
Thus:

> Therefore a biblical theology can never consist in more than a series of
> attempted approximations, a collection of individual exegeses. There can
> never be any question of a system in the sense of Platonic, Aristotelian or
> Hegelian philosophy . . . How can we expound it except by surrendering
> ourselves to the recollection . . . ? Biblical theology (and self-evidently
> dogmatics too) can consist only in an exercise in this surrender, not in an
> attempt to introduce the totality of the biblical witness . . . [12]

*Not* in an attempt to introduce the totality of the biblical witness! Only
'attempted approximations'! Only 'a collection of individual exegeses'! No
question of any sort of system – well, no one really sought or expected something like Plato, Aristotle or Hegel, but there is no doubt, as we have seen, that
'system' and 'a systematic approach' have been among the keywords of Old
Testament theology since Eichrodt and before. Particularly striking, in view of
the 'holistic' approach of much biblical theology, is Barth's sharp turn against
attempted expressions of 'the totality'.

Here is Barth again:

> Because dogmatics is not itself directly concerned with the biblical text but
> with the word of church proclamation founded upon its testimony, it must
> not be expected and ought not to try to achieve what is really the business of
> a biblical theology of the Old and New Testaments (ibid., 821).

Not directly concerned with the biblical text! Barth certainly spoke, but only
occasionally, as if there could be or was a 'biblical theology of the Old and New
Testament' which had different business from that of dogmatic theology. But it
does not seem that this was a very important thing to him. It was something that
was 'not the business of dogmatics'. There is no indication that any results it
could produce would be authoritative or decisive for dogmatics. There is and
was in Barth's theology no place for the importance of a separate subject of
biblical theology which could bring together the biblical material in a holistic
synthesis. Wolterstorff, a sensitive philosopher, expounding Barth, writes:

> The unity of the Bible does not consist in a unified theology or world-view.
> There is . . . 'no Christian view of things', 'no biblical thoelogy'. The unity of
> the Bible consists – so Barth insists – in the unity of its content, in the fact
> that all its parts point, in one way or another, to Jesus Christ.[13]

This latter sentence, following the former as it does, clearly does not provide a basis for biblical theology, but is expressly meant as *something different from* biblical theology.

For Barth the only approach that mattered was the dogmatic. There was exegesis, which could only be partial, and there was theological decision, which could be genuine only when taken on the dogmatic level. The dogmatic operation 'is not itself directly concerned with the biblical text'. Thus a biblical theologian like Brevard Childs, who constantly upholds what he thinks to be Barth's viewpoint, fails to see that in this respect he is quite against the position of both Barth and Brunner. Biblical theology has at times ended up providing a supposed biblical apologetic for the Barthian dogmatic, which Barth himself would have disdained in principle (even if he may at times have relied on it), and in attempting to make a dogmatic out of the totality of the biblical text, which he clearly forbade.

And this is not all. For this means that in that most central element of the Barthian structure, the doctrine of the Word of God, one of the essential pillars upon which it stands is Barth's *rejection* of biblical theology as a mode of procedure – a point clearly perceived by Wolterstorff.

Of course Brunner, and especially Barth, interpreted numerous biblical passages and incorporated these interpretations into their doctrinal frameworks; but that is a quite different thing from supposing that there is, or should be, a distinct operation constituted as 'biblical theology'. And in the case of the Old Testament, as we have seen, Brunner expressly denied that there could be any such thing. Barth, as we see from the second of the two quotations above, did have a notion of what might be 'the business of a biblical theology of the Old and New Testaments', but he appears nowhere to spell out what this business is or to indicate any way in which it might make a difference for his own work, dogmatics. He obviously implies, and rightly as I have said above, that his own extensive work of exegesis does *not* count as 'biblical theology'.

For another expression of a central doctrinal theologian's opinion we may turn to Berkhof. He seems distinctly more favourable towards the results of work in biblical theology. In his *Christian Faith* he is warm towards the main Old Testament theologians and mentions Eichrodt, Vriezen, von Rad and Zimmerli with appreciation. Asking the question whether the 'way of Israel' has a recognizable structure with definite landmarks and a clear direction, he replies that 'the study of the faith has to turn to the disciplines of hermeneutics and the theology of the Old Testament' (229).[15] Eichrodt's exposition of prophecy and its function is 'excellent' (238). The theological dictionaries are cited quite often. There is no stress on the *differences* between the Old Testament theologians; rather, they are generally welcomed and found complementary. He works out compromises between Eichrodt and von Rad over covenant and history (230), and between von Rad and Smend over the existence of a 'centre' (243f.). On the other hand, at least in this book, there seems to be no clear discussion of the 'placing' of Old Testament theology in relation to other aspects of biblical study on the one side and to 'the study of the faith' on the other. There is still no discussion of the theoretical status of biblical theology. The impression given is that biblical theology is one among the numerous ways in which biblical scholarship provides helpful information and guidance to the theologian.

## Does the Bible contain theology?

Another way of putting the question is to ask whether the Bible in fact *contains* 'theology'. Non-theological opponents of Old Testament theology had long made this argument: the material of the Old Testament is not 'theology'. 'Theology' is foreign to it. Jewish opinion, as we shall see, is often the same. Some schools of opinion in the history of religion have also been reluctant to admit the existence of theology in the Hebrew Bible. And even those committed to Old Testament theology often found it necessary to add the qualification that, of course, the Old Testament (and the New) is not 'a theological textbook'. Brunner's strongly-expressed arguments seem likewise to imply that little, if anything, of the Old Testament material should count as 'theology'. To this formulation of the question we now turn.

One who has been cautious about saying that anything in the Bible is actually 'theology' is Gerhard Ebeling in his famous and basic article on the idea of biblical theology:[15]

> A further thing that has become problematical is the application of the concept 'theology' to the actual content of the Bible . . . [From a certain angle] there would be real sense in speaking of theology even in the New Testament, above all in Paul and the author of the Fourth Gospel. On the other hand it would be questionable to describe, say, the preaching of the individual Old Testament prophets as theology. But it is certainly capable of theological explication. From this the conclusion follows that although the Bible for the most part does not contain theology in the strict sense, yet it does press for theological explication.[16]

In more recent times Dietrich Ritschl, under the chapter title 'The Fiction of a Biblical Theology', wrote:

> The question is whether the Bible contains theology in the sense that contemporary theology could get its content directly from it or find a model for

its work in the way in which the Bible presents things. Certainly parts of the biblical writings were 'theology' in a particular way for the believers of their time. But that does not mean that the theological content could be transferred directly to later times or situations. Strictly speaking, most parts of the Bible cannot be transferred. The wisdom literature in the Old Testament and in the New may be an important exception.

Only approximations to theology in the sense of theorizing with a view to regulative statements are present in the biblical writings. Only with qualifications and under certain conditions can we talk of 'the theology of Deutero-Isaiah', of Lucan or Johannine 'theology'; it is easier to speak of Pauline theology because in Paul there are detailed declarations, arguments and definitions that we can follow. And yet even in comparison with the christo-logies, doctrines of the Trinity, doctrines of the church, of grace, of man and so on, the letters of Paul are theology only in the inauthentic sense of the word.[17]

Still less can we seek an overall biblical theology . . .

Not only, then, is much of the Bible not theology: even more, attempts at 'an overall biblical theology' are *particularly* to be discouraged. These remarks indicate serious difficulties for biblical theologians. They have mostly come to believe, and believe passionately, that much of the content of the Bible constitutes theology or can be read as theology – not, perhaps, historical remarks taken in themselves, like the years of the reign of this king or that, but certainly the narratives of patriarchs, the accounts of battles, the religious exhortations, the prophetic speeches of warning; and even more certainly the stories in the Gospels, the teaching of the Pauline letters. Even more, they have mostly thought that by presenting an 'overall picture' of the Bible as a whole they would be expresssing the essentials of its theology. Now theologians tell us that little or none of this material is theology and that individual approximations are better than an overall picture, which should not be sought after. Biblical theologians have often scouted such objections, for they thought that they must come either from historical-critical scholars, a familiar source of error, or from theologians of 'liberal' tradition, who could be trusted to misrepresent the Bible. But here they find that these objections come from theologians of high centrality and of deep concern for the traditional theology of the church. Thus, far from it being the case that biblical scholars, by becoming biblical theologians, are coming closer to the great theological work of the church; they may actually be contra-dicting its most respected leadership.

There are indeed objections which have to be considered. Hans Hübner in his stimulating *Biblische Theologie des Neuen Testaments* has taken up and discussed the points made by Ebeling (see Vol. I, 24ff.). Can one not perceive, he asks, a *theological* conception underlying the narrative representations of the Gospels (26)? These conceptions show clearly theologically reflective and argumentative features, and to such a degree that one can speak of the respective theologies of the individual Synoptic evangelists. 'Naturally the theology of the New Testament authors is not academic theology in the modern sense, but the spiritual achievement of these men is theologically reflective argumentation' (26). He concludes: 'The New Testament is thus a highly theological book' (28).

It seems to me, however, that Hübner is wrong in this and that Ebeling was right. *Of course* the Synoptic Gospels are 'theological': that is not to be doubted. So is the New Testament as a whole. They imply theology and, as Ebeling and Brunner before him said, they invite theological explication. But that a text is 'theological' is not the same as saying that it is *theology*. The content of most parts of the Synoptic Gospels is not theology. Theology may well be implicit in them, but a text is theology only when theology is made explicit in it. One way of expressing the task of biblical theology, or of theological exegesis, is to say that it seeks to make explicit the implicit theology of the texts. But this is needed precisely because the texts themselves for the most part are not theology. If they were theology, in the proper sense, there would be no need for a discipline such as biblical theology.

The distinction between implicit and explicit, as made above, seems to me to be important. If we think of a text as *being* theology, we mean that its theology is explicit. When the theology is implicit, it means that the theology is not *stated* by the text. The theology is in someone's mind, but even there is, perhaps, not explicit. The text may, however, be adequate evidence of the implicit theology.

Where then can all this lead?

The first direction in which it must lead is towards a rethinking by biblical theologians of what they mean when they talk of 'theology' in the Bible. If the biblical material is not (for the most part) 'theology', then what is it? And, what is it that biblical theologians are looking for, or constructing, if it is not 'theology', at least 'in the authentic sense'?

This is not easy to answer. Let me make an attempt. The biblical theologian seeks to study the intellectual and cultural world-image that lies behind the individual texts and their individual meanings. He or she considers the presuppositions from which the writers (and later readers) may have started, the connections with other concepts which have been used elsewhere, or with concepts that might have been used but are avoided, the general world-picture that may have been assumed, the network of connections and indications that may have been involved.

Biblical theology partakes, therefore, of the nature of exegesis rather than that of theology in the proper sense. Exegesis is not, and cannot ever be, a discipline that is purely and only theology: where people seek to make it so, it is likely to be bad exegesis. It is a discipline in which factors of language, of literary form, of history, of environing culture, or knowledge of geography and other *realia*, intertwine and from which theological conclusions may be drawn. Biblical theology belongs to the same category but with two differences: its aim is usually not the sequential following out of the individual text, e.g. Genesis or Luke, but the quest for common factors shared – and usually only partly shared – by a number of texts; and because of this common scope it may come rather closer to the appearance of theology than to the appearance of normal sequential exegesis. The common factors involved, say, in the very various utterances of the Hebrew Bible about 'creation' look a little as if they were a 'theology of creation'. The procedure does not require the assumption that the texts themselves 'are theology' or that all, or even the main part, of the content of the Bible 'is theology'.

Indeed we have to accept the verdict of doctrinal theologians that only very little of the Bible, whether in Old Testament or New, 'is theology'. Religious opinions, expressions and aspirations, however strongly expressed, are not thereby theology. Theology is a reflective activity in which the content of religious expressions is to some extent abstracted, contemplated, subjected to reflection and discussion, and deliberately reformulated. Much of the Bible does not have this character.

This thought opens up a new perspective. *Some parts* of the Bible, we have seen, have a character closer to that of 'theology'. We can therefore, perhaps, trace a movement by which biblical religion gradually begins to formulate itself as something closer to theology. It is noticeable that some of the material which has this character, within the Old Testament, may very probably belong to the later strata: obvious candidates would be Deuteronomy and Deutero-Isaiah, perhaps especially the latter. Parts of the Wisdom literature might also show steps taken in this direction.

It may be likely that a catalyst of this movement was the need to define Hebrew religion as against environing and competing religious trends. 'Self-definition' in this sense (a term of E. P. Sanders) tends to generate something more like 'theology'. Things formerly taken for granted have to be explained, reasons have to be given; arguments against wrong religion give a clearer contour to right religion. In particular, one major stimulant in this direction was Jewish life within the Hellenistic world. A book like the Wisdom of Solomon is much more like 'theology' than the books of the Hebrew canon are. We have to contemplate the likelihood – rather novel to the tradition of biblical theology – that it was Greek thought and language above all that brought biblical religion to the threshold of 'theology'. 'It could be shown,' writes Ebeling, 'that theology arises from the meeting of the biblical testimony to revelation with Greek thinking, and that these two elements are constitutive for the nature of theology.'[18] Similarly Smend, asking whether the phenomenon 'theology' really exists in the Old Testament, writes: 'One will not be able to force the New Testament scholar or, most completely, the dogmatician, whose texts – *overwhelmingly trained on Greek thought* [my italics] – have so much higher a degree of reflection, to answer this question in the affirmative.'[19]

Here again Hübner has reacted against the remarks of Ebeling just quoted, and again, in my opinion, wrongly. Quoting the same passage from Ebeling as I have done, he says that 'for Ebeling two elements are constitutive for theology, namely (*a*) the biblical testimony to revelation and (*b*) Greek thought. Where these two constituents are to be found in the New Testament, one could speak of theology, thus for example with Paul or the author of John' (*Biblische Theologie* I, 25). But Hübner here takes Ebeling as if the latter thought of contact with Greek thought as a *condition* for the presence of theology. I understand Ebeling as meaning it as a mere matter of fact: where we do find theology in the proper sense, it is in fact in connection with Greek thought (and so also Smend as quoted above). This seems correct. Whether contact with Greek thought is a *necessary* condition or not in the later Hebrew tradition, factually it is mostly in contact with Greek thought that we find something like explicit theology.

Ritschl also says of the biblical material: 'Certainly parts of the biblical material were "theology" in a particular way for the believers of their time.' This does not mean that it can be transferred directly to a later time and situation. In its own time, however, it worked somewhat as theology works in a later (and Christian) time. And the biblical theologian may say: yes, that is what we are seeking after, the way in which it *was 'theology' for its own time*. This may justify the existence of biblical theology to some extent. But it justifies it through the introduction of a historical quantifier: *in its own time*. It is as quasi-theology for its own time that biblical theology can evaluate it. But this must mean that historical parameters are necessary for biblical theology – as we have seen to be true from other angles also.

This is important, because it may relativize Ritschl's strictures about the 'fictional' character of biblical theology; and he may have shifted his position since the passage quoted was written. The main criterion he uses in his argument at this point is that of *transferability*. There is no biblical theology in the sense that it can be transferred directly to a later time and situation. We may accept this; but then there may be other characteristics that could justify 'biblical theology'. Might it be that which was *implicit* in the ancient texts: present, yet not made explicit? Might it not deserve the title 'theology' in the sense that, though not 'theology' in the authentic sense, it has features and characteristics that bring it closer to theology in the authentic sense, so that the theorizing process which establishes theology in the authentic sense applies also in this non-authentic area? Which then would be the reason why those who work in 'biblical theology' are persons who also have some experience in 'authentic' theology? Some aspects of this argument will be taken up again later.

We must also raise a question whether it is right to go all the way with Ebeling and to suggest that 'theology' in the authentic sense comes into existence only at the *end* of the biblical period, whether Old or New Testament. Although that understanding of 'theology' as a phenomenon of late stages has been common, we should also recognize the use of the term for very ancient intellectual processes, especially in Egypt. Thus Assmann repeatedly uses 'theology' and 'theological' in his discussion of tendencies of the Eighteenth to Twentieth Dynasties in Egypt.[20] This is not accidental, but may have a connection with the rise of 'theological' decision in early Israel also. I think that implicit theology is present in (or behind, or underlying) texts of very ancient times. This, incidentally, helps us to avoid a simply developmental view, such as would arise if we thought of theology increasing in volume with the passage of time. Yet development – a much disliked term – is not wrong either, for it is the memories of earlier decisions, memories made stronger by the increasing growth of authoritative texts, that make newer decisions richer and more complete.

## Conclusions

1. It must be accepted that most of the material of the Bible is not 'theology' in any direct or authentic sense; biblical theology therefore cannot be validated simply by arguing that the Bible itself is, or contains, theology.

2. 'Biblical theology' is an aspect of exegesis, directed towards individual texts, parts of texts and interrelations between texts, with reference to theological relations and references that they imply and/or express and with openness to questions of truth-values as represented within the Bible, within the environing world cultures, and within the religious/theological traditions that existed before it and were developed afterwards, within Judaism, Christianity and other relevant systems. It should therefore be aware of, and welcome, its difference from what is really theology.

3. It is likely that a certain progression towards 'theology' can be seen within the Bible; a particularly important stage in this movement is marked by contact with Greek language and thought, and is evidenced especially in some 'apocryphal' books like Wisdom, and in Paul and John. But it is likely that in ancient times in Israel, as marked in early texts and as lying even farther in the past antecedent to the texts, decisions were made that also had the character of 'theology'. Both this fact, and the fact that many biblical elements were a sort

of 'theology' for their own time, support the understanding that an historical perspective is necessary for any biblical theology.

4. It should be clearly admitted by those working in biblical theology that the case in favour of their discipline, however it is defined, has not been satisfactorily established and remains precarious, and this from the most central *theological* point of view. Most important are the arguments of doctrinal theologians, who see the enterprise as an amateurish attempt of pious biblical scholars to do the work of theology on the basis of their own biblical expertise alone,[21] and thus as a fundamentally biblicistic illusion. From this point of view it can be argued that biblical scholars would contribute more to theology if they pursued the aspects of biblical study for which they themselves are uniquely equipped and gave less attention and effort to work in the realm that must belong to theology proper. It may well be that these arguments can be overcome, but one should not expect that they will be easily overcome. They will be constantly in our mind as we pursue our subject.

# 16

# 'Christianizing' of the Old Testament?

We have seen that the establishment of relations with the New Testament and the relevance of the Old Testament for modern Christianity have been among the major concerns of Christian Old Testament theologians, though in different degrees from person to person. Nevertheless there has been, most of the time, a counterbalancing trend, which has emphasized the *distinctness* of the Old Testament from the New, and from Christianity in general. This aspect of the distinctness has not been verbalized so fully in the scholarly literature, perhaps because it was thought to be sufficiently obvious, but it is certainly evident on the level of readers and students. Many of them are sensitive to any tendency which they see as a 'Christianizing' of the Old Testament, and they look on such tendencies as unfortunate and unacceptable. Convinced as they are of the authority of the Old Testament within Christianity and its absolute importance as a theological guide, they want to be sure that its Christian character and role is not easily, artificially or tendentiously read into it.

Thus Childs, who emphasizes very much that biblical theology is a Christian enterprise and a part of Christian theology, writes (*Biblical Theology*, 616): 'The aim of biblical theology is not to christianize the Old Testament and thus to drown out its own voice.' A fuller statement is found in his earlier book *OTTCC*, 9: 'the Old Testament functions within Christian scripture as a witness to Jesus Christ precisely in its pre-Christian form. The task of Old Testament theology is therefore not to Christianize the Old Testament by identifying it with the New Testament witness, but to hear its own theological testimony to the God of Israel whom the church confesses also to worship. Although Christians confess that God who revealed himself to Israel is the God and Father of Jesus Christ, it is still necessary to hear Israel's witness in order to understand who the Father of Jesus Christ is.'[1] We shall return later to consider Childs' position in this regard more fully; here I note only that he expresses something that has been very widely felt among the Christian practitioners of Old Testament theology.

The way they often express this is by saying that the Old Testament should be allowed to 'speak for itself'. For Christians, this seems to imply that if the Old Testament is allowed to 'speak for itself', it will produce results which are to the benefit of Christian faith, but, if Christianity is actually imported into it or imposed upon it, the effect will be actually *to reduce* the value of the Old Testament for Christianity and its influence upon it.[2] It should produce Christian results but should not be Christianized. But can this be done?

This has been one of the reasons why Old Testament theologians resisted what they thought to be traditional dogmatic schemes. Eichrodt, turning away from such schemes, urges us to work as best we can 'along the lines of the Old Testament's own dialectic' (I, 33). In similar terms, though addressing a somewhat different issue, in defence against his critics von Rad equally maintains that he is 'letting the Old Testament speak for itself'.[3]

It is not surprising that this 'anti-Christianizing' stance should prevail even among those most anxious to acclaim the Old Testament as a full Christian authority. If the Old Testament is to be a prime source for Christian doctrine and life, the source material has to be really there, and must not be placed there by a process of reading Christianity back into it.

Such a feeling is not without some historical basis, for by the twentieth century many had come to accept that some at least of the Old Testament texts quoted in the New Testament as 'proof' for Christian concepts had had their Christianity read into them. Even many of the most conservative and biblicistic Christians have been aware of this possibility and aware that they had to be on their guard against it. Thus the awareness that Old Testament texts might at times be wrongly 'Christianized' has by no means been a product of anti-Christian or secularist suspicion but can be easily generated on a traditional Christian basis itself. Especially in Protestantism there is a tradition of doubt towards allegorical interpretations and a sense that the literal understandings of passages in the Hebrew Bible are not in themselves 'Christian' meanings.

Not surprisingly, therefore, the Old Testament theologies of this century have for the most part been very cautious of any old-fashioned 'proof-text' approach. Traditional 'messianic' passages like Isa. 7. 14 may be left unmentioned or, if mentioned at all, are integrated into a lengthy contextual discussion and by no means taken as simple 'messianic' utterances, even if they are so used by the New Testament itself.[4] Similarly, although the concept of 'typology' was taken up by a substantial group of central scholars in the mid-century,[5] and especially of course by von Rad, it was made clear that the typology envisaged by them all was no simple repetition of the older scheme whereby Old Testament characters and events were 'types' pointing towards Christ and later realized in him. This newer typology was not a matter of proof-texts but more a doctrine of history in which past events were taken up and reinterpreted. Indeed, taking a very wide view, one might say that all modern Old Testament theology accepted from the start that the older style of taking 'proof-texts' from the Old Testament as links with the New was now unusable. Christianizing of Hebrew texts in that manner was agreed to be a thing of the past, at least for scholarly purposes, even if liturgically and religiously it was still meaningful. What Old Testament theology has been looking for, in this respect, is not texts that will prove Christian beliefs to be true, but rather patterns in history, or conceptual patterns, or organizations of social, legal and religious experience which may prove to be significant when brought into some sort of relation with Christian patterns.

In spite of these attempts to let the Old Testament speak for itself, which should be taken as quite sincere and deliberate, it is difficult to doubt that the handling of the Hebrew Bible by some Old Testament theologians has included considerable Christianizing, though of a more advanced and sophisticated kind than the mere quotation of messianic proof-texts.

It is important, however, to consider in what respect this is done. As we have seen, the intermixing of New Testament material is actually done *less* than one would expect, and less than the principles of the Old Testament theologians themselves would require. Moreover the crude introduction of traditional Christian 'dogmas' is generally avoided: thus we never find anything about the Virgin Birth, even in Catholic Old Testament theologies; seldom anything about the Trinity,[6] seldom mention of incarnation. Attempts to 'prove' that Jesus was the Messiah are on the whole eschewed. Extremely seldom, if ever, do we find references to recherché items of dogma such as the *Filioque* clause, the expression ὁμοούσιος[7] or the *communicatio idiomatum*. Even creation out of nothing, sometimes thought (though questionably) to be a Christian rather than a Jewish idea, tends to be deprecated as something remote from the ideas of Genesis. If concepts such as these are the core of Christian belief, it is hard to say that modern biblical theology has been seeking to intrude them into the Hebrew Bible. Crude 'Christianizing' of this sort, related to the ancient dogmas and credal affirmations, has scarcely been seen.

Most striking of all, in most Old Testament Theologies the aspect of *messianic expectation* is extremely muted. Practically nowhere do we find passages in the prophets interpreted as forecasts of Jesus and his life. Indeed messianism tends to be scarcely mentioned. Childs, in his final chapter of *OTTCC* entitled 'Life under Promise', has just over three pages on 'The Messianic Kingdom and its Messiah' and begins with the two sentences: 'It has long been recognized that the term "messiah" in its technical New Testament sense as the eschatological redeemer of Israel does not occur in the Old Testament itself, but only in the post-Old Testament period. Indeed, one of the important tasks of Old Testament theology is closely to describe the profile of the Old Testament witness without fusing it with that of the New Testament.' Or, to quote another example from Childs in his larger and later work, in Jeremiah the 'messianic theme' is developed 'in terms of raising up "for David, a righteous Branch"', but it seems that this is a minor note, for the next sentence goes on to say that the heart of Jeremiah's promise for the future lies elsewhere (*Biblical Theology*, 178). The next page says that 'Deutero-Isaiah does not make much use of David as a messianic figure' (179). A further discussion of the messianic theme is found in Childs' chapter on 'Christ, the Lord' (*Biblical Theology*, 452ff.), but he argues that 'because the focus of biblical theology lies in the relationship between the two testaments in respect to the messianic hope, the rehearsal of the Old Testament evidence can be brief': in other words, there is a short summary of messianic traditions, which the New Testament later 'appropriates' (455) or 'uses' (title on 456). There is no attempt to suggest that messianic prophecy directed towards Jesus existed. In most Old Testament Theologies written by Christian authors messianic prophecy has only a minor place, and in so far as it is treated, it seems to be implied that the expected fulfilment lies within the future historical life of the people of Israel.

This is not to say that there has been no interest in messianic expectation. On the contrary, important books were written on the subject during our period, such as Mowinckel's *He That Cometh*; but exactly such a book displays a will *not* to become involved in questions of the fulfilment of such expectations by Jesus, and Mowinckel is rightly quoted in this sense by Childs (*OTTCC*, 241). A scholar like Engnell, who stated that the prophets were 'messianists', was rather remote from the world of Old Testament theology. All along this line modern Old Testament theology seems to have departed from the older Christian traditions and adopted more a historical stance, understanding future expectations to have meaning within the historical life of Israel. This is true even of Childs, in spite of his conviction that the Old Testament is just as much a 'witness' to Jesus Christ as the New is. The approach of Wilhelm Vischer,[8] who found Jesus Christ actually present and active within Old Testament times, has been almost totally repudiated, from the time of von Rad's early review onward.

And the same is true, for the most part, of the 'proof-texts' in which the New Testament writers saw the attestation of Jesus, or of diverse distinctively Christian doctrines, by ancient Hebrew writers. A phrase like 'a star shall arise out of Judah' from the Balaam prophecies (Num. 24.17) is studied with deep interest because it was historically understood to be a messianic and eschatological text, but no modern Old Testament theologian seriously supposes that this was a forecast of the coming of Christ. Even a more highly prestigious passage like Isa. 53 is thought of as a prophetic poem, whether concerned with the contemporary present or with the future, around which Jesus may later have moulded his own self-understanding or his sense of his mission, rather than as an actual forecast of his coming (and we may add that doubt has been cast upon the importance of this revered passage for the New Testament writers anyway[9]). Although proof-texts of these kinds are deeply built into the substance of older traditional Christian theology and belief, that sort of thinking has been largely abandoned by the main tradition of modern Old Testament theology. As we shall see, however, there may be some exceptions.

This is not to say that Christianization on a different level has not taken place: I think that it has done so. But it has mostly been of another type or, more probably, of two other types. The two types I have in mind are: first, the use of categories which, while not necessarily part of ancient traditional dogma, nevertheless steer the discussion into a framework suggestive more of Christianity than of the Hebrew Bible itself; and, secondly, the use of categories which are not part of ancient traditional dogma but are significant within *recent* confessional and controversial positions. Both these types, whether distinct or mingled, will be exemplified in what follows.

An obvious and central example is the word *theology* itself. For *theology* is a term of Greek origin, first found, apparently, in Plato (*Republic* 379a), with the sense 'science of things divine' (LSJ). Not only is it not a Hebrew term, nor is there any Hebrew term that covers the same ground, but it is not a New Testament term either. Its greatest use is Christian, and that means in Christianity of the post–New Testament time. Thus it is possible to argue that by applying the term *theology*, and applying it with much determination and emphasis, we are already imposing a Christian pattern and flavour on the discipline. That this is felt by some Jewish scholars is manifest, and this aspect will be considered later. It is possible that this objection can be overcome, but it is not immediately obvious *how* it can be overcome.

An even stronger example of the same kind is *faith*. In my re-reading of Old Testament theologies for the present work this struck me forcibly in several writers, and I was pleased to find the same noted by Westermann in respect of Fohrer and Zimmerli.[10] In both these Theologies, he says, 'faith' is the most frequent word! Yet this hardly fits with the usage of the Hebrew Bible itself, for there one never hears expressions like 'faith in the creator' or 'creation faith'. Naturally one can speak quite neutrally of 'Israel's faith', meaning more or less the same as Hebrew religion. But this is a modern linguistic convention, no longer particularly tied to Christian specifics. Taken in this general sense, 'faith' does not particularly suggest Christianity. However, when 'faith' is taken as a central term, and we hear that 'everything depends on faith' or other such statements, then it is very much a mark of Christianity, being a key word in the New Testament and, most of all, a key term for the relation of believers to Jesus in particular. Indeed it is almost an embarrassment at times to speak of Israel's 'faith', for *faith*, though certainly having some Hebrew background, again shifts the categories towards the Christian ones. Thus when 'faith' is so continually used as a keyword of exposition in an Old Testament theology, it very much suggests Christianizing. Westermann himself does not use this term, but this seems to be the obvious implication of the point he makes.

In von Rad another favourite term is 'confess, confession' (*sich bekennen, Bekenntnis*). This introduces a further complication, for the usage is not only Christian but somewhat sectional within Christianity. It indicates those theological elements which are final and absolute, matters of life and death: the *status confessionis* is the point at which ultimate and extreme decision is expressed. 'Confession' in this sense, though perhaps intelligible, is certainly unusual or abnormal in English; it is familiar only to those accustomed to continental usage, especially to associations in Lutheranism, and in modern times in the 'Confessing Church' in Germany. To those familiar with the terminology, it can lend realism and vividness to the discussion of an Old Testament incident; this may be counted as an advantage. On the other side, it seems a disadvantage, for it obscures the fact that 'confession' in this sense is not a category of the Hebrew Bible at all, or at least not in any obvious way.

Among recent biblical theologians, as we have seen, Childs has been sensitive to the danger of the Christianizing of the Hebrew Bible. He writes (*Biblical Theology*, 616): 'The aim of biblical theology is not to christianize the Old Testament and thus to drown out its own voice.' In a discussion of faith, he recognizes that 'the technical terminology of faith is infrequent' but he thinks that this constitutes a 'problem' for understanding of the Old Testament's theological function. He wants us to 'relate an Old Testament text to its theological reality', but this is a different thing from 'christianizing the Old Testament which is a move in only one direction'. Thus 'the dialectic within the hermeneutical circle involves an understanding of reality which has been formed in part from the New Testament's witness to Jesus Christ. At least the questions which one puts to the Old Testament text arise in part from a Christian stance toward its subject matter.' He summarizes this with the further statement, 'In other words [*sic*], biblical theology seeks to hear each testament according to its own voice, but as scripture of the Christian church.' The arguments are not very clear. What does he mean by saying that Christianizing 'is a move in only one direction'? If the questions one puts to the Hebrew Bible arise 'in part' from a Christian stance towards the subject matter, how does this not form a more subtle kind of Christianizing? If the Old Testament is to be 'heard' 'as scripture of the Christian church', how does that not potentially conflict with the hearing of its own voice? And when Childs tells us, as a central conviction, that the Old Testament, like the New, is 'a witness to Jesus Christ', how is that a hearing of it in its own terms, and how is it other than a profound form of Christianizing? Perhaps Childs can explain this, but he does not do so very clearly. It sometimes looks as if Childs has carefully avoided the crude Christianizing in detail that has sometimes been found, but has done something of the same as a theological totality. This is connected with another point which will be made later: namely, that while to a fair extent he does try to expound the Old Testament in its own terms in the sections specially devoted to it, he also fails in these same sections to provide any textual basis for his claim that the Hebrew Bible 'witnesses' to Jesus Christ, so that his bringing together of the two is an act of pure and sheer dogmatic insistence. Nevertheless his sensitivity in principle to Christianizing is noticeable. Cf. again *OTTCC*, 242: 'one of the important tasks of Old Testament theology is to describe the profile of the Old Testament witness without fusing it with that of the New Testament.'

Sometimes Theologies leave the impression, not so much of a general Christian atmosphere, but rather of a particular or denominational slant. Thus the emphasis on *covenant* in Eichrodt may leave the impression of a Calvinist influence – though it is true that this emphasis came to be very widely accepted by scholars of a large variety of theological traditions: for instance, the interest of Roman Catholic scholars in the emphasis on covenant has been very noticeable. In von Rad on the other hand the emphasis on covenant seems to be lighter. Not that he says nothing about it: his work has many references to it. Thus Deuteronomy, which is often said to be the basis for the von Rad theology, 'is, of course, the outline of a comprehensive covenant theology' (2, 267). He certainly was not convinced by Eichrodt's making it the *centre*. Yet at 2, 412 he acknowledges, perhaps surprisingly, that Eichrodt's 'starting-point in the covenant' had much to be said for it, in comparison with some other approaches such as Köhler's. Where then does the difference lie? It seems that for von Rad covenant is a more *mobile* and *variable* reality. Von Rad is more interested in the *history* of the covenant than in the covenant as an organizing principle. For Eichrodt it does have a history, but at the bottom there lies a fairly fixed structure: 'the' covenant, in very Reformed style. In von Rad's presentation covenants (plural) come up again and again, but the change of circumstance and character is greater. The idea of the new covenant means that 'there is to be a change in the way in which the divine will is to be conveyed to humanity' (2, 213). Jeremiah's new covenant differs from the covenant of Deuteronomy, and this is a 'crucial feature' (2, 269–70). The Chronicler 'does not even know of a covenant theology' (1, 353). God 'dissolved' the covenant but only when Israel said 'No' to Jesus (2, 407). It would be tempting to think that von Rad's position has a Lutheran shape which would contrast with the more Reformed shape of Eichrodt's thought, but I do not see it clearly so: it is easier to see Eichrodt's as Reformed than to give a denominational index to von Rad's. It may be, on the contrary, that von Rad's Lutheran background manifests itself rather in the opposite way, in a seeking to *correct* some traditional Lutheran emphases (see below).

On the other hand von Rad has many other terms that give the feeling of a Christianizing influence: obviously, for example, his heavily stressed depiction of the speech at the giving of the firstfruits in Deut. 26.5–10 as a 'short historical creed', understood by him to be an early document and expressing the primal nucleus of Yahwism. The emphasis laid on this suggests that the analogy of the Christian creeds, especially the Apostles' Creed, was powerful.[11] It is difficult to doubt that the impulse to discover a sort of 'creed' at the base of the Yahwistic development, and to perceive as a high value that it is a 'historical' creed, arises from the influence of the analogy of the Apostles' Creed, with its short articles, its main concentration on historical events in the life of Jesus and its [conceivable] role as a summary of the essential *credenda* out of which the multifarious statements of the New Testament books developed. It is very likely that this analogy was influential in von Rad's perception of the place of the formula of Deut. 26. And here, indeed, later discussion has damaged this aspect of von Rad's approach: on the one hand, as I argued long ago, *if* this was a statement of the nuclear faith of Israel, it was a strangely out-of-the-way place to put it; on the other, as is now widely agreed, the passage is probably of latish date. However, our principal concern at this point is not with these arguments but with the fact that the identification of this as a 'creed' was in itself a sign of the use of Christian categories.

And the same is certainly true of other terms, like *kerygma*. The representation of material as 'preaching' and 'sermons' also gives a very Christian impression. It is true that Rabbinic preaching exists, and Rabbinic sermons; but the degree of emphasis on this concept by von Rad seems very Christian (cf. 1, 221–8). *Kerygma* came into religious language through the claims attached to the coming and work of Jesus; his death and resurrection were the events that were to be 'proclaimed'. In this respect von Rad is followed by Childs, who uses the adjective 'kerygmatic' very frequently and with an impression that it indicates a supreme theological reality and value. Yet surely the tone of 'kerygma, kerygmatic' is derived entirely from the New Testament. Uses of the verb in the LXX are not many, and those of the noun negligible. Admittedly, Childs uses these terms mainly in the New Testament sections of his *Biblical Theology*; but the intellectual effects of 'kerygmatic' principles in interpretation underlie his values in interpretation of the Old Testament also, as is the case with von Rad.

Another case of the same kind is the handling of the laws, e.g. the Decalogue, by von Rad. See 1,190–203, and e.g. the following:

> Israel certainly did not understand the Decalogue as an absolute moral law prescribing ethics: she rather recognized it as a revelation vouchsafed to her at a particular moment in her history, through which she was offered the saving gift of life (1, 193f.).

It is thus doubtful, von Rad argues, whether 'law' is the right term (195). It sometimes feels as if von Rad, perhaps mindful of the long tradition of Lutheran distinction between law and gospel, is trying to modify that tradition by interpreting the Old Testament law as if it worked in somewhat the same way as the New Testament gospel. This would fit in, of course, with his general typological scheme of relating Old and New Testaments (see 2, 388ff., including mentions of Lutheranism, and the emphasis on 'preaching of the law' as a means to salvation).

It seems to me likely that von Rad, with his extensive use of terms like *credo*, *kerygma*, preaching, confession (*Bekenntnis*) and others, does more in the way of 'Christianizing' the Hebrew Bible than any other of the main Old Testament theologians.

But, as we have seen, there is another side to this. Even where some sort of 'Christianizing' can be detected, it is not necessarily a simple *imposition* of a traditional or dogmatic Christian element. Very often, where a Christianizing element can be detected, the Old Testament theologian is seeking some *change* in Christianity, or in his own Christian tradition. He or she is not merely imposing a long-traditional doctrine or exegesis, but rather proposing some sort of innovation, some alteration of focus. A good example is to be seen in von Rad, whose Lutheran context in his handling of the law has just been mentioned. This does not mean that von Rad is simply imposing a Lutheran interpretation; rather, he is proposing an interpretation, based on the Hebrew texts, which he hopes may alter the emphasis of the traditional Lutheran interpretation. He writes: 'There is no basis in the Old Testament for the well-known idea which early Lutheranism exalted to almost canonical status, that Israel was compelled by God's law to an ever greater zeal for the law, and that it was the law and the emotions it evoked which prepared the way for true salvation in Christ' (405). His reason for this is the argument: 'Had the Old Testament writers believed that the law's function was to expose sin they would necessarily have presented sin as easy to understand in theological terms' (405–6). How far von Rad's arguments are right or wrong for his own Christian situation I would not presume to judge. But it seems clear what he is doing: he sees in the Hebrew Bible a resource which can be exploited to steer his own Christian tradition in a direction that seems to him to be more wholesome. And I suspect something of the same is being done with concepts like 'creed', 'kerygmatic' and the rest. In all these we do not have a crude Christianizing of the Hebrew Bible but an application to it of concepts which may affirm such and such a direction, often a somewhat novel one, in Christianity. But even the doing of this, in however subtle a way, may still well be considered to constitute Christianizing.

Very likely the most prominent example of Christianizing, however, lies in the conception of justification by faith. This term itself may seldom appear, but the associated conceptions are very conspicuous. Old Testament theologians often tend to depict characters in the stories as dependent on divine grace rather than acting on their own behalf, as responding to divine acts rather than taking their own initiative. The prime text is Gen. 15.6, commonly rendered in English as something like 'and he believed the Lord and he reckoned it to him for righteousness'. As Oeming writes in the classic modern discussion: 'For Paul this verse is the *locus classicus* in the Old Testament for justification by faith alone without works of the law (Rom.4; Gal. 3.6ff.). For James by contrast it is – with close dependence on Jewish exegesis – in exactly the opposite sense an evidence for justification on the basis of works, and not of faith alone (James 2.14–26).'[12]

The case is a prominent one, for many reasons and in particular because von Rad had written an article on it back in 1951.[13] He called attention to the place of the term *ḥašab* in priestly cultic praxis, but thought that in this particular place the cultic background is broken and 'reckoning' is placed in the area of a free personal relationship of Yahweh with Abraham. This is not a polemic against cultic sacrifice, but a subjectivization and interiorization, with the centre of gravity now lying upon the inner attitude.

Against von Rad's case Oeming directed a fresh examination of the linguistic usage involved, and argued: 'It is an extremely improbable supposition that the tradition-historical background of Gen. 15.6 is the priestly cult-praxis. In fact it is more probable that the subject of "and he reckoned it" is not the deity at all, but the man in question, i.e. Abraham. "Abraham believed the Lord; Abraham counted it to the Lord as gracious help" (the word usually rendered as 'righteousness' may be so understood).' Thus neither the conclusions reached by Paul, nor the opposing ones reached by James, are correct! The mistaken exegesis, so influential in Christian tradition, is explained by Oeming through the influence of the Greek (LXX) translation. We do not have space here to go into the details of this: suffice it that there is very substantial doubt about the common and powerful Christian tradition that on the grounds of Gen. 15.6 God reckoned righteousness to Abraham for his faith.[14]

Now this is not a matter simply of a disagreement over an article by von Rad. His article was influential precisely because it encapsulated a sentiment which had been repeatedly present in Christian work on Old Testament theology. If there was 'Christianizing' in that work, it expressed itself not so much in the often invoked 'dogmas' like Trinity and Incarnation, nor in messianism and the associated proof-texts, but in the sentiment that Old Testament people were upheld through what in Christian terms would be 'grace' and 'faith'. Although the Hebrew Bible not infrequently reports on the *disobedience* and *rebelliousness* of Israel, Jewish readers can be sensitive to the *degree* to which this is emphasized by Christian commentators. Justification by faith is, among the convictions that Christian Old Testament theologians have most often held, the one where they have been most reluctant to give up the 'Christianizing' of the Hebrew Bible.

A familiar example may be seen in Köhler's decision to leave the cult, sacrifices, etc. completely out of his Theology. This could probably be justified on simple grounds of an inability to fit them in. But he revealed a rather serious traditional Christian prejudice in saying that they were 'a scheme for human self-salvation'. Human self-salvation is the negation of the Christian idea of justification by faith. In this the 'liberal' Köhler assumed and adhered to – in a rather crude manner – the 'orthodox' Reformation position.

A more recent scholar like Childs seems to feel no question about Gen.15.6. 'Abraham was pronounced in right relationship with God not because of his obedience in upholding the demands of the covenant but rather his faith in God's promise was reckoned to him as righteousness' (*Biblical Theology*, 496). In Galatians, 'The contrast is not simply between faith in Christ and doing the laws of Moses, but rather is such which excludes any element of cooperation' (495). The exclusion of 'any element of cooperation' is the essential thing, it seems. He repeats this position: 'Paul finds his warrant in Abraham's belief in God which was reckoned to him as righteousness' (543, cf. again 554). Admittedly, these are passages about Paul, placed in a New Testament setting, and Childs does not explicitly say that Paul was understanding the passage of Gen. 15.6 rightly. But in none of these passages does he even hint that this might not be the meaning of the Genesis verse. Nowhere, so far as I can see, does he discuss the question. The chapter 'Biblical Faith' (*Biblical Theology*, 595–613) contains a section 1, 'Faith in the Old Testament and in Judaism' (596–8), but here also there is a paragraph on Gen. 15.6 (absent from the index) which describes it as 'crucial' but still raises no question about the syntax and meaning of the words.[15] The Jewish scholar Jon Levenson, as mentioned above, takes up the exegesis of this passage, choosing as his target some utterances of von Rad and curiously not noting that the same tendencies are repeated in Childs, with whom he allies himself in so many regards.

It appears that the impulse to 'Christianize' of the Old Testament may take two different forms, and these arise from two different principles, both of which are to some extent embedded in Christian tradition. On the one side there is the principle that the Old Testament, though of course a Jewish book, is also fully a Christian book, and if left to itself it will say Christian things. But to encourage it in doing so, the expositor reads into it categories such as those I have mentioned above. On the other side is the principle that the Old Testament will say Christian things; but only if carefully checked and sifted through an application of Christian standards, usually supposed to come from the New Testament. The effect of this may be a kind of 'spiritualizing' interpretation: the Old Testament in itself sometimes says fully Christian things, sometimes on the other hand it says things that are not really Christian, or things that are Christian only when they are taken in a special way, commonly a non-literal and spiritual way. Among Old Testament Theologies something of this may perhaps be seen in Vriezen.

One reason for this sort of variation is that 'Christianity' itself is not a fixed and clearly determined quantity. For some, even though its debt to the Hebrew Bible is fully acknowledged, its real basis is seen in something new, that was not there in ancient Israel. In extreme cases this can produce something in which the Old Testament is a past preparation which, after fulfilment has come, can be largely ignored except as historical background. In the modern Biblical Theology Movement, people who think this way have often been associated with the heresy of Marcion (mid-second century), for whom the God of the Jews was a different and inferior God from the one revealed in Christianity.[16] For others, continuity with that which was there in ancient Israel is of vital importance for Christianity itself. Hence the strongly-marked 'Old-Testament atmosphere' of some Calvinism, producing a Christianity in which the Old Testament seems to be if anything more important than the New. A prominent example was the Dutch theologian A. van Ruler,[17] who thought that the Old Testament was the real Bible, the New Testament being only 'the explanatory glossary at the back of the Old Testament' (Vriezen, 120; for fuller discussion see ibid., 96–8).[18]

With Vriezen the design of his Theology deliberately incorporates a Christian point of view. As we have seen, however, the question remains whether this affects his actual description of Old Testament materials. Vriezen's form of a Christian point of view seems to be that he accepts a certain relativity in the Old Testament. Thus: 'There *is* a line that leads from the Old Testament to Christ; this line is not seen with equal clearness everywhere, but it is a very important central line that runs through the whole of the law, the prophets and Writings . . . but there are also lines in the Old Testament that lead to Judaism and may draw the reader away from Christ' (100). It seems, perhaps, that he tends to Christianize in another way, with a tendency towards spiritualization – 'the spiritual meaning of the material contents of the Old Testament' (93). Though Jesus would not abandon one jot or tittle of the Law, 'because of his spiritual understanding of the law he again and again contradicts the Judaic theology of his days . . . and even repeatedly contradicts certain words of the law. Sometimes Christ used the traditional text freely, and in so doing he showed himself superior to all bondage to the letter. . . he even dared to preach in a critical manner and in this he followed the ancient prophets (cf. Hosea's criticism of Jacob in Ch. 12).'[19] 'Fundamentally the Old Testament teaches nothing other than what was taught by Christ . . . he actualizes the revelation which had been accorded to Israel . . . but Jesus discovers more and other things in God's kingdom than had been revealed in the law and the prophets' (89).

In spite of the Christianizing tendencies which we have seen in various Old

Testament Theologies, however, it would be exaggerated to suppose that these tendencies were so strong as to vitiate completely the work that was done in these contributions. Generally the reader recognizes that terms of von Rad, like *kerygma*, *credo*, 'confession' etc., have to be discounted, and once this is done one can read the Theology in question without troubling about the Christianizing terminology. It seems to depend upon the reader how much he or she is influenced by this sort of vocabulary. If one is clever and used to the style, one can translate it, as it were, into meanings that are more appropriate for the ancient Levites, for Deuteronomy, or whatever it may have been. It does seem, moreover, that the Christianizing tendencies decrease in the later group of Old Testament Theologies. It is possible that they belong to an older era and will be substantially reduced as time goes on. It does not seem to me to be *inevitable* that Christianizing will continue, even where biblical theology is carried out on an expressly Christian basis. After all, as has been said, most or all Old Testament theologians have said that they were against it.

# 17

# Judaism after Biblical Times

One aspect of Old Testament theology that has still to be discussed is its attitude to the Judaism of later times. This may apply to some later strata within the Hebrew Bible itself, or to Hellenistic Judaism as manifested in the 'apocryphal' documents, or – and most of all – to Rabbinic Judaism. Some works of Old Testament theology, as will be shown, have been negative and unfair towards Judaism; and this fact in turn has rebounded upon the subject and done damage to its reputation.

The most obvious example is in Eichrodt's classic presentation. Here one detects a recurrent tendency to depict the religion of later Judaism as one which had lost contact with the main theological structure of the Old Testament itself. According to Eichrodt, antinomies existed which the resources of Judaism were not able to overcome, but which were in fact overcome in Christianity. He points to 'legalism', to 'casuistry', to domination of the religious consciousness by 'fear', to a religion of 'works', to external observance rather than internal attitudes of faith and communion – all of these familiar as terms in traditional Christian disparagement of Judaism. In particular, even when he approves of characteristics of the religion, he sometimes thinks that these characteristics were in some sort of conflict with one another, a conflict which Judaism was unable to resolve. These weaknesses or deficiencies were, he maintains, overcome in Christianity, which on the one hand returned to the original form of such characteristics as they had been back in central Old Testament times, and on the other hand transcended them with some kind of higher realization. These negative passages in Eichrodt's writing often come at the end of a chapter or section, where the writer is finishing his survey of the main biblical period and coming to a conclusion. Thus for example at the end of his section on 'The Personal Relation to God in the Post-Exilic Period', he wrote:

> The essence of the Jewish religion of the Law may therefore be seen as a regulation of the God–Man relationship which exhausts itself in endless casuistry, and leaves the heart empty . . . It is impossible to find clearer evidence of the lack of a unified religious attitude. The fact that Jesus and his Apostles had recourse to the Old Testament in their description of the right attitude toward God witnesses plainly to the fact that in them the inner

schizophrenia of Jewish piety had been overcome, and that the liberation of Man for willing surrender to God had once more emerged into the light of day (II, 315).

'In later Judaism the basis of personal relation to God is fear', declared the beginning of the same passage (II, 313).
Writing about the sacrificial cult, Eichrodt says:

It was the fateful transformation of piety in late Judaism, which made the Yahweh religion into a religion of observance, that first threatened to obscure the soteriological character of cultic action in order to include it one-sidedly within the category of performance and obedience. This was, however, no longer based on the essential nature of the cult as such; rather, it lay in the subjection of it under the alien standard of legalism (*Nomismus*) (I, 177).

Again, after discussing the idea of *merit* and especially the values of the merits of Abraham, Eichrodt ends (II, 464):

Thus at the very heart of the desire for salvation we find once again that inner disintegration of the structure of Jewish faith which continually confronts us ... As religious life was ever more strongly dominated by legal righteousness, and the message of the free gift of God's favour was heavily muffled, the individual's assurance of salvation was subjected to the severest strain, and finally came to a dead end in the utter helplessness of 4 Esdras and Paul the Pharisee.

It is often uncertain exactly what stage of later Judaism is being referred to in Eichrodt's remarks. Some of them probably refer principally to the later sources within the Hebrew Bible itself; others refer primarily to the time of Hellenistic Judaism as documented in the 'apocryphal' books. Thus when he tells us that 'sacrifice lost its original character' or that 'the sense of nearness to God was lost, and its absence is shown in the use of abstract designations for God' (I, 169), he might be referring to tendencies in the later biblical books, or to apocryphal sources, or possibly to rabbinic sources also. When he says that 'in late eschatology the prophetic tension was lost' (I, 262f.), this might most naturally indicate the apocryphal books. When he says that 'the revelatory function of the divine name recedes' (II, 44f.), he seems to refer to both apocryphal and Rabbinic sources, for he continues with the more specific illustration: 'The use of the Name in the Mishnah and in the Similitudes of Enoch, despite the many points of contact between these writings and Old Testament usage, has already acquired a quite different meaning,'[1] and 'only in the New Testament does the divine Name recover its old revelatory significance'. 'A theoretic-constructive element controls the idea of a heavenly dwelling' (II, 194). When he says that 'the new, late angelology is an obscuring of the idea of God' (*eine Trübung der Gottesidee*) (II, 200), influenced by pagan ideas, he is probably referring to apocryphal sources.

Where the reference is to apocalyptic or other 'apocryphal' ideas Eichrodt's judgment will not necessarily be felt so much as a disparagement of *Judaism* (as it finally became). Other passages, however, refer more certainly to Rabbinic Judaism: thus II, 348, which refers to 'hair-splitting casuistry', and here a footnote refers to the Mishnah tractate Shabbat which, he says, 'supplies the best illustration of how real worship of God is bound to be stifled under the heaping-up of detailed commands, from which the spirit has fled'. Eichrodt goes on to comment on the 'deep inner fragmentation' which is the characteristic mark of the Jewish community, and which 'derives from the crucial misunderstanding of God's covenant', but also 'points forward' to a 'creative new foundation of moral thinking and action, to be laid by transposing men into a new total relationship with God, in which the work of grace present in the establishment of the Old Covenant was to come to fulfilment'.

Such negative assessments of Judaism by Eichrodt have come to be increasingly noticed in the last two decades and especially since Levenson's articles of 1987 and after. I have seen that some Christian students, reading Eichrodt's work as a textbook, have expressed their chief response to be not admiration for the theological structure he built up but concern and shame over his attitudes to Judaism. This in turn has been a factor tending to the discredit of Old Testament theology in general.

In spite of these many disparaging remarks, however, it would be hasty to conclude that Eichrodt's picture of Judaism is uniformly negative. On the contrary, at times he considers later Judaism to have a higher standard than the Hebrew Bible. These aspects have not always been equally noted. Thus in the post-exilic community we find 'the comprehensive *repair of the deficiencies of early Israelite morality*' (II, 338). Here he is referring to sexual morality, and he gives examples going down to Ben Sira. Later Judaism in this respect, therefore, had in his opinion a standard *higher than* that of the (canonical) biblical books. According to him, a striving for improvement here had already been going on within the biblical books, e.g. Deuteronomy, Malachi and Job, and this was taken further in Ben Sira. Eichrodt comments that the attitude of Judaism, according to which 'fornication and sexual impurity are felt to be the worst form of depravity', is an attitude 'still influential in the New Testament' (339), and at this point he says nothing to suggest that the New Testament transcended this attitude or overcame antinomies inherent in it. Rather he suggests, though he does not exactly say, that the achievement of Judaism in this respect is the best that can be obtained. 'If nothing like this is to be found anywhere else in the wisdom of the ancient Near East, then credit can only go to the Jewish belief in

the Creator God, before whom man and woman stand in equal responsibility'
(339).

Similarly, in the matter of obedience to parents (339f.), and in that of lying
and deceit, the emergence of ἁπλότης, 'simplicity and sheer straightforward-
ness of conduct', emerges as a basic ethical concept; this is 'the expression of a
matured understanding and incorruptible respect for the duty of truthfulness,
such as ancient Israel had never known' (II, 340). Moreover, he writes that 'this
should warn us not to write off the piety of Judaism, in so far as it encourages
the keeping of the law, as no more than holiness through works . . . the shaping
of life by the Law is equipped with strong safeguards against the danger of
externalism, and constantly leads men back from mere keeping of the
commandments to ultimate personal decision' (II, 303). This last is an important sentence, for it shows that Eichrodt was capable of writing an evaluation
which set the esteem of Jewish religion much higher, and which indeed, if he
had been consistent, would have undermined many of the other judgments that
he himself had written.

It would be mistaken, therefore, to suppose that the sort of statements we
have noticed are necessarily part of a deliberate and consistent tendency. In
many cases they are probably the reverse, because even scholars whom we have
found to say depreciatory things about Judaism can be found also to criticize
depreciatory remarks made by others. Thus Eichrodt, in his highly critical
review of Fosdick's *A Guide to the Understanding of the Bible*,[2] which has been
discussed in another connection above, criticizes Fosdick for making remarks
which would seem to entail an unfavourable view of Judaism. For example, he
criticizes Fosdick for regarding the temple as an obstacle to the universalist
message preached by the prophets, and goes on to say: 'Where one can see the
temple only as an obstacle to the universalism preached by the prophets, then
Judaism too will be valued only as a fall back into the particularism already overcome, along with all the narrow conceptions of the tribal deity' (212f.). Again,
where Fosdick blames Judaism for failing to draw from the prophetic tradition
the 'logical consequence' of 'religion as free, individual choice without dependence on race or nation', Eichrodt suggests that the idea of election in Judaism,
'much as it misses the New Testament's width of vision, may perhaps represent
the more faithful continuation of the prophetic tradition in its *Ausgleich* with the
priestly than a limitless religious individualism can do' (216–17). He goes on to
say that it is 'somewhat too simple to want to define the essence of Judaism with
the idea of racial, national and religious particularism' (217).

A more unfavourable consideration, on the other hand, lies in the fact that
Eichrodt's strictures on later Judaism are seldom adequately based on textual
evidence. When he is writing about Hellenistic times he gives fairly good
references from the apocryphal books,[3] but for Rabbinic sources his citation of

passages is extremely thin, often non-existent, as Levenson has correctly pointed out.[4] Only in very few cases are references given (e.g. II, 74 nn.1,3, and II, 348, referred to above). Occasional references to details, e.g. the mention of Eleazar b. Durdaiah in Aboda Zara 17a (II, 474) and of Akiba (ibid. n.3), also of M. Sota (II, 315 n.), and of Shemot Rabba (400 n.), show that he had the means to do more. He does not entirely ignore the work of Jewish scholars – the prominence of which in biblical scholarship was, of course, much lower at the time of his original writing than it later came to be: for example, the well-known study of Büchler on sin and atonement is quoted at II, 314, 421, 444.

He warmly commended the monograph of R. Sander on fear and love, which appeared in 1935 (II, 314). This work, which one does not see much referred to, is a brief but interesting study. In its first part it surveys the relation between fear of God and love of God in a series of essential sources: 1. Deuteronomy; 2. Nehemiah; 3. the Psalms; 4. Ben Sira; 5. the Testaments of the Twelve Patriarchs; 6. the Psalms of Solomon. Its second part is devoted to the discussion of two rabbinic texts, Mishnah Sota 5.5 and Tosephta Sota 6. 1, in which representative rabbinic authorities discuss the question whether first Job, and secondly Abraham, obeyed the Lord out of fear or out of love. Sander seems to hold that, for the Tannaites named, love is not only the higher motive, but also incorporates a special kind of piety in which it is contrasted with fear (118). One might have expected that this would lead Eichrodt to modify his thesis about love and fear. On the other hand the final statement of Sander's monograph that 'at this decisive point Jewish law-piety points beyond itself to a more profound solution to the question of the relation of fear of God and love of God – to the New Testament' comes closer to Eichrodt's own way of concluding the matter. But at least Sander's thesis was a carefully, textually argued work, containing much detailed information, and Eichrodt clearly admired its qualities. As a whole, however, the fact is that, when Eichrodt speaks of deficiencies in later Judaism and antinomies which were later to be overcome in Christianity, he is usually voicing common Christian generalities and has turned away from the sort of exposition founded on text and evidence which he applies in the main parts of the Hebrew Bible. He seldom cites even the New Testament in this respect, and never subjects it to serious exegesis. There can be no question that for the most part he is not rethinking his material, as he has done in the main part of his book, but is simply giving vent to customary Christian commonplaces that are quite unworthy of the general level of his work.

It is true that he sometimes recognizes that new patterns emerging in late Judaism are produced through following out lines already begun within the Hebrew Bible. For instance, the view of responsibility and guilt taken in the Deuteronomistic and Chronistic works of history leads in a direction which is made firmer in post-biblical Judaism (Eichrodt, II, 293). Nevertheless the main impression, strongly given, is that in spite of differences within the Old Testament itself and similarities between its latest parts and post-biblical Judaism, a general structural unity is perceptible so long as we remain within the Old Testament canon, while post-biblical Judaism is perceived mainly as a disintegration of this structural unity. The New Testament, by contrast, is taken as something like a restoration of this structural unity.

Thus though post-biblical Judaism is not excluded in principle (Eichrodt I, 35), and though its historical mediation of ideas is admitted, the theological evaluation of it within the total scheme is basically negative. There seems to be little attempt to discern any meaning or purpose in this process, disintegration or whatever it may be, whether in itself or as an intermediate stage between Old and New Testaments.

It is interesting, however, that in his general introduction, when considering the material base relevant to his project, Eichrodt (I, 35) considers the question whether it should be confined to the Old Testament documents, 'or ought it also to draw on the extra-canonical Scriptures of Judaism?'. Does he mean here only the apocryphal books? Perhaps, but his next sentence suggests something more, for he goes on to admit: 'there can be no vital objection to bringing within the scope of our study the ways in which later Judaism worked over and appropriated the realm of Old Testament thought', which would suggest the inclusion of all the main Jewish tradition. On this see further below.

Incidentally, and before we pass on to other theologians than Eichrodt, it is interesting to consider the nature of some traditional 'disparaging' remarks. Take Eichrodt's saying, already quoted, that 'in later Judaism the basis of personal relation to God is fear'. While for him this applies to later Judaism, he clearly does not mean it to apply to the Hebrew Bible itself, or to Christianity and the New Testament either. Certainly he intends it to be disparaging. So one may be inclined to deny that it is true, to say that it is quite false to think of 'fear' as a central element. But what if that is true? Curiously, the argument works in the opposite direction from a disparagement. For, purely statistically, the use of terms for 'fearing' God is very prominent in the Old Testament itself, so that, if they are prominent in later Judaism, too, that supports its continuity with the Bible rather than forming a contrast! Moreover, within Christianity itself the idea of 'fearing God' is highly respectable: to speak of a 'God-fearing man', even if uncommon in the language of today, was certainly a term of high respect up to the twentieth century.

'Legalism' works in the same way. Unquestionably 'legalism' in most Christian usage is seen negatively, as an undesirable attitude or policy, and that is what Eichrodt meant. One might therefore want to say in defence: 'No, Judaism is not at all as legalistic as people suppose.' Many Jews have argued in this way, and Christians sympathetic to Judaism have done the same. But what

if it *is* legalistic? Then a quite different counter-argument is possible. My friend
Bernard Jackson wrote a excellent article entitled 'Legalism' to this effect:

> We Jews have in recent years allowed ourselves to believe all too readily that
> the Jewish reply to Christian critics of Judaism, the reply represented by the
> works not only of Jews like Montefiore, Israel Abrahams, Schechter, Heschel
> and Boaz Cohen but also of non-Jews such as Moore and Herford, has con-
> vinced the mainstream of at least informed Christian opinion that Judaism is
> not so bad after all; that it has its inwardness; that it is not obsessed by
> rewards and punishments; that it delights in the law and is not burdened by
> it. But this is selling the pass. It is seeking to justify Judaism in Christian, not
> Jewish terms. Moreover, it has succeeded less fully than some believe.[5]

Jackson goes on to present a powerful analysis of elements in Christianity which
have made it appear that 'legalism' is wrong. On the contrary, it turns out,
legalism is an entirely proper and salutary approach to life; there is nothing
wrong with it. Law should be viewed, he concludes, 'in terms of moderated,
classical warmth' (22). These observations widen the options suggested by
Eichrodt's remarks.[6]

Returning to Eichrodt's ideas in general, we may note that his remarks as
cited above by no means represent extreme or exceptional judgments. They are
at least intended as evaluations of the religious phenomena, and stop short of
saying that Judaism was simply wrong or that it was an example of disobedience
to the will of God. Such more extreme opinions can indeed be found in the
literature. Thus Hans Walter Wolff, a highly esteemed contributor to the discussion of biblical theology, even if he did not write a Theology of the Old
Testament in a complete form, speaks repeatedly not only of a religious defect
but of disobedience to God. In an article on hermeneutics, in a section written
to show that the total meaning of the Old Testament cannot be seen either
through analogy with the oriental religions or through 'its historical connection
with late Judaism and the synagogue' (166), Wolff[7] considers that Judaism has
made the Law into its determinative centre, thus separating the Law from its
context in the historical traditions. The Old Testament itself, he alleges, makes
it clear that this is a 'completely erroneous viewpoint'. He continues: 'The
absolutizing of the law in the synagogue tears it out of the context in the
Pentateuch in which it is firmly surrounded by God's saving deeds for Israel and
his covenant for Israel, and is given as God's help for life' (170). Turning to
another aspect, he adds that the 'philosophical interpretation which regarded
the Torah as the source of all wisdom' was a 'strange honour' which 'completely
silences the Old Testament' (171). 'The synagogue forsakes God's path of life,
which he began in the old covenant, separating God's covenant law from his
covenant acts and seeking in vain to fulfil it in legal casuistry' (176). 'Jesus Christ

restores the connection – broken by the Rabbinate – of the law of God with the covenant of God as a guide for the life of the covenant people' (176). These remarks are distinctly more negative towards Judaism than those quoted above from Eichrodt.

Some other biblical theologians seem to vary back and forwards in their remarks about later Judaism. Take the following passage from Vriezen:

> Thus the relation between Old Testament and New Testament is depicted as essentially one of great tension: in Christian theology neither the historical and spiritual connection on the one hand, nor the historical and spiritual differences on the other, must be neglected. The church must always be willing to admit that 'from the historical point of view the Talmud is just as legitimate a continuation of the Old Testament as the gospel' [the quotation here from H. W. Obbink], without admitting, however, that essentially and spiritually the Talmud is the true continuation and the best interpretation of the message of the Old Testament; between Judaism and Christianity there will always remain a fundamental difference of opinion as to the value of the Old Testament. The Christian Church would renounce her true basis if she did not acknowledge Jesus Christ as the author and finisher of faith (faith in the sense of that relation to God which is exemplified in the patriarchs and the prophets) (121).

Vriezen here wants the church to 'admit' something, but not very much. The Talmud is as legitimate a continuation of the Old Testament as the gospel is, but only 'from an historical point of view', and given the contrast in the previous sentence between 'historical' and 'spiritual' the implication appears to be that from a spiritual point of view (Dutch *geestelijk-zakelijk*, perhaps 'spiritually and in respect of content', 128) the Talmud does not have the same legitimacy.[8]

Vriezen draws our attention to what he considers to be a Jewish conception, according to which there is a 'correlation' between God and the faithful Israelite, a conception which, he says, is to be found in many forms of present-day Judaism (159). Following Miskotte, he declares this view to be 'incompatible with the Old Testament prophetic conception' and thinks that this is 'one of the essential oppositions between the synagogue and Christian theology'. But it is not clear what sort of 'correlation' is being talked about, or where the evidence for it is to be found.[9] Judging from the subject-matter of the previous paragraph, one guesses that the idea is that God and the faithful Israelite are naturally and mutually related, perhaps something like an ontological unity. In comparison with Christian doctrines of grace, this certainly makes an unfavourable impression on the Christian reader. But the passage is too badly presented to be taken very seriously.

On the matter of ritual becoming 'mere observance', a well-known Christian objection to later Judaism, Vriezen is more favourable to the latter. First he formulates the common criticism: 'The cultic ritual gradually gets stuck in mere observance and was looked upon more and more as the highest spiritual achievement, a danger that seems inherent to any legalism and sacramentalism in piety.' But then he gives us the other side: 'We must keep in mind, however, that *rabbinic Judaism* often remained conscious of the relativity of the ceremonial ritual; for them it was a secondary phenomenon, while spiritual penitence was accorded central and primary place' (121, first English ed. 299).

The conclusion of the same chapter, however, rather takes away this more generous recognition. In the end spontaneity disappears from Jewish religion, which sinks into formalism. 'It is this religiosity of the Pharisees and Scribes, depicted in the New Testament, which had to resist in hardness of heart the new, highest revelation of Israel's God in Jesus Christ . . .' (288f., first English ed. 314)

On another well-worn theme, the view of human sinfulness, Vriezen points out that this is 'a very profound difference between Judaism and Christianity' (286, first English ed. 311). 'Judaism has never been able to admit that the will of man is sinful, that sin has affected the essence of human life.' He then explains the good and bad 'inclinations', as everyone does at this point. 'We may therefore say that Judaism recognized both a natural will of man which is weak and inclined to sin, and a good will which directs itself towards the Law and keeps the natural will under control. It is this difference between Judaism and Christianity that makes the former seek salvation by the Law, the latter by God's act of salvation.' All this is familiar enough, and many people have said the same thing.[10] But then Vriezen adds the significant final sentence: 'In the Old Testament we find the seeds of both these views.' This seems to imply that the position found in later Judaism, though profoundly contrasting with Christianity, is a legitimate development from seeds existing in the Bible itself.

In Vriezen also, then, we seem to find an unreconciled conflict between two tendencies: on the one hand at times he recognizes the valid continuity between rabbinic Judaism and the Old Testament, at least historically but sometimes even in terms of theological content; at other points he returns to the familiar description of loss of spontaneity, collapse into formalism, legalism and so on. With Vriezen it is rather more clear, however, that he is thinking seriously about Judaism and trying to find some sort of balance. He quotes Jewish scholars a good deal more than Eichrodt had done.

With von Rad, as we have seen, we have a different kind of theology in which the emphasis lies no longer on religious concepts or religious attitudes, but rather on historical acts of deliverance. Theologies of *Heilsgeschichte*, however, have generally been far from making room for any positive theological importance to be accorded to the development of Jewish tradition. Far from considering this development as an element in the history of salvation, they have tended to exclude it from the latter. Thus von Rad appears to hold that the concentration on the law, its 'absolutization', which took place in later Judaism, involved a sort of cessation of movement in the history of salvation:

> In the post-exilic age . . . Israel now no longer appeared as a people determined by nature and history; it was the law that more and more began to define who belonged to her and who did not . . . what was Israel and what was not became a matter of the interpretation of the law . . . [The] flexibility of Yahweh's revelation, allowing it to gear itself to the place and time and condition of the Israel of the time addressed, ceases. The law becomes an absolute entity, unconditionally valid irrespective of time or historical situation. But this made the revelation of the divine commandments something different from what it had hitherto been. This was no longer the helpful directing will of the God who conducted his people through history: rather it is now beginning to become 'the law' in the theological sense of the word. Up to now the commandments had been of service to the people of Israel as they made their way through history and through the confusion occasioned by heathen forms of worship. But now Israel had to serve the commandments. Certainly the old way of looking at the commandments was still preserved in the post-exilic community for a considerable period. We do not as yet see any legal casuistry proper. But when the law was made absolute, the path to such casuistry, with its intrinsic consequences, had to be followed out. What weighed most heavily, however, was this, that with this understanding of the law Israel stepped outside history, that is, out of the history which she had hitherto experienced with Yahweh. She did not depart from her relation to Yahweh: but once she began to look upon the will of Yahweh as timelessly absolute, the history of salvation necessarily stood still over her. This Israel had no history any longer, at least no history with Yahweh. From now on she lived and served her God in an enigmatic 'beyond history.[11]

Von Rad goes on to trace from this the uncomfortable separation of Israel from the other nations, a loss of solidarity with which there came suspicion and hatred.

Presumably the textual basis von Rad has in mind, though he does not make this very clear, is the difference between the dominantly historical narrative of the Hebrew Bible and the legal-discussion style, coupled with an admixture of anecdote rather than biblical-style history that characterizes the Rabbinic literature. And this difference may be very important. But even if so, we are left with the same question that very often arises in discussions of *Heilsgeschichte* and especially in von Rad's own use of the term. What is the relation between the use of *heilsgeschichtlich* terms of thinking by human beings and the continuance of a factual *Heilsgeschichte* on the part of God himself? Does one continue when the other is absent? Or is there a salvation history only when people are actually thinking that way, in *heilsgeschichtlich* terms? On the level of human thought-forms, no doubt a considerable change can be traced, and along the line suggested by von Rad. The production of fresh historical writings, giving a theological interpretation of the history of the Jews on lines comparable to those of the Pentateuchal narratives or those in the Former Prophets, hardly continues: yet even so, what of I and II Maccabees? The personalities of early times come to be seen as illustrations of the problems and situations of later piety, as if no material historical change in the religion had taken place since the time of Moses, or indeed since that of Noah. But, to pursue my main point, what is lacking in von Rad's statement – which, indeed, is doubtless not intended to be exhaustive – is any hint that this change *away* from a *heilsgeschichtlich* approach on the people's part may itself in a wider sense be part of the working of the divine purpose in history. As a result his statement at least gives the impression that a shift away from *heilsgeschichtlich* modes of thinking on the people's part brings to an end the kind of actual relation with the deity which had hitherto come to expression in *Heilsgeschichte*.

For the present I shall make only two observations about this position. First, in terms of the theological values applied by von Rad himself, this view is again very negative towards Judaism. It depicts it as on the one hand a religion that has somehow slipped out from the essential historical process through which alone the true God is known, and on the other hand as a religion, and the religion of a people, that is somehow bracketed out from whatever is going on in the world. And, of course, traditional words of blame such as 'casuistry' are still here. On the other hand, the whole scheme produces difficulties even for Christian theology; for it is by no means a traditional scheme repeated, but is very much von Rad's own thinking, so far as I know. Is it possible to have a history of salvation that comes to a stop when people cease to use its categories? And is it possible to have a history of salvation that is sometimes going and sometimes not?[12]

I have done enough to indicate that deprecation of Judaism, and failure to recognize its positive importance for all work in Bible and religion, has been present in Old Testament theology and has been a discredit to it. It seems to me likely, however, that in this respect this century has seen a change of spirit within Christian writing on Old Testament theology. The examples I have cited above come from the early great classics of twentieth-century work – Eichrodt, Vriezen, von Rad. As we come on into the post-von Rad generation, it seems that we find less of this sort of thing, less tendency to point out how the great theological insights of the Old Testament came to dry up in later Judaism, to be spoiled, to be overlaid with formalism, legalism and the rest. I hope at least that it is so. And in fact experience makes it certain. I myself took up the matter in a 1966 paper entitled 'The Theological Evaluation of Post-biblical Judaism', versions of which were published in several places.[13] As against those who have depicted the work of Old Testament theology as characterized by anti-Jewish animus and even 'intense anti-Semitism', certainly in the latter part of the century the reverse has been the case: as I wrote in my review of Levenson's book, 'in spite of the faults pointed out, which are not to be denied, the tradition of modern biblical theology, taken as a whole, has been one of the major sources of philo-Semitism and pro-Jewish attitudes in the Christianity of this century. Anyone who has experienced the movement knows this.'[14] By contrast, those who seek to undermine Old Testament theology are likely to create a Christianity that is *more*, and not *less*, critical towards Judaism.

Actually, if one were seeking to identify a locus of negativity towards Judaism, it would be more plausible to locate it in the tradition of *New Testament* theology rather than in that of Old Testament theology. In New Testament theology the figure of Rudolf Bultmann has still a very central place. Räisänen tells us that 'for Bultmann, the old view of Judaism as an anthropocentric legalistic religion (in the pejorative sense of the word) was fundamental to his whole construction', and Bultmann's account of Judaism 'amounts to a vicious caricature and causes his New Testament theology to be incurably lop-sided'.[15] Views of this kind have sometimes been more integral to New Testament theology than they have been to Old Testament theology, where, as we have seen, they have often been rather marginal and marked by inner contradiction.

In fact, in work on Old Testament theology written after 1960 or so there is much less sign of the depreciatory remarks which have been quoted. Quite the reverse can be shown, for example in W. Zimmerli's Sprunt Lectures for 1963, *The Law and the Prophets. A Study of the Meaning of the Old Testament*. Though this is written very much from a Christian point of view, and points forward to a desired complementation in New Testament scholarship and in systematic theology (95), it seems to be completely lacking in disparaging references to the late biblical period or to Judaism. The emphasis is rather on the need for a *dialogue* with Judaism, 'the open, brotherly and listening conversation of the church with Israel', emphasized in the concluding paragraph (96) and also in the Introduction (3). This emphasis on a brotherly dialogue with Israel is something that was lacking in some earlier works, and it makes much difference to the atmosphere in which the discussion is carried on. For a fuller presentation of Zimmerli's thinking see below, Chapter 19. The idea, unfortunately disseminated by certain publications, that Old Testament theology is *necessarily* disparaging towards Judaism, is quite untrue.

There are several reasons why this change of atmosphere took place.

One is that, as has been suggested above, the earlier Old Testament theologians gave higher priority to the establishment of connections with the New Testament than did their later successors (up to a certain point): the more this was emphasized, the more some sort of contrastive picture of Judaism was likely to be implied. At least some among the more recent Old Testament theologians, as has been shown, really said very little about the New Testament at all.

In addition, the last decades have probably seen a more sympathetic study of the *latest* Old Testament period, and coupled with that has been the great interest in intertestamental studies, occasioned among other things by the Qumran discoveries. The idea that late sources are religiously less good is now much less fashionable. The tendency (whether right or wrong) to give a late date, even within the Bible itself, to sources formerly thought to be early is another factor of the same kind.

Moreover, a larger number of Christian scholars have been working in some kind of common context with Jews, and have found it impossible to continue uttering some of the traditional polemical views. In addition, though the terrible events of the war lay back before 1945, it was more like 1960 when full realization of their implications began to be widespread through fresh writing in scholarly literature.

Again, much New Testament scholarship has been questioning the validity of some of the pictures of Jewish religion cast up by the New Testament documents themselves, and this has suggested that relations may have been different from what these documents on the face of them seemed to earlier scholarship to imply.[16]

One or two general points may be added here. Leaving aside for the present the question of post-biblical documents, they concern the evaluation of biblical texts themselves. Undoubtedly the tendency of biblical scholars to see some late texts as marking a deterioration of some kind has given offence to many people. This has been particularly so when it involved the Pentateuchal source P (though it is not clear that any of the three Old Testament theologians mentioned in this chapter, Eichrodt, Vriezen and von Rad, thought that there was any deterioration in P). Other familiar cases are the comparison between Samuel/Kings and the later Chronicles, and matters such as the dissolution of priestly marriages in Ezra/Nehemiah (contrast Joseph's marriage to Asenath in Gen. 46.20, that of Simeon with a Canaanite woman in 46.10, and that of Moses himself to a Cushite woman). All I want to say here is that some kind of deterioration in later stages is not an unusual cultural phenomenon. Literatures may have a 'Golden Age' followed by a 'Silver Age'. The idea that great movements of human culture have in the end a decline, a 'Silver Age', a passage over to a less creative stage, is by no means only a religious idea but is one that is widely used in general studies of cultural awareness. And is it not right? Was

Greek drama at the same level in the first century as it had been in the fifth? Is Italian opera as creative in the twentieth century as it was in the nineteenth? In other words, is it to be absolutely forbidden ever to perceive or to express an opinion that will imply some sort of religious decline or deterioration? If late religious texts should be seen to show some decrease in power or effectiveness, that perception is not necessarily only a matter of prejudice or improper presupposition.

Such a feeling about some later texts is not necessarily a criticism specifically directed at Judaism, for the same perception is in fact very common within Christianity itself. Most people think that II Peter is inferior to I Peter, and Jude (often considered late, though not without contrary scholarly opinion)[17] is not very highly thought of. Moreover, it is generally thought that this fits with the fact that the material written was deteriorating in quality in the later New Testament period, and that this was a reason why a canon was formed at all, to separate the authoritative books from those that came after them. Some disagree with this way of thinking and hold that it is illegitimate to make any distinctions in value between texts, and this may be so; all I say is that it is a way people do think, and confirms that within Christianity there is such a relative evaluation.

It is not likely, however, that the problem will simply go away. As many scholars, both Jewish and Christian, have noted, some kind of serious conflict seems to be involved and in the long run remains ineluctable. What can be done, I would suggest, is for Christian scholarship at least to gain a perception that the post-biblical development of Jewish tradition is a valid – not necessarily the only valid, but at least one valid – continuation of the lines set up in the Old Testament itself. If this could be accepted, it would at least remove the suggestion that Judaism had actually turned against the main current of biblical religion. And, purely historically speaking, it is probable that agreement on this could be obtained. But, in order for it to have real strength and effectiveness within Christianity, it would probably be necessary for resources from within Christian theology itself to be assembled which would convince people that such a line has real meaning from within the Christian sphere of meaning itself. Can such a line of understanding be developed?

The following section takes up again the position I outlined in my articles in 1966 and thereafter.[18] The argument is that, within Christianity, the Old Testament is related to the total work of salvation (and thereby related also to the New Testament) not only through what it is in itself but also indirectly through the tradition of interpretation which grew up from it. A theological understanding of the Old Testament must therefore be not only a theology of the Old Testament, as that term has generally been understood in the developments we have traced, but also a theological evaluation of the interpretative tradition which factually grew from the Old Testament in the centuries following its writing and compilation.

From a Christian point of view, therefore, we could say: Jesus Christ comes in a time when a scripture already exists and a tradition of its development has already developed. This constitutes the setting of his ministry. It is thus not accidental, but positively significant, that Jesus does not come into the situation of Old Testament times themselves, but appears only after there has been a time of ripening or maturation; in this time the heritage of the completed (or almost completed) Old Testament has taken effect in the historical development of the diverse currents of thought within the Jewish people, themselves the historical successors to the people of the Hebrew Bible itself. Thus the New Testament idea of 'the fullness of time' may have a more powerful theological connection with this ripening of Jewish tradition than with the political and technical apparatus of the Roman Empire, which is so often suggested as a connection. The Gospels give much space to the controversies between Jesus and the representatives of the various contemporary Jewish traditions. This is not necessarily because the Gospels reflect *subsequent* conflicts between church and synagogue; it may rather be that the conflict with the established tradition of interpretation is itself constitutive for the nature and concept of Christ altogether. Not only has the work of Jesus to be seen in relation to the Old Testament, but that relation is a dialectical one between two realities, namely the Old Testament itself and the prevailing tradition of its interpretation. This conflict between Jesus and the tradition, as the Gospels depict the matter, is a main cause for enmity against Jesus and rejection of him, even though it remains true that Jesus does not reject the tradition wholly and unequivocally. Thus the conflict with the tradition is a cause leading to the death of Jesus and thereby an agent in the salvation of the world.

The paradox and tragedy in this, however, is much too easily and fatally resolved if we simply consider the post-biblical Jewish tradition to be 'wrong'. Where the Old Testament is valued positively in itself and Christians take sides with Jesus against the interpretative tradition, the effect of this is to throw all the blame directly upon the Jewish tradition. The simplification of these relations is a reason why much Christian scholarship has been alienated from the Jewish interpretative tradition. Even historically there are reasons for holding that the relations were more complicated. Jesus, as portrayed in the Gospels, did something to commend, as well as to contradict, the Jewish tradition. Moreover, as we see it today, apart from the explicit comments about contemporary Judaism, Jesus and the apostles shared deeply in the unspoken general attitudes of contemporary Judaism; and even when they appealed back to the Old Testament against the tradition, that appeal did not make them into men of the Old

Testament itself. The New Testament does indeed see a certain recrudescence of older patterns of experience, such as a sort of revival of prophecy, but the general context remains one separated from the Old Testament (yet also joined with it) by some centuries of history and intellectual development. And, turning to the more theological comparison, we hardly have the right to consider the course of Jewish tradition as a 'wrong' development without also trying to see alternative ways in which it could have gone in this situation. This thought in turn brings us back to a point where theology and religious history meet: for it seems to me that the post-biblical development of Jewish tradition *was* in many ways both a 'natural' one and one which stood in continuity with tendencies already present within the later formative elements of the Old Testament itself. But in general, putting the point in a theological way which will summarize the argument: if there is a 'history of salvation', then the historical development of Jewish tradition, between the Old Testament and the time of Jesus, is part of that history of salvation. And, if between the Old Testament and the time of Jesus, then also between the Old Testament and, let us say, the completion of the Talmud.

If we talk, then, of a theological evaluation of post-biblical Jewish interpretation of the Old Testament, we may begin with a negative point, with an explanation of what this does *not* mean. It does not mean that we make a list of the concepts and attitudes of Judaism in the intertestamental period and then go through this list trying to mark each item as good or bad or as lying close to (or far from) the corresponding Old Testament point of view. This has already been too much done; and when it has been done it has too often resulted in judgments unfavourable to Judaism. It is not the purpose of a theological evaluation, as I envisage it, that we should pass judgment on post-biblical Judaism and decide to our satisfaction which elements in it were good and which bad, which in agreement with the Old Testament and which in disagreement. The significance of post-biblical Jewish tradition for the achievement of salvation in Jesus Christ is not dependent on the tradition's being 'right' or 'wrong': it depends rather on the fact that this tradition is the one that did indeed grow from the Old Testament, as it factually worked upon the minds of the people of Israel, the descendants of those in whose life the Old Testament text took shape. Even if there should be elements in the later development of tradition of which we could say quite certainly that they had departed from the essentials of the Old Testament (and I do not assert that there were such), these elements might still, within Christian biblical theology, have positive meaning through their contribution to the work of salvation; and the same might be true of elements of Persian or of Greek origin which might have entered Judaism in the post-biblical era.

Thus our theological evaluation of the function of post-biblical Jewish tradition does not consist primarily in a judgment of *its rightness or wrongness* by reference either to Christian theological standards or to the position found within the Old Testament itself. The question is rather that of the general theological construction which we put upon the fact that a Jewish interpretative tradition existed at all. Only within such a theological construction can we hope to approach a *theological* answer to questions of the 'rightness' or 'wrongness' of post-biblical traditions, and seen from this perspective these questions may take a form quite different from what we had expected.

The kind of theological constructions which I have in mind might include such elements as the following:

1. The Old Testament is a crystallization of Israel's experience with God, and includes within itself some considerable reinterpretation of earlier stages within that experience. It was the will of God that this process of interpretation should not cease with the completion of the books now held to be canonical, and that his people should continue to interpret and develop their traditions as their own situation grew and changed.

2. This tradition of interpretation, like all biblical interpretation (including the process of formation of the biblical books themselves), was marked by both obedient response and human distortion, yet nevertheless in such a way that the purpose of God continued to be fulfilled. The product of Jewish tradition therefore deserves the respect of Christian scholarship, and indeed of the Christian community as a whole, and the conflicts between Jesus and Jewish tradition do not entitle us to diminish that respect.

3. The degree to which Jewish (and Christian) interpretation is 'valid' or 'natural' is a proper subject for discussion between Jewish and Christian scholarship, the operation being a comparison between the traditions and the texts which they are supposed to interpret. 'Validity' and 'naturalness' are terms which imply the following question: do the forces which led to changes in thought and understanding within the interpretative process have their origin or base within the Old Testament itself? While the subject is a fit one for debate, Christian theology should refrain from general judgments which would prejudice the case against Jewish interpretations. Moreover, judgments traditionally based on sayings in the Gospels or in Paul are today somewhat relativized because we have the opportunity of greater understanding of the historical circumstances in which various traditions arose.

4. The Jewish interpretative tradition constituted the setting for the ministry of Jesus. Among other things, it fixed certain common elements which were unquestioned by the Christian movement; on the other hand, it contained tensions between scripture and tradition which were a central means for the

testing of human insight and obedience, focussing the relation between a revelation acknowledged to have been given and the product which men had made of it.

5. The Christian conflict with the Jewish interpretative tradition is thus a deep tragedy, the sense of which is lost if this tradition is regarded as intrinsically invalid or artificial. The disagreement carries with it a profound sense of *loss*, to which the closest expression in the New Testament is no doubt the Pauline meditation on the destiny of Israel (Romans 9–11).

I conclude with some remarks on consequences which would seem to follow from this approach.

First, this approach implies that the lines of demarcation for the canon of scripture are not identical with the circumference or horizon within which we look for God's revelation or (to use another term) his activity for the fulfilment of his special purpose. Indeed the lines of the canon, as defined for Old and New Testaments, have made it difficult for us to evaluate the 'intertestamental' tradition theologically. It is striking and characteristic for Christianity that a vitally important formative stage lies in a period which the canonical scriptures (and also, to a large extent, the Jewish sources accepted as authoritative in later Judaism) *do not* cover.

Secondly, our approach may help us with some passages in which the New Testament views the Old Testament situation in a way which we as exegetes of the Old Testament can no longer affirm. A clear instance is Paul's concept of 'law'. Though Israel in ancient times may not have lived under 'law' in a sense such as Paul intended, the rise of such a 'law' was a factual historical product of the interpretative tradition through influences continuous from Old Testament times down into later Judaism. The validity of the Pauline conception is thus not destroyed by the fact that we have to see it in a much more indirect way than he could.

Thirdly, our approach might have consequences for general exegetical method. The main emphasis in exegesis – not just in modern times but going a long way back – has been on the coming-to-be of the text, the circumstances which led up to its formation. If texts are related not only to a revelation of God which preceded them but also to the shape which his work would take thereafter, it might be that exegesis should pay more attention to the *effect* that text had afterwards. The difficulty in this is the commentary form, organized according to the sequence and unity of the text. Ancient interpretation commonly did not follow this sequence and unity; texts had an effect not through being expounded in the sequence and context in which they originally stood, but through being built up into the religious structure in ways which the modern critical commentary can hardly hope to follow. In so far as the effect of texts can be followed at all, it may have to be done through a historical account of the rise of a tradition in conjunction with the newer forms of religion which accompany it. If this can be done, it will be a more theologically positive work than recent Old Testament theology has tended to suggest. I shall have more to say about this, however, in Chapter 22, where I discuss Gese's proposals.

It should be recognized that one of the reasons why Christian scholars have tended to perceive 'defects' or 'weaknesses' in some late sources is that they see the same sort of thing in the New Testament. Apart from unyielding biblicists and canonical extremists, most Christians feel that some of the later books of the New Testament are less good expressions of the core of Christianity than earlier sources are. II Peter is not as close to the heart of the matter as I Peter or Paul. The letter of Jude, people feel, does not have much idea of what Christianity is about. This may be unjust: I am not trying to say what is correct in this matter, but to describe what people commonly think. The perception of a deterioration is encouraged by the fact of the canon. The canon itself encourages us to think that the religion was not in so good a shape in early post-New Testament times: people do not think that I Clement or Ignatius stand on the same level. For traditional Protestants, only with Augustine do things get back to a really impressive level.

It can of course be argued that historical description should be entirely neutral: it should simply tell how things were, and the categories of good and bad should be completely absent. Yet few are willing to apply these criteria with complete consistency. If we cannot, in any circumstances, suggest that some particular strand of the Hebrew Bible, or some similar source of the New Testament, presents evidence of a less good religious stance than other, more central, sources, then we cannot say that these central sources are 'good' or satisfactory, much less that they are excellent; nor can we pass moral judgments on the various tyrants and genocidal murderers who also pass across the visual horizon of our subject.

In any case, my proposal is not for such neutrality; it is for theological appreciation of what Judaism has been and is, not just as a factually existing religion, but as a religion behind which Christians also perceive the reality of God. Such appreciation has to remain dominant, even when particular unhappy events or unfortunate choices may have to be observed.

We saw above a passage in Eichrodt in which he at least hinted that literature from post-biblical times might be included in the subject-matter of Old Testament theology. He certainly had the apocryphal books in mind, but possibly Rabbinic texts as well, and his brief continuing sentence 'there can be no vital objection to bringing within the scope of our study the ways in which later Judaism worked over and appropriated the realm of Old Testament thought' would seem to leave room for that wider meaning. I remember giving expression to that same thought in some of my own earlier utterances on the subject. When I did so, people tended to react unfavourably: Old Testament theology, they said, could not possibly have room for all that material, and, as one critic remarked, this would mean that one would be taking in all Jewish literature at least up to the completion of the Talmud! But is the idea so fantastic? Indeed one would not seek to write a Theology of all Jewish literature up to that time (at least I would not); but much of that material, though not exactly subject-matter that must be covered entirely within such a Theology, remains *evidence* showing directions in religion and interpretation, some of which must go back as far as the time of Daniel, or as far as the Dead Sea Scrolls. My idea was not, I think, entirely fantastic.

# 18

# Jewish Biblical Theology?

## *1. General*

The earlier literature devoted to Old Testament theology seldom gave any thought to what Jews might think about the matter.[1] The major interest was an intra-Christian apologetic one: to persuade Christians of the theological importance of the Old Testament, taken as a whole; to provide a dominantly theological interpretation rather than a dominantly historical one; and thus to persuade them not to discount it or ignore it as part of their Christianity. As we have seen, the operation at times involved something of a 'Christianizing' of the Old Testament, and similarly sometimes involved disparaging remarks about Judaism. On the other hand it often included high praise for the Hebrew mind and considerable insistence on the Jewish, rather than the Greek, mentality as the basis for New Testament Christianity. But the terms of the discussion lay for the most part within Christianity. What Jews themselves might think about all this was seldom discussed. It was in the later period – perhaps better, after the watershed of von Rad's Theology around 1960 – that something more began to be said about Jewish opinion. By the 1990s, a great deal more was being said.

Generally speaking, the idea of 'Old Testament theology' has not been welcome to Jewish scholars. Goshen-Gottstein wrote in 1987: 'It would seem that while among Christian scholars much rethinking has been going on' – and here he named some representative names – 'Jewish scholars instinctively shrink back at the very mention of "theology" in the context of biblical studies.'[2] Goshen-Gottstein did not share this feeling (I shall discuss his own views later), but few would doubt that he depicted the situation correctly – with some few exceptions.

'Old Testament' itself is a Christian term. That might be thought to be a superficial matter, which could be overcome by a simple change of terms, let us say to 'biblical theology' (which for Jews would ignore the New Testament) or to 'Tanakh theology' (Goshen-Gottstein's own choice) or to 'theology of Hebrew Scriptures'. More profound, as we shall see, is the difficulty of 'theology' itself. For it too can be considered overwhelmingly a Christian word and some Jews, I think understandably, have felt it so.

The term can, indeed, be used in a wide inter-religious way, as when we talk of 'Muslim theology' or of the 'theology of the Greek philosophers'. As a purely academic concept, applicable to any religion which has some kind of reflective and conceptual core, the term might be justified. But where we are thinking about relations between Jews and Christians, the determinative factual meanings are other. 'Theology' is often felt to be a Christian thing, not something that Jews undertake or that Jewish religion requires, desires, or possesses. If the central intellectual activity of Christianity is theology, the corresponding intellectual activity of Judaism could be reasonably said to be law, along with which one could set *interpretation*.[3] Another way it is sometimes expressed is by saying that for Jews *the Torah* is the limit; to go beyond this and form thoughts about God and his nature is to go too far. So Jews, generally speaking, manage to get along in their religion without either reading Theologies or feeling the need to write them.

Yet this is not entirely true. There is in fact a substantial tradition of 'Jewish theology', with books called exactly this, *Jewish Theology*, some of them written by persons of unquestionable authority. Thus Louis Jacobs, Chief Rabbi of Great Britain, wrote for the *Encyclopedia Judaica* (1971) an article 'Theology' which in a short space displayed something of the richness of Jewish theology through the ages up to modern times, and in 1973 his *A Jewish Theology* appeared. Another work of importance a century back was the *Jewish Theology* of Kaufman Kohler, the 'first major theoretician' (Goshen-Gottstein, ibid., 638 n. 26) of Reform Judaism in the United States. Among major Jewish theologians of the mid-century in the English-speaking world one would have to name Will Herberg and A. J. Heschel, as well as others.[4] And, to go back through time, although the line between theology and philosophy is always hard to draw, it would be difficult to avoid counting Saadiah Gaon or Maimonides as theologians.[5] There is therefore, in fact, a very rich and substantial tradition of theology within Judaism. And an increasing acceptance of the term 'theology' is surely indicated when Michael Fishbane, in a chapter on 'Judaism as an Ideological System', has a section on 'Theology' which begins with the sentence 'The native theology of traditional Judaism is a biblical theology'.[6]

Nevertheless the fact of that tradition does not suffice to overcome that strong suspicion of theology among Jewish scholars which has been remarked. What are the reasons for this?

Central, perhaps, is the feeling that Theologies alone, however loyally Jewish and however supported by the authoritative status of the writer, are not enough to represent Judaism fully and as it is. They tend to concentrate more on ideas, beliefs and intellectual arguments, and less on practices, rituals and observances, than the actual profile of the religion requires. Thus Jacobs' *Jewish Theology* has comparatively little to say about the detailed commandments, the dietary laws or the mode of keeping the Sabbath. Not that these were unimportant to the author: to him they were of first importance. But the fact that he was writing a Theology, the necessary structure of it, led him to give less space to these matters than (say) he had done in his own Penguin book *Judaism*.

Add to this the fact that Theologies, however Jewish, could be religiously suspect. Goshen-Gottstein points out (ibid., 638 n. 26) that 'the term "theology" was quite in vogue among nineteenth-century Jewish liberal thinkers'. After a survey of this he concludes: '"Theology" is thus loaded with doubtful connotations for Jewish scholarship today.'

Moreover, 'theology' may have seemed to suggest a certain element of common ground with Christianity. Even when specific Christian doctrines like the Trinity or the divinity of Christ were denied, as was obviously and invariably done, a lot of what looked like common ground seemed to emerge over matters like creation, providence, anthropomorphism, analogy and the place of metaphor in biblical expressions. In these areas there was some sharing of ideas and tendencies. Maimonides provided valuable material to Christian theologians of the Middle Ages. Kaufman Kohler, though he thought Judaism to be entirely different from Christianity, wrote a Theology which was strikingly similar to what contemporary liberal Christians were thinking. In the time of dialectical theology, Martin Buber was almost canonized by large sectors of Christianity. Will Herberg was seen as a sort of Jewish Barthian. This may also be a reason why the currents of Jewish theology, though respected, are regarded with caution.

There may equally, however, be reasons within Jewish life itself that have nothing to do with Christianity. Professional Jewish scholars are, Goshen-Gottstein writes, 'by training Semitic philologists, historians, or archaeologists' (ibid., 621). But they may exist within a wider constituency in which the Bible is interpreted in a quite different way, based on an educational background in which none of these skills are known or recognized. The mere idea of 'biblical theology' may thus suggest a threat to academic standards through the rise of a radically non-academic approach.[7]

Obviously the definition and specification of 'Old Testament theology' or 'biblical theology' will make much difference. How far is it a matter of a *name*? Is it the *term* 'theology' that is distasteful, and could Jewish scholars undertake the same operations if it was seen that they are not really 'theology' in the normal sense, or if their content was delimited in this way or that? For example, as we have seen, some approaches to Old Testament theology have explicitly defined it from the start as a 'Christian' enterprise, and if that is so, obviously Jews will not want to be involved in it. But this in itself would not logically exclude the creation of a *Jewish* biblical theology. In any case, other Christian definitions of the subject have not so defined it, and then it might be possible that the same undertaking might attract Jewish participation, indeed that

Christian scholars would invite it and hope for it. Again, some definitions of the subject have insisted that its goals would include the establishment of connections with the New Testament; here again, Jewish scholars would feel unable to become involved. But other Old Testament theologians, though Christian, have in fact had little to say about the connections with the New Testament. If, therefore, it were made clear that the establishment of connections with the New Testament were not among the necessary aims of the undertaking, would that make a difference?

The question is not a purely hypothetical one, for, as we have seen, even from the Christian side there have been those who have argued that 'Old Testament theology' is not theology at all, or, alternatively, that, if it is theology, it should not be so. Suppose, therefore, that 'Old Testament theology' were defined or redefined as something like a comprehensive description of implied intellectual concepts, taken within the terms and boundaries of the Hebrew Bible and seen as far as possible within its own self-understandings, where would this take us?

## 2. *Tsevat*

A helpful and attractive article by M. Tsevat takes up some of these points. As he vividly points out in his first paragraph, the idea of a 'theology of the Old Testament' is for Judaism something like a 'zoology of the unicorn' – a non-existent science about a non-existent subject.[8] But a few pages later, looking at the actual content of Old Testament theology, which as he says has remained untested and unclear, he sees a sense in which it can be more positively valued. The Old Testament is a collection of books of different kinds and periods. Its 'theology', seen in a minimal sense, is the attempt to uncover and provide a rational basis for some community of its religious ideas (*eine Gemeinsamkeit seiner religiösen Ideen aufzudecken und rational zu begründen*). People do speak, unacademically, of the Old Testament as the testimony to and representation of special ideas characteristic to it, sometimes even of a unity of ideas. The task of this kind of theology is to investigate these unacademic ideas and, when it is justified, to develop their content. In addition to this, theology lends indispensable services to the understanding of individual texts, whether verses, chapters or books: it is the framework in which isolated, incomplete or unclearly expressed expressions or concepts can be placed in order and find their explanation. 'Thus understood, Old Testament theology is a part of Old Testament philology, and in particular is that part which plays over into the history of ideas.'[9] The same would be the case with Shakespeare or Romantic literature. One can ask: what is the idea of *Hamlet*, and how did Shakespeare develop it dramatically? One can go on to ask, of Shakespeare's entire corpus: what was his

picture of man, his idea of freedom, the nature for him of tragedy? The complicated problems of Romanticism can similarly be compared with those of Old
Testament theology, however it is understood. Old Testament theology appears
to be different because of the long-standing attempt to bring its phenomena and
themes into a systematic or hierarchic order – an effect perhaps of medieval
theology, or of philosophy? Even if this is characteristic of the Bible, it does not
alter the fact that Old Testament theology in this sense has its place within the
literary disciplines (*innerhalb der Literaturwissenschaft*). We do not usually talk of
'theology' in reference to Shakespeare, to Romanticism, or to ancient Greek
literature, and even the study of the Old Testament does not require it.
Nevertheless, in view of the fact that the ideas of the Old Testament are mostly
of a religious kind, refer to God, or for other reasons, the term 'theology' might
suitably be retained for this case.

With this Tsevat moves on to other questions. But we have seen the essential
first point he has made. 'Old Testament theology' in this sense is not really
'theology', but a sort of comprehensive intellectual history which is no more
than a recognized part of 'philology' or literary studies. And, one must say,
though many practitioners of Old Testament theology would have been reluctant to admit it, quite a large proportion of their work has been exactly that. Is
it necessary for it to be more?

Thus, to sum up, Old Testament theology is 'a part of that branch of literary
study which has the Old Testament as object; it is Old Testament philology. It
is objective in the way and in the degree to which scholars of the humanities
(*Geisteswissenschaftler*), in particular those whose main task is understanding,
ensure the objectivity of their remarks. Within the total philology of the
Old Testament, theology is concerned with the understanding of its ideas,
especially, if not exclusively, the religious ideas and those that in the true sense
are related to God' (339). Theology in this sense cannot be avoided by Old
Testament scholarship.

This kind of 'theology' can also be called 'negative theology'. If we turn to the
question of a 'positive theology' in a Jewish sense, it cannot stand upon the basis
of the Old Testament alone. Two bodies of literature are equally essential for
Jewish life: the Hebrew Bible on the one side, and the Talmud and Midrash on
the other. The paths from the Hebrew Bible to Talmud and Midrash are few
and uncertain, those from Talmud and Midrash to the Bible are numerous and
well passable. Thus 'Talmud and Midrash Judaize the Old Testament' (338).
'The Old Testament is absorbed in Talmud and Midrash' (339). So, as I understand it, Tsevat holds that a 'positively Jewish' approach would have to be one
to Hebrew Bible, Midrash and Talmud taken together: there could be no
positively Jewish 'theology' of the Hebrew Bible alone.

So far as this goes, from Tsevat's very illuminating discussion, we should conclude that 'Old Testament theology', so long as it is confined to the first or 'negative' kind, is not theology in the proper sense. It is a sort of comprehensive intellectual history of biblical times, which brings together implications and currents of understanding which are necessary for the interpretation of all sorts of details within the text. Seen in this way, it is not a Christian subject: there is absolutely no restriction of the subject to Christians, Jewish contributions are eagerly desired, and it is not easy to see why Jews should not engage in the same operations.

On the other hand, Tsevat's 'positively Jewish theology' deserves attentive consideration. It is not a theology of the Hebrew Bible, but rather a theology of the way in which the Hebrew Bible is linked with Talmud and Midrash, a linkage which has the effect of 'Judaizing' the Bible. This is quite different from the philological intellectual history which he himself has approved for work on the Bible. It is more like a creative, speculative, theological design of his own, one that can hardly be proved on strict philological grounds and one that would not necessarily be accepted by all Jews or shown to be in agreement with all Jewish tradition: would all Jewish currents accept that the Hebrew Bible was 'Judaized' only through its combination with Talmud and Midrash? Is it not faintly similar to the type of Christian 'theology' which expounds the way in which the two 'testaments' are linked to produce Christianity? Right or wrong, this conception will deserve further consideration at a later point.

## 3. Levenson

A contribution with a very different emphasis is to be found in the work of Jon D. Levenson. His book *The Hebrew Bible, the Old Testament, and Historical Criticism* (1993), a volume containing six essays on the relations of Jews and Christians in biblical studies, is highly critical of Old Testament theology, and especially so in the article 'Why Jews are not Interested in Biblical Theology'.[10] This article, originally published in 1987, has attracted considerable attention.[11]

In many discussions there has been some degree of opposition between historical criticism and Old Testament theology, with scholars supporting one and attacking the other. Levenson overcomes this problem by attacking both with equal severity. He seems, on the other hand, to favour the approach through the history of religion.[12] Here we shall concentrate for the most part on his views about Old Testament theology. For a discussion of the book as a whole I refer readers to my review in *JTS* 47, 1996, 555–60.

The article 'Why Jews are not Interested in Biblical Theology' begins with the story of 'a distinguished Continental biblicist' who had been surprised to find no one in Israel who was interested in Old Testament theology. But is this really true to the reality? It may well be the case that one cannot find books called 'Theology of the Hebrew Bible' written by Jews, as Levenson points out. But that does not mean a total lack of interest. Working for months in the excellent Judaica Reading Room of the Library of the Hebrew University of Jerusalem, I was struck to find a selection of the major Old Testament Theologies there on the open shelves, and obviously in some demand, because the books were quite worn and often were not available because someone was using them. And understandably so, because for certain types of questions in biblical study, where else would students be able to turn?

Naturally, Israeli students would not be interested in some of the aims and purposes of these volumes, such as the search of some of them for contacts with the New Testament. But one can of course disregard that element and use the books as what Tsevat called 'neutral theology', in which respect they continue to act as useful sources, discussion and reference material. The Jewish reader knows very well that these books have Christian interests and Christian assumptions, and when he comes to these he simply skips or ignores them; this does not prevent him from profiting from the remainder. And this is of course how Jewish students use the books, as they themselves have told me. So the lack of interest seems not to have been as total as Levenson's example suggested.

Levenson advances several arguments, some of which we have already touched upon in another context.

First, he takes up the already highly familiar problem of the contrast between the history of religion and Old Testament theology. 'Biblical theology is historical in character,' following Gabler, and so things have to be seen in their historical context (35f.). But Old Testament theology works by the cross-section method (after Eichrodt): it seeks to disengage some 'persistent and distinctive principles' (words quoted from Dentan). Or, quoting John Bright, 'the fact of diversity does not eliminate the possibility of an overarching unity, either in the biblical faith or in any other'. Thus in Bright's work, '"covenant" and "promise" are the twin centrepieces. They run through the whole of the Old Testament and inform all of its parts.'

Levenson, however, regards this as an illusion. Once again the bed of Procrustes appears on the scene. 'The fact is, however, that this cross-cut, indeed any cross-cut, is really a Procrustean bed which cannot accommodate major segments of the book or, to be more precise, cannot regard as major the segments of the book which it does not accommodate' (36). Thus, just as Old Testament theologians tended to emphasize the *unity* of the Old Testament (or of the entire Christian Bible), Levenson emphasizes the diversity. 'Covenant and promise dominate the Pentateuch, but they are missing from Proverbs, Qohelet, and the Song of Songs. The latter books, especially Proverbs, make no attempt to situate themselves within Israel's foundational story; they are unconcerned with the exodus, the revelation at Sinai, and the promise and conquest of the land. Indeed, they demonstrate no awareness of these themes. Bright's claim that in Proverbs "the place of Israel as [YHWH's] people, bound to live under the law, is clearly taken for granted" is specious and circular. One cannot even assume the Israelite origin of all the biblical proverbs.'[13] There are really two points here: first, that the cross-section approach does not succeed in making a real distinction as against the history of religion, and secondly, that the cross-section approach is inherently biased.

> The truth is that Bright's Old Testament theologian – and Bright is typical here – differs from a historian of the religion of Israel in that he or she selects certain themes which appeal to him or her and then presents the entirety of the Old Testament as an expression of only those themes, whereas a historian of religion without theological commitment would frankly acknowledge the diversity and contradiction of biblical thought and feel no apologetic need to concoct a 'unity'.[14]

Levenson then turns to a second aspect. Another way in which Old Testament theology has been established has been that it requires *faith* in its practitioners. 'We may assume,' he writes, quoting Dentan, 'that the Old Testament theologian of today, at least, will be a man of faith.' The modern scholar in some way identifies with the material and takes a 'personal stand in the present, which draws nourishment from the same spring from which the teachings of the past flowed'.[15] Most obviously, this is the case where Christian Old Testament theologians have insisted that the discipline is intrinsically a theological one and requires faith for its operation. Levenson effectively quotes Hasel, who writes: 'What needs to be emphatically stressed is that there is a transcendent or divine dimension in biblical history which the historical–critical method is unable to deal with.'[16] Faith, it seems, is needed before one can discern the cross-section or whatever other central principle is used in Old Testament theology. But the effect of this is that the theology in question would be closer to what in Christian terms is dogmatics or systematic theology than to 'biblical theology'.

Levenson's emphasis, then, is on the *diversity* of the Hebrew Bible. The number of different suggestions of Old Testament theologians about the 'centre' of the Testament itself 'offers ironic evidence for the diversity of theologies in that book' (56). Thus:

> Judaism is somewhat better situated to deal with the polydoxy of biblical theology than is Christianity. Whereas in the church the sacred text tends to be seen as a *word* (the singular is telling) demanding majestically to be proclaimed, in Judaism it tends to be seen as a *problem* with many facets, each of

which deserves attention . . . Most of the Talmud is, after all, a debate, with majority and minority positions both preserved and often unmarked. This is very different from the theological literature of Christianity. A tradition whose sacred texts are internally argumentative will have a far higher tolerance for theological polydoxy (within limits) and far less motivation to flatten the polyphony of the sources into a monotony. What Christians may perceive as a gain, Jews may perceive as a loss.

These aspects of Levenson's article are powerfully argued. If they do not completely convince, it is because of one major feature: no one looks more like a successful Jewish biblical theologian than he himself does. As one of my students remarked to me when discussing these arguments, 'Levenson is one of those who does extremely well what he says ought on no account to be done'. His doctoral dissertation was on *The Theology of the Program of Restoration of Ezekiel 40–48*. Theology? Anyone reading this excellent work would have welcomed it as an important and positive contribution to the theology of the Hebrew Bible, and one that fitted in very well to its style and approaches. No one reading his major work, *Creation and the Persistence of Evil*, would have doubted that it is a work of biblical theology, and welcomed it as such. As he says in the preface:

> First, I believe that there is generally a lack of sophisticated theological reflection upon even such central and overworked aspects of the religion of Israel as creation and covenant. Although it is religious motivation that accounts for the existence of almost all biblical research, the theological significance of the discoveries that the researchers make is rarely assessed, and, conversely, those interested in theology and willing to admit it are often uninformed about philological research, especially into the religions of the ancient Near East. Too often the result is pedantic philology and anachronistic theology. One goal in undertaking this study has been to reassess the biblical theologies of creation in dialogue with the philologists and their discoveries. In so doing, I have tried to avoid the technical jargons of both communities of scholars and to produce a theological study that can be read by any lay person conversant with the humanities (xiv).

It sounds so like the typical Old Testament theologian – or, indeed, one better than the typical! Again, going on to mention the relation of his work to later Judaism, he points out, quite rightly, the 'degree of continuity' between these two literatures, the Bible and the Rabbinic material (xiv–xv). 'Just as I have tried to maintain a conversation with the study of the Near Eastern antecedents of biblical Israel, so have I tried to cast a glance at her Rabbinic successor.' A glance? His discussion, he goes on, should demonstrate that, despite vast changes, 'the biblical theologies at point had a continuing relevance in Rabbinic Judaism'. Of course! And who would have doubted it? In spite of these very proper qualifications, the fact remains that this fine and interesting work operates very largely within the same intellectual framework as much typical Old Testament theology and belongs to the same genre. It certainly looks as if there is one Jewish scholar who is interested in biblical theology after all![17]

It is surprising, therefore, that Levenson in the book now under discussion turns so vehemently against Old Testament theology. Surely there is an inconsistency here. In this respect again, however, he is in good company, for we have seen that many biblical theologians have also set up principles which have not corresponded to the article they have actually produced. In this also, then, he is quite close to the tendencies found within Christian biblical theology.

Several other aspects of his work remain to be remarked on. His awareness of Old Testament theology is often penetrating but is far from comprehensive, as is shown by various misdirected arguments. Thus his opening arguments are against books by Dentan and John Bright; but Dentan's work was a very early venture into modern biblical theology and would not be counted as a strong example, and Bright's *The Authority of the Old Testament* was not intrinsically a work of Old Testament theology, although it did indeed touch upon that subject. It is not clear why at this point Levenson by-passed the much more authoritative works of Eichrodt and von Rad, to which he refers elsewhere. It is quite right that Dentan wrote that Old Testament theology was a 'Christian-theological discipline' (39), but he added a postscript making it clear that Jews could of course take part in it, too, which makes a difference. Levenson writes that 'there is a tendency among Christians to insist that biblical theology requires a measure of faith in its practitioners' (37), and so there is; but he then goes on to argue as if this 'tendency' is a universal agreement, which in this case it certainly is not. He attacks particularly the 'cross-cut' approach of Eichrodt (36f.) and the consequent search for a theological 'centre', but fails to note at this point that Christian biblical theology offered an alternative in von Rad's approach, which he criticizes on other grounds in the same essay, and with which in this respect he would doubtless have some agreement. Von Rad similarly might well have agreed with Levenson, and on a world-wide scale von Rad's opinion would probably be counted as the dominant example of Old Testament theology, rather than Eichrodt's. So the argument strikes only a glancing blow at Christian biblical theology.

The idea of a theological 'centre' is an easy target for mockery, and in much Christian biblical theology it is regarded with scepticism too, though Levenson seems not to know this. Here again he strikes against the Eichrodt tradition and has the agreement of von Rad, though he seems not to recognize this. It is truly bizarre how he rails against Eichrodt's tradition with its 'cross-cut' and its 'centre', thus agreeing with von Rad, when the emphasis on the place of *faith* in Old Testament theology to which he has vigorously objected is far greater in von Rad (and in Childs) than in that tradition. And when he writes that 'the assumption of the theologians who quest after the centre or overarching unity of the Hebrew Bible is that all the books and pericopes therein announce essentially the same message' (55), he is reading into their minds thoughts that suit his own polemic. This was not at all assumed; on the contrary, a 'centre' or 'unity' was sought precisely because it was recognized that the messages of different sources were different.

On the same theme, Levenson, sarcastically reviewing some of the 'centres' that have been suggested, thinks it significant (54) that *duties* do not appear on the list of proposals – but actually the formula round which the recent two volumes of Preuss are written comes very close to that. This is interesting in another respect, in that Levenson has a marked dislike of Lutheranism, with its stress (as he sees it) on faith and its (alleged) undervaluing of duties or deeds: but Preuss was of course a Lutheran himself. An even bigger mistake is when Levenson falls with delight (29) on Gunneweg's support of Baumgärtel's judgment that the Old Testament belongs to a religion totally different from Christianity: 'it is impossible to give a Christian interpretation of something that is not Christian'. Levenson seems to see this as a decisive act against Christian Old Testament theology. 'With these two sentences,' he writes triumphantly, 'Gunneweg has pronounced judgment on two millennia of biblical studies in a distinctively Christian mode. He has fired a torpedo into the prediction fulfilment schema of the Gospels; into Paul's allegories and all their patristic, medieval and Reformation kin; into Wellhausen's historicism, Eichrodt's and Mendenhall's anomian covenantalism, and von Rad's salvation-history; and into much else' – in other words, into pretty well everything in Christianity of all periods and kinds, including a parcel of things that are entirely contrary to one another. This is a wild exaggeration. While this torpedo might have struck one or two of these targets, it was hardly so multi-warheaded as to destroy them all. Perhaps Levenson does not realize that Gunneweg himself was a leading Old Testament theologian (on whom see later in this volume), with a particular special interest in the use of the Old Testament in Christian preaching, and a Lutheran too! Nor, perhaps, does he perceive the reason why the majority of Christian biblical theologians have held back from this same simple and easy solution. The position which Levenson espouses so readily, whether a good solution or not, has been understood to be characteristic of the former pro-Nazi theologians, and on that ground has been avoided by later Christian biblical theology. That the Old Testament belonged to a non-Christian religion and should therefore be totally abandoned by Christianity was a major element in

Nazi pressure on the churches. Does Levenson want Christianity to go along that way?

Levenson's warm support of the history-of-religion approach also raises questions. Unlike the biblical theologian, he argues, the historian of religion would have no difficulty coping with the diversities of the Bible. This seems to idealize the history of religion: granted the theoretical openness of the subject, the fact remains that individual attempts to write a history of religion run very quickly into the same sort of difficulties which Levenson has emphasized for biblical theology. Yehezkel Kaufmann's *History of Israelite Religion*, which is celebrated in a finely sympathetic and also critical section (44), contained many of the weaknesses which have been detected in Old Testament Theologies. Similarly, on the question of the 'centre' and the suggestion of Eichrodt – ridiculed here as in many works of Christian biblical theology – that the covenant was that centre, how was it that Helmer Ringgren, who was the chief historian of Israelite religion in his time and as a historian of religion distinguished himself emphatically from any sort of Old Testament theology, thought that Eichrodt was largely right in this? Again, there seems to be a large misunderstanding in the combination of hostility to historical criticism with easy favour towards the history of religion: for it was precisely its linkage with the history of religion that gave to historical criticism (notably in Wellhausen) the degree of acceptance that it gained. Moreover, Levenson seems not to face the fact that a consequent history-of-religion approach can produce serious problems for Judaism too. Will he really allow it full and free research into the earlier stages of the cult of the God of Israel and his possible association with a female consort, as suggested on the basis of recently-discovered inscriptions? – to quote only one example among many.

A further point: Levenson makes much of the claim that biblical theology 'has been not only non-Jewish, it has been Protestant'.[18] 'A full Roman Catholic embrace of the historico-critical method came about only in 1943 . . . In spite of their rapid ascent to the top ranks of most branches of biblical studies in the last four decades, Catholic scholars have not changed the overwhelmingly Protestant complexion of biblical theology.'[19] He connects this in an interesting and stimulating way with the Protestant polarization of scripture and tradition and the tendency to think of the Bible as the supreme potential source and agent of church renewal; hence 'the motivation to state the Scriptural doctrines precisely and purely becomes paramount'. 'It is this inner-Protestant dynamic that is the mother of biblical theology.' Levenson here interestingly compares Jewish Reform movements, Qaraism and secular Zionism.

These comments are acute and stimulating, but I think they could mislead the reader who is not well initiated in the literature of biblical theology. Roman Catholic Old Testament Theologies have been written by van Imschoot (1954),

J. L. McKenzie (1974, actually quoted by Levenson with some approval, 54), Mattioli (1981, in Italian) and Cordero (in Spanish), and Harrington wrote a Theology of the entire Christian Bible which was published in 1973. Moreover, if one moves away from volumes that are Theologies of the entire Old Testament and considers, as I have submitted we must do, the theological handling of aspects, concepts, particular books and the like, the part of Roman Catholic scholarship becomes much greater in proportion. Consider names like N. Lohfink, D. J. McCarthy, Roland Murphy, J. J. Collins, Botterweck, Fabry and many others.[20] Contrary to Levenson's impressions, in view of the difficulties into which biblical theology found itself falling within mainline Protestantism, I found myself writing not long ago that its main zone of continuing activity was in the Roman Catholic world![21] Thus the crude impression that could be gained from Levenson's arguments – as someone put it to me after reading his article, 'biblical theology is just Protestants saying what they think about the Bible' – needs to be corrected.

In the same vein, he thinks that Old Testament theologies have neglected the place of priests and priesthood (here again he implies a Protestant fault). Correspondingly, he thinks that the prophets are over-emphasized. My own experience was the opposite: one of the things I gained from these theologies from the beginning was a sympathetic understanding of priesthood and priestly thinking, for which I have always remained grateful. As for the alleged emphasis on the prophets, again I thought the opposite: studies in Old Testament theology seemed to call me primarily to the Torah and the historical books, and secondarily to the Psalms.

Levenson also notices the tendency of some Old Testament theologies to paint an unfavourable picture of post-biblical Judaism, as has been discussed above (Chapter 17). He accentuates this into an identification of 'intense anti-Semitism' evident in many of the classic works in this field. With respect, it must be said that this is wrong. Were Walther Eichrodt and Gerhard von Rad intense anti-Semites? What words, then, would Levenson find for a real anti-Semite? There was indeed some unfairness in the depiction of Judaism, and I have already said that this has been a serious fault in some Old Testament Theologies. But to call this intense anti-Semitism is to ignore another side: the field of biblical theology has been one of the main forces tending towards *philo-Semitism* within twentieth-century Christianity. No one who knows the situation within Christianity could doubt it. If it were not for biblical theology, Christianity would be very likely to slide into a position much more alienated from Judaism and the sense of a common Jewish-Christian heritage. That Old Testament theology is basically a continuation of the *Adversus Judaeos* literature of patristic and mediaeval times is too wild an assertion to be taken seriously.[22]

Associated with this is Levenson's discussion of Wellhausen. Here again the

– nowadays common – accusation of anti-Semitism is uttered. Yet Levenson, a learned and brilliant man, remarkably fails to back it up very well. 'From the correct observation that the religion of late Second Temple times and beyond was book-centred in a way in which the earlier stages were not, Wellhausen moves to the questionable judgment that "Judaism" is cut off from its spring of vitality' (42). I agree that it is a questionable judgment, indeed I think it is an erroneous one. But the uttering of questionable judgments falls far short of anti-Semitism, and Levenson's own (unusually) mild language at this point supports that fact. Apart from this, he goes on to quote Blenkinsopp, who points out the appearance of anti-Semitic utterances by other Germans *'within a year'* of the publication of Wellhausen's main book – guilt by association if there ever was! And Levenson goes on to admit that 'his [Wellhausen's] was not a racial anti-Semitism of the kind that flowered in Nazism'. Nevertheless, quoting Blenkinsopp again, Wellhausen's work 'made a modest contribution' to the later atrocities. The fact is, the legend of Wellhausen's anti-Semitism is unjustified: no one would ever have dug this up but for the one fact that he produced a convincing scheme according to which Moses had not written the Torah. The same is true of Solomon Schechter's remark, 'Higher Criticism – Higher Anti-Semitism',[23] also cited by Levenson. I can only repeat what I wrote in this same connection in 1977: 'There was never any proper justification for the deplorable remark "Higher criticism – higher anti-Semitism", a remark that should never have been made by a great scholar, and yet is still sometimes repeated.'[24]

In any case, whatever one is to think of Wellhausen, Levenson's comment is misplaced because, as we have seen, one of the main purposes of most biblical theology was, as its practitioners themselves saw it, to get away from the domination, as they supposed it to be, of the historico-critical method and the fragmenting effects of source criticism on the reading of the Bible. Now admittedly biblical theology was not fundamentalist and did not wish to return to a pre-critical or non-historical approach to scripture; and in that sense it tended to a large extent to hold to a moderately critical assessment of sources and origins.[25] But only in a very limited and remote sense can it be said that historical criticism has been the base of biblical theology or its motive power: on the contrary, the urge to replace historical criticism with some vision of unity was the basic theme. There was extremely little sense in the literature of Old Testament theology that it was developing or celebrating the inheritance of Wellhausen; quite the opposite.

Levenson, like others, is not against historical criticism for every purpose, and he uses it to damage biblical theology. It is not clear why he tries to destroy both historical criticism and biblical theology at the same time, especially when he supports the history of religion. He thinks that historical criticism is disastrous *for religion*, and he is against it when it is thought to be the *only* method, when it is 'awarded a monopoly in the interpretive process' (xiv). But the existence of biblical theology, the very discipline which he has been attacking, proves that historical criticism has not had a monopoly. Biblical theology arose precisely in order to provide something *other than* the historical-critical approach. It would be more correct, for most biblical theologians, to say that they worked with two different methods, the historical-critical and the biblical-theological: they certainly did not suppose that the former had a monopoly.

Levenson's alliance with Childs is another paradoxical element, for Childs is totally committed to biblical theology and considers it an entirely Christian discipline: according to him, the Old Testament is 'witness to Jesus Christ' throughout. Levenson's argument, if anything, should be deeply damaging to Childs. What they have in common is a hostility to historical criticism, though in very different ways. In some ways Levenson in his detailed work uses historical criticism more freely, but *in principle* he goes the other way, asserting that 'the science of history need not *control* biblical study – it need only *influence* it – for the availability of the whole scripture (however delimited) to the traditional religious life to be seriously diminished'. This is surely too extreme for Childs, whose exegesis and theology are both certainly *influenced by* historical criticism even when they object to it, and possibly more extreme than Levenson himself can really mean, for the logic of it would seem to demand the *total* exclusion of all historical considerations from religion. On the other hand, Levenson's confidence in the history of religion is a more serious blow against Childs, for whom the history-of-religion approach counts as totally negative. Perhaps the common factor uniting them is a belief in a traditional, conservative and totally scriptural religion. Possibly also Levenson welcomes Childs' expressly Christian viewpoint about biblical theology, on the ground that it makes entirely clear that Jews can have nothing to do with it?

Levenson leaves us in no doubt that in principle he dislikes biblical theology, though our perception of that is somewhat blurred by his own excellent achievements in what looks very like that same activity. He shows us very well why many Jews share his opinion. One thing his argument seems to lack is any recognition of the 'neutral' or 'negative' sort of biblical theology recognized by Tsevat – a recognition which, I have suggested, might go some distance towards allowing Jewish readers to find Old Testament Theologies useful or informative at least in places. Otherwise two major points, both of them closely connected, should be noticed. First, his arguments seem to imply that there is *no method*, and *no possibility of any method*, by which theological structures within the Hebrew Bible can be responsibly perceived and described. The Old Testament theologian, as already quoted, 'selects certain themes which appeal to him or her and then presents the entirety of the Old Testament as an expression of only those themes'. It is just a matter of personal fancy, or of preferences suggested by a past tradition. And, of course, this is no new idea: theologians themselves say it about each other all the time. But they cannot mean it too seriously without destroying the basis of their own activity. Again, according to Levenson, the debate about the 'centre' is clear evidence that no scholarly method other than the personal faith of the theologian is involved. Levenson presents no real analysis, nothing but pure contempt for people who, he thinks, have no principle except their own personal likings. There seems to be, for him, no possible responsible academic process through which progress in these matters can be made.

And perhaps that is the case. But Levenson's illustration of this situation is hardly a good one. Some of his arguments are very crude. He says that Bright in his *The Authority of the Old Testament* 'refers to Amos five times and to Proverbs only twice, and never to a specific verse, even though Amos is less than one-sixth the length of Proverbs'. So simply numerical a principle hardly increases confidence in the argument. Is there absolutely *no* conceivable good reason why Amos should be mentioned more often in proportion than Proverbs? Must all comment be strictly proportioned to the number of pages per theme or per document? Does Levenson really think that books must give more attention to Chronicles (just over 84 pages of Hebrew text in the accurate Dothan edition) than to Exodus (54 pages)?

Strangely enough, Levenson produces a new argument which might (doubtless against his intention) support a Christian religious use of the Hebrew Bible. His destruction of historical criticism might have effects that are not foreseen. It was always an obvious Jewish argument to say that the prophet Isaiah (or whoever it might be) did not mean what Christians have taken him to mean. This was, in fact, a kind of simple historical criticism. Christian doctrinal theologians like Barth often saw a similarity between the exegesis of Christian historical critics and that of Jewish interpreters.[26] If historical criticism is now blotted out by Levenson, that answer will no longer work. According to him, it is wrong to focus, with the historical critics, on what the original author or speaker meant. The emphasis is on 'recontextualization' – a concept which, Levenson seems to think, lies beyond the comprehension of historical critics.[27] Thus within Judaism itself biblical phrases are recontextualized, after biblical times, in new contexts. But if so, is not recontextualization within the (very different) context of Christianity equally valid?

One final paradox: the reader is surprised by the very *Christian* character of Levenson's argument! In spite of his Jewish learning, he thinks and talks like a Christian theologian. In many places his work reads very like the thinking of a Christian theologian who is, as so many of them are, critical of modern biblical scholarship. Except where Levenson is talking expressly about Jewish life and history, the argumentation seems to be taken over at second hand from

Christianity. His strategy is the same. He brings forward the same points, the same names (Troeltsch for instance, e.g. 119f. – hardly a figure receiving much attention in Jewish tradition!), the same warnings as we have heard from theologians again and again. His time in a Christian divinity school seems to have left its mark. He knows what to say in such a context. Of course he speaks as an observant Jew. He is angry at Christianity for many things, yet on the other hand he has many remarkable points of understanding towards it. Nevertheless the main effect of his argument is to stimulate a legacy of animosity, as if he really did not want relations to become better: if Jews and Christians work together in biblical study, he thinks, they do not do so as Jews and Christians. This is not my view: I think that as a Christian I am called to be with and work with Jews, including hearing them on both religions. On the other hand, in a way his position seems to be less one of Judaism against Christianity, more one of traditionalist religion against modernist religion or irreligion.

To sum up, Levenson makes it clear that he is against [Christian] biblical theology; and, even if some of his arguments have cracks in them, it is very likely that he speaks for many Jews in this. But his arguments are so much directed against Christian biblical theology that they show little interest in even exploring the possibility of a truly Jewish biblical theology. It is not clear what, if anything, he wants to be done on the Jewish side. Perhaps he really wants *nothing* to be done. Perhaps he will accept work on *aspects*, so long as they do not seek to produce a common position for the entire Hebrew Bible; since much, perhaps most, of Christian biblical theology has been of this character, might there be an element of agreement here? Or, perhaps, he would accept a theology which would take the entire Hebrew Bible as long as it also included in its purview the entire rabbinic tradition.[28] But the degree of animosity with which Levenson has discussed the subject has done much to discourage any such exploration. And although he starts out to tell us why Jews are not interested in Old Testament theology, the main impact of his writing may well be to ensure that Christians are not interested in it either. Perhaps this was his purpose. Certainly a main effect of his article over a wide front was to support the turn away from Old Testament theology within Christianity and the turn back towards the history-of-religion approach. Nevertheless it seems likely that new discussion of the possibility of Jewish biblical theology will continue.[29]

## 4. Goshen-Gottstein

Thirdly, we have to consider the position of the late Professor Moshe Goshen-Gottstein, a major Israeli biblical scholar, with a strong basis in Semitic philology and in textual studies, and a close personal friend of mine until his unhappy death.

Goshen-Gottstein approached the subject through a profound course of thinking about the history of biblical studies in general, both Jewish and Christian. His most complete publication on the subject in English is his 'Tanakh Theology' (1987). (For any readers to whom the term is strange, Tanakh or Tenach [or Tenakh: various transliterated spellings are found][30] is an acronym for the Hebrew Bible, based on the terms for Law, Prophets, and Writings [Torah, Nebi'im, Ketubim].) One wonders if a more elegant Hebrew term would not be *Te'ologiya miqra'it* or scriptural theology, biblical theology. Goshen-Gottstein did not live to produce his own Jewish Biblical Theology, and so we cannot know exactly what it would have been like. And there are a number of unclarities in his writings on the matter, especially in his utterances after the catastrophic illness from which he remarkably (or miraculously) recovered but after which his death followed in some years.

The best approach is to quote a key passage in full (slight alterations for clarity made by me):

> It is here that the biblical scholar is faced with a conceptual challenge. It is not just a matter of detailed treatment or better-informed scholarship that puts the volumes of Eichrodt and von Rad in a class of their own, whatever the overwhelming conceptual differences between the two. Perhaps para-doxically – in the light of the severe criticism directed at both – it is this type of attempt at describing and conceptualizing the meaning and message of the Old Testament as a text-reading from within the community of faith, yet away from the traditional mould, that forces the issue on to the student of Tanakh as well. Both Eichrodt and von Rad have struggled – not always successfully – with three major concerns: [1] steering, as much as possible, from [I think he means 'away from', J.B.] the evolutionary-comparative approach and describing the Old Testament in its own terms; [2] remaining responsible to the achievements of critical Old Testament scholarship and to write their work as part and parcel of ongoing academic discussion, and [3] viewing the Old Testament from within a community of faith that will not accept the Old Testament without a New-Testament-directed meaningful-ness. This last issue is ever present and cannot simply be ignored in order to make the work acceptable for non-Christian students of the Bible. Nor will it do any good to pretend that Eichrodt's and von Rad's works should be left outside academic biblical scholarship. In spite of major differences, both works show that the three aspects are interwoven, and this is an integral part of their achievement. We are being offered, for the first time in the past generation, an understanding of the Old Testament analysed from within.

Christian students of the Bible may utter reservations and criticism; Jewish Bible scholarship cannot but attempt to create its alternative position. This is the development within Old Testament studies that in my submission forces us to consider Tanakh theology.[31]

Anyway, the main point is that Goshen-Gottstein considered that, in view of the total past history of Jewish Bible study, it was desirable that Jewish scholarship also should move into a stage of Jewish biblical theology. He undoubtedly shared many of the kinds of opposition which Jewish scholars had directed against Christian biblical or Old Testament theology: his point of view was uncompromisingly Jewish. And some aspects, such as the attempt to make connections with the New Testament, he regarded as self-evidently irrelevant to Jewish research. But he recognized, I think, that Old Testament theology as done by Christians, in spite of its many faults and its deep internal conflicts, furnished something an analogy to which had hitherto been lacking in the Jewish scholarly tradition.

The reader will notice a number of features. There is, first of all, a sense that, given the development of the subject which has already taken place within Jewish scholarship, i.e. the rise of a more or less secular philology, the rise of Jewish history with methods continuous back into the biblical period (and there reinforced by archaeology, a discipline very actively pursued in Israel), and other such factors – creating a certain parallelism with forces active in Christian biblical study – some kind of response to these forces in some way analogous to the rise of Old Testament theology or biblical theology in the Christian world will become desirable in the Jewish world.[32]

Contrary to the common Jewish feeling that 'theology' is a distinctively Christian term, Goshen-Gottstein points out that in origin it is not at all a Christian term: it existed in pre-Christian Greek. Moreover, it was widely used in nineteenth-century Jewish liberalism: for this reason also, he thinks, the term 'theology' is loaded with doubtful connotations for Jewish scholarship today'.[33]

Secondly, Goshen-Gottstein faces the Christian concern with connections to the New Testament – which, of course, he considered religiously entirely wrong – not with plain denial nor with the verdict that this puts the subject outside the academic realm. He fully acknowledged the academic solidity and value of works like Eichrodt and von Rad. If I understand him rightly, he saw their concern with the New Testament as positive, an indication that biblical theology was an utterance that emanated from a community of faith and yet was fully (or fairly fully) integrated with the other disciplines of Bible study such as language, text and biblical history. Jewish scholarship had nothing like another Testament to cope with, but had similar faith-commitments, connections with later authoritative texts, and attachments to the religious community; and therefore a Jewish biblical theology was the natural and inevitable outcome.

Thirdly, Goshen-Gottstein saw both the need for, and the possibility of, some kind of gradation of values which would be needed for Tanakh theology. 'The Tanakh theologian has to examine his texts closely in order to devise a methodology for qualification, not just quantification. It is the overall structure of primary and secondary issues that emerges when we try to take the measure of phenomena that ultimately helps us to deal with the cardinal question "What is it all about?".'[34] I think Goshen-Gottstein is here facing what he sees to be a general *positivism* of the Israeli or Jewish academic scene, and seeking to justify the possibility of a gradation of values which belongs to theology.[35]

Fourthly, he has thoughts about the possibilities of organization of a Tanakh theology. He is opposed to the idea of 'superimposing outside systems on Old Testament *legomena* – such as the reflexes of the traditional triad, theology, anthropology, soteriology (or the same by any other name). It [Tanakh theology] is equally opposed to the transfer of the idea of "Centre" from New Testament theology.'[36] A footnote adds that 'attempts to base Old Testament theology on an alleged centre have been reduced to meaninglessness by successive suggestions'. But then he goes on: 'In a way, Eichrodt's initial *tour-de-force* of forcing all the facts into the mould of the covenant idea was, in retrospect, not as bad an idea as the critics claimed.' And in the end he himself has a sort of scheme which looks as if it would have the same sort of function as the Christian ideas of a 'centre'. 'To get away from the abstract, if the relationship of Israel and the land looms large, in most subcorpuses of the Tanakh, then this is for me a central issue in Tanakh theology' (630). This same nuclear concern, he adds, is a 'minor issue both in the study of religion and in [Christian] Old Testament theology'. The centrality, he says, depends on 'the facts gained by both quantitative and qualitative inquiry, that is, the number and density of occurrences as well as the issues connected with promises and threats concerning the land'. Thus '"theology of the land" is judged solely by facts gained from Tanakh, and it is a question of facts for the student of diachronics if this issue is of the same centrality in the theology gained from halakhic or aggadic sources, medieval systems . . . and the like'. On this example, which at this point is only just a suggestion adumbrated, 'Jewish biblical theology . . . would put forth the double claim of receiving the stimulus for its way of studying facts from its own tradition and of insisting on inquiry into the meaning of Tanakh by strict procedures of quantitative and qualitative evaluation' (631). Thus, in the end, he writes: 'I have my ideas as to how a future Tanakh theology would be organized, based on the evaluation of *legomena* on the relationship between God, people and land, and how such a base line might contrast with later Jewish theologies' (634). The Sabbath is another potentially central theme which he discusses (632ff.), and he goes on to mention messianism and miracles, vengeance and prayer, sacrifice and temple, life and death, and the theology of *mitswot* or commandments (633).

At the moment it must be said that the views of Goshen-Gottstein on this subject have generally not been accepted by the Jewish scholarly public. Whether this will continue to be so, we cannot say. It must be said, from the Christian side, that they are at least a highly relevant set of ideas, which are likely to be very stimulating to all discussion of the subject. Even if nothing is ever to come of 'Tanakh theology', something has surely been achieved by Goshen-Gottstein's very learned and intellectually enquiring approach to the subject on a wide basis. The final words of his article are surely highly significant: 'I can only hope that this essay will help to set the stage for a more realistic and deeply truthful atmosphere in the common work of Christians and Jews in the academic study of biblical religion.'

## 5. Japhet

Far from it being the case that Israeli scholars are not interested in biblical theology, one of the finest works in that area has been written by the Israeli professor Sara Japhet under the title (in its English form) *The Ideology of the Book of Chronicles and its Place in Biblical Thought*. Now indeed the word 'theology' does not appear in the title: perhaps deliberately, it has been avoided, and 'ideology' has been used. (The Hebrew original used 'beliefs and ideas'.) But, whatever one may use as a title, it is very difficult to argue that the actual content is anything different from what one would find in works belonging to (in Christian terms) Old Testament theology. Obviously Japhet is not to be found making connections with the New Testament or with later Christianity: but, as we have amply seen, those portions of Christian Old Testament theologies which deal with Chronicles seldom (to be more exact, never) do so either.

Apart from the use of the term 'theology' itself, the only way in which Japhet's excellent work can be seen as in contrast with the tradition of biblical theology is that it is a work concerned with the ideology/theology of one book only, and not with the ideology/theology of the Hebrew Bible/Old Testament as a whole. This is the sole point at which Levenson's polemical arguments could touch it. But, as we have seen, biblical theology, even Christian biblical theology, is not *necessarily* committed to the production of single volumes containing the one sole theology of the entire testament or Bible. If a group of ten or fifteen volumes, on various groups of books but parallel to Japhet's on Chronicles, were to be produced, how would they, taken together, be anything other than a corpus of biblical theology on Israeli intellectual soil?

For, while Japhet avoids the term 'theology', all the material that concerns theology is here. Chapter headings like 'God's Presence in the World' or 'God's involvement in the History of Israel', plus attitudes to kingship, people and the hope of redemption, when handled with close reference to actual texts, are exactly what biblical theology has been interested in from the beginning. Moreover, though quite properly she makes no attempt to discuss the matter in general, it is obvious from her discussion that she stands within the same general field of scholarship as people like Eichrodt and von Rad, with whom she converses amicably as well as critically, assessing their views, even where she differs from them, as proper and reasonable contributions to the same subject.

## 6. Sweeney

Only at the last moment was I able to include a short mention of the positive and helpful article of Marvin Sweeney, in the volume dedicated to Knierim.[37] Sweeney's discussion is careful, irenic and constructive.

He has taken part in the recent discussions and recognizes that:

> The newly found place of Jewish scholars in the field of modern biblical studies represents an opportunity to appropriate the Bible for Jewish theology as well [as Christian]. This has enabled Jewish thinkers to enter the discourse of the modern Western world on the meaning and significance of the Bible. It thereby contributes to a fruitful Jewish-Christian dialogue which has been engaged since the end of World War II, enhancing the mutual understanding which is fostered by such dialogue. More importantly, the discipline of biblical theology provides an opportunity to define a systematic understanding of the Bible for Jews (335).

Sweeney has mentioned 'dialogue' in this statement, but he is also careful to avoid easy or excessive expectations in this. There are – and this is the centre of his argument – 'two distinctive readings of the Hebrew Bible, determined by the respective canonical arrangements of the biblical books in Judaism and Christianity' (371). The books are the same (not, however, if we consider the wider Catholic canon), but they are arranged in a different way. Sweeney goes on to set out a total scheme implied by the Christian ordering of the books (360–5) and to contrast this with the scheme that underlies the grouping and ordering of the books in the Jewish Bible (365–71).

I cannot properly summarize the schemes as set out by Sweeney, but the following are some aspects. In the Christian scheme, Chronicles and Ezra-Nehemiah 'present the history . . . as one of failure due to particularization . . . The original goal . . . is not realized in that all humanity is unable to take part . . . The inclusion of the book of Esther as the concluding book of this section . . . suggests that God's intention . . . has not been realized because of the increasing separation of the Jewish community from the Gentiles.' In the poetic and wisdom books there is 'a logical progression' through Job, Psalms, Proverbs, Ecclesiastes and the Song of Songs. Similarly the prophetic books, focussed on the future, presuppose the failure of the past and 'point to salvation in the eschaton'. To sum up:

> When viewed in relation to the New Testament, it is clear that the structure of the Old Testament is designed to rehearse the failure of Israel and the Mosaic covenant to achieve God's purposes for the world, to point to the continued need by humans for God, and to project an eschatological scenario of salvation for the righteous that will be fulfilled in the revelation of Jesus as the Christ. It is striking that the structure of the New Testament canon is parallel to that of the Old.

Sweeney's account is well thought out and carefully explained, but I was amazed to read it, for a quite different reason. The problem with it is not that it is *wrong*: it may be quite logical and well-founded. The weakness in it is that, beautiful as the scheme may be, as far as I know it never existed in the minds of Christians, or of most of them. In years of learning in Sunday School and in the hearing of multitudes of sermons and thousands of theological lectures, plus infinite reading of theological books, I never heard of any such scheme. The notion, for example, that the location of Esther at the end of the historical series was understood to indicate 'that God's intention . . . has not been realized because of the increasing separation of the Jewish community from the Gentiles' was totally new to me. I believe that very few Christians, whether lay or theologically trained, have thought in this way. The idea that the ordering of the books precisely corresponded to a total Christian theological scheme seems to me to have been unknown. If there had been such a correlation, it would have made it easier to learn the order of the books, which for us as children was a pretty hard task, but no one ever suggested it. Nor does Sweeney himself give any evidence that Christians, whether theologians, church leaders or people in general, had any such idea. He quotes no one.[38] Even canonical enthusiasts like Sanders and Childs do not deploy any such scheme: perhaps they do so for the grouping of one or two books, like the placing of Deuteronomy in Sanders' thinking, but not for every book in the Bible. The scheme seems to come from Sweeney's own thinking. I did later learn from a student that there are indeed church groups which have a developed theological theory of the ordering of the books, but if this is so, it seems to me that it must count as a sectarian emphasis and is uncharacteristic of the major currents of Christianity. Nor does Sweeney make clear what must be one of the main questions, namely whether, according to the scheme, the books were *intentionally* ordered in this way by church authorities, or whether the scheme is independent of intention and can be simply read off from the facts of the disposition of the present Christian Bible. Or, again, it might be suggested that, even if there was no such intention and also no conscious interpretation of the ordering, the fact of the ordering would subconsciously impress itself upon the Christian reader. There would also be the question, since he traces the ordering back to the Vulgate 'and, prior to that, the order of various Greek traditions', which would surely include the Septuagint, whether the 'Christian' ordering might not go back to an older Jewish ordering in any case – if one can speak of an order of books at so early a time.[39]

The question is an important one, because, with the recent increase of interest in the canon, it is likely that any position emphasizing the ordering of books will arouse interest. Nor do I question Professor Sweeney's account of the Jewish position, which I think deserves to receive much attention from the Christian reader. And I do not question his basic contention, namely that, even if Jews and Christians have the same collection of books, the arrangement of scriptural resources and the diverse ways in which they are used means that they hardly form the same Bible. Or, we may say, the fact that the collection of books is held in common is in itself indecisive, for the collection of books is itself related to a whole series of other questions about how they are used and in what relation to extra-scriptural realities, in which series of questions the ordering of the books is only one factor. This aspect will be taken up again in a later chapter.

Sweeney is right in being interested in Jewish-Christian dialogue and in stressing the difficulties involved in it (372). In this chapter I have been interested in Jewish biblical theology primarily for its own sake and not as a means to dialogue, though that may well be a desirable outcome. I have looked at the matter mainly with the following questions in mind. Is there a field of biblical theology which operates in common for both Jews and Christians? Are Jews likely to develop a biblical theology of their own? Do Jews really want to block Old Testament theology on the part of Christians? Sweeney's well-written article is a significant stimulus to thought along these lines.

## 7. Conclusion

This chapter has surveyed some central contributions to the discussion of Jewish biblical theology, but it should not be supposed that this survey has been complete. There is evidence that many groups, whether Jewish or combined Jewish and Christian, are engaged in discussion of the matter. I remember personally, when questions of 'Old Testament theology' were being discussed at a meeting of the Society for Old Testament Study in England in the 1950s, our venerated colleague Professor Weingreen standing up and saying that all the questions being discussed were not questions for Christianity only, but were equally so for Jews. It is to be expected that many groups will continue to follow this out. Time and patience will be required for misunderstandings and animosities to be overcome.

Whether or not any Jewish biblical theology, so named, ever emerges, the very discussion of it has a significant effect on the Christian conception of biblical theology. For, as we have seen, some Christian Old Testament theologians (notably Vriezen and Childs) have set up as a principle of the subject that it is a Christian theological discipline, 'part of Christian theology', 'requiring the resources of Christian faith', and so on. It would seem obviously to follow that Jews could not take part in this discipline. And this would indeed follow if biblical theologians were logical; however, we have seen that they often are not. When they say that it is a Christian theological enterprise, they are probably making this assertion in opposition to that other side of [Christian] biblical theology that contends – as, for instance, Eichrodt did – that it is a descriptive and non–normative undertaking.[40] In other words, it was not their main intention to exclude Jewish participation (though this is the way, as I have found, that Jewish students often read it); their main intention was to resist *non-Jewish* 'secular' attacks on the academic status of their subject. Admittedly, this shows their obtuseness about the implications of their own arguments. Thus Childs points out that 'it is not by accident that Jewish scholars have not participated in the writing of biblical theologies. (The occasional exception serves to confirm the rule)',[41] and he uses this argument as part of a demonstration that the discipline is an essentially Christian one. Jews don't do it: therefore it is a Christian enterprise – that is the argument (though an obviously illogical one). But the same argument, equally obviously, excludes Jews from doing it even if they want to. The 'occasional exception' – whoever he (or she) was – was poking his nose in where he should have kept it out. Though this was doubtless not meant by Childs,[42] it is the only possible conclusion from his own argument. Probably the same applies to Vriezen: he just did not think of his principle as one excluding Jewish participation.

If Jewish scholars can, in principle, participate in biblical theology, then there is no use or sense in defining it as a Christian theological discipline. Might it be better to say that it is a discipline which Christianity supports and believes to be salutary for its own welfare (and, so far as it can judge, at least potentially for that of Judaism also). In this sense it would be like exegesis itself. Even the most narrow-mindedly 'Christian' of theorists has never supposed that Jews cannot write a commentary on Genesis or that such a commentary should not be read by Christians or consulted as a significant source even on theological questions.[43] In fact, as I have already indicated, many or most of the questions that have been approached by [Christian] Old Testament theology are perfectly within the range in which Jewish scholars can pronounce upon them, and indeed it has turned out to be difficult to cite actual problems in which Christian faith is a necessary heuristic or normative resource.

To sum up, therefore, it is uncertain whether Jewish scholars will ever write works called 'Biblical Theology' or 'Theology of the Hebrew Bible'. But they are already integrated within many of the same set of operations which are essential to [Christian or religiously uncommitted] biblical theology. Christian writers in the field have therefore to keep their minds constantly open to the question of how their judgments in biblical theology would seem to a Jewish readership. This applies whether a Jewish 'Hebrew-Bible-Theology' such as Goshen-Gottstein envisaged ever comes into existence or not.

My latest impressions at the time of writing, however, are that interest in Jewish biblical theology has been stimulated, rather than damped, by the recent discussions. A conference on the subject, organized by Michael Fishbane and Tikva Frymer-Kensky, was held in 1996 at the University of Chicago, and among the papers was a valuable article by Brettler.[44] Isaac Kalimi took part in a conference on the history of Israelite religion in Louvain and spoke in favour of the Jewish interest in biblical theology.[45] The papers of Brettler and Kalimi reached me too late to be discussed fully here.

# 19

# Some Theologies of the 1970s

The completion of von Rad's two-volume work around 1960 marked an epoch in the development of the subject, and for some years no full-size volumes of note appeared to continue the series. By the early 1970s, however, some important new works were appearing. None of these works was of the imposing two-volume dimensions that those of Eichrodt and von Rad had assumed, and there has been a certain tendency in later scholarship to take it that Eichrodt and von Rad form the basic types between which one must find one's way. Thus both Childs and Brueggemann have expressed themselves as if the contrast between these two constituted a 'stalemate' which would suggest the need for the discovery of some quite new approach. This could be misleading, because some works of the 1970s, while less imposing in scale, and while following some of the major lines established by Eichrodt and von Rad, had creativities of their own and may have achieved important modifications of these earlier classics and thus altered the force of the arguments for and against them.[1] Moreover, while some of the Old Testament Theologies of the 1970s can be classed as in the tradition of Eichrodt (so, with qualifications, Zimmerli) or of von Rad (so Westermann), others struck out in interestingly different directions. Of the former we shall discuss both Zimmerli and Westermann, and of the latter we shall discuss three: Fohrer, Terrien and Schmid.

## 1. Zimmerli

Walther Zimmerli's *Old Testament Theology in Outline* was published in German in 1972, in English translation in 1978.[2] It had a background in long consideration of the problems of Old Testament theology, along with extensive exegetical work, the culmination of which lies, perhaps, in his major commentary on Ezekiel in the Biblischer Kommentar series. His Theology, as indicated above, is distinctly brief in comparison with those of Eichrodt and von Rad, and in particular the introductory section 'Approach', in which he outlines his principles and method, is very short (13–15 in the English version). Thus a much fuller impression is to be gained from a series of articles by him which were also published in the early 1970s.[3]

His work deserves to be classed, as we shall see, along with Eichrodt's general type, in that like Eichrodt he has a 'centre'. On the other hand Zimmerli mentions Eichrodt very little and his actual conversation is much more with his near-contemporary, von Rad.[4] Eichrodt's choice of the covenant as centre has ceased to be convincing for Zimmerli, though covenant remains among the 'fundamentals' of his scheme (48–58). His thought is much more aware of the more recent discussions of covenant, for example the use of the Hittite treaties by Mendenhall and by Baltzer, the other arguments of Kutsch, and the review of the whole discussion by McCarthy. In particular, also, Zimmerli is well aware of Perlitt's arguments, which consider the covenant to be a rather late concept, one mainly of the Deuteronomic texts. Zimmerli seeks to limit the force and range of Perlitt's arguments, but obviously for him they affect the alleged centrality of the covenant concept.[5]

However, though Zimmerli thus converses more with von Rad, he distinctly differs from some central positions of the latter. For one thing, he is aware of the questions raised about 'revelation in history' by me, by B. Albrektson and by others.[6] Though Israel had 'a particularly intimate relationship between its faith and its historical experiences', he writes, 'we must still avoid the mistaken assumption that for Israel history as such became the revelatory word of Yahweh'. 'History' by no means simply proclaims Yahweh in the course of events: in catastrophic events 'it is especially urgent that Yahweh's word be heard'.

More important, doubtless influenced by R. Smend's central discussion *Die Mitte des Alten Testaments* (1970), he differs from von Rad's decided opinion that the Old Testament has no 'centre'. Von Rad's work, with its stress on the *variety* of theologies and utterances, falls short, he thought, of providing the *unity* that a theology needed. 'Von Rad's presentation is determined by the cautiousness of the exegete, who knows himself to be obligated only to the text presently before him. It is a theology that refuses to go too far outside the realm of exegesis, and that thus occasionally gives the impression of a multifariousness of utterances that is not fully brought together, in which that which is finally normative remains unclear.'[7] Zimmerli finds the 'central focus' in the Name of Yahweh.[8]

To Zimmerli a name, or at least this name, was more than a mere designation. The Name was basic to revelation. Zimmerli emphasized expressions like 'I am Yahweh' in the Holiness Code, like 'And you [he, they] will know that I am Yahweh' in Ezekiel and elsewhere, and most of all the 'I am who I am' of Exod. 3.14, linked with the 'To whom I am gracious I am gracious, and to whom I show mercy I show mercy' of Exod. 33.19. The whole group expresses the sovereign freedom of the God of Israel. The Old Testament 'firmly maintains its faith in the sameness of the God it knows by the name of Yahweh' (*Theology*,

14). This provides an 'inner continuity'. Moreover, the revelation of the Name is connected with the people Israel and the deliverance from Egypt. The name is thus not a static concept – or, he may have meant, an abstraction or generalization based on other phenomena – but connects us directly with the God whose Name resonates throughout the entire Hebrew Bible. The Old Testament 'refuses to "explain" the Name in a way that would confine it within the cage of a definition. It seeks to express the fact that we can speak of Yahweh only in attentive acknowledgment of the way he demonstrates his nature (in his acts and his commandments)' (21).

The Name thus dominates, especially, the first section on 'Fundamentals' (17–59). Subsections treat of Yahweh as 'God of Israel since Egypt', as 'God of the Fathers' (here touching on the theme of Promise, another of Zimmerli's central interests), and as 'Creator and King'. Another on 'the Election of Israel' follows, and then 'Yahweh, God of Sinai: Covenant and Commandments'.

The next section is on 'the Gifts bestowed by Yahweh', and interestingly begins with 'War and Victory', followed by 'the Land and its Blessings' and 'the Gift of God's Presence'. Then under the heading of 'Charismata of Leadership and Instruction' there are sub-sections on Moses and Joshua, on Judge and Nazirite, on King, Priest, Prophet and Wise Man.

The third section is on 'Yahweh's Commandment' and the fourth, 'Life before God', treats of obedience, worship and wisdom. The fifth, entitled 'Crisis and Hope', is a kind of historical exposition, including in succession the story of the beginnings, the historical books, the great prophets in whose names we have books, and apocalyptic. A brief conclusion on 'The Openness of the Old Testament Message' follows.[9]

Zimmerli was, as it now seems to me, even more passionately committed to a 'centre' of the Old Testament than Eichrodt was with his 'covenant' principle. He was willing to go along with the multiplicity of theologies which von Rad had emphasized, but all these different theologies cited and used the one Name of God, and this united them (he seems not to have been troubled by the very substantial use of names other than Yahweh in certain strata, such as the 'Elohistic' Psalter).[10] The Name expressed the selfhood, the personal character, and above all the *freedom* of the God of Israel, and linked it all with the great historical deliverance of the exodus. God's freedom is reiterated again and again; it was, of course, a central term in Barth's theology. In a sense, therefore, Zimmerli reacted to von Rad's theology by taking the variety which the latter had seen in the Old Testament and bringing it into a unity, in this respect making it more like the unitary aspect which von Rad had considered to apply to the *New* Testament. And this of course made sense: if one can say that Christ is the 'centre' of the New Testament, is it not appropriate to say in the same way that Yahweh is the 'centre' of the Old?

The Wisdom literature is also explained by Zimmerli as closely attached to the centre in the Name (*Theology*,107f., 155–66; *TRE*, 450f.). Since Wisdom does not mention the great historical acts of the Lord, nor the special place of his people Israel, does it bring us to thinking of itself as 'a second source of revelation, independent of the first'? No, because Israel entered into the entire world of creation and 'subordinated the realms it discovered there to Yahweh'.[11] The use of the name Yahweh in Proverbs shows how an international world-view is taken over and directed towards the centre 'Yahweh' (*TRE*, 450). The fear of the one whom Israel has designated as *Yahweh* is the beginning of wisdom. Again, like most scholars he dissents (235) from von Rad's view that apocalyptic is descended from Israelite wisdom.

Like most Old Testament theologians, Zimmerli follows a moderate and widely accepted historical criticism, ordering material accordingly. But this element is not made very prominent and is introduced gradually rather than as a principle at the beginning. The major historical presentation actually comes towards the end, in the last main section entitled 'Crisis and Hope'. This section goes right back to Genesis and leads us on through the historical books and the major prophets, with a final emphasis on Ezekiel and Deutero-Isaiah.

A few remaining points:

First, in view of the stress laid upon the divine Name as the 'centre', it is not clear that that emphasis is sustained through the latter sections of the book. This we have seen to be the case with Eichrodt's 'covenant' also.

Secondly, the history of religion is not neglected, and Zimmerli himself wrote, in about the same period, a substantial survey of work in that area.[12] Thus we have a discussion of the Canaanite 'El' gods (41f.), and of wisdom in Egypt and Mesopotamia (156), and mentions of liturgical aspects in other religions (148–155).

Thirdly, Zimmerli's work pays considerable attention to the actual Hebrew *vocabulary* and thus introduces the reader in a constructive way to the texture of the books, avoiding the abstraction that can otherwise take place. The Hebrew terms are helpfully cited in both Hebrew script and transliteration; unfortunately, many of the Hebrew forms were badly misprinted in the English translation.

As has been indicated above (Ch. 11), Zimmerli's engagement with New Testament material is quite limited. His concluding section on the 'openness' of the Old Testament message does not define this as openness to *Christianity*. That his thinking was deeply concerned with the latter can be seen from the concluding paragraph of one of his near-contemporary articles – not surprisingly for the von Rad Festschrift:[13]

Where this confrontation with the One is recognized without qualification as the centre of the Old Testament, the central question directed to the first half of the Bible by the gospel of Jesus Christ will come to be audible in full sharpness: whether this God – to formulate it in a Pauline manner – is the God of Abraham or the God of Moses.

In his actual Theology as published, however, Zimmerli did not pursue this line of thought.

To sum up, then, Zimmerli's work shows the possibility of a distinct advance which could overcome some of the apparent conflicts of the earlier writers. For the reader who can undertake to read only one Theology and that of moderate length, it can be warmly recommended. Some other remarks about it will appear elsewhere in the present work.

## 2. *Westermann*

Claus Westermann, professor in Heidelberg and closely associated with Gerhard von Rad, produced his *Elements of Old Testament Theology* in German in 1978, and the English translation appeared in 1982. It is of about the same size as Zimmerli's work discussed just above. Westermann also is a very well-known scholar, noted particularly for his part in the hermeneutical discussions, for his work on form criticism and for his very large and detailed Genesis commentary. He has been mentioned above both for his interest in evolution and for his interest in religion as a general human phenomenon, both of them concerns which many Old Testament theologians have passed by.

As mentioned above, Westermann stands close to von Rad, and on his first page he reiterates the position that the Old Testament 'tells a story' and that 'the structure of an Old Testament theology must be based on events rather than concepts' (9). The contrast between events and concepts is basic to Westermann's views and is often repeated; it is linked by him with the contrast between verb and noun. Previous Theologies, he argues, have used terms like *revelation, election, eschatology* and the like, which take us away from the verb-language of the Old Testament itself.[14] Rather than a *Heilsgeschichte*, which suggests a series of acts performed by God, we have a history that takes place between God and man. Its kernel is a deliverance, but it does not remain only a history of salvation, for the character of actions and responses changes as the story progresses.

A basic contribution by Westermann, which carries us beyond von Rad, is his emphasis on *blessing*.[15] Unlike acts of salvation, blessing is something that goes on *all the time* and may apply to all the world. 'It is a quiet, continuous, flowing and unnoticed working of God which cannot be captured in moments or dates'

(103). It is dominant in areas like the primeval history of Genesis.[16] This means, incidentally, that the history-of-religion material is no longer a *difficulty* for theology; rather, it is a positive theological reason for joy (114ff.): all humanity shares in this common element. Nevertheless in Israel the element of saving has the priority: Genesis was 'inserted' in front of the Exodus story (208).

Westermann's approach is also a *structural* one. Deliverance is followed by praise, and the later story in the historical books has the character of a confession of sin. In the prophetic books the structure of the judgment oracle is common to all prophets of judgment, and similar constant factors appear in the Psalms. Wisdom has no place within the original structure, since early wisdom was overwhelmingly secular. Such structures provide a *systematic* character; 'talk about God' remains constant throughout the entire Old Testament (12). With 'constants' one is coming back somewhat closer to Eichrodt.

Certain distinctions are much stressed. One is that between *law* and *commandment* (or prohibition). These are basically different processes. Law pre-supposes an institution with power to punish; command depends on the authority of the one who commands. Commandments therefore should not be subsumed under the concept of law; only secondarily were they so subsumed (21).[17]

Less clear is the distinction between *epiphany*, which 'belongs to God's act-ing', and *theophany*, which 'belongs to God's speaking' (25, 51, 56, 176, 188ff., 199, 213). These are said to be different processes, portrayed in a different linguistic fashion, and they have different histories running through the entire Old Testament. Here as elsewhere we see the result of the emphasis on form criticism.

The *canon* is mentioned from the beginning: it 'shows us the structure of what happens in the Old Testament in its decisive elements' (10, cf. 16, 23f., 31, 194, 217). At the beginning of the last section on the relationship of the Old Testament to Christ, we hear that 'we ought to start from the context of the Old Testament as a whole, the canon in its three parts'. In fact, however, little is said about the canon. The emphasis falls rather on what is form-critically 'original', and little thought is given to the 'final form' of the text. The verb 'choose' is never used in the texts about 'election' and is a late interpretation, 'explained by subsequent reflection' as election (41).

The interest in connections with the New Testament and Christianity, as already remarked, is considerably greater than in most Old Testament theo-logies. The whole Section 6 (217–32) is devoted to this subject, but there are numerous remarks and paragraphs about it elsewhere. Westermann's opinions are sometimes far from traditional. 'In the New Testament only those promises are relevant which are fulfilled in Christ; all others are of no interest and never arise' (19). The constituent parts of the Gospels show a clear correspondence to the structure of the book of Jeremiah (129). Judaism is hardly mentioned:[18] in it the Law is 'absolutized' (24); Paul got his doctrine of the Law from his Jewish teachers and it 'corresponds to the latest usage of *torah* in the Old Testament'. Before this, however, commandments and laws were clearly distinguished, as mentioned above. Paul's usage, important as it may be for his own situation, 'cannot be decisive for' the relationship between the Old Testament and Christ as a whole. Certain aspects of the Old Testament have their fulfilment or correspondence not in the New Testament but in later Christianity (in 'church history', as he puts it): so, for instance, many aspects of the historical books. Westermann scarcely thinks of a non-Christian readership: introducing the subject of creation: he tells us that 'we' consciously or unconsciously approach the matter 'from the first article of the Apostles' Creed' (85).

There is no 'general concept of revelation' in the Old Testament (25), only various processes. The doctrines of the fall and of original sin 'cannot be based on the narrative in Genesis 3'; they come from Jewish tradition as in IV Ezra 7.118 (this, incidentally, seems to be the only Jewish source or apocryphal book mentioned anywhere). 'Death is not punishment for human sins; the punishment for disobedience is rather the expulsion from the garden and thus from proximity to God.'[19] The Sinai traditions 'have nothing whatever to do with' God's saving action, and are thus absent from the 'creed' (following von Rad) (51, cf. 190). The priesthood had no hierarchy in early times, and acquired it only along with the kingship (198); this is said to be significant for the Christian church. Hierarchy is 'not an inherent part of the priesthood as such'.

A number of observations about Hebrew words are offered, some of them leaving a sense of some doubt. There was no term for prayer in the oldest strata, and only in post-exilic times did it emerge (153f.). B*erit*, 'covenant', emerged only in the Deuteronomic period (43). In 'all the world's languages' the word for the genus 'man' is not primitive but is a derivative late arrival (87). All? How can he know this? In similar vein, 'in no primitive language do we find a special verb for "to give thanks"' (157). The verb *lun*, 'murmur', never occurs after the narratives of the wilderness period, and this shows that these stories 'very likely go back to actual experiences' (38). How does this prove it? Words directed to God in worship turn into meditation, devotion leading to theological reflection, and 'this makes it clear why the Hebrew *dabar* embraces both "speaking" and "thinking"' (204). All this is close to the 'word studies' of the older Biblical Theology Movement; but in practically no case does the theological argument depend on them, so that the reader can bracket them out from his consciousness without loss. This does, however, form a point of contrast with Zimmerli, who avoids arguments of this kind.

Westermann, as already indicated, makes more positive connections with the environing religions than most other Old Testament theologians do. This agrees with the rich use of comparative material in his Genesis commentary. In its sacrifices 'Israel's worship participates in one of the phenomena common to all religions' (201). *Cyclic* phenomena, which in much biblical theology had been seen negatively, as a characteristic of paganism, receive a positive evaluation from Westermann.[20]

Interestingly – and a little like Zimmerli in this respect – an important area which one might expect to find early in the book comes near the end, in the chapter on Response: this is 'The Theological Interpretation of History: The Great Historical Works of the Old Testament' (207–16). Here we have the Yahwist, the Deuteronomic History, and the Priestly Writing. The essence of these works is *variety*. 'If God always did the same thing, there would be no history. If God's action and words were definable by nominal concepts, that too would yield no history' (216). How then do they yield a coherent whole? Because God is One.

If von Rad's Theology can be classified as working primarily with tradition-history, Westermann's comes closer to the form-critical pattern. It seeks to overcome some of the difficulties which critics raised against von Rad's work, essentially by modifying and relativizing the emphasis on *history* as used by von Rad, and also through its highly creative emphasis on *blessing*. Although rightly to be classed with von Rad's work, Westermann's book shows numerous points of fresh thinking and originality, in which Old Testament theology was moving ahead in the 1970s. And, apart from his Theology of the Old Testament, the width of his interests and his ability to contribute to problems commonly neglected have been mentioned several times in these pages: for example, on evolution (Ch. 7 above), on natural theology (Ch. 27 below), and on the future of religions in general (Ch. 8 above).

### 3. Fohrer

If Zimmerli and Westermann may be seen as creative advances in the tradition of Eichrodt and of von Rad respectively, some others opened up something of a new line of their own. Georg Fohrer's *Theologische Grundstrukturen des Alten Testaments* (1972) is a good example. It is surprising that the customary surveys (Hayes, Reventlow) say little about Fohrer's work,[21] for it seems to me in some ways to mark a turning point. Although the title would suggest 'basic structures' of a kind similar to those that earlier Theologies had detected, and though Fohrer contributed to the discussion of a 'centre' as the general discussion had done, the content of his Theology is very differently organized and contains some very different themes. An idea may be gained from his chapter titles:

1. Modes of Interpretation of the Old Testament
2. Old Testament and Revelation
3. The Manifoldness of Existential Stances (*Daseinshaltungen*)
4. The Unity in the Manifoldness
5. Force for Change and Capacity for Change
6. Unfoldings (*Entfaltungen*)
7. Applications (*Anwendungen*).

To provide a little more detail:

1. is largely devoted to traditional Christian interpretations, e.g. proof from prophecy, Messianic expectation, plus later dogmatic assumptions, all of which are declared to be more or less wrong. The Old Testament contains numerous different existential stances, which are all typically human and cannot be said to be willed or revealed by God. The Old Testament has to be approached in the same way as any other body of literature, and the understanding of it requires no faith or self-commitment (31).

2. indicates that the various modes of 'revelation' to be seen in the Old Testament are limited, uncertain or unreliable; 'revelation through history' is itself ambiguous and in any case is not a special feature providing distinctiveness as against other religions; revelation to prophets also has many ambiguities, and in particular has its core in a 'secret experience', which cannot be witnessed to or described except by the person who experienced it. The only outwardly perceptible criterion is whether a new 'existential stance' comes from it, and this leads us to 3.

3. There are many of these existential stances. The question of the place of the Old Testament, in view of discoveries in the ancient Near East, has to be answered with an eye to the historical–human side and also to the claims of faith. Only the existential stance can decide this. The existential stance is dominated by the conflict with two powers: magic on one side, wisdom on the other (55).

4. indicates the 'centre' of the dual concepts (*zwei Vorstellungskomplexen*), the dominion of God and community with God (*Gottesherrschaft* and *Gottesgemeinschaft*), and their interrelation. These work out in fear and trust (110ff.).

5. discusses how ancient material can be altered and transformed, how tradition and interpretation work, and particularly how faith reacts upon society and society reacts upon faith (126ff.).

6. 'Unfoldings' contains six sub-sections:

(i) The *personal structure* is manifested by philological and literary features (various words, personal names, stories of individuals, the 'God of the Fathers' in early times). Trust in personal guidance by God is accompanied by a strongly personal sort of ethic. The personal structure of faith is shown also in the conflict with disaster and threats to life, notably in the Psalms, where the thought of sickness is spiritualized and interiorized, the physical suffering being connected to the inward suffering of the soul.

(ii) deals with God's action on peoples and humans – an action not so much in *history* (which would suggest past history) as in the contemporary present. The Old Testament does not give objective representations of past events, but interprets them for the present: often the present interpretation obscures the historical reality. History was not a history of salvation but a history of sin (145); more important, it was always a *history of decision* (147).

(iii) God's work in and through nature also belongs to the realm of religious experience. The promises connected with the gifts of nature go back to a very early time, before the religious-ethical element of Yahweh-faith determined the tradition (151). In this respect the events of Sinai were the turning point (152).

(iv) Correlation between God and man. This is a determining characteristic of Old Testament faith. Various stages and types of this correlation are discussed. Finally, it is clear that the correlation is personal rather than juristic; this again confirms that history is a history of decision (163f.).

(v) Faith as action is also characteristic. Thus series with ten or twelve commandments are not 'laws'; they are commands for action, intended to have an effect on the individual. The inner and outer unity of faith and action is assumed also by the prophets (169). In Jer.31 God does not prescribe his will as a law externally, but lays it in the inner heart of man (171).

(vi) Finally, faith is *diesseitig;* it belongs to this world and not another world (this latter comes into the Old Testament only late, and even it is a development from the here and now of the classic period). After a survey of Sheol and such matters it is observed that the present life is the decisive thing. The man of the Old Testament feels himself threatened by chaos and world catastrophe, but faith upholds him (177). Life in this world cannot flee into an inner or spiritual world and is determined by the demands of the divine will (182). In this world, however, God's dominion is not visible or tangible: rather, it is alive in the believer.

7. 'Applications' contains five sub-sections.

(i) Section 1 is a quite lengthy (185–206) discussion of the *Urgeschichte* or primeval history. The events of this story are meant (204) as an expression of basic human experiences, basically the experience of being 'at the end' and of annihilation. Is there an escape from this? Only divine grace and providence.

(ii) discusses the state and political action, which is reviewed in a roughly historical order (206–31). This leads to comments on the command to love: law and love have to go together (225). The Old Testament is generally critical towards the state and this is the only position that has theological justification; Romans 13 has to be balanced by I Peter 2.13 and Rev.13. The state is not divinely instituted but is an earthly human arrangement. God's ordinance is not the state but the realization of the dominion of God and fellowship with God in the life of the believer (226). The various attempts to realize God's will in political life within the Old Testament fall under the prophetic criticism (230). Political action depends on being called by God, on 'the experience of being placed before God' (231).

(iii) Social life (231–50). Here is discussed the image of God (232f.), the concept of property (233ff.) and work (235), ending up with the problem of wealth and poverty (235–6). These are further discussed in 236–42 and 242–8 respectively. Finally, in 248–50 Fohrer discusses what the message of the Old Testament for our time might be in relation to socio-economic problems. The real cause of trouble lies in the sinful being of humanity, and the Old Testament teaches that the human being must be turned around and transformed, the evil in it overcome.

(iv) 'Human Beings and Technology' (*Mensch und Technik*, 251–60) gives thought to biblical notions of technology: the Tower of Babel, the Rechabites, Solomon's Temple, the involvement with Canaanite culture and the prophetic reaction to it.

(v) 'The Future of Man' deploys three 'models': (*a*) the attempt to ensure the future through renewed legal structures and programmes; (*b*) the 'more or less Utopian solution of eschatological prophecy' and apocalyptic; (*a*) and (*b*) both have difficulties, but with (*c*), the genuine prophetic model (268–73), we have the valid Old Testament model, which starts from the necessary transformation of Israel or of humanity through conversion or redemption and leads to the new-formation of all of life.

To sum up, Fohrer's *Grundstrukturen* seems to carry us back in some ways to the atmosphere of the 'liberal' sort of biblical study against which modern biblical theology had turned. It faces 'apologetic' questions as real problems: did any 'revelation' take place? What if it is a merely personal experience, about which nothing scientific can be said? Fohrer shows a psychological interest, in this respect turning against the fashion introduced by dialectical theology, under which psychological considerations were largely neglected, if not totally banned. And he shows a sociological interest: biblical faith is affected by social factors, and social factors are affected by biblical faith. The political interest is also marked. Not that all questions are handled in a profound manner – consider, for instance, the very naive and inadequate arguments with which he deems himself to have shown that the Old Testament as it lies before us is not revelation (33–5). Nevertheless, his work must count as a fresh departure in many ways. He has no difficulty in mixing in historical-critical studies and insights from the history of religion with his theology, and equally he is ready to tell us, from time to time, what the message of the Old Testament for today is. Some of his basic viewpoints are taken up and developed by later successors in the tradition of Old

Testament theology, such as Gunneweg,[22] who adopts from him the centrality of the *Daseinshaltungen*. As has been said, Fohrer's theology gives the air of a very fresh and stimulating reactualization of something like the 'liberal' Christian point of view. Even when seen with hindsight, it seems to show no signs of Fohrer's own conversion to Orthodox Judaism which took place some years later.

### 4. Terrien

Samuel Terrien's *The Elusive Presence: Towards a New Biblical Theology* was published in 1978. Terrien, a Frenchman, taught much of his life in Union Theological Seminary, New York, and was a highly respected scholar, known especially for his work in the Wisdom literature, e.g. his commentary on Job. He describes his book as an 'essay' which is 'a prolegomenon to a genuinely "biblical" theology which will respect historical complexity within, as well as between, the Old Testament and the New' (xxix). The theme is 'the Hebraic theology of presence', which, it is maintained, is more profound and pervasive than either cult or *Heilsgeschichte* and includes the basis for them both. This theology of presence 'was radically transformed by the experience of the resurrection' (5). From it a genuinely 'biblical' theology may arise. This in turn might bring together the divided currents of conservative Orthodox, Roman Catholic and Anglican Christianity on the one hand and on the other hand 'idealistic, moralistic, sentimentalist, subjectivist and activist Protestants', reminding the former of the need for the 'risk of an insecure and yet secure faith', the latter of the need to know 'that faith cannot live or be maintained from generation to generation without the act of sacramental adoration' (8).[23]

The general approach of *The Elusive Presence* is to state a theme and follow it out through various stages. Beginning with 'Cultus and Faith in Biblical Research', which defines and brings together the two central aspects, the book goes on to Chapter 2, 'Epiphanic Visitations to the Patriarchs', then to Chapter 3, 'The Sinai Theophanies', 4, 'The Presence in the Temple', 5, 'The Prophetic Vision', 6, 'The Psalmody of Presence', and 7, 'The Play of Wisdom' (Terrien's own special area). Chapter 8, 'The Final Epiphany', is a rather short chapter on eschatological expectation. With Chapters 9, 'Presence as the Word', and 10, 'The Name and the Glory', we are in Christianity.

Thus Terrien took a particular theme as central, in the sense that that theme was not only the organizing principle for a wide systematization, but he followed it out, discussed the aspects that were closely akin to it, and left other things aside. Thus he has no substantial discussion of Hebrew law, none of Joshua-Judges and the conquest of the land, none of the succession story of David, nor of some other conspicuous subjects. Yet he thinks that his work improves upon the previous attempts on two sides: on the one side, it is better than the approach through covenant or even through election, kingdom, creation, redemption and other themes, which he considers 'peripheral' or at least 'partial' (472); on the other side he notes the difficulty in 'presenting as Old Testament theology the various testimonies which Israel has recorded on the successive waves of historical challenge and response – however valuable and even brilliant the work of G. von Rad may have been' (ibid.). It is Wisdom that confirms this expectation:

> Does the Hebraic theology of presence provide a legitimate approach to a genuine theology of the entire Bible? Contemporary trends in the study of wisdom as the main source of Christology suggest that this may well be the case. The figure of personified Wisdom brings together the theologoumenon of the name, with its response of the ear, and the theologoumenon of the glory, with its response of the eye (473)

Terrien's approach, then, is more an approach through one theme deemed central, a theme which is said to bring together aspects that might wrongly be considered opposites, than an attempt to synthesize all the themes contained in the Bible. On the other hand his Theology, though distinctly more an Old Testament work than one located in the New, very clearly carries over its line and style of exposition from the Old into the New, and sometimes intermingles the two. In addition, it accords a central place to Hebrew Wisdom, which was a difficulty for some other theologies (Wright, later von Rad, probably others). Though saying comparatively little about post-biblical Judaism, it noted the importance of 'an informed open, and eminently respectful attitude *vis-à-vis* the relationship of early Christianity to pre-Rabbinic Judaism as well as an enlightened rigour of judgment on the exegetical (midrashic) and typological methods used by the first-century church when it read the Hebrew Scriptures' (472). The entire work is poetic in style, in this coming close to von Rad himself, and its theological style is markedly committed and spiritual:

> Biblical theology as the biblical knowledge of God is indeed the object of science, provided that the biblical theologian is also subject to a personal involvement in the 'knowledge' of that God. Biblical theology is thus indissolubly married to biblical spirituality, which in turn remains inseparable from the continuity of the cultic celebration of presence (42).

It fits with the above that Terrien particularly emphasizes the dialectic constituted by the categories of *the ethical and the aesthetic*.[24] The historical and covenantal materials have been too much emphasized, and the theme of presence, which is characteristically 'elusive', is more central. If the 'ethical' applies to the former, the perception of Presence is more an aesthetic matter. The sapiential and hymnic materials of the Hebrew Bible 'are concerned not so much with duty as with beauty' (Brueggemann, ibid.). Moreover, the 'aesthetic' is more characteristic of Terrien himself. His writing betrays his sensitivity to wide areas of the Western artistic and literary traditions.

And in view of the reproach – partially justified as we have seen – that much biblical theology has a Protestant bias or even a particular denominational bias within Protestantism, the widely ecumenical interest of Terrien's theology should be appreciated. He looks for a 'new era of scholarship' in which 'an ecumenical theology of the entire Bible will serve the various families of Christendom now divided' (475). Such an ecumenical theology will 'take the Old Testament with theological seriousness, for it has to reverse the nineteenth- and twentieth-century trend which reduces theology to Christology'. Equally, it will 'discern and describe those elements of theological truth which are common to Judaism and Christianity on the one hand, and Islam and Christianity on the other'. The task of biblical theology, however, is no more than a preparatory one: 'it will not claim to propound a theological elucidation of Christian faith for the end of the twentieth century'. Its scope will be no more than to prepare for the work of the systematic theologian. Many of these values as propounded by Terrien will be values animating this present work also.

On the other hand there seem to be elusive or indefinable weaknesses in Terrien's Theology which have prevented it from attaining a central position in discussion. Is there a vagueness in its near-mystical spirituality, an inconclusiveness in its ability to reconcile differences as 'dialectical' opposites, an impossibility of verifying or proving some of the concepts asserted ('Presence is that which creates a people', 124; 'In biblical faith, human beings discern that presence is a surging which soon vanishes and leaves in its disappearance an absence that has been overcome', 476), which makes it difficult to place it within the mainstream of discussion of biblical theology? Is it perhaps more a personal contribution than a major element in the debate?[25]

## 5. Schmid

Although he has not written a full-length Old Testament Theology, the proposals of the Swiss scholar H.H. Schmid in a group of interrelated essays are highly interesting and may also mark a new turn in the development of the subject. The basic volume, *Altorientalische Welt in der alttestamentlicher Theologie*, was published in 1974, but some of the articles contained in it are earlier.

Contrary to the tendency of earlier Old Testament theology, which emphasized Israel's history as the medium of God's self-revelation and sometimes even reduced creation to a sort of appendix subsequently attached (cf. the thought that the real beginning of the Bible was the beginning not of Genesis but of Exodus),[26] Schmid emphasizes the theme of creation, which is *shared* by Israel with the ancient Near East. Moreover, the theme of creation was not only, and not primarily, an account of the *beginnings* of the world: it was more an account of an *order* under which the world existed and was governed. The order of creation, moreover, was linked with the order of *law*.[27]

In contrast, therefore, with some older forms of Old Testament theology, Schmid is interested in *integrating* the subject with the history-of-religion approach. This does not mean that Israelite faith will be *equated* with the environing religions: on the contrary, understood in this way, it will be revealed what the true *specifica* of Israelite faith are (21).

Moreover, taking up another of the traditional themes of Old Testament theology, Schmid claims that his approach provides essential links with the New Testament. Paul's message of *justification* is an answer to the question of the wholesome *world order* ($ṣ^edaqah$ – δικαιοσύνη).[28] In the same horizon is to be seen the depth of the meaning of *forgiveness of sin* and of the *expiatory death of Jesus*. Other New Testament themes include the emphasis on *peace*, and also the thoughts of the coming final judgment and other apocalyptic expectations, e.g. that of a new heaven and a new earth. Thus the belief in creation, i.e. the belief that God has created the world along with its manifold orders (*Ordnungen*), 'is not a marginal theme of biblical theology but fundamentally *is* its theme'. 'Anyone who wants to have an appropriate understanding of the history of Israelite faith must therefore comprehend in one the polyvalent common-oriental beginning and the continuations worked out in its sequel' (156).

As mentioned briefly above, Schmid's theology also attaches a high importance to the theme of *peace*. The main trend of modern Old Testament theology had given considerable positive emphasis to the place of *warfare* in the Old Testament.[29] Moralistic scruples about its warlike passages were despised as a relic of the older liberalism and branded as a sign of something like Marcionism. Had not Karl Barth written blithely of 'how unceremoniously and constantly war is waged in the Bible'? In particular, Gerhard von Rad, one of the most important Old Testament theologians, had written his *Holy War in Ancient Israel*, which made the tradition of holy war into a very central and positive element of the entire theology of the Old Testament.

Holy war, Schmid goes on, belongs to a nationally limited understanding of God which is closely connected with the ancient understanding of the world (99). The world of the nation is identified, ethnocentrically, as the world as a whole. But on the other side one starts out from the duality of cosmos–chaos. The enemies, the foreign peoples, are basically seen as manifestations of chaos, and have to be repelled in the interests of the cosmos. Warfare thus has a cosmos-supporting function, which is the basis for the positive evaluation of it.

On the other side, however, the Old Testament has also a witness to God as a God of peace. God's peace is the fundamental definition of the world (102); here we have, in contrast with the ethnocentric, an 'identifying' mode of thought. In the course of time, however, the idea of peace is moved increasingly into the future: it becomes eschatological. In the end (109) war and peace are very closely interlinked in the Old Testament. Schmid here (109) passes to the New Testament. It is impossible for us to take every Old Testament utterance about war or peace directly as authoritative for today; between it and us stands the New Testament and the two thousand years of exegesis, especially the approaches of the Enlightenment and their consequences for modern thought.[30] 'The Bible starts out from the position that peace is the real destiny (*Bestimmung*) of the world' (116). This is part of a basic need of humanity to live in a sound, ordered, world.

That this is a very fresh approach, and yet combines several of the accepted interests of biblical theology, is obvious. The giving of priority and basic status to creation reverses the emphasis which dominated much biblical theology throughout this century. Those familiar with the earlier Barth/Brunner debates will not fail to remember that orders (*Ordnungen*) were central to Brunner's conception. It is not surprising that Schmid had to complain that 'anyone who wanted to accord a higher weight to the theology of creation very soon fell under the suspicion of intending a natural theology'. So far as I know, however, he has not taken the further step of saying, Yes, and a natural theology is the obviously right and scriptural outcome of these thoughts.[31]

It would be misleading if I were to suggest to the reader that Schmid's approach has been universally welcomed. On the contrary, it has met with sharp criticism, from F. Crüsemann and especially from J. Halbe.[32] They argue that Schmid has constructed his 'world order thinking' out of a confusion of different things: it is a 'trivial, banal, abstract, unhistorical and history-empty ideologeme' (!). Among other things, biblical law is not based on creation but is derived from the *Privilegrecht Jahwes*, God's own privileged commands.[33] Nevertheless Schmid's approach has also received much more positive comment: see for example the discussion by Reventlow[34] and the balanced assessment by Oeming (100f.). The latter, after acknowledging the difficulties, concludes that 'the world order thinking nevertheless remains a helpful heuristic instrument, with the help of which one can understand broad and central areas of Old and New Testament text as interlinkage (*Anknüpfung*), contradiction and overcoming [of contradiction]'.[35] Moreover, similar thoughts have been expressed by scholars working in the United States. Thus James Crenshaw, the leading specialist in Hebrew Wisdom, has written: 'The dominant background to the thought and belief of the Old Testament is the idea of the all-embracing ordering of the world; that is, creation faith in the wider sense of the term: the creation faith which in some respects Israel shared with its environment.'[36] Equal attention should be given to the thoughts of R. P. Knierim in his major article 'Cosmos and History in Israel's Theology'.[37] He writes: 'Despite the verdict against the theological relevance of Israel's cosmology in the mainstream of Old Testament studies, aspects of this topic have been addressed during the last two decades with various, and so it seems increasing, degrees of attention to its theological significance' (182), and following this he mentions S. Herrmann, O. Kaiser, W. H. Schmidt, K. Koch, H. H. Schmid, C. Westermann and O. H. Steck. For another appreciative recent reference to Schmid's thoughts, see John Barton, *Ethics and the Old Testament*, 67f.:

> For Schmid, the primary horizon of the Old Testament is not God's choice of Israel and the giving to them of the law, but the creation of the world and the moral order that derives from its created character. This implies that morality is first and foremost a matter of human beings recognizing their finite, created status and seeking a way of life which embodies their sense of belonging in the hierarchical universe whose head and origin is God. In other words, the underlying moral system of the Old Testament, on which the tradition of positive law has been superimposed, is more or less the system espoused by Isaiah, and worked out in detail in wisdom writings such as Proverbs.

As an addition to the discussion of Schmid's ideas it will be useful to add a comment on the New Testament scholar U. Luck, who has been associated with Schmid. His basic work, *Welterfahrung und Glaube als Grundproblem biblischer Theologie*, considers *experience of the world* as the basic theme of biblical theology. Its task is to provide an answer to the question 'What contribution does biblical theology make to the understanding of reality?'. Human life meets with dilemmas through the tension between what we expect of life and what we in fact experience. Three ways are offered in the biblical tradition: 1. the institutional way, with justice and law as official order; 2. the historical way; 3. the 'intellectual' way. Each of these meets with difficulties or comes to failure. In the last resort only an apocalyptic hope for a new age of righteousness provides an answer. This is reminiscent of Bultmann's way of understanding the Old Testament through three paths of 'failure'.[38] This cannot be fully discussed here, but the mere existence of such an opinion indicates the variety of recent thinking in biblical theology and the renewed possibility, in recent years, of uttering suggestions which in the earlier period would have been considered impossible.

For the present it is sufficient to say that the three scholars who have been discussed in the latter part of this chapter represent substantially fresh approaches to the whole structure and atmosphere of biblical theology. All of them show originality and new thinking. Though none of them has become, thus far, a leading or dominant figure in the discussion, each of them in his own way marks a dissatisfaction with the classic patterns and a readiness to strike out in a new direction. In a very general way we may say that we see a decrease in the older emphasis on revelation in history or divine acts in history, a decrease in the emphasis on distinctiveness, and an increase in attention to the Wisdom literature, to human experience and perception, and to social and conceptual organization of the world.

# 20

# An Overview of the Older Tradition

This seems a suitable point at which to give some general assessment of the achievement of Old Testament theology, at least as it was up to the 1970s, though I shall not be strictly constrained by that date and may mention some aspects which appear later and which will be mentioned in later chapters. In view of the numerous criticisms which have been directed at Old Testament theology – including, as I have admitted, some by me – and widespread hesitation about its status and prospects, it seems to me right to say firmly that generally speaking, twentieth-century Old Testament theology has done very excellent work and has very substantial achievements to its credit.

Put it this way: supposing someone were to ask for a book which, in one volume or two, presented for the educated but non-specialist reader an intelligible account of the religious concerns of the Old Testament, where else could one turn but to one or other of the main Old Testament Theologies which have been produced? It is practically impossible to think of anything that could compete.[1] No one will suppose that any of the many Introductions to the Old Testament which have been written will do the job: they are concerned with a detailed analysis and history of the literature, but hardly touch on the outlines of the religion. In spite of the challenge offered by the history of religion, that approach has (until very recently, perhaps) produced many specialized studies but few single and comprehensive works that could compete with the Old Testament Theologies, and where such works have appeared, as indicated above, they show a considerable overlap with the latter in any case. Commentaries on biblical books exist in plenty, but by their nature they cannot fulfil the requirements I am making – even if one were to read a commentary on every biblical book, one would still not have achieved the goal. Bible dictionaries can be looked up under various entries but do not present a comprehensively-written account. Nor do scholarly monographs, which obviously confine themselves to a limited area or topic. Relevant works by doctrinal theologians like Miskotte are few.

The Old Testament Theologies on the other hand do undertake to cover the basic material of the Hebrew Bible within one volume or two. They are, with only slight exceptions, written by persons who are trained in the biblical languages, are fully experienced in the range of historical and critical approaches, and are in contact with the current exegetical discussions. They are written for the most part in intelligible and not-too-technical language and can be followed by the non-specialized reader. They are, in short, the best general surveys of the religious message of the Hebrew Bible that have been available in the period under discussion. In view of the many criticisms to which the tradition of Old Testament theology has been subject, there is a need for fresh understanding of some of its strengths.

In this chapter, therefore, I propose to discuss some of the ways in which the older tradition of Old Testament theology may be evaluated and understood.

## 1. *System and Selection*

The Old Testament theology of this century has often been severely blamed for its 'systematic' character. It would be more correct, however, to say that there has been an interesting oscillation between two extremes, which we may call system and anti-system. Both tendencies were commonly present, even in the work of the same scholar.

We have seen that an interest in a 'systematic' operation was basic to Eichrodt's approach. In his view, system provided the antidote to the historical approach which, while perhaps quite right in itself, had ended up by losing its 'feeling for the vital synthesis in the Old Testament and could only see the differing teachings of individual biblical writers' (I, 28). He looked back with admiration on three nineteenth-century scholars, Oehler, Dillmann and Schultz, who 'had attempted to expound the essential content of the Old Testament in systematic form, while at the same time giving full consideration to the newly emergent problems connected with it' (29). Equally, however, he was aware of the difficulties involved in this. 'The unique quality of Israelite religion obstinately resists all efforts to subject it completely to systematic treatment' (32f.).[2] He spoke respectfully of E. König, who in 1922 had produced an Old Testament Theology which attempted to be synthetic as well as historical (31), but the result had not been satisfactory, partly because the historical part squeezed out the systematic, and partly because the systematic part itself went wrong: 'the recalcitrant material is forced [in the systematic section, I think he means] into a Procrustes' bed, because it has been made to fit a dogmatic arrangement foreign to the subject'. System, then, was desirable, but would work only if an arrangement could be found that was intrinsic to the material.

So, in the upshot, Eichrodt continues to require a systematic approach: though insisting on the extreme difficulty of carrying this out, his answer is that it depends on the way you do it. There are therefore two questions: system itself is one, the organizing principle is the other. For the moment I shall concentrate on the idea of system in itself.

Some other Old Testament theologians took the same line. R. C. Dentan described the subject as 'that Christian theological discipline which treats of the religious ideas of the Old Testament *systematically*, i.e. not from the point of view of the historical development, but from that of the structural unity of Old Testament religion, and which gives due regard to the historical and ideological relationship of that religion to the religion of the New Testament'.[3]

In general, however, the main body of Old Testament theologians were hostile to system. George Ernest Wright, for instance, spoke repeatedly against it. 'The biblical language will always be the despair of the precise and exact theologian who above all desires a simple, coherent system' (*God Who Acts*, 32). In the Bible 'the being and attributes of God are nowhere systematically presented but are inferences from events' (57). The New Testament has 'no unified system of doctrinal meaning' (59). God's Word 'is not an abstraction which can be presented in a systematic theology' (83, again 84). Surprisingly, in the end Wright concedes that 'biblical theology cannot be completely unsystematic'; but, he goes on, 'it is not primarily concerned with an abstract "system of thought"' (116). Typically of his argumentation, he attacked system in general but repeatedly shifted his ground and rejected not system but any 'simple', 'abstract' or 'coherent' system.

Von Rad is also opposed to a systematic approach; this is part of his disagreement with Eichrodt. But the way in which he argues seems to concentrate not so much on the wrongness of a systematic *presentation* of Old Testament theology: it is rather that the Old Testament materials themselves are lacking in systematic thinking (1, 116f.). Since the texts are lacking in system, system is an inappropriate way in which to present their theology.

Vriezen pushes this point less hard: 'it is not possible to press Old Testament theology into a complete systematic survey,' he writes (151). The subjects 'interlock in such a way that a systematic classification of the material implies some measure of arbitrariness'. This suggests satisfaction with a systematic approach but awareness that it will not work very well.

More common, however, has been the opinion that no systematic approach is possible in any circumstances. I have heard this view from many scholars and would surmise that it may be the view of the majority of those who take any interest in the subject at all. Among critics of the entire idea of biblical theology, hostility to system and the systematic sometimes becomes shrill and hysterical. Thus Philip Davies writes:

> Mere description of the views of the individual biblical writers does not yield a theology. On the other hand, any attempt to be systematic will involve

value judgments about the differing statements in the biblical books about humanity, god(s), ethics, and so on. Description must yield to evaluation if any kind of systematic account is to be offered. Such a *systematic* enterprise can only serve the Christian religion. I would not *in theory* be able to rule out the possibility of an Islamic or humanistic or Marxist 'biblical theology', but what would such an enterprise serve? The 'Old Testament' is a Christian entity, and no amount of trying to be 'descriptive' will do anything other than deliver a confessional account of its contents (79).

I do not see why a systematic approach must involve evaluation more than a descriptive one, nor why it can serve only the Christian religion. In any case, as already stated, many Old Testament theologians have been anxious to avoid systematization.[4]

It is not so easy, however, to get away from the reproach of 'systematization'. Eichrodt was for it, as we have seen, but with qualifications, and von Rad was against it (at least on the surface). To Goshen-Gottstein, however, these two are still both systematizers: 'Eichrodt and von Rad wrote *opera magna* and worked out systems' ('Tanakh Theology', 625) – though he did not necessarily mean this as a reproach. Something like this has probably been a common judgment.

What is the reason, however, why system has been so commonly resisted? Certainly the term could convey a hint of traditional 'systematic' theology; yet, as we have seen, this affinity was distinctly rejected by Eichrodt and most others. One has the impression that it was something else, and that many writers followed a culturally popular anti-system trend. In contrast to the nineteenth century,[5] when for example Princeton theologians like the Hodges liked to talk about 'the Christian system',[6] in the twentieth century it became popular, if one admired a thinker, to declare that he was *not* a systematic thinker. Plato was not a systematic thinker. Neither was Aristotle.[7] If Aristotle was not, then who was? Thomas Aquinas? No, he was not one either. Hegel? Certainly not.[8] Barth? Of course not. The Old Testament is not systematic. Nor is the New. Nor is the Talmud. Nor is anything in patristic theology. Reality is messy and untidy, and serious thinkers are aware of this. Nothing of note and value is systematic.[9]

One main source of this anti-system seems to lie in an emphasis on *historical* knowledge. People often have simple and ignorant ideas about periods, personages and intellectual trends – for instance, about the Reformation, about Martin Luther, about Hegelianism, about socialism. These simple ideas often have a systematic character. Anyone who has real knowledge knows that all such systems are gross over-simplifications and that the reality was much more complicated, contradictory, changeable over time, and in essence unsystematic. Historical knowledge tends to destroy such ideas. History is essentially untidy.

The increasing emphasis on intellectual history, particularly noticeable in theology, had this effect.

It seems obvious that two or more senses of the term 'systematic' are being confused here. 'Systematic' may suggest an organization so complete that it is supposed to accommodate *everything*. On these terms, a truly systematic theology of the Old Testament will take into account the wife of Cain, the bed of Og the king of Bashan, the question of who buried Moses, the rules for dealing with a woman suspected of adultery, the problem of whether Ezra or Nehemiah came first, and the identity of the 'man' who joined Shadrach, Meshach and Abednego in the fiery furnace, and fit them all neatly into their place in the system. The system will provide, if not an explanation for all these texts, at least guidelines which will be valid for such an explanation, criteria within which all of them will somehow fit. If 'systematic' is intended in this sense, it is not surprising that scholars deny the possibility of a systematic approach.

In fact, when scholars supported a 'systematic' approach, they cannot have intended this sort of thing. They must, in all cases or almost all, have meant something more limited. 'System' must have been intended as something much more limited and much more flexible. It was a sort of inner grid which could be placed within the material and could be seen to provide some degree of basic ordering and coherence. Where substantial failure to cohere persisted, then it might be necessary to bend the system, or to alter it, if necessary to withdraw it and try again. 'System' in this sense is less like the older 'systems' of theology or philosophy (if such systems ever existed) and more like the 'models' of social science, which are used experimentally as a means of locating and 'placing' certain elements within a vast sea of data.

Scholars like Eichrodt had, no doubt, little or no contact with modern social sciences or sympathy with them. When they thought of being 'systematic', their minds turned to the older systematic theology which was still all too familiar to them. In fact, however, they were perhaps unwittingly opening a door into a more modern world.[10] The move from a diachronic perception which explains in terms of origins and changes to a synchronic perception which explains in terms of models and matrices is supposed, rightly or wrongly, to be a significant advance. In fact other aspects of biblical scholarship – most notably and obviously literary criticism – have in the last decades been swift to follow in exactly this shift of perception. It has not been so widely perceived that the same shift has the immediate effect of justifying Old Testament theology, at least potentially and at least in part, against some of the criticisms which had been directed against it. And thus, whether writers like Eichrodt were conscious of this intellectual change or not, those of us who read their work in the 1950s or 1960s or thereafter could hardly fail to observe that the use of a more 'systematic' method rather than a more 'historical' one could well fit in with ways in which we were already thinking. So there is a tendency in modern thinking to accept 'system' as a good and useful term; and if Michael Fishbane can write a whole chapter on 'Judaism as an Ideological System', it is difficult to see why it should be impossible to use the same term for the situation within the Hebrew Bible.[11]

And system in this sense does not profess to cover or to include every detail. One who talks about the 'political system' or the 'economic system' of a country, e.g. 'the American health care system', 'the English class system' or 'the pre-1914 European state system', must be aware that exceptions exist, that tendencies contrary to those recognized in the system are there. The system consists of main structures, within which a variety of contradictory details may fit. This is what happens, or at least may happen, in Old Testament Theologies.

Within Old Testament theology, 'system' has always been linked with *selectivity*. No one ever thought that his Theology included *everything*. 'System' was thus more like a *structure* which had a place within the material, but to which varying detailed aspects were attached in varying degrees of agreement. It was able to some extent to accommodate individual theological differences and also to accommodate diachronic changes. Thus Eichrodt, far from imposing a unitary view of the covenant on all the material, expressly included a significant 'History of the Covenant Concept' (I, 45–69) over several historical stages. In this respect one of the most serious objections levelled at Old Testament theologies, namely that they produced a rigid systematic pattern, has not been generally justified, even if partial manifestations of this tendency have been seen. Following what has been said, I have found it good to use 'structure' rather than 'system'; and *Struktur* is characteristically, and rightly, the term employed in the final statements of the recent Theology by Preuss, which in many ways follows the model of Eichrodt's approach and will be discussed later.[12] It is not surprising, therefore, that when discussing the place of modern structuralism in relation to biblical studies I included the example of Old Testament theology.[13]

This, if true, does something to justify the structural type of Old Testament theology against its critics. Eichrodt and his followers were making the same move from diachronic description of change to (mainly, but not totally, synchronic) detection of underlying structure that was being made in numerous disciplines. Whether fully effective or not, this argument is sufficient to make sense of Eichrodt-type theologies as reasonable academic approaches. What it fails to do, on the other hand, is to justify the claim of such works to be actual *theology*. To suppose that a move from a diachronic approach to a structural one was also a move *to theology* was, in Eichrodt's case, just a mistake. The shift, though probably theologically helpful, was an element in a widespread cultural change affecting the entire Western world. The mistake was caused by the tendency, endemic in the earlier movement of twentieth-century biblical theology, to suppose that there were two contrasting approaches, that of history and that of theology, and that to move from a historical mode to another was to move from history to theology.

On the other side, however, the anxious desire of Old Testament theologians to dissociate themselves from the 'precise', 'coherent' and 'abstract' systems of doctrinal theologians has been deceptive. In this respect, once again they were actually following the tendencies of the doctrinal theology from which they sought to differentiate themselves. The typical doctrinal theologian of the twentieth century might have the title 'systematic theologian', but it was he himself who was anxious to escape from the opprobrium which attached to systems of that kind. G.E Wright, as we saw, thought it impossible to cope with 'the precise and exact theologian who above all desires a simple, coherent system'. He need not have worried. The dominant doctrinal theologians of his time were saying the same thing as he was: indeed the logical basis of his arguments was in fact drawn from them, as his own lengthy and enthusiastic quotations from Brunner make clear.[14] 'Systematic' theology was at the same time making the same sort of anti-systematization noises as biblical scholars were making. It was an illusion, therefore, to suppose that the anti-system feeling among biblical theologians removed them from the area of dogmatic theology; on the contrary, it showed how close they were to it. But even within dogmatics, by the twentieth century, system was not peculiar to theology; it was a part of general cultural thinking.

Whatever be the truth of this, many Old Testament theologians, as we have seen, opposed the (apparently) systematic tendencies of Eichrodt. It is not so certain, however, that they fully succeeded in escaping from them. Be this as it may, we can assert with little fear of contradiction that the anti-system mood has remained dominant, not only in Old Testament scholarship generally, but also among Old Testament theologians themselves. Only late in the twentieth century, so far as I know, does a reasoned support of the systematic approach appear in the writings of R.P. Knierim, with his article 'Systematic Old Testament Theology' (1984).[15]

> Why should 'the telling of the story' (which covers only part of the Old Testament language anyway) be theologically more or less important than language speaking in systematic concepts? Every exegete knows that the Old Testament also speaks conceptually in terms of doctrine.

It is this latter sentence, perhaps, that will leave many scholars doubtful. They will go back to the oft-repeated statement that 'you can't systematize the Old Testament'.

But here a question must be injected, one that is implied by Knierim. Is it really true that systematization is foreign to the Hebrew Bible? People insist that this is so, yet I myself think that there is a lot of systematization in it. An obvious example is the framework of the Deuteronomistic History. The older stories placed within the framework are varied and doubtless less systemic, but the framework is fairly uniform and is applied systematically. The genealogies and chronological information also form a systematic indexing for the narratives: there are of course cracks and disagreements in them, sometimes because more than one system is operative (e.g. there was probably a Priestly chronology, a Deuteronomic one, and other earlier stages).[16]

An important contribution in this respect came from one known best not as a biblical theologian but rather as a linguist and literary theorist, Wolfgang Richter.[17] He begins from the 'small historical creed' of Deut. 26, so essential to von Rad's theology. Following a suggestion from L. Rost, which regards most of the 'creed' as late rather than ancient, Richter enters into a close formalistic analysis linked with fairly traditional source criticism. The formulaic character of many passages shows that they belong to a *schematic* sort of presentation resulting from *system formation*. Literary works, like J, E and various stages of D, 'stand at decisive points of the process of theological systematization' (211). Thus J has the earliest combination of the formulae of 'bringing out' and of 'giving over of the land' in respect of the patriarchs. 'But even this combination should be recognized as the result of an *abstraction* out of more concrete [earlier] traditions' (210, my italics). The detailed argument of Richter cannot be repeated here. Suffice it to say that the article presents a powerful and detailed case for the presence and fundamental importance of system formation within a wide range of basic Hebrew texts.

It looks, therefore, as if the common traditional feeling that the Hebrew Bible material 'resists all systematization' is not so well founded as one might have thought.

Before we discuss this further, however, we have to consider the question of the 'centre', which is a marked feature of the Eichrodt tradition and of many Old Testament Theologies since his time.

## 2. *The question of the 'centre'*

Eichrodt himself actually defined his 'centre' in two ways. On the one hand he expressed it as a group of 'three principal categories': 'God and the People', 'God and the World', and 'God and Man' (I, 33). He divided the three parts of his Theology accordingly. But in addition he took the *covenant* as his central symbol: especially in the first volume (= Part One, God and the People) the covenant is integrated into the title of every section.

It is easy to see the attraction of covenant as a principle: covenant is usually a relational concept, involving two parties, and thus fits relational categories like 'God and People'. Beyond this, in fact, Eichrodt had to incorporate yet a third principle, that of *kingdom*. As we have seen, one of the problems with covenant is its relatively infrequent explicit mention in the New Testament. Since the establishment of connections with the New Testament was one of the central aims of Eichrodt's Theology, as of many others, this looks like a weakness, which he scarcely faced or acknowledged in his Theology itself. In the Theology itself he maintains that 'that which binds together indivisibly the two realms of the Old and New Testaments – different in externals as they may be – is the irruption of the Kingship of God into this world and its establishment there' (26). If this is so, as Spriggs rightly remarks,[18] one might have expected the Theology to be organized around kingship rather than around covenant. In a later article, however, Eichrodt explains that 'covenant was the special manifestation of the kingdom of God in Israel' (thus Spriggs). Seeking to defend this, Eichrodt maintained, as quoted by Spriggs, that kingship language had to be avoided in Israel because of its association with pagan rulers [but surely kingship language was not at all avoided!] and in any case 'the idea of *b<sup>e</sup>rit* concurs with that of kingdom'. Well, maybe, but at best one cannot but see the complexity of the argument. Anyway, for our present purposes, 'covenant' is the central theme for Eichrodt, as is generally agreed.

Many other Old Testament theologians followed some such pattern. Jacob began from 'The Living God: Centre of Revelation and of Faith', and combined this with the themes of the *presence* and the *action* of God. Vriezen held that 'communion between the Holy One and man is the essential root-idea of the Old Testament message'.[19] Terrien took as his central theme the elusive *presence* of God. Zimmerli organized his Theology around the theme of the *name* of God.

There is a striking tendency in the later development of this discussion to produce *double* or otherwise more complicated formulae. Rudolf Smend, though not writing a full-length Theology, made the basic enquiry into this question of the 'centre',[20] and he offered as the best solution Wellhausen's phrase 'Yahweh the God of Israel, Israel the people of Yahweh'. Fohrer proposed a dual concept, with two foci and an ellipse, the rule of God and the community between God and humanity. Preuss in his recent Theology sets forth the rather complex formula: 'Yahweh's electing action on Israel in history for community with his world, which is at the same time an action that places obligation upon this people (and the [other] peoples).'[21] And he builds the sections of his book very much according to this formula and entitles them accordingly.

It is easy to make fun of this question of a 'centre' and use it as a way to ridicule Old Testament theology as a whole. As many as a dozen or maybe twenty 'centres' have been proposed, and this may look ludicrous. On top of this von Rad, commonly thought to be the most important individual theologian, disputed the whole idea of a 'centre' and denied that there was any such thing.[22] Yet the matter is not as foolish as some have been pleased to make it.

First, the denial of the 'centre' by von Rad. Von Rad, as we have seen, thought that there was no single theology in the Hebrew Bible, but many, and so there was no conceptual 'centre'. In this sense he saw a major difference from the New Testament:

> Unlike the revelation in Christ, the revelation of Yahweh in the Old Testament is divided up over a long series of separate acts of revelation which are very different in content. It seems to be without a centre which determines everything and which could give to the separate acts both an interpretation and their proper theological connexion with one another (1,115).

Instead, as we have seen, he emphasized the character of the Old Testament as a 'book of history', in which historical traditions were reinterpreted and reactualized over time:

> If we seek to extract from the bewildering number of these actualizations some characteristic, common and continuing feature, it is this . . . Israel was always placed in the vacuum between an election made manifest in her history, and what had a definite promise attached to it, and a fulfilment of this promise which was looked for in the future . . . The common element . . . was that Israel was poised between promise and fulfilment . . . This continual actualization of the data of the saving history, with its consequence that every generation saw itself anew on the march towards a fulfilment, occupies such a prominent position in the Old Testament that a theology of the Old Testament must accommodate itself to it (2, 414).

In fact, however, it is hard to see how von Rad has avoided the identification of a 'centre': these sentences themselves indicate what the 'centre' was for him. The historical narration, and the reactualization of the traditions, were for him the centre. The difference is that 'covenant' or 'love of God' or 'communion' are, as he saw it, biblical concepts, which he thought inappropriate as candidates for the 'centre'. For him the 'centre' was the method of presentation itself. Moreover, in certain parts of his work, as I pointed out in an early review, he did not succeed in avoiding the sort of 'systematized theological discussions'[23] which he had criticized in Eichrodt and others. Von Rad's opposition to the idea of a 'centre' cannot therefore be accepted without qualification.

Incidentally, there remains the interesting question just what was von Rad's real purpose in rejecting the 'centre' and preferring a multiplicity of different theologies. It has often been thought that this was a return to a historical-critical approach.[24] But I find this difficult to believe. It seems quite unfitted to von Rad's character. I suggest that it was the opposite: it was a theological preference, based upon his picture of the way in which the Old Testament could be connected with the New. It was one of his early convictions, probably formed long before his Theology came to be written. He saw the New Testament as having one unitary theology centred in Christ. That formed the one completion or fulfilment. But the Old Testament contrasted with this, precisely because it had many different stages. All this fitted with the beautiful formulation of Heb. 1.1, which he quoted (*Theology* 1, 115) in exactly this connection.[25] The weakness of the idea lay not in the Old Testament but in the New: at this point he did not properly consider the view, common among New Testament theologians, that the New Testament also had a multiplicity of theologies. Like some other Old Testament theologians, he may have worked with too simple an idea of the New. If the New has several theologies, Christ can still be the 'centre'; but if that is so, then the natural thing would be for Yahweh to be the 'centre' for the Old. And this is close to what Zimmerli achieved in making the Name of Yahweh his 'centre'. However, von Rad was attracted at this point to the idea of the contrast between the many and the one. His reasons were theological. But we must return to our argument.

Secondly, the idea of a 'centre' should perhaps be seen as a kind of hypothesis formation. It is agreed that the 'centre' is not obvious, is not explicitly put forward by the text. This is exactly why it has to be *proposed* or *suggested*. And one cannot simply propose it as an idea on its own. One has to write a complete Theology, or at least a substantial article, in order to explore how far a proposal will work. If existing proposals do not give satisfaction, then one can try another. People sometimes speak as if the various proposals are all definite convictions, each of them at war with all the others. Any profound knowledge of the literature will show that this is not the case. Eichrodt's covenant did undergo a lot of criticism, but most of the other proposals, though different from each other, are not markedly critical of the others. The one that seems to me to have the most passionate commitment of the scholar to it is Zimmerli's centre in 'the Name', but even he does not dispute with other proposals or suggest that his cannot be combined with them, as it very probably can. However, in general one might sum up the discussion with the impression that most of the passages may complement others or indeed may be combined with others. Any that are found to be seriously unsuitable can be discarded without disparagement, as hypotheses that have not worked.

Thirdly, part of the explanation for the 'centre' problem comes from the practical consideration of one writing *a book* which is to present the theology of the Old Testament. The actual theology may be mixed up or chaotic, but a book has to have some sort of organization. A history might be organized on a straight temporal scale (though even that is not so simple), but a theology is usually supposed to be something else. The desire is, usually, not to take the organization out of traditional doctrinal theology. Rather, it should come from within the material itself. But that means perceiving some sort of central structural point or points; otherwise, the book will be a chaos, which is perhaps what some people would like it to be. To write a book with some concept as the 'centre' is somewhat different from insisting that that concept *is* the centre of the theology of the Old Testament itself. There is a difference of nuance. The 'centre' of the book will have to be at least *plausible* as a possible 'centre' for the actual theology, and the writer will have to argue a case for it. But he or she might still write the book while remaining aware that the case could not be proved, or that other possibilities were equally strong. It is probable that some have written with the former intent but have given the impression of a more absolute conviction. In any case, readers may well find that the various proposals enrich and complement one other. Although there was a definite skirmish between Eichrodt and von Rad over the covenant, it does not seem to me that the differences over the 'centre' among Old Testament theologians were in themselves a matter of heated debate or disagreement. On the contrary, there seems to be a sort of evolution in which later proposals take up elements from earlier ones in a creative fashion.

I have mentioned that these questions are connected with the fact of *selection* in the writing of an Old Testament Theology. Some may dislike this, but the only way to avoid it is to adopt the principle that every book on any subject must contain *everything*: all the data, all the interpretations, all the historical facts, and so on – in other words, a plain impossibility, unless one confines oneself to a very narrow topic, which of course some people do. Selection among the facts, data, interpretations and interests is unavoidable, and is a perfectly correct academic procedure.

Thus – to take the most obvious contrasting case – those features discussed above which attach to Old Testament theology attach equally to enterprises such as the history of Israel or the history of Israelite religion. These also have to formulate basic themes around which they gather their data. Thus, for example, the organization of early Israelite religion by Albertz under headings like 'Religious Elements of Early Small Family Groups', 'The Religion of the Liberated Larger Group (The Exodus Group)', 'The Religion of the Pre-State Alliance of Larger Groups', and 'Family Piety in the Later Pre-State Period' are chosen and established by exactly the same sort of criteria as the 'centres' proposed for Old Testament theology, and anyone else trying to write a history of the religion will organize it differently, with other rubrics, just as happens in Old Testament theology. The establishment of 'periods' and the classification of material into groups like 'family piety' are a matter of opinion and debate. The only difference is that Albertz's 'centres' are for chapters or sections, while traditional Old Testament theologies tended to seek a 'centre' for the whole book. But there is no reason why Old Testament theologies should not have several 'centres', e.g. for different periods or for different groups of books.

Moreover, our discussion of Eichrodt's 'centre' may usefully include the following point: in spite of his emphasis on the covenant, many readers have observed that his execution of this principle scarcely continues beyond the first volume of his work. The first volume is actually organized under this concept, each chapter being so named: 'The Covenant Statutes', 'The Name of the Covenant God', 'The Instruments of the Covenant', 'Fulfilling the Covenant'. But the second volume (originally, the second and third) has no such emphasis: the great sections 'God and the World', 'God and Man', are not organized under any such rubric. The term 'covenant' does occur frequently, commonly referring back to what has been said in the first volume, but can no longer be said to be the creative and organizing theme except at limited points, e.g. under Creation (98) or under Faith (288f.). This has sometimes been noted as a sign of weakness in Eichrodt's conception. But on the other hand it shows that he was *not* trying to force everything into a covenantal pattern, and that his 'centre' did operate as I have suggested above.

Looking back, therefore, on the various suggestions for a 'centre' that have been made, rather than submit them to ridicule, one should say that more or less all of them have been reasonable proposals and have represented an important element in the theology of the Hebrew Bible. It should not be our aim to arrive at a definitive solution, and perhaps it should be admitted that no definitive solution can be found. The differences between various Theologies should be seen as different hypotheses. The criteria for judging between them are many and various: degree of emphasis as between different elements in the texts, degree of completeness, degree of sensitivity to various small-scale exegetical possibilities, and so on. In the nature of the case, the *omission* of some elements cannot be a fatal criticism; for, as already pointed out, this cannot stand as an ultimate criterion unless one maintains that any written work must contain *all* data and evidence, which is impossible. To put it another way, the theology of the Hebrew Bible, as a subject or field of activity, contains *all* the data, evidence and exegesis, but a Theology, in the sense of a particular presentation, cannot attempt to do so. Nevertheless an *adequate* representation of all the various trends and tendencies should be required as a standard.

The operation should not be regarded as an attempt to produce the one final and correct theology. On the contrary, it is part of an ongoing discussion, in which new proposals and new directions should be expected, and also welcomed, at any time. Nor should the difference between proposals be depicted as a *contest* from which someone would emerge as 'winner', as portrayed in the sneering and contemptuous words of Philip Davies:

Many Old Testament theologies are taxonomic: one finds the category in which the largest amount of biblical material can be stored (e.g. Eichrodt: 'covenant'; von Rad: 'sacred traditions'; Preuss: 'election'), then, by dividing the drawer into compartments, one fits in everything possible. What doesn't fit has to be ignored or glossed. The winner is the one with the least left over and the neatest drawer. Or a 'middle' or 'centre' point (*Mitte*) is found and the contents arranged round it (79).

All of this is misrepresentation. There is no question of 'storing' the 'largest amount of biblical material'. There is nothing of 'fitting in everything possible'. 'What doesn't fit' can perfectly well be included, and should be, subject to the qualification that there is a necessary limit of space. Talk about a 'winner' is crude caricature.

To sum up the question of the 'centre', it seems to me that the discussion of it has not been a vain waste of breath, as some have thought, and that valuable results have emerged from it, as Smend's pivotal work demonstrated. It is not a matter of reaching a definitive answer, but rather of weighing possibilities for the expression of structure. Whether writers of Theologies define a 'centre' or not, they will very likely have to work with some idea of one (or more?), as a simple necessity for the organization of their work.

How does one estimate the qualities of an Old Testament Theology? Is there a criterion which will enable the reader to grade them? There is certainly no simple criterion, and probably there are many, corresponding to the many ways in which such a work can be constructed. As we have seen, there are many different and possibly competing considerations that may require their proper degree of attention. History of religion? Socio-political questions? Relations with doctrinal theology? History of reception of texts in later times? Perception of current literary-critical trends? Logical consistency? Questions of canonicity? Balance as between different periods? Attention to semantic-linguistic matters in Hebrew? Ability to see the subject as a whole? These are listed in a random order here. Must everything be correctly balanced? I doubt if it is possible.

However, one point of this kind is important for the whole conception of biblical theology: although ability to see the subject as a whole is very important, biblical theology, it seems to me, has to depend upon detailed exegesis and submit to its authority. Thus, to take an example which has already been mentioned, *if* it can be shown exegetically in detail that texts emphasizing the covenant are late – and I leave the question open whether this is so or not – then theologies have to take that sort of thing into account.

There is no question of producing the one right or final theology. Professor Childs in a recent article describes no less than four principal Old Testament theologians as having 'failed'.[26] I do not think that there are 'failures' of this kind (or if so they are few), any more than that there are 'winners' as supposed by Philip Davies. Certainly Eichrodt, Weiser, von Rad and Zimmerli were not among the failures.

# Story and Biblical Theology

## *1. General*

I was among those who from the 1960s onward sought to develop the concept of *story* as a central category for Old Testament exegesis and theology.[1] Others who shared this direction of thought included James Wharton, Hugh Jones and Dietrich Ritschl.[2] A particularly valuable recent study in the same tradition, gathering up the many connections of the theme with various disciplines, is Ingrid Schoberth's book on 'Memory as the Praxis of Faith'.[3]

There are, indeed, many other proposals which have used terms like 'story' and 'narrative': too many for them all to be discussed here.[4] Rather than attempt to survey this complicated terrain, I intend only to give an account of the line of thinking developed by myself and my colleagues and friends as mentioned above, and to concentrate on the significance of the concept of *story* as it applies to possibilities for Old Testament and biblical theology.

First, I quote a section from my own earlier book, *Old and New in Interpretation*, which introduced the concept of story as I have thought it to apply to biblical theology:

> To sum up this section, then: the Old Testament tells acts, events, speeches, thoughts, conversations, and all sorts of varied information, in a highly varied complex. Within this complex, however, certain relations receive particularly clear marking, and one of the clearest is that of temporal sequence. The narrative material has clear, though uneven, marking of temporal sequence. It is characterized by chronological data, by family genealogies, by references back to earlier events, and by an unmistakable progression. It is thus like history, in that it reads in a temporal progression and tells a story which is cumulative from the beginning along a temporal scale. The nearness to history, however, should not be exaggerated. From some points of view what is related is rather a story than a history. The relatedness to history varies from section to section, extending from (let us say) the Flood story, where the relation to history is probably nil, to a story like that of Nebuchadnezzar's capture of Jerusalem, where the relation is quite close.[5] The cumulation of the story, however, is indifferent to this variation. The

sequence contains also speeches and acts of God as it contains speeches and acts of men, and here again the proportions vary from section to section.

The story is both cumulative and variable in another relation also, namely that what is known of God and told about him varies with the progression of the story. Theophany, for instance, is particularly characteristic of the earlier story, under the patriarchs; the giving of the law is mainly concentrated into the time of Moses; under David the narration mainly runs on the human level, yet nevertheless works out the mysterious and tragic destiny of a divine intervention, in which, however, much of the action is not directly miraculous in character but proceeds from normal political and military operations.

In the setting of this progressive narrative, we may say that the acts of God are not really and strictly 'revelatory', except in the trivial sense in which any act done or any thing said may be considered to 'reveal' something of the doer. The acts are, within the story, further acts of one known, of one with whom the fathers have already been in contact and have passed on the tradition of this contact.

To summarize again: this formulation emphasizes the difference between 'story' and 'history', while retaining a positive interest in 'history'. It recognizes the historical features in the Bible which have led biblical theologians to pick on 'history' as its central distinguishing feature. But alongside the features that count as 'history' it recognizes others: myth and legend, for example, but above all divine speech. As I wrote earlier,

> Far from representing the divine acts as the basis of all knowledge of God and all communication with him, [the Old Testament texts] represent God as communicating freely with men, and particularly with Moses, before, during and after these events. Far from the incident at the burning bush being an 'interpretation' of the divine acts, it is a direct communication from God to Moses of his purposes and intentions. This conversation, instead of being represented as an interpretation of the divine act, is a precondition of it. If God had not told Moses what he did, the Israelites would not have demanded their escape from Egypt, and the deliverance at the Sea of Reeds would not have taken place.[6]

This approach emphasizes the beginning, the progression and the culmination of the story as, for certain purposes, more important than the relation between the story and the true historical realities.

## 2. Story and 'history'

The above arguments, among others, may have contributed to what Perdue calls, as the title of his helpful book, 'The Collapse of History'. It is difficult, he writes, 'to point to a single cause behind the collapse of history as the dominant paradigm for Old Testament theology that has led to the present disarray' (7). One way in which we may, perhaps, help to clarify the matter is by noting that 'history' functions as not one single 'paradigm' (if we must use that word) relevant to biblical theology, but as several, as follows:

1. The paradigm of history as basic to the 'historical-critical method', most obviously seen in the separation and dating of biblical sources, identification of authors, description of the development of traditions, combination and redaction, etc.

2. The paradigm of history in the sense of research into the relation of the biblical reports to text-external historical events: e.g. is it historically true that the Israelites under Joshua, as related in scripture, marched round Jericho for seven days, at the end of which the walls fell down? This sort of questioning is often also counted as belonging to 'the historical-critical method', but it is obviously different: questions about the date and authorship of books and traditions can be examined separately from questions about the historicity of reports. They are, however, easily combinable: people may think that if a text is of very late origin, this makes it less likely that it accurately reflects historical actuality of an early time, and conversely. Nevertheless the two are different in principle.

3. The paradigm of history in the sense of the history of the Israelite people, and of course their land, neighbours and environment – the sort of thing one will find in a volume entitled *History of Israel* or the like. This is related to 1 and 2 above, in that the Bible is one of the main relevant sources for the writing of such a history. But the paradigm is essentially a different one, in that material from outside the Bible – inscriptions, archaeology, Mesopotamian and Egyptian, Persian and Greek sources – is very important. Quite apart from questions of historical accuracy, the Bible does not provide any substantial account of certain periods and events.

4. The paradigm of history as the medium through which God acts and makes himself known. God has acted in historical events, events which have a location in past historical time. This is perhaps not the only mode in which God is known, but it is the one most heavily emphasized in the Bible. Moreover, it distinguishes biblical religion from (all?) other religions. It is a common saying that 'Christianity is a historical religion' (Judaism too, but perhaps not so much).

5. The paradigm of history as realized in the 'historical reading' of texts.

Historical reading overlaps with all of those mentioned above but is separable from them. By 'historical reading' I mean a reading which is interested (not necessarily exclusively interested) in the persons who wrote the texts and their thinking, the reality of the persons and events related, the time of writing and its relation to other events and writings of the time, the nature and sequence of divine acts and divine speeches retold, and so on. Historical reading in this sense is not the same as historical criticism, although it has often been the influence which led on towards historical criticism. One may read Deuteronomy with a belief that Moses was the author and with an interest in how it fitted into the situation of his time, and that is still markedly historical reading. Indeed, this is just how historical reading gave the stimulus to historical criticism.

Now if these are different 'paradigms' of history, the ones most centrally affected by the move towards 'story' with respect to biblical *theology* would seem to be, in the first place 4, secondly 5, and to some extent 3. 1 and 2 are also relevant, but more distantly. Perdue gives first mention to doubts about 'the appropriateness of historical-critical method' (7), but I would question whether this is rightly given this prominence here: first because, as we have seen, whatever the case with other aspects of biblical scholarship as a whole, biblical *theology* has been only cautiously and partially reliant on this 'method' and has often expressly distanced itself from it; and secondly because, while it is quite true that the historical-critical method has come more and more under attack in recent decades, it is equally true that recent scholarship has seen what appears to be an increasingly radical and absolute application of that same method, for example in Pentateuchal criticism (affecting 1 and 2) and in the history of Israel (affecting 3). Most of the Old Testament theologians discussed in this volume have, I would think, had in mind a moderately critical position: they will have thought of the story of David as coming from within a century of the life of that monarch; they will have thought of J and E being ninth- and eighth-century or so. They will not have thought of Abraham entering into the tradition only in post-exilic times, nor will they have thought (paradigm 3) that the reigns and empires of David and Solomon may have never existed, but are a product of late ideology. All these highly historical-critical views are now becoming widespread. So historical criticism, though relevant, is not to be thought of in the first place.

Where 'story' in my sense makes a difference in relation to 'history' is primarily in its effect on 3, 4 and 5.

Let us look first at paradigm 4.

To use a term like 'story' was of course by no means original on my part. George Ernest Wright in his *God who Acts* had referred to the existence of *stories*, and their prominence, as a feature of the Hebrew Bible. The relation between God and man, he argued, 'is not developed as doctrine, but rather is set forth as happening in a story'. But he placed a heavier emphasis on the term *history*: it was the action of the God of Israel *in history* that differentiated this God supremely from the gods of other nations.[7] And although in theory he emphasized very strongly the difference made by this narrative or historical character of the Bible, in contrast (as he thought) to the propositional language used by the older conservative theology, there remained the serious criticism, made especially by Kelsey, that Wright in his actual exposition made rather little of the actual story character, the narrative *form* of the texts, so that in effect he fell back into the propositional kind of discourse which he had initially rejected:

> But precisely the *narrative* mode of biblical literature plays no role in shaping the theology. Once this is noted, Wright's initial stress on the narrative features of scripture at the expense of its openly didactic features seems quite misleading. The narrative *qua* narrative does not authorize proposals about God. It simply gives us the grounds for defining biblical concepts which the modern Christian is to take over as his own and restate. The concepts are what is authoritative for theological proposals today, and the narrative from which they are distilled is left behind.[8]

Or, stating it on a different level, in spite of his emphasis on divine revelation *in history*, in practice what emerged as essential was not the narrative material in itself but the *idea*, the conviction or the principle, that God had revealed himself in history.

As already mentioned, von Rad had also strongly emphasized the *narrative* form of the Old Testament material, so much so that he insisted that the design of any Old Testament Theology must follow this pattern. Hebrew thought is thinking in *historical traditions* (1, 117), and we close up our access to its most characteristic core 'if we do not take the world of history seriously in the sequence and inner connections which Israel has laid down for itself' (1, 121). Therefore, in the key sentence, 'the most legitimate form of theological talk about the Old Testament always remains *the rehearsal of narrative* (*die Nacherzählung*)' (ibid.). Von Rad takes this to justify his procedure of following out the historical traditions in one volume and the prophetic traditions, also in roughly historical order, in a second. But in spite of the emphasis on *narrative* or *story-telling* seen at this point, it remains true that the basic theme for von Rad is rather *history* (*Geschichte*) or *Heilsgeschichte*, something that produces problems on which I shall say something later.

And let us agree that the emphasis on history, as a pivotal centre for Old Testament theology, has been salutary and creative. It is, no doubt, the aspect of von Rad's work that made it for many observers the outstanding contribution of the century. It portrayed a world in which *things happened*, and thus created a dynamic impression contrasting with the more static aspect of the work of Eichrodt work and some others. And it is perfectly true of a large portion of the Old Testament that it narrates a history and provides historical data, and that this feature is a striking distinguishing mark in comparison with many other cultures and peoples. In this sense 'revelation in history' was a central conviction of the older Biblical Theology Movement as portrayed by Childs.

Nevertheless these certainties were severely challenged by various forces, among which we must mention especially B. Albrektson's *History and the Gods*, which argued that the gods of other nations had also 'acted in history'. Thus 'The Old Testament idea of historical events as divine revelation must be counted among the similarities, not among the distinctive traits: it is part of the common theology of the ancient Near East'.[9]

This judgment, along with other challenges, was something of a shock to the older biblical theology, and the consequence has been a sharp withdrawal of support from 'revelation in history'. Thus Childs (*OTTCC*, 36) places revelation through history in *third* place, after knowledge of God through creation and revelation through wisdom, but before revelation through the name (of God), a marked difference as against von Rad, who would surely have given first and central place to revelation through history. Certainly divine action in history, being common ground with other cultures and religions, ceases to have 'revelatory' quality in the sense that the mere fact of such divine action places the Hebrew Bible on an entirely different level from the surrounding religious world.

One great advantage of the concept of 'story' is that it sees the story as a whole, while the application to it of the term 'history', though quite proper in some regards, is distorting in others. For one thing, it is inappropriate when applied to elements of myth and legend, which nevertheless form part of a fairly unified story: obvious cases are the stories of the 'angel marriages' where the 'sons of God' took wives from the 'daughters of men' (Gen. 6), or the story of Noah and the flood itself. These are a part of the essential sequence of Genesis, but cannot rightly be described as 'history'. The same applies to tales that are essentially folklore: when Samson caught three hundred foxes, tied their tails together with a torch between each pair, and let them loose among the Philistine grainfields, this belongs to folklore rather than to history. Yet it is part of the characterization of Samson which, taken as a whole, is theologically significant.

Particularly important, from this point of view, is the recognition of the beginning of Genesis, the creation story, as the starting point of the 'story'. Theologies built upon 'history' tended to emphasize events, especially events of deliverance, as the centre from which the material grew, and thus it came to be suggested that the exodus was the real beginning of the Bible, the primeval story or *Urgeschichte* being added on at a later time. Even if this was the case in the history of tradition, the story sequence is different. It begins with creation; the patriarchal story follows, and descent into Egypt and the exodus comes after that.

Within the story, as indicated above, a central place is taken by divine speech, whether spoken by the deity directly or through prophets and other inter-mediaries. In theologies of history there has commonly been a strong emphasis on *events* – one example being the expression 'the Christ-event' in New Testament studies.[10] Events are, in the common parlance of this tendency, the nucleus of divine revelation. What in the story appears as divine speech tends then to be understood as human interpretation of these events.[11] However, as I have argued, in many places the divine speech is not an interpretation of the events but the *precondition* of them. It is essential to the progress of the story. Seen in this way, the emphasis on *events* appears to be more like an apologetic demythologization of divine speech. Some such demythologization may indeed be necessary, as a matter of modern faith and doctrinal theology; but as a representation of the state of affairs within the Bible it is distorting.

We saw above that events in history are not a distinguishing mark of Israelite religion but belong to 'the common theology of the ancient Near East'. But this is true also of divine speech. Not necessarily in all religions, but certainly in some, gods can talk, certainly with other gods, not infrequently with humans also. If there is a distinguishing mark here for Hebrew religion, it must lie not in the mere fact of divine speech but in particular features of its character and content. This aspect has not, I believe, as yet received adequate research within Old Testament theology.

Story, in the sense argued here, certainly represents a shift in terms of paradigm 4 and also paradigm 5. It moves away from schemes of 'revelation in history' (4) and also from the emphasis on historical reading (5). In the latter aspect it brings us closer to a *literary* mode of reading, and this has been widely noted and advocated in various trends of recent scholarship. One reads the work as a story in its own terms as such. Nevertheless, as we shall see shortly, there are limits to this.

But before we discuss these limits, we may note a further advantage in the concept of story, namely in its relation to identity, both communal and personal. The community has a story which is part of its foundation and which imprints itself upon its members and marks their common life. The modern community has its own story, in which the Bible and its later interpretations have a foundational part, and the biblical story is interwoven with more recent story elements. And the individual has his or her own story, in which these elements are again interwoven. The biblical story, interacting with more recent and personal stories, is vital in character formation and psychological realization. As Dietrich Ritschl has said, the neglect of the psychological in much modern theology has been a mistake for which in the end a heavy price will have to be paid (I have already made this point earlier, above 171).

That the story is a totality and to be read as such would seem to agree with the 'holistic' emphasis of many literary and canonical tendencies of today. But the fact that it is a totality does not mean that it has to be swallowed whole, uncritically. If the suggestions made here are accepted without any qualification they can easily begin to have the opposite effect from what is intended. Thus, though reading as 'story' is different from historical reading, that does not mean that historical reading can be dispensed with. For in the modern world (this may not always have been so) the biblical text, taken just 'as it is', turns out to be read above all as a historical record, whether universally (as in more conservative reading) or more selectively (as in more liberal readings). It is only through the presence of historical reading and historical criticism – not necessarily through personal involvement in these operations – that, for most people, the reading as story becomes available. Moreover, this is not only a matter of historical orientation – questions of dates, sources, authors and accuracy of reporting historical facts; much more, it is a matter of theological appreciation. The theologically interested reader finds elements that are clear and others that are unclear, some attractive and some repugnant, some conflicting with others and some that may be universalizable, some that seem to keep step with the progress of the whole and others that seem to go against it. These questions cannot be left to mere taste and untrained impression: they require critical theological evaluation. Evaluation that is theologically critical, and more than theologically passive or accepting, goes in step with the continuance of historically critical reading. And this goes in step with the critical evaluation of the story of the community – Jewish or Christian: a story that comes to people in a form full of historical myths and prejudices, as is the case in persons' awareness of their own personal stories.

For an example of how this may work we may go back to a well-known problem that arose in the discussion of von Rad's Theology. Central to his thinking was the action of God in historical events, of which the Old Testament as 'a history book' was full. But, it was noted, there was a certain distance between the history as related and the history that had really taken place. 'A certain distance' is a mild expression – many would put it as a great deal more. Anyway, such a distance existed. Now von Rad, constantly using the term 'history', expressed his thinking predominantly, if not entirely, in terms of the history *as related*: the history is what we read, and find interpreted, in the pages of the Bible. But it was objected, principally by Franz Hesse, that, if we *theologically* claim that God acted in the history of Israel, then that must refer to the actual history as it took place, whether or not it is correctly reported in the Bible, and even if it is not mentioned in the Bible at all.

Now I would say that the story – and, we can say, the story through which God speaks – is the story as narrated, in this sense agreeing with von Rad; but by using the term 'history' von Rad invited the difficulty which Hesse pointed out, and he was not able to overcome it. The way in which the story is told tells us how the past has been understood in the ancient community. But if we say, as a matter of theology, that God acted or spoke 'in history' – and that might in itself be quite right – then we must, for the sake of theological coherence, mean the history as it actually took place, even if we do not have the resources to know exactly *how* it took place. Otherwise we find ourselves caught in the conundrums of a 'history of salvation' that sometimes went and sometimes stopped, or that went only when people thought in a *heilsgeschichtlich* fashion, and in the weak apologetic argument that, though there is a difference between the biblical narrative and the historical reality, the difference is really quite small. There is a difference here between the interior logic of the story as seen in itself and the application of the universal term 'history', which necessarily carries with it implications that were only partly, if at all, observed within the story.

We can usefully compare this with the familiar case of the quest for the historical Jesus, a quest the fate of which continues to cast a shadow over studies in the Old Testament as in the New. It is widely accepted, as it was in the time of the original quest, that much that is written in the Gospels reflects the post-resurrection understanding of Jesus by the church, and that therefore he may have been somewhat different, or thought differently, or done different acts, or taught differently, in his earthly life. Hence one may seek to imagine what 'the historical Jesus' may have been like. Historical studies may reconstruct the reality. But many have reacted against this quest, and its effect in many quarters has been mainly negative. Historical research does not have the means to achieve this. The texts, it is argued, are not suitable for this kind of investigation. We should accept that we have *nothing* other than the Gospels as they stand, which are the witness of the early church, and it is wrong to seek to go behind them. This argument, generalized, has been a potent force against any kind of critical historical research into the events referred to in the Bible.

Seen from a theological point of view, however, the argument is mistaken. If God raised Jesus from the dead, as Christians believe, then he raised him because of what he had been in his earthly life. God did not need to consult our written Gospels in order to know about this. The prime Christian affirmation of resurrection thus rests upon the reality of the historical Jesus, which we admit may at least have been somewhat different from the existing reports. Whatever Jesus was like, that was why he was raised from the dead. The question whether we can reconstruct him successfully by historical methods is a secondary one. And the argument that it is absolutely wrong even to try to distinguish between probable later layers and probable pre-resurrection layers, should be firmly rejected.

Another way to express this is to point to the importance of *memory*. Note that Schoberth's book, which treats of the concept of story in alignment with some of my earlier suggestions, has 'Memory' as the first word in its title. I find it helpful to borrow the term *mnemohistory* from J. Assmann, *Moses the Egyptian*, 6–22, etc. He writes:

> Unlike history proper, mnemohistory is concerned not with the past as such, but only with the past as it is remembered. It surveys the story-lines of tradition, the webs of intertextuality, the diachronic continuities and discontinuities of reading the past. Mnemohistory is not the opposite of history, but rather is one of its branches or subdisciplines, such as intellectual history, social history, the history of mentalities, or the history of ideas. Mnemohistory is reception theory applied to history (8f.).

In this sense our concept of story can perhaps be seen as belonging to history rather than contrasting with it.

It is not my purpose, however, to develop here all the aspects of the concept of story. More important for my present purpose is another aspect: the 'story' aspect, as I see it, provides an essential linkage between biblical narrative and theology and thus leads us towards an answer to the theological objections to biblical theology which have been discussed above.

### 3. *Story is not theology*

Here I seek to follow the insights of Dietrich Ritschl and Hugh Jones, worked out in co-operation with my own earlier suggestions. Story is not theology, but is the 'raw material' of theology. This helps to make sense of the utterances of e.g. Brunner, who opined that 'there is no theology of the Old Testament', and the similar judgment of Ritschl, quoted above, that biblical theology is 'a fiction'. We can also accommodate here the insistence, expressed for example by Childs, Stuhlmacher, Hübner and Rendtorff, that the Old Testament (or the New) 'is theological'. It may 'be theological' in the sense that it invites theology or calls for it, or requires theological interpretation; but it is not in itself theology. It is raw material for theology. Or it may *contain* theology, in the sense that here and there, at certain places, actual theological decisions come to expression in the course of story. Or, we may say, it may *imply* theology, and then it may be our task to make that theology explicit. But story in itself is not normally theology.

I quote a paragraph from George Stroup's summary of Dietrich Ritschl's thinking:

Narratives may provide the 'raw material' mined from the experience of individuals and communities which the theologian sorts through, reflects on, and criticizes by means of the Christian tradition, but the actual process of theological reflection is not 'storytelling' nor does it take the form of a story. The theologian's task is not to tell or repeat stories but to provide criteria or what Ritschl calls 'regulative sentences' for making critical judgments and comparisons among the different narratives that make up theology's 'raw material'. The theologian's task is not the same as that of the priest or the minister, and while story-telling may be an appropriate means by which the minister proclaims the gospel, the theologian has a different agenda that requires different methods (86).

The importance of this is that it runs counter to the many views, starting with von Rad and continuing in various kinds of 'narrative theology', which suggest that story is itself theology and that therefore, to quote von Rad's words again, 'the most legitimate form of theological talk about God is the rehearsal of narrative (*die Nacherzählung*)'. According to this point of view, not only is story theology, but theology is, or ought to be, story. There is no proper form for theology other than the narrative form. This, I shall suggest, unduly restricts the possibilities and requirements of theology. Theology can be expected to include quite other modes of expression: for instance, affirmation, questioning, argument, hypothesis, speculation, comparison, to mention only a few.

Let us look at some ways in which this may help us. For one thing, it may help us with the fact that though the Bible, as a whole, is not theology, something closer to theology is to be found at certain places within it. Thus we saw, as in Ritschl's basic statement quoted earlier, that 'it is easier to speak of Pauline theology because in Paul there are detailed declarations, arguments and definitions that we can follow'. This, it may be suggested, is why the great Reformers, both Luther and Calvin, granted the certain, and exceptional, freedom of choice that they received through the abandonment of a certain past tradition, through their rejection of allegory, and through other factors, took so explicitly to *Paul* as the source of their regulative interpretative principles. But Paul is not the only relevant case. Ritschl speaks also – surprisingly for many – of the Wisdom literature. We might also think of the Psalms.[12] Again, we should consider that certain *utterances* of personages, divine or human, within the narratives come closer to the nature of theology. We might also think of an increasing presence of something like real theology in some later biblical sources in contrast with the earlier, and this might include books deemed to be 'apocryphal'. We shall come back to these examples.

Another relevant relation was touched on earlier: the relation to later, post-biblical, theology. The traditional biblical theology of earlier this century tended, as we saw, to create a serious gap between the 'theology' of the Old Testament, seen as regulated by the primary source of the Hebrew narrative, and the theology of patristic times. And an analogical statement might be made concerning Rabbinic legal discussions. But this problem arises because the thought-forms of biblical narrative were thought of as *regulative*, or as the true core of the theology of the Bible. Once we see that much of the biblical narrative is not in itself 'theology' but is in essence 'raw material for theology', and once we see that forms of thought and expression that may occur seldom in the narrative, or indeed may be quite absent from it, are quite proper and necessary for theology, then the appropriateness of later theology (and, likewise, of Rabbinic legal discussion) as a mode for making theology explicit becomes more evident.

It may be argued that 'story' is not an adequate term because not all of the Bible is narrative, and from a certain point of view this is so. But in my conception all of the Bible counts as 'story'. A people's story is not necessarily purely narrative: materials of many kinds may be slotted into a narrative structure, and this is done in the Hebrew Bible. Thus legal materials are inserted and appear, almost entirely, as part of the Moses story. In this case they are incorporated into the narrative. Others are more loosely attached: songs and hymns of the temple and of individuals, mostly collected in the Book of Psalms but some slotted into the narratives as in Samuel, Kings and Chronicles. It does not matter much what weight we place on the 'Solomonic' authorship of Wisdom books: whether because they came from Solomon, or because they were general lore of Israel, they are part of the story also.

In the New Testament the letters of great leaders, and an apocalyptic book like Revelation, form part of the story, along with the more strictly narrative writings. Thus in general, although not all parts of the Bible are narrative, the narrative character of the story elements provides a better framework into which the non-narrative parts may be fitted than any framework based on the non-narrative parts into which the story elements could be fitted.

One reason for differentiating between story and theology is that story, as manifested in the Bible, is often theologically vague, obscure, ambiguous or non-committal. This is, after all, just what Brunner had in mind when he wrote: 'It is often difficult to know what the doctrinal content of Old Testament passages is at all.'[13] His remark, however, is not equally true of *all* Old Testament passages: as he himself said, it is 'often' true. What, after all, is the 'theology' of the stories of Abraham and Isaac with their wives taken into the house of a great potentate (Gen. 12, 20, 26), or of Jacob's manipulations with the sheep and goats of Laban (Gen. 30–31)? Maybe there is a theology there, but one cannot claim that it is obvious, or that it is actually stated by the text. People have been able to think of such a theology, but in order to do so they have had to go outside the text itself, turning either to another passage (which, usually, is more explicit theologically) or to later interpretative tradition. For such interpretations, the text itself is raw material. The old principle that the clearer passages are there to explain the less clear worked in this way: the 'clearer' passages were commonly the ones that were theologically more explicit – hence once again, as indicated above, the primacy of Paul in Reformation theology.

Story, then, is often theologically unclear. Moreover, among the various genres and types found in the Bible, this is particularly true of story. Doxological texts like hymns, or wisdom texts, or letters, are often more explicit theologically. Thus, though story is rightly singled out as the most prominent feature of the Bible, story is a feature that is, much of the time, distinctly removed from the precise statement of actual theological content.

This is particularly so in the portions of the story which seem to come closest to history, most obviously the story of David. Is the story, as some maintain, a glorification of David and an ideological support for the dynasty? If so, why does it spend so much time relating things that are to the discredit of David? Is it, as others think, an ironic or tragic tale, bringing out the hidden ways in which God works through the doings of sinful people? But, if so, how does it fit with statements that the Lord was 'with David', e.g. II Sam 5. 10? The fact that such different impressions can be formed is evidence that the theology of the narrative is not made explicit. Von Rad writes: 'This historian . . . is none the less a theologian, a theologian even with a very well-defined idea of God's relation to this history. There are, admittedly, only three places where he speaks of God explicitly. But these are of fundamental importance' (1, 314). Of course explanations can be suggested. Overarching conceptions can be deployed. But these tend to fail to explain, or to take account of, all the detail of the story.

The same is true of the larger-scale, more 'political', history, now commonly called 'the Deuteronomistic History', which covers the period of the kingdoms from Solomon down to Nebuchadnezzar and the end of the kingdom and temple. This central and important corpus of text does indeed contain a constant refrain, which forms the framework within which older stories are fitted (so at any rate it is commonly understood). Disasters come upon the people because of one same thing: the 'high places' were not removed – these being understood to be local sanctuaries other than the one central one as required by the reform programme of Deut. 12. There is something unsatisfactory about this as a theological explanation for national disasters. Even more disquieting is the account in II Kings 17 of how, when (northern) Israel was exiled to Assyria, the Assyrian king brought peoples from various Mesopotamian localities who took possession of Samaria. To begin with, they 'did not fear the Lord', and the Lord 'sent lions among them, which killed some of them'. The king of Assyria was told of this, and he commanded that a priest (one only!) from the Israelite exiles should be sent, to teach them 'the law of the god of the land'. The passage goes on to tell of the religious aberrations of these peoples, who in the end, it is told, 'feared the Lord but also served their own gods', and this goes on to the (then) present day. That trouble caused by 'lions' should be reported to the king of Assyria and have brought about this change in religious policy must have some sort of reality behind it, but must also be remote from a convincing description of whatever that reality was.

One common and traditional approach is to say that, in the end of the whole matter, God has been in control of history. Köhler, for example, has a chapter so entitled: '§32. God Directs the Course of History' (92–5). This was not so original a thought, for the same has been said in churches for centuries, no doubt. Von Rad distinguishes more subtly between various strands in this:

> For the Deuteronomist the divine guidance of history is established beyond all doubt; but that it is by his word that Yahweh directs history, this is practically hammered into the reader. At the same time the author of the Succession Document shows that he himself understood this history as the fulfilment of an explicit word of Yahweh, since he sets the whole complex in the shadow of the Nathan prophecy (II Sam. 7) (1, 342).

But the divine guidance or control of all history seems to be poorly indicated in the narrative. Often it seems more as if history is conducted by humans, and God sometimes reacts. He 'raises up' adversaries in response to bad behaviour by Solomon (I Kings 11. 14, 23). Jeroboam, who turns out to be more successful and more of a long-term threat, is not 'raised up' but given the stamp of approval by a prophet – yet this only temporarily, since he soon turns in the wrong direction. The 'word of the Lord' is certainly seen as a factor in history. Such a word, through Jehu ben Hanani, says that Baasha and his house will be utterly swept away, and sure enough this happens some time later (I Kings 16. 3–4 and 11–13). But it is hard to conclude from this that everything reported, or everything that took place, in the history was controlled by God. Thus at 16.21:

> The people of Israel were divided into two parts: half of the people followed Tibni ben Ginath, to make him king, and half followed Omri. But the people who followed Omri overcame the people who followed Tibni the son of Ginath; so Tibni died, and Omri became king.

Did God control this decision? The text gives no idea. Omri, indeed, is disapproved of, and reported as doing evil a few verses later; but would Tibni ben Ginath have been any better? The text gives no idea.

We thus come to another idea of Dietrich Ritschl's,[14] the implicit thesis that God does not 'guide' or 'make' history but interprets it and criticizes it.

There is much that is true in Günther Klein's critical summary[15] of exegetical insights that conflicts with the idea of God's government of the world, taken in a direct and naive sense. Jewish and Christian believers cannot with good conscience and on biblically-supported theological grounds maintain that God guides history. In the light of his commands and his promises, history happens to a large extent against his will.

Thus to say that God 'willed' the destruction of Jerusalem by Nebuchad-nezzar, the ending of the Davidic kingdom and the desolation of the temple is too far-fetched to be considered, as is, of course, any idea that Auschwitz and the destruction of the Jews of Europe, and likewise other manifestations of genocide, are examples of God's 'control of history' – a problem that has exercised many Jewish thinkers in the last decades.[16] As Ritschl remarks,[17] the question of divine providence and the divine government of the world comes to us only indirectly out of the Bible, and much more out of Greek philosophy, especially out of Stoicism, for which it was a matter of great importance to understand the total framework of the cosmos and of life in general as guided by world-reason. This is not to say that God is indifferent to history. Ritschl uses the terms 'criticism and interpretation'. God 'interprets' history (Ritschl himself uses the quotation marks), and his interpretation effects changes; it even, in part, 'makes' history – now through the speech and action of Jews and Christians, as then through the mouths of prophets and apostles. For the understanding of the Hebrew prophets and the biblical reporting of historical events all this is very important.

Another aspect is the making of 'summaries': shorter statements which attempt to summarize the essentials of a longer text. A good example is the passage from Deut. 26.5ff., 'A wandering Aramaean was my father', a recital which belongs to the presentation of first-fruits. As is well known, von Rad took this to be an early and original 'small historical creed' which expressed the central elements, later expanded into the great historical statement of Israel's faith. But it is now more generally thought to be itself a later document, and a summary of what were seen, for this purpose, to be the essentials of Israel's story. This is not to say that short statements are *never* more original than the full-blown story. They may well be so. We can have a lengthy story which is summarized and also brief central statements which are expanded. Thus it would be quite possible to imagine that the quite complex story of Moses and the exodus did indeed grow from some small nuclear memory that 'we were in bondage in Egypt but the Lord set us free'. Both expansion and summarization can have taken place, sometimes both together. And so creeds, which distinctly belong to theology, can be thought of as (very concentrated) summaries of the gospel story, as well as possibly expansions of certain elements in that story.[18]

Theological summaries are not to be thought of as only post-biblical credal formulations; they are found within the biblical text itself, for instance in remarks by one of the characters, or in editorial comments. A familiar case is Joseph's comment:

> As for you, you meant evil against me; but God meant it for good, to bring it about that many people should be kept alive, as they are today (Gen. 50.20).

This was noted by von Rad, who wrote:

> This is the wisdom teaching of the Old Testament at its most distilled, and the sum total of the whole story is expressed when the opinion is given that all human life is under the sovereign sway of God (1, 440; cf. also 1, 172f., 454).

In this case the summary is part of the original story, but in others it is probably often an editorial comment.

The making of theological summaries of a story is a markedly ambivalent activity. The summary almost necessarily leaves out much of the detail and colour of the original; on the other hand, without it the story itself would be more difficult to interpret. In central currents of Christianity, it is thought that the creeds are necessary for the understanding of the Gospels; and yet the Gospels themselves undoubtedly continue to enjoy a greater reverence and a wider use.

I have talked, thus far, primarily as if theology came *later* in the story process, or *after* it, but we have also to consider theological forces, pressures and decisions as coming *before*, as 'guiding' or 'steering' (Ritschl's word is *Steuerung*) the formation of stories. I quote from a forthcoming article of my own:

> Dietrich Ritschl, in his essay kindly contributed to my Festschrift,[19] began by announcing an interest in the '*Vorher*', the 'before' of biblical texts, as well as the '*Nachher*' or 'After'. The present tendency in biblical scholarship is to emphasize the 'After'. The alleged over-emphasis of older critical scholarship on the *origins* is frequently pilloried in recent writing. According to this tendency, it is more important to know about what came 'after': the *final form* of the text, the end of the process, the latest stages, the *Wirkungsgeschichte* or history of reception. Where this emphasis is carried far enough, it begins to appear that what is 'before' begins to be neglected. 'Origins' and 'background' come to be laughed at. Where this happens, as it does in some 'canonical' styles of biblical theology, we seem to find a reversal of the insights which drove the older biblical theology. In it the emphasis was on that which came before: 'revelation in history' meant a revelation in historical events that took place before the text was created, and the text was a record of, or a response

to, these events. There were weaknesses in these formulations, as most have seen, but the emphasis on that which was 'before' was salutary: the text was a response to pre-textual realities and stimuli of some kind. Where this insight is lost, we tend to come back to a position where the achievement of the final form of the Bible, plus its subsequent effects, becomes in itself the greatest of all controlling events. But can people really want this to happen?

Though it is important that theology, in the sense of explicit theology, grows within the Bible and is more clearly discerned within later stages, it is mistaken to suppose that theology, in the sense of regulative expressions which 'steer' stories and texts, must be absent from quite early materials. If the term 'theology', even in an explicit sense, can be properly used of Egyptian phenomena of the second millennium BC,[20] how can we be prohibited from using it, at least in an implicit sense, of the axioms that guided stories about Abraham or about Moses, even if the present form of these stories comes from post-exilic times (the present fashion, for which one would not wish to risk one's life)?

# 22

# Gese and the Unity of Biblical Theology

Professor Hartmut Gese of Tübingen is a distinguished scholar in the areas of ancient religion and biblical exegesis and theology.[1] Although several of his works are available in English, his thought has not yet had in the English-speaking world the full discussion it deserves.

We have seen that although much or most Old Testament theology set out with the purpose of building (or repairing) a bridge towards the New Testament, rather little was actually achieved in this respect, and the same may well be true of New Testament theologies. It may well be felt that their main achievements lay within the world of one Testament rather than the other. Precisely because these theologies took one, or the other, as their principal base of operation, their essential material, criteria and modes of thought tended to come from that one Testament and it proved difficult for them to give anything like complete coverage to both. Thus even when they insisted that the connection with the other Testament was central to their task, this connection tended to be a by-product and in the end to be less than fully convincing. Why did so few scholars attempt a Theology of the entire Bible? The motivation for bringing the two Testaments together, however, remained. Surely there should be a way in which a theology of the whole Bible, what I have called a pan-biblical theology, could be worked out?

The sense may thus have arisen that the particular task of stating the unity of the Bible could not be fulfilled by starting from the basis of one Testament or the other; it could be fulfilled only if one started on the basis of the entire Bible and took the establishment of its coherence as the *primary and central*, not as a peripheral or additional, goal. Along with this there may sometimes go a certain feeling that there is something wrong with the whole separation between Old Testament studies and New Testament studies. They should really be one thing, not two; and it is sometimes said that they would have always been one thing but for the rise and ascendance of historical method, which forced the distinction between the two and made them separate. This brings us to the sort of position taken as a starting point by Gese: the mutual relationship of Old and New Testaments is fundamental to all biblical theology.[2]

Given that this is all-important, the next question for Gese is how to proceed in order to determine the relations between the two. There are various old and traditional approaches which he examines, and all of these have difficulties.

1. Allegorical and typological approaches run the risk of losing sight of the original Old Testament meanings.

2. A scheme of prophecy and fulfilment leaves the Old Testament, once the fulfilment has come, without much intrinsic importance.

3. Even the particular statements of the New Testament itself about the Old, e.g. Paul's contrast between letter and spirit, cannot be taken as definitive guides, because these contrasts apply only to certain theological conceptions and cannot comprehend the enormous variety of the literary texts of the Old Testament. These traditional *aporia*s are noted by Gese and passed by; the search for a method has to find something better.

These different possibilities thus proving defective, Gese's choice falls decisively upon the history of tradition, and in this he starts out from the pattern set forth by von Rad. There is no definable theological 'centre' in the Old Testament; rather, it exists in the form of manifold currents of tradition, and this form lies open for the coming of the new tradition of the New Testament. The novel step in Gese's thinking is that unlike von Rad he insists that the Old and New Testament together form *one closed corpus of tradition*. The entire Bible is one complete continuum, within which change and growth or development take place. Behind this growth of tradition, also, the history of revelation goes on. God reveals himself through the process of the history of the biblical tradition. The New Testament presents itself as the completion of this process, the τέλος.

This approach, as Gese develops it, carries consequences for the idea of the *canon*. The canon of scripture is important because its existence relates to the totality of the tradition process. It is quite wrong therefore to look for anything like an inner canon or a 'canon within the canon', since only the totality of the canon represents the totality of the process of tradition and revelation. In this respect there are certain similarities between the thought of Gese and that of Brevard Childs, which will be discussed in the next chapters: the canon itself and as a whole signifies and corresponds to the contours of the process of revelation.

But Gese views the detailed form of the canon, and also its relation to revelation in general, in quite a different way from Childs. As Gese sees it, in New Testament times there was still no complete or closed Old Testament canon: the Law and the Prophets were already fixed, but the third part of the canon, the Writings, was still 'open'. The New Testament accepted as scripture documents of late apocalyptic such as the Book of Enoch. Still more, it was the New Testament itself that – for the church – brought about the closing of the Old Testament canon; hence one of the most remarkable and memorable of Gese's sentences, 'it was through the New Testament that the Old Testament came into being'. Christianity created its Old Testament.[3]

It follows, consequently, that the Protestant churches were mistaken in deciding to accept the books of the later, authoritative, Jewish canon, or the books of the Masoretic Text, as their Old Testament canon. There was no good theological reason for the abandonment of the books that Protestants now call 'Apocrypha'. It took place, Gese maintains, partly because the church had lost possession of the Hebrew Bible and had to recover it from the synagogue, with the effect that only the books of the then Jewish scripture came to be recognized, and partly because the spirit of Renaissance humanism sought out the 'earliest' and 'most genuine' tradition and was therefore ready to cut out the apocryphal books as 'non-genuine' ('Schriftverständnis', 13). The apocryphal and apocalyptic books are an essential part of the stream of tradition, and the omission of them from the canon causes a serious distortion of its testimony to that tradition.

These points, then, form the essentials of Gese's approach to the unity of the two Testaments. What are we to say about it?

The core of Gese's very interesting position seems to lie in his judgment that *tradition history* is the essential mode by which biblical theology might attempt to deal with the problem of the unity of the Bible. The principle behind this may perhaps be stated thus: on the one hand biblical theology means theology that seeks to express the unity of the entire Bible (as contrasted with theology of the Old or New Testaments or of portions of either); but on the other hand biblical theology means theology that works on the Bible by means, methods and techniques such as biblical scholars use. This forms a distinction from systematic (or doctrinal or dogmatic) theology. Biblical theology is indeed theology, but it is theology that is done by biblical scholars and thus has a continuity with their methods of working and thinking.

This is particularly clear in the case of tradition history. Tradition history proved to be a powerful approach to the literary and structural analysis of the Old Testament in the hands of the great school of Alt, Noth and von Rad.[4] It was important for questions of history and literature, and succeeded in analysing the layers and strata of growth within the Old Testament books. Starting from there, essentially the same method was extended to become a method, indeed *the* method, of Old Testament theology in the hands of von Rad, of pan-biblical theology in those of Gese.

The method, therefore, belongs distinctly to biblical scholarship and is based on the successful application of it in historical and literary questions: it does not derive from dogmatics or belong to it. In this sense the choice becomes readily intelligible. If one first accepts that it is on the plane of biblical scholarship and by methods workable on that plane that the unity of the Bible is to be established, then it follows that the choice of tradition history is a very natural consequence, even if it is not the only conceivable possibility. There would be, however, the possibility of a quite different decision: one might decide that the unity of Old and New Testaments was in essence a dogmatic matter, to be handled on the doctrinal level, and not one that could be adequately demonstrated or elaborated on the level of biblical scholarship at all. If this were so, however, it would not necessarily follow that tradition history was the central mode of tackling the problem. We shall come back later to the questions arising from these choices.

From the side of biblical scholarship, the initial question that faces Gese's conception seems to be this: can the Old and New Testaments really be understood as forming together one continuum of tradition? Against this conception the obvious first objection is that the New Testament itself does not conceive of itself in this way. It does not present itself as being really a continuation of ancient Jewish tradition, or as the closing or termination of such a stream of tradition.

At this point a great deal depends on the level at which we pose the question. Are we predicating our statements upon the conscious intention, the self-understanding, of the New Testament texts, upon the way in which they themselves expressed their position? Or are we arguing from the way in which modern scholarly discussion may read and construe the implications of what they said? Looking in one of these ways, we may be led to favour Gese's view; in the other, we may find we cannot agree with it.

If we look at the level of actual historical development, as scholars see it, we may perhaps rightly notice and emphasize the continuity of the New Testament with a long development of Jewish tradition going back to the Babylonian exile and coming right down to the first century AD. The recognition of this continuity is entirely salutary and right: it corrects the Christian tendency, encouraged particularly by the Protestant canon of scripture, to recognize only the two customary Testaments but not the tradition that links them together. The New Testament belongs to this tradition just as the Qumran sect does, and just as do also the writers of books like Jubilees, Enoch, Wisdom of Solomon and the rest, along with the traditions later assembled in Pirqe Aboth and all sorts of materials that later came to have their place in Mishnah and Midrash. Without this tradition of interpretation many things in the New Testament would have been impossible or at least very unlikely. It was Wisdom and other 'intertestamental' books, and not the Hebrew Old Testament, that identified the disobedience of Adam as the uniquely calamitous 'fall' which brought sin, corruption and death into the centre of human existence.[5] It was the apocalyptic development, mainly in the second century BC and only thinly represented (by Daniel and various other fragments) within the canonical

Hebrew Bible, that provided the background and the intellectual basis for much eschatological expectation. It was the interpretative conventions of these various traditions that were used by Jesus and the New Testament writers, and by means of them they were able to establish that Jesus was the fulfilment of that which the prophets long ago had said. In these and other similar ways the New Testament stood in continuity with a long and varied development of Jewish tradition. Gese's conception takes all this well into account.

It remains a question, however, whether the New Testament actually understood itself in this way. Its own self-understanding, as expressed in its own writing, may have been substantially different from the way in which scholars, for themselves quite rightly, see it. Perhaps the New Testament sees itself not as the completion of a long development of tradition coming right up to its own time, but as the fulfilment of an *ancient* scripture? For the New Testament that process of Jewish tradition which we as scholars recognize so well had already crystallized as *scripture*. There was indeed ongoing tradition, but the New Testament does not recognize it as authoritative: on the contrary, it suggests that, at least in some places, human beings have made the word of God ineffective through their tradition. The scripture/tradition conflict is already there in New Testament times. Scripture is authoritative but post-scriptural tradition is not.

In the New Testament, as I sense it, the Old Testament is felt to be already rather far away. The prophets were men of ancient times: it was *long ago* that they had spoken and written. God had spoken πάλαι, long ago (Heb. 1.1). According to Josephus, prophecy had ceased several centuries before his time, and I do not know any sign that the New Testament differed from this opinion. There is not, for instance, any explicit mention in the New Testament of the Maccabaean period and its events. There are of course very probable literary influences, but that is not the same thing; what I mean is that there is no explicit mention of the events of that period. Recent events, yes; that is, events of the Herodian and Roman period, like the tower that fell upon people in Siloam, or the Galileans savagely treated by Pilate (Luke 13.1–4), or the various brigands who had caused trouble, yes, but hardly events of the second century BC or before. Of course there were books that came from this time, as we know; but the people of the New Testament did not see them as so recent. Daniel, as *they* saw it, was a book of Babylonian and early Persian times. Tobit and Judith were even older, being set in Assyrian or early Babylonian times. Wisdom was doubtless a writing of Solomon himself, a thousand years back. Jubilees, if known, was written by Moses himself, as it itself expressly states. The Testaments of the Twelve Patriarchs went back to before Moses. Enoch – largely, as we see it, actually a second-century BC work – was certainly known, and was quoted in the New Testament as authoritative prophecy, but had been written by Enoch himself several thousand years before, which must mean, if you think about it, that the Book of Enoch is the first book of any kind to have been written by man, apart from any works penned by Adam and Eve themselves. Among our present 'Apocrypha', perhaps only Ben Sira and the Books of Maccabees would have been understood as works coming from a post-Ezra period.

The New Testament ideas of 'the end of the ages' or 'the fullness of time' seem therefore to fit well with the idea of a longish waiting period. God made his basic revelation to Israel and then there was a sort of gap, a period of quiet, a 'silence in heaven', during which that revelation matured and its fulfilment was awaited; and then quite suddenly and unexpectedly that fulfilment came. This would fit in with ideas of the Qumran sect: it was 390 years after the time of Nebuchadnezzar that God visited Israel, then there was a short period of twenty years during which they groped for the truth, and then at the end of these twenty the Teacher of Righteousness was raised up (CD 1.5–12).

The numbers of years in themselves are not so important, but they are symptoms of the important fact that for the New Testament the authoritative spoken revelation of God to Israel was already in scriptural form and was understood to have been so for a long time; and this scriptural form was already fairly sharply distinguished from ongoing tradition and interpretation. Thus the idea that the Old and New Testaments are linked through forming one continuum of tradition may well be a proper modern scholarly way of describing the situation, but does not seem to be a correct statement of the way in which the New Testament itself understood that situation. We can, I suggest, think in either of these two ways, but we cannot mingle them without risk of confusion.[6]

Now this, if right, has a further implication. If we follow this modern scholarly mode, the first of the two as stated above, then it may well give us good reason to perceive a continuum of tradition; but so long as we reason on this level, it is not clear how we can say that the New Testament *brings this tradition to an end*. On the contrary, if taken in that way, the Judaeo-Christian tradition seems to continue smoothly enough – even if in two very different streams, the Jewish and the Christian – through the Rabbis into the modern world or, respectively, through the New Testament into the Fathers and from there into the mediaeval church, the Reformation and indeed into the present day. On the other level, by contrast, that of the actual thinking of the New Testament, we do have a definite consciousness of an *end*, a completion, a final stage, but it seems to be not the completion or ending of a continuum of tradition; rather, it is the completion of a series of events of salvation, the fulfilment in Jesus Christ of God's purpose for humankind, or, more correctly, the completion of one central series within the events of salvation (for there are others to come). Thus the idea of the New Testament as a τέλος belongs to a different context and a different level of argument from that on which we can, quite legitimately, identify a continuum of tradition to which both Old and New Testaments together belong.

With these thoughts in mind, we can return to one or two of the questions that have been mentioned. First, the separation between 'Old Testament' and 'New Testament'. This question is not posed in exactly these terms by Gese himself, but it will occur to many as another formulation of the problems taken up by him. In recent years it has often been complained that this conventional division of scholarly areas is a harmful one. There ought to be only one scholarly field, namely the Bible. In particular, some may argue, the division is an effect of the domination of biblical scholarship by the *historical* approach. According to this argument, when people came to see the Bible historically, Old and New Testament were driven apart.

I do not think that this argument should be accepted. I leave aside one argument, namely the fact that we have had some very good scholars who were in fact highly distinguished in both Old and New Testaments: in Great Britain I think of H. F. D. Sparks, F. F. Bruce, Barnabas Lindars. I would indeed admit that in most of these cases the level of distinction is higher in one Testament than in the other; nevertheless, I have not conceded the claim that one must be either an *Alttestamentler* or a *Neutestamentler* but cannot be both.

But, leaving aside the arguments from the facts of scholarly history, the question of principle is interesting. It is not clear to me why *historical* considerations as such could have caused the split or separation between Old Testament scholarship and New. If the difference of historical period is the point, it would more naturally have led to the placing of the division in the *middle* of the Old Testament. And this is, of course, exactly how it works in most Jewish historiography, where 'the Second Temple period' is one historical unit, running from the rise of the Persian Empire down to the late first century AD and including the rise of Christianity. This was also the time in which most of the available sources came to be in Greek, in contrast to the Hebrew of the Old Testament. The New Testament would have been one element among others in this historically–defined unit. If *historical* considerations had been in control, such a division would have been more natural and obvious.

The fact is that there was no essential reason in *history* for the establishment of the major scholarly division between Old and New Testament. Historically speaking, there is absolutely no obstacle to the idea of 'biblical studies' as a unified field and no reason against it except the purely practical problem of mastery of so long a period, involving such a variety of sources, cultures and languages. From that point of view, the professional historian's viewpoint would be that at least 'Old Testament' was much too large an area to allow for normal standards of competence, and even 'New Testament' might well count as too large also.

In fact the separation between Old and New Testaments as academic fields is not the product of an historical approach, but came about naturally and on Christian soil, for it followed easily from traditional theology. Theologically seen, the contrast between Old and New Testaments was always the greatest and the most obvious of the many contrasts and dividing lines that run across the fabric of the Bible. It is one that is abundantly recognized explicitly within the New Testament itself and is expressed in the canonical structure of the Christian Bible. Thus the separation between Old and New Testament studies, which in any case should not be ultimate or final, is not something dictated by a historical approach but rests upon the realities of the subject–matter, or at least upon traditional theological perceptions of them.

Next we should come back to the matter of the Old Testament canon. Gese is right in saying that for the people of the New Testament the extent and the demarcation of ancient scripture were rather vague and undefined. In this sense the acceptance of the books considered by Protestants as 'Apocrypha' is closer not only to church tradition but also to the position of the New Testament itself. But I do not think that this settles as much as Gese thinks it does. His point is that there is a continuity of tradition which includes both Old Testament and New, and that these books symbolize that continuity. Yes, but it seems to me that they do not symbolize it very well. On the one hand, most of the apocalyptic literature, which we agree to be very important in this tradition, not only did not find its way into the (Protestant) canon, but did not find its way into the Apocrypha either. Important books like Jubilees and Enoch were scarcely known except in remote traditions; as far as I am aware, the Testaments of the Twelve Patriarchs, an important example, though widely copied and circulated, seems not to have been in any demarcated canon that we know. Moreover, many of the apocryphal and pseudepigraphic works that we know give a peculiar picture of Jewish tradition as it was in the period 300 BC–AD 50. Many of these books are better understood not as interpretation of scripture but as a continuation of it, even as an improvement on it. Scripture being wonderful, why should one not produce even more of it? One improved upon scripture by re-writing the books in a better or more modern style or by adding other books of the same general kind. In this sense these books come closer to the concept of *scripture* than to that of post-scriptural *tradition*. They were mostly books *of biblical type*: consider Judith, Tobit, Wisdom, Ben Sira, IV Ezra; this could have been a factor in the acceptance of them. Thus the main churches which accept the books known to Protestants as the Apocrypha do not regard them as an additional but separate section, coming between the Old Testament and the New and thus symbolizing the intertestamental continuity; they regard them rather as part of the Old Testament, just as (say) Chronicles is, which is a work of rather similar type. But documents of more specifically 'interpretative' type, like the Qumran *pesharim*, are not found in our Apocrypha anyway. Nor did any Christian canon include documents of the 'oral tradition' such as (say) Pirqe Aboth. So the question of the Apocrypha and their acceptance is not as important as Gese suggests. If like Protestants we do not accept them as canonical, we still have to perceive by imagination this proliferation of Jewish tradition, most of which lies outside the Apocrypha anyway; if like Roman Catholics we accept them, we then have a larger Old Testament, but the presence of these extra books has still not done very much to symbolize through the canon the nature of the intertestamental process of tradition.[7]

Two other remarks before we leave the matter of the canon. First, it would be possible that Gese was wrong about the historical fluidity of the canon at the time when Christianity began, and that the Jewish canon had in some sense been fixed perhaps in Maccabean times.[8] But even if this were so, I think his position could be adjusted to allow for the difference. He might, for instance, simply say that, even if the Hebrew canon in its present form was decided on (by some persons or groups) in the second century BC, it still remained open for many deviant groups, among which the origins of Christianity are to be found.

More peculiar, and a major problem in his thinking, is his evaluation of what he calls the 'Pharisaic reduction' of the material of tradition (*Sinai*, 17f.; 'Tradition', 323f.; cf. also 'Schriftverständnis', 13). In this, according to his account, from the widespread variety of materials, through anti-apocalyptic, anti-sapiential and possibly anti-Christian motives, the body of the then 'Writings' was *reduced* by expelling everything possible.

Gese seems to understand this – assuming that things did take place historically in this way – as something quite different from the 'completing' of the tradition-stream by the New Testament. Pharisaic Judaism 'reduced' the canon to a minimum in the third section, the Writings, but made no attempt to 'complete it' (*verzichtet auf eine Vollendung des Traditionsprozesses, Sinai*, 18), in order to start off a new tradition process on a different plane. This is a very peculiar argument. He seems to mean that the New Testament completed and ended the tradition process, incidentally creating the (completed) Old Testament, but that the Pharisaic canonization of the Hebrew Bible was not a 'completion' of the Old Testament at all: partly because it expelled part of the tradition, and partly because it commenced a new stream of tradition on a new level. (At this point it is difficult to know if one is understanding Gese rightly.) The acceptance within (Protestant?) Christianity of this Jewish view has produced a great deal of trouble ('Tradition', 324); in particular, it has destroyed the continuity between Old and New Testaments.

If I understand Gese correctly at this point, I would have to say that his evaluation is very peculiar. He seems to mean that the two religions, Judaism and Christianity, are typologically quite different in respect of the place of tradition. In Judaism the old stream of tradition is erroneously 'reduced', and a new stream of tradition is begun. In Christianity, the contrast seems to imply, the New Testament completes the old stream of tradition but there is no 'new stream of tradition on a different level'. But is it certain that this is true of Christianity? If Christianity in canonizing its scripture did indeed, whether by intent or by implication, license the inauguration of a new stream of tradition on a different level, then it seems in this respect not to be typologically different from (normative or Pharisaic) Judaism. I do not know, but I would guess, that Gese would have to say: in Christianity post-scriptural tradition is purely exegetical and thus subsidiary to scripture; it thus carries no substance of its own as tradition had done within the biblical period. But then: is this *historically* the case, or is it rather a theological statement of how it ought to have been?

We return, therefore, to the general picture of a pan-biblical theology built upon tradition history. Now there may well be no question of the value and importance of tradition history as an approach within biblical scholarship. The question is whether it has the power to answer this particular problem and thus to demonstrate and display the theological unity of the Old and New Testaments. It has been argued that, if this method is to carry out this task, it will work only if the entire period from the beginnings of the Old Testament to the end of the New is regarded as one continuum of tradition. But, at least on the basis of Gese's argument as an example, the attempt to do this produces some considerable strain. It does not seem to fit the New Testament material very well. It produces some very odd evaluations of the decisions made about the canon. If one is to ask what is the fundamental reason for these difficulties, the answer that occurs to one is that a method suited to biblical scholarship is being asked to do work that belongs to dogmatic theology, and because it does not do this without strain, judgments that really belong to the dogmatic level are being fed back into the decisions of the method.

This becomes explicit at another point in Gese's discussion. In order to provide a satisfactory account of the unity of the one biblical tradition, tradition history has to be reflected on, or transferred to, the dogmatic (or even metaphysical?) level as well. The history of tradition is accompanied by a history of revelation (especially 'Schriftverständnis', 23ff.; 'Tradition', 324ff.; *Sinai*, 21f., 24ff.). This seems to mean that the intellectual process of the formation of tradition has behind it an 'ontological' process (this is the term used by Gese himself). Gese strongly emphasizes the dynamic and historical aspect of this. Here he follows the history-of-salvation emphasis of the older biblical theology, even though in some other aspects he departs from that kind of thinking. Revelation is a historical process. But it is not just the process of the events that is narrated in the Bible, though some of these do have a key place; there seems rather to be a process in which truth itself develops and reaches its fullness and completion. In the event of the death and resurrection of Jesus, 'the boundaries of being and not-being fall down. Being comes to be and truth became historical.'[9] Thus we have something like truth coming to its full realization or actualization in a process which corresponds to the tradition-history of the Bible. And so, though Gese begins by seeking to realise the unity of the Bible on a level controllable by biblical scholarship, it now seems that he has to create a sort of dogmatic correspondent that stands behind his concept. I wonder if it would be similar to an idea which I myself have expressed: namely that the biblical tradition is not only a process of the recording and transmission of a (previous) revelation, but is a full part of the process of revelation itself. God did not just elect Israel; he elected into existence the tradition of Israel.[10] Something like this may be what he meant by speaking of an 'ontology' at this point.

Now this side of Gese's thinking has been subjected to a good deal of criticism. People have said that it transformed theology into a 'phenomenology' of tradition-history (so H.-J. Kraus), and others have seen in it a Hegelian idealism, an unfortunate biological analogy of growth, and other faults. Whether these alarms are justified or not I shall leave aside. Instead I shall make only this observation: that the problems of these dogmatic images and observations seem to arise naturally from the biblical framework which has been set up and into which the answer to the problems is supposed to fit. Once it has been laid down, on the level of biblical scholarly methods, that the whole biblical tradition is one continuum, moving and increasing *without major interruption* towards its final point in the New Testament, then it is natural that the dogmatic ideas associated with this will be terms of growth towards a completion. On the other hand, since the revelation is viewed as a holistic reality correlated with one indivisible continuum of tradition, and since the revelation is not in the events reported but in the tradition process itself, it is not surprising that the essence of revelation comes to be stated in ontological terms, as 'being coming to be' and as truth becoming historical. These may be metaphysical terms, but they are metaphysical terms chosen because the choice of them satisfies the needs of the tradition-history model with which we began. I do not suggest that these are insuperable difficulties, but difficulties they do seem to be.

Gese's ultimate answer seems to be that there is no alternative. But let us suppose that there *is* an alternative.

Let us consider the possibility that, in order to handle the question of the unity of the two Testaments, we have to move outside the scope of biblical theology as it is usually understood, so that the question stands really on the doctrinal (traditionally: 'dogmatic') level. If this were so, then it would not be surprising if the various biblical theologies of either Old or New Testament had not really succeeded in providing a full account of how the two Testaments interrelate. Such an apparent failure would not be a true failure, but would be a proper response to the realities of the situation. Can we give reasons why this should be so?

One might argue as follows: the coming of Christ into the world is not just a step upward in an already existing process of revelation; nor is it a new or final interpretation of a revelation previously given; nor is it an intellectual solution in which all the pieces of a puzzle suddenly come together into one pattern. It may be some of these things incidentally and in part, but in principle it differs in that with the coming of Christ there is a new substance of revelation, something that was not there before, even if intimations and premonitions of it are to be seen all through earlier times. The New Testament events are not just a completion of the Old, or a completion of a preceding continuum of tradition, or a fulfilment or final interpretation of these, but a new substance of divine presence that had not been (fully?) there before, and one which does fulfil the Old Testament but is not fully explained by being taken as such a fulfilment.

This I take to be an agreed principle of Christian faith. There are, however, differences in degree. Some currents give more stress to the newness of that which comes with Christ, others more to the continuities that bind this new substance to the old covenant. There is a difference of stress not only according to denominational tradition, but also according to scholarly specialization. Much Old Testament theology has come from the Reformed tradition (Eichrodt, Vriezen, Jacob, Zimmerli): the Reformed tendency to magnify the Christian importance of the Old Testament is reinforced by the professional specialism of the Old Testament scholar, anxious to demonstrate the fullest possible significance for his subject within Christian theology. Some New Testament theologians, on the other hand, certainly acknowledge the Old Testament and Jewish interpretation, as well as the Graeco-Roman world, as background, but on the level of biblical theology tend to suggest that the New Testament can be quite well interpreted in itself. And on the accepted levels of biblical theology, the New Testament theologians may be more in the right than Old Testament scholars tend to admit. But as a dogmatic matter it is impossible for Christianity to rest content with that. For Christianity, as a matter of belief it seems essential that the Father of Jesus of Nazareth was the One who in ancient times was the God of Israel, and that the matter of the Old Testament is a valid testimony to the being and nature of that God. Thus when people say 'You can't understand the New Testament without the Old or apart from the Old', it seems that this is true not only on the more trivial level of background and historical connection, which no one disputes, but also on the dogmatic level, because that is necessary for Christian faith – at least according to the main traditions of it,

However, it is not clear that this is also workable on the level of biblical theology as usually understood.[11]

These observations are strengthened when certain other factors are taken into account. The first is the difficulty of establishing common ground in terms of common ideas or common theological content between the two Testaments. It was precisely because this was difficult on the level of express statements that the older biblical theology sought so hard to establish it on the level of word meanings and logical and conceptual patterns. And on this level, even if many arguments used in that attempt must be said to have failed, there is nevertheless a real continuity. But the fact remains that, when after a long immersion in the Old Testament one returns to serious concern with the New, one feels it a very strange and very different world of thought. Influences of Hellenism cannot be ruled out, as so much of the older biblical theology sought to do; and even the genuinely Hebraic elements of thought often belong to the world of post-biblical Judaism rather than that of the canonical Hebrew books.

Along with this goes the fact of the modes used by the New Testament to express its fulfilment of the Old: the scheme of prophecy and fulfilment on the one hand, the handling of individual Old Testament texts on the other. These connections depend on meanings that are perfectly understandable given the interpretative possibilities of the time, but are remote from direct meaningfulness within the Old Testament situation itself: this is no new idea, but is widely recognized and acknowledged. Even if we take into the schema the development of interpretative tradition between Old Testament and New, this still does not seem to give us means to say that the New Testament assertions of fulfilment truly fit with the Old Testament situation. Yet these fulfilments and interpretations are both very pervasive and quite essential. Perhaps we have to admit that their validity cannot be established on the level of biblical theology. It is when we work on the level of doctrinal theology that we become free to recognize that such fulfilments and interpretations, linguistically and exegetically dubious as they may often be, nevertheless function as effective indicators and testimonies to the event of New Testament revelation to which they are attached.

Before going farther, it may be useful to note one particular aspect characteristic of Gese's thinking (and of Stuhlmacher's after him) which may be suitably mentioned here: the emphasis on the 'Zion Torah'. The Zion Torah is no mere quantitative expansion of the Sinai Torah, but passes over into something of quite different kind.[12] Unlike the older Sinai revelation, the Zion Torah is an eschatological revelation directed to all peoples. Late Judaism sought to remove this eschatological emphasis and development of the tradition, while Christianity fitted on to a positive continuation and completion of it. 'The time was fulfilled. Jesus of Nazareth entered into the Being opened out by the history of revelation.'[13] One can see how, given Gese's general ideas, the sketching out of such a development would seem to be natural. From the other side, however, the biblical evidence which he uses has been quite otherwise interpreted, and his entire approach through the 'Zion Torah' has been seen as a mistaken construction. We have no space to follow this out farther: let it suffice that it stands as a good example of the way in which the doctrinal level and the biblical theology level may interact.

To resume my own argument: the third consideration lies in the unevenness of the relation between Old Testament and New. Large elements that are theologically very prominent and important in the Old Testament are scarcely taken up or even noticed in the New. Contrariwise, elements that become all-central in the New may have a comparatively limited footing within the Old. Messiahship and messianism is the most obvious case; and what about the complex of Adam, fall, sin and death? Thus, it seems to me, any theology that works on the principle of following the logic and the priorities of the Old Testament and accords attention to its materials in proportion to their prominence and importance is bound to have difficulties in establishing connections with the New.

Now, it is nothing new to notice these and other such points. Gese himself notices some of them (*Sinai*, 11f.), and he uses them to show the many difficulties that stand in the way of accepting traditional connections between the Testaments. He then goes on from this to argue that nothing is left but tradition history to provide the required connection. But this is valid only because he assumes that the connection must be proved from within biblical theology as distinct from doctrinal theology. As soon as one considers that the connection does not stand on the level of biblical theology at all, at least not in its most important and comprehensive aspects, then these same arguments point in a different direction. They become positive pointers to the fact that the interrelation of the two Testaments stands on a different level.

If they are handled on a doctrinal rather than a biblical-theology level, these three aspects can be handled more positively. First, the differences of ideas and theological content as between Old and New Testament: for doctrinal theology this is no novel question, and it has been traditional to deal with it through such schemes as the sequence of different covenants or the dialectic of law and grace. These traditional formulations would have to be modified today in order to take account of the greater complexity of biblical material as now understood; but the approach would remain a doctrinal one.

Secondly, the explanation of Old Testament texts within the New Testament: these ancient texts can be validly re-used in relation to doctrinal affirmations, even where they cannot be deployed on the level of biblical theology. To take a very simple example: St Matthew's use of Isa. 7. 14 in its application to the birth of Christ can be deployed as part of the doctrinal understanding of christology, even if that meaning cannot well be associated with the Old Testament meaning of the same text on the biblical-theology level.

Thirdly, the displacement of emphasis as between the Old Testament and the New is something that has always been accepted on the level of doctrinal theology. Dogma was never equally associated with everything in scripture. Some of the most important dogmatic *loci* were always connected with areas that had comparatively little prominence in scripture: for instance (again) the virgin birth, similarly inspiration of scripture, perhaps also predestination. On the other side there were always large and prominent areas of scripture that generated little or no doctrinal attention: think, for instance, of the prophets' speeches against the foreign nations, which fill up dozens of pages; or the significance of the splitting of the people Israel into the two nations and king-doms Judah and Israel, which is clearly a central theme of the Old Testament, and yet doctrinal theology has on the whole left it on the side – not necessarily rightly, of course.

To sum up, then, the affirmation and explication of the ultimate unity and coherence of the two Testaments may belong to the operations of doctrinal rather than of biblical theology. For this reason, the existence of a 'gap' between the Old Testament and the New, even if it does breach a certain continuum of tradition, is not a serious fault or problem. Thus the striving of biblical theology to establish coherence and unity, even if it is viable up to the level of the entire Old Testament or the entire New Testament, involves essentially doctrinal questioning if it is to be carried up to the level of the entire Bible, and the effect of this is to put in question the existence of biblical theology as an operation independent of doctrinal theology.

One final remark: the establishment of biblical unity on the basis of a con-tinuum of tradition seems to carry with it difficulties in the evaluation of Judaism. This seems to be clearly visible in Gese's thinking. He seems to think that Old and New Testament form one continuum of tradition, but Judaism through the nature of its canon process breaks or 'reduces' the tradition and then (illegitimately?) starts on a new process of tradition. It is difficult to see that these conceptions are other than unfair to Judaism. They seem to imply that Judaism, at least in the form in which it has come down to later times, had no real Bible in the sense in which the church has a Bible (a body of completed tradition, the New Testament having created the Old and completed the whole), and similarly that in permitting the growth of tradition on a 'new' level, parallel to or additional to canonical scripture, Judaism was doing something improper or illegitimate, at least as seen in comparison with what Christianity (in Gese's conception) has done. These considerations are apart from the main argument presented above: but it may be reasonable to claim that, if an argument in biblical theology results in what appears to be an unfair, distorted, or at least implausible picture of Judaism, that is an additional reason why such an argument should not be accepted.

In conclusion, then, to sum up: the thought of Hartmut Gese represents an interesting and novel approach to the interrelation of Old and New Testaments, an interrelation understood as central to *pan-biblical* theology as distinct from the theology of one Testament or the other. His approach, however, remains a controversial one: influential both in itself and through the adoption of it by Stuhlmacher, it has also had much negative reception.[14] On the one hand it may be questioned whether detailed biblical materials, and historical processes like the formation of the canon, have been satisfactorily treated. On the other hand, while like any other proposal in this field it involves relations between exegetical and doctrinal operations, it leaves the discriminating reader with much doubt as to whether these connections have been rightly established.

In any case Gese's proposal is likely to remain prominent in all discussion of the theme 'biblical theology' for some time to come. It makes a determined effort to see Old and New Testaments as a single continuum. It provides integration with the history of religion while preserving a high degree of perception of the distinctiveness of the Bible. It rightly sees the importance of the 'post-biblical' religious continuity in Judaism, even if its final expression of this is defective. Unlike most biblical theologies, it takes up the question of the apocryphal books in a serious and original way. It has a strongly 'canonical' emphasis, which is nevertheless sharply distinct from other canonical approaches like those we shall examine in the next chapter. Even where criticisms of it are offered, as they are offered above, one must acknowledge the original and stimulating quality of Gese's ideas, along with the great learning of their author.

One further note in conclusion. We have noted the way in which initiatives established by Gese have been taken up and followed by Stuhlmacher.[15] This is of interest because the general approach of the two appears to differ considerably. Gese, as noted above, has a background of concentration in the history of religion, and his idea of the 'continuum' makes sense within this frame of reference. I have not seen a discussion by him of the 'historical-critical method', but it may probably be assumed that he feels at home within that approach. On the other hand he combines these insights with elements of a distinctly speculative-dogmatic theological point of view. Stuhlmacher, on the other hand, while also very theological in his approach, finds that this drives him into an anxious effort at balance between a justification of historical criticism and an insistence on its limitations.[16] His thinking has a strong church emphasis, which comes to expression in a longing for the exegesis of texts to be in agreement with the confessional documents of the later church. This particular emphasis is not present in Gese's work, as far as I know.

# 23

# The Canonical Approach: First Stage

## *1. General*

In approaching this subject, I have to begin by expressing my gratitude to my friend Professor Brevard Childs for the stimulus that his thinking has been to me in the entire field of biblical theology. Though I have come to disagree with almost everything in his proposals about the subject and in the values with which he has approached it, I realize how very much I owe to him, in that his thinking has been the catalyst for much that has become my own. I believe that there are some who have a particular vision, and that they are called to follow out that vision and explore it to the utmost. Whether it finds favour with others or not, that is their vocation and their service to those others. Whether or not I agree with what they do does not make any difference to this. I am not sure whether Childs himself thinks in this way: it seems to me more as if he wants to stop people from thinking in any deviant ways. But to me it is important. The following out of such a vision to its fulfilment can be very costly, in time and work but still more in isolation and in estrangement, which cannot but be painful. Without the stimulus of his work I would not have come to many of the perceptions, whether right or wrong, that are in this book.

The positions developed by Childs were not entirely novel; rather, they developed out of older stages in biblical theology, out of the 'Biblical Theology Movement' as he himself called it. At an early time he wrote: 'One of the persistently weak points of the Biblical Theology Movement was its failure to take the Bible seriously in its canonical form.'[1] It is doubtful whether this is correct. Much is left vague, of course, by imprecise terms like 'take seriously'. As I see it and remember it, the main current of biblical theology has been canonical from the beginning, even if the words 'canon' and 'canonical' were not much used.[2] The entire emphasis on the *internal* relations of biblical material implied the canon as the boundary. There was a common body of biblical thought, which extended throughout the Old or New Testaments and, going farther, through both Testaments taken together. This common body of biblical thought was to be distinguished from external currents of ideas: from environing religions, thus from polytheistic and mythological paganism, from the mystery religions, from 'intertestamental' Judaism, from Greek thought, from philosophy, from later theology. Biblical theology might be interested in the development of Israelite historiography, but that came to an end with the latest biblical books: for most people and most of the time, it did not go on into I and II Maccabees. In the New Testament field, it might be interested in a development of (say) ideas of sin and salvation, but the relevant development stopped short with (say) II Peter and did not include I and II Clement or the Didache on the same basis, still less Justin or Irenaeus. Biblical theology thus had the *exclusive* characteristic of a canon, separating what was within from what was without.

And it also worked *inclusively*: the idea of 'seeing the Bible as a whole' was complemented with the notion of 'taking the Bible as it stands'. Differences between sources, and analytic perceptions of that kind, were not denied, but were not valued very positively. While sources might differ, there was, it was hoped, a sort of common theology which provided and evidenced a unity of the whole. This did not necessarily deny that each book or source or period might have its own individual theology; but even in their variety the theologies of the canonical books displayed, or implied, or built up into, some kind of impressive unity. The diversity of books and sources was thus to some extent by-passed, or this was at least hoped: texts and judgments from every source worked together to provide a total theology. This too is a sort of 'canonical' position.

The canon, then, in both these senses, represents an emphasis that underlies much of twentieth-century Old Testament theology, even when this terminology was seldom directly used. What Childs did was to emphasize both these aspects more heavily and to focus them more deeply (though not more clearly!) by infinite repetition of the word *canon*.

In New Testament scholarship also, we may add, a consciousness of the importance of the canon was lively. In 1970, the same year in which Childs' *Biblical Theology in Crisis* appeared, Ernst Käsemann edited a volume entitled *Das Neue Testament als Kanon*, which contained contributions from a variety of viewpoints, mostly originally published in the 1950s and 1960s, along with a new critical analysis and concluding summary by the editor. It is unfortunate that this volume, the contents of which are of very high quality, has not thus far been translated into English. The articles betokened a fresh interest in the canon, a change of balance as compared with the older stages of Bultmannian leadership.

One who was aware of this change of interest was Krister Stendahl. We have already looked at other aspects of his famous article on 'Biblical Theology' in the *Interpreter's Dictionary of the Bible* (1962), but it is proper to add here that he also included in it a substantial section entitled 'The Significance of "Canon" for Biblical Theology' (428b–430b), which has not attracted as much attention or discussion as his distinction between 'descriptive' biblical theology and hermeneutically perceived meaning for today. In the descriptive operation Stendahl seemed in the first place to see no significance for 'canon'. It had no historical status, and materials that lie outside the later canons were fully relevant for biblical theology. When one turns, however, to the hermeneutical task for later times, however, the canon becomes all-important:

> The question as to the meaning of the Bible in the present – as distinguished from the meaning in the past as stated by descriptive biblical theology – receives its theological answer from the canonical status of scripture. It is as canon, and only as canon, that there is a Bible, an OT and NT as well as the whole Bible of the church as a unity (429).

Such a statement is remarkably like a foundational utterance for the canonical criticism which was soon to arise, and from which Stendahl was later to distance himself so sharply. Moreover, Stendahl was not able, it seems, to keep the canon entirely apart from his descriptive ideal:

> But when the descriptive task is addressing itself to the interplay between different parts of the Bible, as, e.g., the NT understanding of the OT, it naturally takes cognizance of the limits of, as well as of the very idea of, canon.

It seems, then, that a variety of interests within biblical scholarship of many kinds, and biblical theology in particular, had been leading towards a concern for the canon, and this was to express itself in more explicit form from about 1970.

## 2. A canon within the canon?

One aspect which may conveniently be slipped in at this point is the idea of an inner canon, a group of books or a body of texts within the Bible to which higher authority or dominance is to be ascribed. The idea is not a new one and had appeared in discussion over a century or more.[3] But the rise of Old Testament theology in its modern form evoked the question in a new way. In so far as theologians sought to state and describe what was the central or essential theology of the Old Testament, it was always possible that their statement would have the effect of casting doubt upon certain sections, books, or groups of books which failed to preserve these essential characteristics intact. In view of the very common opinion that revelation in history was a central theme, or *the* central theme, it is not surprising that the Wisdom literature, in which this theme seems to be muted or absent, should draw some criticism and be regarded as deficient or inferior in authority to the rest of the canon.

The thinking of George Ernest Wright provides a good illustration. In his

*God Who Acts*, as already mentioned, he found the place of Hebrew Wisdom to be 'the chief difficulty', and declared that it remained 'near the pagan source of wisdom'.[4] This might be understood to mean that the Wisdom books should be excluded from the canon. Goldingay takes it so,[5] but I do not think Wright meant this, at any rate in this passage. It seems to me, rather, that he is trying to *explain* the contribution of the Wisdom books and thus to overcome this 'chief difficulty'. In his very next sentence he goes on to say that 'in the canon of scripture, Proverbs has the important function of supplying an explanation of the meaning of the law for individual life',[6] which suggests that Proverbs, in spite of its theological weaknesses, rightly remained in the canon and remained fully functional there. Previous paragraphs had offered similar positive explanations for Job and Qohelet, in spite of Wright's judgment that the wisdom teachers 'lacked the peculiarly Israelite doctrine of society'.[7]

In his following words, however, Wright goes on to say that 'in order to survive as a living force in Judaism and Christianity the wisdom movement had to undergo a more thorough acclimatization to the doctrines of election and covenant'. This is done, he says, 'in the apocryphal Wisdom of Solomon', and he goes on to refer to Ben Sira (Ecclesiasticus). This gives the impression that he thought that the full value of the wisdom tradition was realized only when the two main 'apocryphal' wisdom books were taken into the reckoning; and this might suggest that it would be wholesome if these two books were within the canon. However, he does not actually say so. Thus, to sum up, Wright's position in *God Who Acts* seems rather to be that the Wisdom books have certain theological defects but with proper explanation can be seen to be a salutary force within the canon.[8] His view is rather typical of that of the Biblical Theology Movement in general: theological virtues, when perceived, show that it is good for a book to be within the canon, and, conversely, the presence of a book within the canon makes it likely that its theological virtues will be perceived.

Wright entitled his final chapter of his later work *The Old Testament and Theology* (1969) 'The Canon as Theological Problem'. Here he is doubtless aware of the rising trend of interest in the canon. Thus he is already launching out in the fine style of canonical criticism when he scolds the RSV for putting the longer ending of Mark into fine print (169f.). 'Should we not openly confess that our putting verses 9–20 of Mark 16 into fine print, so that they will not be used in the churches, rests upon a kind of primitivism which supposes that only the original words of the Gospel are to be considered Scriptural?' – a sentiment really quite characteristic of Childs.

Later in the chapter, however, he came to the question of the canon within the canon. He devoted a short historical sketch to it, which indicated that at all times – in Judaism, in the New Testament, in the Middle Ages, in the Reformation and in modern times – there has in fact been a canon within the canon. The inner canon is defined or constituted by the regnant theology of a time. 'The canon within the Scripture will be those portions of the literature which are conceived best to express what the theology believed to be most important and relevant for its particular era. The remainder of the Bible will be partially ignored, partially reinterpreted in the light of a theology's central interpretative position, and partially held in tension with what was deemed of central importance' (182). Thus 'the truth is to be found in actual usage, and here the actual theology of the user provides the interpretative principle whereby the canon within the canon can be discerned'.

It is often said that Wright 'advocated' a canon within the canon, but this seems not to be the case, at least in the major books quoted here. He makes no suggestion here – or elsewhere so far as I know – that would define the inner canon. All he says is that there will inevitably be one.[9] And he does add that 'the formal canon imposes certain limits', so that complete relativism does not follow.

To clarify this, we should add that, when people talk of a canon within the canon, they may mean several different kinds of thing. They may mean an inner group among the biblical books, such as the earlier prophets, or Paul, or the Gospels; but they may also, and commonly do, mean an aspect of content, or a theological principle.[10] It may be 1. a particular book or group of books (the most obvious and direct sense); 2. a key theme like justification by faith; 3. the essential underlying theological structure; or 4. something to which or someone to whom the scripture refers (e.g. the history of salvation, or Jesus Christ). (In Wright's sketch, referred to above, there is some mixing of these types.)

Moreover, while the canon in the customary sense is public and legislative, hard and fast in the form of a book of printed words, unless it is reified by some sort of legislative action, a canon within the canon is more like an idea, a reference, and it may be more personal and more casual. To say that everyone works with an inner canon may be a personal reference: everyone at any one time is doing this, but it may change as time goes by. It does not necessarily indicate that all must do the same, or that religious organizations must legislate in such a way.

The point made just above, that an inner canon may be a reference to the actual theological realities to which the texts refer, is particularly significant: it is as if one says that God is the canon within the canon, or that the covenant is it. Within Christianity, many have been attracted by the thought that the New Testament is the inner canon within the Bible as a whole. Such a view is put forward by James Dunn, and can be rephrased to say that Jesus Christ is the canon within the canon: 'The New Testament witness to Christ serves as the . . . canon within the canon by which to measure and interpret the rest of the canon – the Old Testament.'[11] Or again, 'Whatever the theory of canonicity, the reality is that *all Christians have operated with a canon within the canon.'*[12] Set within a book that demonstrates the high *diversity* of New Testament Christianity, this leads on to the paradoxical but suggestive proposal that the unity within the diversity *is* the canon within the canon. The unity of the New Testament 'canonizes Jesus-the-man-now-exalted as the canon within the canon'.

The question of an inner canon within the New Testament itself should also be mentioned here, for it is perhaps a clearer instance than that of the New Testament within the entire (Christian) Bible. The volume *Das Neue Testament als Kanon* mentioned above contains good examples. Important comments are made by W. G. Kümmel, by Käsemann himself as editor, and by Herbert Braun.[13] I cite the position of Braun: the inner canon consists in the preaching of Jesus, in Paul and in the Fourth Gospel. This block forms a unity in the way in which man is seen in his situation before God. Within this block the central and essential theological conceptions are made clear. The basic phenomenon of the New Testament is the *event character* of the challenging and questioning of man through Jesus; this is the canon within the canon, by which true canonicity is to be measured. Here and there indeed there are exceptions. The various sources at times slip into unfortunate deviations: Jewish or Hellenistic ideas, for instance, rather than true Christian ones. But such deviations are not *typical* within them.

The canon within the canon, this basic event that flows out of the centre of the preached New Testament, is to be validated in open and critical hearing as against the New Testament itself. The circularity involved in this – the standard emerges from the New Testament and turns itself against the New Testament – is unavoidable, because the canon carries within itself the oppositions which have been named above.

So, Braun goes on, 'one can read the canon of the New Testament rightly only when one knows – through the New Testament itself – of the canon within the canon' (230).

We cannot follow out all the fascinating aspects of this German discussion here. From Braun's opinion as quoted only two things need to be noted: first, the fully *theological* character of his argument. The criteria are not at all historical or historico-critical; the block selected is chosen because it has the right theology at heart. Secondly, however, Christians may question parts of Braun's argumentation, few can doubt that the books he has chosen are (within the New Testament, leaving aside the Old, which did not come into the discussion here) the books by which, overwhelmingly, the church and Christians in fact live.

Clearly, then, the discussion of a canon within the canon has been evidence at least of the fact that people have been conscious of the canon and interested in its reality and function.

When we turn to those who strongly oppose all talk of an inner canon, it is not difficult to detect their arguments. They are outraged by the idea of an inner canon and insist that there is only one canon, given by God and authoritatively recognized by the church, and that it is utterly destructive even to think of expressing preferences within the totality of Holy Scripture. The whole point of a canon is that *all of it* belongs together. The church never set up a canon of scripture with the idea that one might thereafter select an inner canon from within it.

There seem to be two arguments in this. The first is from the idea of a canon itself: the canon is the selection of a *totality*, intended to be collectively authoritative, so that the lines of connection back and forward across the canon determine the interpretation of all its parts. According to this view, the church established the canon, but certainly did not establish a canon within the canon, nor did it invite believers to establish such an inner canon on the basis of their contemporary theological needs or trends.

The second argument, and probably the more important, is that against *subjectivity* or, as Wright expressed it, for he was well aware of this counter-argument, *relativism*. People who held this view were, one may suspect, not so much hostile to the *elevation* of certain texts to a dominant place (many of them, probably, secretly supported the elevation of the Pauline texts about justification by faith to such a place); what they were really hostile to was anything that looked like the *downgrading* of any canonical texts to a secondary position. For Old Testament specialists this has been specially important, because they fear any kind of downgrading of certain Old Testament books, or of the Old Testament as a whole. The canon, and the canon as a whole, seem to be solid and established facts; any talk about an inner canon opens the gates to sectarian opinions and individual fancies, and thus destroys the solid foundations that the canon itself provided.

A third set of arguments came from late-twentieth-century intellectual movements: from structuralism and from the 'New Criticism'. As against the older historical investigation, which had sought to distinguish older and later elements within a text, to identify 'original' meanings, and to trace the redactional developments which had led to the 'final form', these trends emphasized the final form and led people to ignore the past history, the origin, the development of a text. Likewise they were interested in a text as a whole and not in the history of its parts. Obviously, this could lead to the reading of a major text like the Pentateuch or the book of Isaiah as one single document; going farther, it could lead to the reading of the entire Hebrew Bible, or the entire Christian Bible, as one single text, the lines of connection within which provide the essentials for its own interpretation.

Such, in simple form, are the lines of confrontation in the question of the 'canon within the canon'. All of these are taken up, with variations and in varying degrees, within the movement of 'canonical criticism' to which we are leading. Childs is adamantly against any idea of a canon within the canon and aligned himself more or less with all the arguments against it as set out above; to these he set another, which can be said to be his creative contribution to the whole matter. Sanders, on the other hand, sought to combine both positions: after outlining the position of Wright, in the quotation cited above in n.9, he went on 'and my indebtedness to that view of the Old Testament pervades this book'.[14] However, his next sentence is: 'But Childs is also right: the problem of authority must be broached in full canonical context.' To anticipate somewhat, the new contribution made by Childs is this: he not only rejected any inner canon but made the canon, as defined by him, into the primary and supreme guarantor of rightness in exegetical method and the ultimate basis of rightness in biblical theology.

For the present, it may be useful to state my own position on the question of the 'canon within the canon'.

The position, exemplified above from Wright and especially from Dunn, to the effect that 'whatever the theory of canonicity, the reality is that *all Christians have operated with a canon within the canon*', seems to me to be right in essentials, although it is misleading to use the terminology of a 'canon within the canon.' The only case which is really something like an inner canon is the Torah in the stepped canon of Judaism, and to a very limited extent perhaps the Gospels in those traditions which give them liturgical pre-eminence. Only these form a specially defined and publicly known group of books within a wider canon. Another possible case would be the New Testament, in those Christian views in which it is thought of as the inner canon regulative for the understanding of the whole: but this would seem to me rather to be a sort of private opinion, however widely held, rather than something with the public and ecclesial character that the term 'canon' implies. Most of the other cases are not canons but groups of favourite passages, preferred because they are thought to express regulative theological conceptions. As Wright correctly put it, these are 'those portions of the literature which are conceived best to express what the theology believed to be most important and relevant for its particular era'. Here the regulative status of the passages is not dependent on a *canon* but on a theological preference, which is different. But where a theological preference comes to concretize itself in the form of a defined group of books considered to be essential, this is in effect an internal canon. This can be illustrated practically: soldiers and sailors in wartime might often have with them a small volume which usually might contain the four Gospels and the Psalms: for their existence, as seen by whoever supplied the books, these were the essential biblical texts, the effective canon.

It is also significant that, in spite of these many shifts in emphasis between preferred scriptures, attempts to alter the ecclesiastical canon have been rather few. Much the most important has been Luther's relegation of James, Hebrews and Revelation to a secondary status on the ground of their failure to support justification by faith. What really happened was the reverse: not the making of a dominant inner canon, but the tacit loss of interest in various books and strata, so that they came to be little noticed. This happens already within the Hebrew Bible, and in modern times it is widespread. People often do not want to read genealogies, geographical and tribal lists, or obscure passages from some prophets. The neglect of the Old Testament as a whole in many Christian traditions usually has this character: people do not want to change the canon so as to remove it; they simply let it fade out from sermons, from liturgies, from general usage.

A central criterion in this is the New Testament, and here again it seems to me undeniable that Dunn is right in general. Even if the Hebrew Bible canon as we now have it existed then, the New Testament people had no idea of using it *as a whole*, as a complete canon which had to be interpreted in every area. Numerous books of it are not quoted at all. Christians chose from it elements which were useful and fruitful for the needs of their own Christ-centred faith. But I would express this less as a *canon* which regulated their choices, and more as a neglect of the large areas which did not interest them much. But if we must use the term 'canon within a canon', then the New Testament's use of the Old does seem to belong to this category. This will be strongly opposed by all those who insist on the one complete canon, within which no selection or preference is permitted. But the evidence of the New Testament makes this position very probable, while the arguments against it are too obviously driven, for the most part, by the dogmatic conviction that no inner canons or such entities should be allowed.

Why, after all, has the argument of Wright and others from the continual existence of a 'canon within the canon' been so strongly resisted? Because, one supposes, the more and the longer the periods in which religion has got along with an inner canon, the more difficult it becomes to assert that no inner canon can ever be tolerated. Was there ever a time or a place where church and exegesis were governed by the one canon of scripture and no interior selection? Is it the idea that Calvin's Geneva provides the needed example? Or do people think that, even if there has always been a 'canon within the canon' in Wright's sense, there still remains a possibility that one can find a way to do without it and to work with the one exterior canon only? Is not the modern canonical movement in exegesis and theology an attempt to carry this out? Very likely it is so.

Perhaps the most serious counter-argument, however, is that over sub-jectivity. If people can choose their inner canon according to the theological fashions of the time, in what sense can the Bible be considered to be authoritative at all? To this, however, there is an answer. As we have seen above, the various 'inner canons' did not stand upon their own intrinsic authority as canons but were dependent on theological preferences which expressed themselves through these groups of books or passages. The same theological preferences, however, still operate where all inner canons are denied and only the one total canon is accepted. The one total canon contains a great variety of material, richer in choices than most of the inner canons have been; its material can be weighted, cross-compared and understood in many ways. Theological preferences, which are regulative for the inner canons, are equally regulative, or even more regulative, when only the outer or total canon is accepted. Sub-jectivity, in other words, if it is a problem, is equally a problem under both sets of conditions.

This is probably not accepted by canonical theologians in the modern sense of the term. They think, roughly speaking, that the canon itself provides a frame which, if accepted for biblical exegesis, results in a solid and definitive interpretation such as other approaches fail to provide; and they think that, taken as the basis for biblical theology, it produces a theology that fits with the Bible as a whole and brings its parts together in a total perspective. Is this credible? Or is it an illusion?

These considerations are by no means final. We have still to enter into the main positions of canonical theology. However, the discussion of the 'canon within the canon' has provided a suitable introduction to the questions that lie ahead.

### 3. *The approach of Childs: first stages*

Clearly, then, most biblical theology has presupposed, often tacitly, an interest in the canon as the boundary of scripture.[15] This being so, the question of an inner canon within the total canon of scripture came to be discussed. Only in the later 1960s or so, however, did the concept of canon come to be the trademark of a particular and strongly individual approach to biblical theology.

It was James Sanders who called his *Torah and Canon*, published in 1972, 'an essay in the origin and function of canon . . . an invitation to formulate a sub-discipline of Bible study I think should be called canonical criticism'.[16] Sanders' approach will be discussed later. Meanwhile, Brevard Childs had started the publication of a linked series of books which launched a 'canonical method' or, as he later preferred to call it, a 'canonical approach'.

The first book was his *Biblical Theology in Crisis* (1970). It fell into sharply distinct parts. Its first and main part was a well-written and discerning account of what Childs called the 'Biblical Theology Movement' – mainly in the United States, though some, justifiably, doubted his assurance that it was so exclusively American.[17] It was in fact an internationally-linked movement; what seems important about its American basis is that in America it fell more distinctly into 'crisis', while (say) in Germany this is hardly true. Anyway, to sum up, Childs wrote:

> The Biblical Theology Movement underwent a period of slow dissolution beginning in the late fifties. The breakdown resulted from pressure from inside and outside the movement that brought it to a virtual end as a major force in American theology in the early sixties.[18]

However, for Childs this was not the end of the matter. 'The need for biblical theology in some form is greater than ever' (92). 'One of the soft spots of the Biblical Theology Movement lay in the failure to develop the area of biblical theology as a rigorous discipline . . . Often one gained the impression that what distinguished biblical theology from the disciplined study of the Old and New Testaments was a homiletical topping' (93). So, in order to lay the foundation for a new biblical theology, the first step is to establish the proper context for interpreting the Bible theologically (97). All sorts of ideas of 'context' have been sculling around. 'As a fresh alternative, we would like to defend the thesis that the canon of the Christian church is the most appropriate context from which to do biblical theology' (99).

Context, in fact, had been a matter of 'great confusion' in the Biblical Theology Movement (98). This was now to be cleared up, the canon forming the one sole and absolutely authoritative context. With this, Childs argued, went the 'acknowledgment of the *normative* quality of the biblical tradition' (100). The canon also provided an adequate hermeneutical position. I return to my original quotation, adding the important following sentence: 'One of the persistently weak points of the Biblical Theology Movement was its failure to take the Bible seriously in its canonical form. It accepted uncritically the liberal hermeneutical presupposition that one came to the biblical text from a vantage point outside it' (102). Notice this point, for it is probably symptomatic for Childs. The idea (unexplained) that this was the hermeneutical presupposition, and that it was also *liberal*, and that the only alternative to it lay in the canonical principle, explains much in Childs' later development. The Biblical Theology Movement 'shared this hermeneutical uncertainty', hence 'it was vulnerable to every shifting wind that blew'.[19] The 'confession' of the Christian canon claims that the theological data do not lie 'in some form of positivity behind the text'. The attempt to get at some sort of other reality lying behind the text is the fatal mistake.

But on the other hand (103), the canonical reading does not read the text 'on the flat'. The church always insisted on 'relating the text to the reality to which the text pointed'. The text does not have 'an authority separated from the reality of which it speaks'. There are important questions here to which we shall have to return. Furthermore, the Biblical Theology Movement suffered from 'a total failure to come to grips with the inspiration of scripture' (103–4).[20] All these aspects, already adumbrated in Childs' work of 1970, continue to be expressed in his later writings.

Biblical theology, he argues, is needed for practical reasons. 'Christian pastors continue to do their own biblical theology' (95). 'The real question is not whether to do biblical theology or not, but rather what kind of biblical theology does one have!' The breakdown of the Biblical Theology Movement has left these people in uncertainty. 'It is imperative that direction be given to these pastors,' Childs asserts. Curiously, he never seems to consider that, if biblical theology is in confusion, they might just study theology, or Christian theology, or dogmatic theology, or historical theology. He writes as if nothing but biblical theology is any use for them. Why can they not read Tillich, or Schleiermacher, or Reinhold Niebuhr? Does he mean that they will not accept any theology, or be interested in any theology, unless it is explicitly *biblical* theology? Is that Childs' idea?

The remaining chapters of the book contain soundings in the possibilities of a canonical approach, 'Testing a Method' (Part III). It must be said that these chapters leave a very vague and uncertain impression, in comparison with the critical history of the Biblical Theology Movement in the first part of the book. In themselves they are only soundings, but they are far from convincing as indications of what may follow.

A larger-scale test of Childs' proposal was provided by his Exodus commentary (1974). The preface to this substantial (650-page) volume tells us: 'The purpose of this commentary is unabashedly theological. Its concern is to understand Exodus as scripture of the church' (ix). 'It will be immediately clear from this perspective,' the author goes on, 'that a different understanding of the role of biblical interpretation is being offered from that currently held by the majority of scholars within the field.' The introduction opens with the statement that: 'The aim of this commentary is to seek to interpret the book of Exodus as canonical scripture within the theological discipline of the Christian church' (xiii) and continues by telling us that 'the author does not share the hermeneutical position of those who suggest that biblical exegesis is an objective, descriptive enterprise, controlled solely by scientific criticism, to which the Christian theologian can at best add a few homiletical reflections for piety's sake'. These sentiments agree with what we have already seen to be Childs' thinking.

As Childs explains (xiv–xv), the format of the work is such that each section (e.g. VII on the Plagues of Egypt, 121–77) comprises six elements:

1. A translation with some textual and linguistic notes.

2. 'Literary, Form-Critical and Traditio-Historical Problems', a section which discusses the 'early forces at work in the shaping of the oral tradition' and the history of redaction.

3. 'Old Testament Context', the 'heart of the commentary' (xiv), 'attempts to deal seriously with the text in its final form', to understand it 'as a piece of literature with its own integrity', and especially so because this is canonical text and 'much of the frustration which the preacher experiences in using commentaries stems from the failure of the interpreter to deal with the text in its canonical shape'.

4. 'New Testament Context': this 'attempts to describe how the early church understood the Old Testament scripture in the light of the new confession of Jesus Christ'.

5. 'History of Exegesis': 'No one comes to the text *de novo*, but consciously or unconsciously shares a tradition with his predecessors.' This section seeks to broaden the focus of discussion beyond a few names in recent scholarship.

6. Theological Reflection. These are not to be 'random homiletical ruminations' but are intended 'to develop a more rigorous method of actualizing the text for the church's present task'.

This format, however, is not rigidly adhered to: some sections, for instance, omit the Theological Reflection or combine it with the History of Exegesis (e.g. XVIII, 488–96, on the Statutes and Ordinances of the Covenant; this section has no New Testament element either), and in some it is very brief, e.g. less than a page on XXII (599f.). In effect only just over half of the sections have a separate element on Theological Reflection. The New Testament element is lacking in others, e.g. XV on the Jethro incident or XXII on Exodus 33. There are also Introductions to the Wilderness Wanderings traditions and to the Sinai traditions, and there are two Excursuses on the Hardening of Pharaoh and the Despoiling of the Egyptians (170–7).

A full review of this large commentary cannot be attempted here. The following remarks may, however, be helpful.

First, Childs here puts into effect his conviction that critical scholarship has placed too much emphasis on the origins of texts and too little on their reception, effects and subsequent development. Elsewhere he mentions with sympathy the opinion of David Steinmetz that 'pre-critical' exegesis is superior.[21] He pays much attention to the way in which mediaeval Jewish commentators, and theologians of the patristic and later periods, have dealt with the text both in its details and in its general effect, and this aspect has been considerably praised. It certainly makes a difference in comparison with the customary critical commentary.

Nevertheless my main feeling when, already well knowing Childs' general views, I first used the book in teaching a class on Exodus was how little the real difference was. It was surprising to find that the analysis into J, E and P, in great detail down to half-verses and quarter-verses, is still there and takes up a lot of space for discussion, continuing all the dullness and sterility that Childs has frequently pointed out in this phenomenon.[22] The canonical approach, it seems, does not *start from* the final form of the text, but from the earlier stages and processes of redaction. Even if 'the study of the prehistory has its proper function within exegesis only in illuminating the final text' (xv), this is not how it works out in the commentary. In a case like the Plagues section, after extensive source analysis a detailed description is given of the J source, the E source, and the P source as wholes (133–42), and this is quite interesting and helpful. The focus is supposed to fall on the skilful way in which these have been combined,[23] but in fact what happens is the opposite: little is said to show how the combination is skilful, and in many cases it is the 'Old Testament Context' element, supposed to be 'the heart of' the commentary, that is dull and platitudinous and comes rather close to the 'homiletical ruminations' which have been castigated above.

It seems to me that it is not the canonical approach in itself that makes this commentary different from most others: the difference is made mainly by the presence of the material on New Testament and History of Exegesis. Both the Old Testament material in itself, including its 'canonical' stages, and the Theological Reflection seem to me to remain rather close to both the virtues and the defects of what traditional scholarship had already produced. In fact the newer elements in the commentary tended to have the opposite effect on me from that which had been intended. Thus on the Plagues of Egypt the differences between J, E and P turned out to be *more* interesting than one had expected, while the final-form effect and the theological reflection seemed dull, rather obvious and platitudinous. The history of exegesis also often turns out differently from what one might expect. To learn how seriously Luther and Calvin disputed about whether the Hebrew midwives told a lie to Pharaoh only shows how the stupid moralism about anything in the Bible, which was still normal into the twentieth century and which one might have blamed upon Victorian moralism, was already there with the Reformers and before them.

Against this expansion of content, on the other hand, one must set the contrary judgment: once the vision of a commentary is expanded to include all this, how can it fail to include a great deal more? How out of all the mass of human thought directed upon a biblical book and its effects over two or three millennia can one rest with the opinions and ideas that Childs has seen fit to include? How does he escape the suggestion that he has included exactly those effects and comments that are congenial to his own ideas and his own approach? How can he escape from the thought that his own sympathy for pre-critical exegesis is only a product of his own obvious and continually voiced hatred of the Enlightenment?

Thirdly, as Mark Brett has well expressed it in the best discussion published,[24] Childs markedly fails to follow out consistently the interpretative methods upon which he himself insists. In his actual discussion of texts he vacillates between arguments akin to an ahistorical 'New Criticism' reading and others of a traditionally historical kind. As Brett puts it, in this book Childs is 'constantly swapping hermeneutical hats'. Brett distinguishes (esp. 41f.) between 'hermeneutical pluralism', which would admit that there are different types of exegesis, depending on different interpretative goals, and 'hermeneutical monism', which would argue that 'all results should be commensurable in the end'. Childs tends to favour monism, but is incoherent when he does so; 'he is much more coherent in his pluralist moments' (45). For examples see Brett, 40–52.

The work on Exodus is intended as a theological commentary; no one will question that. And theological commentaries, as we have seen above, should count as belonging to the general field of biblical theology. But this leaves vague the question of the other kind of biblical theology: the production of a work that professes to be 'an Old Testament Theology', i.e. an attempt to bring together in one or two volumes a conspectus of the theology of the Old Testament (or, of course, of the Bible). Indeed, Childs later attempted both of these tasks. But one might also ask the question: if one were to write a commentary like his Exodus volume on every book of the Bible, what would there be left that an Old Testament Theology in the other sense would have to do? Might not the theological needs of these pastors be met by the theological commentaries?

On the other hand, it is right to note that the Exodus commentary, in spite of its avowed departure from the style of biblical scholarship in general, remains rather close to that style and respectful of what has been accomplished through it. Thus in his section on the Call of Moses (47–89), the Textual and Philological Notes (49–51) are very similar to what one would have found in any other commentary of the same size and format. The following sections on form criticism and such questions are quite respectful to what others have suggested. Again, in the section on the Divine Name (6off.), various proposed solutions are quite equably discussed. Albright's view is 'undoubtedly the most forceful recent argument'. Freedman's view 'encounters a number of difficulties'. That of Cross has 'certain difficulties'. The form-critical analysis and the stylistic and thematic analysis on 64–71 also seem to continue on the normal tone of scholarship. Even the criticism of Cross for seeking a 'reconstructed tradition' instead of 'taking seriously' Israel's own tradition is introduced gradually and mildly. One has the impression that the commentary remains on terms of reasonable mutual understanding with other currents of Old Testament scholarship. In Childs' later works, as we shall see, this degree of mutual understanding tends to disappear – to put it mildly. And even the final section of each chapter entitled 'Theological Reflection' does not amount to much – just the same fault which had been blamed on the inadequate theological character of previous critical commentaries.[25]

The situation changes in this respect with the *Introduction to the Old Testament as Scripture* (1979). Admittedly, this is not explicitly a work of biblical theology, but in it the canonical approach appears in its developed form, which is supposed to be continued in essentials in the succeeding two volumes which are Theologies.

I have written extensive reactions to this work elsewhere,[26] and will restate some of these in summary form. Generally speaking, as I wrote in 1980: 'In terms of ideas this large book is a very simple one. Every one of the forty-one chapters says the same thing. A review of critical scholarship leads up to the elements of progress and of disagreement that result. It is then explained that all this work has been inadequate because it has not sufficiently emphasized the canon or canonical form. New solutions, and new visions of the meaning of the book, based upon the canon are then outlined.'

To elaborate upon this simple introduction:

1. As compared with his earlier writing and the Exodus commentary, Childs now distances himself much more drastically from critical scholarship. Its failures and confusions, real or imagined, are not only mentioned but form the *vital* substance of argument. The denigration of past scholarship is not only present, but has now become the *essential* step in the argument of each chapter.

2. One reason for this lies in the double sense of the term 'canon' already mentioned above. Childs' argument in earlier works like *Biblical Theology in Crisis* mainly emphasized 'the canon as context'. This meant, basically, the total corpus of the Bible as the context within which the individual text should be seen. But in the *Introduction* there is also a greatly increased emphasis on the canon as the 'canonical form', i.e. the final form of the text. Exegesis should be of the text as it stands, the final form as it emerged from the process of redaction and canonization. Increased emphasis on this means increased hostility to any and all exegesis that seeks in any way to penetrate back to an earlier stage. The worst of all offences, it now appears, is to try to 'reconstruct' an 'original' text or an 'original' form of the tradition. Thus historical investigation moves from being something that is dubious and unreliable to something that is in principle wrong and destructive – for theological understanding (Childs admits

that historical investigation may be legitimate for other purposes, but it is quite irrelevant and damaging to theological understanding). Thus almost anyone who seeks a background in the past for a text, or a previous context outside of the biblical tradition, is demolished for 'reconstructing' speculatively a context other than that of the canonical form.

The use of the word 'canon' for two quite distinct entities (actually for three, as we shall see later) has damaging effects. For the canon, in the sense of the list of books recognized as authoritative scripture by a church, is a public, legislative and objective fact. Indeed its objectivity is one of its main attractions for the devotees of the canonical approach. But when 'canon' is also used as the principle of final-form exegesis for individual books, this is not a public, objective or legislative fact: it is only an opinion, a proposal, a method which might be good or not so good. When 'canon' is also a 'construal', whether of the whole or of a part, it is really an interpretation: it is not a datum from which one may start, but the result of someone's exegetical imagination, whether right or wrong.[27]

Later Childs produced a parallel work on the New Testament, *The New Testament as Canon.* He surveys New Testament scholarship over a wide field and seeks to show that, like work in the Old Testament, it is full of antinomies and failures, all of which are the result of failure to observe the canonical principle. This work, though large, gives a secondary impression in comparison with the Old Testament Introduction.[28] The writer has obviously only a second-hand familiarity with New Testament scholarship, and the degree to which scholarly argument is replaced by dogmatic assertion of principle becomes greater.[29] Two aspects of this should be noted. First, there is an obvious intellectual favouritism in the survey of scholarship: anyone who says anything about the canon or who seems to make Barthian noises is greeted with warm respect, while those who do not are often depicted as prone to 'easy' solutions, lacking in subtlety and depth. Secondly, a similar bias in the matter of theology itself becomes evident. No one has demanded more than Childs that scholarship should be 'more theological'. But what happens when scholars *are* theological and their theological preferences are made evident? Then Childs uses their theology *against* them. Thus of Vincent Taylor, the author of a respected, though admittedly dull, commentary on Mark, Childs points out with disdain that he has 'a free church theology'.[30] Well, why should he not have a free church theology? Obviously, by Childs' own principles that is what he ought to have. In fact this begins to reveal what later becomes glaringly evident: that Childs' warm advocacy of 'theology' applies only to his own theology and a small group of others approved by it, and that 'theology' is a good thing only when it conforms to certain very limited patterns.[31] And this, of course, is the fact that justifies many biblical scholars in doing exactly what Childs laments, namely, steering clear of theology altogether. He cannot both demand that scholars 'be theological' and blame them because they are so. This may sound extreme, but is amply evidenced, as we shall see, in the two volumes on biblical theology which form the culmination of the 'canonical approach'. To these volumes we now turn. In the following chapter we shall take them together, though our main attention will go to the larger of the two, the *Biblical Theology of the Old and New Testaments* (1992).

## 4. Childs' Biblical Theologies

We shall look in the first place at the organization of material in the two works, and first at the shorter *Old Testament Theology in a Canonical Context* (1985; here abbreviated to *OTTCC*). This is, by Childs' standards, a comparatively slight work of some 250 pages. Nor does he seem to make it clear why two works were published or how the first is intended to relate to the second, since the later and larger *Biblical Theology* in its Old Testament sections perforce goes over much of the same ground again.

Now the question of the organization of an Old Testament theology has been one of the central questions during much of the century, and considerable controversy has taken place about it. Writers of Theologies have generally felt it necessary to include a substantial section to explain and justify their organization of the material. In this work of Childs, to the surprise of the reader, this element is almost entirely lacking. *OTTCC* has a very brief section (15f.) which begins by going back to the difference between Eichrodt and von Rad with their 'systematic' and 'traditio-historical' schemes of organization. Childs writes: 'I suggest that both of these alternatives arise from a view of a closed body of material which is to be analysed descriptively.'[32] When Old Testament theology is viewed canonically, he then tells us, 'the issue of organization is sharply relativized. At times the shaping process introduced systematic features; at times it structured the material historically.' In an unaccustomed burst of pluralism,[33] we hear that 'there are innumerable other options' and that 'the real issue lies in the quality of the construal and the illumination it brings to the text'. In other words, if it is good it will be good and if it is bad it will be bad, but there is no guidance to tell us, in this respect, how to make it good.

This seems to mean that the organization of an Old Testament Theology is no matter of concern: you can do it any way, so long as your approach is canonical. This is, somewhat surprisingly, rather like a return to the easy-going, indifferent attitude of Köhler. And this is confirmed by the result, for the chapters are strung out in a sort of common-sense order, with absolutely no

argumentation to say why it should be or must be in this order and not in some
other. If anything, the order is of the kind used by Köhler and many others,
and criticized by many as being a dogmatic order, though I have argued above
(39f.) that it was no more than a common-sense order, even if much used in
dogmatics.

   The sequence of chapters is as follows:

    1. Introduction to Old Testament Theology
    2. The Old Testament as Revelation
    3. How God is known
    4. God's Purpose in Revelation
    5. The Law of God
    6. Knowing and Doing the Will of God
    7. The Theological Significance of the Decalogue
    8. The Role of the Ritual and Purity Laws
    9. The Recipients of God's Revelation
   10. Agents of God's Rule: Moses, Judges, Kings
   11. The Office and Function of the Prophet
   12. True and False Prophets
   13. The Theological Role of Priesthood
   14. Benefits of the Covenant: the Cultus
   15. Structures of the Common Life
   16. Male and Female as a Theological Problem
   17. The Theological Dimension of Being Human
   18. The Shape of the Obedient Life
   19. Life under Threat
   20. Life under Promise.

   Thus, although 'canonical shaping' is frequently mentioned in the various
chapters (e.g. 156ff., 238f.), the canon seems to have no shaping function in
relation to the organization of a biblical Theology. The order is just the same as
any non-canonical person might have used: surely a reason for disquiet. It is,
moreover, a big departure from Karl Barth, for whom one had to have strict
theological reasons for the *order* of presentation of doctrines. It already suggests
something that will develop more fully later on: that as Childs comes to his theological presentations, the importance of the canon is beginning to fade and the
importance of doctrinal rectitude is beginning to increase.
   The much larger and more complicated *Biblical Theology* has seven major
sections, thus (I shall not enumerate the many smaller chapters in detail):

    1. Prolegomena (mainly on the history of the subject)
    2. A Search for a New Approach

3. The Discrete Witness of the Old Testament
4. The Discrete Witness of the New Testament
5. Exegesis in the Context of Biblical Theology (two major examples: Gen. 22.1–19 and Matt. 21.33–46)
6. Theological Reflection on the Christian Bible
7. A Holistic Reading of Christian Scripture.

The key to the presentation lies in the three sections 3, 4, and 6: the Discrete Witnesses of the Old Testament and of the New, and the Theological Reflection on the Christian Bible. A chapter on 'Canonical Categories for Structuring a Biblical Theology' (91–4) begins by telling us that 'the specific characteristic of the canonical shaping of the two testaments into one Christian Bible lay in the preservation of two distinct witnesses to a common subject matter who is Jesus Christ. The peculiar nature of the Christian canon derives from the joining of the Old Testament witness in its own integrity with the New Testament witness in its own integrity' (91). This provides some kind of explanation for the organization of the three great sections as stated above. The rest of the chapter, however, does not go on to explain or justify the internal organization of these sections. In fact section 3 on the Old Testament follows a common-sense semi-historical organization such as one could find in any critical introduction, working through the periods from creation through the patriarchs, Moses, the possession of the land, the monarchy, exile and restoration, and then going on to groupings such as the prophets, apocalyptic, wisdom and the Psalms. Similarly, in the New Testament we have an introduction, then the earliest proclamation, Paul, the Gospels, Acts and 'the Post-Pauline age', again a semi-historical presentation. The content of all these passages contains ample polemic about the damage done if the guidance of the canon is not observed; but the actual *shaping* is exactly what the canon does *not* provide. It is a plain historical-critical principle, and the complete denial of 'canonical shaping', to treat Paul *before* the Gospels.

Section 6, 'Theological Reflection on the Christian Bible', is even less shaped by the canon. It is organized in a thematic way like any theological textbook: The Identity of God, God the Creator, Covenant and Election, Christ the Lord, Reconciliation, Law and Gospel, Humanity Old and New, Biblical Faith, God's Kingdom and Rule, and Ethics. Most of these contain, roughly speaking, an Old Testament portion, a New Testament portion, a united 'Reflection' on both, and a final section connecting the whole to doctrinal theology. Especially these last portions often bring in mentions of modern controversies, e.g. God and Sexuality (376ff.), Liberation Theology (406ff.), the Ecological Crisis (409ff.), various ecclesiastical disagreements (526–9), and ecumenicity (529). Often there is considerable overlapping, since the same subject can come up again in two or more of the major sections. Lack of cross-references and of an index of themes and concepts make it more difficult to follow these arguments.

But the main point about the organization is that in it the canon falls into the background. The organization is increasingly thematic and not at all canonical, especially so in section 6. This fits with what we have already observed: the concern of this large book, which might have been or should have been the consummation of the canonical approach, is elsewhere: its concern is the rightness of Childs' personal theological views. We shall turn to this shortly.

Meanwhile, here are one or two remarks about the literary character of the books, which affect their usability by readers. The reader should be aware of one difficulty in using Childs' works for thorough study and comment, namely that the indexes are very bad. Some of this is simple carelessness: in the *Biblical Theology*, for instance, the indexing has missed dozens of mentions, so that, for instance, the name of Karl Barth (or, indeed, my own) is cited in the text at numerous places which have been overlooked in the index. A more important reason, however, lies in the organization of bibliography. Childs places bibliographies at the end of every individual section, and this is of course quite proper. But his indexes then register not only the names referred to in the text, but also all the names of writers whose works are listed in the bibliographies. The effect is that the indexes list under the names of scholars not only the places where something is said about these scholars but also all the places where one of their articles or books has been listed. Since the same book or article is often listed in several bibliographical lists, multiple listings may occur when in fact very little comment on the scholar concerned appears in the book. Thus in *OTTCC* Vriezen's name is indexed for four places but three of these four are in mere bibliographical lists and there is only one mention of Vriezen's name in the text of the book (4). Zimmerli's name is listed for twenty-five places, but most of these are in bibliographies and only ten or so are actual comments. In the *Biblical Theology*, though the index contains ten entries for P. Stuhlmacher, most of these refer to bibliographical lists or the barest of mentions, and in fact nothing substantial is said in the entire book about this important scholar, who as it happens has made contributions rather similar to those of Childs. In addition, while there is an index of persons and of biblical passages, there is none of concepts, so that the reader has difficulty in finding the places at which terms like sociology, trajectory, feminism, Pelagianism and so on are mentioned.[34] Since the structure of the books means that references to such subjects recur at many points and in different connections, it is difficult for the serious worker to trace the relations between different mentions. The reader is compelled to make up his or her own index. This is no mere technical matter, because the reader will want to judge the degree of consistency between various passages. Has the author changed his mind at certain points? Thus, to take a very obvious case, in

*Biblical Theology* (377) we read that 'within Christian theology it is very difficult to find a justification of the feminist insistence on the use of "inclusive language" in reference to God', and this is part of a wide-ranging attack on feminist attitudes, which are interpreted as contradicting trinitarian orthodoxy. But in *OTTCC* he has already 'judged it quite appropriate' to use 'inclusive' language (40). Has he changed his mind, or has he forgotten what he said earlier?

The place of James, mainly in relation to Paul, is discussed at least six times (302–7, 500f., 547f., 611, 700, 705). We read: 'There is a wide consensus that James reflects a very different theological world from that of Paul' (306). Perhaps Childs does not share this view, but if he does not, he does not make that clear. He tells us: 'Obviously James is sounding a different note from Paul respecting his understanding of faith and works' (501). But on 547f. we find something more like a traditional harmonizing interpretation: James and Paul were agreed but were speaking from different perspectives. 'James and Paul appear to be addressing different questions from very different perspectives which should not be easily harmonized' (548). On 611, after asking 'How is one to explain its [James's] harsh contradiction of Paul', the same paragraph goes on: 'it seems clear that James is not debating directly with Paul. In fact his actual opponents correspond only vaguely with Paul. The Pauline emphasis on faith encompassing works of righteousness within a new eschatological existence seems strangely lost in the debate'. Childs then tells us that James 'attacks an obvious misunderstanding that faith alone apart from works is sufficient' (700), exactly the easy harmonization which was rejected on p. 548. Then, appealing to the Book of Concord, he approves the decision of later Lutheranism to correct Luther on all this: Luther was wrong (705). Few of the references in this section are registered in the indexes. In a case like this it is not that the variety of comments makes it difficult for the reader to understand what Childs means; it is rather that the reader is left uncertain whether Childs has remembered and taken into consideration what he himself has written earlier. If he had made his own index of concepts, this difficulty might have been overcome.

There is also unclarity at times in his references to other scholars, which are often given in simple parentheses without any clear explanation of how the person relates to the problem under discussion. Thus a sentence like this from *Biblical Theology*,

> By the end of the nineteenth century the impact of various concepts of historical evolution became pervasive (cf. Schultz) (6),

leaves it vague whether it is Schultz (who will be unknown to most readers) who embodied this concept of evolution in his work or whether it is Schultz who has pointed out the presence, and the disadvantages, of this concept. Allusions of this kind are tolerable where they concern highly familiar figures such as

Bultmann, but given Childs' very wide reading they can be quite opaque to the average reader.

Finally, the style is dull and repetitive, and bizarre clichés like 'the hermeneutical issue turns on whether' and 'the basic hermeneutical issue at stake turns on the fact that' (42) or 'the final problem turns on the issue of' (*Exodus,* 325) are repeated to a maddening degree. That 'the complexity of the theological issues have been overlooked' (63) and that other scholars' ideas are 'simple' and 'flatten' the 'witness' of the text and do not really 'touch to the heart of the theological problem' (14) are reiterated to the point that the reader ceases to pay any attention to them, knowing that they will recur continually.

With this we turn to the main discussion of Childs' two main theological volumes.

# 24

# Childs' Theologies

## *1. General*

Professor Childs writes as if he was the only theologian in the world, or at least the only one among living biblical scholars. He uniquely knows what is and what is not theology. Thus he can sovereignly declare which approaches are theological or useful for theology and which are not. He has definitive knowledge of what the church wants and needs. He writes as if he sat above the discussions and debates of normal scholarship, 'transcending' them (one of his favourite words). In almost every section the highest point is reached when he gives his own declaration: 'my opinion', 'my judgment'. His personal theological certainty and his assurance of standing well above the level of his exegetical colleagues is one of the outstanding characteristics of these two books, and especially of the later and more important one of them. As we shall see, in many respects this book is neither a work of biblical theology nor one of canonical theology; it is more like a personal dogmatic statement provided with biblical proofs.[1] Its presupposition is the rightness of his own theology, and its purpose is to demonstrate that same rightness.

No one who knows modern theology will doubt that this entire work is a manifestation of one particular offshoot of Barthian theology. There are indeed three heroes of the work: Luther, Calvin and Barth, in ascending order. The opinion that most of modern scholarship is in a poor state, which might have some truth in it, is coupled with the converse notion that the Reformation had the right answers all along, a pious delusion which even Childs does not seek to demonstrate. Anyway, the three heroes are pretty well always in the right, or would be, except when they differ among themselves. Then there is a definite pecking order. When Luther differs from Calvin, it is Calvin who is right. Sometimes Calvin is superior to Barth. Barth's exegesis can be poor in comparison with Calvin's (e.g. 621, where Barth's chapter on faith is 'almost listless' while Calvin's is 'strong and magnificent'), which would make it look as if Calvin was the top hero. On the other hand, the Calvin of this book is very much the Calvin created by Barthianism, so that it turns out that Barth is the top hero in the end. The very vocabulary used by Childs comes straight out of Barthian rhetoric: 'struggle', 'wrestle', 'utterly', 'grounded in', 'at the very heart of', 'christologically', 'hammered out'. Yet there are qualifications to this, as we shall see.

The technique used in the author's Introductions to the Old and New Testaments was a simple one. Section by section addressed some problem of biblical introduction or exegesis. Various suggestions and solutions by scholars were reviewed, their defects were uncovered. In almost every case the answer was the same: the defects and dilemmas had been caused by neglect of the canonical setting, and attention to the canonical setting would put everything right. Childs transcends the narrow, stumbling, prejudiced world of scholars, their simple minds darkened by (most commonly) the assumptions of the Enlightenment.

Exactly the same technique is followed in the *Biblical Theology*. A topic is taken up – let us say, 'The Role of the Old Testament within the Early [Christian] Proclamation' (225ff.) or 'Paul's Understanding of the Law' (542ff. + elsewhere). Scholarly approaches are described, sometimes fairly sympathetically but more often contemptuously; opposing opinions are registered, and then the judgment is delivered: the actuality is deeper, more subtle, more complex. The opinions of scholars are superficial, their methods are not theological, their exegesis is 'flat', they do not 'wrestle' or 'struggle' with the text and its problems. So where is the deeper, more subtle, more complex answer to be found? Childs is the one who has it. He is the one who knows the 'deep' and 'complex' character of the texts and the problems.

The approach is thus strikingly narrow and self-centred. Enormous reading in the literature has been carried out. But, of all the scholars mentioned, apart from Barth and Barthian heroes (and not all of them), almost *everyone* is in the wrong. In many cases Childs does not even bother to give reasons why someone's ideas are defective: he just hands down a minimum grade, like a professor who issues a C minus without any explanation of how the student could have done better. For example, the highly respected American biblical theologian Samuel Terrien took 'elusive presence' as the theme of his work which, among biblical theologies written by Old Testament scholars, at least extended its scope into the New. Childs writes of him that his rubric 'may illuminate the Old Testament to some degree, but, in my judgment, seriously obfuscates the New' (15). Why so? What is wrong with it? No answer. He returns to the theme and denies that 'elusive presence' is an inner-biblical category (551). But why?[2] How does it differ from 'the reality of God-with-us' which according to Childs himself is all-important (478f.)? Again no explanation. To me this handling of Terrien, who after all has been one of the few to write a major work of biblical theology in the United States this century, is improper.

This is no isolated case. Literally dozens of such judgments are to be found in the text: it is in fact the author's standard method. *Everyone* but himself is wrong! And in many cases they are not only wrong, but are portrayed by Childs as basically stupid: lacking in subtlety, prone to 'easy' solutions, ready to swallow any current opinion rather than 'wrestle' with the real problems. He expects us to believe, for instance (543), that both E. P. Sanders and H. Räisänen 'fail to take seriously' the possibility that Paul is 'wrestling' with the reality of the Old Testament law. His mode of replying to criticism is often of the same kind: when reviewers have suggested that there is some inconsistency or failure in his method, he thinks it enough to reply with the equivalent of a brusque 'No, there isn't!' (e.g. 104 to Brueggemann and others). His book might well have adopted as sub-title the title of Edward de Bono's work *I am Right and You are Wrong*.

The overwhelming impression given, therefore, is one of the *isolation* of the author. As he himself says, 'this volume has carried on a sustained polemic against other positions within the field which have been judged as inadequate, misleading or outright erroneous' (722). He never wrote a truer word. Apart from the three heroes of the book, Luther, Calvin and Barth, he agrees with practically no one. Of course polemic against wrong viewpoints is proper: but Childs gives the impression that there is practically *no one* in current biblical theology with whom he is in any sort of sympathetic conversation.

Take the example of his Yale colleagues. Many have thought of Yale as a centre for a 'post-modern' style of theology following something of the Barthian lines of thought, a line into which Childs' thinking would fit very nicely. For example, the closeness of Lindbeck's theological work to the principles of Childs has been widely noticed.[3] Not so in this book: Lindbeck's approach, though 'stimulating', is on the wrong track (21ff., 723) and not a single good word is said about it. Meeks is 'sophisticated' (23) and has 'remarkable exegetical skills', but the result of a two-page discussion (666–8) is entirely negative: 'From the perspective of faith, what Meeks is describing is at best an empty garment without a live body' (668). Kelsey is a noted theologian, whose views have attracted many modern biblical scholars (81), but if he were right 'the task of providing a bridge between biblical and dogmatic theology would be doomed from the start' (592), and a longer discussion on 661–3, while admitting certain advantages, ends up overwhelmingly negative: Kelsey 'undermines' a fundamental theological distinction; his view is 'erroneous' and the discussion concludes with an imputation of 'Pelagianism'. Dahl, formerly at Yale, seems to be the only Yale scholar who gets a favourable write-up.

Thus the absoluteness of Childs' judgments is striking. I personally do not feel that I have been unfairly treated by his comments: what he says about my own work is cautious and respectful even when mistaken. But the attitudes he expresses about his scholarly contemporaries in general seem to me to cast a deep shadow over his claims to speak for theology, biblical or other. Most of his judgments against approaches that seem to differ from his own are not on matters like exegetical details or linguistic facts, where hard evidence might settle an issue: they are questions of theological values where discussion could often disclose unexpected common ground, where compromise is often possible, and where in any case both parties have the same basic purpose and interest, namely the theological interpretation of the Bible. It is, curiously, just at this point, where both parties have the same purpose and interest, that Childs becomes most completely negative. I have already quoted his earlier opinion about Stendahl, one of the great exegetical thinkers of America, that his thinking 'destroys from the outset the possibility of genuine theological exegesis'.[4] This is Childs' typical style of comment, and it continues in this new volume. The opinions discussed are not just unbalanced, mistaken or misleading; they are totally destructive; they are *trash* that must be utterly rejected. Contrary opinions do not just display a misguided theological judgment, but *completely destroy* any possibility of theological interpretation. Thus in the same style John Barton (!) is described (173) as guilty of 'cynical reductionism' which 'renders impossible any serious theological use of scripture'. Paul Hanson's work is 'unabashed propaganda for modern liberal Protestant theology' (18).

Particularly striking, therefore, is his inability to accept kinship or support even from those who stand very close to him and endorse the general direction of his thinking. He seems to feel specially threatened by anyone who might be an ally or a help, and especially by Americans. This impression is not a new one: from the beginning of the canonical approach his inability to admit common ground with James Sanders, the other chief canonical critic in North America, was noticeable (see now *OTTCC*, 136f.). Here the same tendency is greatly extended. The German New Testament scholar H. Hübner has written with great appreciation of Childs' approach, but also with constructive criticism;[5] however, Childs writes that Hübner's approach 'destroys the theological integrity of the Old Testament and silences its canonical witness' (77). That is, Hübner's approach is not just mistaken in its emphasis, but totally destructive and disastrous.[6] This is not unusual, but is typical of Childs' tone in his judgments on exegetical work. Walter Brueggemann, vainly seeking to accept much of the canonical approach and yet to modify it for the better, is brusquely snubbed and repelled (72f.): his thoughts are 'predictably' a 'radically different construal' and display him to be 'a most eloquent defender of the Enlightenment' – association of anyone with the Enlightenment is, it seems, the very worst Childs can say about them. The length to which Childs can go with this is well illustrated in his judgment that Käsemann's approach to the 'hermeneutical problem of critical reconstructions' brings out 'the heart of the methodological issue' (213), yet 'his manner of setting up the problem is clearly a legacy of the Enlightenment and not that of the Reformation, which skews the

basic theological issues from the start' (215). This, if it is seriously meant, is a
clear statement of principle that *any* theological thought that does not start from
the Reformation is wrong.

Moreover, in spite of the clear intellectual nepotism in favour of those who
represent the inheritance of Karl Barth, it turns out that in the end they do not
do very well either. It is not as if Childs is at home with his fellow-Barthians.
Most of them have gone far astray. T. F. Torrance's work on faith and science
does not provide 'fresh illumination of the biblical text' (406). Paul van Buren's
opinion is swept aside as 'idiosyncratic' (242). H.-J. Kraus's work is 'impressive'
(521), but Childs remains 'uneasy' about it, not surprisingly when Kraus has
gone off in the direction of a liberation theology (25) 'which seems to flatten
everything in its path' (a phrase which might with justice be applied to Childs'
own product). Unlike Barth, Kraus produces 'no memorable exegesis' (648) – a
judgment which Moberly later, in an otherwise generally appreciative review,
turned back on Childs himself, saying that there is no memorable exegesis in *his*
work either.[7]

Moltmann, who certainly learned from Barth, has got some things right but a
lot of others wrong. 'The crucial theological issue turns on what is meant by
faith', concludes Childs (406–9), implying that Moltmann is wrong about faith.
If he is wrong about that, he is far wrong indeed. Worse, in the section on 'The
Ecological Crisis' (409–11) it emerges that Moltmann is in deep trouble. Childs
is bothered by his 'ideological bias which passes for a historical explanation of
the roots of the crisis and shares a heavy flavour of European romanticism'.
Further, 'a theology of creation which underplays human sinfulness runs the
risk of replacing the biblical hope of a new creation by a fanciful utopian dream
of human imagination'. Not only so, but Moltmann seems responsible for 'a
Pelagian theology' (411).

In other words, according to Childs' depiction, Barthianism produced upon
the theological scene a ghastly bunch of failures and heretics. Even the revered
Hans Frei, certainly one of Childs's own major sources of inspiration, in one of
his last essays 'moved in a direction, in my opinion, which for Christian theology can only end in failure' (20). Is it not shocking to say this about Frei? Do
not these numerous errors within the Barthian tradition suggest that there was
something seriously wrong with Barth's inheritance? How can it be that, out of
so many, only Childs has got it right?

## 2. *Childs and Barth*

Childs is not, indeed, totally uncritical towards Barth. On the key subject of
faith, as mentioned above, he thinks Barth's section is 'almost listless' in

comparison with Calvin (618). Barth's exegesis of the image of God in humanity is 'strained' (568). On the other side, Barth's suggestions can be 'intriguing', like his connecting of Genesis with the Song of Songs, but there is 'no canonical warrant' for such an idea (*OTTCC*, 193).[8] Indeed, Barth's exegesis can at times be contrary to scripture! (We are amazed to hear of 'areas in which Barth's interpretation stands in considerable tension with scripture itself' [521f.] – why are we not informed what these areas are, so that we could do something about it?) Childs seems hesitant over the rightness of Barth's political judgment in the post-war period (56of.). In other words, Barth himself was not all that good. Thus one can, in theory, improve upon Barth. But Childs, it seems, will not allow anyone else to do it except himself.

As I have said, it is transparent that this work does not really belong to biblical theology but is a biblical apologetic for a Barthian dogmatic stance. And a number of features which have been mentioned confirm this. In some respects the personal imitation of Barth is very close. This would include the combativeness, the extreme terms of the condemnations issued, and the need to dominate. It would also fit with the extreme inability to accept help and support: Brunner in his famous controversy with Barth was falling over himself in his attempts to agree with Barth, to support Barth, to say that Barth was entirely right except for a smallish modification; but Barth would not have any of it.

It would also fit with one of the most obvious features of Childs' work, namely his inability to accept any other position on equal terms for discussion. This is exactly Barth. To reason with an alternative position would be to accept that there was common ground, and that would be about as bad as to accept natural theology. Thus, in the early reviews of his *Introduction*, when I asked him for the *reason* for something about the canon, he replied with the statement that 'the acceptance of the canon as normative does not function initially as a derivative of reasoned argument', and he went on to claim that the asking of the question brings us into the conflict of reason and faith.[9] I would have thought that anyone with a theological sense would have known that to talk of reason or reasoning in this context means *reasoning within faith*, which is what goes on in theology, or should do so.

After all, on the key subject of the canon, his three heroes, Luther, Calvin and Barth, had very different opinions. Luther made radical alterations in the canon, removing several books from full canonical status on the grounds of theological content, forming an obvious 'canon within the canon', something that Childs sternly forbids anyone else to do or even to think of. Incidentally, how can he claim a Reformation basis when his principles exclude Luther so sternly? Anyway, Calvin did not follow Luther in this. As for Barth, he expressly asserted that the church could in principle alter the canon, something that would surely have been condemned by Calvin.[10] How do we decide between them (leaving aside even more aberrant opinions) without asking for a reasoned explanation of grounds and evidences? With the absence of reasoning, 'theology' becomes a mere assertion of personal convictions, compounded with the apologetic assemblage of biblical proofs and the labelling of contrary opinions with the names of heresies and trends in the past history of ideas (notably the Enlightenment). Here we see the deep sickness of the 'kerygmatic' principle, which is endlessly appealed to. When unqualified, it can quickly degenerate into a language that is purely assertive. So it is not by chance that much of the content of these volumes is described as 'theological reflection' and not 'theological discussion': reflection is something one can do by oneself; discussion requires two parties and some sort of equal basis.

The unwillingness to reason on equal terms also explains the tendency to condemn scholars' opinions without giving any reasons. It is a little bit like Kafka, who in the early days was sometimes compared with Barth. The evildoer is condemned without a trial, without any evidence, without any defence. We here see the 'kerygmatic', assertive principle carried to its extreme.

Another and a very essential Barthian aspect is Childs' sense that he can rule on what is theology and what is not. Since, in his scheme of things, theology is the ideal, and interpretation that is not theology is automatically inappropriate, to say the least, this is strategically very important. One line in the heritage of Barth – whether intended by Barth himself or not – worked in this way. 'Theology', being strictly the science of the knowledge of God, is built upon God as he has revealed himself. 'Theology', therefore, analytically (in the Kantian sense of the word) means Barthian theology. Entities like 'liberal theology' are not theology, even if they use the name. This seems to be the presupposition for Childs' stance. Other approaches to the knowledge of God do exist but, because they differ from this conception, they are in essence *not theology*. Thus Childs never seems to treat liberal 'theology' as a *different* form of theology with which one has to enter into discussion: it is a foreign body, which should not exist at all.[11]

Further, it is commonly labelled as 'ideology', a dangerous practice to which we shall return. Entities like the history of religion are therefore not theology, and not being theology they are not eligible as considerations within theological exegesis. Let us admit that this is one possible model; but at best it is only one opinion among others. Childs takes it, however, as an absolute.

A Barthian aspect is also to be seen in the sense of intellectual superiority which is so obvious in this stage of Childs' writing. Anyone who lived through the period of Barthian ascendancy will recognize this. Barthianism was said to be built upon good theological principles like faith and revelation: so in theory at least. In practice it was different. Barth's own position was worked out in large measure through a deep study of the history of ideas, particularly of theology.

In this sense its basis was historical. It is to the credit of the Barthian movement that it stimulated intense study of the older doctrinal traditions and made them potentially meaningful for modern times. But there was a negative side to this. Barthians had an answer to everything.[12] Their (supposed) knowledge of the history of ideas was a weapon continually used in controversy. Barth disdained apologetics, but in practice a Barthian apologetic grew up. Its unspoken principle was: Barthianism is right because Barthians know more than other people and have superior intelligence. Childs' enormous industry in the history of exegesis and theology, coupled with his contemptuous assessment of the minds of contemporary scholars, reproduces this situation exactly.

It would also fit with Childs' oft-repeated claim to speak for 'the church'. Often, when Barth had formed some quite novel and quite individual hypothesis, he went on to declare that it was the teaching of 'the church'.[13] The church was essential to his theology, but on the whole there was little *input* from the church. Childs emphasizes that the church is the *context* for interpretation, and this may be entirely right; but he wants all the interpretation to come *from* the canonical approach *to* the church, not much to come *from* the church (as it is) to the canonical approach. He condemns without hesitation utterances of what the church actually thinks, as in the case of the Presbyterian Confession of 1967 (527ff.). There is no reason to suppose that Childs is any closer to the life and needs of the church than any other average biblical scholar. Childs' 'church' is not the actual church in which we live: it is a fictitious body of people who are crying out for more Barthianism and more canonical criticism. It is a projection of his own theology, an instrument for intellectual persuasion. As I wrote before, biblical scholars do not need to be instructed about the church by the canonical approach.[14]

### 3. Childs differing from Barth

But there are also several ways in which Childs' interpretation of Barth is simply wrong, or, putting the same thing in another way, places where he goes seriously against the intentions and principles of Barth.

First, Childs' work is in fact an overwhelmingly *conservative* interpretation of Barth, in which the many progressive, liberal, socially-minded and theologically critical aspects of that great theologian are systematically filtered out.[15] It is most unlikely that Barth would have sympathized with Childs' almost unqualified opposition to almost any sort of social work on the part of the church, his deep lack of sympathy with feminism, or indeed his increasingly severe hostility to historical work upon the Bible. In all this Childs comes closer to the conservative Barthian tradition which has been powerful in certain circles in the

Anglo-Saxon world. Like these circles, he seems to see the essence of Barth's work, as a matter of theological history, in its rejection of *liberalism*. We noted how right back in *Biblical Theology in Crisis* Childs had come to the conclusion that 'biblical theology was still liberal in method'. This could mean either of two things: that method in biblical theology could not be other than liberal, so that biblical theology should be accepted as part of the liberal heritage; or that a method had to be found that would expunge the traces of liberalism from biblical theology. The latter seems to be closer to Childs' mind. When the word 'liberal' occurs in his writing the reader knows that this is something very bad – as in his judgment on Hanson's work cited above.[16] He is looking for an approach in which every tiniest vestige of 'liberalism' is removed.

Yet in this very respect, if Childs hopes through his canonical approach to strengthen the cause of Barthian theology, he may well be wasting his time. If he hopes to establish his conservative, anti-critical, version of Barth as a powerful theological movement, he is likely to be disappointed. Among the many enthusiasts for the canonical approach that one meets, only very few if any know or care anything about Karl Barth, and in so far as they do know about him they think he was largely wrong. They are interested in the canonical approach not because of the true lines of Barth's thought, of which they will mostly never know anything, but for the sake of an apparently anti-historical approach to the Bible, which is what they want and will gain from Childs' work.

Childs frequently contrasts the extremes of the theological left and right (e.g., 'The threat of domesticating[17] the Word is equally present on both the right and the left of the spectrum', *OTTCC*, 6), and this again is a familiar Barthian pose. He pictures himself as occupying the middle ground, as walking the narrow tightrope between the abysses of conservatism on one side and liberalism on the other. This, however, is self-deception: though some effort is made to keep a distance from *extreme* conservativism, the balance of the two Theologies falls entirely on the conservative side, while anything that seems to be 'liberal', with few exceptions, is totally repudiated. In any case, it is all an illusion: probably all theologians, whatever their views may be, have the same sense of occupying the middle ground. In this Childs is just the same as the rest of us.

And it is not only theologically conservative but socially conservative too. Here he parts company with Barth and stands on the opposite side. Of liberation theology he admits rather grudgingly that 'a powerful biblical note has often been sounded' (560) and he notes the Barthian influence in the matter. But he is obviously upset by Kraus' interest in it and returns to it several times (24f., 521f., 646ff.). He tells us that Kraus' work is 'dominated by a form of Liberation Theology which seems to flatten everything in its path and to level the whole of the Bible to one refrain'. His stance is 'ideological' and the excessive use of the terminology of freedom and liberation is 'oppressive' (649). Well, maybe so; but of course liberation theologians, as Childs must surely know (though he shows no sign of it), will be quick to say that Childs himself would do better to be sparing with accusations of ideological bias, since he himself is a glaring example of it. This aspect will have to be considered later.

We see it particularly in the section on reconciliation. Childs is quarrelling with a recent Presbyterian document. As against the emphasis of the document on reconciliation between humans, he writes, citing Calvin: 'The ministry of reconciliation does not consist in any human extension of Christ's reconciliation but [Calvin says] "the application consists entirely of the preaching of the Gospel"' (528). 'God's reconciliation is different in kind from human . . . The ministry of reconciliation committed to the church is quite clearly to proclaim the good news of what *Christ* has done.' The Christian is called to serve his neighbour, but this has nothing to do with reconciliation, which comes purely from God to man and cannot be extended into a human service of reconciliation. Surely this is a straight theological endorsement of social conservatism, which Barth, I think, would have condemned. Note also how on this question Childs departs from *biblical* theology. His appeal is to Calvin; but, even if he is right about Calvin, was Calvin right about the Bible at this point? On this sort of question he could easily have been wrong, influenced perhaps by his anti-Catholicism. Quotations of Calvin cannot be decisive for biblical theology.

On the matter of feminism, conservative tendencies are again dominant. (Here for the moment we leave Barth, but it follows what I have just been saying.) Childs in his nostalgia for the Reformation cries: 'Would that God would raise up in the new generation of the church's scholars a Ms Calvin or a Martina Luther!' (24). Unfortunately, it seems that this is what God has already done. Though not known as a feminist, and partly agreeing with some of Childs' strictures against 'inclusive language' and the like,[18] I found that his arguments against feminist positions, on the ground that they imply modalism in place of sound trinitarian doctrine (377f.), only had the effect of making me feel more favourable to the feminist view. No feminist will find this argument other than laughable. He wants serious reflection on this 'pressing challenge' (483), but seems to have no idea how to set about it (cf., however, *OTTCC*, 188–92). Above all, I suspect, he wants feminism to 'break out of its initial identification with liberal Protestant theology' (24). Maybe this is right, and I do not dispute that it might be better so; but in the context of Childs' theology it only strengthens the impression that at every point he stands for conservatism on social issues. Barth, by contrast, might have been much more easy-going about feminism, in spite of the absurd hatred that some feminists have thought it right to pour upon him.

Related to this is Childs' absolute insistence that the 'God of the Bible is without sex' (374, cf. *OTTCC*, 39f.). 'How do we know that God is not masculine?

We know it from the very Bible which speaks of God as "he"' (377). Childs' attempts at a linguistic proof of this seem to me to be valueless. To me it seems obvious that the Old Testament, with some qualification in some few segments, represented God as male; later in the tradition it may have been different. The change of perceptions involved in this is one of the most important aspects of biblical religion and theology. The fact of this change is entirely obliterated by Childs' argument, which makes the later, demythologized, position standard for the Bible as a whole.

A further difference from Barth lies in the position accorded to historical criticism. One of the main reasons for the (partial) success of dialectical theology in its various forms lay in its ability to return to a Reformation type of theology while leaving room for the acceptance of historical criticism and thus avoiding a merely conservative return to older orthodoxy. Many Barthian exegeses thus rested upon accepted critical positions. For instance, Barth took it as obvious that Genesis 1 was a different story from Genesis 2–3, and formed his exposition of the creation theme accordingly. Again, his rejection of natural theology was facilitated by the widely accepted view that the 'Paul' of the Areopagus speech in Acts 17 was not Paul at all, so that Acts 17 was disjoined from Rom. 1–2, reducing the indications of natural theology in the latter. Most important of all, Barth's desire to avoid 'the annulling of the results of biblical scholarship in the last centuries' is not only his opinion, but a foundational element in his great achievement, his threefold structure of the Word of God.[19]

Certainly Barth was at times irritated by historical criticism – more correctly, irritated by the attitudes of critics, rather than by the principle of historical criticism – but he by no means rejected it as a serious hindrance to theology. Indeed, the insights achieved by it formed a basic element in his own theology of revelation.[20] To him it did not matter enough to be counted as a serious enemy. To Childs, on the other hand, it does matter a lot and it does count as a serious enemy. Although from the beginning of the canonical approach his position was that criticism was legitimate in certain contexts but for most theological purposes irrelevant, his hostility to it has obviously grown more bitter since that time. His efforts to say that he integrates it usefully with his theological work (e.g. 416, 722) do not alter the general impression made, namely that *any* intrusion of a critical historical perspective is destructive to any attempt at biblical theology.[21] Childs does assert (ibid., 722) that his use of historical-critical methods is quite in accord with his general theological theory, and thus seeks to turn aside criticisms for inconsistency in this respect. But it is hard to doubt that real inconsistency, or repeated change of mind, is present here and that Childs is both often dependent in his exegesis on the very methods which he most condemns, and often condemnatory in the comments he makes on an approach which he says he allows. The explanation for this lies in his philosophical weakness and refusal of reasoned argument, to which I have already referred.

More important is the matter of the canon itself. As I pointed out,[22] the whole emphasis on the canon as a guide to interpretation is rather foreign to Barth [I could have added: rather foreign to Calvin, too].[23] How did he get through all these thousands of pages, including masses of exegetical discussion, with hardly any mention of the canon? Already Stendahl in his famous article had mentioned that Barth laid little emphasis on canon but much on inspiration. I would think it more correct to say: little on canon but much on revelation, for I do not see that inspiration was so central in Barth. Anyway, the fact remains that Barth, unlike Childs, got through hundreds of pages without feeling any need for the word 'canon'. Thus in spite of his own constant invocation of Barth, Childs is taking a line which in this respect is entirely innovative in relation to Barth. In reply to this criticism of mine he writes:

> Although it is true that Barth makes infrequent mention of the function of canon in his *Church Dogmatics* largely in reaction to its traditional Catholic misuse, nevertheless an appeal to a correct theological role of canon is actually very compatible to [sic] his theology.

But this is again a mere assertion with no explanation and no argument. I have no idea what he means by 'its traditional Catholic misuse' and know of no evidence that any such misuse would have caused Barth not to mention the canon. It certainly did not stop Childs mentioning it. In any case, it may be that Childs' emphasis on the canon is *compatible* with a Barthian theology, but of course only at the price of changing its balance and nature very substantially. The same is the case, as we have seen, with the idea of biblical theology itself. At the least we may say: since Childs in spite of his complete Barthian loyalty has made substantial changes of balance as against Barth himself in both these regards, he might show more tolerance for others who, equally influenced by Barth, have moved in other directions which may be also 'compatible'.

## 4. Biblical theology and doctrinal theology

We have not yet, however, come to the major assessment of Childs' work. In essence, what he has written is not a biblical theology: it is a dogmatic theology with biblical proofs, or more correctly, it is a personal religious confession accompanied by claims that alternative religious positions are to be rejected. In essence, the work does not belong to *biblical* theology at all.

Naturally, the boundary lines between dogmatic (in my terms, doctrinal) and biblical theology are not easily drawn. Childs seems to approve the position argued by Avery Dulles: 'biblical and systematic elements are inextricably inter-twined' (*Biblical Theology*, 8), and that is a quite convincing position, as far as it goes. They are certainly intertwined in Childs' own work. But, even if they are necessarily intertwined, can they not be distinguished, so that one would say: at this point my argument lies on the plane of biblical theology, at this point it lies on that of systematic theology?[24] With Childs one must say that such distinc-tions are seldom, if ever, made. Systematic considerations are used to block out biblical evidence, and biblical evidence is used to limit or delimit systematic possibilities. It is seldom or never made clear which of these is happening. The ultimate result is that the work is a mishmash of biblical and systematic claims. It is not a biblical theology: at some points the Bible falls into the background, as we saw in the case of the Presbyterian document on reconciliation.

In addition, this is the most important of the aspects in which Childs departs from Barth. That Barth did much to stimulate the rise of modern biblical theology is beyond doubt. But the practitioners of that discipline, perhaps just because they were themselves mainly biblical scholars, often failed to realize that Barth was not with them in the lines that they drew out from his stimulus. Childs is a powerful example of this. He likes to depict Barth as 'doing biblical theology' and he seems to have no inkling of the possibility that Barth would not particularly support his own programme. In this he shows that he does not know Barth so very well after all.

Childs wants biblical scholarship and doctrinal theology to come closer to one another. The value of this is diminished, however, by the fact that, like most other modern biblical theologians, he does little or nothing to define what doctrinal (dogmatic) theology is and how it differs from biblical theology as he understands it. He offers the feeble and platitudinous advice that doctrinal theologians should do more work on the Bible and biblical scholars should pay more attention to doctrinal questions (89). He finds it deplorable that some doctrinal theologians write as if they could work apart from the Bible. He thinks that biblical theology should 'function as a bridging discipline to dogmatic theology' (19, 592, 721). One gains the impression that doctrinal theology is the same thing as biblical theology but for being expressed in longer and more mod-ern or more mysterious words.

This is in fact a considerable misreading of Barth. I have already shown in a preliminary way that Barth, like his contemporary Brunner, had a sceptical atti-tude towards the twentieth-century 'revival' of biblical theology and in no sense felt indebted to it or dependent on it. Barth had no theory of biblical theology, and scarcely ever mentions the term in the long pages of his *Dogmatics*. For Barth himself there were two entities: theology (which could only be dogmatic theology) and exegesis (which was also really dogmatic). There was no place or need for a 'biblical theology' which lay between the two and which formed a necessary intermediate discipline or bridge.

In particular, one of the main purposes of biblical theology as conceived by most modern biblical theologians, the 'holistic' vision of bringing the entirety of the Bible together into a unity, was something that Barth not only did not need but actually forbade. Thus, as we have seen (above, 244), Barth wrote:

> Therefore a biblical theology can never consist in more than a series of attempted approximations, a collection of individual exegeses . . . Biblical theology (and self-evidently dogmatics too) *cannot consist in an attempt to introduce the totality of the biblical witness* . . . (my italics).[25]

This admonition is a serious blow to the holistic aspirations of many styles of biblical theology and of canonical criticism in particular.

When Childs talks of Barth, or likewise of Luther and Calvin, as 'doing biblical theology' (e.g. 589, etc.), he is reading his own concepts into their minds. As Stendahl rightly argued,[26] for Augustine and Luther, as for Calvin and for all classical theology, there was no such thing as 'biblical theology'; there was only 'theology', and Barth stood rightly in that tradition in all that he did.

Secondly, and again in biblicistic style, Childs tries to make theology totally dependent on the Bible in a way that results in something quite different from Barth. He chides theologians for not working from the Bible and, quite wrongly, deems it 'an assumption of the Enlightenment' that 'the theological enterprise has other avenues to truth than the Bible' (370) – in fact such a view, including a major place for natural theology, was normal to classical theology long before the Enlightenment. By insisting that theology has *nothing* to work on other than the Bible he assumes a markedly biblicistic pose which is quite other than that of Barth himself.[27] I repeat a crucial passage, already quoted in Ch. 15:

> Because *dogmatics is not itself directly concerned with the biblical text* [my italics] but with the word of church proclamation founded upon its testimony, it must not be expected and ought not to try to achieve what is really the business of a biblical theology of the Old and New Testaments.[28]

Thus, in so far as Barth draws any line of difference between doctrinal and biblical theology, it is in the terms that the former is *not* directly concerned with the biblical text, while the latter is. This is in agreement with the position taken by me in this book, as also in previous writings.[29]

That Childs is confused about this can be shown from one striking illustration (*Biblical Theology*, 588f.). Barth had 'argued that the sequence relating to Adam and Christ should actually be reversed to that of Christ and Adam because Christ is the measure of true humanity', etc. Bultmann opposed this: Adam was first, Christ came after. 'The great strength of Bultmann's interpretation,' Childs writes, 'lies in his close attention to the literary structure of Paul's argument.' Yet, 'it is a question whether Bultmann really understood what Barth was doing exegetically'. Barth, according to Childs, is seeking 'to pursue Paul's witness beyond the text itself to reflect theologically on the substance (*res*) which called forth the witness'. This is clearly inconsistent, for the alleged 'substance' is the direct opposite of the 'witness'. But that is not the main point. The main point is Childs' next sentence: 'in a word, Barth's exegesis is an exercise in biblical theology'. Obviously the reverse is the truth. It is Bultmann whose approach represented biblical theology. Barth's approach is not unarguable, but is arguable only on the grounds that it represents valid and possible *dogmatic* theology. This fits in with what I have said elsewhere: there is no doubt about Bultmann's status as a biblical theologian, just as there is none about Barth's status as a dogmatician.

That Childs' theology is dogmatic rather than biblical is shown by two of its main intellectual pillars. The first is the idea of 'witness', seen just above. This is repeated endlessly, starting on p. 9: 'The role of the Bible is not being understood simply as a cultural expression of ancient peoples' (who interested in biblical theology ever supposed that it was *simply* that?) 'but as a testimony pointing beyond itself to a divine reality to which it bears witness.' Certainly. Whoever in theology supposed otherwise? But as a methodological statement this definitely belongs in the dogmatic realm. Either we know the divine reality from the words of the text, in which case exegesis tells us what it is saying about that reality, and the bit about 'pointing beyond itself' has no significance; or else the divine reality is something that is hypothesized and then identified as the object to which the text 'points'. This latter is the doctrinal approach (or, at least, one doctrinal approach). The dogmatic theologian forms a hypothesis of the 'divine reality' – Barth's whole theology is a gigantic hypothesis of this kind – and then indicates the ways in which individual textual items fit in with, indicate or 'witness to' the various elements of this hypothesis. As used by Childs, the 'witness' terminology belongs to the dogmatic realm. In his work no passage of scripture, whatever it says, ever 'witnesses' to anything other than what Childs already believes.[30] Thus no passage is ever found to 'witness' to natural theology, although several passages make express statements which – at the very least – might be so interpreted. Why do they not so 'witness'? Because as a good Barthian Childs does not believe in natural theology. The 'witnessing' approach, applied in this way, is an obvious mode in which the biblical evidence is fitted into the mould of the scholar's personal convictions.

More evidence that Childs' work is really dogmatic in character is his use of the category of heresy. In systematic theology it is traditional, and may perhaps be justified, to judge opinions as 'Pelagian', 'Sabellian' or the like. But in biblical theology such judgments are not appropriate.[31] The use of them implies the supposition that biblical theology must be orthodox by traditional systematic categories, and no doubt it is true that some biblical theology has worked with such a supposition. But the true situation is the reverse: anyone working with the idea of a 'biblical' theology has to accept the likelihood that by traditional systematic categories elements of biblical theology will be unorthodox or even heretical. 'Heretical' opinions should be welcomed: they are signs of the fact that biblical theology is different from doctrinal theology. Thus Stendahl rightly pointed to the fact that 'adoptionist' positions have a place in the christology of the Bible alongside more 'orthodox' ones.[32] Seen in this way, Childs' approach at a number of points negates biblical theology.

Equally central is Childs' difficulty with the idea of referentiality (a term introduced into biblical theology, so far as I know, largely by me). On the one hand he is against any historical referentiality: it is wrong, given a 'historical' narrative, to seek to know what 'really happened',[33] what the actual referent was; this is one of the basic errors of historical criticism. This anti-referential position can make sense and has the advantage of being related to much that is thought in the modern literary approaches to the Bible. Attacks on referentiality go down well in the modern world. But on the other hand Childs' entire 'witness' theory goes in the opposite direction: it is entirely referential. In order to understand, you have to know the *objects referred to*, the divine realities to which the text refers. He insists on this again and again. Thus Childs is stuck with two theories, a non-referential one for historical matters and a strongly referential one for theological matters. Failing to reconcile these obviously contradictory stances, or, more correctly, not even trying, he uses one or the other *ad hoc* for various problems as they come up. For, to take the most obvious difficulty, some of the most 'theological' statements of the Bible are its most 'historical' statements, as the whole tradition of biblical theology was emphasizing not long ago. So to oppose historical referentiality can cause deep theological problems. Left in that way, it could lead to a biblical story which is a total myth or fiction, relating 'events' none of which ever happened. As I wrote some time ago, there is no doubt that Jesus 'canonically' rose from the dead; the important question is whether he rose in any sense external to the text that tells the story. And Childs probably agrees with this; so in *OTTCC*,148, he produces a modification of his theory. Though he has been 'highly critical of a historical referential reading', the 'reverse construal' of a completely non-historical reading is just as unsatisfactory. 'The canon makes its theological witness in numerous ways in relation to historical referentiality.' Sometimes there is only a very loose connection, at others 'a genuinely historical component belongs to the heart of the witness'. So what was the point of the attack on historical referentiality? And: how do we know when the canon, among its 'numerous ways', is 'witnessing' to a historical referent and when it is not?

## 5. *The relation of three theologies*

As we have seen, the main elements of Childs' *Biblical Theology of the Old and New Testaments* are three great sections: the 'discrete witness' of the Old Testament, the 'discrete witness' of the New, and 'Theological Reflection on the Christian Bible'. How was this arrangement arrived at and what is its purpose?

We may perhaps start at p. 77, where we hear that 'emphasis has fallen on the unity of the one composition consisting of two separate testaments. The two testaments have been linked as Old and New, but this designation does not mean that the integrity of each testament has been destroyed.' We should note this word 'integrity', which occurs often in Childs' writing and yet is nowhere, so far as I have seen, explained or defined. What he means, I think, is that each section (here, each testament) performs its own function in its own terms, which then contributes to the totality, but without being modified in order to fit into the totality. Thus we go on to read:

> The significance of emphasizing the continuing canonical integrity of the Old Testament lies in resisting the Christian temptation to identify biblical theology with the New Testament's interpretation of the Old, as if the Old Testament's witness were limited to how it was once heard and appropriated by the early church (77).

And here he goes on to argue against others, like Gese and Stuhlmacher, who (according to him) see the witness of the Old Testament as 'limited to its effect on subsequent writers'. Where this is so, he says, 'the Old Testament has thus lost its vertical, existential dimension which as scripture of the church continues to bear its own witness within the context of the Christian Bible'.

Thus 'both testaments make a discrete witness to Jesus Christ which must be heard, both separately and in concert' (78). And so, after further elaboration, biblical theology has the task of reflecting on the whole Christian Bible 'with its two very different voices, both of which the church confesses bear witness to Jesus Christ'.

Now we have already seen that this theory of witness, which in Childs' *Biblical Theology* has become much more important than the much-advertised canon, is confused and contradictory. Not that Childs is without justification in saying that the Old Testament is thought within Christianity, rightly or wrongly, somehow to bear witness to Jesus Christ; but it can do so only by completely breaching the rules of Childs' theory, for such a belief is (allegedly) *res* without any *verbum*: it can be proposed, but only as belief without textual foundation, as dogmatic hypothesis and not as scriptural reality. This may sound harsh, but is fully supported by Childs' own work: in the 110 pages

(97–207) of the 'discrete witness of the Old Testament', Jesus Christ appears nowhere to be mentioned. Childs seems not to believe his own theory.

Moreover, when we come to Childs' section on the New Testament the atmosphere is very different. The emphasis on 'growth' and 'trajectories' is manifestly greater. 'Tracing growth' or similar terms (e.g. 'describing the formation', 225) appear again and again (222, 224, 263f. etc.), and 'trajectories' are everywhere (notably 216f., 262ff.). Throughout the main central part of section 4, 'The Discrete Witness of the New Testament', rather little is heard of the canon or the final form: often one can read twenty pages and think 'Surely he's forgotten all about the canon'. Much more is heard about the *original* form of the witness and the various stages through which it passed. It looks as if an apology to historical criticism and a farewell to canonical criticism would both be appropriate. Such a judgment, however, would be a hasty one.

The first sentence of the New Testament section tells us that 'our major concern will be to describe briefly the main lines of the growth of the New Testament's witness to Jesus Christ' (211). Describe! Growth! And trajectories! 'The approach is that of tracing traditio-historical trajectories *from within the tradition*' (my italics) by contrast to 'a history-of-religions perspective which strives for an allegedly objective description of religious phenomena'. The essential point is 'within the tradition'. What this seems to mean is: you can go back within the tradition and discover and enjoy its earlier stages and its developments, so long as at every stage you are accepting towards the tradition and, in particular, do not see it or explain it in any way other than the way in which the tradition sees itself. In particular, you must understand it at all points as 'kerygmatic' and 'theological' and not see it or explain it at any point as a product of a history-of-religion development or as a result of sociological or political or other non-religious forces.

This question is elucidated in a discussion mainly with Käsemann over the question of the historical Jesus (212–16). Käsemann is respected by Childs for his theological seriousness (262) and for his recognition of the 'kerygmatic' character of the New Testament.[34] But he wanted, in Childs' words, 'a rigorous historical-critical analysis of the kerygma in order to "discern between the spirits" and to establish the authentic kerygma apart from its many distortions and harmonizations'. This is condemned by Childs, because Käsemann 'transported to the study of the kerygma the same critical tools which function in the realm of *Religionsgeschichte*, evaluating the truth of the gospels from the perspective of historical probability, logical consistency, and cultural relativity'. Thus 'it is one thing to trace the different levels of witness within the New Testament. It is quite another to reconstruct historical levels apart from the world of faith on the basis of general rules of human rationality or cultural development.'

It is not surprising that Käsemann is one of the scholars with whom Childs engages in a running battle, coming to the surface repeatedly whether over the same or different matters (cf. 247, 262, 309, 485, 496ff., 510, 610). At this point the conflict is because Käsemann thought that the tradition of Jesus had been maintained 'in a shattered form,[35] distorted by its reception, and misunderstood as much as understood' (Childs, 214). It is 'a mixture of true and false witness to the gospel' (215). He is 'therefore committed to recovering the genuine gospel . . . by means of a *Sachkritik*'. To Childs it is illegitimate to attempt this. But why? He does not take the position that scripture is totally perfect: 'all scripture suffers from human frailty; there is no untainted position'. He adds the cheap and silly remark, ascribed to Barth, about being 'more critical than the critics'. What Childs really seems to mean is that you can penetrate back into various stages of the tradition, but not in such a way as might discover that the tradition had at an earlier stage been, theologically, substantially different.

Childs' handling of Käsemann seems to me to be unfair and intemperate. On the one hand Childs has no proposal for *methods* that will discover earlier stages of the tradition other than the methods that Käsemann or anyone else will use. There *are* no methods for discovering the history of tradition that are fundamentally different from those used in the history of religion: or, if there are, Childs has not explained what they are. He offers no criteria for the differentiation between what is historical and what is not, and in this sense his 'history of tradition' is not a history at all.[36] On the other hand he seems to think that, because it is agreed that scripture is 'kerygmatic', the nature of the kerygma must be (at all previous stages) what it is in the final New Testament text, and also that it must be, at all stages, what he, Childs, believes it to be, because he personally thinks that it is kerygmatic. Käsemann's argument is that the exact form of the original kerygma is unknown and has to be discovered. Childs will allow it to be discovered, so long as it is in essence the same as what the final form of the text has thought it to be all along.

We see, therefore, that Childs' return towards the historical and the dia-chronic is only apparent. He seems to want 'historical' trajectories but is ready to deny the validity of historical evidence about what they may contain. Thus some of the 'trajectories' seem not to be *historical* trajectories at all: they are logical or pseudo-logical derivational statements. Though dressed up as if they were diachronic, they are really hypothetical logical connections within the writer's own theology. Thus an utterance such as that 'the doctrine of justification by faith is a derivative of Paul's christology' (245) is not a diachronic statement but a (logical/theological) hypothesis stated as if it was a fact.[37]

Equally important in this section is the relation between the two 'discrete witnesses'. That Childs should want to state the separate witness of the Old and of the New seems to me not unreasonable in itself. He is here touching on the question, which we have already partially discussed above, whether the Old Testament just as it is, and in complete form, operates as scripture in Christianity, and he wants to answer 'yes'. This, with reservations, is also my opinion. But there is more to it than that. As he himself so often says, the issue is deeper and much more complex. He wants to be sure of rejecting all those opinions according to which the Old Testament is authoritative, for Christianity, only as it was received within the New (Hübner), or only where it fitted in with specific Christian needs (Dunn), or only in a mode where the Old is actually criticized by the New (so Vriezen, cf. above), so that it is authoritative only with modifications resulting from such criticism. I think, partly with Childs, that the Old Testament as a whole is authoritative within Christianity (though one must add that authority is relative to the possible modes of interpretation, which will make a difference). But I think that these contrary opinions, which he wants to avoid, are far more convincing for the New Testament situation itself, and that by presenting the Old Testament as a 'discrete' witness Childs enables himself to evade this probability.

For what he fails to do is to present the theology of the Old Testament *as it must have seemed to a person of the first century*. What he presents is a theology of the Old Testament as an educated canonical critic of modern times may see it. But, even if this is the theology of the Old Testament taken as a whole, that does not mean that it is the theology as the canonizers may have seen it. Still less is it the theology as the New Testament people may have seen it. That theology was vastly different from that which a modern canonical critic may deduce from the canon of the Old Testament. Things that may be central to such a critic may have been peripheral at that time, and vice versa. Childs gives us a good example with *monotheism*. The term 'monotheism', he tells us, is 'theologically inert and fails largely to register the basic features of God's self-revelation to Israel' (355, cf. 360). That, however, is only an expression of his own present-day theology. In the first century, I would think it likely that monotheism was far more important than all the salvation history, kerygma and canonicity which are so much emphasized in this volume, and that natural theology also had a much more creative role, compared with total negativity towards it on Childs' part. Thus the 'trajectories' pass through a vacuum and register nothing of what may have been central for the actual transition between the Testaments.

Another uncertain area lies in the 'newness' of the New Testament. Its 'discrete' character means that it is not just an appendix to the Old, or a midrash on it, or 'simply the last chapter of a story' (211). Nor did the Old Testament 'flow by inexorable laws' into the New – as if anyone ever supposed that it did (Childs thinks of this as an example of 'merely historical categories'). Positively, 'the decisive feature of the New Testament is the element of newness over against the past' (212). Yet 'this new revelation of God's will has been made consistently and immediately in terms of its relation to God's prior commitment to Israel'. This 'astonishing' fact, he goes on, constitutes 'the rationale for the theological enterprise of a Biblical Theology of the two Testaments' (212). I do not see anything astonishing about it.

Anyway, the dependence of the New Testament upon references back to the Old is thus an essential element in Childs' argument. 'It is a basic characteristic of the four gospels, not only to regard the earthly Jesus from the perspective of Easter, but also to describe every phase of Christ's ministry through the lens of scripture' (264). *Every* phase? Can this really be proved (cf. also 78f.)? Again, 'the most striking feature of the New Testament is that it bears its witness to the radically new in terms of the old' (93).

But these strong claims are soon counter-balanced. Thus: 'There is an equal need to investigate those cases in which the New Testament made no use of the Old Testament, but stood at a great distance from its tradition history. There will be times in which the New Testament's use of the Old Testament is highly selective, or one in which a single component is employed as a critical norm against other major streams of tradition. Only after this descriptive (sic!) task has been done will it be possible to turn to the larger task of trying to engage in theological reflection . . .' (94).[38]

In principle Childs is quite right in this. But the principle is not carried out in his execution of his project. This last passage, early in the book, certainly leaves room for consideration of the material in which the New Testament ignores the Old, or uses it selectively, or uses part of it as a critical norm as against another. But this theme, though certainly present in Childs' book, seems to me to be drowned out by the opposite impulse, namely the desire to show that the New Testament has regularly, indeed almost always, expressed its message through reference to the categories of the Old. Thus of Acts (290ff.) he begins by telling us that 'for Luke the content of the Christian message is largely defined in terms of the Jewish scriptures'. But then what about the Areopagus speech, which has no quotation from the Old Testament but contains one from a Greek poet, and to which Childs makes no reference at all? In a paragraph about the Prologue to John (367f.) there is stress on the 'Old Testament images' in the passage, but no mention of the possible Greek background of λόγος. There seems to be no reckoning with those substantial Pauline passages which offer a sort of mainly philosophical argument in which Old Testament references are rather marginal, like the very central I Cor. 15.

To sum up, anxious on the one hand to avoid the suggestion that the Old Testament works for Christianity only as transmitted and interpreted by the New, and on the other to emphasize the use of Old Testament categories by the New, Childs fails to give any proper account of what the New Testament is like in these respects. He does not give anything like a serious picture either of how the Old Testament was seen by the New Testament people or of how the New Testament people expressed these 'new' elements, the existence of which he himself admits. The connection between Old and New Testaments in his presentation turns out to be (*a*) basically purely dogmatic and (*b*) empty of convincing detail. The idea that the two 'discrete witnesses' are to the same thing is purely dogmatic and has no textual evidence, nor does he offer any; the strategy of offering two 'discrete' sections only ensures the emptiness of any living connection.

### 6. *Abandonment of the canonical approach?*

I have argued that Childs' *Biblical Theology* is not really a biblical theology at all. While including elements that are something like biblical theology, it is basically a personal dogmatic theology with biblical proofs. But we now go on to see that it not only is not a *biblical* theology, it is not a *canonical* theology either. We have seen already that Childs – surely to the surprise of most of his readers – made no attempt to fashion the ordering and organization of his books on a canonical basis and simply listed topics on a loose, thematic, traditional common-sense basis. We have also seen that his mode of relating the three theological surveys which form the main part of the book is not canonical either. In fact, both the volumes on theology contain various methodological sections which are fairly strongly canonical, and numerous occasional outbursts which are canonical and concentrate on condemning any other methods; but the main body of their presentation is not distinctively canonical at all.

Thus when we start section 3 of the *Biblical Theology* we read in the first sentence that the task is that of 'tracing the growth of the Old Testament traditions as a theological witness' (97). *Growth?* What has this to do with the canon? Surely it is the opposite of what we have learned to expect from a canonical approach? For the whole tenor of the canonical arguments has been that one has to deal with the final text as it stands, and not spend time on considering how it got there, which is a matter of 'reconstruction' and speculation. On reading this, canonical enthusiasts are stopped in their tracks, astounded that the approach from which they expected so much has looked back towards the burning Sodom of historical criticism. And this mention of 'growth' is not an isolated phrase. Only a few lines later we hear that a goal of the analysis is 'to establish the *initial* setting of a witness within the *history* of Israel' (my italics); but an interest in the initial or original or pristine has been repeatedly attacked by Childs in the earlier pages of his approach. And so Childs goes on (99), in introducing his 'new approach', to say that it is 'largely irrelevant' whether one calls it 'canonical', 'kerygmatic', or 'post-critical'. Thus Childs has in effect admitted what I have said: he is commencing a line of thought which is *not* distinctively 'canonical' after all. He is pulling down, it seems, much of the structure he has built up.

In this latest book Childs seems to make a distinct effort to create some room for the historical or, as he often calls it, the 'diachronic'. He wants to defend himself against criticisms made on the ground that the canonical approach 'has no use for the diachronic dimension and is basically a static handling of the biblical text' (104, referring to opinions of Brueggemann, Hanson, B. W. Anderson).[39] 'Nothing is farther from the truth,' he replies indignantly, goaded perhaps by the term *static*, notoriously a bad word in biblical theology. On the contrary, he says, the diachronic element is positively important. 'It seems obvious that this final form can be much better understood, especially in its crucial theological role as witness, if one studies carefully those hundreds of decisions which shaped the whole. Thus it greatly sharpens one's vision of the final form of the Pentateuch which is the goal of exegesis if one first distinguishes between earlier and later levels within the witness . . .' It is good, 2. 'if the various stages in the growth of Israel's witness can be historically correlated . . .'. 3. 'It is theologically significant to see to what extent early stages of the tradition became normative for particular groups . . .' 4. 'Biblical texts from different ages, even when given a subsequent normative canonical form, continue to reflect a quality of their original life' (216–17).

These remarks, if really meant, are a straight acceptance that everything that has been said in favour of traditional historical criticism is true. But can one accept that Childs really means what he says at this point? How can it be reconciled with the facts of his own books, with their endless wearisome polemics against historical study of the Bible? How can it be reconciled with his own article, published after the *Biblical Theology*, which goes systematically through a series of major Old Testament theologians and argues that they all went wrong for one reason, namely that they thought they had to take account of historical criticism?[40] The key sentence reads as follows:

> The painful lesson which has emerged in the last fifty years is that the many serious attempts at a theological compromise which would build a confessional Old Testament theology directly on the foundation of historical critical methodology (Weiser, Eichrodt, von Rad, Zimmerli) have also failed, at least when measured by the theological call of the 30s.[41]

Later on, in the first chapter of the main New Testament section, we hear again of 'the proper function of the diachronic',[42] and now there are added further statements such as the following: 'In spite of the inadequacies of the use of the historical critical approach as an exegetical tool, I would strongly argue for the usefulness of recovering a depth dimension within the kerygma which does not fall victim to the persistent pitfalls of critical scholarship since the Enlightenment' (216). 'The recovery of the historical dimension within the kerygma can aid in correlating the witness to the concrete life of the early church,' and similarly it 'helps the interpreter understand the range of kerygmatic diversity as well as establishing the nature of its unity' (217). This leads on to a positive section on 'historical trajectories' (262ff.) within the Gospels. Asking the 'difficult question' 'what is the need or legitimacy of reconstructing historical trajectories within the four gospels? . . . Why try to recover a stage prior to the final form of the text when the text has already been described as kerygmatic, that is, as witness?' (262), he answers:

> Nevertheless, I would maintain that there are important exegetical advantages in recovering a historical trajectory within the gospels which need not fall into this hermeneutical trap outlined above [reference to Käsemann and his ideas]. It is certainly possible critically to trace the growth of levels of tradition within each gospel. Moreover, the recovery of this depth dimension within the canonical witness offers important insights toward understanding the final form of the text.

The 'trajectories' have already been briefly discussed. Those that appear in *Biblical Theology* seem to be of two kinds. Some are fairly innocent things, like the 'growth of levels of tradition within each gospel', which Childs thinks can be traced critically (263). Others, though dressed up as if they were diachronic, are really hypothetical logical connections within the writer's own theology. His objections against Käsemann in this regard, in so far as they have value, have the same destructive effect on Childs' own trajectories.

Nevertheless, Childs' turning towards the historical requires some further comment. One reason for it lies in the fact that he realizes he has other opponents than historical criticism to deal with.


*7. Modern 'literary' reading*


A clear example lies in his disappointment with the modern styles of interpretation on the basis of literature and language. He tells us that the 'move from history to language' (204) has not been a success. 'The new focus on language in biblical studies has already run into profound problems, indeed far more quickly than the historical paradigm which it sought to replace' (205). The emphasis on language can 'domesticate the Bible theologically just as quickly as the excessive stress on history did'. The danger of rendering the biblical text 'mute for theological reflection' has not been diminished.

Again, looking back to the time when he wrote his *Introduction to the Old*

*Testament as Scripture* (1979), Childs tells us that the major obstacle to serious theological reflection then seemed to him to be 'the diachronic legacy of nineteenth-century historical criticism. Consequently I greeted as an ally the growing twentieth-century appeal to narrative theology as at least a move toward recovering a holistic reading of the Bible' (722). Subsequent experience, however, has disproved this expectation. 'The threat lies in divorcing the Bible when seen as literature from its theological reality to which scripture bears witness. When the focus of the analysis lies in the "imaginative construal" of the reader, the text is robbed of all determinative meaning within various theories of reader response. The effect is to render the biblical text mute for theology and to deconstruct its tradition in a way equally destructive as the nineteenth-century historicists' (723).

This directs us to a series of paradoxes in the whole matter. The relation of the canonical approach to various kinds of modern literary appreciation has been excellently discussed in John Barton's widely appreciated book *Reading the Old Testament* (1984). Childs' canonical reading can be well appreciated in the context of structuralism, New Criticism and reader-response ideas. Thus some leading literary critics like Frank Kermode have warmly turned to Childs' support.[43] Kermode couples this with substantial criticism of my own critique of Childs. But, as Kermode possibly did not realize, this was getting things rather upside-down. Childs probably does not want this sort of support, and it is likely to be an embarrassment to him. For he wants to have his approach purely theologically based and must be aware that – from his own point of view – it is weakened through support from 'secular' trends of dubious theological affiliation. In fact I am more positively interested in the literary developments involved than Childs is, and contributed an article and part of a book on the subject back in 1973.[44] On the other hand, though I thought then, and still think, that these developments are positively significant for theology, I also thought and still think that, if applied alone, they will have serious limitations for theological appreciation.[45] I thus largely agree with Childs in his negative judgment of much that has come out of these trends.[46] And in particular, these trends are unlikely to be positive for the sort of theology that Childs represents. But why did Childs not see this long ago? It was obvious to anyone with a theological sense. Is his admission that he backed the wrong horse in this respect not an admission that his hostility to historical study has been so undiscriminating as to unbalance his theological judgment?

## 8. *Relations with earlier biblical theology*

A remarkable feature of Childs' presentation is his failure to converse with the past development of biblical theology itself. Considering the size of the two volumes when put together, it is astonishing how little note is taken of the Old Testament Theologies written by predecessors, such as Eichrodt, Vriezen, von Rad, Fohrer and Zimmerli. All these scholars are mentioned ('my unforgettable teachers', he writes of Eichrodt, von Rad and Zimmerli in the preface to *OTTCC)* and come in for some discussion, but for the most part there is no presentation at all of the way in which their theologies were conceived and organized. Their names do occur in the indexes, but, as already explained, many of the occurrences are references only to bibliographical lists and do not indicate that anything is said in the text about the scholar concerned. Once we subtract these, the actual references are remarkably few, and of them the great majority refer to other works by these scholars than their Theologies. Actual references in the *Biblical Theology* , leaving aside bibliographical lists, are: to Eichrodt 4, to Eissfeldt 2, to Fohrer none, to Vriezen 1, to Zimmerli 7. Only von Rad does better, with about 21. *OTTCC* has more index references for some people, but the situation is the same. In it Zimmerli has 25 references, but only 9 of these are to actual remarks in the text, and only 1 (108f.) to the principles and plan of his actual Theology. There are probably some more because of omissions from the index, but this gives one an idea. Though these scholars are referred to, there is practically no discussion of their general ideas, the principles on which their Theologies were organized or the nature of their presentation. From Childs' volumes one would not learn anything substantial about the variety of Old Testament Theologies that appeared in the modern period.

The reason for this is easily seen. Childs is convinced that biblical theology cannot be reinstated except by the canonical approach as advanced by him. Over against this he needs to categorize all other approaches as dominated by a historical approach or other faults. If this were to be a valid argument, he would need to show that all the earlier Old Testament theologies, e.g. those of Eichrodt, Jacob, Vriezen, von Rad, Zimmerli and others, were hopelessly deficient because of their acceptance of historical criticism, or whatever other error-inducing factor, probably the Enlightenment. Here and there he does of course criticize some of these works, and quite properly. But he does not make the criticism that is necessary to his general argument: in other words, he does not even try to show that they made a hopeless mess of the whole thing because they accepted some measure of historical criticism or otherwise neglected the canon. 'The field has run into a stalemate', he says, with some mixture of metaphors, *OTTCC* 5. By 1985, when *OTTCC* was published, this was far from being the case.

In this he is in a difficult dilemma. He is an enthusiast both for biblical theology and for his own canonical approach. The absolutism of the canonical approach is so great that it would logically lead to a condemnation of everything done in any other way. But, while willing to go to extremes in negativity towards historical approaches to the Bible, he cannot easily be so negative about the past tradition of biblical theology, which like himself has commonly been seeking to escape from the purely historical, even when admitting a historical element. He respects the older theologians like Eichrodt, Vriezen, von Rad and Zimmerli, but they may be an embarrassment to him. For, the better the work they have done, the farther they go towards proving that the canonical approach was not necessary after all. It is not surprising that he says little about them in his Theologies. In his later article of 1994, however, as we have seen (above, 423), he judges them to have 'failed' because they hoped to build upon a historical-critical foundation. I do not think, however, that they 'failed' any more than Childs himself has 'failed'. I do not consider that theologies 'fail' or 'succeed', nor do I think that they built upon a historical-critical foundation any more than he himself does. All of them, like him, sought to do something greatly different from what historical criticism had done and was doing; his own involvement in historical criticism, as we have seen, is, in spite of his assaults against it, very substantial.[47]

In fact the major similarity of Childs is to von Rad: the ambivalent position towards historical criticism, partly using it and partly seeking to circumvent it; the emphasis on the connection with the New Testament; the involvement of the personal faith of the scholar in the interpretative process.[48] Both of them uttered words of apparent desperation, von Rad at the end of his second volume, in saying that, if his work had not established the relation with the New Testament, it would be no more than a history of Hebrew religion, and Childs, when he writes that:

> If the canonical approach is conceived of as a closed system by which to handle biblical revelation, it is also doomed to failure and should rightly be rejected *(OTTCC, 26)*.

## 9. Other questions

On detailed points there are many errors, some of which may derive from haste; however, others must reflect a serious lack of critical attention to what he was saying. Thus discussing σῶμα, 'body', he tells us that it designates the whole person and is 'inseparable from life' (580). It is 'never used of a corpse, but serves to identify the subject as an I (I Cor. 13.3)'. Actually it is commonly used of a corpse: Matt. 27.58, 59; Mark 15.43; Luke 23.52, 55; 24.3, 23; John 19.38, 40; 20.12; Jude 9, etc.

The desire to use a rigorous method and to avoid homiletic and apologetic pseudo-solutions was also part of Childs' programme from the beginning (cf. above, 388). But not a few explanations of this type remain. Many of the concluding 'reflections' in both Theologies seem to me to be very like customary religious platitudes and homiletic/apologetic explanations, much more so than expressions of a vibrant new theological vision.

One apologetic argument, in a different area, is seen when we are told of 'the striking fact that the New Testament does not *cite as scripture* any book of the Apocrypha or Pseudepigrapha. (The reference to Enoch in Jude 14–15 is not an exception, *Biblical Theology*, 62.)' In the absence of any *reason* why the reference to Enoch should not be an exception, this remains a mere reiteration of traditional apologetic for the accepted (Protestant) canon.[49]

More important are questions of argumentation and interaction with other scholars. Considering the vast amount of literature read by Childs, he might have done better to give more attention to scholars who are actually commenting on his own canonical project. Thus (*OTTCC*, 6, cf. 148) he tells us that 'it is a basic misunderstanding to try to describe a canonical approach simply as a form of structuralism (*contra* Barton)'. This reaction is typical of Childs' extreme sensitivity to any comment that appears to classify his thinking as being in the same category as any other comparable trend. The 'simply' of his sentence, however, is entirely untrue, as indeed is the whole sentence. Barton did not say that it *was* a form of structuralism, simply or otherwise: he said that it ought *logically* to be seen as a form of structuralism '*if it is to be more than merely redaction criticism in an advanced form*' (my italics, *Reading the Old Testament*, 133). Since in Barton's opinion the canonical approach *is* more than merely an advanced form of redaction criticism (Barton, 102), which is Childs' own opinion, too, he is not calling it 'simply a form of structuralism': at most he is saying that, if certain conditions were fulfilled, it would necessarily have some common ground with the latter. Barton made it clear (again 133, cf. 101ff.) that the price of adopting a structuralist theory of reading 'might prove too high' for Childs. In other words, the conditions were not fulfilled, and canonical criticism took a somewhat different direction. In fact Barton repeatedly states that Childs' approach is something entirely new, which is what Childs really wants to hear in this regard (Barton, 90, 100: e.g. 90: 'Any criticism of [Childs' approach] which assumes that it is merely a minor addition to existing methods will be bound to miss the mark').

Similarly, it is untrue to say that I 'rejected the canonical proposal out of hand' (72), for I found it interesting and stimulating in its earlier forms, as I said (*JSOT* 16, 1980, 12–23). Childs says that I 'sharply denied any hermeneutical significance to the canon'; but this is not at all the case: what I said, and clearly, was that it *sometimes* had this effect, sometimes not. 'Canons are not particularly hermeneutical in their character,' I wrote, and the illustrations which I adduce in the following paragraph are, I think, undeniable; in any case Childs says nothing about them. Moreover, my remarks at that point concern 'canon' in its usual sense, i.e. the canon of books in the Bible. If we consider 'canon' in the other sense used by Childs, i.e. the final form of books as distinct from earlier forms, I think that it may of course have a hermeneutical effect and have frequently used it in this way. I think, however, that it is one potentially useful approach among many, but not a universal rule nor one that should dominate over all other considerations.

## *10. General overview*

At first sight the canonical approach looked as if it might solve some of the problems of biblical theology, or, more correctly, might simply and automatically eliminate the existence of them.

Thus the history of religion simply disappears from view, since nothing other than the canonical documents are to be considered. Sections of a book like Proverbs may have been adapted from an Egyptian source, but that is of no interest: the canonical document says nothing about any such origin, and only the book as it stands deserves to be considered. Within the canon, of course, there is also history of religion: religion changed between Moses and Elijah, between Jeremiah and Ezra. But religion and religious change are simply ruled out on the ground that the study of them is not part of theology. Thus, in discussing an essay by von Rad on creation, Childs mentions several critiques of it, among them one by H.H. Schmid. But all he says of the latter is that 'Schmid simply substitutes a history-of-religions schema for von Rad's form-critical analysis of Israel's theological witness without ever addressing the problem' (109). The nature of Schmid's material and argument is ignored. The principle seems to be this: if it can be classified (by Childs) as belonging to history of religion, it can be ignored.

Again, on the question of Hebrew or biblical mentality, this basically does not matter any more. Earlier writers who 'strove to discover inner-biblical categories' (*OTTCC*, 15) are 'not to be disparaged', but are not of central importance. One should not 'attempt to discover from linguistic conventions a special Hebrew mentality' (*BT*, 572). The principle seems to be: if it is within the canon, then it is authoritative theological material, whether it is peculiar to Israel or not.

And this could seem to be a certain advance. Thus Childs ceases for the most part to worry about Greek thought and its opposition to Hebrew, which could be an advantage for one who goes on into the New Testament as he does (not that he uses this advantage to any degree).[50] It also enables him, as already mentioned, to some extent to push aside the objection to patristic theology on the grounds of its underlay of Greek philosophical thinking. 'No one would defend the terminology of ὁμοούσιος as biblical, but the theological question is whether it is a faithful rendering of the biblical witness in the face of proposed alternatives' (482, cf. also 378, where this same term is mobilized in order to keep the feminists in their place). Childs passes on to us the assurance of T. F. Torrance that ὁμοούσιος is a proper word to use: 'far from imposing an alien Hellenism on the Gospels', such terms were 'adapted' to allow the New Testament witness to come through 'without distortion through an alien framework of thought'. But even if this is true, this 'adaptation' would never have taken place but for the important role of natural theology among the Fathers. And is the claim true anyway, or is it just a wish-fulfilment dream of orthodoxy? Can Childs himself validate what he quotes?

There is reason to think that he cannot. For, if 'inner-biblical categories' are not so essential, and if ὁμοούσιος is a faithful and totally non-distorting category, it would seem that any set of categories from any philosophy will be perfectly appropriate for expressing the 'witness' of the biblical material. This, however, is not how Childs handles other scholars. Kelsey is attacked (592f.) for accepting a modern philosophical consensus as a basis for theology, similarly others. McKane is reproved for applying the categories 'secular' and 'religious' to Hebrew Wisdom: they are 'quite alien to wisdom' (188f.).[51] But they are not more alien than ὁμοούσιος was. Natural law would be 'heavily encumbered with philosophical meaning foreign to the Old Testament' (684). Aristotle's notions of 'virtue' and 'character' cannot be found in the Psalms or in Paul (706). Ebeling's handling of the relation between the Jesus of history and the Christ of faith 'appears to many to be derived from a modern philosophical construal', which apparently shows that it is wrong (604). It is wrong, again, if ideas about humanity are organized 'according to philosophical lines of thought' (59). All the people who used such schemes doubtless did so with exactly the same assurances in mind as Childs offers to us for ὁμοούσιος. The openness of Childs' position in this respect is thus only apparent: it is applied selectively, with favouritism extended to those who are orthodox in Barthian terms. Again, the contrast between 'ontic' and 'noetic' revelation 'is a non-biblical formulation', but 'this formulation does correctly describe a central biblical stance towards the identity of Jesus as the exalted Christ' (466). If non-biblical formulations are acceptable, then one cannot blame other scholars for using them.

Another traditional question was that of the 'centre', and it also automatically disappears: the organization provided by a 'centre', which first had to be identified, is now replaced – or might be replaced, because, as we have seen, this is not in fact done in Childs' version of the canonical approach – by the *boundary*, which is there, is present, and does not have to be identified. But Childs' strange decision not to *organize* his theology on a canonical basis means that he offers no alternative solution. His adoption of the facultative do–it–any–way–you–like solution avoids the question of the 'centre', but also shows that the canon, as interpreted by him, has no answer to that question anyway.

The question of natural theology scarcely enters into Childs' mind: it is too remote to be worth even the constant pillorying to which he subjects many other approaches. At the crucial New Testament places, e.g. Acts 17; Romans 1–2, he never even mentions it. But if natural theology has really to be considered as an exegetical possibility, it blows apart not so much his argumentation – for he does not trouble to argue against natural theology – but the whole system of values which he assumes as authoritative throughout. For it shows that the whole Barthian system was far from justified in its claims to take account of the *totality* of scripture: on the contrary, it deliberately pressed for the elimination of certain emphases which are – with a high degree of probability – present within the Bible. While a non-canonical approach to scripture, say one based on a preference for certain sources like the genuine Pauline letters, might perhaps be able to hold its own against any admission of natural theology, a canonical approach which claims to express the *totality* of scripture will be unable to do so. Or, putting it in another way, a Bible seen as devoid of natural theology would be yet another canon within the canon. And the – surely unthinking! – acceptance by Childs that St Thomas Aquinas was 'a serious biblical theologian' and 'a model for biblical theology' proves that a biblical theology wholly built upon a basis of natural theology is perfectly possible and indeed desirable in Childs' eyes, however little he says to make this positive valuation evident.[52]

Only apparently, therefore, has Childs' canonical approach dealt with the problems. Most of them remain.

*11. General intellectual concepts*

There remain a few questions about what appears to be Childs' ultimate weapon, namely his view of the history of ideas. This affects several of his terms, all of which are used as extremely negative symbols: Enlightenment, historicism, positivism, religion, ideology.

## (a) The Enlightenment[53]

Childs' intense hostility towards the Enlightenment, and his use of it as a means of disproof of almost any modern interpretation of scripture, is too evident to require further exemplification. But the question then arises whether this fits with his extreme Barthianism.

Barth certainly had his idea-base in the Reformation, and was critical of the Enlightenment, as almost all Christian theologians have been in greater or less degree. However, his writing about it, as in his history of Protestant theology,[54] is not only witty and ironic but also appreciative and not unsympathetic. By contrast, Childs demonizes the Enlightenment: to him it seems to be pure evil, the latter-day Antichrist, the universal source of absolute ruin to all Christian thinking.[55] Would Childs, with Barth, be tempted to see in Rousseau 'one inspired by a touch of the hem of the mantle of the prophet Amos'?[56] I very much doubt it. Childs' use of the term 'Enlightenment' is thus entirely different in tone from Barth's; it is in fact identical with the way in which some American fundamentalists use it.[57]

Here, however, he is hoist with his own petard, for it seems to me that a good case can be made to the effect that Barth himself was essentially a product of the Enlightenment and that he knew this very well. Thus the marked contrast between reason and revelation, central to Barth's views, is an obvious aspect of the Enlightenment, as well as of the Middle Ages. Barth's musical tastes were, notoriously, directed towards that monument of Enlightenment taste, Mozart. And, coming back to the Bible, an essential element in Barth's reasoning towards his view of scripture and revelation was his desire to avoid the 'annulling of the results of biblical scholarship in the last centuries':[58] what were these last centuries but the period of the Enlightenment and its aftermath?

Again, we can argue that Barth's philosophical position is very close to that of Descartes.[59] I quote an important passage from Professor William Abraham. Considering Barth's 'quest to liberate Protestantism from its enslavement to the cultural norms of the modern period', he goes on:

> It should be clear by now, however, that this is an illusory liberation. Despite all Barth's warnings about the need to eliminate any trace of Cartesianism from our thinking, in terms of epistemology Barth is thoroughly Cartesian in outlook. Like the Reformers who inspired him, he was wedded to an exclusivist foundationalism which sought to track every idea back to the Word of God. This affinity with Descartes should not, of course, surprise us; for Descartes may well have indirectly imbibed his exclusive foundationalism from the very Reformers to whom Barth turned for epistemic inspiration. Descartes and Barth are both totally enmeshed in the same epistemological soil. They share the same epistemic sensibilities. Once we make allowances

for the fact that Barth's interests were confined to theology, while those of Descartes were more general, we can discern that they are both wedded to the same fundamental ideas. They both hold that there is only one foundation for knowledge; they both believe that this foundation must provide certainty; they both insist that every effort needs to be expended to ensure the right foundation; and they both believe that all other foundations lead to epistemic disaster. Both Barth and Descartes occupied the same epistemic territory. Differences in their material positions do nothing to undercut this claim.[60]

If this is so, or is even partly so, Childs's ultimate weapon has self-destructed. And from this it follows that Childs himself is just as much a child of the Enlightenment as all the others to whom he applies this undesired epithet. *All* Childs' arguments against scholarly positions on the ground that they depend on the Enlightenment should therefore be disregarded.

### (b) Historicism

This is confirmed by another argument, namely the historicism of Childs' thinking. Childs over-uses the bogey of 'Enlightenment' to the extent that it becomes simply laughable. Among those dominated by the Enlightenment, and therefore obviously wrong, are Käsemann (215), Brueggemann (73), the main part of all the older biblical theology (9) and many others. With this we are entering the realm of real nonsense. What can have moved Childs to so extravagant a departure from reality?

The answer is that, in spite of his own strong opposition to 'historicism', his own approach to the understanding of biblical scholarship is entirely historicistic in character. Historicism, for this purpose, is the idea that, in order to understand something, the essential mode is to get at *its origins*. The historicist is never satisfied with the thing as it is; he or she has to understand it by discovering its past. This is Childs' approach. He thinks – in my opinion wrongly, but that is not the central question here – that the origins of critical biblical scholarship lie in the Enlightenment. He therefore thinks that the assumptions and presuppositions of the Enlightenment control what is thought and done by scholars in that tradition. As I have written elsewhere:

In other words, in approaching this important matter, he *clearly and openly professes his own adherence to the simplest and most obviously erroneous form of historicism.* To understand a phenomenon like modern biblical criticism, you have to go back to its earliest beginnings and see how it developed out of these, allegedly out of the Enlightenment. Exactly, in other words, the historicist programme which he himself has excoriated whenever it was applied by biblical critics to anything in the Bible. The arch–anti-historicist is himself a historicist![61]

Even if biblical criticism began with the Enlightenment, this is largely irrelevant to the understanding of what it was like in the nineteenth century or is like in the twentieth. Modern biblical criticism has to be understood and evaluated either (*a*) philosophically, through a reasoned discussion of its logic and procedure; (*b*) pragmatically, through an analysis of its aims and its results; or (*c*) biographically, through an investigation of what particular biblical critics actually think or thought, what their loyalties and values are or were. Such a biographical investigation, one may suspect, would show that allegiance to the Enlightenment had a very small place in their thinking, while loyalty to the Reformation had (among the Protestants, who were the majority) a very large one. The depiction of scholars like Käsemann and Brueggemann as fanatics for the Enlightenment proves nothing but an inability to understand anything of the personalities of scholars who take a different point of view from one's own. In any case, any investigation of modern biblical criticism has to be synchronic and explain it in terms of what it is today. The real nature of the critical movement is greatly distorted by the historicist attempt to explain it in terms of its origins – even if this account of these origins is in some sense historically true – which I think it is not.

To sum up, therefore, that critical scholarship is to be traced back to the Enlightenment is a theme continually repeated in these works. That this argument is invalidated by the logic of Childs' own attacks on historicism (when applied to the Bible itself) is manifest. His argument that scholarly traditions can be undermined through their connection back to the Enlightenment is invalidated by his own attacks on historicism, even if his account of the history is a correct one.

### (c) Positivism

Like Enlightenment and historicism, positivism is also a bad thing for Childs. He sees it as an aspect of historical criticism and that sort of thing – the desire for a 'positivity' behind the text, to be found by research. The fact that he characterizes this research as 'speculative' and 'reconstructive' shows, however, that it is the opposite of positivistic. He seems unaware of the most obvious thing about positivism where it exists within theology: positivism is an aspect of *conservative* tendencies.[62] Fundamentalism has strong positivistic tendencies. So has Barthianism, and Bonhoeffer wisely blamed Barth for a 'positivism of revelation'. Childs' hostility to hypothesis and reconstruction marks his thinking also as clearly positivistic. Here again his own arguments confound his own product. The attraction of the canonical approach is itself an attraction to positivism.[63] To this we may add:

### (d) Theology and religion

Nothing is more evident in Childs' work than his identification with 'theology' and his idealization of it, coupled with a very negative view of religion. But in the end it seems that the reverse is the case. Childs does not seem to be a theologian, nor does he think theologically. The theology he presents is almost entirely second-hand. Simply retailing a form of popular conservative Barthianism does not constitute theological thinking. Although Childs lets us know what his opinions about a variety of theological questions are, hardly anywhere does he develop a serious theological argument of his own. He seems to be a historical scholar with a set of strong theological convictions, rather than a theologian who thinks things out and explains them to others. In a percipient review Margaret Davies wrote of *OTTCC*: 'What this book seems to this reader to provide is a response to the Hebrew Scriptures which ignores both history and rationality . . . and which finds solace in a religion of the heart.'[64] Yes, indeed. This is parallel with the development of Barthianism in general, which in its earlier days was interested in the secular, in atheism and the like, and 'seemed to value these as honest reactions to reality, unlike the reactions of religious people which were dishonest and unreal. But in its latter stages Barthianism forgot most of this. It came to favour piety, religiosity and the like more than the lively stimulus of critical thought. Its tendency ended up with privilege for pious people.'[65] Or, putting it another way, to be hostile to 'religion' seemed very good in the days when the opposition was thought to lie in Schleiermacher, in Harnack, in liberal theology; but the same people who so bravely espoused these values, when they came to meet logical positivism, or analytic philosophy, or modern sociology, very quickly reversed their direction: religion was what they stood for and what they depended on. This is true of Childs' canonical approach throughout. Thus his *Introduction* argues:

> It is constitutive of Israel's history that the literature formed the identity of the *religious* community which in turn shaped the literature. This fundamental dialectic which lies at the heart of the canonical process is lost when the critical Introduction assumes that a historically referential reading of the Old Testament is the key to its interpretation. It assumes the determining force on every biblical text to be political, social, or economic factors which it seeks to establish in disregard of the *religious* dynamic of the canon (41, my italics).

It is the *religion* that makes the essential difference.

*(e) Ideology*

I have already remarked on Childs' readiness to stigmatize other people's opinions as 'ideology' or 'ideological' and pointed out that this is very dangerous ground to tread upon. Moltmann is 'ideological', so is Kraus; so is Paul Hanson. In connection with Kraus we have to beware of 'the ideological stance of modern liberation theology' (649). Not only are scholars influenced by ideology, but (perhaps even worse!) they give the impression that the biblical writers themselves were influenced by it, indeed were full of it. Barton's view of the prophets leaves little that 'was not seriously contaminated by ideological bias' (173). It is 'a disaster for theology to interpret it [the New Testament] as a collection of human ideology' (526). After the Enlightenment, Childs believes, scholars thought that the biblical writers were just uttering their own ideologies.[66]

What then is 'ideology' for Childs? Is it just anything that he disagrees with, any world-view that differs from his own? Ultimately, yes: there is the true theology, which is pure from all contamination by ordinary human ideas based on reason, experience, mysticism, or indeed religion, or which if it has ever used such ideas has transformed them so that they serve its own needs. But these human ideas, if they are built up into some sort of world-view, are an ideology which pretends to the status of a true theology. It is characteristic of Childs' thought that this becomes worse in more modern times. It was all right for the Fathers to adopt terms from Greek philosophy, for they were faithfully interpreting the gospel; but after the Enlightenment it becomes different. In fact it is obvious that when Childs talks about 'ideology' he has in mind 'liberal Christian theology' with its linkage with historical criticism (cf. the linkage of arguments on 525f., and the characterization of Hanson's views as 'a highly ideological construal of theology . . . which frequently turns into unabashed propaganda for modern liberal Protestant theology', 18), and likewise liberation theology (cf. *OTTCC*, 49).

And here Childs might have thought about the damage that he is likely to do to theology itself. Here is a first-rate, theological, biblical scholar, intent on the primacy of 'theology' within biblical study. But what he does is to condemn and reject one theology after another as a form of 'ideology'. He may except his own theology from this judgment, but others will not. What they will conclude from his writing is that *all* theology is ideology. And in some senses that could be argued: but not by Childs, for whom 'ideology' seems always to be a pejorative term.

In throwing about accusations of ideology, Childs has assimilated himself to the ideology of our time: for all of us can do this, and many are doing it. Those devoted to liberation theology are experts in it, far more than Childs is, and will not require five minutes to dismiss his entire work as a mass of ideology. Which ideology? They will probably say: the ideology of white American male conservatism (this is not my own opinion, however, see below). Childs may not be aware of this, but this does not make any difference: one is not normally aware of one's own ideology. The fact that he thinks it is lively, kerygmatic, biblically-based Christian faith only shows how ideological it is. This may be quite wrong and unjust, but it is Childs' own fault that it will happen. He does not have enough respect for the exegetical and theological convictions of others to make him avoid the usage of 'ideology'.

And I think that it *is* ideology, though not necessarily the one that people will identify. Let us return to Barth for a last time. There is one thing that Childs seems not to have learned from Barth, namely, that it was good and proper, for those who learned from Barth, to laugh at Barthians and Barthianism. All the good Barthians learned this and Barth himself encouraged it. The people who followed Barth like sheep and had a Barthian answer for everything should be thought ridiculous. In other words, to go a little farther with the same principle than was usually done: Barth was a great theologian, but Barthianism was an ideology, or could easily become one. I think it was one.

### (f) Fundamentalism

Gunneweg wrote, correctly, that Childs is not a fundamentalist in the normal sense, and of course that is true.[67] The traditional fundamentalism, based on historical accuracy and inerrancy, is remote from Childs' viewpoint.[68] But Gunneweg thought it more accurate to speak of a 'canonical fundamentalism'. As I have argued, however, in the later developments of Childs' writing the importance of the canon seems to diminish. What it looks more like, if we are to use terms of this kind, is a 'theological fundamentalism'. The biblical traditions can be traced back and we can see differing forms of the 'witness', but it must always be 'theological', which for Childs seems to mean *pure from contamination* by any thoughts based on ordinary human reason, imagination or experience. As we have seen, he is completely upset when someone like Käsemann suggests that the Gospel traditions are 'mixed', containing some valid expressions of Christ and others that are in varying degree distorted. In other words, while historical criticism, though often damaging, can be tolerated, *theological* criticism is virtually or totally excluded. There is thus a kind of theological inerrancy. All of scripture is to be interpreted for its 'theology'; anything else that is there can be neglected. The means for interpretation that are permitted are such as to rule out all methods and all kinds of evidence that could make the scripture say, theologically, something other than what Childs believes.

*12. Conclusion*

Childs' publications in biblical theology are likely to do great harm to the
subject and its prospects, particularly because they confirm the most significant
suspicions of the enemies of biblical theology, who will see it as a mode for the
enunciation of personal convictions and for the advancement of existing and
established modern theologies. Even for those devoted to the advancement of
biblical theology Childs offers little. He does not offer a method which can be
followed by others, especially if they do not share his views in full. The whole
work, as already stated, is an apologetic for the rightness of his own methods and
his own personal theology; and his arguments consist in large measure of ruling
out as illegitimate all methods and evidences that might lead to a different
exegesis than his and all theological values that differ from his.

  Even for those most devoted to a conception of a canonically-based biblical
theology his work must be a disappointment, for it contains numerous compromises with those same methods and ideas which he himself has so vigorously
condemned.

  Nevertheless it is unlikely that the canonical impulse in biblical theology will
die away. Childs touched on aspects which for many are religiously very important, and these are likely to produce other expressions in the future. In the next
chapter we shall consider briefly some ways in which this might come about.

# 25

# Other Canonical Possibilities

## 1. General

The most obvious way in which a theology might be written on 'canonical' principles but differently from Childs' approaches would be to organize its *content* around the patterns of the canon. Thus such a theology might very naturally have three great sections, covering Torah, Prophets and Writings, or perhaps better four, accepting the later division of the Prophets into historical books and prophetic books. It might also have sub-sections under individual books, and smaller divisions where appropriate, as with individual Psalms. It might well also discuss special groupings of books, most obviously the Twelve Minor Prophets as a composite but unitary work, and equally the Megilloth.

One of its advantages would be that the starting point of the whole might be clear: the beginning of Genesis. This would in any case be in accord with my concept of 'story' and is not peculiar to a canonical approach. But in any case the work could continue cumulatively: what has been achieved by the end of Genesis, what new perspectives are added in Exodus, what in Leviticus and Numbers, how the perspective changes in Deuteronomy and so on. In the historical books or Former Prophets one would have to decide how far historical discussion was to be included or not, and if it were included, whether it was to include only biblical source material or take into account other sources of information. Presumably comparative discussion would be permitted, and one could then discuss the theological differences between an account in Kings and one of the same event in Chronicles, or similarly between Kings and Isaiah. Prophetic books like Isaiah – or, say, the Minor Prophets as a single block – might be handled as unitary works. But one could also incorporate cross-cut comparisons, such as the view of the priesthood in several different books, or the treatment of covenants, or the roles of women characters. At its best it could be very good; it could also turn out to be another one-volume commentary combined with a sort of Bible Dictionary. But at least this would be the obvious way in which the work might be undertaken. Doubtless, however, other patterns may well emerge.

Another possibility would be to follow the general pattern used by Childs, and to remain 'canonical', both in the sense of emphasizing the canon of books and in the sense of final-form exegesis, but to eliminate from the work some of the great weakness from which it suffers in its present time, namely its inability to co-operate with any other methods or to accept support and agreement from others who basically want to go in the same direction.

First, such a theology would be open to a variety of possibilities and not be tied as Childs' is to a particular and personal system of beliefs. It would certainly be open to Jewish scholars and to Christians of all denominations and approaches, and indeed also to scholars of other religious affiliations and of none. It would hope not to extract from the Hebrew Bible support for any one existing theology but to discover and explain a really 'biblical' theology that would be novel and creative for all.

Secondly, instead of using the idea of the canon as a force to attack the tradition of historical criticism and modern scholarship in general, it would ally these two sides. Nothing can be known of the circumstances and purposes of canonization except through historical investigation, and final-form exegesis is best considered as an aspect of historical criticism, one which at most may have been undervalued in the past.

The whole hostility between canonical and historical exegesis should be recognized as unnecessary, as is shown by the continual dependence of canonical exegesis upon the historical, and forgotten.

Thirdly, a theology built upon a canonical approach must certainly group its materials in some sort of canonical manner, e.g. by what is in a particular book,[1] what is in the Torah, what is in the Prophetic Books, and so on. In this one would have to consider differences made by different plans of canon, for instance traditional Jewish, 'sectarian' (Qumran) Jewish, Samaritan and two or three kinds of Christian.

Fourthly, what one gets out of this, if it is a theology, is a theology extracted from the patterns of the text and abstracted from the persons, the events and the reasonings which produced the text. It remains a question what use such a 'theology' is to anyone. If the theology has to give some account of the factors and reasons *why* the text is as it is, there is no alternative to a historical investigation of these persons, events and reasonings. That is to say, the theology would have to be complemented with historical investigation and especially the history of religion. This is necessary if we are to know even only the minds, intentions and procedures of the redactors and canonizers themselves. If so, we would have come back to where we are, the only difference being perhaps some enrichment through insights gained while passing through the stages outlined above.

It is likely that approaches to the theology of the Hebrew Bible along these lines will soon appear.

## 2. *Sanders*

Space must be given to the thoughts of James A. Sanders, who was actually the first in the United States to publish a serious canonical analysis and to propose a discipline of 'canonical criticism'.[2] His work would deserve more space in this book, were it not that he does not do much to claim that it leads towards an 'Old Testament theology' or a 'biblical theology'. The emphasis of his thinking is more on a *hermeneutic*. As Childs puts it (*OTTCC*, 137):

> [Sanders] assumes that the situation of the modern interpreter of the Old Testament stands in close analogy to that of the ancients. We also stand between the biblical text and a historical moment, and we also strive to adapt our tradition into the changing context . . . By studying the Old Testament and its hermeneutics, we can learn how to apply a correct hermeneutic in our time.

Childs agrees that behind Sanders' position there lies 'a strong theological concern'. But here once again, with Childs, the fact that it is 'theological' does not help. It is a 'classic move of liberal Protestant theology' – but I do not see how it is 'classic', since the canonical proposal seemed to be a new thing, nor do I see how it is 'liberal'.

It is true that Sanders has certain terms which recur and seem to function as central theological principles: 'monotheistic pluralism' is one, 'theocentric' is another.

Sanders' views have much to commend them. Unlike Childs, he is able to work within existing scholarly patterns and add his own perspective to them. He provides a mode which may well be effective for preaching and church interpretation. He furnishes some very useful corrections to the canonical movement: for instance, when he points out that the older usage of the Bible in the church was largely 'oracular' rather than canonical, which I think is entirely true and very important. This is one of his great contributions, and we shall return to it below. But as it stands at the moment, it looks as if he thinks in terms of *interpretation* of the individual text or of blocks of text, rather than identification of the *theology* that lies behind the corpus as a whole.

## 3. *Rendtorff*

The most prominent figure on the horizon at present is that of Professor Rolf Rendtorff. But since we have so far only short articles to explain his plans, it is difficult to embark on a discussion of what may appear. The following brief points may be made:

1. Rendtorff clearly allies himself with the 'canonical' emphasis and sympathizes with the general direction of the work of Childs. Indeed, if anything, he goes farther in this direction than Childs does. As Rendtorff sees it, though Childs talks about the canon a lot, he does not really build his Theology around it; as we have seen, he seems to forget about the canon over considerable stretches of his book. Rendtorff wrote: 'I consider Childs' *Theology* to be much more "systematic" than "canonical".'[3] This agrees with my own opinion as stated above. Rendtorff, we can expect, will build his future Theology more distinctly around the *shape* of the canon. On the other hand, whether we agree with Childs or not, it is more clear *why he* wants his approach to be canonical: it is built into the whole complex of his views about theology and theological history, about preaching and the needs of the church, about historical criticism, about the history of religion and so on. In Rendtorff's case this is not so clear. Why does he want an Old Testament theology at all? What does he think that it is? It does not seem to have the churchly objective of Childs' work. It certainly wants to stay close to Judaism and Jewish exegesis, but what motive does it have on the Christian side? Granted that [Christian] Old Testament theology does exist, one can understand that Rendtorff wants to steer it in a certain direction. But if we go back to its basic rationale, he has not made it clear why he thinks it should exist at all.

In one article – admittedly, a very brief one in a semi-popular periodical – he seems to maintain that theology and reading the Bible are simply the same thing:

> As 'biblical theologians', how should we approach the Hebrew Bible? What questions should we put to the text? Again, the answer is very simple. We should look for the questions in the text itself. I mean that in a very strict sense: by *reading* the Hebrew Bible. By reading, not by distilling ideas.

He goes on to point out that biblical theology has too often taken its ideas and topics from outside the Hebrew Bible.

> When we select our topics and questions from sources outside the Old Testament, we get answers only to those questions. But these are not the questions to which the Hebrew Bible attempts to provide answers.
>
> We can learn what those questions are only by reading the Hebrew Bible on its own. Our point of departure must be first *to read the Hebrew Bible in its given form as a theological book*. If it is not theological on its own, then it cannot be theological at all. And if it is not theological, to try to uncover a 'biblical theology' would be to misuse the Hebrew Bible for a purpose alien to its own intention. But if it is a theological work – as it surely is – we can expect to be able to find the biblical authors' intentions in their work; they had no reason to hide them; they wanted the reader clearly to understand their

message, and therefore wrote their texts in a way that would certainly be understood.[4]

A very simple argument is also found when he tries to state the basic relation (or, rather, non-relation) of the Hebrew Bible to Christianity:

> My point of departure is the simple fact that the Hebrew Bible came into existence, and more or less assumed its final shape, before Christianity emerged. Therefore, for simple historical reasons and for the sake of intellectual honesty, it seems to me to be impossible to measure or to evaluate the Hebrew Bible from the viewpoint of theological conceptions that came into being only after it. If we refuse to accept this conclusion, we must assume that the Hebrew Bible had no meaning at all before Christianity appeared (42).

Something similar seems to apply to his interest in the canon itself. In his article 'The Importance of the Canon for a Theology of the Old Testament',[5] the main reasoning seems to lie on two levels: first, the relationship to Judaism, and secondly the intellectual grounds within recent (critical) scholarship. Thus on the first: 'it becomes necessary to see the whole of the Old Testament in the light of its final canonical form as an expression of the self-understanding of postexilic Judaism' (55); and, secondly, a survey shows how important lines *in Old Testament scholarship* have increasingly been interesting themselves in the final form (51–2). Specific *Christian* theological reasons for the canonical emphasis seem to be less prominent. And, of course, in respect of the relation of the 'final form' to Judaism, this raises the further question: is the tripartite division of the canon, with its corresponding degrees of weighting, to be normative for Christian theology because it operates so in Judaism? And, if not, how does the canonical form provide a common basis for Jewish and Christian thinking?

2. Rendtorff makes clear his sense of loyalty to the heritage of Gerhard von Rad, as do all those who worked with him. But there is also a major shift, in that von Rad's central emphasis on *Heilsgeschichte* has little or no reflection in Rendtorff's present position. Von Rad's emphasis on history as a theological medium was followed up, but also much transformed, by the Pannenberg group, and Rendtorff was the Old Testament specialist in that group. But he came to believe that this *heilsgeschichtlich* tradition had really operated as a means of taking the Hebrew Bible away from the Jewish people and appropriating it to Christianity, and Rendtorff dissociated himself from this line of thinking.[6] So he is really seeking to take a direction that will necessarily be very different from that of von Rad.

This shows up in another connection. Having started in a canonical direction, Rendtorff wants to suggest that von Rad himself had something of a canonical approach. He has a section entitled 'A Canon-related Survey (Gerhard von Rad)'.[7] And as I have said earlier (378ff. above), most of the main tradition of Old Testament theology implied a sort of canonical interest. But beyond this rather general and unfocussed interest I do not see that it is true of von Rad. He seems to me to be *less* canonically focussed than many other Old Testament theologians. It is quite true, as Rendtorff points out, that, contrary to his own theological viewpoint, according which the exodus is the real starting point, he begins the main part of his Vol. 1 with Genesis and the primeval history. But only in a limited way is this a canonical move: I would say that it is much more a *heilsgeschichtlich* move, partly mixed up with historical-critical considerations. In this series he follows the *historical stages*; he places Genesis at the start because the first stages of the history of salvation are to be found there, but Chronicles at the end because it is a *late book*. In the second volume, in the Prophets, he follows the *historical-critical* order, separating off Deutero-Isaiah and so on. This is the reverse of a canonical approach. [Since the above was written, Rendtorff in the Knierim FS alters the emphasis, saying now that von Rad's approach was not 'canonical' in the strict sense but rather 'canon-oriented'. This is a distinct improvement. But I do not really think that it was 'canon-oriented' either.][8] For von Rad, he writes, Deutero-Isaiah 'represented the absolute peak of Israelite religion . . . the exile is the great caesura – afterwards there was only decline'.[9] Rendtorff would wish to dissociate himself from this view: if Deutero-Isaiah worked during the exile, that was – in his opinion – just the *beginning* of the great period!

3. Particularly prominent in Rendtorff's thinking is his high sensitivity to Jewish exegesis: indeed it seems at times that the favouring of Jewish exegesis, rather than the production of a theology, is the principal element in his plan. In this respect he stands at the opposite extreme from Childs' 'pan-biblical theology' and other relations with the New Testament are to be avoided.

> Reading and interpreting the Old Testament in its own right excludes the claim that Old Testament theology is only possible as part and parcel of 'Biblical Theology' embracing both Old and New Testament.[10]

Such a statement does not exclude pan-biblical theology as a project for Christians, but it does not give much encouragement to such a project either. What if Christians are canonically minded and insist that their reading must be guided by the totality of the Christian canon? Rendtorff's emphasis, for Christians working on the Old Testament itself, lies on the achievement of a theology which will be acceptable to *Jewish* scholarship.

Here again he is distant from von Rad. As already indicated above, von Rad's positive emphasis, at least in his intentions, was markedly Christian and directed towards contacts with the New Testament. Judaism was seen, not so much negatively, but as if lying in a sort of vacuum unrelated to the great historical acts of God.

There is also a question if Rendtorff, as it appears, looks for a kind of common Jewish-Christian theology of the Hebrew Bible, along with a total acceptance of Jewish exegesis. In this, much depends on just how much he has in mind. That the modern study of Old Testament theology (and New Testament theology too) should be fully open to Jewish scholarship has been entirely affirmed by me in this book. Moreover, that traditional Jewish exegesis should be deeply respected, and should be more studied by Christian scholars than has lately been normal, is absolutely right.[11] But at times Rendtorff seems to go farther and to say that traditional Jewish exegesis must be *accepted as right*, at least on a broad front, if not in all details. But, it seems to me, traditional Jewish exegesis is entirely tied into the whole system of Judaism as a religion; and the consequence is that such an approach will in effect exclude the *possibility* of even considering a Christian interpretation. Once we reach this point we have not done much to achieve a common Jewish-Christian theology.

4. Rendtorff would, I think, shape his Theology around the order of the books in the Jewish canon, and would begin with Genesis and creation – which latter point I think is right, whether one follows a canonical principle or not.

5. In matters of source criticism and the like, Rendtorff has been a main initiator of the move away from the traditional J, E and P to a 'new paradigm': such people as 'the Yahwist' never existed, and the Pentateuch belongs in essence to a late date.[12] In this respect Rendtorff remains on the whole quite happy with historical-critical method, but thinks that it leads to quite different conclusions. His demolition of 'the Yahwist as theologian' and his various associated textual proofs work entirely by historical-critical methods, but argue that they demonstrate the errors of the traditional historical-critical 'results'. The older critical approach wanted to find the earliest sources, the earliest theology; the newer idea is to find the latest of both. This assists Rendtorff to see the Hebrew Bible as closely connected with post-exilic and later Jewish life.

There is a difference, however. Rendtorff's work on the Pentateuch is highly historical-critical in one sense, namely that he perceives numerous stages of 'working over' (*Bearbeitung*) to which story complexes have been subjected. Editorial additions, glosses, combinations are found very frequently. Nicholson writes of him that he 'finds evidence of several stages of development in the promise of land, of an earlier and a later formulation of the promise of blessing for others through the descendants of the patriarchs, and of two mutually independent groups of formulations of the promise of numerous progeny'.[13] This is very like the common picture of historical criticism, reconstructing numerous sources and positing numerous stages of redaction, stressing the separateness of elements and the failure of the text to provide cohesion. On the other hand

Rendtorff, as Nicholson notes, is much less interested in *origins*, which are supposed to be the obsession of historical critics. He seems less concerned to go back to the beginnings. The reconstructed editings and connectings of material seem to lie at a late period, leading up quickly to the final form.[14] On this side he is closer to the canonical ideal as seen by Childs.

Here again, then, we have a contrast with Childs: Childs accepts and uses the traditional source analysis, including an early J and E, but is deeply distrustful of the whole mechanism of historical criticism. In these respects Rendtorff is free and open in a way quite absent from the thinking of Childs: he laughs at Childs' orthodoxy, his heresy-hunting arguments, his demonization of the Enlightenment; all that type of argument is quite absent from his approach. His picture of the total shape of Christian theology remains somewhat obscure, at least to me at the time of writing: the great emphasis is on the turn away from all past anti-Semitism (which he perceives as pretty widespread) and the affirmation of Jewish tradition, Jewish exegesis, the Jewishness of the Hebrew Bible.

6. On the other hand Rendtorff's approach seems to be 'canonical' in that the prehistory becomes irrelevant for him. His theology, if I understand him rightly, will be based on the text, not on the persons involved or on the events (if any) which took place in early Israel and are related in the text or otherwise known from extra-textual sources. As I mentioned above (115), Rendtorff at one stage spoke regretfully of the absence of attention to the history of religion in German theology and seemed to sympathize with a renewal of it and with its integration into the curriculum. It is not clear how this goes with his present plans. The impression one now gains is that, if the history of religion were ever to prove that there were at some time such phenomena as a female consort for Yahweh or a sort of semi-polytheism, for Rendtorff's theology as now projected these would lie back in the past: all such phenomena had disappeared before the books were written and before the biblical canon was completed, and so can be ignored for the purposes of theology. If this is so, then he would seem in this to be closer to Childs. He does not, however, have that aversion in principle to the history of religion which Childs has; he knows and recognizes its importance, but thinks, perhaps, that a theology *of the Hebrew Bible* should not go into that sort of thing.

7. What remains unclear to me is just what in Rendtorff's mind is the motive and intention for a theology, or indeed just why the theme of the canon is so important to him. But such uncertainties will doubtless be resolved when more of his work has been published. Certainly it is likely that Rendtorff's Theology, when published, will be the most consistent representative of the canonical direction for the next decades.

There follow here two short sections, not on particular biblical theologians of canonical tendency, but on general aspects which are relevant and deserve to be mentioned.

## 4. Reception history

One aspect of the canonical movement has been an emphasis on the history of the *effects* of writings rather than on their origins, and I have myself written in favour of this interest, as also have canonical theologians. More should be done to investigate the history of reception: in German also *Wirkungsgeschichte*. This is quite right and is mentioned again elsewhere in this volume. But it seems to me to lead in a somewhat different direction from what is now often said.

First, canonical theologians often speak as if this is an innovation on their part: no one thought of this before. Reception history has been neglected, and should now be given more attention. The 'historical–critical method' directed scholars towards *beginnings*. People have to be turned away from their sinful quest after 'origins', a speculative enterprise which will never produce certainty, and direct their gaze towards what was done with texts *after* they were composed, after they were finalized.

This is fine, but it comes too late to be innovative. The movement in this direction has been in full swing for some time. I personally know many scholars in Hebrew Bible who have no great interest in the dates and circumstances of origin of the biblical texts. To them the Bible, complete, is a datum: what interests them is the later interpretation. The meaning of the Bible in itself, or as it was in its composition, is of interest to them only as an occasional resource for elucidation of the later interpretations. In my experience this is common. People read the Habakkuk scroll because of what it may have meant in the second or first century. To them, what the original prophet may have meant is only of marginal interest. But those who form their scholarly path in this way are not necessarily interested in the 'canonical' movement and especially not in its theological motivations. In many cases they adhere much more to the 'purely historical' view of scholarship and remain sceptical of theological values. In this respect they show that the supposed 'obsession with origins' is not intrinsic to the 'historical–critical method'.

Moreover, plentiful works of research in this area are being produced. Thus one may point to the series of *Beiträge zur Geschichte der biblischen Exegese* and *Beiträge zur Geschichte der biblischen Hermeneutik*, often very detailed works, devoting, for example, an entire volume to the history of reception of one Psalm or some other passage. Massive composite works like M. J. Mulder's *Mikra* and Magne Sæbø's *Hebrew Bible/Old Testament. The History of its Interpretation* are impressive evidence.

The argument for the need for reception history is therefore no particular argument for a canonical approach to biblical theology. On the contrary, reception history points in the opposite direction. For reception history is explicitly and emphatically a *historical* operation. First, it depends on *evidence*. If there is no evidence for the reception over a century or two, then there is nothing one can say about it. Unquestionably the discovery of the Dead Sea Scrolls has been an enormous stimulus to this mode of research, for until they were discovered there was very little evidence to tell us how biblical books were interpreted over some vital centuries. The canon, and canonical form, in themselves tell us nothing. Looking at the final form of a biblical book tells us nothing about how it would be interpreted two centuries later. Only after evidence of the reception has been found can one begin to see and appreciate how the tradition lived and worked. Reception history, therefore, valuable as it may be for theological interpretation, points very distinctly in favour of a historical, evidence-based, operation.

## 5. *Afterthoughts about the canon*

Having already written far too much about this subject, I apologize for trying to add even more: but it is basically only one point, namely the question whether the canonical approaches really restore something that was in the tradition of the churches. For it seems to me that they do not.

What strikes me, on thinking about it, is the notable *passivity* of the canon in church life. Of course, it decides which books are in the Bible. But in the regular daily life of the church this does not seem to matter so much. In the synagogue it is different: there the entire Torah is methodically read through in sequence from beginning to end, and certain other books and portions are read in conjunction with certain festivals. But there is little comparable to this in the churches. I have heard of churches which read the entire Torah in sequence, imitating Jewish practice, but this must be highly exceptional. There are lectionaries which prescribe readings day by day or Sunday by Sunday, and these may try to 'represent' the entire canon, i.e. to have some portion from every book, but they do not generally – if ever – try to read the whole Bible. Lectionary practice in general is to make selections. The Gospels would be by far the most prominent, but even there it must be uncommon to read all four in full – not surprisingly, since there is considerable overlap. The one book that is really read methodically in its entirety is the Psalter – and even this only in certain church traditions. Thus in Scottish Presbyterianism, where love of the Psalms has traditionally been intense, particular Psalms were normally chosen at will for congregational singing and a regular progress through the 150 poems was unusual, if it ever occurred. In fact, the usual thing was that certain Psalms were favourites and were used very frequently, others being neglected – the opposite of a canonical procedure.

When one turns to sermons and the like, once again much of the older tradition was non-canonical. It is only in very modern times that we have come to use the word 'text' of an extended passage like a chapter of a biblical book, or even of an entire book like Genesis. In my childhood such a usage would have been strange or unintelligible. A 'text' was a short phrase, seldom more than a sentence in length, generally shorter. A preacher would 'give out' a text for his sermon. It might be taken from a passage of the scripture read, but not necessarily so. It would be a combination of words which would convey a religious or spiritual message. It could be something like 'Thou, God, seest me' or 'Deep calleth unto deep'. Naturally, attention might be given to the context, to the passage as a whole from which it was taken, but this was by no means necessary and was often not done. Similarly, in some church traditions there is a prescribed 'text' for weekly preaching, usually a short pericope, one that in older times was thought to be highly significant. There is nothing against such a procedure, but it is something quite different from a 'canonical' approach: it is more like a 'canon within the canon', a set of basic passages to which one must turn again and again.

The point of this is to reinforce the important observation made by James Sanders, namely that much of the older use of the Bible was an *oracular* one rather than a canonical one. Any portion, however small, could be taken in itself and formed a word from God. This was deeply entrenched in Jewish interpretation and also in the use of Old Testament passages by the New. And its effects survive down to the present day. It is often pointed out with indignation that the historical-critical method split up the unitary scripture into small pieces. In so far as it did so, it was fitting into this oracular procedure, long established in Judaism and in the church. Actually, since the oracular procedure only served in the long term to highlight the contradictions between the different oracles, it was the historical-critical procedure – contrary to common present-day opinion – that was holistic in effect, creating totalities such as J, D and P which could be seen each to share a common theological outlook.

Not that people in older times did not know the fuller contexts, especially the stories. Of course they knew them, at least those found in the books made more prominent by liturgical reading or (notably in the Old Testament) by narrative interest, like the stories of Samuel, David or Elijah. And of course the New Testament writers knew these larger and wider contexts. But this did not stop the oracular method from working and continuing.

The canon did, of course, have a part in the life of the church, but it seems to me that it was not in the first place in the life of worship, liturgy and preaching.

That life worked mostly with selections. The canon worked more obviously in other aspects. One was that of *study* – Bible-reading, whether personal and devotional, or more academic and professionally theological. One might read *the whole Bible* and try to know it in its entirety (even so, one suspects that certain portions were commonly skipped over). More distinctly, the canon would function as the total source for the *proof of doctrine*. Any verse from the canon could be a proof; no words from outside – not being inspired – could have the same force. For all theological debate the canon was decisive. But for the life of worship, of devotion, of preaching, of evangelism, the canon stayed in the background and was rather passive, as I have said. The church worked for the most part with selections. Doubtless 99% of active church-goers have never heard the word 'canon' – and this was so in older times, too.

Nor does it seem that the 'canonical' approaches of the present day are bringing us back to an older world, like the world, perhaps, of the Reformation. On the contrary, the Reformation seems to me to have initiated some of the same movements against which modern canonical criticism has most protested.[15] Thus Fohrer in that same Theology which was discussed above began with a series of passages from Luther which emphasized the essential character of knowing *the historical background*:

> For expounding the prophet one needs a double kind of knowledge. The first is grammatical, and this can be counted as most powerful. The other is even more necessary, namely the knowledge of the history . . . When we first have the grammatical knowledge, we have at once to go on to the histories, that is, what these kings, under whom Isaiah prophesied, did, and these histories have to be carefully learned and investigated.[16]

And again:

> Take the last book of the Kings and the last of the Chronicles, absorb them both well, especially the histories, speeches and events (*Zufälle*) which have taken place under the kings who are named in the titles, up to the end of the books. For it is necessary, if one is to understand the prophecy, that one should know how it was in the country, how things were, how the people thought or what proposals (*Anschläge*) they had with or against their neighbours, friends and foes.[17]

Luther's commentaries on a passage like Genesis 22 show many features very similar to those which have been most complained of in historical-critical work. The historicism of the Reformation approach can be well seen in his chronological work, on which I have written.[18]

That Calvin doubted the Petrine origin of II Peter on stylistic grounds, and suspected that certain Psalms might be of Maccabean date, is also historical-critical in style, but does not particularly touch the canonical question. More important from this point of view is the fact that in two of the most important areas, the Mosaic Laws and the Synoptic Gospels, his commentary was written on *a harmony*. The significance of this has not always been realized. For a harmony is the reverse of the canonical values. A harmony means that the commentary abandons the final form of the individual book or Gospel: it comments on what Moses legislated, on what Jesus did and said. In other words, it goes 'behind' the texts to the things that, on the basis of the texts, 'really happened'. This was, to a certain degree, easier, because the texts were historically inerrant; yet that principle was not as helpful after all, since the texts, even if inerrant, at times did not agree with one another. In essence, a 'harmony' was a *reconstruction* which was hypothetically formed and in this respect was a forerunner of all that the later historical critics were to do.

# 26

# Some Recent Theologies

As mentioned above, it is by no means the case that production in biblical theology has fallen off or atrophied. Certainly in Germany a lively discussion has continued, and productivity of new work has been very strong. This chapter will review briefly three recent works, those of Kaiser, of Gunneweg and of Preuss.


## 1. Kaiser

Kaiser's highly original Theology, which G. W. Anderson hails as 'this exhilarating volume' (at the time of writing I have seen only the first volume),[1] might well have been conceived as a refutation of much that has been said about the subject. On the one hand it is perhaps more integrated with 'historical-critical' analysis than any other Theology of the modern period has been. Thus its Section 3, part 1 (157–212) has two chapters, entitled 'God, People and Land in the Post-Priestly History (JEP)' and 'God, King, People and Land in the Deuteronomic and in the Chronistic Histories'. These would be difficult to read without a fairly good mastery of the critical analysis, and such an analysis is in fact explained by the writer at the start of each chapter: see for example his introduction to the documents J, E and P (157–62). Kaiser shows none of the distrust of historical criticism which has animated some biblical theologians: he accepts it fully, including those modifications in the critical picture which recent discussions may have brought about (see for instance his discussion of the dating of J, 6of. and n. 4). He does not see the fact of lively modern discussion and probable reformulation of the older critical 'results' as reason for doubt about the approach: rather, it is a ground for full confidence in its rightness, and in its applicability to the task of theology, which in this connection is 'to show the unity of the testimonies to God in the Old Testament in the midst of their differences' (158). Without the recognition of differences which the critical approach provides there would, it is implied, be no room for biblical theology to operate in.

Equally clear is Kaiser's involvement in the history of religion. This is an area in which Kaiser is a distinguished expert, and he probably moves in it with greater ease than most Old Testament scholars. He has a deeply cultivated understanding of Greek culture and religion and is lacking in the naive and often ignorant negativity towards classical culture from which many other biblical scholars suffer.[2] §7 is entitled 'The World of the Gods', and its first paragraph begins with the expression 'concerning the difficulty, and the necessity, of understanding the world of the gods as the background for the rise of Yahweh to world dominion' (90). Thus for Kaiser the history-of-religion material is not just a 'background' to the rise of Hebrew religion or a contrast to set against it, but a process in which the concept of the Israelite God is actually involved and out of which his shape and outline is developed and becomes clear. Aspects and developments in Egyptian, Mesopotamian, Ugaritic and Greek religion are thus positively interrelated with the religious history of Israel and the presentation of Israel's God. On p. 111, for instance, the final paragraph has the title of 'The Conflict between Yahweh and Baal or the Birth of the Personality of God and Man'. Thus history of religion is taken in Kaiser's work as a positive and creative part of the task of biblical theology – and rightly so, as I have already indicated.

If some of the commonly made arguments had been valid, one would have to expect that Kaiser's work, thus integrating into his Theology both historical criticism on the one side and history of religion on the other, would have produced a result that was purely historical and descriptive, unrelated to the New Testament, to Christianity and to needs of interpretation within the modern world. Exactly the reverse is the case. Kaiser's Theology is entirely written as a *Christian* Theology and its sections on method and purpose are studded with extensive quotations, especially from Martin Luther. §6 (75–89) sets out to handle the relationship between Law and Gospel and seeks to preserve 'the unity of the scripture of the Old and New Testament in the midst of their differences, showing forth the analogies that exist between them and the naturally assumed (*selbstverständlich*) presuppositions common to both, while not obscuring the differences that exist between them'.

Moreover, for the modern world an existential interpretation is commended. With this we can do more justice to the Old Testament than with a 'mere description' (88), and such an existential approach will facilitate the relating of the work with the New Testament, for the latter 'in view of the manifoldness of its christological approaches and eschatological ideas attains its unity only through existential interpretation'. Again, with respect to the idea of canon, Kaiser has an important proposal. For him, if there is to be a 'centre of scripture', that centre is not to be found in a particular theological concept or idea which has to be identified and described theologically. Rather, the 'centre' of the whole is the Torah itself – something *given* as the controlling element by the organization of the Hebrew canon itself. Thus §7 works out in sequence how the Torah is the foundation document of Judaism, the essence of prophecy, related both to the historical books ('Former Prophets'); to the Prophets in the general sense; to the Writings, specifically to the Psalms, the Wisdom books, the Song of Songs, to Esther, Daniel and Chronicles; and to the deutero-canonical writings. The emphasis on the Torah as 'centre' is thus not only canonical in style, but is also, in view of Kaiser's explicitly Christian and Lutheran stand-point, a sign of a friendly openness towards Judaism, which was only to be expected in view of the writer's many remarks in his other writings.

Again, the historical-critical approach has often been criticized on the grounds that it looks primarily for origins and for the earliest evidence, and fails to give proper attention to the final text. In Kaiser's case it does both: it emphasizes both origins and the final form. Thus if §13 takes nineteen pages to treat the 'Form of Appearance and Character of Old Testament Prophecy' (*'Erscheinungsform und Eigenart der alttestamentlichen Prophetie'*), it is followed by §14, in which over thirty pages are devoted to the passage 'from the prophetic word to the prophetic book', and here we read, for example, of the meaning of the complete Book of Isaiah (233f.), of the Book of Jeremiah 'with its fifty-two chapters' as 'above all an aetiology on a grand scale of the fate of exile', and of the Book of the Twelve (Minor) Prophets as 'a compendium of prophecy and a history of Jewish eschatology'.

Kaiser's achievement is thus a tangible proof that many of the strictures passed upon Old Testament theology have been mistaken, or at least that, even where they were deserved in relation to certain past attempts, the weaknesses of these attempts could be overcome. This is not to say that his own work is beyond criticism. Certain aspects of it are likely to evoke dissatisfaction.

One such aspect is the overwhelmingly Lutheran tone that Kaiser gives to all his expressions of 'Christianity' throughout his work. In view of the wide-ranging perspectives in all other aspects of his study, it is remarkable that he did not see fit to express the 'Christian' insights in a more ecumenical way. His Theology is written as if it were a work expressly for Lutheran students, and little or no consideration is given to the sometimes very different insights of the Roman Catholic, Eastern Orthodox, Calvinist or Anglican reader. Especially in view of the emphasis on Law and Gospel, which is made central to the *Christian* perspective of the work, some engagement with the very different Calvinistic understanding would have been desirable; and this is particularly so in view of the fact that much work in Old Testament theology, indeed perhaps the majority of the older works in this century, has had a distinctly Calvinistic colouring. Not that this makes Kaiser's position wrong, but it does mean that his argumentation fails to cover all the ground.

Equally, questions are likely to be asked about Kaiser's apparently complete acceptance of the Bultmannian view of the Old Testament as a *history of failure* (*Scheitern* – literally 'shipwreck'), and along with this of the general existential interpretation and the scheme of demythologization (87–9). In this latter respect he tells us that: 'The thought of the Old Testament in spite of its Deuteronomic rationalism is of a nature that lies within myth. It takes the metaphors with which it speaks of God's being, continuing and acting, as realities' (88). This leads on to a philosophical discussion, from which it emerges that 'the appropriate interpretation of mythical texts is therefore functional and existential'. 'The anthropomorphic mythologemes and the grandiose history-myths stand directly or indirectly in the service of the interpretation of divine promises and demands, or respectively of law and gospel.' Such thoughts are indeed profound and interesting, but it is likely that many will feel doubts about their being taken as so completely basic to the interpretation of the Old Testament and its relation to the New.

However, to sum up, we cannot but agree with H.-P. Müller's tribute to Kaiser as 'a scholar who in spite of all his detailed historical and exegetical work has advanced the fundamental theological and philosophical questions of Old Testament scholarship as hardly any other has done'.[3]


## 2. Gunneweg

The late Professor Antonius H. J. Gunneweg (1922–1990) included in a distinguished career a deep interest in the theology and hermeneutics of the Old Testament and in its place in Christian preaching and church life generally. His *Vom Verstehen des Alten Testaments. Eine Hermeneutik* appeared in 1977 and an English translation *Understanding the Old Testament* followed in 1978.[4] His major theological work, entitled *Biblische Theologie des Alten Testaments. Eine Religionsgeschichte Israels in biblisch-theologischer Sicht*, was published posthumously in 1993. Among other relevant works one may notice the Festschrift presented to him in 1987: M. Oeming and A. Graupner (eds.), *Altes Testament und christliche Verkündigung*, a volume particularly devoted to the relations between the Old Testament and Christian *preaching*.

A brief survey of the earlier volume, the Hermeneutic, will indicate its scope. The organization is partly historical and partly thematic. After a brief introduction to 'The Old Testament as a Hermeneutical Problem', Chapter 2 goes on to 'The Old Testament as a Heritage'. This is concerned primarily with the patristic period: the break with Judaism, principles like typology and allegory, the idea of the 'Old Testament' itself, the unity of Old and New, and the dogmatic 'suppression' (*Verdrängung*) of the problem. Chapter 3 is on 'The Old Testament in the Light of the Reformation and in the Fire of Historical Criticism'; in fact it goes beyond what this title would suggest, for it comes up to the rise of modern Old Testament theology and looks briefly at prospects for the future. Chapter 4 has the title 'The Old Testament as Law and Covenant Document' and introduces the themes of law, rejection of 'Jewish law', relativization of the law by the prophetic movement, and so on. Chapter 5 undertakes the sensitive subject of 'The Old Testament as Document of an Alien Religion'. Unlike many other scholars, who simply recoil with horror at any suggestion that the religion of the Old Testament is an 'alien' religion (alien, that is, to Christianity), Gunneweg takes the formulation very seriously.[5] Chapter 6 is on 'The Old Testament as a book of History' and handles the familiar questions involved in this. The final Chapter 7 is entitled 'The Old Testament as Part of the Christian Canon'. It is plain that many of the major themes and problems of Old Testament theology are handled here.

We saw already that the anxiety to hold biblical theology and the history of Israelite religion clearly apart, which had been an important principle for some earlier biblical theologians, had come to be considered less important, or even to be totally ignored, by some later workers. Nowhere is this clearer than in the title of Gunneweg's later work, according to which the same book is a 'Biblical Theology of the Old Testament' and at the same time a 'History of the Religion of Israel within a Biblical-Theological View'. Moreover, this work, we are told on the back cover, 'considers the Old Testament consciously in the context of the Christian canon'.[6] So here once again we have a work that brings together the elements which one had formerly thought it necessary to hold apart: theology, history of religion and biblical canon can all combine together.

As is the case with the study on hermeneutics, the organization of the volume is basically a historical one, apart from the opening chapter which sketches the rise of modern Old Testament theology, recent proposals, and the plan of the present work. Thereafter there are chapters on: 2. The Environing Ancient Religions, especially the Canaanite; 3. The 'Pre-Israelite' or Patriarchal Period; 4. The Origin of the Main Religious Themes in the Early-Israelite Period; 5. Israel's Religion in the Epoch of the Tribal Confederacy; 6. Religious Innovations in the Epoch of Existence under the State; 7. The Great Prophetic Movement of the Time of the Kings; 8. The Babylonian Exile and Radical Religious Change (*Umbruch*); 9. The Jerusalem Restoration and its Prophets; 10. The Late Post-Exilic Period.

The general structure therefore very much suggests a history of religion. A glance at the content, however, will show that the purposes and interests of a Theology are central throughout and thus justify the main title of the book. Although the framework may be organized through temporal description of religious history, the discussion and the questions raised belong much more to theology: theology 'in the sense of reflection and afterthought about religion, of spiritual interpenetration of faith and as an attempt to make faith

expressible and also to proclaim faith' (147). We begin with the primary assertion that:

> The object of a theology of the Old Testament is not the revelation of God
> which took place in Israel/Judah, nor is it God in this history of Israel; for
> God is not the object of an academic discipline but is the 'over-against'
> (*Gegenüber*) of faith. The object [of such a theology] is rather the under-
> standing of God, the self-understanding – with Fohrer the *Daseinshaltung*
> or attitude to existence – of Israelite/Judaean people who are the (mainly
> anonymous) authors of the Old Testament texts or of those to whom these
> texts are directed (34).

It is interesting to note how Gunneweg stands close to Fohrer in his use of the
concept *Daseinshaltung* (34).

Theology (here I follow p.176) as a historical science cannot decide the
questions of truth. It can work out the original sense, intention, direction, and it
can interpret the results for the present meaning; but whether one identifies
oneself with these utterances is an existential decision of faith. This is the
difference between exegesis, science and theology on one side and preaching on
the other. This view, we note, is markedly different from many Anglo-Saxon
viewpoints, which tend to put exegesis and historical studies on one side and
theology along with preaching on the other.

Secondly, the historical character of the understanding of God and self must
not be forgotten. The relation between past and present is not a subject-object
relation but a dialogical subject-subject relation. Historical understanding is a
dialogical process: there is mutual and retroactive action between past and
present, between modern interpretation and the understanding of ancient
times, between explaining and being explained. According to Gunneweg, this
dialogical relation exposes as false the dilemma between objective history of
religion and committed or believing theology; this *aporia* can be overcome.
Compared with this insight, the question whether the representation of the
material is chronological or systematic is one of secondary importance and has
only practical or didactic significance.

Thirdly, a theology of the Old Testament has to avoid assuming that the Old
Testament is a *Vorstufe*, a preliminary stage to the New. The Old Testament is
not dependent on the New, and Judaism also can rightly appeal to it as its basic
document. The Old Testament 'closes itself' against the traditional schemes of
prophecy/fulfilment, type/antitype, law/gospel, and also against schematiza-
tion on the lines of Christian dogmatics.

Fourthly, nevertheless, Old Testament theology has to prove itself as a part
of Christian theology. 'This certainly cannot mean that the Old Testament is to
be interpreted in a Christian sense. What is pre-Christian cannot be interpreted

as Christian.' The historical discipline of Old Testament theology is Christian theology, in that it takes into account the historical fact of the Christian canon of Old and New Testament.

How does it do this? This is a critical question. Gunneweg's answer is:

It does this by confronting the Old Testament self-understanding or *Daseinshaltung* or the knowledges of faith and their changes and disagreements with other possibilities of the understanding of existence, of the world and of God and also measures them evaluatively by the standard of the central knowledge-in-faith and *Daseinshaltung* of the New Testament (35).

This he claims to be a scientific and controllable undertaking. It is equally possible to carry out the converse operation and ask how far the New Testament represents a degeneration from authentic Judaism; the answer to this could be that Jesus belonged within Judaism while Paul had broken with it. All this is strictly scientific; but faith, not science, determines the decision between the two preferences and thus, for example, makes the decision whether the Pauline letters should be rejected as post-biblical and unbiblical, or whether they belong to the essential content of Christianity.

Fifthly, for the reception of the Old Testament in the church the New Testament is the criterion. The New Testament structure of faith is the 'canon within the canon' (161). Gunneweg resists the 'Calvinistic over-estimation' of the Old Testament (*Understanding*, 7), setting it in parallel to, but in reversed direction from, the Marcionite rejection of the Old Testament. Wherever the attitude to existence of the Old Testament shows itself equal to this criterion, the Old can be directly accepted as Christian, preached and taught, without the reading in of any Christian or christological interpretation. This is in fact what has been done all along. The church has always used the Old Testament critically in the sense of the church's own criterion and has thus always factually used it in the form of selections.

Sixthly, this selection complements the Christian message, because the latter itself assumes it from the beginning: examples are monotheism, creation, the idea of election, the conception of a people of God among the heathen, and the Psalter, a selection used as the prayer book of Christianity.

If Kaiser has shown that a Theology may combine historical-critical study with the history of religion and still be an actively Christian undertaking with a strong canonical emphasis and a deep interest in interpretation for the present day, a similar effect is exercised by Gunneweg's work.

It is clear that Gunneweg has a strong and clear set of principles, many of which will be controversial. He is close to other Old Testament theologians on certain points, but departs from them on others. Thus his emphasis on the Christian character of Old Testament theology and on the New Testament as the final criterion reminds one of Vriezen; both of them agree that the New Testament and Christianity have used the Old Testament critically and selectively, and rightly so. On the other hand Vriezen insisted on revelation as the object of his theological study, while Gunneweg declared this to be out of reach and thought that only human ideas and human existential attitudes were accessible.

Other aspects of Gunneweg's thinking include the following. He expresses quite strong opinions on various detailed points. The covenant concept with the formula 'Yahweh God of Israel, Israel people of Yahweh' is not a bad choice for something like a 'centre' (71). If so, it applied exclusively to Israel, and was not a relation between God and man. But this covenant conception was not received or continued in the New Testament (here he was following Grässer).[7] Gunneweg argues this vigorously (72), entering into the combination of texts and vocabulary customarily used to connect 'covenant' with the early church. In place of the exclusiveness of the covenant with Israel, genealogically and nationally definable, there now stands the *inclusiveness* of the 'many', for whom Jesus' blood was shed. It is thus 'flagrant heresy' ('*eklatante Häresie*') when church authorities sometimes say that the new covenant includes the comprising of the Gentiles within the covenant of Israel (73): this is just as bad as the opposite error of the 'German Christians' in making Jesus into an Aryan and calling for the abrogation of the Old Testament. The new διαθήκη creates a new reality (105), an *Existenz* in this world but not of this world. If the Christian church falls back into the pre-Christian attitude to existence it loads itself with all the pre-Christian apories and tragedies to which Israel was a victim.

Some of Gunneweg's ideas seem rather traditional. He is fully aware of recent trends which move the 'Yahwist' down to a late date or abolish him altogether, but he stoutly defends a fairly early date (149). Von Rad's 'Solomonic Enlightenment' is still here (236), but slightly qualified. Some popular sociological approaches to the early history of Israel are dependent on a 'Marxist-socialist ideology which was already out of date when it originated' (90). The notion that Canaanite culture was dominated by the *cyclic* rhythm of nature has by now become questionable; but Gunneweg rather emphasizes it, repeating it several times and making it a key point of opposition between Canaanite and Israelite religion (43, 93,102). The idea of the amphictyony, on the other hand, though used quite a lot, is treated with critical caution (89f, 96f., 105). Some thoughts may seem to the reader to be rather incongruous in this setting: so for example the doctrine of the two kingdoms, which is obviously very important to the author and is repeated twice (118f., 197). Again, he follows common German opinion in emphasizing the secondary place of creation as compared with exodus and redemption (139, 142).

Others of Gunneweg's thoughts are very original and provocative; some of these have been quoted above. Another appears on p. 95: it is commonly argued that the God of the Old Testament is also the God of the New and the Father of Jesus Christ, and that this fact is sufficient to guarantee that the Old and New Testament belong together. Gunneweg points out, surely rightly, that this infinitely repeated argument deserves to be treated with some reservations.

Unless 'one returns to a massive verbal inspiration', it is a justified concern to investigate the psyche of the Prophets (174). Yet this is not likely to succeed (176); nevertheless we must come back to it again and again (179).

By contrast with many other Old Testament theologies, detailed engagement with the New Testament is quite extensive in this book (see for example 72ff., 82ff., 137f.). The term 'faith' is very frequently used when speaking of Old Testament situations. That faith is not a work of man but the reception of that which God does, is emphasized (151, 157). The reception of the Hebrew Bible is of high importance. Much emphasis is given to the use of κύριος (82–4). The Christian God does not have a name. In this connection the LXX wording ἐγώ εἰμι ὁ ὤν at Exod. 3.14, which is described (79) as 'inappropriate and rather philosophical-sounding' (as it is in almost all scholarly works) is soon afterwards (81) given a more positive interpretation: 'linguistically, it was inexact, but it was for all that none the less meaningful theologically and at the same time philosophically'. There follows a mention of tendencies in Ben Sira and especially in the Alexandrian Jewish philosopher Aristobulos, who held the Jewish tradition to be the true philosophy and the Jews to be a people of philosophers, and then a long quotation from the honoured older New Testament scholar Schlatter, who tells us: 'None of the ancients seemed to let himself merge with the biblical convictions as easily as did Aristotle' – an utterance that would have been unheard-of in all earlier biblical theology! Jewish theology began with Aristotle.

*Scheitern* (failure, originally 'shipwreck'), and aporia are frequent terms (e.g. 196f.), suggesting a Bultmannian background. But the use of them is qualified. Thus:

> Karl Barth, who wanted to understand human religion exclusively as a 'work' of man ... and therefore as sin, was just as wrong in this one-sidedness as was Bultmann, who wanted to read the entire Old Testament as a book of shipwreck and as the paradigm for our own personal shipwreck (130).

'Demythologization' also appears, but is mainly used not for a modern interpretative method but for a mode in which ancient Israel demythologized myths like the conflict with the primitive dragon (142, 155) or institutions like kingdom and state (148f.).

Gunneweg's introductory section on the modern history of Old Testament theology (20–33) gives most space to the discussion of Eichrodt (24f.) and especially von Rad (26–9), who is deeply respected by Gunneweg but against whom he levels a notable series of criticisms (28). Debate with von Rad, or at least interaction with his opinions, continues at various later points (e.g. 142, 236, 245). There are also paragraphs on Zimmerli and Westermann, but a rather longer appreciation of Fohrer is particularly notable:

> It is regrettable that Fohrer's crystal-clear and scarcely refutable reflections have not found more notice in the discussion. Starting from Fohrer's approach, the old dilemma between history of religion and theology of the Old Testament is no longer impossible to overcome (30f.).

A final page (32f.) is devoted to Childs, and some objections to the canonical approach are raised there. The importance of the canon is by no means to be underestimated. But, in particular, while the 'final form' has its own meaning, so have the many and varied past traditions which have gone to make up the canon: thus the final form of the prophetic books does not make the original significance of the prophets unimportant. As mentioned above (Ch. 24), Gunneweg thinks that Childs 'successfully avoids vulgar fundamentalism, but only with the help of a new, more canonical, fundamentalism'. He also adds, rather enigmatically, that the reception as such (that is, of the Old Testament as part of the two-part Christian canon) 'poses its own questions to the Pharisaic canon of the Hebrew Bible' – here rather similar to Gese's thinking?

In fact, in spite of the phrase 'in the context of the Christian canon' on the back cover, there is not much about the canon in the book: its final section is on 'Eschatology and Apocalyptic' and there is no section on canon formation or the like. Probably the phrase is to be taken as a reference to the interaction with the New Testament, which, as we have seen, is a very real element in the work.

In spite of its arrangement as a history of Israelite religion, the originality and significance of Gunneweg's work seems to lie primarily on the side of theology. Here he offers many rich and suggestive insights, especially in the interrelation between the Old Testament and the New, or between the Old Testament and Christianity.[8] He is not so much collecting and restating the theological material of the Hebrew Bible; rather, ultimately speaking, he is discussing the theological matrices within which that material is to be grasped.

## 3. Preuss

Horst Dietrich Preuss's *Old Testament Theology* appeared in two substantial volumes in 1991 and 1992 (English translation by Leo Perdue, 1996). The first chapter, entitled 'Determination of the Standpoint', furnishes a brief history of the subject and discusses the possible approaches to be taken. Preuss briefly reviews the modern discussion of a 'centre' around which Old Testament theology may suitably be arranged (I, 21ff.). Seeking to provide an adequate answer, he arrives at the rather complex formula, difficult to express in English: 'Yahweh's electing historical action upon Israel for community with his world, which is at the same time an action that puts obligation upon this people (and the other peoples)' (German '*JHWHs erwählendes Geschichtshandeln an Israel zur Gemeinschaft mit seiner Welt, das zugleich ein dieses Volk (und die Völker) verpflichtendes Handeln ist*', 29).

The reasoning behind this includes the following. In the Old Testament we do not have before us the revelation of God as such; rather, we have testimonies to it and answers to it – in this respect a position rather like that of Gunneweg described above (27). The 'facts' are there only in the 'kerygma'. The Old Testament witnesses primarily not to God's being but to his action. God's action is primarily upon Israel and is an action which *elects* a group to community (*Gemeinschaft*) with him; in doing this he places *obligation* upon this people. The basic election is in the exodus from Egypt, but this then serves as the basis for future action. Action that both elects and imposes obligation is thus the typical thing in the Old Testament, the 'basic dimension of Old Testament faith'.[9] The Hebrew Bible thus demands an essential interpenetration (*Ineinander*) of 'systematics' and of 'history', of synchrony and diachrony, and it also makes such an interpenetration possible through the recognition of this its basic structure.

The main and central structures of the Old Testament, Preuss believes, must align themselves with this 'centre'. But, quoting Smend, 'the centre of the Old Testament is not the totality of the Old Testament', and the setting up of a 'centre' must necessarily mean that the various books and texts have to be 'placed' in their varying degrees of nearness to this centre (24). Moreover, there are some bodies of text within the Hebrew Bible which may be said to have sought to unfold a 'theology' of their own – he thinks of Deuteronomy, Deutero-Isaiah, perhaps the Priestly document – and obviously one will have to keep particularly close to such materials.

Here one comes on to the connections with the New Testament on one side and with Jewish understanding on the other. One will have to ask whether this perception of basic structures within the Hebrew Bible is open to the possibility of pan-biblical theology as a Christian concern; if it is so, then it must avoid seeking to deprive the Jews of their Bible or even giving a possible impression of so doing. Yet (here more in agreement with Childs) the Christian interpreter can scarcely read the Old Testament as if he or she had never heard of the New. To sum up this point, Old Testament theology is not in itself pan-biblical theology, nor is it normative Christian theology; as Old Testament theology it is not to be measured by the standard of the New (here against Gunneweg).

Positively, however, Old Testament theology would wish, 'precisely through its historical-descriptive asking after the basic structures of Old Testament faith', to *prepare the way for* pan-biblical theology. Preuss concludes this careful statement of his plan with the hope that Jewish readers would also find the comprehensive view of the Hebrew Bible attempted here to be an appropriate one (I, 25).

Following this decision, the total structure of Preuss's work has four great sections, two in each of the volumes:

I. An overview (§2) of the election passages of the Hebrew Bible, and following this a full discussion (§3) of the choosing of the people and the placing of them under obligation.

II. Yahweh as subject of the electing action in history. This includes (§4) the names of God, his 'working powers' (spirit, face, angel, name etc.), his 'revelation' (clearly treated as an uncertain subject, and so marked by him in inverted commas): 'The Old Testament knows no *concept* (*Begriff*) of revelation, certainly not a sole or fixed one' (I, 200), God as creator, and the question of utterances about the 'being' or 'essence' of God, including eternity, holiness, jealousy, the living God, and anthropomorphism. §5 is entitled 'God's world and the world far from God', and here we find the dwelling places of YHWH, the ark, the tent of meeting, groups like the cherubs and seraphs, demons, Satan, and the underworld – perhaps a somewhat incongruous group.

The second volume includes:

III. The outworkings of the original election and the further thinking out of it: the further objects of the electing action of YHWH in history. This includes sub-sections on such subjects as the patriarchal narratives, kingdom, temple, priesthood and prophets.

IV. Results and implications of the experienced historical election. Here we will find 'the Israelite and his relation to God' (anthropology), the life of the chosen (basic questions of ethos and ethic), the divine service of Israel (cult), the future of the people of God (future expectations, eschatology, apocalyptic) and 'the chosen people of God and the nations'.

Preuss has written with great competence and consistency, both in exegesis and in theology. His work is dense and rich in information. It has very ample notes (nearly 200 pages of them) and thus gives the reader a wide sweep of information about the present and recent exegetical scene, much more than any other book in modern Old Testament theology; unlike Childs, who also has read extensively and quotes widely, Preuss gives the impression that the scholarly discussion has been positive and helpful to him. The book is perhaps somewhat heavy to read, partly because biblical references, which are very numerous, are cited only with chapter and verse numbers and have to be looked up every time by the reader.

Looking back on his work at its end (II, 307), Preuss sees it as 'historically oriented and purely descriptive' and thinks that it cannot in the end be left like this. 'Old Testament theology will have to join in the endeavour within Christian theology to produce a "biblical theology".' The orientation backwards to the Old Testament [as provided by Old Testament theology, I think he means] will ensure that in such a combined theology the important message of the Old Testament does not come off too badly'.[10] On the question of *how* the Old Testament is to be treated within this other 'biblical theology' he seems to offer no suggestion.

Basically Preuss's book seems to be an affirmation and a continuation of that classic line which began with Eichrodt.[11] One hears an echo of that earlier scholar in the first paragraph, where the purpose is defined as the attempt to offer 'an overview of the world of faith and witness of the Old Testament' (*'eine Zusammenschau der Glaubens- und Zeugniswelt des AT'*). Although difficulties in this approach have been seen, later experience suggests that the line taken by Eichrodt, and here followed by Preuss, may be the most practical approach to be seen thus far. But a consequent problem will be mentioned shortly.

Some recent proposals looking in a more 'canonical' direction (he mentions Clements, Childs, Martens, Goldingay, Rendtorff) are discussed (I, 17–19), but seem to be considered as being too vague so far. Less attention or none at all, on the other hand, is given to those who think that the whole project of an Old Testament theology is conceptually incoherent, inherently anti-Jewish (Levenson), theologically undesirable, or else simply impossible to put into practice. Apart from the introductory discussion of recent interest in the canon, little interest in the canon is shown, and indeed it is seldom mentioned. One such case is the following.

It was only from later times, looking back, that it could be seen who was a 'true' prophet and who a 'false' one (II, 86): the framework of understanding was set by the canon. 'That the problem for earlier hearers had been set quite differently was now more seriously lost from view through the fact that the prophets had become scripture.'

The apocryphal books receive rather few mentions. Sirach receives a paragraph (II, 251) for its more positive relationship to temple, cult and priesthood. Parts of Enoch may be earlier than Daniel (II, 280), and incidentally von Rad was wrong in associating apocalyptic with wisdom (II, 277). A positive role assigned to Sirach and Wisdom in developing and enhancing the Wisdom tradition after Job and Qoheleth (II, 207) will be mentioned below. Rabbinic Judaism is scarcely mentioned, if at all.

At this point it is relevant to notice that on historical matters Preuss seems to take something of a traditional critical point of view. The 'ancestors' like Abraham were brought together in a linear succession, possibly by JE (II, 10), and thus are figures of tradition rather than historical personages. Once we come to David and Solomon, however, it seems that we are dealing with real people. Likewise in the prophets it seems that the books tell us more or less what Amos or Jeremiah were like and what they said. Preuss is aware of recent trends in criticism that maintain that the books present a late ideology rather than a reliable historical picture, but on the whole he seems to pass that tendency by.

Particular interest attaches to his use of the Wisdom literature. As has been mentioned, he has elsewhere considered this material to be unsuitable for use in Christian preaching,[12] and it is interesting to ask how far this evaluation has made a difference to his descriptions of it in his Theology. In fact – contrary to what one would expect on the basis of common current assumptions – there is little sign that this evaluation has affected his work. In this particular respect, it seems, convictions about present-day values and relevance have, to the author's credit, made little difference to historical description. Thus see his discussions of the relations between wisdom and creation (I, 227–31), between wisdom and humanity (II, 126–34), between wisdom and ethics (II, 203ff.), between wisdom and the cult (250), all of which seem to treat the wisdom traditions quite positively. 'Limitations' of the ethics of wisdom are noted (II, 207), but these limitations are already to be seen within Proverbs and are made completely clear by Qoheleth and Job. Then 'the further development of Israelite wisdom (Sirach and the Wisdom of Solomon) shows that this wisdom necessarily underwent many alterations and enhancements for its preservation and continued corroboration'.

Among many other points of interest we may note the secondary place of creation: 'Yahwistic faith is primarily election faith on which is based faith in salvation' – statements about creation are additions to this original basis (I, 237). In this Preuss follows familiar tendencies of German theology. 'Creation theology, like the monarchy, the kingdom of God, the temple, and the agrarian festivals, belonged to the elements of the piety of a sedentary civilization which were later assigned to Yahwistic faith' (ibid.) On the other hand, H. H. Schmid's thoughts about a creation theology, closely entwined with ancient Near Eastern thinking about order, are mistaken (ibid.).

Some further points of interest: Abraham's 'faith' is not as constant as one might suppose, but Gen. 15.6 turns out to be faith all the same, after a rather complicated argument (II, 160ff.).[13]

On the place of women, the Hebrew Bible, we are told, is not helpful to the cause of women's emancipation (II, 109). In the same section, Preuss offers us his explanation of polygamy 'allowed because numerous progeny were sought in order to increase the family's labour force and because this provided a support system for as many women as possible as well as for aged parents later on' (104): this looks like an idea of his own rather than anything that could be proved from the Hebrew text (and how could it work unless there were twice or more as many women as men?).

Like some other Old Testament Theologies, Preuss's work contains quite considerable amounts of material which could be considered to belong equally to the history of religion, and he notes it as a defect in von Rad's work that this consideration is largely neglected there (I, 20). Thus there is a full discussion of the faith of the ancestors as 'an El religion' involving the amalgamation of El with Yahweh (II, 9, etc.) and there is likewise a recognition of the deities Sedeq and Shalem in Jerusalem (I, 173f.; II, 42, etc.), with their further incorporation into Yahweh.

Like many Christian Old Testament theologians, Preuss continues from time to time, at the end of a major section, to slip in some sort of mention of Christianity or hint at it. In his work, however, such mentions are few and slight. Jesus is mentioned at II, 208 and Luther is quoted (II, 252); at II, 184 we have mention of Paul and justification: 'Already in the Old Testament it is clear that within the particular, fundamental structures of Old Testament piety there already exists what Paul calls the justification of the sinner' (cf., however, 370 n.622, which gives evidence of a contrary view); the sentence 'the Word became flesh' (John 1.14) is mentioned as a fitting summary to end the discussion of Hebrew language and its connection with Hebrew thought (II, 135–140).

On the other hand, in a number of places there are remarks which show Judaism in a favourable light. Thus II, 214 has the welcome comment that one cannot say that the ancient Hebrew cult represented works, not grace (a note here refers back to Köhler). Another conclusion to a section tells us:

> The Old Testament awaits the sovereignty of God, even as Judaism later on awaits it as well. Christianity awaits this sovereignty together with both of these and offers the prayer 'Thy kingdom come' (II, 283).

And a chapter conclusion says: 'In the tension between the priests and the prophets, there is ultimately a tension between the God who has come and the God who is to come' (II, 66).

To sum up, outside his introductory pages Preuss's references to aspects of the New Testament and Christianity are few and slight.

Preuss's work is competent and comprehensive. If it continues the line established by Eichrodt, it must also be said that it succeeds in avoiding some of the weaknesses that were to be found in that earlier work. But there remains one basic question, and that is whether the book gives us enough of a *theological* lead. I leave aside the introductory chapter which discusses the history, methodology and structure of Old Testament theology (I, 1–26): the theological understanding that animates this section is clear. But when we come to the main body of this very compact and comprehensive book,[14] we cannot avoid at times the feeling that it presents us with the *necessary material* for a theology rather than a theology itself. This is of course no new criticism, and was classically stated by Karl Barth about critical scholarship in general. But in Preuss's work it seems at least in places to be valid. Take for instance the suggestions, which may well be quite correct, that at some early stage Yahweh was combined with El, and later again with Sedeq and Shalem, deities of Jerusalem. One does not dispute the fact, and it seems important: but how does one understand such a process theologically? If it is true, does it not make a great difference to our idea of the God of Israel? Or take another very minor example: in his section on marriage (II, 103–5) Preuss mentions the institution of the levirate. Everyone knows about this: but what theological conception does it convey? In respect of really *theological* initiatives, the much shorter books of scholars like Fohrer, Kaiser and Gunneweg seem to offer more.

Unease about things like this remains with the reader after Preuss's exemplary work. It brings us back to criticisms of Eichrodt that were made by Vriezen and von Rad in different ways. Or does it mean that Preuss is quite right, and that a strictly *biblical* theology, or an Old Testament theology, just cannot deal with these problems, and that a preparatory, ancillary, role is the only function it can have?

## 4. Conclusion

A number of recent presentations of the problems of Old Testament theology have concentrated their attention on the more familiar and earlier 'classics' of the field, normally in fact on Eichrodt and von Rad, as if these formed the two basic types and as if a 'crisis' or a 'stalemate' was created by the difference between them. I think that this was mistaken, and that important advances were made by the work of the 1970s and especially that of the 1990s. Works like those of Fohrer and Gunneweg do not have the massiveness of the two classics named, but they certainly put new possibilities before us. Kaiser's work cannot be fully evaluated because it is unfinished at the time of writing. That of Preuss fully equals the massiveness of the older works, and may well have succeeded in avoiding some of their weaknesses.

# 27

# Natural Theology within Biblical Theology

## *1. Central biblical sources*

The subject of natural theology has been mentioned at several places within these pages, and Chapter 10 in particular described the intellectual background and the way in which biblical theology allowed itself to become a servant of that rejection of natural theology which had become dominant in the twentieth century. As I said there, if it turns out that natural theology is actually present within the Bible, or is at least supported by it or even only possibly implied by it, the effect is to overturn a large proportion of the assumptions and values which have underlain modern biblical theology. This present chapter, as much as any other in this book, is therefore likely to have an innovative impact on the subject.

In approaching it, for the present I will take for granted the traditional terms of the question, such as 'natural theology' and 'revelation'. It is by no means my purpose to show that we must use the expression 'natural theology', and a number of scholars have pointed to the unclarity of the terms and made alternative proposals. At a later point in this chapter I shall return to this, but for the present I assume the customary terminology.

Now I do not have to spend much time in 'proving' that the Bible contains, implies and supports natural theology, since I have provided full argumentation for this in my Gifford Lectures.[1] A short summary will suffice. I began from the New Testament. Paul's speech on the Areopagus (Acts 17.22–34) is the prime example. The argument starts from creation and the opposition to idolatry, both prime aspects of Judaism and especially emphasized in its Hellenistic documents. There is no mention of the people of Israel, of the patriarchs or the prophets, or of the law of Moses. No Old Testament text is cited, though the substance of some is incorporated; the only 'scripture' quoted is, explicitly, from a Greek poet, a good representative of that Stoic universalism which was later to become so influential in Christian theology and notably in Calvin. The emphasis is entirely universal. God has no needs for which he is dependent on humanity, but he has given life and breath to all in the hope that they might feel after him and find him. Such a hope is not a remote fancy, for though transcendent, God is not far from each of us: 'we' includes all humanity, and God is the medium which envelops us all. In the past he overlooked human ignorance about the essential matter, namely the wrongness of worship of images, but now he commands all to repent. The argument comes back to the resurrection, which had been mentioned also in the conversations beforehand (v. 18). Judgment and resurrection were customary themes of 'special' revelation, but the *way* in which Paul presented his argument is a typical natural-theology approach. The various arguments against this are discussed elsewhere;[2] suffice it here to say that I consider them mistaken.

The one serious counter-argument is the historical-critical one to the effect that this is not Paul himself at all. Seen in this way, Luke as author of Acts foisted on his 'Paul' a sort of natural theology that seemed to him, Luke, to be fitting for the scene at Athens, but this was at best a misunderstanding of Paul. As stated above (169f.), the existence of this critical argument made it easier for those who denied natural theology. And of course the historical-critical argument could be quite right, though I do not myself think it to be wholly so; in any case it makes no difference to my position. For, even if Luke's piece of natural theology is a misrepresentation of Paul, the fact remains that this piece of natural theology is there in the Bible and has to be taken seriously by anything professing to be biblical theology. One can indeed take the view that the genuine letters – or the genuine thoughts – of Paul are the true centre of authority within the Bible (perhaps many biblical theologians think so), but, even if so, the natural theology which Luke *thought* to be Pauline has to be recognized as a factor in any theology of the New Testament or of the Bible.

In fact, even if Luke misunderstood Paul, it seems to me that he misunderstood something that was genuinely there in Paul. Romans 1–2 contains a series of arguments that at the very least are very similar to natural theology. In 1.18–32 Paul (if we may take it that it *is* Paul this time!) explains the wrath of God against human wickedness on the grounds that 'what can be known of God is plain to them, because God has shown it to them'. Ever since the creation of the world his invisible nature has been clearly perceived *in the things that have been made*. They are therefore without excuse. Having failed to recognize God in the created things, they worshipped the created things in place of God. Therefore they were given up by God to evil and to 'unnatural' sexual practices. That is, just because 'natural revelation' was disregarded, and 'natural' things were worshipped in the place of God, the punishment that fell on humanity included 'unnatural' evils.

Again, in 2.12–16, though Gentiles do not have the 'special' law of God, as revealed to Moses, they may nevertheless 'by nature' do things that come under the function of that law. They 'show the work of the law written in their hearts, their conscience (συνείδησις) witnessing together [with it?] and their thoughts accusing or defending'. In both these passages 'nature', φύσις, is not an incidental factor but a central theological criterion. The term *conscience*, with its distinct Stoic background, is equally notable. Now there are indeed arguments which try to show that these passages do not involve or imply natural theology, but they are exegetically very weak, and show strong evidence of the extreme bias against natural theology that has been dominant throughout most of the twentieth century. And of course the passages are not natural theology in the fully developed and philosophical sense which we see in the Cappadocian Fathers or in the Middle Ages. But they do appear to imply that there is something validly known of God, revealed through his created works, which is accessible to all human beings through their being human, and which through the law 'written in the heart' forms a resource for moral decision. And even if that is not natural theology in the developed sense, it is closer to the basis of natural theology than it is to the revelation-centred, kerygmatic, theology that has been dominant in most of the twentieth century.

And this means, incidentally – for it is not essential to our argument – that it is more likely that Luke's portrayal of Paul in Acts 17, though perhaps a misunderstanding or an exaggeration, was a portrayal of something that was really there. Paul did use – even if only occasionally – arguments which in the later church were *rightly* understood to point towards and lead towards the development of natural theology. This will doubtless be disputed. But even if it is disputed, the case of Acts 17 alone is enough. By it the situation in biblical theology is immediately changed. For it means that there is at the least a possibility that natural theology is a factor within biblical argumentation and proclamation. Biblical theology therefore can no longer rely on the supposition that natural theology is certainly unbiblical, unless it simply rules out from authoritative status those texts in which it may appear. And those I have mentioned are the absolute minimum: large additional possibilities within the New Testament will be mentioned shortly.

My own discussion went, however, from Paul to the Wisdom of Solomon, for it contains arguments which are very close to those of Romans. Whether Paul knew the book or not – it is, actually, an excessive scepticism to suppose that he did not – he, and he in particular, used arguments that were either drawn from it or were created by someone who thought in very much the same way. Among these are: 1. the use of the story of Adam and Eve to explain why *death* entered the world; 2. a concentration on *idolatry* not only as the primal sin but also as the source from which *all moral evils* flow; 3. an emphasis on *creation*, in the sense that the beauty and wonder of the created things should have led people to a recognition of the creator; 4. natural theology:

> From the greatness and beauty of created things
> the Creator of them is by analogy perceived (Wisdom 13.5).

The first three are all characteristic of Paul, and much more lightly, if at all, represented in other New Testament documents; it becomes much more likely that he, in Romans, used the fourth also.

The importance of the Wisdom of Solomon in this connection immediately raises other questions for biblical theology: for here we are saying that a Greek book, and one outside the Hebrew canon, had a central importance for the thought of Saint Paul and thus served not only as a link in transmission but also as a creative and transforming force in the passage of ideas from the Hebrew Bible to nascent Christianity. Later in this chapter we will return to the questions that arise from this.

Passing to the Hebrew Bible itself, Psalm 19 was always a traditional passage for natural theology:

> The heavens declare the glory of God
> and the firmament proclaims his handiwork.

And this tradition was quite right. Those in modern times who rejected natural theology attempted exegeses that would eliminate the signs of this, but the arguments are strained, specious and not worth spending time upon.[3] There is no good reason for rejecting the presence of natural theology in this poem. At the utmost, one might cast doubt upon the extent and importance of it; but one could not legitimately deny the strong case for it. Knierim writes finely:

> Many Old Testament texts make it clear that Israel, together with its environment, knows about the cosmos and its life, not only from the Torah but also from the observation of the natural which has even flowed into the Torah. In this respect, Israel shares with its environment the common knowledge of God's creation of the world, and of the knowledge and the praise of God.[4]

There are, then, some biblical materials which, while hardly constituting natural theology in its developed patristic or mediaeval sense, belong more naturally to the side of natural theology than to that modern trend which has rigorously excluded natural theology. Even the presence of these few examples would be enough to upset the value system of that modern trend. I do not suppose that one can 'prove' from a few texts, however central, the validity of an important theological position. But these few texts, as I have argued, are only the tip of the iceberg: they are the indication, only seldom made explicit on the surface, of something that underlies large areas of the Bible. We have therefore to go on and look more deeply into the elements that might be relevant. It is no longer a matter of quoting texts, but rather one of identifying elements which would make a difference in the construction of biblical theology as a whole. For this, we begin with the Hebrew Bible.[5]

## (a) Creation

The creation stories of Genesis 1 (and others in the Hebrew Bible) are surely the essential starting point for our theme. God created the world and living beings in an ordered manner and sequence, finishing up with humanity, and rested on the seventh day when all this was complete. But how did the writers of the text know that it all happened in this way? Unlike many other passages, it has no rubric saying 'Thus saith the Lord', no statement that the passage was spoken by God, none even that it was spoken by Moses on behalf of God (the Torah contains no claim that as a whole it was spoken by Moses, although this came to be generally understood. Contrast Jubilees 2.1: 'And the angel of the presence spake to Moses according to the Word of the Lord, saying: write the complete history of the creation, how in six days the Lord God finished all his works and all that he created . . .'). Genesis in itself contains no hint of from where all this knowledge about the six days and their contents came. It simply relates that these were the facts. God did the acts of creation, but did not issue the report about them. Perhaps the creation in itself was a revelation of God, but the report, the story, was not. From where then did it come and why was it believed?

Stories of creation were not unique to Israel but were widespread, and were known especially in Mesopotamia, the area which has left its traces in many features of Genesis.[6] Such stories typically involved the gods, but the stories themselves were human wisdom, or myths, as we may call them. From the beginning Israel probably had such stories in many forms (Genesis 1 is only the most prominent among several in the Bible), or received them from other peoples. It moulded them into a new shape, corresponding to the Hebrew conception of God: in particular traces of polytheism and theomachy, if there were any, were reduced, and the result at least in Genesis 1 was the magnificently monotheistic (even if with some qualifications!) depiction which we now have. But what were the forces that impelled this formation of the story? On one side there were the religious conflicts and religious convictions of Israel; on the other there was the effect of continual human experience of living in the world. The carefully-thought-out sequence with its eight works in six days, and with the two stages in which first the outer physical constitution of the world was established and then the animate creatures were brought forth, ending up with humanity, is a classification that sought to make sense of man's experience of the world. It is often said that Genesis should not be read as a scientific textbook, and of course *we* should not so read it; but for those whom it addressed it had a function quite close to the function which science has in our modern world. To them it *was* a sort of science.

Now this does not prove that it was natural theology, nor am I trying to say that. Genesis does not say, as later natural theology, both in Wisdom of Solomon and in Paul, argued, that God was known through the works which he had created. To Genesis God was known from the beginning: there was no problem or question in the knowing of God. So it is not a matter of how God was known or could be known. I *am* saying, however, that the story of creation derived from human knowledge: from myths and their modifications on the one side, and from the experience of the world as modified through Israel's particular religious conceptions on the other. The later employment of the creation stories as the prime basis for natural theology was certainly an extension of their intrinsic nature and function, but it was not an unnatural extension. If the basis for natural theology is 'anterior knowledge', i.e. knowledge of something about God that is anterior to some further and perhaps more complete revelation, then the creation stories are anterior knowledge and intended as such.

The place of creation as the starting-point should be emphasized. It was surely a great mistake to say, as Westermann said in the tradition of von Rad, that 'the beginning of the Old Testament is not the beginning of Genesis but the beginning of Exodus'.[7] The Bible therefore began with a great act of deliverance, and the creation theme was added on later. Or, as von Rad put it, Old Testament faith was election faith, i.e. 'primarily faith in deliverance': the coexistence of a creation faith in the Bible was therefore for him a *problem* which had to be solved.[8] There may have been some traditio-historical basis for this: it is quite true that many old statements emphasize the exodus from Egypt and say nothing about creation. But as a theological picture it derives its apparent strength from the modern Christian idea of the theological priority of redemption over creation and likewise, analogically, from the emphasis on special revelation and the rejection of natural theology. Any theology emphasizing creation was, after Barth, suspect of leading to natural theology: not surprisingly, for that is what it does lead to, but it is right and not wrong that it does so.

The priority of the exodus may thus have considerable importance as a significant stage in the theological development. But if we see the material as a *story*, the reverse is much more important. The starting-point is all-important. What is said at the beginning sets the stage for that which is to follow.

### (b) Law

On the surface, the legal material of the Hebrew Bible gives the impression of belonging almost entirely to the sphere of revelation.[9] Almost all the laws stand under the rubric 'and the Lord spoke unto Moses, saying . . .'. Biblical law is thus represented as something verbally pronounced by God on Mount Sinai; it is not represented as a group of norms that existed in society or that had evolved in order to meet changing social conditions. But it is likely that the latter was the reality: it was the convention in Israel that, where law was recognized as religiously binding, it was put under the rubric 'law given to Moses at Sinai'. Extremely little legal material exists that does not come under this title.

Within the Bible itself, however, it is extremely likely that law was revised and developed in the course of time. Social conditions changed, unclarities in older laws had to be clarified. Thus over central elements like manslaughter or slavery it is reasonable to trace a development, some texts being later than others and amplifying or modifying the older ones. Few scholars doubt that this is so. But this makes it likely that some legal elements were developed by normal human social processes and came later to be recognized as revelational.

The biblical text itself shows examples of this. Moses received instruction from Jethro his father-in-law, who told him that he was administering the people wrongly and that he must delegate matters to others, keeping to himself only the most special cases. This was good common-sense advice, and was accepted as such; but it was not based on revelation, nor was it represented in the text as being so based.

Particularly decisive, however, is the body of Mesopotamian law, much of it doubtless older than the biblical laws can be. Good examples are the law of the goring ox (Exod. 21.28ff.) and the law of the Hebrew slave (Exod. 21.1ff.). If an ox kills a person, the ox is killed; but if the owner has been warned that it is dangerous and has not restrained it, then the ox is killed and the owner is killed too. A Hebrew slave (probably enslaved through debt) works for six years and then goes free; in the Hammurabi laws the period is three years, but the basic structure of the law is very similar. What God thus 'revealed' through Moses is at most only a variation on something that already existed as a social norm. 'Biblical law, thus understood, comes closer to the operation of natural theology than to that of purely revelatory theology.'[10] One can go on and say that the Bible took this material and made it into revelation, so that in its biblical form it is revelatory: but even so the process is more akin to that of natural theology. Natural theology does not deny revelation; rather, it maintains that revelation can and does take place on the basis of what is already known, of anterior knowledge.

The field of biblical law is thus one which shows a high degree of affinity to the operation of natural theology. When later Jewish apologists explained and defended the laws on the ground that they were in accord with 'nature' or with the structure of the world as contemporary philosophies saw it, they were responding to something that was in the nature of the laws themselves, at least in some cases.

*(c) The prophetic word*

At first sight the prophets would seem to be, of all ancient institutions, the most revelatory in character, the most dependent on the direct word of the Lord, and in all the most remote from natural theology.[11] The prophet was inspired by the Spirit; he had a word from the Lord which he had to speak. But exactly what this word was like, and how it functioned, is a difficult matter to understand.

Yet within the prophetic movement there are aspects which are closer to natural theology than would at first appear. One lies in the adoption, e.g. by Amos, of a sort of common ethical basis, a recognized national or international morality, which was taken to be common ground.[12] Again, the use of *reasoning*, perhaps on the model of a law-court, suggests something very different from mere denunciation, something more like a rational debate. Reasoning of this kind took a central part in the conflict against polytheism and idolatry in books like Isaiah 40–55.

Central to the question, however, must be the way in which the divine word received by the prophet is supposed to have worked in relation to his (or her) own psyche and personality. It is difficult to obtain a clear idea of what most biblical theologians think about this. The psychology of the prophet was a matter of keen interest in older scholarship, and Wheeler Robinson's *Inspiration and Revelation in the Old Testament* (1946) is doubtless the last notable study along this line in English. One of the effects of dialectical theology was to place a sharp *Verboten!* across this track: one had to state the *theology*, not poke into the mental state of biblical people. But merely stating the theology (if that can be done) leaves it vague *how this theology was attained*, which is the problem now concerning us. Biblical theologians, commonly ready with explanations, seem to be coyly taciturn at this point. None of them, so far as one can see, takes the terms quite literally, as if to say that in communicating with prophets God enunciated the precise sentences, in Hebrew and with the correct grammar, vocabulary and phonetics necessary for intelligibility (and these would of course have to be synchronically correct!), and that the prophet merely repeated what he had audibly heard.[13] But if not this, then what?

Perhaps many think that the deity made some sort of non-auditory or sub-sonic communication, which the prophet 'heard' and then passed on. The question then is how far the prophet's own mind, experience and perception of the contemporary situation entered into his rendering of the (originally non-articulate) message. Or the other possibility is that the message came from the prophet's experience and his perception of the situation in the first place, that he or she perhaps piled up a strong heap of violent reactions and sentiments, and then let them burst forth with the deep certainty that the resultant message was the Word of God. I suspect that most theologians hold this latter view but do not like to say so outright. Concentration on the 'theology' of the prophet's utterance can leave delightfully vague the question 'Did the prophet simply get this message from God, so that his thoughts had no part in it?' or 'Was it formulated through his own situation and experiences, in which case he may have worked some of it out by a process akin to natural theology?'. In the latter case the message is still the word of God; the only difference is that the content comes through the mind of the prophet. Even conservative people, who are emphatic about the word coming from God, probably accept this, since they do not want the prophet to be a mere human phonograph.

Thus biblical theologians tend to think of the prophets as persons with moral and theological discrimination – in fact, as rather like biblical theologians themselves. They perceive the deep religious and social dangers and abuses of their times, they foresee coming disaster; they warn the populace and rulers; they demand social justice. They can diagnose the deep structures of evil that underlie religion and society. From the resources of ancient tradition they can summon up images which help to recall the people to ways of righteousness. Quite right. But the more the prophets are seen in this light, the more their greatness and their contribution are seen to lie in *their* perception of their world. And, after all, is it not notorious that the earlier prophets show little sign of knowing the resources of Moses and his law, of Sinai, of the covenant? May it not be, therefore, that their perceptions, out of which their form of the Word of God was formed, came in part – no one supposes in entirety – out of their perceptions of the world and the common moral and religious values which they shared? And if so, a little closer to natural theology than one might have thought?

### (d) The Wisdom literature[14]

The Wisdom literature will probably form a less controversial area, for it will be widely accepted that it has a certain similarity to what later came to count as natural theology.[15] Indeed, the impression of this has been so strong that a number of scholars have found it difficult to accept that the Wisdom literature could really be accepted within Old Testament theology. G. Ernest Wright, for example, had difficulties in this respect,[16] and H.-D. Preuss explicitly argued that the 'act–and–consequence sequence' characteristic of Wisdom was 'a piece of natural theology' which represented 'the way in which the so–called natural man thinks and wishes God to be'.[17] F.-J. Steiert, beginning a survey of the question whether Israelite Wisdom is a 'foreign body' in the Old Testament, describes Preuss's position and makes the judgment: 'In the background of Preuss's thinking is the fear of meeting here with a new form of "natural theology".'[18]

Most scholars have not taken the drastic step of abandoning the Wisdom literature, and have hoped somehow to retain its theological vision within their ideas of Old Testament theology. Nevertheless for many this has not been easy, and, as has been mentioned, von Rad himself seemed to have difficulties in incorporating Wisdom within the framework of his major Theology. The reason is not far to seek: Hebrew Wisdom did not easily accommodate itself to the common parameters of biblical theology, heavily influenced as they were by dialectical theology.

This applies in varying ways and degrees to all three of the major Wisdom books of the Hebrew canon, Proverbs, Job and Qoheleth. These books are in general lacking in the sort of material deemed to be most characteristic of the 'special revelation' of the rest of the Hebrew Bible: the promises to the patriarchs, the covenant, the exodus, the prophets. Connection with history is extremely thin. The name of the God of Israel occurs in Proverbs (87 times), and he is to be trusted and feared, but narratives about him scarcely occur. In Job the name occurs only in the prose framework and not in the poems except at 12.9, said by some to be a proverb, by others to be an insertion in the earliest stages of transmission;[19] God's part in the debates is his speeches in 38–41, and these again are about creation and its wonders.

The Proverbs are another case of the same kind. Most of the proverbs are human comments on human experience, advice on how to behave, warnings against foolishness and recklessness. Much of this material is not at all Yahwistic. Certainly there are also passages that celebrate how Wisdom comes from the Lord, how it was there when he created the world; and in the individual sayings the name of the Lord is sometimes quoted. Quite a large number of the units may well not be Yahwistic; Levenson points out that substantial sections may not have been composed by Israelites at all.[20] A substantial section follows the Wisdom of Amen-em-ope so very closely that it is generally believed to have been adopted in its entirety. Mentions of the name of Yahweh are very unevenly distributed: often there are only two or three in a chapter, as in 11, 12, 14, while 15 has nine in all and 16 begins with eight in the first nine verses, 19 has five and 20 has six. 13, 26, 27 have none at all, and 30 and 31 only one each. Once again I am not suggesting that Proverbs is merely a book of natural theology: few such books exist. But that it is a mixture in this respect is an obvious way in which the understanding of it may be approached. The paucity of suggestions along this line in the scholarly literature is surely an effect of the deep bias against natural theology which has been endemic in this century. When Childs (*Biblical Theology*, 189) writes that the poem of Proverbs 8 'raises the whole issue of wisdom as a mediator of God's self-revelation in the world', what is that 'whole issue' other than the issue of natural theology? I quote again from J. J. Collins:

There are certain fundamental aspects of the sages' approach to reality which are common to natural theology in all ages. Specifically the sages attempted to discern the religious dimension of common, universal human experience without appeal to special revelation or the unique experience of one people. This religious dimension was correlated with the distinctively Israelite tradition but it was not subordinated to it.

Ecclesiastes (Qoheleth) is also close to the questions of natural theology.[21] His reaction against the expectation that traces of God might be found through study of the world as it is is in itself evidence that the Wisdom tradition had encouraged that expectation. Moreover, he does not turn to revelation to solve his difficulties: he looks more to the limitation of man's life and of his knowledge outside his immediate environment. Again, whether or not he engaged with actual influence from Greek philosophy, more than any other person in the Hebrew Bible he was something of a philosopher, one who had, in Martin Hengel's words, 'the *critical individuality* of an acute observer and independent thinker'.[22]

We leave aside for the moment the 'apocryphal' books and other Hellenistic Jewish sources, in which the presence of natural theology is normally unquestioned.

### (e) The New Testament

When we come to the Gospels, we have something that is of paramount importance for Christians. The parables, I wrote, have a clear 'grounding in' (I used the Barthian cliché advisedly) publicly available knowledge and in that sense they come close to natural theology.[23] To quote a few lines from the next page:

> The teaching by parables is important because it is a clear choice to appeal to a source different from the revelatory chain communicated through pre-existing authoritative scripture. Jesus' teaching was visibly his own, and differed in this respect from that of the scribes, who depended on previously given authorities. This is not accidental but is an important clue to the basis and approach of his ministry.

It is not difficult to offer a theological construction which will give a place to this. From a Christian viewpoint Jesus is the centre and culmination of God's presence with human beings in the world. At this point a mode of speech develops in which ancient scripture, though authoritative and the Word of God as always, is left in the background and the truth is communicated on the basis of common experience, experience greatly exaggerated, indications from people's behaviour and from the world around us; this is highly appropriate for incarnation. Here again I am not thinking of 'pure' natural theology, if there ever was such a thing, but of a situation where the distinction between revealed and natural theology is overcome. We might say that there never should have been such a distinction. But the distinction was not important as long as both types were affirmed: it was only a classification that helped in methodological clarity. However, once the total denial of natural theology was not only announced by Barth but made into the distinctive mark of right theology, it became positively damaging. And, of course, in the matter of the parables we seem to have Barth at long last on our side:

> The New Testament parables are as it were the prototype of the order in which there can be *other true words* alongside the one Word of God, created and determined by it, exactly corresponding to it, fully serving it and therefore enjoying its power and authority (my italics).

This is not the end of material in the Gospels, for one would have to consider the possibility that the Johannine Prologue is also a place where a natural theology of the Logos was smelted together with the Old Testament terms of revelation and creation. Whether this is so or not is of course a question for detailed expert exegesis. All that I say is that, from a theological point of view, the possibility is completely open. During this century opponents of natural theology have busily sought to show that every detail of the Prologue comes out of Old Testament tradition and terminology.[24] I find this difficult, in particular because, while it looks obvious that λόγος was a common rendering of *dabar* and would suggest derivation from it (though the actual distribution in the LXX makes this by no means so clear),[25] the peculiar locution ὁ λόγος in this syntax is hardly paralleled in the LXX of the canonical books and seems very odd for Hebrew. Perhaps this is not certain; anyway it is certainly wrong that the question should be foreclosed because of hostility to natural theology.

I have already discussed the obvious cases in Paul and Acts, but these in their turn open the way to much more. As was mentioned above,[26] it is quite proper that the numerous Old Testament quotations in the New should be studied and evaluated, and this has been done in some excellent ways. It is equally important, however, to balance this by the quotation and study of the many places where matters are decided without the use of scriptural passages or with only minimal effect from them, and where therefore some sort of philosophical or common-sense argument is used. A striking example is the lengthy and important passage about the resurrection, I Cor. 15.35–57, where the substantial quotation in vv. 54f. comes in after the main argument is over. Just before this, at v. 33, we note the affirmative use of a Greek proverb, attributed to Menander, who was no channel of special revelation; cf. the Greek quotation, already mentioned, at Acts 17. 28.

The same may apply to some of the passages of ethical instruction, sometimes known as *Haustafeln*, in the Epistles. For instance, Colossians 3.1–4.5 appears to have no biblical quotations, though it does have some references. This does not mean that all the content is natural theology. Most of it is doubtless derived from Christian teaching. But many of the ethical terms are strikingly close to terms of Greek popular philosophy.

The above paragraphs refer to various *books* or *passages* which may be relevant for our theme. It may also be affected, as was briefly touched on above, by semantic questions about the meaning of words, especially theological terms of the New Testament. In the time of the Biblical Theology Movement (in Childs' sense), word studies and lexical investigations were a major way in which attempts were made to prove, against 'Hellenistic' interpretations which might have pointed in the direction of natural theology, that such words, though outwardly Greek, had Hebrew meanings and thus were 'grounded in' the 'special revelation' of the Old Testament. In fact opinion has swung the other way. I quote again the judgment of Link, following Bornkamm:

> It cannot be disputed that Paul received the thoughts of the Greek tradition, not only eclectically and through a mere borrowing of their vocabulary, but thoroughly in their inner coherence [*Zusammenhang*] and in their framework of reality. He thus positively accepts an internally cohering thought-framework of Gentile natural theology.[27]

But even if opinion has thus changed, it cannot be said that the movement has as yet been sufficient to alter the approach of Old Testament theologians.

A good example might be the terms 'faith' and 'believe' – which take me back to my *Semantics of Biblical Language*, for it was in the study of these terms, which came to form Chapter 7 of that book, that my approach first formed itself. In those days, in the time of the Biblical Theology Movement, it was an obvious approach to insist that 'faith' and 'believe' in the New Testament had received their 'content' from biblical Hebrew. How this was to be explained was not clear, but it was certain that to do so would count as a great advantage. By contrast, any attempt to explain the terms out of the Hellenistic usage would be unwelcome.

A book like the *Greek Rhetorical Origins of Christian Faith* by James L. Kinneavy would therefore have been regarded as the rankest heresy. According to Kinneavy, there is no significant Old Testament background for New Testament 'faith'; on the contrary, the true situation in life from which the latter has arisen is Greek rhetorical practice, with the basic sense of 'persuade, persuasion'. Now it is no part of our purpose here to decide whether Kinneavy is right or not. His book begins at something of a disadvantage, the author admitting from the start (4) that like Shakespeare he has 'small Latin and less Greek' and, we may presume, no Hebrew at all. Nevertheless the small representation of relevant terms in the Old Testament, whether in Hebrew or in the LXX, provides serious support to any theory like Kinneavy's. All I wish to say here is that theology, including biblical theology, should make no attempt to bias the discussion in one way or another.[28] Kinneavy quotes D. M. Baillie, who writes that a hypothetical reader coming to the Old Testament from the New and expecting to find faith 'mentioned on every page' would then be surprised to find, 'to put it roughly and broadly – that the Old Testament never mentions faith at all'. If D. M. Baillie, certainly a distinguished theologian, should be right in judging that 'the Christian notion [of faith] did not come from either Jewish or Greek analogues',[29] then that will be of great theological importance.[30]

It is not my purpose, however, to assemble long lists of passages in order to prove that something akin to natural theology exists in the Bible or is implied in it. I have long ceased to believe that any amount of biblical evidence will convince people against their theological convictions. They have to see a way out, an alternative path for them to take, before they will recognize the biblical evidence for what it is. More important therefore is to consider the ways in which the element of natural theology, if it is there, will change and affect the prospects of biblical theology. Before we go any farther we may turn to the chief explicit discussion of natural theology by a central Old Testament theologian before 1990.

## 2. *Westermann*

The most important utterance about natural theology to appear from any Old Testament theologian before the 1990s came in an article by Claus Westermann in 1987 entitled 'Karl Barths Nein. Eine Kontroverse um die theologia naturalis. Emil Brunner – Karl Barth (1934)'.[31] He begins with a look back at that earlier time:

> Half a century after this controversy, which was then a high point in theological discussion after the seizure of power by the National Socialists, it is worth while, in a completely changed situation, but one in which *creation* has again achieved a special significance, asking how this controversy appears today. When as an Old Testament scholar I look back on this controversy between two systematic theologians, I am particularly occupied by the question of speech about the creator and about creation, then and now. When Barth's article with its provocative title 'No!' appeared – and at that time every number of *Theologische Existenz Heute* was awaited with excitement – enthusiasm among the younger theologians reached a high level, and the article received practically 100% agreement.

So what were Westermann's impressions as he looked back?

It is often said that biblical scholars, in comparison with doctrinal theologians, are naive and uncritical in their use of concepts: they use terms unthinkingly, without asking what they mean; they fail to define or to justify their terminology. Doctrinal or systematic theologians, by contrast, are careful to define and justify their usage, to make clear what they are talking about, to make sure of covering all the possibilities.

Not so! says Westermann as he reconsiders what was then said, and that by two of the most renowned theologians. They were – both alike, it seems – slack and inexact in their argumentation. Both of them 'presuppose' the concept 'natural theology', and neither of them asks from where this concept comes, what it means and how it is to be adjudged on the basis of the Bible (389). 'As an exegete,' he writes, 'one is amazed that so problematic a concept did not induce questioning in either of the two writers.'

Later he goes on to the subject of revelation in creation or *revelatio generalis* (391). Here again it becomes clear 'that the two articles are based on concepts which were formed in the dogmatic tradition but have not been tested (*nachgeprüft*) on the basis of the Bible'. Barth insists passionately that revelation of God is only in Jesus Christ, and that this excludes any possibility of 'natural revelation' or *revelatio generalis*. In the situation of the time this may have been right; but there was a weakness which could scarcely be perceived then. Following the dogmatic tradition, Barth presupposes that one can speak of 'revelation in creation' or of *revelatio generalis*, even if only in order to reject them sharply. In this he assumes an overarching concept of 'revelation' which can comprehend both the coming and work of Christ and also something such as revelation in creation. Such a generalized and abstract concept of revelation can perhaps be derived from Romans 1–3. But apart from this one passage the Bible 'knows no such general, abstract concept of revelation' at all. 'When the Bible elsewhere speaks of creation, it never calls this revelation, and it never speaks of "revelation in creation"' (392). 'It follows from this that the concept of revelation cannot be used at all to apply to the work of God the Creator, and that this work of creation must be spoken of in another, more appropriate, language.' There is no biblical basis for the subsuming of the work of creation under the concept of revelation.

When we pass on to the concept 'knowledge of God' the same thing happens. 'It is astonishing that both [Brunner and Barth] assume the concept "knowledge of God" in this connection as if it were *eo ipso* clear what is meant by it' (393).

Not only so, but both dogmaticians agree that creation did not take place for its own sake: Brunner thought it took place so that man should have a natural knowledge of God; Barth thought it took place as a preparation for the revelation in Christ. Both alike nowhere talk of an action of God upon the world as a whole and on humanity as a whole. That in the Psalms and Deutero-Isaiah all creatures are called to praise along with the worshipping community means little or nothing for either of them. [Brunner, he admits, mentions the praise given by creation, but only once.] Human responsibility towards the created world, and the task of protecting the created world – all this is ignored. The making of man in the image of God is treated only under the one point of view: what it means for human salvation. That creation in the image of God gives to *all humans*, of all peoples, races and religions, the dignity of being God's creatures is said by neither Brunner nor Barth.

Westermann, then, is far from willing to remain within the terms of the discussion of 1934 – on either side. He emphasizes – somewhat in line with my own distinctions – that the Bible contains no *doctrine* of creation. What it gives us is a *story* of creating. Only through its story character is the Bible's speech about creation *living speech*.

> In Genesis 2 what belongs to man is living space, food, community, language, relatedness to God: in Brunner all the talk is abstract, about reason, the human, being a person, the *imago dei*. What we usually call *nature*, non-human nature, appears in both these theologians only in this same concept, *nature*, not in the rich fullness of its concrete reality. For them nature is only a means to an end: therefore they debate whether anything can be *known* from it or not (391).

Westermann, then, does not exactly give an answer to the question of natural theology. He refrains from coming down on the side of either Brunner or Barth. His position is rather that if we start from the biblical creation stories we are led to a different set of concepts and questions altogether. This is how he ends his article:

> That human beings and the world were created by God or by a god was said all over the world in the early history of humanity, in whatever form. In all these creation narratives, myths or epics the aim (*Ziel*) is simply the existence of the world and of man. The fact that they exist is referred back to the action of a god. The creation stories of all mankind agree in this, and the same is true for the creation stories of the Bible. The special character and uniqueness of the latter lies in the fact that they are brought into connection with the history of a people, the people chosen by God, and that this history again leads on to the story of a saviour, a son of this people, through whom God brought deliverance to humanity as a whole. The peculiar meaning of talk about creation, that it is a matter of the existence of the world and the existence of humanity, which God created and whose Lord he is, up to the goal to which he will lead world and humanity, remains the totality of the

action of God, in the midst of which stands God's act of salvation in Christ (394f.).

It is not clear how in the end Westermann would answer the question of natural theology, except for his saying that the question was wrongly put. But that in itself may well be a very substantial contribution made by a biblical theologian to a central question of all theology.

## 3. Revelation

We saw above that Westermann questioned the use of the term 'revelation' in the controversy between Brunner and Barth. The Bible has no general term for revelation,[32] and when it talks of creation it talks in quite other terms. Equally, he thinks, the concept of 'knowledge of God' is not used in the biblical stories and is not applicable to them. In the Bible, creation is an idea about land, food, species, birth and life. 'Revelation' comes out of the dogmatic tradition: most recently, out of the Enlightenment controversies. Quite so. As I said above, the according of a central place to 'revelation' by Barth identifies him with the Enlightenment approach. I had similar ideas when I addressed the problem in *Old and New in Interpretation*, and before that in my early short article 'Revelation', in the preparation of which I went through all the relevant biblical vocabulary.[33] For instance, though it might often be said that God 'revealed himself' in his mighty acts of the exodus, there is not a single certain case where a word 'reveal' is used of these events. The term 'reveal' in the Bible applies to a considerable number of different and quite limited sorts of action, so that, as Westermann says, there is no 'biblical concept of revelation'. Nothing like 'reason' or 'nature' was ever thought of in connection with, or in opposition to, revelation.

'Revelation' is thus a 'second-order' (or third- or fourth-!) term: our use of it as a general term for God's action and communication is an abstraction and generalization, and used in this way it may not be damaging. But I would point out that central theologians have taken a similar position to my own or indeed have gone farther in the same direction. Thus Dietrich Ritschl writes:

> There are serious doubts not about the origin but about the use of the overall term 'revelation'. They are concentrated on the almost inevitable danger that this produces two-storey thinking or reality, a double truth and also a devaluation of secular wisdom and empirical knowledge. The history of theology demonstrates that the church and its theologians have largely succumbed to these dangers. The overall term 'revelation' should be avoided in theological arguments and in the doctrine and proclamation of the church,

because the explanation of its complicated logical derivation, needed if mis-understandings are to be avoided, cannot always be given when the term is used . . . I think it must be possible in the theology of the future to get on without the classical concept of revelation. This classical concept arose first in the Christian church when it came into contact with the gnostic view of the world and God. [34]

On the matter of terminology see Childs, *OTTCC*, 20ff., on 'revelation' as discussed by myself and (independently) Downing.[35] He thinks that these pro-posals offer 'simple, common-sense definitions' (22), and that the knowledge of God in the Old Testament (and in the New) involves a great variety of things far transcending these 'definitions'. He goes on to say that 'revelation' is an *inadequate* shorthand expression which seeks to encompass an enormous range of activities connected with God's relation to his people. And 'no better term has emerged which even begins to convey the full range of meanings associated with the disclosures of God in the Bible'. But this is exactly the reason why we should *not* look for *one term* which will encompass this enormous range of activities.

In so far as it is a matter of terms only, my sense is the following. 'Revelation' is essentially an *inexact* term; it is one that has grown up in the philosophical and dogmatic traditions, and even in these mainly at a rather late date; there is no sound basis in the Bible for the very general meaning in which it is now normal. And as an inexact term for all and any of the ways in which God speaks, does anything, communicates, inspires and so on it may be easiest to let it continue. The point at which it becomes positively harmful is when it is used in a more technical sense, to *discriminate* within the complex of acts, events, words, speeches, books, inspirational experiences and so on, and attempts are made to separate out, to define, to deliminate what is revelation as against what is not revelation. When we use the term in this way we soon find ourselves lost, or else forced back on uncritical reiterations of older dogmatic assertions. This happens, for example, when we begin to ask whether the contents of the Bible 'are revelation' or not. For many of the things that are in the Bible are there not because God uniquely put them there, or caused humans to put them there; many of them are there because they were already common knowledge. That Josiah was eight years old when he began to reign in Jerusalem and his mother's name was Jedidah (II Kings 22.1) is there because everyone knew this to be the case. How is that revelation? The same is true, by extension, of many other cases, including human persons 'revealing'. Thus when 'revelation' becomes, as it has for many persons, an indispensable sign-word for faith, it leads to serious misunderstandings.[36] And the same may be true, as Westermann points out, of 'knowledge of God' and other time-hallowed expressions.

My own proposals in *Old and New in Interpretation* took as central the model of cumulative tradition. This received attention from H. Berkhof, who provided a helpful comparison with Pannenberg:

> Whereas Pannenberg wants to make the concept of 'history' central [in revelation], J. Barr rejects this, seeking to replace it with the model of the cumulative tradition . . . He thinks that in this respect he is far removed from Pannenberg, but their results show a remarkable convergence. The core of Barr's argument is 'that the growth and development of tradition is soteriologically functional. We do not have a series of divine acts, the interpretation and presentation of which constitute the tradition; we have a growth of tradition, the existence of which provides the matrix for the coming divine acts and the impulse for their very occurrence' (p. 156). I have tried to continue in the converging paths of Pannenberg and Barr. In my opinion the thus far current concepts of 'salvation history' were trailing behind the insights in the biblical disciplines.[37]

Hence Berkhof arrives at his own decision: 'We choose the description: *revelation consists of a cumulative process of events and their interpretations*' (62).

Central to our problem is the conception that revelation essentially belongs to the past: the principle 'no revelation after Ezra', as Ritschl calls it.[38] 'This means a distinction between ordinary times and revelatory times or events.' The result is to give 'a metaphysical or trans-historical character to revelation before any clarification or definition is attempted'. '"Ordinary world history" is of another, lower quality than revelatory history.'[39]

However, not all these problems have to be solved for my present purpose. They come to a climax in the fact that Karl Barth not only rejected natural theology but rejected it as an essential element in a theology in which revelation had 'prolegomenal' status, in other words was built into the foundations of everything before anything else had been clarified or worked out. Berkhof writes: 'The danger existed that the revelation concept was too easily used as a Prolegomenon, without sufficiently investigating the correctness of the choice and reckoning with the problematics that it entails' (45).

## 4. Christology and the question of natural theology

The most hostile reactions to any discussion of natural theology come from the thought that Jesus is the sole channel of revelation of God and that to recognize something like natural theology in the Bible is to eliminate the centrality of Christ and to talk as if other modes of relation to God can be worked out by humanity, he then being fitted in as a sort of complementation or addition.[40] This is felt to be little other than the total destruction of Christianity.

But, according to this same point of view, true knowledge of Jesus Christ is available only through the criterion of the Bible, both Old and New Testaments. If the Bible contains material that lies close to, or points towards, natural theology, then one has simply to enlarge one's picture of Christ so as to accommodate that fact. Refusal to do so is to deny the realities of the Bible in order to sustain one's dogmatic convictions. Moreover, again according to the same point of view, there is an all-important linkage between Christ and creation. If that is so, then it may be that natural theology is one of the forms of that linkage.

There are in fact a number of ways in which this can be done. Thus W. J. Abraham, hardly a liberal, a historical–critical biblical scholar, or a doubter of vital Christianity, writes:[41]

> It is simply false to say that someone committed to the possibility of natural theology is logically committed to a denial of the potential status of divine revelation, or to the denial of justification by faith, or to a denial of the crucial significance of the witness of the Holy Spirit in the life of faith. All one is committed to in exploring the possibility of natural theology is the investigation of the soundness and validity of various arguments for the existence of God . . . It is one thing to argue for and against the cogency of the teleological argument; it is another to argue for or against justification by faith. Barth was so enmeshed in his version of canonical foundationalism that he could not perceive this kind of obvious distinction.

And again:

> Barth simply begged crucial questions about the nature of the grace of God working in creation and in the human subject. Engaging in natural theology can be interpreted as an activity made possible by God's common grace working in creation or as an expression of the image of God in the human mind without strain. It could equally well be expressed in terms of a doctrine of creation which speaks of the working of the Holy Spirit. Natural theology can well be interpreted as one means which the Holy Spirit uses to bring people to commitment to God. It is only if one is committed to a certain doctrine of sin or to a certain pneumatology that these claims will be called into question.

Again I quote from Berkhof:[42]

> The belief that Jesus Christ is *the* way, the truth, and the life, and that no one comes to the Father except through him, seems to lead to the conclusion that there is no real revelation apart from him. But, at the same time, that same belief pushes us in a seemingly opposite direction: If in Jesus Christ the Father is revealed who is the creator of heaven and earth, then in Christ also

the ultimate mystery of created reality must be manifest. Then it must be so that in the Word-made-flesh there is revealed *that* Word by which all things were made (John 1.1–14) and that all things were created by and for Christ (Col. 1.16). But then it is impossible that this reality, which inalienably remains God's creation, should not in all kinds of ways, no matter how fragmentary, incidental, or broken, bear witness to the purpose of its creator.

And again:

> Expressed positively we must say: *the divine revelation in Christ is indeed normative, but not exclusive.* The indiscriminate use of both these adjectives has caused much confusion. That Christ is *the* truth does not mean that there are no truths to be found anywhere outside of him, but it does mean that all such truths are fragmentary and broken unless they have become integrated in him as the centre . . . So the Christian belief in revelation stands necessarily in a dialectical relation to the beliefs in revelation as these are found in the world around . . . This dialectical character is clear in the biblical data . . . [43]

These statements express exactly what I mean. Just as, in traditional Christian faith, Christ brings together norms and concepts inherited from the Hebrew Bible, so he also – even if only secondarily – brings together norms and concepts that have come to expression by a different pathway; all the more so since substantial material within the Bible has already gone through exactly the same process – not only within the Bible, but within the traditions that animated the Bible and interpreted it, some of them no longer represented within our scriptural canon.

## 5. Ecology

That the matter of natural theology has something to say about the ecological concerns of our present time seems obvious, and I mentioned it briefly in my *Biblical Faith and Natural Theology* (18, 83, 149, 159, 180). Perhaps the essential point is this: although awareness of the world and of its relation to the creator God has been taken up – in part from natural theology – into what the religions see as divine revelation, this awareness belongs to humanity as such and is not specific to the biblically-based religions. The religions have shared in the consciousness of ecological problems but cannot be said to have taken the lead in awareness of them or the initiative in doing something about them. Indeed it has been argued that the Abrahamic religions have been signally backward in this respect and that the biblical emphasis on human 'domination' of the world has been a major factor in promoting the present ecological crisis. I do not agree with this in principle[44] – claims that Buddhism and other religions have done better are often imaginary fancies[45] – but it cannot be doubted that for certain large groups the biblical material has indeed historically worked in favour of a human-centred and potentially destructive perception of the environment. This was not, of course, the case in biblical times themselves.

And this is what makes the difference. The presence of a natural-theology world-view within the Hebrew Bible (or, likewise, the New Testament) does not mean that this world-view has to be adopted as eternal and unmodifiable truth. Rather, the fact that it was there means that it may be modified or even replaced. (It is often said by admiring scholars, in conformity with their own values, that the creation story of Genesis 1 is 'dynamic' rather than 'static', and within the Hebrew Bible and biblical theology that may be quite true; but its long-term impact on human world-view was of course a static one.) Even within the Hebrew Bible very different pictures exist. The speeches of God in Job 38–41, for instance, furnish not a classified account of creation, but rather a set of riddles posed by the variety and remoteness of life and existence.

It was inevitable that the Greek world-view would enter into competition with the biblical views: not because Greek philosophy was necessarily better than biblical theology, but because the biblical and Jewish traditions had nothing at all to offer over large areas where Greek science and other Greek thought had worked. A symbiosis of Jewish tradition and Hellenistic thinking is evident in many – not necessarily all – currents of Judaism and early Christianity. Greek natural theology was at the same time accepted, combated, and transformed in the main lines of patristic orthodoxy, as has recently been described by Pelikan.[46]

But equally it made sense that the heritage of the Graeco-Roman world, which the church had thought it part of its duty to preserve, came to be challenged. Luther's attack on Aristotle is the most vivid element in this.

But after the Reformation, natural theology grew and changed in parallel with developments in natural science. Biblical and religious motivations were of first importance in figures of the Enlightenment like Descartes, Locke and Newton. In England leading expressions of natural theology by Butler and later by Paley were influential. But a natural theology like Paley's has long ceased to fit with the way in which people think, and has become only historically significant. As I suggested earlier, the expansion of scientific knowledge made it easier and apparently more 'natural' to reject natural theology altogether.[47]

The point of this is not to tell the history in detail, but to make clear the central implication: the presence of natural theology within the Bible does not mean that its natural theology is engraved in stone, to be accepted for all eternity; it is rather that just as the Bible received elements from natural theology in its own time, so elements from changing natural theologies must affect present-day belief and action. As I wrote before, the older world-views had no idea of a world in which 'nature' could change, no idea of the fact 'that human agency through scientific and technological skill has the power, and also the duty, of moulding to some extent what "nature" is to become'.[48] The world was stable, except in that in extreme cases God might destabilize it and reverse the process of creation; but human action, whether good or bad, did not have that power. Ecological theology becomes necessary today because we know that we do have that power.

It is in this way that I see the natural theology of the Bible providing the basis for a natural theology for today which takes into account the scientific and technological realities – along with their social and political corollaries. Not that all modern views calling themselves 'ecological' are to be accepted without question: some of them are doubtless enthusiastic (in the bad sense), ill-informed and half-baked. But a critical involvement in such a task is obviously an essential part of a theology for the present time. For Christians – and, I would think, for Jews also – such involvement would necessarily include the integrating of this natural theology with the central theological themes which used to be called 'special revelation'.

On the other hand such a 'natural theology' with ecological purport would remain 'natural', in the sense that it is not, and should not be, a special preserve of Jews or Christians. For ecology, like natural theology, belongs to all people.

And this takes us back to the wise words of Claus Westermann which were quoted above. Looking back at the controversy between Barth and Brunner, he noted that they paid no attention to an action of God upon humanity as a whole, or upon the praise given to God by the created world itself. These omissions need to be rectified. Similarly to be corrected are such traditional sophistries as the idea that natural theology may give knowledge of God but this knowledge is 'not saving knowledge': 'saving knowledge' does not come into the matter at all, at least in the sense originally meant, i.e. something that makes a difference between true believers and other people. If 'saving' means saving from famine and cancer and destruction, then of course it is indeed saving knowledge that we are talking about.

## 6. *Morality*

Natural theology, as here conceived, is not only a study of the question whether God exists or not: that is only one part of it. Another is the question of the moral sense of humanity. This is involved in one of the chief traditional biblical passages, Rom. 2.15, with the use of the term 'conscience' and the argument that the Gentiles, who do not 'have the law', may 'by nature' do what the law requires and then are 'a law to themselves'.[49]

Christians generally affirm that, while there is a human moral sense, it is distorted by sin and re-established only by true faith; which of course is so, except that even when one has true faith the distortion by sin seems to continue. But, distorted or not, an existing human morality is presupposed, and might easily be supported through connection with the image of God in all humanity. And, of course, one can turn to the Torah as the basic source of right moral judgments. But that leaves the question: are things right and wrong because they are so decreed in the Torah, or are they in the Torah because they were recognized to be right and wrong in any case? The latter is the case at least for some moral questions. After all, the legal principles of non-Israelite peoples did not generally enjoin murder, theft and adultery as desirable practices, as one would imagine on the basis of some arguments that one hears. Even some of the Ten Commandments can thus hardly be thought of as introducing novel rules, never heard of before.

Moreover, there are areas of morality which are regarded as extremely important but which are comparatively little emphasized in express law-giving such as we find in the Torah. An obvious example is offered by the case of lies. Lying is generally regarded as a shameful dereliction of morality. Yet the express instructions of the Torah mention it comparatively little. The prohibition of 'bearing false witness' in the Decalogue is not a prohibition of lying in general: it is a prohibition of false accusation of another, which might make another a criminal and bring punishment upon him or her. This is why it is classed along with capital crimes like murder. False accusation in this sense is noticed and placed under severe retribution, for the false witness will be punished with the punishment that would have come upon the one accused (Deut. 19.16–21). But lying in other senses, in other words lying in general, is seldom mentioned in the law codes (Lev. 19.11). Yet the wrongness of lying is something of which the prophets are well aware: see many cases in Jeremiah, for example, and in the narratives. The wrongness of lying was probably recognized in the culture, and included in Leviticus for that reason. 'Natural' morality is taken up into the Bible.

This is only one instance among many. But it means, as I have argued previously, following Stewart Sutherland, that:

> A religious belief which runs counter to our moral beliefs is to that extent unacceptable.[50]

Not that this is in itself a final solution. For our moral beliefs are not cast iron and may undergo change through the influence of religious beliefs. Conversely, and more commonly, we seek to argue that things which at first sight seem contrary to our moral beliefs are really quite moral. But this latter argument itself implies and confirms the authority of our moral beliefs.

There is, then, no simple and direct way in which our moral beliefs can be brought to bear upon material like the content of the Bible. All I affirm at this point is that the 'natural' moral beliefs of humanity do constitute a powerful norm: not the only one, but certainly a powerful one.

### 7. Genocide?

In my *Biblical Faith and Natural Theology* I took as an example the extreme case of the extermination of the Canaanite population (207–20). Dr Hiebert in his excellent review (*Interpretation* 49, 1995, 300) wanted me to say more about 'how I would deal with' this problematic material. I shall not repeat the exposition of my previous book but will try to show how it fits in with the arguments of the present work.

The question depends on several variables:

(*a*) Historically, different assessments of what took place in the events represented in the biblical text as the conquest of the land by Israel;

(*b*) Exegetically, different explanations of the purposes of the traditionists who formed and handed down the traditions both of the commands to exterminate and of the carrying out of the commands;

(*c*) In a sense of biblical theology, differing possible accounts of the theology of the *ḥerem*, the theology of the practice of ritual destruction (whether such practices were carried out or not);

(*d*) Within biblical theology, the difference between those who consider it to be descriptive and those who consider it to be evaluative (Ch. 12 above);

(*e*) The difference between story and theology;

(*f*) The difference between biblical theology and doctrinal theology.

The case is a good example of this last difference. Within biblical theology, the whole matter seems to me to be of prime importance. I remember that when as a young teacher I first taught a course in Old Testament theology, in Edinburgh in 1955, fired up with enthusiasm from von Rad's book on Holy War, my first lecture in the series was on the holy war and its traditions. And though further study has changed the focus of the question in many ways, the subject remains a central one. If there was a theology of the Old Testament, this command and practice, strange and offensive as they may be to us, do much to shape the character of the entire text and must have a central position.

As a matter of doctrinal theology, on the other hand, I think it has to be simply repudiated. As a matter of the past, some sense can be made of it; but as a matter of guidance for present belief and action, it cannot be accommodated. Even taken in the rather absurd allegorical sense, where the Canaanites become the temptations and sins that beset us, it is a very dangerous association. This provides us, however, with a good illustration of how biblical theology differs from doctrinal.

It may then be objected: one cannot remove the destruction of the Canaanites without upsetting the balance of the Hebrew Bible as a whole. These commands and narratives are part of the canon. Certainly so. But the presence of texts within the canon of scripture is only one of the norms that count; their presence may maintain the balance of scripture, but it certainly does not sustain the balance of modern doctrine. Moral implications are another norm.

We discussed earlier the contrast between the descriptive and the evaluative approaches to biblical theology. It is often presented as if the descriptive mode restricts the theological core of the text, while the evaluative recognizes it and opens it out into relevance for the present day. In this particular case the reverse is true: the descriptive mode can give full value to the theological basis and implications of the practices described, while the evaluative will necessarily move them to a marginal position.

The difference between story and theology can also perhaps be useful here. The destruction of the Canaanites is certainly part of the story and cannot be eliminated from it. And, as I have suggested, there must have been a sort of theology behind the practice, or even behind the idea of such a practice. Yet, on the other hand, any theology which is also evaluative, or which seeks to present what comes out of such a story for the modern world, must pass judgment on such an element.

As already indicated, much depends on the detailed exegesis. One approach that has been discussed in recent years is the suggestion that the command of destruction, and the execution of it, was for the most part not historical but rather ideological: the real intent was the purity of the religion, through the elimination of practices represented as Canaanite. Reformers, intent on purity of religion, developed and used the images of extermination of peoples. If this should be right, then the events may not have happened as depicted. But is this an improvement? For the command to destroy remained. The existence of such commands in a sacred text is a serious and fateful matter. Keel and Uehlinger remark on the tragic irony it would be if two or three millennia before Auschwitz Jewish reforming purists introduced such an ideology into a sacred text.[51]

Our guide in modern doctrinal theology, H. Berkhof, *Christian Faith*, 248–9, gives considerable thought to these questions. He has used, he says, 'the phenomenological-historical method', looking for 'the structures of Israel's relationship to God and their developments in history'. Only so, he continues, 'could we track down the theological core of the Old Testament'. He goes on to say that one method is not enough: we have to elucidate the Old Testament also from a socio–economic and political-sociological perspective. This would

greatly enrich the sketch he has presented but would not 'alter the basic theological lines'.

The same, however, 'cannot be said easily of the cultural-historical approach'.
Its disregard through a 'wrong doctrine of inspiration' has caused much confusion and misunderstanding'. Berkhof goes on to outline aspects of change and
development over time. Then:

> At first Israel thought of the wars she had to wage against her neighbours as
> simply wars of Yahweh. In accordance with Oriental ethics, Israel saw herself
> obliged to devote captured cities to Yahweh by means of the 'ban', that is, by
> massacring the inhabitants. For ages her thinking was wholly or mainly
> collective: only the people as a whole is important, and the individual only as
> a part of that whole. Therefore sin could be punished in an entire (innocent)
> group or in the descendants to the third and fourth generation.

Other examples follow: the future of the individual after death; marriage and
polygamy. 'Israel gave shape to its faithfulness to Yahweh within the cultural
traditions of its environment and times. As such this is nothing unusual; we do
the same. The normativity of the Old Testament (the same holds for the New)
does not lie in its forms of expression but in what these forms were meant to
express, or, more correctly, in what these expressions pointed to, namely God
in his acts.' The [later] demise of these forms 'makes it clear that the purposes
of this God came through inadequately in these forms'. And so, returning to a
final summary:

> It will not do to conclude that the Old Testament preaches a bloodthirsty and
> immoral God and that therefore it must be rejected. It will not do either to
> canonize, for instance, the wars of the Lord or the casting of lots (and why not
> then polygamy?).

The verb 'canonize' here means, obviously, not 'to recognize as part of holy
scripture' (for in that sense these elements cannot be other than canonical) but
'to recognize as authoritative for a central function in doctrine for today'.


## 8. Conclusion

The most important reality, it would seem, is this: there is, within the Bible, an
element which points towards a theological source or reality that lies *outside* the
Bible. Biblical theology – not only in its 'canonical' forms – has tended to be a
very closed, inward-looking discipline. Its connections with historical criticism
and with history of religion opened it up somewhat, but the more modern trends
have in part reduced these forces. The main attraction has lain in gaining the

maximum concentration of all the possible biblical aspects, for the Bible's theology is right there, inside the Bible. The witness of the elements close to natural theology is that this is not so: the Bible itself points to things that come from outside and – at least sometimes – welcomes these resources. There is therefore no closed organism of biblical theology: it is not self-contained, it is open, perhaps in various directions. This makes a great difference to the whole way in which the subject is approached.

This does not mean pointing to something that lies outside the range and being of the one God, the God of Israel. Nor, if we should use the term 'revelation', does it mean 'denial' of revelation, as people are quick to suppose. It means that certain realities lying outside the 'special' zone of revelation are taken up into that revelation and constituted as revelatory. There is no choice about it, for to deny this thesis is to deny the evidence of scripture itself, which sometimes explicitly and often implicitly points in this direction.

Secondly, it makes a big difference to the history–of–religion approach, at least to that element which concerns the influence of environing religions on Israel. Thus Proverbs contains a longish piece (Prov. 22.17–23.12 at the least) which has a large degree of verbal agreement with the Egyptian Wisdom of Amen-em-ope. This is widely accepted. Now it was always said, in the spirit of biblical theology, that while these things were taken over, of course they were transformed through being put into their new setting. Maybe so, but this argument is pretty weak in its application to the group of Proverbs concerned. For one thing, transformation of this kind was normal in all natural theology: it was always transformed by being placed in its new setting, as is clear in all Christian natural theology. Its being transformed makes it not less like, but more like, normal natural theology. But the point is not so much that such materials were transformed (if they were) but that it was judged possible to undertake a work of transformation on them in the first place. This was material that had come from a foreign land, composed under other gods, viable within a totally different religion – how would anyone with an exclusively boundaried sense of biblical theology suppose that anything of such a text could be transformed at all? The fact that such material was considered to be transformable indicates a feeling akin to that of natural theology: a certain underlying common ground which could be accepted for use within a Hebrew sacred text.

To end with, here is a recent comment on the subject:

Affirming this universal and objective revelation of God in creation, the ecumenical consensus opposes Barth's view . . . This emerging ecumenical natural theology seeks to do greater justice to the continuity between God's authority as creator and redeemer, and it is often more trinitarian in depicting the totality of God's self-revelation . . . At the same time, current natural theology appropriates something of Barth's christocentric understanding of revelation in a way allowing for a greater appreciation of God's grace always undergirding creation.[52]

# 28

# Oeming

One of the most important and creative works on our subject in recent years has been Manfred Oeming's *Gesamtbiblische Theologien der Gegenwart* (i.e. *Pan-biblical Theologies of the Present*, original publication 1985). Though it is not in itself a Theology either of the Old Testament or of the Bible, it is important for many reasons. First, it offers an unusually penetrating analysis of von Rad's attempt to connect the Old Testament with the New, distinguishing various different intellectual 'models' with which he worked. Second, it connects the co-existence of this group of models with the philosophy of Gadamer. Thirdly, it shows how the various models were further pursued after von Rad by various scholars, and this analysis furnishes a particularly clear and helpful map of recent scholarship in the field, mainly in Germany. Fourthly, it includes a significant evaluation of the work of Childs. Fifthly, it concludes with an outline of a programme for pan-biblical theology which may well overcome some of the antinomies that have cut across it. Sixthly, it is significant for its conscious integration of philosophy with biblical theology. The work, a Bonn University dissertation, has not yet become well known in the English-speaking world, and one fears that it may never be translated into English as it deserves to be. I venture therefore to provide a summary of its rich argumentation, a summary which necessarily had to omit numerous aspects: I trust that I have not thereby damaged the impact of a book which has meant very much to me.

After a brief statement of the problems and a brief history of previous approaches, which emphasizes Bultmann's apparently self-contradictory attitudes to the place of the Old Testament in Christianity, Oeming begins his work with a descriptive analysis of 'the pan-biblical models of von Rad'.

## *1. Von Rad's four models*

Von Rad, in the third and final section of his second volume, sought to provide a new foundation for the unity of Old and New Testaments. In so doing he did not try to bring together the manifold different materials through the use of systematic categories, as Köhler and Eichrodt had done. Rather, he sought to take the results of historical criticism seriously and from these to advance exegetically to thoughts about the unity of the Bible. An attentive analysis will indicate something that had been by-passed in most of the secondary literature: namely, that in this procedure von Rad has combined several quite different models of thought. According to Oeming, these are:

(*a*)  The promise-history model;
(*b*)  The tradition-history model;
(*c*)  The salvation-history model. Under this are subsumed two aspects:
       (i) The structural analogy of the two Testaments;
       (ii) The unity of God's history;
(*d*)  The language-history model.

Oeming exemplifies these in a short study of two or three pages each. He then indicates a list of hermeneutic premises which appear to underlie each of them. I will give a brief example of what von Rad had said, and follow it with a summary of the premises as identified by Oeming.

## (a) The promise-history model

Von Rad thought, on grounds of plain exegesis, that the Old Testament can be read only as a book full of *expectation* (von Rad 2, 329ff.). It is therefore no interpretative trickery to read it as a prophecy directed towards Jesus. Nevertheless scientific, historical-critical study cannot *show* that Christ was the fulfilment of precisely these expectations. Christological interpretation therefore has the charismatic character of a *venture* which cannot be methodologically controlled. Nevertheless there are some elements which can have methodological control: the Old Testament context must be fully investigated, that which is typical has to be perceived, and it can be perceived only within the space of the total history that finds its goal in Christ.

## (b) The tradition-history model

Von Rad argued that Israel again and again reactualized the older traditions in the light of new saving arrangements (*Heilssetzungen*). This was a 'charismatic-eclectic' process.[1] There was thus a continual filtering process within the Old Testament itself. Von Rad extended this to include the New Testament. Realization in Christ was the final 'hermeneutical transformation'.

## (c) The salvation-history model

There is a real history, God's intervention in the process of the world: 'History becomes word and word becomes history'. The historical action is basic, but the historical fact is known only through word and interpretation.

New interpretations show that the history is open to the future and look for new application in new situations of the salvation history. 'History' here, however, is not the history of modern historical science. To go back to our 'positivistic' question about what is historically credible would be the end of profitable work on the Old Testament, because its historical texts 'do not let themselves' be handled in this way. An appropriate handling of the text must avoid dividing word and act of God, just as it must avoid playing off the kerygmatic against the historical-critical.

Within the salvation-history model von Rad, according to Oeming, used two subsidiary models. First, he saw a structural analogy between the two Testaments. The correspondence between them lay not in the religious-conceptual (*im religiös-Begrifflichen*) but in the salvation-historical, because in Jesus Christ we see the same interweaving of divine word and historical fact that we know so well from the Old Testament. The emphasis on the future is likewise analogical. The typological approach thus fits into the salvation-historical as well as into the promise-historical model.

Secondly, the older salvation history of earlier times had thought of an objectively existing and continuous process from creation to the end of the world, with Christ as mid-point. Von Rad rejected the objectivity implied in this idea: the Bible knew nothing of objective facts. On the other hand he was much more conscious of *discontinuities* in the history of salvation. Persons or objects of the ancient stories were not types of Christ; everything depended on the *events* that took place, their gradients and contours, and each event from time to time gives its witness towards Christ. Thus the New Testament salvation history is the *prolongation* and *conclusion* of God's history in the Old. The unity of God's history brings together the salvation-history and the tradition-history models.

### (d) The language-history model

'This model of the unity of the Testaments rests upon a quite specific conception of language' (Oeming, 31). Every language owns and presents a quite specific world-view. 'To the quite different apperceptions of the reality of life there corresponds the difference of the languages' (von Rad, 2, 353). Language is an organic totality and every part of it expresses itself only as a part of the whole.

Oeming is certainly right in saying that this is closely related to the philosophy of language developed by W. von Humboldt, though von Rad may not have named him expressly. 'The religious language of Israel corresponds to a reality which was open on all sides to God . . . This language is appropriate (*sachgemäss*) because it knows how to name appropriately the realities created by God's speaking' (von Rad, 2, 353: the sense is somewhat obscured in the published English translation). And von Rad went on to claim an 'unbroken continuity' between the language of the Old Testament and that of the New: in spite of the fact that the former was Hebrew and the latter was Greek, 'in a higher sense' it was one unitary language (von Rad, 2, 354).

According to Oeming the following premises can be seen in these models.[2] The first three are attached to the promise-history model:

1. Historical-critical exegesis is indispensable for Christianity, because it gives essential insights into the theological content of the individual texts and also into the theological contours of the Old Testament as a whole. Nevertheless a merely historical-critical consideration is not sufficient, for the Christian faith of the exegete must come into play as a factor in exegesis.

2. The history of reception and effects (*Wirkungsgeschichte*) has to be taken into account, since the individual text gets its true meaning only from the totality of the Bible. Exegesis has to communicate that which is *typical* and is analogical in both Testaments.

3. Typological exegesis is in the last resort beyond methodological control: it is a charismatic act. There can therefore be no absolutely valid exegesis: every period has to hear for itself, and all exegesis is historically conditioned.

The next four are attached to the tradition-history model:

1. In spite of many changes the Old Testament tradition process is a continuum which extends into the New Testament.

2. The process is one of adaptation to new situations and coalescence of the Old within the horizon of the present.

3. The tradition process is one of critical selection. What is really obsolete and has lost value is not reactualized but quietly abandoned.

4. This process of hermeneutical transformation and critical filtering is not methodologically controllable but charismatic and eclectic.[3]

The next two premises (three in Oeming, collapsed by me into two) are attached to the salvation-history model:

1. Historical thought in the Old Testament rests upon a non-distinction between fact and interpretative word (*kerygma*). It does not recognize the difference between objectively real history and its application for the present in faith. 'Such a distinction is dead positivistic abstraction.'

2. The interpreter has to work within these thought-structures of the texts themselves.

Oeming does not attach any identified premises to the language-history model.

## 2. *Gadamer and von Rad*

The above material is not complete but may be enough to give an indication of the sort of approach that Oeming undertakes. What it leads up to is the question: taking together the set of hermeneutical premises implied by von Rad, and, in particular,

1. The transcending of 'merely' historical-critical exegesis;
2. The inclusion of the subjective assumptions of the exegete, in this case his or her faith, in the exegetical process;
3. The high valuation of tradition as a filtering process;
4. A certain philosophy of history; and
5. A dependence, perhaps unconscious, on W. von Humboldt's philosophy of language,

Oeming asks whether the grouping of these aspects in von Rad's work is a purely accidental conglomeration, or whether it suggests a close contact with an existing philosophical position. The answer is the latter and the position suggested is that of H.-G. Gadamer. Oeming's next chapter (his Ch. 3) is thus a statement of Gadamer's views, emphasizing the aspects important for pan-biblical theology.

There follows (Ch. 4, 42–4) a comparison between Gadamer and von Rad. It is significant, and a point that few theologians can have noticed before Oeming's book, that already in the period 1967–1974 one of the leading Gadamer experts, Pierre Fruchon, had noted in detail the close similarity between von Rad's *Theology* and the thought of Gadamer,[4] and Oeming is able to corroborate this from biographical data and from von Rad's own later writing, in particular a paragraph added to the Preface of the fourth (1962) edition of his Theology (p. 12 in the original; not present in the ET, which was done from the first edition).[5]

Oeming next proceeds to a critique of Gadamer's hermeneutics. He by no means seeks to discredit Gadamer, but he points out, rightly, that Gadamer's thought has received very strong criticism (Ch. 5, pp. 45–57). As I have pointed out before,[6] theologians who have relied on Gadamer's thinking (James Robinson, Andrew Louth, Mark Brett)[7] have often talked as if it was above and beyond criticism. His ideas, it appeared from their writings, did not require to be justified or defended against alternative views. All that was needed was to quote Gadamer and the argument was finished. This is entirely unacceptable. Gadamer's ideas must be respected, but their probable weaknesses have also to be acknowledged.

Three particular areas of weakness are picked out by Oeming. First, Gadamer's contrast between 'truth' and 'method' suggested that only a subordinate area in the humanistic disciplines could be controlled by *method*. There is an experience of truth which transcends the control area of academic method (quoted by Oeming, 47). Against this it can be argued that 'truth' which is not controllable by academic method simply has no status within the academic world.

Second, Gadamer attaches a very high value to tradition. If a thought or an institution has proved itself through the tradition process as worthy of adoption, then this 'proves' its superior appropriateness. However, it may be objected, tradition itself is not a unity but contains deep contradictions. These cannot be used or evaluated except by critical rational processes.

Third, Gadamer's philosophy of language seems to make language more real than reality. 'All being that can be understood is language' *(Wahrheit und Methode*, 450). In this form of linguistic idealism language becomes an active power, like a personal subject (Oeming, 55). The discovery of truth is 'not a methodical activity of the subject, but an action of the thing itself . . . which "undergoes" or "suffers" (*erleidet*) the thinking'. But today, in Germany as elsewhere, a conventional-instrumental sign theory holds the field, and Gadamer and others who represent the Humboldtian inheritance are 'anachronistic idealistic outsiders' (Oeming, 76–7).

Oeming does not dismiss Gadamer or reject his ideas totally. Summing up the discussion at this point (57), he points to the 'ambivalent impression' that Gadamer makes. On one side Gadamer appears as the remarkably radical and critical theoretician of knowledge, who has uncovered the excessive methodologism of the Enlightenment and brought tradition and language tradition back to their true power and light. On the other he is the totally uncritical romantic who wants to rescue the good old times from the destructive analysis of rational method. The main point is that Gadamer is no unquestionable support for biblical hermeneutics but at best a highly uncertain, ambiguous and deeply contested source of assurance. The importance of this will emerge shortly.

Oeming now proceeds (Ch. 6, 58–80) to a criticism of von Rad himself under the heads of his four models. These criticisms will not be summarized here, since they overlap considerably with comments of my own in this book and elsewhere. But Oeming's final summary (77–80) is important.

> If one considers von Rad in the light of the history of his reception and effects, one obtains the same ambivalent picture as with Gadamer: here the picture of the radical critical exegete, a true pupil of Albrecht Alt, who strictly applied to the Old Testament the form-critical and the tradition-critical methods and achieved considerable success therein; there the picture of a conservative charismatic, who out of pious commitment seeks to read a testimony to Christ into the Old Testament, and who does not shrink back from a *sacrificium*

*intellectus* when it comes to defending the Christian and churchly nature of the Old Testament (77).

In particular, Oeming goes on, the different models are too seriously mingled with one another and their systematic disposition is unclear (78f.). They cannot easily be combined with one another and can even represent opposite poles. Thus for instance the promise-history model wants to understand the Old Testament as directly aimed towards Christ, while the language-history model avoids any idea of an original christological intention and understands the Old Testament as language material, with the help of which the novel Christ event can be expressed. And so also when we compare other pairs among the models. It was the remarkable linguistic and literary art of von Rad that enabled the various models to be held together. Not surprisingly, most of those who followed in his inheritance found themselves pursuing one or another of the models rather than the combination of them all.

## 3. *The models as developed after von Rad*

Thus Oeming continues his study by identifying and presenting a 'further development' for each of the four models used by von Rad.

1. Under 'Further Development of the Promise-history Model' he begins with the note that in von Rad himself, promise history and typology are closely interwoven, but that among those who followed his lead in this respect the two come apart and either one or the other is pursued. Under promise history he mentions the work of K. Schwarzwäller, C. Westermann and D. L. Baker as attempts that brought nothing essentially new after von Rad, and adds as original approaches the thought of the Jewish writer H. J. Schonfield and of Ulrich Mauser (81–91). Under typology he records that almost all later opinion turned against von Rad's judgment, quoting especially J. Barr, P. Vielhauer and G. Fohrer. The only exception named as one who still supports typology is Baker,[8] and even he only in a very restricted way.[9]

An alternative to be added, however, is 'typology of existence' or *Existenztypologie* (the term coined by Preuss). This typology exploits analogies (not identities!) in human existence before God as in the Old and New Testaments. Our steps toward Christ are thus prefigured: the Old Testament maps out the life situations on the basis of which the message of Christ comes and where it has meaning and relation. This typology does not attach narrowly to Christ, to 'the second article', but extends over all domains of life and experience, and particularly in areas where the Old Testament goes beyond the New, e.g. in ideas of creation, in erotic experience, in scepticism. This approach was closely connected with questions of Christian preaching of the Old Testament and, according to Oeming, it has had a wide positive reception.

A kind of 'existence typology' may also be represented by the thought of H. H. Schmid and the New Testament scholars U. Luck and D. Lührmann. This is discussed briefly elsewhere in the present volume (see Chapter 19) and will only be mentioned here. There is a universal idea of a world order, which permeates both Old and New Testaments and the ancient Near East alike. Experience, however, does not fit with the world order which is believed to be right and proper. The basic problems of the biblical tradition process are the basic problems of modern humanity. Biblical theology may thus become a theological interpretation of experience in general.[10]

This model has received warm acceptance, e.g. from Henning Graf Reventlow and P. Stuhlmacher. On the other hand, as mentioned above, it has been subjected to very strong criticism, from F. Crüsemann and especially from J. Halbe. Oeming offers a partial defence of Schmid's position.[11]

Oeming concludes this section with a reference to the ideas of M. Hohmann, who sought to combine Tillich's principle of correlation with Bonhoeffer's understanding of the Old Testament. The many-dimensioned character of human existence should be illuminated by an inner-biblical correlation.

2. For the 'further development' of the tradition-history model Oeming finds his chief example in Hartmut Gese, followed by P. Stuhlmacher. I have already discussed Gese's work at length (see Ch. 22), and mentioned Stuhlmacher in that connection. Oeming ends this section with a discussion of ideas of the French scholar Henri Clavier (then, in 1976, already elderly).

3. For the further development of the salvation-history model the principal interest falls upon the 'Pannenberg circle'. The motif of salvation history, so emphasized by von Rad in relation to his own strongly kerygmatic theology, was here taken up by a circle of his own former students and developed into a contrary model. God revealed himself indirectly through history rather than directly through his Word. Complete revelation is still to come. Hence the strong emphasis on apocalyptic as the framework for the New Testament. Along with this goes the emphasis of Pannenberg on universal history: not a particular series of historical events, but only the entirety of history can fully reveal God. Moreover, history is seen as factual: the facts are open to anyone who has eyes to see, and faith is awakened through the perception of them.[12] These ideas were met with recognition as important but also with considerable opposition: the high-point of the latter (Oeming, 141 and n.6) was the 'fistfight' or 'exchange of blows' (*Schlagabtausch*) between Günther Klein and the members of the Pannenberg group.

The full unfolding of Pannenberg's theology has been discussed elsewhere and lies beyond the scope of our present work. For biblical theology specifically it is of interest to note that while the emphasis on *history* in the group arose from the Old Testament, through von Rad himself and through Rendtorff, who was the leading Old Testament specialist of the group, questions about whether the Old Testament was so very 'historical' came quickly to be asked (Knierim, Barr, Smend, Perlitt). In 1981 Rendtorff himself revoked his support for the salvation-history programme, claiming that salvation history was a specifically Christian construction used for the purpose of a Christian taking over of the Old Testament from the Jews, and one that could not be found or supported in the latter. Far from the emphasis falling on the *end* of history, it should fall at the beginning, with creation.

A second development from the salvation-history model lies in Franz Hesse's strong opposition to von Rad and denial of the existence of salvation history in the Bible. Rainer Schmitt replied with a defence of von Rad's ideas on a somewhat different level. Oeming concludes this section with some pages on salvation-history ideas outwith German Old Testament studies (159–62).

4. Fourthly, we come to the further development of the language-history model (163–81). Beginning with a comment on the enormous growth in the interest in the theme of *language* within the theology of the last forty years, Oeming goes on to discuss the work of H. Haag, H.-J. Kraus, and especially A.H.J. Gunneweg. Since Gunneweg's Theology is treated separately in the present volume, I refer the reader to that chapter. Here, however, it should be noted that Oeming himself tells us that he had long thought that Gunneweg's thoughts formed the best solution, but he now thinks that further elaboration is needed (168f.). Criticisms of Gunneweg by P. von der Osten-Sacken, K. Schwarzwäller, F. Mildenberger, W. Zimmerli and S. Wagner are all taken into account. Finally it is mentioned that P. Stuhlmacher also has found language history to be 'an eminent factor for the creation of unity between the Testaments' (180).

Oeming's next chapter is a short discussion of the concept of a 'centre', both for the Old Testament and for the New (182–5). Following this is a chapter on the 'canonical approach' of Childs (186–209). Oeming is very critical of this approach, along lines similar to those taken by me in Chs. 23–24 of this book.

A short Ch. 13 on 'Psychological Models' follows.


*4. Oeming's own proposals*

Chapter 14 is entitled 'Attempt at an Interim Balance (*Zwischenbilanz*)' and presents a series of theses with discussion following. The first three concern the historical-critical method and can be left aside for the moment. The conclusion should, however, be recorded, namely that 'the historical-critical method ought to be the sole appropriate methodological basis for pan-biblical theology' (221).

More novel and more important for our present purpose is Thesis 4, which asserts that 'essential points of principle, about which the various biblical theologies conflict, are not primarily theological, but in the first place philosophical, questions' (222). Thus, for example, in respect of the philosophy of history there is a conflict between a universal-linear and an existential-punctual approach. In respect of the philosophy of language, there is a conflict between a conventionalist theory and an idealist theory, the latter ascribing to biblical language a power that is unsurpassable and not replaceable. Thus in general hermeneutics there is a rational, methodologically orientated type of thinking on one side and on the other a type of thinking that emphasizes a charismatic, not methodically controlled, understanding.

Oeming concludes by saying that it may be a banal insight to recognize this, and indeed it may be so. But, he goes on, and rightly, very few in the debates about pan-biblical theology have really thought back over their own philosophical implications. That this is so has already been indicated in these pages; once again it is a part of the unwholesome inheritance of dialectical theology, which tended to develop philosophy as a polemical instrument to be used for the analysis and destruction of others but not as a means through which any positive truth relevant for theology could be attained.

Oeming's Thesis 5 asserts that 'systematic-theological decisions enter essentially into the formation of pan-biblical theologies' (223). Here he offers three 'loci' *De revelatione*. When revelation is seen as having its exclusive place in the Christ-event, this has quite a different effect from what happens when other points of revelation are accepted. Again, when revelation is seen in apocalyptic fashion as special knowledge, this produces a quite different picture from an understanding in which revelation is not a supernatural insight into salvation-historical processes but a directly relevant address, to be understood only in the *Vollzug* of *Existenz* (a phrase hardly to be rendered into pure English; perhaps 'the consummation of *Existenz*', J.B.?). The relevance of these questions for the matter of natural theology – not noted by Oeming here, or indeed, so far as I see, anywhere – is obvious. The other two *loci* are *De Israel* and *De Christo* (224).

In Thesis 6 (225), Oeming concludes that pan-biblical theology in the sense of a unitary doctrine constantly witnessed by the entire Bible does not exist and cannot exist. Thesis 7 goes on to emphasize the quadruple plurality that has to be taken into consideration: the pluralities of

1. Philosophical premises;
2. Doctrinal premises;
3. Old Testament theologies;
4. New Testament theologies.

This state of the problem cannot be simplified through assertions of the allegedly obvious, or leapt over by dogmatic assertion.

Oeming's concluding Chapter 15 (226–41) is entitled 'Contours of a Biblical Theology as Value-Relating Exegesis'. Here he presents his own theoretical basis for future pan-biblical theology. Such a basis is necesssary unless we are to fall into sceptical resignation or 'flee forward'[13] into 'post-critical' exegesis. Oeming therefore chooses to explore the resources of the thought of the Neo-Kantian philosopher Heinrich Rickert (1863–1936) as adapted by Max Weber. History is not a valuing, but a value-relating discipline. The procedure of value-relating is not an arbitrary, subjective act but comes under strict logic. The measuring of an individual historical situation by the standard of values is a rational act which can be expected of any being who is gifted with reason and capable of judgment. Through the differentiation between practical valuing and purely theoretical relating to values, historical science achieves objectivity and universality.[14] The full argumentation cannot be restated here, but the following are some of the essentials as they bear upon biblical studies:

1. Exegesis is primarily interested in the most precise possible comprehension of the *individual* text. 'Crosscuts' or ideal-typical comparisons have only a heuristic function (232).

2. The content thus comprehended must be related to a *value*. From the Christian point of view this value can only be that which is Christian (*das Christliche*), as witnessed to in the New Testament (this last is later somewhat modified; see below). This theoretical value-relating of the Old Testament text to the New Testament witness is *a logical act, an accomplishment of the power of judgment that is totally independent of faith or unbelief.* Through this value-relating to that which is Christian the significance of the Old Testament text to Christian faith comes to be known (232).

Things, however, are more complicated, for the standard 'Christian' is by no means unambiguous. The New Testament presents a wide spectrum of Christian theologies and, as with the Old, these are varied and nuanced according to confessional allegiance, philosophical premises, political convictions and so on. This 'factual pluralism' has to be built into the model. This leads on to four further considerations:

1. Precisely because of the inter-religious and inter-confessional co-existence of possibilities, the act of value choice must contain an element of commitment (German *Bekenntnis*) and decision. A 'pure exegesis' that claimed to arrive at a universally authoritative theology on the ground of historical exegesis alone is impossible because of the inner-biblical pluralism. As long as the exegete's decision is open and is not represented as universal or the only one possible, this

element is desirable and necessary. It gives profile and relative clarity to the presentation of the biblical testimony. Thus a Catholic, a Protestant and a Jewish position are all alike good and proper.

2. The concept of a 'value' needs to be made more explicit. Familiar terms like 'justification' or 'kingdom of God' require a wide explication, and for this a systematic-theological way of thinking is necessary. The separation between historical exegesis and systematic theological penetration and evaluation destroys an organic unity to the hurt of all. What is 'Christian' is not a known quantity but has to be worked out.

As the value 'Christian' thus unfolds itself as the 'canon in the canon' for a proposal on the doctrinal level, it is accessible and understandable to one who does not share it, and is thus intersubjectively communicable and discussable. Everyone is in principle in a position to enter into the thinking of the other, to use for himself or herself the premises of the other. This is of enormous importance for the ecumenical discussion.

3. Historicity (*Geschichtlichkeit*: should we rather say *historicality* here?), which means that the theory-formation of pan-biblical theology is changeable and may become obsolete, does not lead to relativism but demands a fresh and living understanding for each present moment. The act of preaching is the point at which the need for this is most pressing and obvious.

4. A peculiar *ambivalence* attaches to many Old Testament texts, and the openness of many concepts is essential for a wholesome Christian reception of them. Decisive questions remain undecided. For instance, was Abraham chosen by God on the basis of his special achievements or potential abilities, as Genesis 22 might make probable, or was it God's unmotivated grace towards this particular man, who had no special merits of his own? Questions of this kind are *fruitful semantic ambiguities*. Value-relating exegesis has to make clear the manifold possibilities of the linguistic material of the Bible. The same applies to Jewish, Muslim and other hermeneutics.

Finally Oeming addresses himself to 'the particular value (*Eigenwert*) of the Old Testament' (Ch. 15.2, 237–41). Given the theoretical basis that he has laid down, the practical execution of it cannot be a mere discovery of a line of historical continuity in the sense of the tradition-history and salvation-history models. 'The historical-factual must rather be questioned for its Christian validity.'[15]

In particular, pan-biblical theology does not consist in a measuring of the Old Testament by the standard of the New. On the contrary, the New is to be measured by the standard of the Old, and the witness of both is to be thought through under systematic-theological aspects. Pan-biblical theology is thus neither a merely historical nor a merely doctrinal discipline, but both at once.

The meaning of the Old Testament thus varies from text to text and from theme to theme. Total judgments about *the* value of the Old Testament are therefore faulty. But its voices are always to be heard with care and attention, for three reasons:

1. Even where the result of value-relating is a *Sachkritik* or critical assessment of the content, the material thus criticized remains as a constant question and a fact that continually calls for a fresh justification of the position taken. The canonization of the Old Testament in the church has thus institutionalized continual reflection over values.

2. In those parts where the Old Testament is analogous to the New and equal in value, the value of the Old lies in the explication not of christology but of that which is Christian. The vividness (*Einprägsamkeit*) and plasticity and even at times the coarseness of the narratives makes them very well adapted to the concretization and unfolding of that which is Christian. Some are analogous to New Testament materials and do not contain anything basically different, but they are expressed in a quite different way: for example, the place of man between animal and angel, the position of the seventh day as a day of rest. Without the richness of the Old Testament in pictures the Christian kerygma would be seriously poorer.

3. The irreplaceable peculiar value of the Old Testament is clearest in those places where it represents a plus as against the New and thus complements the latter: aspects such as monotheism, creation, the personal conception of God, the language of prayer, joy in nature, in husband and wife and children, in good eating and drinking – and also in deep scepticism and desperate accusation against God. And (a key utterance of Oeming's): 'It is not the New Testament but the Christ-event that is the comprehensive, all-sufficient event of salvation.'

## 5. Discussion

Oeming's analysis of von Rad's work is helpful and illuminating; particularly helpful is the way in which the identification of the various models leads on into a mapping of the various streams of scholarship which have each in their own way exploited and followed up initiatives found in von Rad. His depiction of the contradictory forces operating in von Rad's work is convincing and enlightening.

Perhaps one might add this as a final impression. To von Rad it was obviously a matter of extreme devotion and importance to bring out the deep connections between the Old Testament and the New, in other words to build the groundwork of a pan-biblical theology. His choices in exegesis were heavily

influenced by this aim. As I have already mentioned,[16] his rather pathetic
concluding paragraph lamented that, if he had not succeeded in establishing this
link with the New Testament, then all his work could in the last instance be no
more than a history of the religion of Israel – a phrase that implied the low
evaluation of history of religion which we have seen to be common in much
biblical theology. But, much as one must appreciate the pathos underlying this
passage, as an appreciation of his own achievement it was surely quite wrong.
Surely no one could seriously take von Rad's work as 'merely' a history of
Israelite religion. The linkage with the New Testament, on which he laid so
much emphasis, is probably the aspect of his work that has had the least effect
in the long run. Not only Jewish readers[17] but Christian readers also tend to skip
these passages. What he really achieved, and what he is most esteemed for, is a
Theology of the Old Testament and arguably, as Oeming says, the best single
book yet to be devoted to this subject.[18]

More important for us here is the disclosure that von Rad's thinking was so
closely allied with Gadamer's philosophical position. In the paragraph added to
his Preface in the Fourth Edition,[19] he wrote that 'in the urgently necessary
revision of our outworn conceptuality in the philosophy of history, we exegetes
should not despise the help of present-day philosophy, for it is much more in
movement (*beweglich*)'. Gadamer, he goes on, concerns himself under the theme
of *Wirkungsgeschichte* with phenomena which come very close to the actualization process as set out in his own Theology. According to Gadamer, the real
meeting with a historical work or a historical tradition lies in this history of
reception and effects lies. Much as his historical objectivism may conceal the
reality, the modern interpreter is a last link in this chain of those who understand. What von Rad most gained, he thought, from Gadamer was 'his critique
of an uncritical positivism'.

Whatever we may think of this, it does show that von Rad was willing to
express, if not his philosophical dependence, at least his readiness to accept
philosophical aid. It is equally characteristic, however, that even this was done
only *afterwards*: he did not think of making it explicit in his original writing. The
idea that a philosophical *foundation* for a biblical theology had to be worked out
and stated at the beginning was as remote from his thinking as from that of
almost all biblical theologians. Moreover, one can well understand why von Rad,
even if conscious of the affinity of his thought with Gadamer's, may have preferred to be reticent about it in the original presentation of his Theology. For a
philosophical support is a double-edged instrument: if Gadamer is right, then
that is a source of strength, but if Gadamer is wrong or even only controversial,
then a reliance upon him is a source of weakness.

Again, given that von Rad felt, and rightly, this closeness to Gadamer, it
remains a question whether for him this really meant an involvement of

philosophy in the work of biblical theology. Did von Rad enter into an open philosophical debate, in which Gadamer's ideas were compared with those of other philosophical directions, arguments on both sides were heard, and a decision was reached? If the philosophical decision had gone against Gadamer, would von Rad have altered his theological methods? Or had he already formed an opinion, basically on theological grounds, for which he was pleased later to find a confirmation in Gadamer? The latter would be more in the normal style of biblical theology.

Nor does von Rad or, so far as I know, any other biblical theologian go as far as Oeming does with his perception and declaration (in his Thesis 4, 222, quoted above, 506) that the basic conflicts visible within biblical and pan-biblical theology are philosophical in character, coupled with his own willingness to take up a philosophical position, expound it and say how it would work out in a biblical theology. If this is true, it must mean a substantial change of course for biblical theology.

Naturally, as was completely predictable, Oeming was blamed by critics for doing this, and in his second edition he gives his reply (270). There is a problem here, for one can of course 'import' implications which do not fit the subject-matter and cause distortion. Oeming's modest reply is that he has looked around and found no better scheme than the one which he has used.


## 6. Conclusion

It is not my purpose here to express agreement with every detail of Oeming's searching argument. Everyone interested in the field will have some disagreement with his judgments at one point or another. Nevertheless his study represents a very important step forward and provides suggestions which will open the way for progress in numerous regards.

On the one hand his analysis of the heritage of von Rad by the identification of the various models is in itself a valuable step forward: not simply because the models may be rightly identified, but because the entire mode of working, by proposing models as hypotheses and testing them against the material, is a significant innovation within traditional biblical theology. The models represent a useful way of thinking, which lies somewhere between the systematic approach of some and the more historical, heterogeneous, disorganized approach of others.

Secondly, there is much of value in Oeming's formulation of a mode in which objective historical understanding and committed value-relation are seen not as contraries but as combined. If right, this would overcome one of the great antinomies of traditional biblical theology (cf. above, Chapter 12). If the

Rickert-Weber view of this should prove defective, then perhaps another can be found that would prove satisfactory.

Thirdly, there is enormous promise in the way in which Oeming has built *pluralism* into his conception. In the past, when people have talked of a personal commitment or involvement, this has often been expressed exclusively: you can't do this unless you are a Protestant, or a conservative, or a Barthian, or whatever. In the end this line of thinking leads to a hopeless solipsism: no one can talk about anything except what they themselves believe. On this basis theology would come to a stop: no orthodox theologian could talk about Gnosticism, no Protestant could talk about anything Catholic, no Christian could talk about anything Jewish. This may sound absurd and exaggerated, but it is the obvious and necessary implication of arguments that have been repeatedly used in biblical theology. In the past, when it has been said that biblical theology could not be pursued without entering into the doctrinal or 'dogmatic' realm, this has often been understood in a narrow, sectarian, way. Oeming's vision is the reverse: Jews can enter into Christian 'dogmatic' thinking, Catholics into Protestant, and so on, and precisely this is the value of the exercise. I think this is absolutely right, even if the terms might have to be defined somewhat differently.

There remain questions about Oeming's study. For instance, can Gunneweg's strong development of the language-history model really stand in view of Oeming's own criticism of the same model as used by von Rad and Gadamer? Is the emphasis on *preaching* as the point where biblical-theological considerations become most critical really justifiable? Can the role of philosophy in biblical theology be properly justified without bringing in the further question of natural theology, of which Oeming appears to say nothing? Is it enough to say that biblical theology must include a 'dogmatic-systematic' element without explaining what this element could be like and how it would work? And is it realistic to expect many biblical scholars to accept this extension of their scholarly scope without much extended justification? Despite its salutary and completely positive character, about which I entirely agree, is the 'historical-critical method' really the basis (*Grundlage*) of pan-biblical theology (221)? Is this statement not just the one most likely to provoke indignant denials, which, one may suggest, could have been avoided? In spite of these and other questions and uncertainties, I remain certain that Oeming has a very great achievement to his credit and one that can be expected to move biblical theology creatively forward.

# 29

# Mildenberger

Some readers may be surprised that here I present a work that falls into a very different class from those discussed so far: the *Biblische Dogmatik* of Friedrich Mildenberger (3 vols, 1991, 1992, 1993).[1]

Mildenberger has been mentioned earlier in this book, but only marginally. He might be classed as a dogmatic theologian, but his work has included much that comes close to our own field of interest. In 1964 he wrote a shortish work (148 pp.), the title of which might be translated as *God's Act in the Word. Considerations on Old Testament Hermeneutics as a Question of the Unity of the Testaments*.[2] This followed soon after the publication of von Rad's *Old Testament Theology* and also took account also of numerous important articles of the 1950s, especially in journals like *Evangelische Theologie*. It forms a significant part of the discussion among Old Testament scholars following the appearance of von Rad's main work, and also includes numerous references to doctrinal theologians such as Miskotte, van Ruler, Ratschow and Ebeling. Towards von Rad himself it would seem to be on the whole appreciative, but also critical. It is regrettable that this work is little known in the English-speaking lands. I am sorry that it was unknown to me when I wrote my *Old and New in Interpretation* (1966).

In 1967 another shortish (99 pp.) work was published, the title of which in English would be, perhaps, *Half the Truth or the Whole Scripture? On the Conflict between Faith in the Bible and Historical Criticism*.[3] A short passage from the second page will give an example of the content:

> The inability of historical exegesis to transform the historical facts into validity for the present day shows unmistakeably the limits of the historical method. It cannot by any means claim that it works out the right interpretation of the Bible according to which the practice of the church would have to be directed. Wherever such a claim is made, it must be energetically opposed. For in the end result this would lead to the situation that only the historical expert could understand the Bible rightly; everyone else would be dependent on his results, which they would have to take over, more or less without any testing.

This – in itself a very familiar position – does not mean that Mildenberger totally rejects historical exegesis; not at all. He is quite friendly towards it, while repeatedly insisting on its limitations. But he emphasizes the need for a consideration of the position of *the church*:

> Academic biblical exegesis and the practical life of the church must not lose contact with one another . . . A biblical scholarship isolated from the church will distort the essentials of the text with which it deals, while conversely a church-only, edification-centred, exegesis will be unable to span (*abzuschreiten*) the wide horizon of the Bible. Biblical scholarship and practical church life must find each other.

Also relevant is his shortish book on the doctrine of God, published in 1975.[4] This does not directly address questions of biblical theology, but has significant discussions of such matters as how God is known, natural theology and related matters.

I shall not discuss these earlier works here, but proceed to the much larger, and very recent, work, the *Biblical Dogmatics*. The subtitle of the whole is 'A Biblical Theology in Dogmatic Perspective'. It may be felt that the title of a 'Biblical Dogmatics' places the work outside the frame of biblical theology. In fact, however, it takes serious cognizance of biblical theology, uses the expression frequently, and enters into detailed discussions with biblical scholarship and especially with biblical theologians, including several of those who have been mentioned in this book. It is at least possible that a work of this kind may offer suggestions for future biblical theology or provide patterns which it will be stimulating to discuss.

The work is lengthy, dense and heavy, and I am not expert in every area touched upon, so that I may have misunderstood some things. In any case I cannot pretend to give more than a brief sketch of its character and its thought. There are three volumes, each of them of increasing length (the first has 281 pages, the second 433, and the third 496). There are good indexes, however, which help the reader to find material, especially the general index of concepts at the end of Vol. III. Each chapter ends with a summary which helps the reader to grasp the basic argument, a real blessing at the many points where the total in detail may prove difficult to master.

Many readers may find the subtitles for the three volumes baffling. They are, in German:

1. *Prolegomena: Verstehen und Geltung der Bibel*
2. *Ökonomie als Theologie*
3. *Theologie als Ökonomie.*

I shall translate these in a peculiar way, since in this context *Theologie* is not exactly what we mean by theology, still less is *Ökonomie* to be rendered by 'economy'. I shall translate the terms with theologia and oikonomia, using these Hellenic forms to follow the usage of the Greek Fathers, from whom the usage comes. In Mildenberger's usage the two elements, theologia and oikonomia, are both parts of theology as we usually use the term; indeed, they are more than parts: together they form the great overarching distinction that dominates his organization of theology.

The first question, then, obviously is: what does Mildenberger mean by theologia and oikonomia? This is not too easy to answer, since the terms are clearly ancient and technical. They come from older theology, but Mildenberger adapts the use to his own modern outlook. Roughly speaking, theologia is the doctrine of God in himself; oikonomia refers to the aspect when, as it were, God goes out of himself to handle exterior realities. In the Greek Fathers, Mildenberger tells us, oikonomia was more or less synonymous with the incarnation. Perhaps the English 'administration' would give an idea of the derivation of oikonomia – it is what is done *by God*, outside himself, as it were, to put things back as they ought to be.

Mildenberger explains his own usage on I, 230ff. Theologia includes the doctrine of God, of the Trinity, of creation, of the rational creatures (angels and humans), of providence and of the beatific vision: he sums these up as the 'constitution of reality in God'. Oikonomia by contrast is the 'restitution of reality by God', i.e. through God's outward action in Jesus Christ and in the Holy Spirit.

Though these terms are of ancient origin, Mildenberger takes into account the ways in which their content has developed in more modern times. A key reference point for him is the thought of David Hollaz, a theologian of late Lutheran orthodoxy, whose *Examen theologicum acroamaticum* was published in 1707, in a time of interaction between orthodoxy and Enlightenment. Hollaz is first introduced on I, 13 and is, I estimate, mentioned more frequently in the volumes than any other human being, Schleiermacher being the nearest competitor. But in spite of his frequent reference to Hollaz, Mildenberger is not one to be thought of as a mere repeater of ancient orthodoxies. On the same page, I, 13, where he first mentions Hollaz, he writes the important sentence:

The perspective under which I handle the biblical texts is determined on the one side by the Reformation tradition, on the other by the Enlightenment.

And, as we shall see, much space and dense discussion is devoted to more modern theology: notably to Kant and Schleiermacher, and in the twentieth century to Barth and Tillich. Among living theologians, Pannenberg and Jüngel are perhaps the most often mentioned. Moreover, while some sections seem to be deeply sunk in church tradition, a very different impression is given by Chapter 1 §3, 'Models of Usage-Orientated Exegesis of Scripture'. This has three sections on: 1. Psychological Exegesis, 2. The Bible in Liberation Theology, and 3. Feminist Exegesis of the Bible (72–90). A welcome of a certain peculiar kind is given to all three. They are forces that can be positively valued for their critical contribution, and they thus have an influence on theological understanding. Yet, to take the feminist case as an example, its insights as a whole 'certainly cannot be integrated into the undertaking of a biblical dogmatics' (I, 89). Yet dogmatics cannot be untouched by the feminist criticisms and must be watchful for defects to which these criticisms call attention.

Returning to theologia and oikonomia, there follows a short but dense historical account of how these two were 'broken apart' in the Enlightenment (I, 231–6) and how they are 'interlocked' (the noun is *Verschränkung*) in modern dogmatics, in which Schleiermacher, Barth and Tillich are particularly discussed (I, 236–43). In a section on the methodological consequences for a biblical dogmatic (I, 243–6) he then explains how this will work out (especially I, 245), and this brings us to the titles of Volumes II and III:

'Only by the way through the restitution of reality by God can the God be comprehended in whom reality is constituted' (I, 245). This forms Vol. II: Oikonomia as Theologia or as Leading to Theologia. And: 'The constitution of reality in God is biblically described only in that it is comprehended as the reality restored through God's action' (I, 245 again). This gives us Vol. III, Theologia as Oikonomia.

I apologize for this difficult phraseology, but it is necessary if one is to understand Mildenberger's reasoning and the structure of his book.

The way to realize this is complex. Dogmatics provides something of a skeleton or framework. Biblical material attaches to both theologia and oikonomia. There is a complex *Ineinander* of theologia and oikonomia, which means that the representation depends on a very subtle relating of biblical materials to the questions, an interconnection more complex than in any previous dogmatic outline. Patience and attention are therefore requested of all readers by the author (I, 246 and elsewhere), a very necessary requirement, as readers of the present summary will well understand.

In his summary (I, 246), Mildenberger makes several essential points. First, he will not follow the ordering of a biblical theology, which he takes to be a temporal ordering by earlier and later. On the other hand the traditional dogmatic outline will not do either. The question is how to link theologia and oikonomia together in such a way that the completeness of doctrine is preserved. A quick summary of Schleiermacher, Barth and Tillich follows, and it is concluded that none of these models provides a practicable outline for a biblical dogmatic.

The reader may ask: Where does the biblical material come into this? Does it belong to theologia or to oikonomia? How does it fit in? The answer seems to be that the biblical material belongs to both, but the questions come to the biblical material in a different way in each. It is essential to see that the dogmatic content is not first laid down and the biblical evidences added on (I, 247). Rather, dogmatics is conceived of as posing the questions to which the biblical texts are to be discussed as *answer*. However, the interlocking of theologia and oikonomia means that oikonomia has to be presented as theologia and theologia as oikonomia. Hence an all-important sentence: *the basic questions of dogmatic theologia should find their answers in the biblical oikonomia, while conversely the questions of dogmatic oikonomia must find their answer in the biblical theologia.* 'Only so' (the fatal *nur so* of German theological argument! – rather frequent in Mildenberger's style) will the statement do justice to the unavoidable dogmatic problematic on one side and to the proper weighting (*Eigengewicht*) of the biblical utterances on the other' (ibid.).

All this may seem obscure to the biblical scholar, but it is necessary to explain it if one is to understand the characteristic *ordering of material* in the work. To the simple mind of the biblical scholar it may seem odd that creation comes as the *last* section of the last volume, and that it is *preceded* by a section on *the world*, while matters of sin and atonement come still earlier, in section 2 of Vol. II. This follows from the dialectic of theologia and oikonomia.

At least we do not have here the simple order God-man-sin-redemption that has been so often disapproved of. Biblical theology, as we have seen, has often worried over the ordering and organization of material, and has wanted to avoid a traditional dogmatic order. Here, with Mildenberger, is an order that may be dogmatic, but is certainly not *merely* traditional and clearly has a powerful process of reasoning behind it.

How then do we know where the biblical material is going to appear? As the author has explained, not in the temporal order of before and after. Nor, it seems, in any obvious scheme, like the order of books or a canonical order. It appears, it seems, where, and if, the dogmatic questions require it.

But there is plenty of it. Attention to biblical material can be dense and detailed. Thus in Vol. III, within a section entitled 'the human constitution in relation to God', the first subsection is entitled 'the chosen deliverer' and consists entirely of a seven-page exposition of the Samson story (III, 113–19), with very considerable annotation, most of it referring to recent and serious exegetical work. On the other hand, the index seems to indicate that the same volume contains no reference to any part of Judges outside this section, and indeed Vol. II has only very few references, Vol. I none at all.

Before we go farther, it will be helpful to indicate that Mildenberger engages in substantial conversation with at least some of the work in biblical theology which has been discussed in earlier chapters of the present book. Gese's ideas are discussed quite a lot (see especially I, 101f. on his basic ideas for biblical theology; also II, 112–15 on his views of atonement; III, 409f. on the gods of Canaan). The position of Childs also receives consideration at a number of points. His canonical approach receives a two-page general discussion (I, 256f.), and this will be taken up again below.

Among modern Old Testament specialists Westermann is much the most discussed. His view of the blessing and saving actions of God is related to the balance betweeen theologia and oikonomia, in fairly long notes (II, 106, 109; 116, again III, 243, 301 n.99). Mildenberger has obviously tangled with Westermann's views in the past (II, 116 n. 99).[5] In Volume III (216 n.115) we have the dispute over the distinction between command and law, and still more over creation (III, 408–10).

Von Rad is also mentioned, but distinctly less: central matters include von Rad's conception of *Nacherzählung* (I, 160); the historical credo (I, 170 n. 33); and typology (I, 197).[6] But there is no *general discussion or assessment* of von Rad's position in Old Testament theology. This may be because Mildenberger feels he has dealt adequately with von Rad in his earlier book, mentioned above. In particular, he favours the use of the term 'God's history' (*Gottesgeschichte*).[7] On this concept see particularly §23, 'Gottes Name als Inbegriff seiner Geschichte' (II, 385–406).

Zimmerli is little mentioned; surprisingly, not at all in the long section on the Name of God (II, 363–404). Preuss comes in for his views on the connection between act and consequence (*Tun-Ergehen-Zusammenhang*) and its negative consequences for Wisdom (I, 143, 145f.; III, 334 n. 59, 416; on his 'structure-analogy' see I, 46 n. 45, 222 n. 67; on experience II, 261 n.68; 263 n.74. Fohrer appears at I, 103 n. 37, 258–9, but more as an example of a common attitude than for the sake of his own Old Testament theology; other mentions are of detailed exegetical opinions.

The concept of story with which I have been concerned and which is discussed in Ch. 21 above is mentioned or discussed here a number of times: I, 171f.; II, 203 (critically), 374 n., 393 n., 400 n.; III, 120 n.59, 423 n.79. On the ordering of theological elements compare a reference to D. Ritschl, *The Logic of Theology* (I, 244 n.). He is said to make the passage *twice* from oikonomia to theologia: there is first ecclesiology, which leads to the trinitarian doctrine of God; then follows christology, which in a fourth stage leads on to anthropology. Relatedly, my own *Old and New in Interpretation* in its German form is appreciatively discussed at I, 253 n.22, and described as 'a book that in many regards loosens up some hard confrontations'.

The older Old Testament theologians are mentioned very little: Eichrodt and Jacob appear nowhere in the index, Koehler and Vriezen only very marginally (I, 228 n.4). H.-J. Kraus is mentioned, but more for his exegesis of the Psalms than for his work on biblical theology.[8] Of New Testament specialists significant for theology, after Bultmann, those mentioned are mainly Käsemann and Stuhlmacher. Stendahl appears nowhere.

Of particular interest to me was the *limited* emphasis given to the concept of *revelation*. The passage II, 389ff. is concentrated on *difficulties* that arise from the revelation theology of Barth; here there is an emphasis on the thought of E. Jüngel. Again, I, 165 works on Pannenberg's ideas of 'revelation as history', and I, 25ff. describes traditional formulations of 'reason and revelation'. I, 142–51 is an entire section entitled 'Soteriology and Wisdom or Revelation and Reason'; it is by no means an insistence on 'revelation' as the answer to problems. II, 166 is about the special case of the 'revelation of God's anger'; it notes (167) the 'intolerable nature (*Unzuträglichkeit*) of the traditional dogmatic handling of scripture, which turns it into an arsenal, out of which ideas drawn from elsewhere can then be demonstrated'.

Discussion of *natural theology* continues at many points through the book. Mildenberger thinks of the opposition between 'natural theology' and 'revelational theology' as something that is very intensely discussed at the present time – not my impression for biblical studies, at least in the English-speaking realm, or for biblical theology anywhere. He is disturbed by the loose terminology and lack of exact definition as seen in this discussion, which indeed may very well be right (I, 230). He earnestly pleads for the use of his own terminology instead of these misleading concepts (I, 231). This is, at any rate, something different from an outright condemnation of 'natural theology'.

What Mildenberger condemns more seriously and consistently is metaphysics and 'metaphysical thinking'. In this respect he is often critical of the past dogmatic tradition, which has accepted too much of metaphysics, but in a mixed and disordered way: see for example the treatment of Law and Gospel (I, 233f.), where we are told that 'a metaphysical understanding of law has stood in competition with the theological understanding'. Metaphysics is connected with the supposed 'normality' that would exist if sin had not entered the world. To this we must add: Mildenberger lays much emphasis on the distinction between a Parmenidean metaphysic, concentrated on the distinction between necessary and contingent being, and a Cartesian metaphysic, concentrated on the distinction between (thinking) subject and object (constituted through thinking). These, Mildenberger thinks, have often been confused in theology, and he uses the distinction heavily. For the central presentation of the matter see the large section §13, 'The Crisis of Metaphysical Thought about God' (*Metaphysiches Gottesdenken in der Krise*), II, 12–43. Roughly we may say that in his thought the damage done by 'metaphysical thinking' seems to take the place of the customary contrasts between 'natural' and 'revelational' theology, and this may well be a step forward.

Strikingly for a 'Biblical Dogmatic', there appears to be no mention at all of Hebrew thought or Hebrew mentality, or indeed of anything like 'biblical thought' in general. Naturally this may be considered a wise omission, since these concepts have been shown to have underlying traps in them. But it remains peculiar that when a subject like 'metaphysical thinking' is discussed, it is mainly discussed in terms that go back to Greek philosophy and forward to patristic, Reformation and modern theology; the possible place of the Bible, or of particular elements within the Bible, in relation to this or in contradistinction against this, seems mainly to be left aside. There is no shortage of biblical *material*: but it is mainly introduced in a different place and context. For after all, what if some traces of Greek metaphysics found their way at some stage into some part of the Bible? If so, this would help to explain how they got into the theological tradition later on. But Mildenberger seems to treat these questions as part of the theological framework, into which the biblical passages are introduced as a separate part of the operation. In all this respect he seems rather remote from the sort of thing that has been characteristic of much biblical theology – whether with success or not.

Somewhat parallel to this is another aspect. Right at the start Mildenberger introduces the distinction between 'simple God-talk' and academic (*wissenschaftlich*) theology (I, 14ff.). This is important to him because it relieves theology from the task of having to prove (*bewahrheiten*) its own speech about God to be well-founded, and it provides a 'present reality' to which theology has reference. But when he comes on to discuss the 'place' of simple God-talk, he at once names 'the church' as that place. Simple God-talk is related to the Bible. That which confronts us, requiring a response (I cannot think of a better rendering for *das Anstehende*),[9] and the Bible do not 'come to speech' independently, being thereafter conjoined; only when they are both present together is either expressed or understood (I, 18). Moreover, an important section (§8.3, 'The Biblical Texts as Language of Simple God-talk', I, 195–203) expounds this. I wonder if this would have some correspondence with my distinction between *story* and *theology* (see above, Chapter 21).

As was mentioned above, Mildenberger gives substantial reference to the canonical approach of Childs. His major discussion and assessment (I, 256f.) concludes that Childs lays too much weight on the normative function of the canon:

> The normative function of the biblical texts is derived from their primary function in simple God-talk and from the experience which is had with

these texts here. Dogmatically expressed, the scripture as means of grace has precedence over the scripture as *principium cognoscendi*. It is not the distinguishing function of the canonical decision that is primary; on the contrary, this comes *after* the use [of the texts] (I, 257).[10]

Other points connected with the canon are as follows: Childs' final-form exegesis of Habakkuk is seriously considered on II, 274f. in relation to a later and contrary assessment by E. Otto.[11] Mildenberger sees the two contrary views – Otto's one more historical, the other more 'abstract' (Otto's opinion of Childs' view) – as less distant from each other than they would seem at first. More in the style of Childs, Mildenberger sees the Psalms as having been separated from their original situation in life and having gained a new life of their own as Word of God (II, 263). Childs' thoughts about the canonization of the Song of Songs receive a lengthy but also critical footnote (III, 245). A footnote also criticizes Childs' assessment of Qoheleth in his *Introduction* (III, 332 n. 51). In general, Mildenberger comes close to Childs in being unsympathetic to any kind of historical 'reconstruction'.

Some other aspects that have interested us in the present book are lacking from Mildenberger's presentation. There is little mention of Judaism: I, 111 notes that the problem of acceptance of the Old Testament in the church is less serious today than that of making Christian use of the Old Testament legitimate in Jewish eyes. For this he passes us on to a study by F.W. Marquardt.[12] Judaism is a factor in the problem of the canon (I, 255). 'Late Judaism' as a designation appears on I, 259. The church, he says, does not have to dispute *other* forms of speech about God, for instance in Judaism (I, 29f.).

The idea of 'Jewish biblical theology' seems not to be discussed anywhere. In this regard the approach is entirely Christian. The unity of scripture, which is much emphasized (see I, 92–115), is axiomatically the unity of the *Christian* scripture of Old and New Testaments. This would seem to imply, though I have not seen it expressly stated, that there cannot be *any* Christian 'Theology of the Old Testament [alone]'.[13] Among the scholars discussed in the present book this, I suppose, might fit particularly with Gese's conception. Others, like von Rad and Westermann, were deeply concerned to establish connections with the New Testament, but however strong the efforts they made in this direction, the fact remains that what came out was a theology of the Old Testament rather than one of the [Christian] Bible. Indeed, I think this remains true of Gese's project also, in its actual outcome, if not in its original plan. So it remains slightly strange that Mildenberger, while certainly disagreeing with a scholar like Westermann on many theological points, still converses with him as one who is within the field of relevance for 'biblical dogmatics' in his own sense. Similarly with Childs, who in spite of his emphasis on the relations between Old and New still remains very obviously an Old Testament man, and achieves his biblical theology of the Old and New Testaments largely by *juxtaposing* two *distinct* theologies which, as it happens, support each other thoroughly. With Mildenberger, on the other hand, the distinction between Old and New Testaments is little emphasized. It is dealt with in an important chapter of the prolegomena (I, 248–54) but plays little part in the detailed work of the two succeeding volumes. Like Childs, Mildenberger thinks that it is wrong not only to consider the Old Testament 'inferior' or the like, but even to consider that it has to be understood 'through' the New. Here he has to argue with other Lutheran dogmaticians, W. Elert and P. Althaus, as well as with M. Oeming, whose work has been discussed above. It is fatal to suppose that the New Testament can be understood for itself (I, 252), and so it cannot serve as mediator of the thoughts of the Old. There is a truly biblical question about Old and New, before and after, but this should not be mixed up with the relation between the two Testaments (I, 254). When the dogmatic tradition talked of the Old and New 'Testaments', he says, it had in mind not the two corpora of *text* but *two different dispensations* (*Setzungen Gottes*).[14] In this respect it would seem to imply – though he does not say this – that Childs' method does not observe the 'unity of scripture' and indeed is imperfect as Christian theology.

Or, to put it in another way, Mildenberger, in spite of his very excellent contact with so much in biblical theology and exegesis, seems not to make any contact at all with Old Testament theology as it has been, and with the tradition of its development. He brings in all these people, von Rad, Westermann and so on, and discusses their views on this or that text or on some important problem, but nowhere seems to give a proper account of any of them and what they were trying to do. Nor does he seem to show, or even to try to show, how his own product could provide for the need that they were trying to fill. Perhaps he thinks there is, or should be, no [Christian] Old Testament theology at all; but if so, he does not make this clear, and his constant interaction with parts and elements taken from such theologies suggests that he does not think so, in principle anyway.

This is a puzzling element. From the beginning Mildenberger thinks that there is biblical theology. This is not disputed. It stands in some sort of distinction from dogmatics (I, 11, the very first page). Indeed, biblical dogmatics, his own project area, stands 'between biblical theology and dogmatics'. Biblical dogmatics is to do something that neither dogmatics nor biblical theology can do, namely provide a presentation of a 'pan-biblical theology'. This is not to be a historical description, but an 'actualization' of the pan-biblical connections for the present-day church situation. Therefore, he says, the perspective of dogmatics is regulative for the comprehension of the biblical texts, even where historical and exegetical questions are included in the discussion.

Central, however, to his conception of biblical theology is his idea that it is totally dominated and controlled by 'historical reconstruction', by the 'historical-critical method'. But he does not show this to be the case, does not even argue for it, and seems to have no idea that this is a contested notion within biblical theology itself. Perhaps he thinks that it has been demonstrated in his own earlier writings, but it is certainly not demonstrated here. Within biblical scholarship, generally but not universally, the opposite impression prevails: people think of biblical theology and 'the historical-critical method' or 'historical reconstruction' as contrary entities. My own view is that while most biblical theology has *accepted* historical criticism as a valid approach to *analysis*, its *synthetic* task has been approached in an entirely different way, and it is only this latter that makes it into 'biblical theology'. It is therefore characteristic of most biblical theology that while accepting historical ranging of the material, it goes on to a synthetic operation, synchronic or otherwise, that is quite different and works on different principles. Mildenberger thinks that for biblical theology the distinction between 'earlier' and 'later' is decisive, but he makes no attempt to prove this. It would be hard, in view of the common opposite accusation against biblical theology that it fails in precisely this aspect and piles together things that belong to quite different historical periods.

Mildenberger's arguments against historical criticism come within the context of a section on 'The Critical Questioning of the Unity of Scripture' (I, 93ff.). He proceeds, as many others have done, to examine the 'presuppositions' of this approach (I, 95). But his analysis is very weak, because he takes on only one single example, namely Georg Strecker's arguments against the proposals of Gese and Stuhlmacher for a biblical theology (in my terms, a pan-biblical theology).[15] Strecker maintains: 1. that historical thought has discovered very different theological concepts in the scriptures and this has made 'suspect' [even Strecker does not say 'impossible' or 'totally false'] the unity in content of the Old and New Testaments; 2. the integrity of the biblical canon could not remain untouched, because the biblical texts stand in relation of form and content with the contemporary and intertestamental literature; 3. the 'identity of scriptural teaching and dogmatics' has been broken up by historical criticism since the Enlightenment, so that there is a historical and theological gap between the Bible and the utterances of dogmatics. All these claims might well be accepted, Mildenberger goes on, if it is accepted that the Bible can be satisfactorily understood with the universal methods of historically-operating science and if it is also accepted that the experiences with the Bible which are had in connection with 'simple God-talk' have no meaning for the understanding of the Bible. He sums this up: in other words, '*if every form of inspiration is denied*, because academic understanding must in principle claim the universality of its ways of thinking'.

Whatever one may think of these arguments, what is said by the one Georg Strecker in the course of one argument about one question is not enough. Nor is it necessarily true that the assumptions thought by Mildenberger to underlie Strecker's statement are really held by Strecker. Still less likely is it that Strecker's view represents the opinion of every scholar who works with historical criticism. But most important: even if the claims made by Strecker and the interpretations given to them by Mildenberger are true, the latter is surely wrong in suggesting that they necessarily mean the denial of 'every form of Inspiration'. On the contrary, it seems to me comparatively easy to maintain all of Strecker's rather radical statements and still hold to a view of biblical inspiration, even of verbal inspiration.

Mildenberger does not seem to care about the production of a synthetic theology of the Old Testament; and of course this is the tradition of many great doctrinal theologians, as I have maintained in the face of considerable incredulity and criticism. Of course doctrinal theologians will and must interpret biblical passages; but a synthetic account of the Old (or of the New) Testament as a whole is just what they do not feel they need. What biblical theologian would ever get away with an account that talked about the 'chosen deliverers' and took only Samson as an example? The doctrinal theologian may interpret much of the Bible, but does so in a selective way. Even when the Bible is understood as a unity and as a whole, this is still the case. The ordering of the framework, which is dogmatic, poses the questions, and suitable biblical passages are chosen for their answers to these questions. Passages from the Bible may also indicate that the framework has to be adjusted, and Mildenberger has shown ways in which this has been done and can be done.

Again, at certain points Mildenberger speaks as if he was quite negative towards historical-critical method; yet on the other hand he seems to consider that dogmatics and biblical theology have corresponding, but opposite, tasks, and fit very well together (I, 12). Over wide ranges of questions he seems fully to accept the customary historical-critical analyses. Thus in the important section §17 on 'The Jealous God' he starts out by telling us that this theme is no longer controversial in the Priestly work of history but belongs above all to Deuteronomy and the Deuteronomistic history, all this backed up with references to M. Noth, H. Weippert, O. Kaiser, R. Smend and others (II, 120ff. and notes). Long and detailed interchanges with biblical scholars are carried out, and in general these totally lack the complaints, endlessly reiterated by Childs and others, that the work of these scholars is defective because of its historical basis, its lack of canonical emphasis, or the like. Moreover, unlike Barth, who in his arguments with biblical scholars tended to cite scholars like Gunkel of an era already falling into the past rather than those like Noth and von Rad, who by his own time already had the leadership, Mildenberger is frequently in contact and discussion with *recent* exegetical opinions, and is really *interested* in them. For those who hold that biblical scholars and doctrinal theologians should work together, Mildenberger provides a very serious paradigm for our time.

He has also taken seriously the history of religion, though he handles it rather marginally. Thus on II, 122 he has a long note (n. 22) on questions of mono-theism and the like. He finds the discussion – very reasonably – contradictory and indecisive; but there is no sense that the approach through history of religion is simply rejected in principle or considered to be irrelevant. He inter-acts very seriously with the thoughts of Sundermeier, mentioned above (II, 213f. n. 47). A very positive confrontation with the question of 'the religions' (plural!) appears in §35, 'The Mediation of Jesus Christ in Creation', and in particular in §35.3, 'The Universality of the Creation Mediator and the Religions' (III, 444–51). Here he touches on the Wisdom literature, which, he says, indicates the direction in which one should look for answers (III, 445). 'Wisdom speech does not have to be genuinely biblical, but at least in its origin *can* point to the common features between the speech of the chosen and that of those "passed over"' [this last is his term, which takes the place of the harsh 'rejected' of much older theology]. A footnote (n. 88) says: 'It is a natural assumption (*Selbstverständlichkeit*) of historical exegesis, which cannot be dispensed with, that a comparative-religion exegesis of biblical texts is possible. It indicates such common features of religious speech, but must naturally also attend to the change which takes place in the canonical context' (III, 445 and n. 88). Incidentally, he finds practically no place in his thinking for the concept of *development* (and I suppose this would include evolution also).

I have found Mildenberger's book fascinating, both in itself and because it makes contact at many points with questions that have arisen in our discussion of different proposals within biblical theology. His ideas would appear to offer satisfaction to impulses which we have noted in the work of several others.

Thus there is no doubt about the *church-centred* aspect in Mildenberger's approach. It is *in the church* that the 'simple God-talk', basic to the start of the approach, is to be heard. Not only the creeds and the Reformation confessions, the great theologians of earlier and of modern times, are to be heard, but even practical details of official church organization and such matters. Yet, if 'validity for the present day' is the desired goal, as implied in the passage quoted above, 513, one gains little impression from Mildenberger of any sort of *new directions* in which the church is to be pointed: rather, one gains an impres-sion of a system by which the church is to be *regulated* so that it stays the same.

Moreover, while Mildenberger certainly *integrates* biblical exegesis with doctrinal theology, and to an amazing degree, his way of doing it means a con-siderable departure from the aims and values that have hitherto animated biblical theology. For, like much or most biblical theology, he emphasizes the *unity* of the one scripture. But the way in which he does this seems to be entirely dogmatic: he does not try to *demonstrate*, from the material of scripture, that it has a unity, nor does he have that commitment to a 'holistic' reading which has attracted many. On the contrary, for him the unity of scripture is a dogmatic *axiom*. Far from its meaning that his work will gather together all the material of (say) the Psalms or the Judges, this means that he can *select* and *use* particular key passages, with the assurance that what they say will also fit for the others, subject always to their correct placing within the great scheme of theologia and oikonomia. But what if there are biblical passages which do not fit within the scheme?

This would seem to be the central question. The assumption appears to be that from the Bible itself the early theologians advanced to their recognition of theologia and oikonomia, and this was further clarified in the Reformation and treated in various ways by more recent theology. This being established, one can look back on the Bible and see how it gives answers, or adjustments, or reinterpretations, to the questions raised in the great theological scheme.

Some will say that this fails to give space for the final authority of the Bible. The thinking is dominated by the great theological scheme, and even if that scheme is derived from the Bible (which has hardly been shown, and might be difficult to show), it is difficult to see how the Bible might be able to free itself from the control of the scheme. The total theology then, rather than the Bible, might be regarded as the supreme controlling factor. On the other hand one might say that Mildenberger's work is a gigantic hypothesis, integrating biblical and doctrinal materials and conceptions. Such a hypothesis cannot be proved right from the Bible alone. Rather, the Bible itself cannot function theologically without being placed within such a scheme. This hypothesis can claim to offer as much as any other now in existence.

A work like Mildenberger's might offer a good fulfilment of the interests of that sector of biblical theology which drew its inspiration from Karl Barth. For the structure is quite different. Barth's *Church Dogmatics* is essentially a dogmatic structure, within which large amounts of biblical exegesis are incorporated. Mildenberger's is much more a *biblical* dogmatic: even if we think that the dogmatic structure controls the biblical, the focus of interest is on the biblical element in a way quite different from Barth's. And Mildenberger, in spite of his reservations about biblical scholarship, is actually far more closely in contact with the modern forms of it than Barth ever was. It is therefore interesting that he draws back from the Barthian emphasis on *revelation* and uses the concept sparingly.

I mentioned above that Mildenberger surveyed the ways in which the relation between theologia and oikonomia was seen by three major theologians,

Schleiermacher, Barth and Tillich, and concluded that none of these models provides a practicable outline for a biblical dogmatic. Striking from our point of view is the way in which Mildenberger gives equal consideration to Barth and Tillich, in view of the massive presence of biblical exegesis in Barth and the contrasting thinness of it in Tillich. From a methodological point of view, as he sees it, this does not matter.[16] Here is his summary of this question:

> Karl Barth and Paul Tillich in the general shape of their dogmatics or systematic theology follow the traditional structure: prolegomena, doctrine of God, creation, reconciliation, redemption. In each portion attention is given to the interconnection between theologia and oikonomia. With Barth this works in such a way that he always approaches each of the individual elements of content from the angle of God's revelation in Jesus Christ. In Tillich theologia and oikonomia are tied together as question and answer in the method of correlation. Neither of these models of a modern dogmatic, appropriate to its time [*Keines dieser Modelle einer modernen, zeitgemäßen Dogmatik* – this applies to Schleiermacher also, whom I have not included in my quotation – J.B.], seems to provide a practicable outline for a Biblical Dogmatics.[17]

This is an important point, because many may have thought that the Barthian outline was closer to biblical theology, purely on the ground of the amount of exegesis and reference to the Bible that it contains. Not so in Mildenberger's thinking:

> Nor can the thinking of the *Church Dogmatics* of Karl Barth be repeated once more. If we wanted to follow him in all his unusual decisions, we would be left with a Barthian scholasticism rather than a meaningful and fruitful thinking out of the area of problems (I, 244).

Again, that most memorable and most effective Barthian formulation, even if it is untenable in the long run,[18] namely that the Word of God exists in three forms, the Word preached, the Word written, and the Word revealed [stated in this order by Mildenberger], is criticized here (I, 117).

On the other hand, it is strange to go back to Mildenberger's earlier book, as quoted above, and to read there that a dependence on biblical scholarship, historical in character according to his conception of it, would mean that only the historical expert could understand the Bible rightly, and everyone else would be dependent on him. For Mildenberger's own solution means that only the trained and sophisticated theological expert can understand anything rightly; and the reasonings of historical criticism are child's play, which the intelligent lay person could master in half an hour, by comparison with the esoteric interrelations of theologia and oikonomia.

My final assessment of Mildenberger's fascinating work is that it is a theology-driven, rather than a biblically-driven, proposal. The scheme is one constituted by the post-biblical theological tradition, and the biblical material is fitted into that scheme. It would be wrong to suggest that Mildenberger does not consider the question whether there is biblical material that does not fit into the scheme, but though this question is doubtless in his mind, there is little or no positive engagement with it, no discussion of ways in which the use of the Bible within the scheme may be *assessed*, *verified* or *falsified* on the basis of the biblical texts themselves. But if the Bible cannot *disconfirm* the scheme, then it cannot *confirm* it either. Nor is there any attempt to begin from a theology developed from the biblical texts taken as a whole. Though treated extremely seriously, they are chosen and discussed *selectively* according to the questions addressed by the scheme itself. This means that the assurance of the unity and authority of the *entire* Bible actually operates *negatively*, producing the assurance that what is true for one part of the Bible will be valid for the entirety. And thus, although Mildenberger converses well with particular judgments of individual biblical theologians, he seems not to see the point and purpose of most biblical-theological work. This is partly because he classes biblical theology as basically a diachronic, historical-critical operation, which is therefore in his opinion unable to deliver regulative guidance of any kind.

Complementary with this is the strong *church-relatedness* of Mildenberger's thought. The Bible will assuredly fit in with the church tradition, as it has been in the Fathers, in the Reformation and above all in its confessions of faith, in Lutheran orthodoxy and in a path carefully picked out through the mazes of more modern theology. I do not say that he *forces* the Bible to fit in; but the fact remains that it does in the end fit in. And this means that the authority of the Bible is in the end diluted, for its accord with the tradition, properly understood, is so central.

This leaves an impression that while the church has to be *regulated* by the system, it is so regulated that it will stay the same, secure in the joint support of the Bible and the creeds and confessions. Thus it is striking that at certain points where novel suggestions come in, as with feminism and liberation theology, Mildenberger does not reject them or say that they are wrong, but honestly admits that he cannot find a place for them in his Biblical Dogmatics. Similarly, while questions are raised by the religious pluralism of our time, the 'whole approach of biblical dogmatics' forbids the offering of any answer (III, 445). The same type of argument appears on III, 410: 'The entire tenor of my thinking in this volume, which started out from election, must lead in this direction.'

Nevertheless, in spite of these criticisms, Mildenberger's work provides valuable lessons for us. For there are many within biblical theology who have expressed values similar to his – unity of all scripture, church-relatedness, attention to the later interpretative tradition, guidance by the creeds and confessions and so on. Mildenberger's work presents, I suggest, a more consistent working out of these concerns than we have had from others. And it is possible that something along the lines of his work, perhaps more closely combined with lines developed within biblical theology, will emerge as a favoured option in the future. For those who think of a specifically Christian biblical theology of both Testaments taken together, this might be the best available example to follow. Nevertheless it is difficult for it to overcome certain weaknesses indicated above.

# 30

# Räisänen

A complete contrast with Mildenberger's viewpoint will be found in the thought of the Finnish scholar Professor Heikki Räisänen. Though some New Testament theologians have been mentioned in this book, I have made no attempt to discuss the work of any of them in a general way. I propose to make an exception with Räisänen. His short book *Beyond New Testament Theology* (1990) is not in fact in itself a theology of the New Testament; its title is deliberately chosen to indicate that the author seeks to go 'beyond' New Testament theology as it has been practised, and to enter into something that will be different, but built upon what it has achieved. In any case some of the thoughts that it presents may be very relevant for Old Testament theology, and offer suggestions that have not hitherto been fully expressed within that area.

Räisänen, though officially a New Testament scholar, has carried out important research in other fields. He wrote an important monograph on the Muslim understanding of Jesus; he explored the hermeneutics of Mormonism; his most recent book, entitled *Marcion, Mohammed and the Mahatma*, brings together a remarkable range of themes, all of them of primary importance for present-day religion.[1] Within New Testament studies he is known particularly for his work on the subject of Paul and the law;[2] he is one among a number of recent scholars whose work on Paul has emphasized the need for fairness in the understanding of Judaism and who have produced a picture of Paul's relation to the religion within which he began substantially different from that which has been common. Moreover, he argues against the common view that Paul, though admittedly difficult to understand, was distinguished for his 'clear, cogent and penetrating theological thought'.[3] On the contrary, Paul was far from consistent. I quote one short passage:

> It seems to me that almost any early Christian conception of the law is more consistent, more intelligible and more arguable than Paul's – whether you take Matthew or Luke, Hebrews or James, Marcion or Justin . . . Even though I have my roots in a church alleged to be the most Lutheran in the world, it seems to be impossible to make Paul's theology *the* norm with which one can measure everything else in the world of early Christianity (not to speak of Judaism).[4]

The first part of Räisänen's book (3–90) is a survey of the past tradition of New Testament theology, including some works that are not exactly Theologies but come close to it. His reviews are concise and clear, and cover a very large variety of scholars who have sought to contribute to the subject. There is an obvious interest in, and sympathy for, the position of W. Wrede, who early this century offered the classic argument for the abandonment of 'New Testament theology' in its customary form and its replacement by 'early Christian history of religion'.[5] Räisänen states his own general position thus:

> I would argue that New Testament scholarship made a fatal mistake when, in the aftermath of the First World War, it turned its back on the liberals and the history-of-religions school and succumbed to the rhetorical-theological appeal of dialectical theology (xv).

I shall return to this sentence and attempt to reconsider its value for biblical theology as a whole. I shall not enter here, however, into Räisänen's analysis of the past tradition of work on the New Testament; my interest lies rather in his Part Three, 'Outline of a Programme', which occupies the remainder of the book (93–141 plus notes). Though Räisänen's argument refers almost entirely to New Testament scholarship, much of his thinking may well be equally relevant to the problems of Old Testament theology which form our main subject.

A good starting point is the question of the *ecclesial* setting of Old Testament theology. We have already touched upon this point once or twice, but here it reappears in a somewhat different way. That Old Testament theology had something to do with 'Christianity' or with connections with the New Testament has already been discussed, but to say that it must have its context 'in the church' or that it should 'be ultimately a function of the church'[6] is to go somewhat farther. Many Old Testament Theologies, even if they had thoughts in this direction, said little about it. More recently, however, stronger assertions of the church-involvement of the subject have been made. Thus we have seen that, not only within an Old Testament Theology, but in a commentary on a biblical book, Childs wrote that 'its concern is to understand Exodus as scripture of the church' (*Exodus*, ix) and that: 'The aim of this commentary is to seek to interpret the book of Exodus as canonical scripture within the theological discipline of the Christian church' (xiii). Its sections on 'Theological Reflection' are intended 'to develop a more rigorous method of actualizing the text for the church's present task'. The emphasis on the church in Childs' two Theologies has already been mentioned above.

To return briefly to the New Testament Theologies, a position somewhat parallel to that of Childs is there taken by Peter Stuhlmacher. He too emphasizes the history of reception (*Wirkungsgeschichte*) of the texts, but in this, Räisänen writes:

> He [Stuhlmacher] gives a fruitful starting-point an ecclesiastical bias. His history of influence is less interested in all the influences the texts may have exerted than in the fact that they had an influence on the rise of the creeds of the church. Stuhlmacher infers that the texts therefore ought to be read in the framework of those creeds (methodologically, a *non sequitur*) (81).

Stuhlmacher tries to avoid total negativity towards historical criticism,[7] yet on the other hand seeks anxiously to avoid any results that could call in question the authoritative church documents. Räisänen writes of the 'desperate struggle of church-oriented exegetes (notably Stuhlmacher), kicking against the goads of historical criticism and trying to avoid presenting "negative" (or merely negative) results' (97).

He perceives that this ecclesial emphasis has been dominant. It has been present even among scholars who are perceived as 'radical' and 'purely academic', and it has come to the surface in work on biblical theology, in a way that has not been apparent in works of specialized research. 'Most often New Testament theology has been understood to be ultimately a function of the church . . . Even relatively radical exegetes who have encountered much opposition from their churches have wanted to work in a church context (J. Weiss, Bultmann, Conzelmann, Käsemann)' (93). Specialists, he says, 'increasingly work without necessarily paying any attention at all to theological questions in the strict sense' (and here his note cites my own *Scope and Authority of the Bible*, 1980, 22f.) – but in spite of this, 'all syntheses and most of the reflection on principles connected with them – or even short general statements on what the discipline is all about – have been governed by the conviction that New Testament study has an ecclesial-theological task . . . Synthesizing seems to possess a philosophy of its own, distinct from that which governs monograph production.'

In spite of this, in recent years voices have been heard demanding with increasing vehemence that exegesis should be done in a church context and for the needs of the church – some of them since 1990, when Räisänen's book was published. Thus a collection of essays called *Reclaiming the Bible for the Church* edited by Braaten and Jenson was published in 1995, including a contribution from Childs.[8] To this should be added several writings of Francis Watson. As I noted above in passing, Philip Davies obtains a dramatic beginning for the argument of his *Whose Bible is it Anyway?* by quoting from the front flap of Watson's *Text, Church and World* the challenging words 'should biblical studies continue to exclude theological concerns from its agenda?'.[9] The question – for which the author of the book may not have been responsible[10] – shows a hysterical mode of exaggeration which forms an ideal gift to the severely anti-theological arguments of Davies.

Räisänen analyses cleverly some of the arguments that are commonly used. 'There is no separation between learning and life,' writes Käsemann. So far, so good. But then, Räisänen goes on, 'with astonishing ease, "life" is simply narrowed down to "Christian life" or "life in the church"' (94). 'Life', properly, has to be seen in a broader way. And so:

> To confine oneself to serving a church is – to exaggerate only slightly – comparable to a social scientist's or a historian's confining himself to serve a certain political party (or a certain nation) with his research (95).

And he goes on to quote the work of Gerd Petzke, who has argued that 'in a post-Christian society exegesis should be orientated on the concerns of society rather than those of the church'.[11]

Moreover, Räisänen goes on, an orientation towards society is no more than a first step. 'The truly appropriate horizon today for biblical study . . . is humanity as a whole' (96). This fits, we may remember, with the ecumenical perspective which, as we saw above,[12] was one of the potentials and one of the attractions of biblical theology at an early time, but has not always been kept in mind thereafter. For ecumenicity cannot be confined in the long run to the limited zone of the traditional Christian communions. If this is important for New Testament theology, it seems even more important for Old Testament theology, where the same scripture is shared with the very different religion, Judaism, resulting in the various problems that have already been discussed in part above.

These thoughts lead Räisänen on, very properly, to the question he phrases as 'Proclamation or information?' (97). 'Exegesis orientated on a world society cannot aim at a kerygmatic goal.' The global perspective 'demands that the task be conceived in terms of critical information rather than proclamation . . . In this process both one's own tradition and those of others have to be understood with *empathy* . . . The history of the discipline of New Testament theology tells us that most often a kerygmatic way of conceiving the task has been accompanied by a caricature of rival systems. Thus the Judaism of New Testament times has been blackened, so that the light of the gospel may shine forth all the more brightly. On a smaller scale, this is surely true of the treatment of Stoicism and Gnosticism as well' (99). (The same, of course, can be said of the Canaanites in Hebrew Bible studies.)

We have already seen that an emphasis on preaching has been a significant element in the tradition of Old Testament theology, so much so that its efforts have sometimes been stigmatized as no more than homiletical elaborations and ornamentations. One does not have to go all the way with Räisänen – I doubt whether some of the religions will ever stop preaching, however global the view of society, and maybe it is wrong to try to stop them doing it – but surely he is entirely right in urging that these kerygmatic principles are out of place in biblical theology. For, however much preaching and propaganda may be indigenous to a religion and unavoidable within it, they are certainly improper as between biblical scholars or biblical theologians. Kerygmatic approaches distort the possibilities of discussion and undermine the academic theological character which it might otherwise have had.

It should be emphasized that Räisänen is not hostile to church-orientated scholarship. 'It is not my intention,' he writes, 'to do away with church-theological study of the Bible. My point is simply that we may not have always realized how very different such a task is from a historical interpretation of the material' (96). In fact, he claims, 'many members of the churches welcome a broad perspective' [such as he himself proposes] 'or are engaged in pursuing it themselves'. But, he goes on, 'My point is simply that the traditional interests of the churches, which are still often assumed in an authoritarian and aprioristic way, cannot provide the orientation for a synthesis.' This last point could be put more strongly, for orientation to 'the church' very commonly turns out – as we have seen – to be orientation to one particular church and its parochial theology, its confessions, its traditions, its view of the canon and so on, or indeed to one particular school of the theology of a particular church, or indeed to the theology of an individual. And the converse could also apply: much of what is written in exegesis or in biblical theology, whether 'historically' or more 'doctrinally' conceived, is more orientated to the *conflicts* existing within and between churches and theologies than to making the Bible understood to those who stand outside these conflicts.

Equally to be noted is the question whether, even where scholarship is indeed church-orientated, the churches are likely to absorb much of it: for, as Räisänen notes, 'the churches notoriously accept and appropriate much less of the flood of exegesis than is available' (98). The proliferation of commentaries on biblical books is, he adds, 'a survival from the good old days when exegesis could still be seen as normative'.

Räisänen's criticisms of the orientation to preaching are very well taken and should be accepted. Of all forms of persuasion, preaching is the most remote from the academic. The preacher knows the truth and is always right, and he or she seldom spends much time on the fair explanation of contrary opinions. This may be quite necessary and quite salutary for religion, but it does not provide a good analogy or setting for anything seeking to be biblical theology.

Some others of the questions discussed by Räisänen are more specific to the New Testament and may be left aside for the moment. But two of them are very close to the concerns we have been discussing. He sees a 'New Testament theology' as limited to the canonical documents, while a work on 'early Christian religion' would include all relevant sources whether canonical or not. For the

New Testament the question has been made more obvious because there is a larger number of potentially relevant texts from close to the time of the canonical texts: no such body of material has as yet emerged for the Hebrew Bible. Thus Räisänen gives a sympathetic evaluation of Helmut Koester's major work, his *Introduction to the New Testament*, in which 'Romans, Ephesians and Colossians each receive roughly as much space as the Gospel of Thomas and the Shepherd of Hermas' (84). In practice, however, he admits, 'much history-of-religions work has also been done in church-oriented New Testament Theologies' (102), as exemplified by Bultmann. But, he argues, 'attempts to sketch *historical* lines of development on the basis of *canonical* texts alone (such as Kümmel's) are methodologically hybrid . . . The narrowness of the perspective renders truly historical work impossible at the outset' (102).

On the other hand, Räisänen is 'personally still inclined to maintain some continuity with traditional "New Testament theology" in focusing on a discussion of religious *thought* in early Christianity' (105). The question involved here goes back again to Wrede, who protested against the concentration of New Testament theology upon the intellectual or theological component, which for him is only one among the several that make up a religion.[13] When Räisänen decides nevertheless to continue with a sort of 'theology', his decision is a pragmatic one: one has to start somewhere, and a comprehensive history of *all* early Christianity would be too immense a task to be realistic (105). Nevertheless, thought must not be studied in an isolated way, neglecting historical, psychological and social realities, the experiences of individuals and groups.

To sum up, then, Räisänen opts for Wrede's vision in a modified form:

> The canon cannot be the starting point in exegesis oriented on society. Therefore the objective of the synthesis should not literally be 'New Testament theology' but early Christian thought. By contrast, scholars of the church can, in a church context, concentrate on the canon and outline theologies of the New Testament or, more consistently, of the whole Bible, in the light of their respective confessions.

Räisänen's many interesting and provocative points cannot be discussed here in full, but certain aspects provide a useful complement to our earlier discussions. We may begin, perhaps, with his general statement, quoted above, that:

> I would argue that New Testament scholarship made a fatal mistake when, in the aftermath of the First World War, it turned its back on the liberals and the history-of-religions school and succumbed to the rhetorical-theological appeal of dialectical theology.

Part of this is in agreement with the position taken in this book, namely that Old Testament theology allowed itself to be guided excessively by dialectical theology: indeed, even now it is only slowly and painfully extracting itself from that embrace. On the other hand, Räisänen's statement might well be improved by the addition of an acknowledgment that the liberals and the history-of-religion school did not do so very well either. That either of these currents, or both of them taken together, were on the way to providing a complete and satisfactory exegesis seems too much to claim. But they certainly both provided materials, and elements of necessary interpretation, which were solid and essential, and which continued to be known and taught in educational institutions throughout the period when liberalism and the history-of-religion school were in eclipse, because it was impossible to do without them. And in Old Testament scholarship, whatever was thought of liberalism, the presence and influence of the history of religion continued to be felt at least in some countries, a necessary consequence of the close connection of the subject with Semitic languages, Near Eastern studies, Assyriology and Egyptology and so on.

Nevertheless, in the specific area of Old Testament theology scholarship did indeed to a large extent, in Räisänen's phrase, 'succumb to the rhetorical-theological appeal of dialectical theology'. Even though there were few who became pure partisans of Brunner and Barth,[14] and some limited criticism of these directions did emerge (e.g. from G.E. Wright in his later work), most work in Old Testament theology over the central decades of the century did follow these principles. And that their appeal was 'rhetorical' as well as 'theological' is rightly put by Räisänen. That biblical theology gave a sort of 'homiletic' air was widely perceived, as we have seen.

For Old Testament theology, one of the great factors likely to alter this is, as we have seen, the fact that the Hebrew Bible is shared between Jews and Christians. Whether a Jewish biblical theology becomes possible or not, and whether the subject leads to new forms of communication between Jews and Christians or not, the mere fact that these questions are discussed imparts an inter-religious character to the subject. This certainly comes short of making it a subject directed towards society as a whole, as Räisänen hopes, but it at least makes it something other than a subject completely bounded by the perspectives of the church. Or, to put it more positively, the sharing of the same scriptures with Judaism *is* one of the perspectives of the church, and one the importance of which has been widely recognized in the last decades. And here the 'kerygmatic' exchanges have already come to be replaced in considerable measure by the character of 'information' for which Räisänen hopes; or we might speak of a 'sisterly' sharing of convictions, as some have done.

A related question in his thinking lies in 'church-related' scholarship. Here he associates church-related studies with the biblical canon, while history-of-religion researches pay no attention to the canonical boundaries. I am doubtful, however, whether this distinction can stand. Certainly church-related studies can be called 'Theology of the New (or, of the Old) Testament' or indeed 'Theology of the Bible' (if that can be written) and that can be quite honestly meant: such a work is intended to give theological guidance within the church about the material of the canonical books. But I do not see that, even for the most church-related purpose, and even for the most 'canonical-thinking' of readerships, it is possible to pursue these objects while *excluding the information to be gained from non-canonical documents.*

Räisänen's questioning of current claims to the 'church-related' character of biblical theology (and indeed of any theology) also deserves to be carried farther. It is of course considered 'the right thing' to say that biblical theology, and indeed all theology, 'belongs within the church' or 'must be carried out in the church context', and, as Räisänen observes, this is obediently repeated by scholars whose own normal work appears not to have this character in any very direct sense. One does not wish to upset this estimable sentiment. Yet in what sense is it realistic and in what sense is it sincerely meant?

Central to the reality is a plurality: theologically speaking, there is only one church, the church of God, but for practical purposes, including the making of theological decisions, there are many churches, and these have different theological standards and traditions. Moreover, in each church there are different currents of theological thinking. There is no such thing as 'the' church for the purpose of theological decisions; and the many actual churches find it difficult to make such decisions because of the different currents running within each of them. The nearest one can come to 'the' church is through the ecumenical endeavours and the academic institutions of our time. It is only through these that the work of scholarship actually reaches 'the' church.

Comparatively little creative theological work, exegesis and biblical scholarship is really done 'in the context of the church'. Theology and biblical scholarship do indeed serve the church, but they serve it principally through one particular context, namely the context of *education.* The central power-house for this purpose is the context of *the university.* There are of course excellent institutions belonging to a particular church, seminaries and theological colleges and so on, and these have a life specially related to their own church; but their ideas, teachers, books, courses and methods do not essentially differ from the universities in which theology is taught. And even within individual parishes or localities, organizations like Sunday schools, lay Bible-study groups and so on are also part of an educational process. And of course pastoral experience, personal devotion, worship and prayer are also fountains from which the waters of theology flow. Nevertheless, for most people it is within the educational process that most theological thinking, Bible study and exegesis are done.

And this is also true of those who most vociferously assert that the place of theology and biblical exegesis lies properly 'within the church'. To a large extent they are themselves academics, and at least at some times they use 'the church' as a card to play in what is really an academic and intellectual argument. Of the nine who contributed to a recent booklet entitled *Reclaiming the Bible for the Church*,[15] every one is a professor or holds a similar academic post. As we have seen in the case of Childs as discussed above, it is far from likely that those who argue in this way are willing to entrust theological and exegetical decisions to the churches to which they belong, much less to the immense variety of the churches of the world. For the churches not only have different theologies, but they have very different ideas of the role which theology – and biblical exegesis – ought to play within the total life of the church. Very often the demands that biblical theology should belong within the church are not an acceptance that the church can handle the questions of biblical theology: rather, they are attempts to *alter* the church, to make the church something other than it in fact is: for example, to make it more identified with the authoritative confessions or to make it, in a nostalgic longing, more like the church of some former era. The argument that biblical theology belongs within the life and discipline of the church ought to be fully respected; but it must also be perceived that at times it is a device to gain an intellectual point at issue which could not be gained by straight intellectual discussion.

Moreover, we have seen that biblical theology is not the same as doctrinal theology, or at least may not be the same. The fact that doctrinal theology is integrated with church life and maintained in some degree by church authority does not mean that biblical theology has the same character.

Räisänen's thinking has some obvious contacts with that of Albertz discussed above. Both of them lay the emphasis on the history of religion, and both alike notice the damage done by the rise of dialectical theology and its effect upon biblical theology. Both alike emphasize the modern situation and the need to provide a response to it. But Albertz continues to see his work as justified and undergirded by the church's needs, while Räisänen breaks away from this and looks toward a wider horizon altogether. Biblical theology should be orientated towards *society* as a whole. The point he makes, that when the location of biblical study 'within the church' is emphasized, this is often done in an 'authoritarian and aprioristic way', is very important; to this could be added that the interests of 'the church' are very often related to some past stage of the church, say to the Reformation confessions or to the church of some other past period, and poorly related to what the actual churches and their people are like today, in relation to the world in which they live.

Of central importance, however, is this thought, which complements my arguments above:

Bultmann accepted Barth's starting-point: one can only understand a text if one has an inner relationship to its real message. This statement may be accepted, if 'inner relationship' is understood in quite general terms (so that 'critical sympathy' or 'genuine interest' will qualify); for Bultmann, however, 'faith' as a religious and existential commitment was at stake. But the claim that a Christian can never 'understand' a Muslim text, or vice versa, is simply obscurantist.

With astonishing naiveté, 'faith' always seems to mean *Christian* faith in these hermeneutical discussions. Not even the existence of Jewish faith has been taken seriously (not even in Old Testament theology, until quite recently). But Jewish faith will produce a very different picture of the New Testament from that drawn by Christian faith . . .[16]

The claim that one can understand a text only if one identifies with it in one's own personal faith is certainly destructive and should be rejected from interpretative theory. For, followed out in its implications, it must mean that no one can speak of, or can understand, any position other than his own personal convictions. Just as a Jew cannot understand a Christian text, a Christian cannot understand a Jewish text. Moreover, an orthodox Christian theologian cannot understand Gnosticism or explain a Gnostic text, since for that one would have to be a living Gnostic, or to have one present. A Christian preacher cannot explain passages from the prophets, since he or she cannot understand the syncretisms and Canaanite practices to which the prophets refer. The position, in other words, is one that leads to an impossible solipsism, and signs of this have been present in much of the theology of the century now ending.

Räisänen is right to reject this. And here his argument is by no means 'merely' a reaction coming from the history of religions. It is an indispensable condition for theological work of any kind. And in the present-day world it is fortunately being realized to some degree. I am delighted that my excellent colleague Amy-Jill Levine is a Jewish professor teaching New Testament to Christian students, just as I dare, in spite of inadequate knowledge, to teach Mishnaic texts and other authoritative texts of Judaism. We *must* be able to do this; if we cannot, we are imprisoned in the walls of our own beliefs and cannot even defend them or explain how they differ from others. In all this Räisänen's thinking runs parallel to much that has been said above in my discussion of the descriptive approach and faith-commitment.

There is a weakness in Räisänen's position, however, in that he ends up (rightly, in my opinion) favouring an approach through biblical theology, or at least a continuity with it (105). But he could, I think, offer stronger reasons for this than he does. The pragmatic reason that 'one must begin *somewhere*' is hardly enough.

Perhaps we could start from his proposal and think of a historical study of 'early Christian thought'. But within this, which would include a mass of material of all kinds, it might then be possible to mark out and distinguish those elements and implications which would particularly deserve to be thought of as 'theology', elements which not only existed at such and such a stage but which were then taken to be regulative, whether they were thereafter treated as normative, modified, developed, or indeed in due course abandoned and forgotten. A theology of this kind would lie within his history of early Christian thought and be subject to clarification and checking by it, but would nevertheless have a certain independence. Though controllable by historical methods, it would look for implications, along the lines mapped out above for historical theology, and would require a kind of analogy with general theological thinking.

# 31

# Brueggemann

Walter Brueggemann is a very well-known and central scholar, among the clergy perhaps the most widely-known Old Testament specialist in the United States. He has written on very many different aspects of biblical study, and is notable also for his outstanding work as a series editor, in which he has power-fully assisted other, especially younger, scholars to have their work published. Very notable for our purpose is the series Overtures to Biblical Theology, which has included such important works as Phyllis Trible's *God and the Rhetoric of Sexuality*, Gammie's *Holiness in Israel*, Balentine's *Prayer in the Hebrew Bible* and Perdue's *The Collapse of History*, to name only a few. These works repre-sented a wide variety of opinion and by no means constituted a 'school', so that Brueggemann's editorial support to scholarship has been noticeably open and catholic.

And he himself has been one able to innovate and to realize important changes of mind. A good illustration, from his earlier work, came when the positive interest in Israelite wisdom began to increase markedly after the 1960s.[1] Brueggemann was one of the first to welcome this newer trend and to give it expression on the wider stage of biblical theology. In 1972 a study of his was published with the provocative title of *In Man We Trust: The Neglected Side of Biblical Faith*. And this was about Wisdom; indeed its essential basis lay in the one book of Proverbs. Describing himself as a 'son of neo-orthodoxy', Brueggemann enthusiastically embraced the fresh perspectives that this change of emphasis had brought him:

> The man of Proverbs is not the servile, self-abasing figure often urged by our one-sided reading of Scripture in later Augustinian-Lutheran theological tradition. Rather he is an able, self-reliant, caring, involved, strong person who has a significant influence over the course of his own life and over the lives of his fellows . . . Proverbs . . . has no patience for a god who only saves sinners and judges sins. The God affirmed here trusts man, believes in him, risks his world with him, and stays with him in his failures.[2]

The picture of Jesus himself was affected. 'The theology of the wisdom teachers,' Brueggemann declared, 'is consistent with the major thrust of Jesus' teaching.' Conventional terms of incarnation and atonement are not adequate for the fullness of his person and work. Rather, Jesus

> embodies . . . the teaching of the wise men about how one lives as a life-bringer . . . He is the manifestation in a human life of the kind of style the wise urged upon people. He also enables people to attain that style . . . Jesus of Nazareth may be the culmination of other traditions but he is no less the culmination of the wisdom tradition.[3]

This certainly shows a flexibility of viewpoint. When Brueggemann produces a *Theology of the Old Testament*, therefore, as he has done in 1997, we can expect some fresh insights and approaches.[4] He had already had published a collection of essays entitled *Old Testament Theology*, edited by Patrick D. Miller, in 1992, and these have been briefly mentioned above, but his complete Theology is a massive work of 777 pages and deserves a substantial discussion of its own. However, since it appeared only at the last possible moment for consideration in this book, this chapter has something of the character of an appendix, and could not be integrated with the foregoing discussions.

In Brueggemann's Theology, somewhat as in the Book of Job, there is a Prologue and Epilogue (though not so called) and a central presentation in four great parts. The Prologue is entitled 'Retrospect' and is itself in two sections. The first of these discusses the development of Old Testament theology from beginnings in the Reformation up to the 'generative period' of Eichrodt and von Rad and the changes that came with the 'collapse of history' in Perdue's term, the sociological emphasis, and above all the rise of rhetorical approaches. The second part is on 'The Contemporary Situation' and emphasizes post-modernism, pluralism, rhetoric once again, narrative and imagination, drama and metaphor, intertextuality, and various other models that have come to be tried out. There are surveys of four 'centrist' theologians (Childs, Levenson, Barr, Rendtorff, 89–98), and of others who are more 'at the margin' (Trible, Pixley, Mosala, 98–102). The chapter ends with 'Four Insistent Questions': historical criticism, church theology, the Jewishness of the Old Testament, and 'public possibilities'.

What I have called the Epilogue is Part V: 'Prospects for Theological Interpretation'. Here Brueggemann considers 'what may come next in Old Testament theology'; the first sub-heading is 'Disestablishment: from Hegemonic Interpretation to Pluralism', and this title gives a good idea of what the whole is like. The author comes back to 'Some Pervasive Issues', namely the relation of the Old Testament to historical criticism, to the New Testament and church theology, to Jewish tradition and the Jewish community, and to 'The Problem of Justice'. The final paragraph of the book affirms that 'acknowledgment of Yahweh requires reordering of everything else'.

To many of these matters we shall return. But first I shall describe the core of the book and its structure. The basic theme is Israel's *speech* about God: 'the speech is the reality to be studied' (118) , and the way to understand speech is to see it as *testimony*. This leads us to the basic metaphor of 'the court'. 'The proper setting of testimony is a court of law.' The court 'cannot go behind the testimony to the event, but must take the testimony as the "real portrayal". Indeed, it is futile for the court to speculate behind the testimony' (121). 'For Old Testament faith, *the utterance is everything*' (122). Thus Israel's speech about God is imagined as testimony before 'the court', and as such it falls into four great sections: Israel's 'core testimony', her 'countertestimony', her 'unsolicited testimony', and her 'embodied testimony'.

The core testimony is identified by the 'grammar' of 'full sentences' that are 'organized around an active verb that bespeaks an action that is transformative, intrusive, or inverting' (123). God is the characteristic subject; there is an active verb (notably of the *hiphil* stem), and a direct object. In this 'complicated' grammar (125) 'we are close to the core claim of Israel's faith'. The various chapters that follow distinguish different forms of testimony in verbal sentences (God who created, who commands, who leads, etc.), in markings with adjectives, in noun testimony, and finally in a chapter entitled 'Yahweh Fully Uttered', which answers the question: 'What does all of this add up to as a presentation of the character of Yahweh?' (267).

The countertestimony, the second major element, is like a cross-examination. There is in Israel 'an uneasiness about that marvellously positive testimony'. The basic testimony is therefore probed and questioned, 'partly in the utterance of Israel and partly in the alleged utterance of non-Israelites' (317). Israel's faith 'is a probing, questioning, insisting, disjunctive' faith'. Here, then, we find questionings of Yahweh's presence, the sense of abandonment, his hiddenness, possible abuses and contradictions, 'covenantal sanctions' or curses, psalms of complaint, theodicy, and of course Job, Qoheleth and Psalm 88.

The third element, the 'unsolicited testimony', comes from the fact that Israel gives additional information, extraneous to its speech about God, which is the only thing that 'the court' considers relevant (408). Israel likes to talk; it sketches in additional information; it sees connections which impinge upon Yahweh but come, as it were, from outside him. He never comes 'alone', but in relation, and the parties in relation are here called 'partners'. Successive chapters discuss Israel, the human person, the nations and creation as 'partners', and all this is summed up in a 'drama of partnership', which affects Israel's total 'articulation of Yahweh' (556ff.) and leads on to a 'metanarrative', the articulation of which is the work of Old Testament theology (558).

The fourth element is essentially about *mediation* (so the titles of each chapter) but comes as a whole under the name of 'Israel's embodied testimony'.

The author admits that here he is stepping somewhat outside his governing metaphor of 'the court', and his explanation is obscure. 'Israel can find no way in its testimony to resolve the jaggedness of a relationship marked by both incommensurability and mutuality' (567). This is why 'the relatedness of Yahweh is so problematic'. In fact creator and creature *do* make contact: there are 'practices that give the testimony *concrete embodiment*' (568). So, after considering the unmediated presence of Yahweh, we go on to chapters on the Torah, the king, the prophet, the cult and the sage as means of mediation, followed by some general conclusions.

These four aspects of 'testimony', then, form the framework within which the theology of the Old Testament is presented.

It may well be that this fourfold organization is the great and original contribution of this work; for, as we have seen, there has been much desire to avoid organizing a Theology on the basis of a traditional dogmatic scheme. But if so, what sort of scheme is there to be found? Brueggemann's scheme is not dictated either by Judaism or by Christianity: it seems to come from his own intuition and imagination. It enables the reader to see different directions in the total biblical text, to distinguish them and also to correlate them. The image of 'the court', on the other hand, is less happy, as we shall see.

The outstanding characteristic of this work, however, is its being centred upon *rhetoric*, to an extent nowhere near approached, so far as I know, by any other major Old Testament Theology. 'Our postmodern situation, which refuses to acknowledge a settled essence behind our pluralistic claims, must make a major and intentional investment in the practice of rhetoric, for the shape of reality finally depends on the power of speech' (71). Yet more: 'Speech constitutes reality,[5] and who God turns out to be in Israel depends on the utterance of the Israelites or, derivatively, the utterance of the text' (65). Again, and in sacramental language: '*I shall insist, as consistently as I can, that the God of Old Testament theology as such lives in, with and under the rhetorical enterprise of this text, and nowhere else and in no other way*' (66, author's italics). Most extremely of all, we come close to the suggestion that Yahweh is created or 'generated' by Israel's rhetoric. '*The rhetorical mediation of Yahweh in the Bible is not a disembodied, ideational operation*' (574). 'Yahweh is generated and constituted, so far as the claims of Israel are concerned, in actual practices that mediate . . . it is a question of characteristic social practice that generates, constitutes, and mediates Yahweh in the midst of life' (574). Yahweh is 'given to Israel in practice' (575) , but this practice is a part of 'rhetorical mediation'. This is said to fit with Lindbeck's view 'that religious reality is constituted and generated by actual, sustained, concrete, communal practice' (574).

Now this huge emphasis on rhetoric can be creative. It can lead us into a careful examination of the texture of passages, and Brueggemann follows this out, providing extensive quotations of biblical passages and identifying some of the verbs or other words that are used. Unfortunately, he leaves the passages in English, which considerably reduces the effectiveness of the method. But basically this may be a step forward, in comparison with the identification of central ideas and concepts. And, of course, in principle, one can say that the God of Israel is 'generated' or 'constituted' by the texts of Israel – but only in a certain sense, and with strict reservations. Is there really a God like the God of Israel, or will Brueggemann rule out the question on the ground that even to ask it is 'essentialism'? Brueggemann is often carried away by his own rhetoric (as distinct from the rhetoric of Israel) and fails to make these qualifications or to make them clear.

It is Brueggemann's rhetorical emphasis that correlates with his markedly non-historical approach. On the one hand, for a scholar so open to various trends of scholarship, he is extremely negative towards historical criticism. This is surprising. Leo Perdue as recently as 1994 looked forward with anticipation to Brueggemann's 'theology of imagination': especially important, he argued, would be 'the inclusion of historical criticism, social-scientific analysis, and newer literary methodologies'. This theology, he believed, 'would not polarize scholars but rather should allow for the engagement of most of the work that students of the Old Testament currently do'. Moreover, 'history and historical questions would once again have an important role in theological discussion'.[6]

In fact little or nothing of these hopes are realized in Brueggemann's larger Theology. He does declare at the start: 'The gains of historical criticism are immense, and no informed reader can proceed without paying attention to those gains' (14). But the reverse is what develops in the rest of the book. Historical criticism is almost entirely neglected, and almost all mentions of it are entirely negative. 'Historical-critical judgments' carry with them 'theological presuppositions alien to the material itself' (45). Criticism can (perhaps) be tolerated in a marginal way, but must be 'held under close scrutiny' (103) , scanned with extreme vigilance and suspicion. On the other hand, the rhetorical exposition to which Brueggemann accords such positive importance is noticeably unhistorical. It is not only that historical *criticism* is neglected or rejected: *history altogether* is very largely ignored. The absence of historical location makes the rhetorical emphasis more central and determinative. The passages quoted are strung out without any indication of the time from which they came or, in most cases, the historical situation. The rhetoric is a function of the conjunction of the words and sentences. There is, indeed, a theoretical emphasis on the 'concrete' setting, even more on the political implications, but this 'concreteness' is often itself an abstraction, for nothing is done to determine what the 'concrete setting' was.

There is another side to this rhetorical emphasis. That other side is the fact that Brueggemann is so very much a rhetorician himself. The preaching, homiletic, element in his style is so much more obvious than the reasoning, the argumentative. His use of language is exceptional, and this works in two opposite ways. At one end of the scale it can be vivid, poetic and evocative. It can be lively, as we saw in the quotation from a review some pages back.[7] At the other it seems to be mesmeric, using long words where a short one would be better, creating weird coinages which few readers can be expected to understand, failing to explain what is meant. 'Reductionism', we already saw, was used as a term of reprehension by Childs. But where Childs with this weapon slew his thousands, Brueggemann slays ten thousands, if not millions. The word occurs everywhere. It applies to the Enlightenment (of course), to biblical criticism (naturally, 14 etc.), but also to church interpretation (2, 10) and church theology (107, 528), to Eichrodt and others who follow his style (28) , even to Childs (85, 732). Brueggemann even worries that it is present in himself (738). There is 'ontological reductionism' (19) and other kinds; some people 'have known only a reductionist Bible' (106). In fact, almost everyone who has ever said anything about anything is a reductionist, except for the Hebrew Bible, and it only when understood through postmodern interpretation.

Though the book often emphasizes the 'concrete', it is the abstract that is prominent in its diction. Why can he not use plain words? 'Old Testament theology, when it pays attention to Israel's venturesome rhetoric, refuses any reductionism to a single or simple articulation; it offers a witness that is enormously open, inviting, and suggestive, rather that one that yields settlement, closure or precision' (148). All too true, particularly the last word: the lack of interest in precision is very evident. Who can make sense of a title like 'The Density of Nouns of Sustenance' (277)? Why must we have words like 'equanimous' (604) and phrases like 'I will exposit those nonnegotiable awarenesses' (559; cf. 'the nonnegotiability of neighbourly obedience', 582)? Who can make sense of this: 'while the incommensurability of Yahweh would seem to require that they do not [make contact], Yahweh, in mutuality, moves out of incommensurability (kenosis) for the sake of contact; but it is contact that does not compromise Yahweh's sovereign incommensurability' (568)? This kind of talk may be rhetorically effective, but not in the sense that it makes the matter clear to the reader: rather in the opposite sense, that it surrounds the matter (if there is any) with a cloud of vagueness induced by mystifying abstracts and unfamiliar neologisms. And this, combined with a marked tendency to *exaggerate* (a well-known rhetorical technique, sometimes dignified with the title of *hyperbole*), leaves a distinct impression that the long vague words are there for another reason: to enable the author to back away from some of his more extreme statements when someone asks if he really means them! We shall see some examples later. In a word, the emphasis on rhetoric may be in part a right identification of what is essential in the biblical material; but it is also very much an imprint of the author's self, and of his own way of doing things. There is a preacher's style, more than an academic's style, in much of the work, and it looks as if it was intended for just such an audience: no wonder that Perdue's *Collapse of History* is welcomed. Preachers know about rhetoric and politics, which are stressed here; they are more distant from history, perhaps also from theology when it is conceptually clear.

To put it in another way, rhetoric is a double-edged instrument. Certainly, as Brueggemann has perceived, rhetoric is in fashion in modern academic and semi-academic speech. One notices how people now say 'your rhetoric' where they once would have said 'your arguments'. But Brueggemann seems blind to the other side of this: that rhetoric is *despised*. One may be influenced by the rhetoric of politicians and preachers, but very suddenly there comes a moment when one says 'It's only rhetoric'. There is nothing behind it. Even if there is no essential reality behind one's speech, the rhetorician has to claim, or pretend, that there is such a reality, for his rhetoric to be effective. This is the trap to which this book comes too close.

Brueggemann's work has certain connections with my own. His emphasis on *utterance* is related to my emphasis on divine speech (46). He seeks to follow my insistence on the importance of words in context (123). His perception that some biblical narratives 'do not intend to be "doing theology"' (367) is akin to my distinction between story and theology, though he makes less of it than I do. He leans, at first perhaps hesitantly but certainly in increasing measure, towards an acceptance of my interest in natural theology (157, 162, 336n., 455, 529n., 592n., 681). And he has many detailed insights which I very much favour: for instance, it is often said that, after the Bathsheba incident, David was forgiven 'because he repented'.[8] Brueggemann rightly sees that the text says nothing either of David repenting or of his asking for forgiveness; according to Nathan's words, he had *already* been forgiven, and the reason is God's favouritism towards David, which creates a real theological/ethical problem; this in turn is very proper matter for the 'countertestimony'.

I was complimented by the attention he has given to my work, which is friendly and charitable throughout. It will be proper, however, to clear up certain misunderstandings at this point. I certainly never took 'a lean or reticent stand toward the theological claims of the Old Testament' (96); nor do I consider the historical-critical tradition 'as an emancipatory movement'; though that may well be an element in its historical effects, I do not think that this was an important part of the motivation of the critical tradition, and certainly it is not my reason for supporting it. I just think that it discovered truth and therefore cannot be discounted. Since it discovered truth, theologies that reject it are, in that respect, false theologies. Brueggemann is entirely mistaken in talking of my 'polemic against the entire Barthian programme': I do not think Barth was always wrong, but I do think that he was sometimes wrong, and one of the things about which he was mistaken was natural theology. And, since he made that in so many ways the touchstone of his 'programme', this does affect everything in some degree. However, I do not think he was wrong in everything and, as this book shows, I have considerably followed his guidance throughout my approach to biblical theology, in this respect contrary to common 'Barthian' opinion (95–7). Nor have I ever had any conflict with 'church theology' (105f.), since, as far as I know, all that I have argued lies well within the boundaries of approval by church theology, which of course, to take the same example again, permits and encourages historical criticism and does so rightly. I do know scholars who have suffered from 'church theology', but I cannot say that it has been my fate in the slightest. Much depends, of course, on the question of which church one belongs to, and which country. Nor do I accept the distinction between the church and the 'academic guild' (97): and, as mentioned above,[9] the fundamentalist question, as I have handled it, is entirely a church problem. So Brueggemann's situating of his 'centrist' theologians in relation to the various problem areas, though well-meant and suggestive, needs some revision.

It will be natural to continue with some comparisons between Brueggemann's work and that of Childs. They share many features, from general overarching concepts down to common features of vocabulary and style. But the differences are more outstanding.

Starting from the most mundane level, one element Brueggemann has in common with Childs is the absence of an index of subjects or concepts. How is any reader to find the – quite interesting and potentially valuable – insights of the author on, say, homosexuality? There is no index and the table of contents gives no help (the answer is: 194ff.). It seems to me that, within works of biblical theology, indexes of biblical passages are survivals from a past era and could easily be omitted, but indexes of concepts are necessary. How does one find the references to feminist thinking? You have to read the whole book to find out (try, to begin with, 244, 264f.).

Like Childs, Brueggemann is totally negative towards any idea of finding out 'what happened' (e.g. 714). And just here his crowning metaphor of 'the court' breaks down. The 'court' *must accept* the testimony and cannot '"speculate" about "what happened"'. This court apparently has no place for *evidence* and no interest in examining its probability. Surely this is absurd! How would this work in an accusation of murder or fraud? What sort of 'court', whether in ancient Israel or in the metaphor-world of this volume, is *bound* to accept the testimony it hears and cannot decide whether person A had killed person B, because that would be 'speculation'? Brueggemann's court must be a sort of inquisition, a court interested in thought crimes only.

A good illustration of Brueggemann' s distance from Childs is over the place of 'ideology'. To Childs it is abhorrent to speak of 'ideology' within the Bible, while Brueggemann finds it quite frequently. Solomon's prayer at the dedication of the temple 'has an implicit ideological component' (142). Isaiah reflects the 'royal ideology' (624). The monarchic period is built on ideology, from David and Solomon to the end (639). Yet there seems to be a selectiveness in the perception of ideology. It is applied to matters of royalty and temple, but not to the Ten Commandments (183–86) or to practices like the jubilee year, which is a 'wise and cunning provision' and a 'radical vision' (189f.), but is not described as ideology. Nevertheless ideology within the Bible is recognized without embarrassment. Perhaps thinking of those like Childs who attack anyone who perceives ideology in the Bible, Brueggemann writes that 'indignation against ideology' will get us nowhere (711). This, again, is a common postmodern way.

A more important difference is over relations with Judaism. Here Brueggemann has much more to say than Childs. Old Testament theology is conceived of not as Christian but as common to Jewish and Christian interpreters, and Levenson's work is particularly recognized. References to Jewish-Christian relations occur at many points (longer passages include 107–12, 733–5). Brueggemann is anxiously apologetic and full of goodwill; he repeatedly insists that it was wrong on the part of Christians to perceive Judaism as 'legalistic'. In this respect it might have been more tactful not to identify Moses as the initiator of a religious authoritarianism which later (even if within Christianity) leads on to infallibility and the Inquisition (579)! In particular, he declares himself much against Christian 'supersessionism' – again one of these long words, nowhere clearly defined and likely still to be unfamiliar to many readers, where a great deal depends on just how much it includes or does not include.[10] What really can Christians claim? What exactly have they to stop thinking? If Christians abandon 'supersessionism', what view of their relation to the Hebrew Bible are they to adopt?

Brueggemann's emphasis is on the 'openness' of the Old Testament message, so that a Christian reading should not 'preempt or foreclose' or 'crowd the reading of the Old Testament into a confessional corner' (109, cf. 380). But then what *can* a Christian reading achieve? Although this large book contains many references to the New Testament, Jesus and Paul and so on, on the whole it seems to treat the Old Testament as a complete corpus in itself, for Christians as for Jews. 'Acknowledgement of Yahweh requires reordering of everything else'; but then, if so, does believing in Jesus reorder it entirely again? It seems to me that Brueggemann has here taken the Christian belief that with Christ the whole world is made totally different, and applied it as if it was valid for the Old Testament in itself. Following the declarations of Vatican II, we are moving towards a recognition 'that Jews and Christians are co-believers' (112). This may be a good idea for Christians; but I am not sure that Jews *want* to be 'co-believers' with Christians.

Brueggemann is not shy of bringing in New Testament materials, and there are quite frequent mentions of Jesus and Paul. He argues that it is quite legitimate 'for Christian interpretation to draw the Old Testament text to its circumstance, namely to its life with Jesus' (734). This is legitimate 'because the text permits such evocative construal of its polyvalent quality'. Again:

> The Old Testament vulnerably and willingly tolerates such [Christian] use, for which it seems to present itself (732).

(Brueggemann sometimes writes as if the text was a living person, who can decide how it is to be treated, 'presenting itself' for this and 'refusing' that, 'closing itself' to something else. All these, surely, are really Brueggemann's own decisions, not those of the text.)

Christian interpretations and analogies are *possible* and *legitimate* because the text is open and 'elusive'. But he never claims that they are *the right ones*. Here there is a striking disagreement with Childs (732). Against those who insist that a Christian interpreter can write only a 'biblical theology' [a pan-biblical theology in my words], on the grounds that the Old Testament is not available except in the presence of the New, Brueggemann reacts vigorously:

> If the Old Testament text is as polyphonic and elusive as I take it to be, then such a procedure is inherently reductionist, because it reduces the polyphonic, elusive testimony of the Old Testament to one single, exclusivist construal, namely the New Testament-christological construal, thereby violating the quality of generative openness that marks the Old Testament text.

This will lead on usefully to the question of the *canon*, which in turn brings us back to questions of Jewish-Christian relations. Between Brueggemann and Childs there is an obvious difference in the degree of emphasis on the canon. Brueggemann sometimes mentions the canonization process in a style very reminiscent of Childs: thus, noticing two different 'strategies of presence', the Priestly and the Deuteronomistic, he notes with emphasis that 'the canonizing process retained both, assigned both to Moses, and refused to choose between them' (673). Nevertheless mentions of the canon in his book are in fact rather few. His many quotations of text are quotations of *passages*, and he is seldom concerned to show how far these passages conform to the final, canonical, form of the book. In working thus with selections and quotations he may well be closer to the older church traditions than the canonical movement has been, as suggested above (Chapter 25). Speaking generally of Childs' programme, he notes that it steers clear of the dangers of 'modernist criticism' and 'takes up theological themes that modernist foundationalism [What is this? – J.B.] must eschew'.

In the end it seems that the questions of canon are not very important for Brueggemann's approach. Canonical considerations may be useful at times, especially as an antidote to historical criticism. But the rhetoric is visible and effective in limited parts, and the boundaries between books, their 'integrity' in Childs' term, the need for 'holistic' reading, all these do not matter very much. On the other hand Brueggemann can perhaps be thought of as being *more* canonical than Childs, in that Childs so often and so obviously *starts out from* historical criticism and seeks to progress to the canonical reading, while Brueggemann for the most part, though condemning historical criticism if anything even more absolutely, in the handling of actual texts simply ignores it from the start.

But his final judgment on Childs seems to be on somewhat different grounds. It is not because Childs is wrong about the canon, but because he has subjected the Bible to 'church theology'. His method has in the end 'generated a reading of the Old Testament text in and through the categories of Christian systematic theology' (85). This approach 'features its own reductionism, which in turn overrides and distorts the specificity of the text'. The canonical project is 'massively reductionist' (92). It does not 'allow for what I regard as most Jewish in the utterance of the text' (93). The distinction between Jewish and Christian readings thus once again becomes paramount. The basic passages on this are 107–12 and 729–33.

> The truth of the matter, on any careful reading and without any tendentiousness, is that *Old Testament theological articulation does not conform to established church faith*, either in its official declaration or in its more popular propensities.[11] There is much that is wild and untamed about the theological witness of the Old Testament that church theology does not face. It is clear on my reading that the Old Testament is not a witness to Jesus Christ, in any primary or direct sense, as Childs proposes, unless one is prepared to sacrifice more of the text than is credible (107).

Again, in the second major part of Childs' *Biblical Theology* 'the Old Testament is enveloped in New Testament claims and nearly disappears' (731). Here again it is emphasized: 'it is so clear that the Old Testament does not obviously, cleanly, or directly point to Jesus or to the New Testament.'

This comes back, therefore, to Brueggemann's strong sensitivity to questions of exclusion, of 'supersessionism', of anti-Semitism, of Jewish-Christian dialogue. To insist, as Childs has done, that Old Testament theology is and must be a *Christian* affair and part of *Christian theology* is to offend against these sentiments. Brueggemann in an important part of his text insists that Christians and Jews do read the same Bible:

> It is my judgment that, theologically, *what Jews and Christians share is much more extensive, much more important, much more definitional than what divides us* . . . There is something diabolical, in my judgment, in parting company whenever and wherever it is possible for us to do theological reading together . . . It appears to me that the waiting of Jews (for Messiah) and the waiting of Christians (for the second coming) is a common waiting that stands against a despairing modernity (108–9).[12]

Thus Brueggemann concludes a section with the question: 'Must we make allowances in our interpretation in response to the long history of anti-Semitism that has marked the Christian use of the Bible? My answer is a positive one.' There is 'no doubt that' Reformation interpretation was profoundly anti-Jewish. With this he joins 'nineteenth-century developmentalism'. A 'theological supersessionism which breeds practical anti-Jewishness, which is rooted in the absolutist claims of Christian theology, must be reexamined'. And so: 'While the open future of the Old Testament can and has been taken up by Christian claims, the Old Testament itself does not mandate that outcome to a specifically promised future. Much must therefore be left open, more than in the past' (112).

To sort out the claims and counter-claims involved here would require a book in itself. Brueggemann is right in saying that the Old Testament text does not univocally point to Jesus, and Childs had no textual evidence to support such a claim, which was based on purely dogmatic assertion. On the other hand, as stated above (310), Childs' insistence that Old Testament theology was a 'Christian theological' operation was intended not so much to exclude Jews but to exclude the supposedly 'secular' investigations of (mainly Christian) historical and sociological critics. It was the narrow restrictions of the theology he followed that caused him to express his own attitudes in this matter wrongly. Childs' own work, as in his Exodus commentary, shows very well that he is happy to read along with Jewish commentators. His trouble is not that he cannot read along with Jews, but that he cannot read along with Christians who think differently from himself. Nor would I say that he subjects the Hebrew Bible to 'church theology': the defect is rather that he restricts church theology to one narrow stream represented mainly by himself along with an idealized picture of the Reformation. Brueggemann at this point attacks Childs for the *narrow authoritarianism* of his theology, which in itself is quite true and is also a good postmodern viewpoint, but not for its being a *wrong* theology, both contradicting biblical evidence and being a partisan opinion rather than 'church theology', which is my own opinion. As for his enveloping the Old Testament in the New, to the point that it virtually disappears, I think something could be said on both sides. On the problems of past anti-Semitism, supersessionism and the rest, I do not believe that Childs is any less sensitive to these than the rest of us are. Unquestionably, however, Brueggemann has placed them more in the foreground of his theology. On the other hand, he has not sufficiently probed the question whether it is possible for Christianity to be satisfied with the mixture of 'elusiveness' and 'openness' that he proposes for us.

Historical criticism has been mentioned several times, and this may lead us back to the Prologue, for it is there that Brueggemann mainly discusses the subject. Here again we may note a difference from Childs. As we saw at an earlier point, these two scholars appear to compete for the prize to be given to whoever can blacken the Enlightenment the most. Both of them alike depend on a particular view of intellectual history (Brueggemann emphasizes 'episte-mology' quite a lot), and the two seem about equal in their hostility to the Enlightenment and are very similar in the way in which they apply this picture of intellectual history to modern biblical studies. They share a certain idealiza-tion of German thought in the 1930s, Childs more so, but Brueggemann seeks also to pin the driving impulse of his subject to that time.[13] But there is a key difference. For Childs the Reformation (recast in Barthian terms) remains the ideal, and though he occasionally makes some appeal to postmodern positions, hoping that they will undermine the Enlightenment,[14] his ideal lies entirely in a pre-Enlightenment world, reappearing only for a brief moment in the Germany of the 1930s. Brueggemann, on the other hand, seems rightly to perceive that the Reformation is just as full of traps and defects as any other period in intel-lectual history, and is in any case itself deeply implicated in the Enlightenment (5–9). His opposition to the Enlightenment is thus, or tries to be, expressly a postmodern one.[15] He identifies himself almost entirely with the styles of the present (and, perhaps, of the future?). His writing is full of the fashionable vocabulary of the times: pluralism, hegemony, privilege, elitism, closure, marginal, metanarrative (which he says he does not like, but uses anyway). Anti-Enlightenment utterances from anyone are accepted without criticism, however dangerous or wrong-headed they may be: thus Gadamer's opinion that the Enlightenment had 'a prejudice against prejudice' is accepted without question (14) – oddly for a theologian who elsewhere strongly attacks Christian anti-Jewish prejudice! If prejudice is a good thing, why should we not have more of it? Anyway, in the way it ends up, it seems that Brueggemann is really the greater hater of the Enlightenment and should win the prize. For, as I shall elaborate later, though Childs uses the evils of the Enlightenment as a sort of weapon to discredit the ideas of other scholars, it does not make so much difference to him in the long run, since his aspirations go back to before the

Enlightenment; while in Brueggemann's case the wrongness of the Enlightenment provides much of the *theological substance* which he perceives in the
Hebrew texts. His implicit reasoning seems often to be: all wrong perceptions,
all hegemony, supersessionism, authoritarianism, developmentalism, autonomy
and the rest derive from the Enlightenment. Postmodernism destroys the
Enlightenment perceptions. Therefore any postmodern interpretation is right
and, as it happens, coincides entirely with the intention of the biblical text
and its rhetoric. In this way the anti-Enlightenment argument is an essential
mechanism for his theological perception. This is why Brueggemann, who
seems just as Enlightened as the rest of us, is so dependent on his endlessly and
tediously repeated arguments (or rather rhetoric) against the Enlightenment.

Now it is not for us to argue about intellectual history in the Enlightenment
period. I will just say for Brueggemann, as I have said for Childs, that I simply
do not believe their accounts to be historically true. Far from being valid
historical accounts, which then have an impact on theological decisions, I think
that they are accounts basically generated out of apologetic, partisan, theological
drives, and are full of ill-informed popular misconceptions of people like
Descartes, Locke, Kant and equally of the way in which theology, biblical study
and church life were interlinked in the relevant times. In this respect Childs
seems to do better: for, even if I do not believe him, he has unquestionably done
enormous readings in the literature of the relevant periods, while Brueggemann
seems much of the time just to repeat popular stereotypes of anti-Enlightenment hatred, combining the pre-Enlightenment arguments of Childs with the
(often quite different) postmodern hostilities against the Enlightenment. Look
at this (one example among many): 'Historical criticism affirmed in its practice
that the Old Testament, in its faith claims, is superseded by Enlightenment
rationality and its accompanying autonomous objectivity' (15 n.). Notice
*autonomy*, which for Brueggemann is a deadly enemy, frequently to be attacked.
Or take this sentence, from his earlier essays:[16]

> It is, nonetheless, increasingly clear that historical criticism is no objective,
> disinterested tool of interpretation, but it has become a way to trim texts
> down to the ideology of Enlightenment reason and autonomy and to explain
> away from the text all the hurts and hopes that do not conform to the ideo-
> logy of objectivity. In the end, the text is thereby rendered voiceless.

Historical criticism, this seems to mean, makes Moses into an earlier Kant,
David into a Voltaire, Isaiah into a Rousseau and Ezekiel into a Hume. To
borrow one of Childs' favourite phrases, nothing could be further from the
truth. The main impact of historical criticism, as felt by the earlier twentieth
century, has been to emphasize the strangeness of the biblical world, its *distance*
from the world of modern rationality.[17] There were indeed, in a movement such

as the (older) Quest for the Historical Jesus, some who sought to make Jesus into a person of modern mentality; but it was historical criticism that showed the erroneous character of that attempt.

One striking difference lies in Brueggemann's friendly and sympathetic inter-action with wide reaches of modern scholarship. While Childs mentions most modern scholarship only in order to condemn it, Brueggemann repeatedly expresses his gratitude for the help and insights he has received, often from scholars who, he must know, are by no means at one with his own theological convictions. Only very occasionally is he condemnatory, as for example (330 n. 23) towards Allan Bloom's 'elitist' *The Closing of the American Mind* – and this, of course, is not a work of biblical scholarship. Brueggemann's work can thus be said to be much less an individual production than that of Childs and more a work that is, for all its own very real originality, informed by contact with a consensus of present-day scholarship. On the other hand, this presents something of a contradiction with his own severe disparagement of the whole post-Enlightenment heritage out of which, according to him, most of modern scholarship has grown. Childs is thus perhaps more logical in condemning the whole lot together. For Brueggemann, friendly and catholic as he is in associating himself with so many trends of modern scholarship, fails to reckon with the problems of consistency that this raises.

First, he often fails to note that the same scholars on whose support he rightly relies are quite against the general positions that he himself adopts. An outstanding case is that of Albertz, whose works are quoted numerous times, and with approbation. But nowhere does Brueggemann seem to note that this same Albertz wants to discourage all Old Testament theology and is a warm advocate of history of religion, which Brueggemann sweeps aside with hardly a mention (on p.727 he says that it 'resists theological metanarrative' and 'resists any notion of Yahweh as an agent in Israel's life'; on p. 744 he admits its acceptability, but only outside the church/theology context).

Here are two more cases of the same kind. Brueggemann gives warm accep-tance to the ideas of H.H.Schmid about a theology centred in world *order* (numerous references, e.g. 336, 338, 456, 461, 532, and with no apparent element of criticism). And he himself praises the elements of 'order' and 'beauty' in the Priestly tradition (336f., 665). But he later goes in the other direc-tion: in full postmodern style we read (738) that it is 'the benefactors [he means "the beneficiaries"] of the status quo, those who are advantaged by present political, economic, and legal arrangements', who 'believe that the maintenance of "order" ⁻ that is, the present order – is a primary function of Yahweh'. 'Order', therefore, means hidden privilege, and is to be absolutely denied. But this contradicts his own approval of Schmid's theology.

The same is the case with Moltmann. Moltmann is cited in about a dozen places, and all of them favourably. But then what about the fact that Moltmann thinks the Enlightenment was in many ways a good thing and very much in line with elements of the Christian message? How can Brueggemann continue with his endlessly repeated condemnations of the Enlightenment without even noticing the existence of theologians of whom he himself approves and who think differently?

The same thing happens with other themes. Development and developmentalism are roundly condemned, without any discussion. But this ignores the fact that development of doctrine has a respectable history and status within theology.

A word more about the history of religion, mentioned above in my comments on Albertz. Is not Brueggemann's strong dismissal of this approach – just at the time when it is coming to be far more widely accepted within biblical theology! – another inconsistency? For what can the *pluralism*, so fully affirmed here, mean if one can write a book about one religion without giving a moment's thought to the others? Why must *the Hebrew Scriptures*, and not some other source, be the ones to which one must turn? Is this not another case of the hegemonic privilege that we are being urged to abandon? Surely postmodern pluralism will demand equal treatment for all religions? Brueggemann may well agree with that: but, if so, his complete avoidance of comparative remarks (except between Judaism and Christianity) leaves all other religions (including the Canaanite) out in the cold, and implies the privilege-assumption that the Old Testament can be considered alone, without reference (even adverse reference) to other religions.

Again, there is a question of *quality*. Brueggemann insists that anything like historical criticism has to be looked at with the utmost suspicion and approved, if at all, only after severe examination. But for anything that is postmodern no such suspicion is required, and so anything coming from the fashionable postmodern sources is fully accepted with only very occasional critical examination. Not surprisingly, the utterances of Foucault are treated with grave respect, while Derrida is, if not canonized, at least warmly welcomed, and indeed integrated into the central movement of Yahwism. He, we are told, 'is engaged in a thoroughly Jewish enterprise of reading at the edge' and 'his deconstruction reflects an ancient Jewish commitment to iconoclasm' (330, cf. 740). 'Derrida is appealing back to the centre of the Mosaic revolution' (740). Alone among post-biblical thinkers, Derrida comes close to Moses himself. And the same applies to less well-known persons. Second-rate and third-rate opinions, as long as they seem postmodern in tone, are cheerfully quoted with approval, while Descartes and Kant, especially the former, are treated like fools. Plato, being an elitist, is much inferior to the Sophists, who – guess what? – were rhetoricians (54, 64,

119 n., 330 n.). Where did this idea (repeated at least four times!) come from, and how did it come to be an authoritative principle for Old Testament theology? Thus Brueggemann seems to stand for a total surrender to the post-modern *Zeitgeist*. Only once have I noticed an element of criticism and resistance, and that only in a footnote (711 n. 13), where he suddenly and surprisingly talks of 'the interest ["interest" in his terminology means "self-interestedness"] driving postmodern perspectives' and goes on to express his suspicion that 'such perspectives, in rage and resentment against theological authoritarianism, constitute an unwitting lust for Cartesian autonomy', the uncritical embrace of which is 'as costly as the alternative of authoritarianism'. But this welcome moment of critical reflection about postmodernism does little to relieve the impression that Brueggemann has here undermined his own book as a whole. There is no use in putting the blame on Descartes. As I have written before, the ideologies that are a danger to us are not those of the Enlightenment or of the nineteenth century, but those that are popular and influential in our own time.

The rhetorical approach means that Brueggemann quotes texts extensively, and this is an advantage for the reader in one way, as compared (say) with Preuss, who gives only the chapter and verse numbers and leaves it to the reader to look the text up. On the other hand, the greater the emphasis on the rhetoric, the greater the need to have the texts in Hebrew, while in fact they are quoted in English. At certain points, indeed, notably in the section of *verbs* in the 'core testimony', the reader is given in parenthesis a note of the root or word used (e.g. 27), or a grouping of the roots is provided (e.g. 145–52), but little of this practice is continued after the first part of the book. An emphasis is placed on the areas where 'testimony' is centrally in verb form, or in adjectives, or in nouns. Thus there is an attempt to bring vocabulary and grammar into the presentation. But in fact possibilities of this kind are very little followed out.

It would be natural, once a historical approach is so completely rejected as it is here, to proceed to a synchronic linguistic procedure involving tests, matrices, paradigmatic substitutions, statistics, pragmatic relationships with speakers, length of speeches and alternation in conversations, and so on; but nothing of this sort is attempted. Though James Kugel is quoted four times, his book on poetry and rhetoric is nowhere mentioned, nor is Adele Berlin, nor Eskhult (E. J. Revell's *The Designation of the Individual. Expressive Usage in Biblical Narrative*, 1996, was of course too recent to be usable). Lowth and parallelism, formulaic patterns and word-pairs scarcely appear. In this respect Brueggemann, avoiding a historical approach, just fails to provide any sort of *method* which he can lay before the scholarly community, other than that of complementing the Bible's rhetoric with his own. There is no sort of method or procedure by which one can *evaluate* the terms Brueggemann applies to words and texts: how can we determine when a text is 'dense' or a noun is porous or a word 'elusive' or otherwise? And Brueggemann's complete disregard of *comparison* lets him down here: for if words are 'dense' or 'elusive' in the Hebrew Bible, how does this differ from what they are in Arabic, or Greek, or English? Density, porosity and elusiveness may well be present in all religious speech, and indeed in all poetry as well.

There are another two problems about rhetoric as here presented. First of all, considering the numerous passages quoted at length in Brueggemann's book, one notes that they are far from equally representative. In particular, *narrative* texts are seriously under-represented. The majority of those quoted are *speeches* – speeches of prophets and psalmists, sometimes speeches of God; and perhaps this is deliberate policy in a book that stresses speech and utterance. But the Hebrew Bible contains a wide array of other types of text, which are very little represented here. Where do we see examples of legal passages, of sacrificial rituals, of Gideon's campaigns, of the Deuteronomistic formulas for kings, of designs for temples, of genealogies and lists of cities and boundaries, of tribal poems like Gen. 49? Song of Songs is quoted only once (342), while Qoheleth receives a quite detailed consideration (393–8). Thus very large areas of Israel's traditions are under-represented. This may be deliberate policy – perhaps on the lines of my own argument that story is not theology, while speeches of persons within story may be theology. Or perhaps it may be a consequence of the choice of *testimony* as the basic category; if so, the result puts in question the adequacy of *testimony* for this purpose. In any case, in view of the large size of the book, the unequal representation of the types of Hebrew literature is startling, and should have had some explanation or justification.

Moreover, within this area, most of those who have thought about a 'rhetoric' of the Hebrew Bible have emphasized that its outstanding aspect is its being above all a *historical rhetoric*. It communicates by telling of past events, or supposed past events. Naturally, this view can be pressed too far, and has come under criticism. But it can hardly be said to be so completely discredited that it can be totally ignored. Yet Brueggemann seems not to address it, not even to mention it as a possibility against which he has to argue. Is this the carrying of his non-historical approach to extremes?

And here we come to two other weaknesses that damage this book: both result from the will to keep clear of 'history'. First, practically nothing ever *happens* in it: it is all about thoughts and utterances and attitudes. Even events, like the exodus, are not told as things that happened (remember: it is wrong to ask what happened) but as elements in a rhetorical presentation. This is strongly insisted on: there is *no going behind the witnesses* (206). And, likewise, there are hardly any *people* in this book. There is no biographical sketch, no depiction of a personality. Nobody does anything. Practically no one ever has a theological idea. There are only texts, which rhetorically render a depiction of God. This is particularly noticeable in the case of the prophets. Little is said about their lives or anything they did (622–49). We indeed hear of a 'Mosaic revolution' (644, 735–40), but what sort of revolution was this? What happened in this revolution, and when, and how do we know about it? Perhaps there *was* no revolution. Indeed, this approach may fit very well for some books such as Job: no one worries much whether there was a real Job or when he lived. But to present the entire Hebrew Bible in this way – the absolute negation of von Rad's approach – cannot be satisfying.

Looking back on his work from near its end (714), Brueggemann expresses the feeling that he may in the end regret his concentration on 'speech' . And, as a reason for his choice, he goes on to cite 'two temptations that characteristically vex Old Testament interpretation'. The first is the temptation to look for *history*, to want to know 'what happened'. Even von Rad, he says, 'could not escape the modernist trap of history'. But this is not so. Von Rad, though emphasizing history as the milieu of God's action, was far from identifying it with 'what happened'. Notice the use of the term 'modernist': in true 'postmodern' fashion, 'modern' now means that which is antiquated. Brueggemann's solution is to abandon all concern for history altogether. There is no use in distinguishing the more true from the more false, the somewhat biased from complete propaganda. Having made this point, he goes on to Childs. Seduced by the ancient Hellenistic lust for Being, Childs 'reaches for "the Real"', for an 'ontological reference behind the text'. If this is what Childs is doing, I am pleased to say that I think he is right at this point.

Both Jewish and Christian religions read the text as being strongly history-related and as referring to something that is ontologically Real. Attempts to evade this are clever sophistries. What Brueggemann seems to be expressing at this point is his complete acceptance of the anti-essentialism of the postmodern fashion (cf. also 485).

The real fault in Brueggemann's work seems to me to lie, however, in its Prologue and its Epilogue. The Prologue sketches out the history of the subject and establishes the categories that Brueggemann will use, again and again, for his assessment of biblical material. On the history of biblical theology he provides some good assessments and much useful orientation; yet there is something incongruous in the sudden transition from Barth (15–20) to Alt, Noth, Albright, Wright and Mendenhall (20–7). It is surely a misunderstanding of Childs to say that he 'mounted a critique' against the Biblical Theology Movement: he recorded its rise and decline, with sadness and with the purpose of reviving it.

More troublesome, however, is Brueggemann's depiction of the Enlightenment and its relation to biblical criticism (he always says 'historical criticism', as if all biblical criticism was historical in character) . He thinks, like Childs, that historical criticism claimed 'objectivity' or, as he often puts it, thought itself to be 'innocent' (innocence, like disinterestedness, is a bad word in this book: it means a hypocritical pretence of innocence, when one is in fact grabbing a piece of the hated 'privilege'). 'The gains of historical criticism are immense' (14) – but (stressed in italics) *'What has not been noticed is that such scholarship is not as innocent as it imagined itself to be.'* Not been noticed? What Brueggemann says has 'not been noticed' has been the infinitely repeated speech of innumerable commentators for the last fifty years. What has 'not been noticed' is the dominant fashionable ideology of wide currents of our time, and Brueggemann is simply accepting, and taking as an interpretative guide, this widely accepted point of view. To say that it 'has not been noticed' indicates that rhetoric can go too far.

Exaggerations of this sort can at times be serious. 'It is fair [sic] to say that, by the end of the nineteenth century, the Old Testament had ceased to be a part of Scripture with any authoritative claim for the church.' I think this is just ludicrous: it is so far from my own experience that I cannot believe Brueggemann had seriously thought about it. Certainly in Presbyterianism, and I believe in many other churches, the Old Testament continued to be absolutely mandatory for education, preaching and doctrinal discussion, whether in 'liberal' or in 'conservative' currents, right up to the Second World War, after which time it was receiving renewed support from the same Barthian currents which Brueggemann correctly relates.

One of the arguments about biblical theology, as we saw, has been that it should provide interpretation for the modern world situation. Many biblical theologians, however, have not done much of this. But Brueggemann enters into it with vigour, presenting his diagnosis of the modern world situation, which he tends to name 'military consumerism' (explained on 718, 741), 'late capitalism' (485), 'technological despair' or the like. The answer to this is 'distributive justice' (736f.): 'the intention of Mosaic justice is to redistribute social goods and social power'. This is quite admirable in itself, but some of the biblical examples given are doubtful. The borrowing of silver and gold from the Egyptians, never to be returned (737), seems a poor pattern for distributive justice and one likely to evoke amusement rather than obedience. The equality in the amounts of manna (737 also) is not a very strong example either. The year of Jubilee (189f.) is also dubious: as far as I can see, under its principles a rich family which had squandered its wealth on riotous living would get it back again, while a poor family which had worked and saved in order to gain more land would lose it all again.

*Advocacy* is of supreme importance (e.g. 63), but what does Brueggemann really advocate? Does he advocate that there should be no immigration control at all (741)? Probably not. Does he advocate the annulment of the Constitution of the United States, surely the most important document of the Enlightenment, which has *fixed* its values eternally (though fixity, like closure, is something he is strongly against) upon the centre of world power? Given his opposition to the Enlightenment, it would be the logical course; but one doubts if he means it. When distributive justice is to be 'concrete, material, revolutionary, subversive and uncompromising' (745), are we to think of Brueggemann as a real bomb-throwing, Kalashnikov-waving revolutionary? Probably not. It's only rhetoric, after all. As in many churchly attempts to pronounce on social matters, there is no consideration of the practical politics involved.

The main fault in this book is the constant reiteration of the error of the Enlightenment, to which is added every sort of vice such as 'supersessionism'. With this goes a vast over-emphasis on the importance of epistemology, manifested in the continual and wearisome denigration of Descartes. It leaves the idea – as with Childs at times – that a new post-critical Enlightenment has dawned, in other words that all the faults of Enlightenment and liberalism, in accepting the trends of modern times, are now to be repeated.

And it is not so clear in any case that Brueggemann has stayed clear of the temptations of the Enlightenment. Nothing is worse, according to him, than *autonomy* (expressly forbidden by Yahweh, 556). But then, if so, why is *hegemony* so bad a thing? Because it infringes the autonomy of others. So autonomy is the basis of the whole set of values after all. (Perhaps Childs perceived this when he said that Brueggemann was 'a most eloquent defender of the Enlightenment', a judgment that previously struck me as absurd.)[18] Actually, it is not so clear that ancient Israel objected to hegemony so very much. There were, indeed, people who objected to the authority of Moses, and thought that everyone should have the same share of influence, but the Bible does not sympathize with them. Brueggemann is worried about the fact that not everyone had equal access to the temple, 'for access is privileged entry to power' (659 n.24). This is a true postmodern concern. It comes straight out of modern American experience: denial of access is discrimination. But what evidence is there that anyone in ancient Israel had these worries about the temple?

This is the final criticism of Brueggemann's vast and thoughtful work. It leaves the impression of a total surrender to postmodernism: not so much to postmodernism in all its forms, as to the sort of liberal/postmodern mixture influential in the so-called 'liberal' churches and theological schools, where the gospel is a combination of altruism, egalitarianism, anti-elitism, pluralism, multiculturalism and political correctness.

Readers would be best advised, in reading this book, to avert their minds from everything said about the Enlightenment, and to direct their attention to the solid presentation of the rhetoric of texts, which is the author's real aim. He has succeeded in showing that flexibility of mind which was referred to earlier, and he has offered a real alternative to some positions which have previously attracted most notice. He has given a solid and suggestive answer to some problems in the relation between the Hebrew Bible and Christian theology. He has given a major lead in his selection of rhetoric as his theme. He has created, imaginatively, a stimulating organization of the 'testimonies', which might suggest other new approaches for others to follow. The whole could, surely, be vastly strengthened if it was expanded to include more of these very qualities which Perdue hoped to find in it.

# 32

# Apocryphal and Other Non-canonical Books

Already in discussing Gese's contribution (Chapter 22 above), I noted his view that the so-called 'Apocrypha' form part of the total continuum of tradition and that it was a mistake on the part of the Protestant Reformers to remove them from their place in the biblical canon. We have seen the increasing interest in the canon of scripture, not only in Gese's work, and it is clear that in due course any such interest is bound to raise anew the question of the books which might have been, or possibly have been, part of the Bible but have come to be regarded as outside it.

First, let us remind ourselves of five basic things about the books that are commonly called 'the Apocrypha'.

1. They are Jewish books which come from the time after the main part of the Hebrew Bible was complete but before the beginnings of Christianity.[1]
2. Though some of them were written in Hebrew or Aramaic, they have survived mainly in Greek or other translations, and others were written in Greek from the start. More recently, however, portions of Hebrew or Aramaic texts have been found among the Dead Sea Scrolls, making clear that a number of these books had Hebrew or Aramaic originals, which were later translated into Greek and other languages.
3. Although all of them are Jewish books, written by Jews,[2] for the most part they did not become part of the mainstream of Jewish tradition – the main exception is Ecclesiasticus or Ben Sira, which was quoted with respect by the Rabbis, but nevertheless was not preserved in full by them – and thus they were preserved for later ages through a Christian channel of transmission.
4. They are, roughly speaking, books which up to the Reformation were part of the Christian Bible, and still are so in the Catholic and Orthodox churches, but which after the Reformation were separated off and moved into a sort of appendix, or (more commonly) excluded from the Bible altogether.
5. Alongside the 'Apocrypha' so defined, there are other books of the same general kind. However, these were not part of the Roman Catholic or Greek Orthodox Bibles, but were accepted as canonical in more remote

regions (e.g. in Ethiopia, in some Syriac-speaking churches, or in Slavonic cultures) or whether they counted as canonical or not, can be loosely classed in the same general group. These other works are often called 'Pseudepigrapha'; the most obviously important among them, if only in respect of their size, are the Ethiopian Book of Enoch, the Book of Jubilees and the Testaments of the Twelve Patriarchs. For our purposes the distinction between Apocrypha and Pseudepigrapha is not important and will be ignored here for the most part.

A sixth point is less commonly noted and has special importance for our subject. Many of the books concerned give the impression not so much of books that look back upon the Bible and comment on it: rather, they seem to *continue* it, to offer a rewriting or updating of it, to seek to be a new edition of it. In a certain limited sense they can be said to interpret the Bible, but in a more profound sense they seek to *continue* the movement of the writing of scripture itself. In many cases their genre is not the genre of the commentary; it is the genre of the scriptural book itself. Thus Ben Sira and the Wisdom of Solomon very obviously follow out the general pattern and style of the biblical Proverbs. The author of 1 Maccabees 'modelled his work on the historical books of the Old Testament'.[3] The Book of Jubilees is certainly a rewriting of Genesis/Exodus. Vermes applied the term 'rewritten Bible' to cases of this kind.[4]

Moreover, some of the 'apocryphal books' are in fact different editions, or parts of different editions, of books that are in the 'canonical' Bible. It is well known today that some books existed, even in Hebrew itself, in more than one edition. Jeremiah is the prime example. The Greek text of Jeremiah is about one-sixth shorter than the standard Hebrew text.[5] This is not to be thought of as the result of shortening in the process of translation into Greek. On the contrary, the Greek text was made from a different, and shorter, Hebrew text of this book. On the other hand the material of Baruch, Lamentations and the Letter of Jeremiah were apparently collected together to form a larger Jeremiah corpus, and may be regarded as another expansion of this book, different from that which produced the other, also expanded, text of our MT. In books like Daniel or Esther additions which went to make up a longer text of the book stand in our English Apocrypha as separate pieces of literature. I Esdras again is a different edition running parallel to various parts of our standard biblical text.

In other words, the production of many 'apocryphal' books is akin to the production of scripture itself. The composition of books we now know as 'apocryphal' was to a considerable extent *continuous* with the process of literary editing and the finalization of the books we call 'biblical'. In at least some important cases, the production of these writings belonged to the same literary process as had produced the 'biblical' books. Some of them may well, indeed, have been composed before the finalization of the 'canonical' books was complete. In this respect they tend to differ from works of comment and exposition, and also from works of Rabbinic tradition.

I mentioned above the important part played by the Reformation in sharpening the distinction between 'Apocrypha' and the canonical scriptures.

However, there was a difference between the beginnings of the Reformation, the Reformers themselves, and what came later. The original position of many Reformers was that, though these books did not have full authority for proof of doctrine, they were basically good books, good to read and religiously instructive. Article VI of the Thirty-Nine Articles of the Church of England (1562), a very Protestant document, says of these books that:

> The Church doth read [them] for example of life and instruction of manners; but yet doth it not apply them to establishment of doctrine.

Luther similarly took a moderate position, depending on whether he personally liked this book or that: he said, in his vigorous way, that he would be happy to drop II Esdras into the River Elbe, but on the other hand he respected the Letter of Manasseh and included it in the appendix to his Bible translation. He included the books in question (except for I and II Esdras) as an appendix in his German Bible (1534) and in his preface allowed them to be 'useful and good to be read'.[6] Calvin also, especially in his earlier period, showed serious respect to some of the apocryphal books and continued to be willing to use them in theological argument, though often with some caution and hesitation.[7] Particular respect was attached to Ben Sira, which Calvin, following patristic opinions, took to have been written by Solomon (even though the text itself at 50.27 names 'Jesus son of Sirach' as author).[8] In controversy, where Roman Catholic opponents quote these books, even where Calvin notes their lesser authority in comparison with the agreed canonical books, he remains unwilling to let his opponents have their persuasive power on their side, thereby admitting that they have some demonstrative force.[9]

Later, however, to take one example among many, the Westminster Confession (1647), a basic document of Presbyterianism, severely stated:

> The Books commonly called Apocrypha, not being of divine inspiration, are no part of the canon of the scripture; and therefore are of no authority in the Church of God, nor to be any otherwise approved, or made use of, than other human writings.

In other words, not being inspired, they were no better for religion than today's copy of a newspaper or a trashy novel such as one might buy at the airport. The fullest expression of this attitude came in the early nineteenth century, when the

British and Foreign Bible Society decided not to distribute any Bibles that included the Apocrypha.[10] Only recently has it once again become accepted within much of Protestantism to publish Bibles containing these books.

This same attitude has entered into our common speech. When we say, 'that story is apocryphal', we mean that the story is a fiction, that it is not genuine, is not true, has been falsely attached to the person or subject referred to. Though apocryphal stories may be amusing, they are not read for their truth value. The same attitude spills over into our valuation of religious books. If they are 'apocryphal', what value can they possibly have? They are *pretending* to be holy scripture when they are nothing of the sort. This is of course why people generally do not read them.

Not long ago I mentioned the Wisdom of Solomon in a discussion and a man stood up and said, 'Why not *Alice in Wonderland*?' At first I did not understand, but then I saw what he meant. He thought: if you can quote the Wisdom of Solomon, why not assign the same authority to *Alice in Wonderland*? Well, the answer to that is obvious, if you think about it: no one ever supposed that *Alice in Wonderland* was part of the Bible, but the 'apocryphal' books *were part of* the Bible for fifteen hundred years, during which most of traditional Christian doctrine was worked out, and still are so in large areas of Christendom. The question therefore is not: If we consider the apocryphal books to be theologically relevant, how can we refrain from dragging in all sorts of uninspired and frivolous literature? It is: Did the Reformation have good ground for removing from the Bible a group of books which had hitherto counted as authoritative scripture? After all, most of those who today would oppose the acceptance of the Apocrypha as canonical would also rise up in anger against any proposal that we should remove from our present (Protestant) Bible two or three of the books that are within it. Yet this is exactly what was done in the case of the Apocrypha.

The result is that people on the whole do not read the apocryphal books and do not know them. If in earlier days one read the Bible because it was religiously authoritative, by the same principle one avoided the Apocrypha. Thus though the apocryphal books have had a considerable influence upon our culture, much of it has been through the indirect channels of art, literature and music, rather than through religion itself. Art lovers know of Judith holding the head of Holophernes, music lovers know Handel's *Judas Maccabaeus*, and many have been delighted by James Bridie's play *Tobias and the Angel*, but they still do not read the books from which these famous elements came.

Indeed the Apocrypha can at times serve as a useful avenue for a kind of non-religious religiosity. I once taught in a university that was rather proud of its secular, non-religious and non-denominational character. But at important ceremonial occasions it was felt proper to have a reading of something solemn that sounded like a Holy Scripture. To read from the New Testament might suggest a proclivity towards Christianity, and to read from the Old might imply a favour towards Judaism. The Apocrypha provided excellent neutral ground, and a favourite reading was the 'Praise of the Fathers' from Ben Sira (Ecclesiasticus) 44:

> Let us now praise famous men
> and our fathers in their generations . . .

This is a source replete with fitting sentiments, and one that has the advantage of hardly mentioning God at all. All good fun and beautiful language, but it confirms what I have said, that people's liking for the Apocrypha, in so far as it existed at all, was not deeply based in religion.

Now opposition to the full canonical status of these books did not begin with the Reformation. The most important opposition came much earlier, from St Jerome, about AD 400. Jerome was the translator of the Latin Bible, the Vulgate as it came to be known. (There was an earlier Latin Bible before Jerome, now usually called the Old Latin, Vetus Latina; its Old Testament had been translated from the Greek and not from the original Hebrew.) At a time when few Christians knew Hebrew, Jerome knew it quite well; he lived in the East, he talked with Jews and consulted them about the meaning of words. He insisted that the Old Testament must be translated from the original Hebrew, the *hebraica veritas* or Hebrew truth, as he called it. This policy then affected not only the language but the books of the Bible: for Jerome considered that only the books that were in Hebrew and that were canonical for the Jews should count as definitive scripture for the church. The other books, which already existed in the church's Bible, should not have the same status. This may be taken as the starting point for question of the Apocrypha. But, though Jerome was venerated as a saint and scholar, his opinion was not generally accepted in the church. In particular, Augustine, his even greater contemporary in the Latin church, resisted the plan for the new Bible, and the 'apocryphal' books remained within the Bible until the Reformation raised the question once again. However, Jerome's views continued to be known, and on this question the Reformers appealed constantly to his authority.[11]

But why did the Reformers or their followers take the step of actually demoting these books from full biblical status and placing them in an appendix or outside the Bible altogether? Gese, as we have seen, explained it through the effect of Renaissance humanism with its principle of *ad fontes!*, the appeal to the *earliest* sources, and no doubt that was a factor;[12] but there were other reasons which derived more directly from the nature of the biblical or semi-biblical material. However, the reasons were mixed and mutually contradictory; it seems that they employed a confused medley of arguments. There were ancient traditions, for it was known that various biblical books had been disputed in the ancient church: for example, it was known that Revelation was long disputed in the East, notably by Eusebius. There were arguments that authorship proved canonicity: thus if Solomon wrote a book, that made it canonical. But equally, canonicity proved authorship: thus if II Peter is canonical, that proves that Peter wrote it, while if it had not been canonical, its 'claim' to be by Peter would not have counted, just as the 'claim' of II Esdras to be by Ezra proved nothing, since the book was not canonical. There were arguments that historical errors disproved authority: I Esdras has numerous discrepancies as compared with the canonical books Chronicles, Ezra and Nehemiah, and this, it could be argued, proved its inauthenticity. Finally and most important, there were personal preferences based on theological content – this last especially with Luther.

Now there are weaknesses in these arguments. The first is that the apocryphal books could be seen by Christians to provide some good links between the Old and New Testaments, which were now broken: for instance, the close connection of Paul's arguments with books like the Wisdom of Solomon and IV Ezra. Christian argumentation about the linkage of the Gospel with previous scripture was actually being damaged by the relegation of these books to an appendix, and still more by their total rejection. Moreover, it was familiar that the New Testament had quoted such books as authoritative sources: thus Jude 14ff. quoted Enoch as an authoritative prophecy.[13]

The second weakness is a theological one. No previous authority was more important to the entire Protestant position than St Augustine. It was he who supplied the essential basis for the fundamental Reformation theology of grace, of justification by faith, of predestination. In the ancient church, he was the hero of Protestantism. But, as I have already mentioned, he was quite against the proposal of Jerome that the 'apocryphal' books should be demoted from full biblical status. Not only so, but in his own theology, to which Protestants so continually appealed, he had again and again used passages from these books as doctrinal proofs. Thus Wisdom 9.15 reads:

the corruptible body weighs down the soul
and the earthly habitation presses down the sense thinking of many things.

To Augustine this was a key text, and it is quoted, in whole or in part, eighty-two times in his works.[14] The passage is not marginal, but forms part of the path by which important Platonic elements were introduced into Western doctrine. Again, to prove an important point in marital ethics, he quotes the prayer of Tobias at his wedding (Tobit 8.7–10; *de doctrina Christiana* III, 18). Many other cases can be added. If these books were as weak and misleading as was being claimed by Protestants, how could this do other than discredit the entire Augustinian theology upon which the Reformation position rested? How could

Augustine be right when he did not accept the boundaries of the Bible as Protestants insisted they must be?

The third weakness is that, in the question of the canon, the Reformation did not have a united voice. As we have already seen, there was the division between those who said that the Apocrypha, though a subsidiary part of scripture, were still good for religious reading, which implied that they had some sort of divine inspiration though weaker than in the other books, and those who thought they were of no use at all to religion.

Most important and serious, however, was the position of Luther, who was not worried too much, one way or the other, about the Apocrypha in our usual sense of the term, i.e. the Old Testament Apocrypha, but who *created within the New Testament* a sort of new Apocrypha, though that name was not used for it. For in the New Testament, acting on his principle of justification by faith, he pronounced the Letter of James to be an 'epistle of straw', theologically weak or defective, and removed it, along with the Letter to the Hebrews and the Book of Revelation, to a kind of Appendix at the end of the Bible. This produced the odd result that Luther, though fairly 'orthodox' about the Old Testament canon, was taking analogous action in the New Testament to what had been done by others in the Old. The principle, however carried out, that books could be demoted from the long-established canon on the grounds of theological deficiency cut across the whole foundation of the canon and had effects that were still being heard into the twentieth century.

Moreover, Luther's position, whether we judge it right or wrong, upsets the claims of modern canonical theologies to be 'in keeping with the Reformation'. Luther's principle, that on the grounds of justification by faith, based on certain arguments of certain biblical books, one can demote from full canonicity the entirety of other books which fail to share this theology, conflicts with the idea that the canon as such provides the guide to interpretation. On the contrary, the guide to interpretation is provided by one part of the canon, and in consequence of this some other parts of the canon are demoted from full authoritative status. This is closer to the condemned 'canon within the canon' approach than to a 'canonical' approach. In any case, whether Luther was right or wrong in this, it means that the recent 'canonical' approach cannot claim to be 'in keeping with the Reformation'. Childs, following the logic of his point of view, writes:

> The much attacked Lutheran Book of Concord was fully justified in correcting Luther's disparaging evaluation of the book of James because it appeared to contradict Paul (705).

Very well: Luther was wrong. But if Luther, in one of his most famous and decisive judgments, was wrong, how can one pretend that the canonical approach represents a 'Reformation' point of view? At the most one portion of the Reformation, less than half, is being affirmed here.

The real reason, I suggest, why later Protestantism effectively removed all the apocryphal books from the canon was one that was not consciously expressed at the time: it followed as a necessary corollary from the orthodox Protestant view of Holy Scripture. Through the way the orthodox Protestants saw authority, they needed a Bible that had no fuzzy edges. There had to be a clear-cut division. Every word counted. What was inside was inspired; what was outside was not inspired. For this the canon had to be absolutely and clearly defined. But in that time there was only one canon that was absolutely and clearly defined, and that was the canon of the Hebrew Bible, the Bible of the synagogue. The exact limits of the other books, the 'Apocrypha', were not defined and not definable. All the Christian canons which included 'extra' books had fuzzy edges; there was no absolutely definite boundary – hence still today the confusing boundary between 'Apocrypha' and 'Pseudepigrapha'. For instance, how many Books of Maccabees were there? The traditional Apocrypha of the English Bible had two, but in Greek there were three or four. Even the Roman Catholic canon was not entirely precise: only fairly recently (at that time) the book called IV Ezra (II Esdras 3–14 of the English Apocrypha), which had been part of the Vulgate canon, had been removed and placed in an appendix as a result of debates in the Councils of Florence and Trent. (It is still there in modern editions of the Latin Bible.) As for the churches of even remoter parts, such as Ethiopia, in so far as anyone knew anything about them, they had within their canons even more out-of-the way books, such as Jubilees and Enoch.

Moreover, some of the materials which came to count as 'Apocrypha' were not separate 'books' at all, but additional pieces of text for 'biblical' books, which in the Greek Bible amplified the material of the Hebrew books of Esther and Daniel. In the midst of all this variation of opinion the only clearly defined text was that of the Jewish Bible. Once it was felt that only an exactly defined text could support the conception of a precisely bounded divine inspiration, there was no alternative to following the Jewish Bible and relegating other texts to the status of Apocrypha. This, I suggest, is the ultimate and underlying reason why most Protestant opinion, some time after the Reformation, came to adhere to the Hebrew canon and placed the other books in a lower status.

Actually, the orthodox Protestant view of inspiration logically demanded – though this was seldom perceived – not only a precisely defined *canon* (of books) but a precisely defined *text* (of words). Hence came, later, that well-known phenomenon, the sanctity of the King James Version in English. For the strict inspirationist it is uncomfortable to hear that it is uncertain whether the longer ending of Mark, or the story of the woman caught in adultery in John, are authoritative scripture or not. For the Old Testament the problem was again one familiar to Jerome. He knew very well that the Greek and Latin texts in existence and used by Christians had considerable variations between them. The Jews, by contrast, had not only a clearly defined canon but a highly uniform *text*. *Hebraica veritas* obviously made a good practicable basis for his Vulgate, and still more for the numerous vernacular translations of the post-Reformation period. In fact, however, the difference was not absolute: even the tradition of the Masoretic Text has variations and discrepancies; but they are very small in proportion to the traditions of other texts, and most people were not conscious that they were there at all – as is still the case today.

Now whether it was intended or not, the virtual absence of the 'intertestamental' books brought about a weakness in later religion. For Christianity, it opened up a serious gap between the Old and the New Testaments, a gap of several hundred years if one counted Daniel as a book of Babylonian/Persian times, as readers of older times did. What, if anything, was God doing in all this time? Why were there no scriptures to communicate his voice? The existence of this gap created the impression that the New Testament writers got their ideas either from the Old or from direct new divine revelation; they had got nothing from the intervening tradition of interpretation.[15] In fact the opposite was the case: the Wisdom of Solomon, for instance, was a vital source upon which essential parts of Paul's doctrine depended. Much in Christianity depended on that intervening tradition: if the apocryphal books had been there for Protestant Christians to read, they might have well symbolized that dependence. Far from introducing false doctrine, at certain points they were sources upon which the New Testament itself may have depended.

One of these, already mentioned, is the role of something like natural theology in Wisdom, and that subject need not be taken up again here. Wisdom also provided an entry by which Hellenistic views of humanity, soul and body and the like, came into Jewish tradition, and this of course is what I have been describing above in the case of St Augustine. The advice *quod tibi fieri non vis, alii ne feceris*, 'what you do not want to happen to yourself, do not do to anyone else', is a part of Tobit's speech to Tobias (Tobit 4.15),[16] and is doubtless related to the well-known formulation of Hillel and to the words of Jesus (Matt. 7.12).

Particularly striking, however, is the case of interpersonal forgiveness. To quote from a valuable article by David Reimer,

> To sum up on the New Testament: Christian tradition places forgiveness squarely at the centre of its identity, believing that in doing so it faithfully follows the Bible's united witness on the subject.

But:

> It comes as something of a surprise, then, to discover that interpersonal forgiveness is virtually absent from the Hebrew Bible.

It is in Ben Sira that we find:

> Forgive your neighbour the wrong he has done, and then your sins will be pardoned when you pray (28.2).[17]

Reimer provides more material which I therefore do not have to repeat, and goes on to add examples from the Testaments of the Twelve Patriarchs. In addition, he goes on to argue that biblical theology requires an approach 'that incorporates ancient Jewish and Christian nonbiblical writings' (282). Thus he writes:

> The advent of 'canonical criticism' in its several guises has pushed the canon to the foreground of biblical theology. But, somewhat ironically, affirmation of the canon must itself bring approval of tradition, since it is tradition (or the believing community) which authorizes canon. Brevard Childs's own interest in the history of interpretation was motivated out of just such concerns. Far from excluding extracanonical writings from the exercise, this means that not only Augustine, Luther and Calvin are of interest, but ben Sira, Tobit, and Enoch much more so . . . The weight which a canonical approach accords to *tradition* has the unintended effect of relativizing canonical boundaries (264f.).

There was of course one matter on which the Reformers were quick to find 'false' doctrine, and that was the question of purgatory, atonement after death and prayers for the dead. Protestantism was sternly against all this: prayers for the departed were sternly prohibited in the stricter currents. Judgment is immediate after death, and nothing can alter the decision then made.

On this matter the basic text was in II Maccabees 12. It tells of a battle in which some Jewish soldiers lost their lives. On the next day Judas and his men 'went to take up the bodies of the fallen and to bring them back to lie with their kinsmen in the sepulchres of their fathers. Then under the tunic of every one of the dead they found sacred tokens of the idols of Jamnia, which the law forbids the Jews to wear. And it became clear to all that this was why these men had fallen' (v.40). So they prayed that the sin which had been committed might be blotted out. Judas collected money, two thousand drachmas of silver, for a sin offering and, it is said, 'in doing this he acted very well and honourably, taking account of the resurrection. For if he were not expecting that those who had fallen would rise again, it would have been superfluous and foolish to pray for the dead. But if he was looking to the splendid reward that is laid up for those who fall asleep in godliness, it was a holy and pious thought. Therefore he made atonement for the dead, that they might be delivered from their sin.'

Now nothing is more characteristic of traditional Protestantism than its negative view about prayers for the dead or atonement after death; nothing more seriously differentiates it from Catholic life and culture. It cannot be doubted that this passage, from II Maccabees, which was widely used in arguments from the Catholic side, was a more important factor than any other single passage in the Protestant rejection of the Apocrypha.

Yet here again the Protestant position was uncertain, even on the most highly canonical ground of the New Testament. For Paul himself, arguing about death, resurrection and baptism, invokes 'baptism for the dead' as a reality upon which arguments may be based (I Cor. 15.29): 'Otherwise, what do people mean by being baptized on behalf of the dead? If the dead are not raised at all, why are people baptized on their behalf?' Exactly what was intended by baptism for the dead, I do not know and would not wish to speculate about. But it is clear that there was such a practice, and that Paul takes the factual reality of it as evidence for the reality of resurrection.

Yet even this example illustrates the fact that the canonicity of the book need not have been felt as decisive. Even if it was necessary for Protestants to deny absolutely any atonement for the dead, there were other ways in which this could have been done than by removing II Maccabees from the biblical canon. It could have been explained otherwise. Most obviously, it could have been said that this was a Jewish practice which under Christianity was no longer operative – exactly what had been done with dozens of other practices laid down in the canonical Old Testament.[18] Seen in this way one could have said: the passage is good exemplary teaching for Christians, for it emphasizes the belief in the resurrection of the dead and its value for human life, but the actual practice of 'atonement for the dead' is no longer to be carried out.

For, as we have seen,[19] whatever is done or not done with the canon of scripture has to be balanced by the canon of theological preference which is applied. Where Luther demoted the books which by his principle fell short, Calvinism with its theological preference of predestination had the same effect. The canon is only one of the forces which affects the nature of theology, belief and preaching. When I deployed some of these arguments in the Sprunt Lectures,[20] an objector said: 'You are telling me I ought to preach from the Catholic canon!' The answer to this is twofold. First, I have no idea of changing anyone's canon or of making any proposal of such a kind. But, secondly, the answer should have been: 'Even if you were to preach from the Catholic canon, you would still be saying exactly the same things that you are saying now from the Protestant canon.' For, from the viewpoint of modern preaching, the differences between the two canons are distinctly marginal. From the viewpoint of biblical theology, on the other hand, they may be more important. We should now look at some aspects of this.

In his *Old Testament Theology in Outline* (1978, German original 1972), Zimmerli wrote a first page on 'Purpose and Scope' which is really about the canon. It ends with the sentence 'The following presentation of Old Testament theology is based on the Hebrew-Aramaic canon.' In subsequent discussion I expressed some regret about this sentence.[21] Not that there was anything intrinsically wrong with it; it could have been printed within most Old Testament Theologies. But the need to express this decision seemed to me to imply, or at least to allow, the judgment: that the content of a Theology must be constrained by the exact boundaries of the canon followed, so that a Theology based on a different canon would be substantially different. To me this seems to depend on which books are 'omitted' or 'added'. The omission of Exodus or Job would be a grave deficiency which would damage a Theology irretrievably. But if a canon that included (say) Judith and Baruch were adopted, the chances are that these books, canonical or not, would not be mentioned anywhere anyway. Thus Zimmerli's book, according to its index, appears nowhere to mention Obadiah or Ruth; on the other hand, in spite of being based on the Hebrew/Aramaic canon, it includes fairly substantial theological points based on II Maccabees (35, 236) and Ben Sira (80, 158), and I think quite rightly so. But this means that *precise* co-ordination of the theology with the canon boundary was not attempted – again, I think, rightly.

On the other hand, some of the Old Testament Theologies written by Roman Catholics use the 'apocryphal' books (to them, of course, not really apocryphal – except that they tend to use this term anyway!) quite a lot. A glance at a typical page of van Imschoot, for instance, will show the difference: in the French version consider I, 41 or II, 105; but he commonly distinguishes them under a rubric of 'late books' or the like, and so on:

> This eschatological mode of hope appeared clearly only in the latest books of the OldTestament and the apocryphal books (the citations following are from Wisdom and Maccabees, II, 105).

In another respect, an interesting case is provided by the Wisdom literature. In several of the great sections of the Hebrew Bible, the canonical divisions correspond in a clear and convincing way to *completeness* in a chronological or thematic sense: so obviously the Pentateuch and likewise the historical books from Joshua to Kings, while the collection of the Prophets is likewise a total assembly of the books of prophetic sayings. All these collections, one might say, are not only 'religious' canons but are also literary and historical canons. In this respect the Wisdom Literature is different: Proverbs, Job and Ecclesiastes hardly constitute a totality of the same kind. By contrast, the five books brought together when Ben Sira and the Wisdom of Solomon are added provide a very satisfying completeness of the same kind as we have with the Pentateuch, the historical books, and the Prophets. They are a literary canon. This has been noticed in a number of Old Testament theologies: it was implied by G. E. Wright (see above, Chapter 23), and von Rad in his *Wisdom in Israel* devoted a whole chapter to 'The Wisdom of Jesus Sirach' (240–62, plus abundant mentions elsewhere in the book). In his Chapter 14 on 'The Divine Determination of Times' he includes substantial reference to Sirach, Enoch, IV Ezra, the Testaments of the Twelve Patriarchs and Jubilees.

Towards the Wisdom of Solomon von Rad is cooler. He thinks that this book, though 'otherwise, in many respects, a reliable custodian of Palestinian tradition – was the first to abandon . . . the line which had been adhered to hitherto and take a decisive step along the road to a mythical, speculative deification of wisdom' (cf. the quotation from D. Georgi in von Rad's n.31). On the other hand, von Rad's last paragraph,

> Sirach was aware that he stood in a line of succession. Or did he sense that the main work had really been completed before him? (262),

might indicate a feeling that Sirach's contribution was in the end subsidiary. Childs writes near the end of his *Biblical Theology*:

> Especially in terms of wisdom literature, one senses the contribution of the larger Christian canon represented in the Apocrypha. It is significant that the most important modern treatise on the theology of wisdom by G. von Rad (*Wisdom in Israel*) should also include an extended treatment of Sirach (711).

This appears to sympathize with von Rad in including this section in his Theology. Childs also follows von Rad in including positive remarks about the contribution of Sirach and Wisdom (*Biblical Theology*, 189ff.). We may compare his section on pp. 63–68 which avoids a definite decision for the Hebrew canon and ends up telling us that 'perhaps the basic theological issue at stake can be best formulated in terms of the church's ongoing *search* for the Christian Bible'.[22] Part of the task of Old Testament theology is to participate in this search. But if that is so, one would expect Old Testament theologies to spend much time and space discussing the advantages and disadvantages of one canon as against another. This is not the case, however, in Childs' own work, or in any other so far. He notes that no great difference in the normative function of the Bible is to be seen as between the inclusion of the Apocrypha in the Geneva Bible and the removal of them from the Authorized Version in the nineteenth century (66). In fact the general impression given by his Theology and the works leading up to it is that the Hebrew canon is the final basis, and that there is no need for any further 'search'. What other solution could one find that he would approve? 'The theological issue at stake,' he argues, 'is the maintenance of a common scripture between church and synagogue as witness to Jesus Christ, which is threatened if the Hebrew text is abandoned as the normative Old Testament text by the church'.[23] On the other hand, in the matter of the *order* of the books, while arguing for the priority of the Jewish tripartite division, he says that 'the order of the Hebrew canon has no historical or theological claims for the Christian Bible' (ibid., 667). In general, he seems to show a wise hesitancy in this matter, though he couples it with the absolute statements just quoted.[24]

We saw above that these questions touched not only the *canon* (i.e. which books were authoritative) but also the *text* (i.e. which words were in the books). The Septuagint or Old Testament in Greek not only contains books that are not in the standard Hebrew Bible but also, in the books which are common to both, has many differences of wording, in other words a different text. This is also true in some degree of other ancient versions, but the Septuagint has paramount importance for our purpose, since, at least in many places, it was the form of the ancient Jewish scriptures that lay before the early Christians and is quoted in the New Testament and indeed throughout later Greek-speaking Christianity.[25] It is not surprising, therefore, that voices have been raised from time to time arguing that the Septuagint should still be the basis for the Christian Old Testament. On the one hand, translations for Christian use could be made from the Greek rather than from the standard Hebrew text, and/or, whether such translations are generally used or not, theologians should take the Greek text as their authoritative text for interpretation.

Arguments in favour of taking the Septuagint – not only its canon, but its text – as the Old Testament for Christians have been increasingly deployed in recent years. The leading Septuagint scholar Dominique Barthélemy wrote two articles.[26] One of them, arguing mainly from the ancient history of conflict on this subject in the church, ends up by proposing that the 'original form' of the Christian Old Testament should be a Bible in two columns, with the Septuagint in one and the standard Hebrew in the other. Barthélemy ends by invoking the canonical principle as stated by Augustine:[27] that which was read in the principal apostolic sees – at Antioch, at Rome, and at Alexandria – is canonical (126).

The second has perhaps a wider and more theological message. Its title is 'The Old Testament Matured at Alexandria'. Here Barthélemy leaves the ground of history and straight textual criticism and turns to biblical theology itself. According to the central figure of von Rad, ancient traditions expressed themselves in new perspectives: this was the essential process of 'actualization'. Faith in Yahweh, through being expressed anew, came to itself all the more, was freer and more self-conscious. If there was a problem of Canaanization, was there not on the other side a successful 'Yahwehization' of Canaanite conceptions that had been taken over? The same applies to 'Hellenization'. There was a resistance to the idea of putting the Bible into Greek, but 'the translation of the scriptures into Greek Judaized the *koine* more than it Hellenized Judaism. It charged words that had formerly been profane and pagan with resonances that were typically Israelite'(134–5). Barthélemy follows this with relevant arguments about Alexandrian exegesis and the allegorization of Homer. But we pass on to his conclusion:

> Christians do not have to keep in step with Israel, beating retreat after the attempt to enter into dialogue with Hellenism that the Septuagint was, and stabilizing defensive lines on the Masoretic Text. The church is the inheritor of the great openness towards the nations that the Septuagint was.

And again:

> If the Septuagint has to be the *last actualization* of the Mosaic message in face of the nations *before Pentecost*, it is the canonical and therefore original form of the Old Testament of the people of Pentecost.

As against the 'retreat' to the Masoretic Text he argues:

> Some imagine that it (the MT) represents *the* Bible of Palestinian Judaism in the epoch of Jesus. The Qumran discoveries prove that it is nothing of the kind. The MT is only a sclerotic and archaizing text-form, the dictatorship of which, imposed after the coming of Jesus, had the effect of drying up the proliferation of textual transformation (*devenir*) which was in full evolution up to that time.

More recently the subject has received fuller attention from studies published in Denmark. The Danish scholar Mogens Müller wrote an article called 'The Septuagint as the Bible of the New Testament Church', and followed it up with a book on the subject, *The First Bible of the Church. A Plea for the Septuagint*. Another Danish scholar, K. Jeppesen, commented on this in another article, 'Biblia Hebraica – et Septuaginta. A Response to Mogens Müller'. Jeppesen ends his discussion with a feeling that the church should still use a translation based upon the Hebrew text; but 'in biblical theology there is much to say in favour of letting the Septuagint have the same weight as the Hebrew text – therefore in this case *Biblica Hebraica and the Septuagint*'.

'Canonical' theologians have also addressed this question, at least in passing. Childs, as we have seen, strongly but with some hesitations supported the Masoretic text, apparently saying that it was essential to have the same text as that used by the Jews. It is, of course, a precisely defined text and in that sense fairly 'final', which agrees with the general emphases of canonical criticism. (For the New Testament, by contrast, there never was any completely authoritative *text* corresponding to the MT in the Old. New Testament texts exist in forms that in substance and meaning have much greater diversity than the comparatively uniform MT.) Reacting, no doubt, to arguments like those of Barthélemy, Childs writes (*Biblical Theology*, 665): 'It is a false biblicism to argue that, because ancient Christians often used a Greek text, a warrant is thereby provided for dispensing with the Hebrew text'.'

Rendtorff, on the other hand, considers that :

> It makes no essential difference here if we stress that it was not the Hebrew canon of rabbinic tradition that was adopted as component of the Christian Bible, but the Hellenistic canon of the Septuagint; for in the Septuagint, too, the Holy Scriptures are summed up as 'the Torah and the Prophets', as New Testament citations show.[28]

Now where does all this lead us? First, we have to acknowledge that the arguments with which the older Protestantism rejected the Apocrypha were weak and internally contradictory. Secondly, we observe the cultural and religious change which has brought the Apocrypha back anyway into many of the Bibles we see on sale. Basically, much religion is no longer convinced that every word in every sacred book is equally essential: so long as people have the absolutely essential group of books, their religion will not be substantially altered if they have, or do not have, one or two marginal books extra. Thirdly, the absence of the Apocrypha made it easier for Protestants to forget about the part played by post-biblical Jewish tradition in amplifying and interpreting the Old Testament. It has often been said that Christianity was damaged through its inadequate appreciation of Jewish tradition. Within the Christian context, neglect of the Apocrypha was one of the reasons why this took place. Fourthly, there is the perennial question of fundamentalism, which may be becoming the greatest problem for religion in our time. For fundamentalists of any religion, the existence of apocryphal books is a permanent threat to their idea of scripture, one which they avoid only by taking it as axiomatic what the canonical books are, and thus by avoiding all attention to the question.

What arises from this is that theology is not really built upon the canonical books. It is built upon what was *thought*; its base lies *behind* the canonical books, in the life of ancient Israel. No theology of any value can be built purely upon the information given by the canonical books, and thus, as we have seen, such central workers as von Rad, Zimmerli and Childs do in fact attend to the material of 'apocryphal' books and build it into the structure of their arguments.

Questions about any possible alteration of canons are essentially unimportant.

Canonicity of books is something that seems to belong to the past: it was decided back there, and nothing can be gained by altering it today. It is built into the history of our religions. In Christianity canonicity is like heresy: it is a historical concept. To say that some view is 'heretical' is to say that it has a similarity with something that 1500 years ago would have been classed as heretical. But to say that it is really heretical today is meaningless, for generally speaking the churches have no idea how to deal with such a question. Some change in canons could be made, but very strong reasons would have to be put forward for it, and since it would have to have a very large measure of agreement it is unlikely that any such proposal would succeed.

In the same connection, however, it follows that no canon is, or should count as, a Christian 'confession'. Christian confessions imply the existence of holy scripture, but the canons of Christianity are various and the ways in which their contents are deployed are even more so. It seems quite improper to regard particular Christian canons or views about the canon as having the status of 'confessions': they are no more than sectional opinions. Even for those Christians who adhere to the (Protestant) canon of the Old Testament, the existence of the apocryphal books must mean a relativization of the precision of canonical boundaries. There is no such thing as 'the' Christian canon, except in so far as we take 'canon' in a rather vague and imprecise sense.

This does not exhaust the potential importance of the questions arising from the Apocrypha. For biblical theology there is another of still greater significance. We have seen above that it is a real question how far the biblical books contain anything that can count as 'real' theology. Though, as I have argued, implicit theology was there from an early stage, explicit theology is something that appears occasionally, particularly at times of religious crisis. It *grows*, or at least may grow. Also, as we have seen, the articulation of something like theology has historically been connected with contact with Greek language and culture. What this means is that a phenomenon like the Wisdom of Solomon may be a symptom of a very important stage in the rise of theology towards prominence, a prominence that it did not fully attain in Christianity until after New Testament times. Thus an 'apocryphal' book like this has special importance, not just as an example of Jewish tradition in its period, but as an epoch-making stage in the growth of theology towards explicitness. This consideration gives added importance to the whole question of the Apocrypha. For our subject, however, the question is not whether these books are to be read in churches or not, but what part they play in any biblical theology.

As we have seen in the discussion of Gese's ideas above, the books of the traditional Apocrypha, even if they are accepted as canonical, still give us only a very limited idea of Jewish tradition in the relevant period. A much larger and more varied scene opens out to us when we take the Dead Sea Scrolls into consideration[29] – and Gese would of course agree with this. I shall not attempt to provide examples or detailed discussion here. Suffice it to say that the Scrolls make clear to us the extent of a Jewish *sectarianism*, and thereby a world of conflict and criticism, closely linked with the transmission and interpretation of biblical and other authoritative religious books. This is a setting in which it makes sense to see the scene of new and radical religious and theological departures. Writing of the 'sociopolitical and religious contexts' of the Scrolls, Brooke tells us:

> The theological basis of the worldviews of the individuals and groups belonging to those contexts cannot be definitively derived solely from the canonical texts; even the theological principles of those who determined the final extent of the canon cannot be derived solely from those texts (75).

The Dead Sea Scrolls, therefore, must be part of the 'canon' for biblical theology, whether or not they are part of the canon of any religious institution of today. But, as already suggested above,[30] if we come down to this time – and after all the canonical Daniel brings us down to it – we can hardly fail also to include the earliest beginnings of the traditions which were later to mature in Rabbinic tradition.

# 33

# The Distribution of Resources and
# Pan–Biblical Theology

Some chapters back we noted the interesting position of Professor M. Tsevat. He found a place for a theology of the Hebrew Bible which would be a sort of comprehensive intellectual history, a kind of companion to philology or indeed a part of it. He called this 'negative theology'. Alongside it, however, he had ideas of what would be a 'positive Jewish theology', which, to repeat my words above, is not a theology of the Hebrew Bible, but rather a theology of the way in which the Hebrew Bible is linked with Talmud and Midrash, a linkage which has the effect of 'Judaizing' the Bible. 'Talmud and Midrash Judaize the Old Testament' (338). Thus, if I understand it rightly, there can be no positively Jewish 'theology' of the Hebrew Bible alone. A 'positively Jewish' approach would have to be one to Hebrew Bible, Midrash and Talmud taken together. What we are looking at here, it seems, is not a *biblical* theology, but a theology of the way in which the various documentary resources of Judaism are distributed, within the structure of that religion.

Would there not be a place for something similar that would apply to Christianity? Such a work would be, in traditional Christian terms, something like a *Christian doctrine of the Old Testament*.[1] Its task would be to consider, define and explicate the way in which Christianity uses, selects from, evaluates and understands the Old Testament, in relation to other resources – not only the New Testament, but tradition, theology, ethical judgment and so on. Within Christianity such an approach would have to be critical, selective and evaluative. Its ultimate criterion would not be the texts themselves but the ultimate theological realities as Christian faith understands them. As between Judaism and Christianity it would be essentially comparative – not necessarily seeking unity or agreement, but certainly seeking understanding in the midst of differences of different magnitudes.

There are several reasons why such a work could be creative. First, one of the problems of traditional Old Testament theology is that it has often tried to solve questions which, properly speaking, cannot be solved within the horizon of the Hebrew Bible itself and within the boundaries of its resources. Even if one tries to achieve a position about the relation between the Old Testament and the

New, that relation cannot be securely established even with the combination of them both, for the relation between them is something established by *Christianity itself*: differently in its different forms, and not by the Bible in itself. Too often Old Testament theology has been used as a means to achieve solutions to problems which lie beyond its reach.

Secondly, there do exist, of course, many formulations, traditional or more recent, about the place of the Old Testament, and these deserve to be heeded. But many of these tend to derive from older classical theologies, from the patristic period or from the Reformation, and have to be reconsidered from the viewpoint of newer knowledge.

Thirdly, and in particular, the traditional formulae tend to be ill-informed (to put it mildly) and hostile in relation to Judaism. Any new approach would have to incorporate present-day appreciations of Judaism, along with the vastly increased knowledge of its history. Moreover, the entire discussion would be designed with comparative discussion with Judaism in mind.

Fourthly, it is likely that an undertaking of this kind would be aware of some of the same questions which have animated the recent 'canonical approaches'. The reason why I call attention to another possibility is that, for me, the canon is one, but only one, and not *the* only one, among a number of factors involved here and, in my opinion, by no means the most important one. For me, what may be called the 'theology of distribution' has been, and remains, far more powerful than the canon is or can be.

Fifthly, this undertaking is religion-specific. That is, the differences have their basis not so much in the text itself, but more in the resultant religion which follows after the text and considers itself to have a base within it.

Along with this goes the recontextualization of the text, upon which Levenson laid emphasis.[2] He did not pretend that meanings in Rabbinic Judaism were identical with those of the Bible in itself. In Rabbinic thought and practice the text was 'recontextualized', setting the meanings within a new complex.[3] Indeed. This was also done in the Qumran community and, if so, in Christianity too. Of course texts were set within the context of a religion and theology that were substantially different. The explanation of this in terms of recontextualization means that there is nothing unnatural in the process. The traditional Jewish objection, namely that Christian uses of Hebrew texts did not mean what the authors had meant, ceases to be effective. Christianity indeed has quite a different structure, but given this structure, the adoption of ancient texts within it is just what we should expect to happen, and is not essentially different from what happened within currents of Judaism itself. Thus Christian exegesis, both within the New Testament and after, is a perfectly proper topic to be included for consideration within biblical theology, even biblical theology of the Old Testament alone, just as Jewish exegesis is. If we accept for consideration the after-effects of texts, then both alike are fully relevant. However, after-effects, as has been pointed out, cannot be discovered by looking at the biblical texts themselves; they can be known only through the study of later interpretative texts – and this depends on the existence of such texts.

But then we have to take into account the effects of recontextualization. Recontextualization is not a matter of merely quoting texts or reusing their vocabulary. That is a minor aspect. The really important thing is the total theological scheme within which they are now placed and located, and its difference from the total theological scheme or schemes within which they stood during the period of the Hebrew Bible. Each such scheme has its own way of mobilizing and utilizing its resources. This means, as I see it, that the canon of scripture in itself, however it may be organized and differentially weighted, cannot be the decisive instance. Rather, I agree with Dr David Reimer when he writes that 'the real "canon" for religious purposes is not the canon of scripture but the linkage between scripture and interpretation'.[4] That linkage depends not on the canon itself but upon the total pattern of the theological, religious or legal system under which the interpretation is being carried out. Each such system, Jewish (and Samaritan!) – and there were certainly more Jewish systems than those that left their mark in the traditional Judaism of later times – and Christian of various kinds and currents, might evaluate the 'canonical' books in one way or another, the difference in emphasis as between the Torah and the Prophets being the most obvious case. The contents of the group of authoritative books could be different. More important, each would have certain principles of priority and emphasis which applied, not to this or that book or group of books, but to this or that theological idea or conviction, this or that past or future event, this or that person or group of persons. Thus the theology was much more important than the canon. Or, if we wish to use the word *canon* in the sense of *authoritative criterion* – as is done by my friend Professor Abraham – then we say that it is the theology that is the real canon.

Is early Christian theology – say, that of the New Testament – really quite different from that of the Old, or is it really basically the same? Our answer must be that both are true. As I said above, a theology centred upon a Christ who came from God, was crucified and resurrected, and has brought new life and new creation into the world, is deeply different from any totality of Old Testament times, even if elements of similarity are to be found here and there. Yet equally, Christian faith has absorbed into itself enormous areas of categories, memories and story material, primarily from the Hebrew Bible, though not from it alone, and primarily from parts of it rather than equally from every part. This is not surprising; on the contrary, it was to be expected.

As we look, from the Christian point of view, at the possibilities of a 'pan-biblical' theology, one thought dominates my mind. People are anxious, as the term itself suggests, to create a theology of 'the Bible', of the two corpora the Old and New Testaments. As people say, the Old Testament cannot be understood without the New, and equally, the New cannot be understood without the Old. So let us have one theology of this one great twofold corpus. I have nothing against this in principle, though I see two big difficulties in trying to carry it out: first, the sheer size of the theological differences between Old Testament and New; and secondly, the peculiar fact of the temporal gap between them, especially where the apocryphal books are more or less ignored.

But beyond this I see a larger objection. Most of those who call for a pan-biblical theology seem to me to suffer from an inner contradiction. On the one hand they want to bring together the total corpus of Christian Scripture, because it is the closed area of original revelation. As such it must all belong together. But in fact a theology of the whole Bible, strictly built upon that corpus exclusively, will not provide what these Christians want. The Old Testament as interpreted by the New, and the New as read in the light of the Old, taken together, will still not provide an adequate Christian theology. For the New, taken in itself with the Old, has many vaguenesses and inconsistencies, and at the best still does not provide anything like an adequate interpretation of the whole of the Old; nor does the New, even taken with the Old as a closed corpus, provide anything like a secure and adequate Christian theology.

What is commonly wanted by those who seek a pan-biblical theology is something else, something that depends on the argumentation of *post-New Testament* theology and interpretation. They need the work of post-New Testament commentators who (unlike the New Testament) went into *every* corner of the Old and interpreted it in a Christian sense. Still more, they want, they need, the arguments of anti-Marcionite and anti-Gnostic writers; they want and need the developed christology and trinitarianism of the fourth century. All of these are still not provided if one sticks to the biblical corpus. What this leads to is an essentially apologetic exegesis, seeking to prove at every point that Paul was a consistent thinker, that Marcion was wrong about Paul,[5] that Gnosticism was remote from John, that nothing could be understood except on the basis of the later orthodoxies. But the New Testament, taken for itself, even when joined with the Old as one corpus, does not provide these assurances.

It is quite understandable that such assurances should be sought; but what they mean is that the boundaries of the closed corpus of the authoritative Christian Bible are being overrun. We are now looking, not at a theology of Old and New Testament taken together, but at a theology of Old Testament, New Testament, *and* orthodox theologians up to 400 or so. The operative canon includes not only the New Testament, but the anti-Marcionite and anti-Gnostic writers of the second century as well (and Justin too, according to Watson).[6] So pan-biblical theology in this sense does not work. And the sense of this, though seldom thus expressed, is part of the reason why Christian doctrinal theologians of this century were doubtful about the project of biblical theology from the beginning.

At this point we may usefully think back to Gese's idea of the continuum. The continuum of theology in biblical (and intertestamental) times made good sense, but it did not come to an end, as Gese thought, with the New Testament. It runs on into the patristic period, as in Judaism into the Rabbinic traditions. But this means that Old Testament theology is one section of the continuum, New Testament theology another, the time of the Apostolic Fathers and the Apologists another. These can usefully be studied separately; but 'separately' does not necessarily mean 'in isolation from each other'.

Gese, in developing his idea of the continuum which included both Old and New Testaments, linked it with an emphasis on the canon. However, the Christian canon, making 'Old Testament' a separate unit from the 'New', curiously – and especially when the apocryphal books are disregarded – has usually had the opposite effect: the two appear more as separate blocks, where a certain shading of the boundaries between them could well be more correct.

'Old Testament theology' as a separate subject is valid because there was something like theology in Old Testament times, either driving and steering the story material or implied by it, and expressed in certain utterances here and there. The Old Testament is not only a holy text from which in later circumstances theology can be distilled; it is the manifestation of a theological process that was actually going on in biblical times (i.e. Hebrew Bible times), and that was very probably substantially different from the theological impressions that the same texts made when later recontextualized within a profoundly different theological system.

If there were to be a Jewish biblical theology – and that is not for me to say – it would have the same possibilities. It could be, as Tsevat suggested, a theology of the interlinkage between the Hebrew Bible and the later authoritative sources and interpretations. But it could also be a theology of the concepts and interrelations that existed in biblical times – whether in the actual authors, or in the previous world out of which their past experience came, or in the later rewriters, or in the hearers and readers – and such a theology would be a real and valid subject in itself. How far it would agree or disagree with an Old Testament theology as written by Christians we cannot yet tell.

# 34

# David Brown

As has been suggested above, work in biblical theology cannot insist on dominating the thought of doctrinal theology. But it can furnish indications and suggestions to doctrinal theology; and likewise it can indicate, among the many options of doctrinal theology, those which are amenable to its own work, and provide a space and a conceptual area which gives room for its own operations. This chapter outlines one particular approach of general doctrinal theology which appears to me to offer a very congenial framework for the biblical theologian to have in mind.

It is a special pleasure to cite the work of David Brown in this respect. He and I were inducted as Fellows of Oriel College, Oxford, on the same day in 1976, he as Chaplain and I as Oriel Professor of the Interpretation of Holy Scripture. He is now Van Mildert Professor of Divinity in Durham University.

## *1. General*

Brown would not, I imagine, think of himself as a 'biblical theologian', and there is no mention of biblical theology by that name in the portions of his work that I have used. Entitled *Tradition and Imagination*, it emphasizes the total growth of tradition through biblical times (both Old and New Testaments) and on through the two millennia since then.[1] Tradition, however, is not a pedantic antiquarian matter 'without any deep religious life in it'; rather, biblical stories have been 'subject to imaginative rewriting, both within the canon and beyond', and this rewriting has to be taken as seriously as that which nominally lies on the biblical page. 'One of the principal ways in which God speaks to humanity is through the imagination.' Thus Brown's book emphasizes the appropriation and development of biblical themes within the *art* of later eras, an important aspect upon which I will not be able to dwell here.

His first chapter is entitled 'Tradition as Revelation', and he unfolds his basic conviction

that, so far from Christianity being undermined by post-biblical developments in its self-understanding, it has been hugely enriched by them. Not of course that this was always so, but I do want to challenge the view that later reflection that deviates from its scriptural roots must necessarily stand under divine judgment. Indeed, it can sometimes, I shall argue, not only be positively enriching but actually act as a critique of the scriptural text. A Christianity that confines God's revelatory acts to the narrow compass of Scripture, even when this is expressed in terms of the effect of that Scripture upon us in the here and now, I find less and less plausible, the more one becomes aware of the historical situatedness of the text. It seems odd to postulate a God without revelatory impact upon the history of the church when that history is not significantly different in fallibility and conditionedness from the history of the biblical community itself.

## 2. *Enlightenment*

After this, I shall follow Brown's development of his theme roughly in the order in which the elements important to my present work appear.

Of primary importance, in view of things that have been mentioned above, is Brown's fairly positive assessment of the Enlightenment, though post-modernism is discussed and some elements in its critique are accepted. As against the view that the Enlightenment was 'fundamentally orientated towards the undermining of religious belief', he notes the positive Christian values which animated such figures as Descartes, Newton, and even in a way Voltaire.[2] Thus 'when Hans Frei and his successors in the Yale school of narrative theology accuse the Enlightenment of being responsible for the abandonment of the Bible as narrative', this is true only with qualifications. The Enlightenment quite properly 'gave added impetus to the search for appropriate historical narratives' and it is quite mistaken to suppose that 'relatively objective historical writing [is] an impossibility'.[3]

Later Brown continues:

The history of the formulation of Christian doctrine is a history of sustained indebtedness to Greek thought, and for those who would jettison such borrowings, I would add that the same seems to me no less true of the history of scripture in relation to the surrounding cultures.

Or, to quote the same thought in another form:

[My objective is] to challenge the common assumption that the power of revelation is necessarily undermined if external material from the surrounding culture is used to illuminate or even to rewrite its story.

## 3. Judaism

Brown's Chapter 3 is entitled 'Learning from Judaism and Islam'. We read:

> It is Enlightenment values that force us towards the recognition of the historically-conditioned character of Scripture, Enlightenment values too that require us to take seriously religions other than Christianity.

Such an opinion, taken out of context, might look like a characteristic expression of religiously 'uncommitted' modern relativism. Coming as it does, however, from one deeply committed to rather orthodox and tradition-centred Christian values, it has a quite different effect.

> Though I write as a Christian, it seems to me not implausible that sometimes at least God might have spoken more effectively through the history of faiths other than one's own.

> If God is to speak to humanity at all and be persuasive, he must speak within the particular restraints of specific social contexts.

Particularly relevant to our purpose, in view of Chapters 16–18 above, is the warm sympathy with which Brown handles the Jewish tradition. His reflections on it are undoubtedly not only more profound but more extensive and more textually-based than most Old Testament theologians could have produced. Thus, for instance, in the matter of work forbidden on the Sabbath, he follows out the different kinds of work that came eventually to be prohibited.

This brings us quickly to the topic of 'legalism', already discussed above (Chapter 17). Christians, Brown writes, 'are too quick to see such developments as no more than the growth of legalism'. On the contrary, he argues, they 'tend to forget that when the law is fully accepted as a framework for life and internalized as no mere external, burdensome imposition, it can be truly liberating'. 'The real heart of Sabbath legislation has been described as *imitatio Dei*, while the insistence upon three meals as part of *Oneg Shabbat* ("Sabbath delight") indicates its essentially celebratory character'.

There is no necessary incompatibility between Christians endorsing their own tradition and at the same time viewing the development of the Jewish tradition in this way as also part of divine providence and revelation.[4]

Not that Brown avoids making distinctions between Jewish and Christian ideas and practices. Thus he speaks of 'the move of the New Testament away from the deontological, rule-bound approach of the Old Testament towards a teleological or goal-oriented morality'. Christianity is thus significantly different; but the values of Judaism are still to be recognized. Brown not only recognizes them but goes into considerable detail in researching them. See for instance his sensitive treatment of the Kabbalah.

Not only is Brown sympathetic to Jewish tradition and practice; even more significant for our purpose, he is able to acknowledge that, at points where Christian doctrine has been built upon interpretations of the Hebrew Bible, these interpretations have sometimes, or often, been mistaken, accidental or otherwise dubious or a minority position. Not only have they at times been distant from the original meaning within ancient biblical times, even in later times the dominant Jewish interpretation has had more in its favour than the Christian one as used in the New Testament. Thus, on the important case of Paul's interpretation of Gen. 15.6 (Rom 4.3), he argues that 'the Jewish interpretation is the more natural'; at the core of the narrative 'lies the question of obedient action, faithfulness, rather than Pauline faith'.[5]

So taking the Abraham story in a more general way, he writes:

> Paul so fundamentally alters the original meaning of the Abraham story that greater respect for comparable degrees of change within Judaism and Islam is required, if Christians are not to find themselves committed to condemning their own tradition.

This does not apply only to the use of particular proof-texts. It applies to the larger issues as well. Talking again of Paul's handling of the Abraham story, Brown writes:

> There is something unsatisfactory in exegesis which not only leaves much of the Old Testament deeply problematic but also seems to force Christianity into an antagonistic attitude towards Judaism . . . What I shall argue is that Paul uses a christological criterion to impose a harsher interpretation of Jewish tradition than Christianity in fact requires.

And again, of Galatians 4.21–26:

> It is hard not to convict Paul of an exegesis that is strained even by midrashic standards, as well as one that seems inevitably, once more, to force Christianity into a contemptuous attitude towards the history of Judaism.

Once more, on the central question of whether Jesus continued in obedience to the law or did something to abolish it, and whether Paul followed him in these or not, Brown tends to the view that Paul's position was internally contradictory. Matthew's version of a saying looks more likely to be what Jesus may actually have said. 'My point is not that Matthew always gets it right, but, that, despite his apparent inconsistencies, he deserves more credit as a theologian than he is normally given'; and so, he continues:

Paul may in fact be much more confused than Matthew. Certainly, in his search for an adequate justification for going beyond Jesus' explicit teaching he resorts to a bewildering variety of arguments against law.

Here he adds his judgment that Räisänen 'presents a powerful case for the view "that Paul's thought on the law is full of difficulties and inconsistencies" and that, in so far as he was "an original and imaginative thinker", he is best understood as working by "intuition" rather than by careful, reasoned argument'.[6]

Not that Brown is to be understood as anti-Pauline. He summarizes his position well in the sentence: 'That Paul was extraordinarily perceptive on a large range of issues surely does not entail that he must have been equally insightful in everything'.

He continues:

To look at Paul alone might easily mislead one into supposing that Paul invented a wholly new Christian position on the subject, whereas Matthew demonstrates that there was no radical discontinuity but a continuing, developing tradition. Indeed, it was a trajectory that continued beyond the canon, as elements in his own [Matthew's] writing were themselves subject to reinterpretation.

## 4. Islam

Even more striking is Brown's sympathetic discussion of Islam. It exhibits 'a similar pattern of creative development through tradition as we have already suggested applies in respect of Judaism and Christianity . . . Muhammad's insights were built upon the work of earlier prophets, among them Moses and Jesus, while any detailed investigation of *ḥadīth* would force the conclusion of continued developments subsequent to Muhammad's death . . . Nor should Christians be dismissive of what Islam has achieved . . . Although Christianity too has its egalitarian streak, Islam seems to me, on the whole, to have been better at preserving that insight.' One specific example where the Qur'an is 'morally superior to a Christian gospel' is cited:

In Luke 1.20 Zechariah is punished for disbelieving the angel's promise that his wife Elizabeth would bear him a son (John the Baptist). By contrast, in the Qur'an (19.10), the version Muhammad reports is of a three-day dumbness specifically requested by Zechariah as an immediate sign that God would indeed do as he promised. Is the Qur'an not, here at least, morally superior to a Christian gospel?

But it should not be thought that Brown's consideration of Islam is confined to the short extracts quoted above. 'Even what comes later than Christ in another religion can still illuminate and inform one's own'. This sentence introduces a learned and sensitive discussion of Sunna, Qur'an and Ḥadīth, which leads on to other terms and concepts of revelation and tradition. Islam exhibits 'a similar pattern of creative development through tradition' to that which obtains in Judaism and Christianity.

## 5. Greek religion and culture

If Brown's openness towards Islam is striking in a Christian theologian, his understanding towards the religion of ancient Greece is even more important in relation to the question of biblical theology. There was revelation in Greek religion (contrary to common opinion);[7] its myths were not static or devoid of religious content. Homer was a sort of 'canon' which later writing used as a standard but also developed. Greek religion was not at all lacking in religious devotion (109). 'It will not do to treat biblical mythology as profound, while continuing to be dismissive of myth in all other contexts'. 'The power of such transformation [of older traditions] is well indicated by the extent of their incorporation into the new religion of Christianity'. Sometimes this was a thin veneer, 'but more commonly Christian and classical values were thoroughly integrated. Zwingli even promised King Francis I that he would one day see both Adam and Hercules in heaven . . .'[8] The acceptance of pagan prophets came early in Christianity, partly because of Jewish interpolations in the *Sybilline Books*'. There follow more detailed studies of Odysseus, Iphigenia, and Helen and Ganymede. For example, the story of Odysseus is traced through Sophocles, Virgil, Dante, Fénelon, Pope, Tennyson, Joyce and Kazantzakis. 'Just as the journeys of Abraham had their good and bad aspects and so prompted further thought about life's pilgrimage, so those of Ulysses also elicited further reflection on the patterning of readers' lives.' Similarly, 'for much of Christian history the sacrifice of Iphigenia has been almost as well known as that of Isaac . . . I fail to see why God should not have used a similar story to help illuminate how the scriptures can themselves be appropriated'. Helen and Ganymede have something in common with the story of Joseph and Potiphar's wife. Each of these stories is traced out with a rich apparatus of detail in the history of art, literature and interpretation.

Even more centrally, introducing the argument of the second part of his book, Brown writes:

Appearances notwithstanding, the biblical stories of the patriarchs can be seen to exhibit many of the features of the formative narratives of the classical world.

Again, the New Testament can only be properly understood if due account is taken of the assumptions of the ancient world. Thus, as one example:

> Nowadays, Jesus' miracles are most commonly read as demonstrations of his divine power, but this ignores the frequency of belief in similar miracles not only in the subsequent Christian tradition but also in the ancient world, particularly at the shrines of the pagan healing god, Asclepius.

'The Apologists owed a great debt to pagan thinking', and 'the same is no less true of the origins of Christian art'. Christ was depicted, riding into Jerusalem, in the garb of Asclepius:

> Extensive use was made not only of pagan philosophy (particularly Platonic and Stoic) but also of pagan myth. Indeed, one of the fascinating features of the period is that, whereas the modern argument tends to be that if there are pagan parallels (for example for the Virgin Birth) it cannot be true, the ancient argument was that such myths proved the conceivability of God acting in this way.

## 6.  *Limitations of scripture taken alone*

Brown fully affirms the authority of scripture, but he holds that its authority is exercised only when scripture is seen together with subsequent interpretation. This agrees with the fact that there was a development within scripture itself: later texts corrected earlier ones. The church 'improved on the contents of the original narratives'; or, to quote the sentence more fully:

> just as the story of Jesus' birth was rewritten towards the end of the first century by the evangelists to reflect the significance now found in Jesus, so the later church continues this process, and in so doing improved upon the contents of the original narratives.

> Christian theologians often write as though the Bible should be given the first and last word. Certainly as revelation it needs to be given the first word, but if even the gospels themselves are an evolving tradition in which not only does Matthew correct Mark and John Matthew but all even the perceptions of Jesus himself, why should that evolving tradition have ceased?

This was so already in Old Testament times:

> Even though later writers had no doubt that Abraham was a historical figure,

nonetheless their dissatisfaction with the story as it stood led to major alterations in the way it was told.

And so:

> Though of course the various writers concerned never explicitly say so, since for them the meaning they discover is actually already present in the text, it seems clear that the motivation for new readings [of older texts] lies at least in part in dissatisfaction with the apparent theological content of the Genesis narrative.

This applies even in very central doctrinal matters. Among the Gospels, 'Only John makes the claims to full divinity [of Jesus] explicit (and even then he remains subordinationist in his theology)'.

> Raymond Brown has claimed that the historical Jesus would have endorsed John's judgment on himself. That is a claim which I do not find plausible. It is only the exalted Jesus who would, like the church, have understood the full significance of who he was. The incarnation was a real kenosis that necessitated gradual development in the understanding of who Jesus was . . . John immeasurably advanced that process, but even he needed correction not only from the synoptics but also by the later church. When the council of Nicaea condemned Arius in 325, it also by implication condemned even John's christology as inadequate in some respects. All elements of subordinationism were now removed.

And thus, more in general:

> We need . . . to admit candidly that it was only from the church's later history that a critique could be thrown back upon scriptural assumptions through a refocused understanding of the full implications of the incarnation . . .[9]

In other words, scripture does not have an absolute normative superiority to later tradition:

> While not denying the right of scripture to critique later elements in the tradition, there is also in my view an equal right of later tradition to critique scripture, and this is what makes it inappropriate to speak of one always acting as the norm for the other. Instead, a dialogue must take place, with now one yielding, now the other.

More generally: there has at times been a 'failure to acknowledge deficiencies within the text itself', deficiencies which led theologians of the past towards acceptance of an allegorical meaning. On the contrary, there is need for 'full and frank acknowledgment of the limitations within the text itself: that the Bible contains that from which we may now legitimately recoil'. The destruction of the Canaanites as described in Joshua, or the ending verse of Ps. 137, should not be taken as allegories of the future defeat of evil. Such allegories

> fortunately considerably lessened the impact of the morality they conceal, but the only sure-fire way of guaranteeing the elimination of such sentiments from Christianity would be proper recognition of the fact that the texts were after all intended literally, and as such significantly fail as acceptable religious expression.

## 7. The 'intertestamental' period

It might be argued that 'the stream [of revelation] seemed to stop once for several centuries with the closure of the Old Testament and so, if once, why not again?'.

Brown answers:

> Here the most obvious reply is that, while such a response might have once seemed plausible (through most of Christian history), modern biblical scholarship has made it quite untenable. As a Christian it is tempting to suppose a natural continuity between the Old Testament and the New, but, if Old Testament scholarship has shown one thing, it is that that continuity is very much weaker than commonly supposed. An excellent illustration . . . is the way in which the attempt which the New Testament writers make to forge the link through Old Testament 'prophecies' has been shown, more often than not, to be creative misreadings rather than anything to do with the original meaning of the passages concerned.

Or, to continue:

> It would nowadays be widely acknowledged that no adequate comprehension of the New Testament is possible without some understanding of what went on in the intertestamental period. That of course does not necessarily make that intervening stream of itself revelatory, but it does mean that it contributes at the very least to the formation of revelation in much the same way as for many a modern Christian great tracts of the Old Testament contribute towards the intelligibility of the New rather than themselves being revelatory.

Thus, to give more concrete examples, 'eschatology (and with it apocalyptic) plays a major role in the New Testament but only a peripheral one in the Old'.

For messianic expectations one would do better to turn to the Qumran writings or the Psalms of Solomon than to the Hebrew Bible; similarly, for 'Son of Man', more can be gained from I Enoch.

Likewise, Wisdom and Sirach 'exercised a marked influence on the christology of the New Testament, particularly in Paul and Matthew'. In the Letter of James, Job is treated as an example of patience, but in the Old Testament Job was anything but patient, 'whereas that description corresponds exactly to what emerges from the intertestamental rewriting, *The Testament of Job*'. James's view of Abraham's sacrifice of Isaac almost certainly reflects the influence of Jubilees. Other examples are added.

The quotation of I Enoch as scripture – it 'prophesied' – cannot just be dismissed as a wild aberration.[10]

> Books like I Enoch and Jubilees were engaged in the task of reinterpreting earlier scripture in a similar way to Chronicles' treatment of Deuteronomy or Deuteronomy's of Exodus. The fact that they sometimes wildly erred does not mean that they could not also sometimes improve upon what they read, just as the later canonical writings are a similar mixture of bettering and worsening.

This has an effect on the question of canon and Apocrypha, which will be taken up in the next section.


## 8. *The Septuagint*

The importance of the LXX as a translation fits in with the above. The place of 'creative misreadings' in the use of passages from the Hebrew Bible has been mentioned. A vivid example follows: the place of the animals in the Christmas story owes its origin 'to reflection on the Old Testament, and to two verses in particular':

> An early verse of Isaiah declares that 'the ox knows its owner, and the ass its master's crib', while Pseudo-Matthew helped mediate the Septuagint's mistranslation of a verse from Habakkuk: 'you will be made known in the midst of two animals'.[11]

'Creative mistranslation' is mentioned again later. An important example is mentioned in a discussion of Isaac taken as a type of Christ, which was certainly a common interpretation in later Christianity. Brown writes:

> The degree to which the connection is already made in the New Testament is a matter of some dispute. Paul's talk of a God 'who did not spare his own Son'

might be an allusion, but if so it is surprising that he does not take advantage to give added force to the comparison through any use of the Septuagint description of Isaac as the 'beloved' son.[12] Similarly, even where this phrase is used – in the baptismal narrative – one observes that Luke took it as a reference to Psalm 2 and not Genesis 22. So the development of the comparison may be much more strongly post-biblical than is often assumed:

Following these values appreciated in the Septuagint, Brown sympathizes with the publication of Bibles containing the Apocrypha, which he describes as 'the restoration of former Protestant practice'. He rightly thinks, however, that for any real revision of the canon 'the possibility of ever achieving consensus on the matter may well be past'. What he asks for is 'a more sympathetic consideration of this intertestamental literature, whether or not it finally achieved canonical status':

> If the Greek additions to the book of Esther make it a more profound book which at least secures a reference to God within its pages, or the alternative title for Sirach – Ecclesiasticus ('The Book of the Church') – indicates how much more spiritually rewarding it is than the canonical book of Proverbs, there is surely nothing to be lost in going further and conceding the presence of insights in the intertestamental literature that on occasion advance upon the canonical text. Indeed, such a conclusion would seem forced upon the Christian, where those insights appear to have decisively shaped similar perspectives within the New Testament itself.

## 9. Historical criticism

To Professor Brown the historical-critical approach seems not to constitute a major problem or a source of concern for theology. He does indeed note that within biblical studies confidence has declined 'as apparently assured results have come under attack', and cites as examples 'changing attitudes to source hypotheses for the Pentateuch or the existence of Q in gospel criticism'. In particular, he recognizes 'that such studies seem to be doing little to advance appreciation of the value of scripture, as scholarly consensus and use in church grew ever wider apart'.

Nevertheless his own approach seems to have a considerable kinship with the historical-critical one: not so much in any attempt at positive identification of sources, dates or authorships, but rather in his own strong emphasis on 'the historical situatedness of the text' (cf. above, 587) and on the rewriting of earlier scripture by later biblical writers (as also by post-biblical traditions). Thus:

The reason why narratives retain their power in different circumstances is because readers either give new prominence to hitherto neglected aspects of the text or because they resolve to tell the story in a new way . . . This indicates the need to see narrative in a continuing process of re-presentation, as also to examine why this should be so. If the division of the Pentateuch between J, E, D, and P has become less fashionable in recent years, even without any delving beneath the biblical text there remains for all to see an example like Chronicles' rewriting of Kings. Equally, in the New Testament we have the alterations made by Matthew and Luke to Mark, and John's radical rewriting, whether or not in conscious awareness of the details of the narratives of the other evangelists.

Thus, unlike some other modern scholars, Brown's strong emphasis on the *later interpretation* of texts does not mean that interest in *the original* can be ignored or regarded with contempt. Thus:

Some parts of the Old Testament assume the existence of other gods, just as in at least one passage the actual existence of the great sea-monster Leviathan appears to be accepted. Though these are, I think, the natural reading of the author's intention, the gods can without much difficulty be reinterpreted as a council of angels, just as Leviathan can become purely a mythical symbol for the future, complete victory of God. But something is lost in our understanding of the history of the tradition, if we simply assume the later reading and do not acknowledge the pressures that led to it. To give a rather different example, so prominent is modern Liberation theology's exegesis of the Exodus as an act of divine liberation that it is very easy to conceal from ourselves that the focus of the original authors was significantly different. For, while the Israelites groaning under bondage may be the occasion of God hearing them, he responds because 'God remembered his covenant with Abraham, with Isaac and with Jacob' (Ex. 2.24). In other words, the primary reason is not compassion at all but because God has a nation to establish, and that is presumably why the final redactors of the Pentateuch found no incongruity in retaining an earlier account of a Hebrew mother (Sarah) abusing an Egyptian slave (Hagar) with God's full and explicit endorsement.

Once we are talking about 'earlier accounts' and 'original authors' we are remaining within some kind of 'historical-critical paradigm', as the ghastly jargon of our time expresses it. And this is not occasional, but happens repeatedly in Brown's work. The historical development of tradition *after* biblical times makes sense because it fits in with a similar development that is discernible *within* biblical times. In view of this it seems that Brown is expressing his own general position when he says that, apart from tradition, 'the other three major resources for Christian reflection have all been transformed – the Bible through the critical method' (the other two are reason and experience: readers can look up the rest of the passage for themselves). Amid these transformations, Brown goes on, 'tradition has remained largely out in the cold'. But it can be argued that it was biblical criticism, more than any other influence, that established the recognition of tradition as central to the Bible;[13] or, if it has not done so, then Brown's own presentation is likely to make it more so. In the older discussions, tradition was very often that which *followed* the Bible, not what took place within it.

Another good example appears in a discussion of the universalism or otherwise of the blessing to Abraham. Brown notes again that source criticism is under attack, but he begins with it and shows how the story could have been understood in one way under J, writing perhaps under David or Solomon, how it would have had a different purpose under E ('perhaps in the eighth century in the northern kingdom'), and again otherwise later under P ('in post-exilic times'). Though source criticism is now less popular, very similar conclusions 'seem forced upon us even if we confine our attentions to the internal logic of the Genesis narrative as a whole'. So the source-critical approach may be subject to doubt, but it does not matter so very much, since a similar interpretative result can be reached without it.

Certainly Brown, if quite properly reserved towards historical criticism, is also critical towards some of the modern alternatives that have been offered. Thus he discusses Karl Barth, who asserts 'that he has nothing whatever to say against historical criticism' but goes on to contrast modern scholars unfavourably with Calvin, who, in the famous phrase, 'wrestles' with the text 'till the walls which separate the sixteenth century from the first become transparent'. Brown objects:

> But the problem is whether a meaning for today can be extracted that simply through close attention to the words; whether in attempting thus to bypass historical criticism Barth does not in fact distort the range of meanings which can be derived from the biblical text and thus how it may best be appropriated for today. Thus, suppose that scholars such as Stendahl and Sanders are right that the real thrust of this epistle for Paul was other than justification by faith,[14] do we not need some argument from Barth or his successors that the way in which the Reformation appropriated the epistle to such a view was a legitimate development? In other words, my point is not that Barth's readings of scripture are necessarily wrong or unhelpful, but that we need some justification of how the church came to read the text in a rather different way, and that would seem to raise acutely the whole question of tradition.

Brown goes on to complain that Barth 'offers us only a brief, dismissive reference to tradition'.

Brown also discusses other interpretative methods that differ from the historical-critical, e.g. those of Ricoeur. I shall not enter into these, except to quote one judgment on Gadamer, who like Brown places a strong emphasis on tradition:[15]

> Gadamer fails to acknowledge how often it is that what we most need is release from our 'prejudices', not their reinforcement. As the history of Christianity well illustrates, even tradition itself needs first to be undermined before it can acquire a capacity for further development.

## *10. Canonical interpretations*

Brown is aware of the recent movement towards canonical approaches. It would seem, *in part*, to fit in with his own emphasis on the later rewriting of an older text. Thus 'no biblical scholar could now possibly deny how deeply a developing tradition has helped shape the thinking of the biblical writers', and, in a footnote shortly after, he cites, quoting Childs, 'how the addition of Amos 9 transforms the unrelieved stress on judgment and doom in the original prophet's message'. Yet only in part does this fit with the canonical approach, for its emphasis is not on development, but on finality.

Again, we could expect Brown to sympathize with the emphasis of the canonical approach on the later *reception* of biblical texts and to support Childs' interest in the history of exegesis. But here again there is a sharp contrast. For Childs, however valuable the later exegesis may be, it is the canonical form that for ever remains the norm; Brown's idea that the later exegesis could be new revelation, possibly transcending or even reversing the sense of the biblical form (whether pre-canonical or finally canonical), would surely be impossible for Childs.

In an important passage Brown expresses his purpose 'to identify some of the triggers that have led to changes in social perception'. Huge transformations have taken place, 'for instance within the Old Testament in respect of the importance of law, personal responsibility and the after-life, or in the New on the status of Christ or expectation of the end'. Not all such developments have to be seen as positive:

> But, if historical fact is not the only form of truth, there is no reason in principle why they could not be, and charity would seem to demand that we at least take seriously the motives under which such changes have been wrought. Moreover, if all thought is conditioned, it would seem inevitable

that certain issues will not have been faced adequately by the scriptural writers. That being so, it would seem scarcely credible that the last significant change that required a fresh imaginative application of the tradition occurred in the first century of our era . . . This is why the Yale approach seems to me so inadequate, with Childs in effect suggesting that the canonical text already has all the necessary checks and balances for subsequent reflection, or Hans Frei that the existing, unaltered narrative has the power in itself to shape the life of the Christian in any age.

To sum up, 'The written text is not the final control'. 'Christian self-reflection operates with a considerably less static canon than is commonly assumed.' Revelation is 'a process that continues well beyond the closure of the canon'.

## 11. *The historical Jesus*

No reader of Brown's work could doubt that he writes from within a traditional Christian, trinitarian and incarnational, standpoint. It is therefore all the more significant that he makes serious use of a picture of Jesus as he historically was, a picture that differs in important ways from many traditional Christian views.

> Modern biblical scholarship has forced upon us a very different understanding of the nature of the incarnation from that which prevailed through most of Christianity's history.[16] Gone is the incarnate lord who remained transcendent to the ambiguities of history and in his place has come someone so thoroughly shaped by the social setting in which he found himself that in retrospect we must declare some at least of his beliefs false. It is not just a matter of easily containable error such as the three-decker universe or the authorship of the Pentateuch and Psalms but also some beliefs which helped profoundly to shape the very substance of his message. Probably he thought that the end of the world was imminent, and as a corollary he may well have died disappointed or in despair. Perhaps also he presumed continuing obedience to Jewish law. Most significantly of all, he had no consciousness of his own divinity. Such admissions are often thought to carry with them the automatic demise of orthodox Christian belief. But . . . it will be my contention that, so far from this being so, such discoveries can instead be very effectively employed towards the actual strengthening of incarnational doctrine.

It is implied, I think, that the older arguments about the historical Jesus were intended to disprove Christian beliefs about him, to make him, put simply, an ordinary human with a religious genius; but it was a mistake when theologians leapt to the opposite conclusion and thought it necessary to claim that nothing whatever could or should be said about the historical Jesus, and that absolutely nothing should be attempted that would get us behind the canonical text. Certainly historical study does not have absolute objectivity, but some degree of relative objectivity is both possible and necessary, as Brown has pointed out. And in any case, he argues, the study of the historical Jesus is not at all a threat to incarnational belief but actually an enhancement of it.

## 12. Natural theology

I have not noticed the actual term 'natural theology' within the pages of Professor Brown's book, and that may be an advantage because of the sense of many scholars that the expression is a bad one for what is meant. But I have quoted a number of passages which suggest a sympathy towards what has usually gone under this name. As we saw, he holds that 'the history of the formulation of Christian doctrine is a history of sustained indebtedness to Greek thought', and this would be likely to include the influences of Greek philosophy which have commonly been taken to be basic to natural theology.

Moreover, Brown extends this 'indebtedness' back into scripture itself and its relation to the surrounding cultures, which is just what I myself have argued, and for the Hebrew Bible as well as for the New Testament. With his theologically positive evaluation of ancient Greek *myths* and *religion*, Brown goes even farther in this direction than most supporters of natural theology have thought to go. Any kind of interreligiosity in texts or in practices, as we have seen, brings us near to something like natural theology. And finally, with his emphasis on *tradition*, one may expect that Brown would see the tradition of natural theology as part of the total Jewish and Christian tradition and therefore as a positive element. Not that everything that has gone under the name of natural theology has been right: it certainly has not. But with its ups and its downs it has been part of the tradition; the breakers of the tradition have also often been the deniers of natural theology.

## 13. Biblical theology?

As I have said, Brown appears not to use the term 'biblical theology' and not to see the concept as a necessary one for his work, so far at any rate. And it is not difficult to see why. For revelation, as he sees it, though unquestionably first accessible through the Bible, continues through all tradition thereafter, up to the present day, and, while the Bible can be a sort of 'norm' against which later tradition is to be evaluated, later tradition can also provide norms against which aspects of the Bible can be evaluated. In this sense it would appear that a theology of the Old Testament, or of the New, or of the total Christian Bible, would be a theology of one stage, or a group of stages, in the total tradition. A theology of one stage, e.g. the Hebrew Bible, would not be – so far as I can see – more important or more essential than a theology of a sub-stage, e.g. a theology of Deuteronomy or a theology of the period of the return from exile. There might be some advantage in summarizing a longer period, but there might be some loss through failure to bring in the smaller details, such as a study of a shorter period or a smaller set of texts would provide.

The essential difference would be that many views of biblical theology have expressed or implied that the one great block of the Bible corresponds to the one total process of revelation; and that a theology of the Bible would thereby furnish the one supreme norm, in so far as any written document can do so. It would no longer be just this one text or that other text – which even historical criticism might be able to handle; it would be a statement of the total impact of the entirety.

Here in particular Professor Brown's argument seems to go in the opposite direction. A decisive discussion arises when he comes to deal with the iconoclastic controversy – a subject very relevant for one to whom religious art is so important. He tells us:

> Now that the Reformation arguments about the destruction of images in churches are for most of us firmly in the past it is very easy to lose sight of how uncompromising the biblical attitude in fact is . . . The sculpting of images is condemned unequivocally . . . this generated much anxiety in the later middle ages . . . The truth, in my view, is that, if we rely on the general thrust of scripture alone, the iconoclasts were right.

The New Testament, he goes on, provides no qualification in this respect to attitudes based on the Hebrew Bible and Judaism.

> We need therefore, in my view, to admit candidly that it was only from the church's later history that a critique could be thrown back upon scriptural assumptions through a refocused understanding of the full implications of the incarnation . . . For a proper assessment of human creativity we must go beyond scripture. *The letter of scripture misleads; so does its general thrust* [my italics, J.B.]. Only by contemplating God's sketch or portrayal of himself in the incarnation, as did later Christianity both explicitly and implicitly, can we arrive at the truth. Continuing revelation has now taken us well beyond the canon of scripture.

Not only the letter of scripture, but also its general thrust, misleads! A serious challenge, surely, to the holistic ethos of much biblical theology. And a reason, perhaps, why doctrinal theologians have, as I have argued, been less desirous of biblical theology than biblical theologians have expected them to be.

Nevertheless I believe one can see how a theology of the Hebrew Bible could well fit into a general scheme such as Brown provides and supplement it usefully. In his book, the Old Testament, broadly speaking, functions mainly as the starting-point: its narratives and images provide the first stage of material, upon which the later development of tradition is built. An Old Testament theology would go back more into the earlier network of stories, concepts, assumptions and conflicts which underlie the production of what eventually became the text itself. This, one might hope, would further enrich the already many-coloured picture of tradition which Brown has provided for us.

## *14. Conclusion*

I think that David Brown's work is quite magnificent, but it is not my purpose to evaluate it as a whole; indeed, I could not do so, partly because, as already stated, I have not seen one half of a work that has yet to be published, and partly because, as I am well aware, I have concentrated on those aspects which are most central to the themes and problems of my own present work. I have deeply appreciated large areas of his discussion, especially in the field of Christian art and later literature, but have left them aside for the present purpose. My purpose has been to show that among the various current approaches within Christian doctrinal theology there are options which offer space and concepts for the sort of directions in biblical theology that emerge from my own discussion above. For this purpose Brown's work has been an ideal example. I do not say that biblical theology *must* ally itself with an approach like his; I do suggest that it should see in it a possibility for its own development. It remains possible that biblical theologians will wish to keep free from any sort of alliance with doctrinal theology of any kind; I only suggest that in doing so they might first of all make themselves aware of what this line of theological thinking, closely interlinked with biblical exegesis, actually provides. And from its distinctly Christian position, its understanding approach towards Judaism (and Islam) and to Greek religion (and thus in principle to the history of religion) ought to be significant, even if only as a pointer in a direction along which one may go.

Undoubtedly many biblical theologians will find difficulties in Brown's line of thinking. Some will want to keep their work entirely distinct from doctrinal theology; more will find the emphasis on tradition too great to be acceptable.

Partly from their position as biblical scholars, and partly from their own theological traditions, they will want the Bible to be the supreme norm, one superior to tradition, however highly one recognizes the force of the latter. They will ask how an approach so deeply founded in tradition makes room for those who, while belonging to the same tradition, have broken with tradition, or denied its force, or understood it in some quite other way. I am sure that these questions can be answered, but it is not immediately obvious how it can be done.

# 35

# Conclusion

I began by noting that the concept of biblical theology is a *contested* concept, and this is likely to remain so; it is not to be expected that this book will have settled all the questions. But I can perhaps summarize some areas in which progress may have been made, and note others in which questions will have to be put in a different way in the future.

Perhaps the clearest transformation deriving from recent discussion is the return of the history of religion to centrality through the work of Rainer Albertz. Contrary to the total discounting of the history of religion by some Old Testament theologians, it is Old Testament theology that is now very much on the defence, its clothes having been entirely stolen by the opposing party. Even the theological arguments used in the past on behalf of Old Testament theology have been turned against it. In spite of this it remains likely, however, that Old Testament theology will survive and continue. But it will have to accept an over-lap with the history of religion. Just how this will be defined will have to be discussed. Certain uses of evidence and certain types of argument will have to be changed. But the idea of a strict separation between religion and theology must be completely abandoned. Such a separation, it should be remembered, was never maintained by what Brueggemann calls 'church theology': it was never more than a personal or partisan opinion. Since this separation is an obstacle to our work on the Bible, doctrinal theology also should consider abandoning it, in so far as it is still upheld.

The 'canonical' movement, in so far as it aims at a theology of the Old Testament, is of great interest but is likely to split up in several ways. That its arguments, and its gains, in Childs' form of it were literary rather than theological was noted at an early stage by John Barton.[1] Theologically, it is likely to split up because the theologies of leading figures like Childs and Rendtorff are massively contradictory with one another, as far can be told at the present time. Internally, it is likely to split up, because the various senses of 'canon' in Childs' work lead in different directions. 'Final-form exegesis', for instance, can be carried out without any commitment to a 'canonical' sort of theology, and will often turn out to be nothing more than a variant of historical criticism, done with the eyes looking in the other direction. I have done many examples of it myself: for instance, one showing how the two creation narratives of Genesis 1

# Abbreviations

| | |
|---|---|
| *ArPh* | *Archives de Philosophie* |
| *ATR* | *Anglican Theological Review* |
| *AUSS* | *Andrews University Seminary Studies* |
| *BJR(U)L* | *Bulletin of the John Rylands (University) Library* |
| BWANT | Beiträge zur Wissenschaft vom Alten und Neuen Testament |
| *CBQ* | *Catholic Biblical Quarterly* |
| CD | Covenant of Damascus |
| *CD* | *Church Dogmatics* (Karl Barth) |
| *CJT* | *Canadian Journal of Theology* |
| CTSA | Catholic Theological Society of America |
| *DBI* | *Dictionary of Biblical Interpretation* |
| *EKL* | *Evangelisches Kirchenlexicon* |
| ET | English Translation |
| *ExpT* | *Expository Times* |
| *ETR* | *Etudes théologiques et religieuses* |
| *EvTh* | *Evangelische Theologie* |
| FS | Festschrift |
| *HBT* | *Horizons in Biblical Theology* |
| *HTR* | *Harvard Theological Review* |
| ICC | International Critical Commentary |
| *IDB* | *Interpreter's Dictionary of the Bible* |
| *JAAR* | *Journal of the American Academy of Religion* |
| *JBL* | *Journal of Biblical Literature* |
| *JBR* | *Journal of Bible and Religion* |
| *JBTh* | *Jahrbuch für Biblische Theologie* |
| *JJS* | *Journal of Jewish Studies* |
| *JQR* | *Jewish Quarterly Review* |
| *JR* | *Journal of Religion* |
| *JSOT* | *Journal for the Study of the Old Testament* |
| *JSS* | *Journal of Semitic Studies* |
| *JTS* | *Journal of Theological Studies* |
| *KuD* | *Kerygma und Dogma* |
| LSJ | Liddell-Scott-Jones, *Greek-English Lexicon* |
| MT | Masoretic Text |
| *NTS* | *New Testament Studies* |
| *NZSTh* | *Neue Zeitschrift für Systematische Theologie* |
| OBO | Orbis Biblicus et Orientalis |

| | |
|---|---|
| *OTE* | *Old Testament Essays* |
| *OTS* | *Oudtestamentische Studiën* |
| *OTTCC* | *Old Testament Theology in a Canonical Context* (Childs) |
| *PSB* | *Princeton Seminary Bulletin* |
| *RHPR* | *Revue d'histoire et de philosophie religieuses* |
| *RS* | *Religious Studies* |
| *RSPT* | *Revue des sciences philosophiques et théologiques* |
| *RSR* | *Religious Studies Review* |
| *RThPh* | *Revue de Théologie et de Philosophie* |
| *SEÅ* | *Svensk Exegetisk Årsbok* |
| *SJOT* | *Scandinavian Journal of the Old Testament* |
| *SJT* | *Scottish Journal of Theology* |
| SOTS | Society for Old Testament Study |
| *TDOT* | *Theological Dictionary of the Old Testament* |
| *THAT* | *Theologisches Handwörterbuch zum Alten Testament* |
| ThB | Theologische Bücherei |
| ThExH | Theologische Existenz heute |
| *ThPr* | *Theologia Practica* |
| *ThR* | *Theologische Rundschau* |
| *ThZ* | *Theologische Zeitschrift* |
| *TLZ* | *Theologische Literaturzeitung* |
| *TRE* | *Theologische Realenzyklopädie* |
| TSF | Theological Students Fellowship |
| *USQR* | *Union Seminary Quarterly Review* |
| *VT* | *Vetus Testamentum* |
| *VTS* | *Vetus Testamentum Supplements* |
| *VuF* | *Verkündigung und Forschung* |
| WMANT | Wissenschaftliche Monographien zum Alten und Neuen Testament |
| *ZAW* | *Zeitschrift für die alttestamentliche Wissenschaft* |
| *ZTK* | *Zeitschrift für Theologie und Kirche* |

# Bibliography

Abraham, W.J., *Canon and Criterion in Christian Theology* , Oxford: Clarendon Press 1998

Ackerman, R., *J. G. Frazer. His Life and Work*, Cambridge: Cambridge University Press 1987

Albertz, R., *Persönliche Frömmigkeit und offizielle Religion. Religionsinterner Pluralismus in Israel und Babylon*, Stuttgart: Calwer Verlag 1978

——, 'Die Stammesreligionen', in *Fides pro mundi vita. H. W. Gensichen FS*, Gütersloh 1980, 159–64

——, 'Interreligiöses Dialog und die "Stammesreligionen"', *NZSTh* 23, 1981, 225–37

——, *A History of Israelite Religion in the Old Testament Period* (2 vols), London: SCM Press and Minneapolis: Fortress Press 1994, ET of *Religionsgeschichte Israels in alttestamentlicher Zeit* (2 vols), Göttingen: Vandenhoeck & Ruprecht 1992

——, 'Religionsgeschichte Israels statt Theologie des Alten Testaments! Plädoyer für eine forschungsgeschichtliche Umorientierung', *JBTh* 10, 1995, 3–24

——, 'Hat die Theologie des Alten Testaments doch noch eine Chance? Abschliessende Stellungnahme in Leuven', *JBTh* 10, 1995, 177–88

——, Müller, H.-P., Wolff, H. W. and Zimmerli, W., *Werden und Wirken des Alten Testaments. Westermann FS*, Göttingen: Vandenhoeck & Ruprecht 1980

Albrektson, B., *History and the Gods*, Lund: Gleerup 1967

Albright, W. F., 'Return to Biblical Theology', *The Christian Century*, 19 November 1958, 1328–31; reprinted in his *History, Archaeology and Christian Humanism*, 287–300

——, *From the Stone Age to Christianity: Monotheism and the Historical Process*, Baltimore: Johns Hopkins Press 1940; paperback, New York: Doubleday 1957

——, *History, Archaeology and Christian Humanism*, New York: McGraw-Hill 1964

——, *Yahweh and the Gods of Canaan*, London: Athlone Press 1968

Amir, Y., 'Die Begegnung des biblischen und des philosophischen Monotheismus als Grundthema des jüdischen Hellenismus', *EvTh* 38, 1978, 2–19

——, 'Der jüdische Eingottglaube als Stein des Anstosses in der hellenistisch-römischen Welt', *JBTh* 2, 1987, 58–75

——, 'Die "Mitte der Schrift" aus der Sicht des Hellenistischen Judentums', in M. Klopfenstein et al. (eds), *Mitte der Schrift?*, 217–36

Amsler, Samuel, 'La Politique d'édition des Sociétés bibliques au XIX$^e$ siècle et le canon de l'Ancien Testament', in Kaestli and Wermelinger, *Le Canon de l'Ancien Testament*, 313–38

Anderson, A. A., 'Old Testament Theology and its Methods', in *Promise and Fulfilment. Hooke FS*, Edinburgh: T. & T. Clark 1963, 7–19

Anderson, B. W. (ed.), *The Old Testament and Christian Faith. A Theological Discussion*, New York: Harper & Row and London: SCM Press 1963

——, Response to M. Tsevat, 'Theology of the Old Testament – A Jewish View', *HBT* 8, 1986, 1–59

Anderson, G. W. (ed.), *Tradition and Interpretation*, Oxford: Clarendon Press 1979

Angus, Samuel, *The Mystery Religions and Christianity*, New York: Scribner 1928, reissued New York: Dover Publications 1975

Armstrong, A. Hilary, 'Karl Barth, the Fathers of the Church, and "Natural Theology"', *JTS* 46, 1995, 191–5

Assmann, Jan, *Re und Amun. Die Krise des polytheistischen Weltbilds im Ägypten der 18.–20. Dynastie*, OBO 51, Freiburg: Universitätsverlag 1983

—, 'Arbeit am Polytheismus. Die Idee der Einheit Gottes und die Entfaltung des theologischen Diskurses in Ägypten', in H. von Stietencron (ed.), *Theologen und Theologie in verschiedenen Kulturkreisen*, Düsseldorf: Patmos Verlag 1986, 46–69

—, *Moses the Egyptian*, Cambridge, Mass.: Harvard University Press 1997

Auld, A. Graeme, 'Can a Biblical Theology also be Academic or Ecumenical?', in R. P. Carroll (ed.), *Text as Pretext. Essays in Honour of Robert Davidson*, Sheffield: JSOT Supplement Series 138, 1992, 13–27


Baillie, D. M., *Faith in God and its Christian Consummation*, Edinburgh: T. & T. Clark 1927

Baker, D. L., *Two Testaments, One Bible*, London: Inter-Varsity Press 1976

Balentine, S. E., *The Hidden God. The Hiding of the Face of God in the Old Testament*, Oxford: Clarendon Press 1983

—, 'Prayer in the Wilderness Traditions', *Hebrew Union College Annual Review* 9, 1985, 53–74

—, 'The Prophet as Intercessor: A Reassessment', *JBL* 103/2, 1984, 161–73

Balentine, S. E., *Prayer in the Hebrew Bible*, Minneapolis: Fortress Press 1993

—, and Barton, J., *Language, Theology and the Bible. Essays in Honour of James Barr*, Oxford: Clarendon Press 1994

Balla, P., 'Does the Separation of History and Theology destroy New Testament Theology? Räisänen's Challenge', in P. Balla (ed.), *Teacher, Scholar, Friend. John O'Neill FS*, Budapest: Faculty of Theology of the Károli Gáspár Reformed University 1996, 87–100

Barnes, Jonathan, *Aristotle*, Oxford: Oxford University Press 1982

Barr, J., 'The Problem of Old Testament Theology and the History of Religion', *CJT* 3, 1957, 141–9

—, review of H. H. Rowley, *The Faith of Israel*, in *JSS* 2, 1957, 397–9

—, 'The Problem of Israelite Monotheism', *Transactions of the Glasgow University Oriental Society* 17, 1957–8, 52–62

—, 'The Meaning of "Mythology" in relation to the Old Testament', *VT* 9, 1959, 1–10

—, 'Theophany and Anthropomorphism in the Old Testament', *VTS* 7 (Oxford Congress Volume), 1960, 31–8

—, *The Semantics of Biblical Language*, London: Oxford University Press 1961

—, *Biblical Words for Time*, London: SCM Press 1962

—, 'Recent Biblical Theologies: VI. G. von Rad's *Theologie des Alten Testaments*', *ExpT* 73, 1961–62, 142–6

—, 'Hypostatization of Linguistic Phenomena in Modern Theological Interpretation', *JSS* 7, 1962, 85–94

—, 'Revelation through History in the Old Testament and in Modern Theology', *Interpretation* 17, 1963, 193–205; also (with slight differences in text) in *Princeton Seminary Bulletin* 56, 1963, 4–14, and in *New Theology*, no. 1, ed. M. E. Marty, New York: Macmillan 1964

—,*Old and New in Interpretation*, London: SCM Press and New York: Harper & Row 1966, ²1988

—, 'Den teologiska värdering av den efterbibliska judendomen', *SEÅ* 32, 1967, 69–78

—, 'Judaism – Its Continuity with the Bible', The Seventh Montefiore Memorial Lecture, published by Southampton University 1968

—, 'Le Judaïsme postbiblique et la théologie de l'Ancien Testament', *RThPh* 18, 1968, 209–17

—, 'The Old Testament and the New Crisis of Biblical Authority', *Interpretation* 25, 1971, 24–40

—, 'Man and Nature: The Ecological Controversy and the Old Testament', *BJRL* 55, 1972, 9–32; also in D. and E. Spring (eds.), *Ecology and Religion in History*, New York: Harper 1974, 48–75

—, 'Semantics and Biblical Theology – A Contribution to the Discussion', *VTS* 22 (Uppsala Congress Volume), 1972, 11–19

—, *The Bible in the Modern World*, London: SCM Press and New York: Harper & Row 1973

—, 'Reading the Bible as Literature', *BJRL* 56, 1973, 10–33

—, Review of Hasel, *Old Testament Theology*, and of Harrington, *The Path of Biblical Theology*, in *JTS* 25, 1974, 182–6

—, 'Some Old Testament Aspects of Berkhof's *Christelijk Geloof*', in *Weerwoord: Reacties op Dr H. Berkhof's Christelijk Geloof*, Nijkerk, Netherlands 1974, 9–19

—, 'Trends and Prospects in Biblical Theology', *JTS* 25, 1974, 265–82

—, 'Story and History in Biblical Theology' (Third Nuveen Lecture, University of Chicago), *JR* 56, 1976, 1–17

—, 'Biblical Theology', 'Revelation in History', and 'Scripture, Authority of', in *IDB Supplement Volume*, Nashville: Abingdon Press 1976, 104–11, 746–9, 794–7

—, Review of G.J. Botterweck and H. Ringgren, *Theological Dictionary of the Old Testament* 1, Grand Rapids: Eerdmans 1974, *Interpretation* 30, 1976, 186–90

—, 'Some Semantic Notes on the Covenant', *Beiträge zur alttestamentlichen Theologie. Zimmerli FS*, Göttingen: Vandenhoeck & Ruprecht 1977, 23–38

—, *Does Biblical Study still belong to Theology?*, Inaugural Lecture at Oxford, 26 May 1977, Oxford: Clarendon Press 1978

—, 'The Language of Religion', in L. Honko (ed.), *Science of Religion: Studies in Methodology, Proceedings of the Study Conference of the International Association for the History of Religions, Turku, Finland, 1973*, The Hague: Mouton 1979, 429–41, with reports on the following discussion, 458–83

—, Review of D.H. Kelsey, *The Uses of Scripture in Recent Theology*, Fortress Press and SCM Press 1979, in *Virginia Seminary Journal*, 30.3 and 31.1, November 1978 and March 1979 (one number), 39f.

—, Introduction to British edition of P. Stuhlmacher, *Historical Criticism and Theological Interpretation of Scripture*, London: SPCK 1979, 9–12

—, Review article of B.S. Childs, *Introduction to the Old Testament as Scripture*, in *JSOT* 16, 1980, 12–23

—, *Explorations in Theology* 7: *The Scope and Authority of the Bible*, London: SCM Press 1980; American title *The Scope and Authority of the Bible*, Philadelphia: Westminster Press 1980, containing three articles already listed above, viz. 'Story and History in Biblical Theology', 'Does Biblical Study still belong to Theology?' and 'The Bible as a Political Document', plus the four which immediately follow:

—, 'Historical Reading and the Theological Interpretation of Scripture'

—, 'Has the Bible any Authority?'

—, 'The Problem of Fundamentalism Today'

—, 'The Bible as a Document of Believing Communities'

—, 'Some Thoughts on Narrative, Myth and Incarnation', in A.E. Harvey (ed.)., *God Incarnate: Story and Belief*, London: SPCK 1981, 14–23

—, Review of Paul Ricoeur, *Essays on Biblical Interpretation*, in *Theology* 84, November 1981, 462–4

—, Review of B.L. Hebblethwaite, *The Problems of Theology*, in *New Blackfriars* 63, no. 740, February 1982, 91–2

—, Review of Patrick Henry, *New Directions in New Testament Study*, in *Virginia Seminary Journal*, April 1982, Vol. 34 no. 1, 69–70

—, Review of William J. Abraham, *Divine Revelation and the Limits of Historical Criticism*, in *The Times Literary Supplement*, 24 December 1982, 1422f.

—, 'Bibelkritik als theologische Aufklärung', in Trutz Rendtorff (ed.), *Glaube und Toleranz. Das theologische Erbe der Aufklärung*, Gütersloh: Gerd Mohn 1982, 30–42

—, 'Jowett and the "Original Meaning" of Scripture', *Religious Studies* 18, 1982, 433–7

—, *Holy Scripture: Canon, Authority, Criticism*, Oxford: Clarendon Press and Philadelphia: Westminster Press 1983

—, 'Jowett and the Reading of the Bible "like any other book"', *HBT* 4/2–5/1, 1983, 1–44

—, 'Hebraic Psychology', in Rom Harré and R. Lamb (eds), *The Encyclopedic Dictionary of Psychology*, Oxford: Blackwell 1983, 266–7

—, 'Allegory and Typology', in Alan Richardson and John Bowden (eds), *A New Dictionary of Christian Theology*, London: SCM Press 1983, 11–15; also article 'Semantics', 535–6, reprinted unchanged except for new bibliography from Alan Richardson (ed.), *A Dictionary of Christian Theology*, London: SCM Press 1969, 311–12

—, Review of W.J. Abraham, *The Inspiration of Scripture*, in *JTS* 34, April 1983, 370–6

—, Review of W.J. Abraham, *Divine Revelation and the Limits of Historical Criticism*, in *SJT* 36, 1983, 247–50

—, *Escaping from Fundamentalism*, London: SCM Press 1984 (US title *Beyond Fundamentalism*, Philadelphia: Westminster Press 1984)

—, 'Biblical Language and Exegesis – How far does Structuralism help us?', *King's Theological Review* 7, 1984, 48–52

—, Review of R.E. Brown, *The Critical Meaning of the Bible*, in *JTS* 35, 1984, 146ff.

—, Review of J. Muddiman, *The Bible: Fountain and Well of Truth*, in *Theology* 87, 1984, 58f.

—, 'Paul and the LXX: A Note on Recent Work', *JTS* 45, 1994, 593–601

—, 'Why the World was created in 4004 BC: Archbishop Ussher and Biblical Chronology', *BJRUL* 67, 1985, 575–608

—, 'The Question of Religious Influence: The Case of Zoroastrianism, Judaism and Christianity', *JAAR* 53/2, 1985, 201–35

—, 'Anthropomorphism', 'Monotheism' and 'Polytheism', in *Harper's Bible Dictionary*, San Francisco: Harper & Row 1985, 32, 652, 806f.

—, 'Biblische Theologie', in *Evangelisches Kirchenlexikon*, Göttingen: Vandenhoeck & Ruprecht, Vol. 1, 1985, cols. 488–94

—, 'Exegesis as a Theological Discipline Reconsidered – and the Shadow of the Jesus of History', in Donald G. Miller (ed.), *The Hermeneutical Quest: Essays in Honor of James Luther Mays on his Sixty-fifth Birthday*, Allison Park, Pennsylvania: Pickwick

Publications, 1986, 11–45

—, Review of John Barton, *Reading the Old Testament*, in *JTS* 37, 1986, 462–5

—, *Biblical Chronology: Legend or Science?*, Ethel M. Wood Lecture, London: Athlone Press 1987

—, 'Words for Love in Biblical Greek', in L. D. Hurst and N. T. Wright (eds.), *The Glory of Christ in the New Testament. G. B. Caird FS*, Oxford: Clarendon Press 1987, 3–18

—, 'Delitzsch, Friedrich', in *Encyclopaedia of Religion*, New York: Macmillan 1987, 4, 276–7

—, Review of R. Lauha, *Psychophysischer Sprachgebrauch im Alten Testament*, in *JTS* 38, 1987, 459

—, 'The Authority of Scripture: The Book of Genesis and the Origin of Evil in Jewish and Christian Tradition', in *Christian Authority: Essays in Honour of Henry Chadwick*, Oxford: Oxford University Press 1988, 59–75

—, 'The Bible and its Communities', in *Harper's Bible Commentary*, San Francisco: Harper and Row 1988, 65–72

—, 'The Theological Case against Biblical Theology', in G. M. Tucker, D. L. Petersen and Wilson (eds), *Canon, Theology and Old Testament Interpretation. Childs FS*, Philadelphia: Fortress Press 1988, 3–19

—, 'Mowinckel, the Old Testament, and the Question of Natural Theology', The Second Mowinckel Lecture, Oslo 1987, *Studia Theologica* 42, 1988, 21–38

—, 'La Foi biblique et la théologie naturelle', *ETR* 64, 1989, 355–68

—, 'Biblical Exegesis and Natural Theology', *Svensk Kyrkotidning* 7–8 (4195–6), 85th year, 17 & 24 February 1989, 85–91 and 101–7

—, 'The Literal, the Allegorical, and Modern Biblical Scholarship', *JSOT* 44, 1989, 3–17

—, 'Biblical Scholarship and the Unity of the Church' , Nineteenth Lecture of the R. T. Orr Visitorship, London, Ontario: Huron College 1989

—, 'Literality', *Faith and Philosophy* 6, 1989, 412–28

—, 'Do We Perceive the Voice of the Heavens?' , in J. C. Knight and L. A. Sinclair (eds.), *The Psalms and Other Studies on the Old Testament Presented to Joseph L. Hunt*, Nashotah House Seminary, Wisconsin 1990, 11–17

– 'Luther and Biblical Chronology', *BJRUL* 72, 1990, 51–67

—, 'Biblical Law and the Question of Natural Theology', in T. Veijola (ed.), *The Law in the Bible and in its Environment*, Publications of the Finnish Exegetical Society 51, 1990, 1–22

—, Review article of Brett, *Biblical Criticism in Crisis?*, in *JTS* 43, 1992, 135–41

—, Notice of Brett, *Biblical Criticism in Crisis?*, in *SOTS Book List 1992*, 101f.

—, *The Garden of Eden and the Hope of Immortality*, London: SCM Press 1992

—, *Biblical Faith and Natural Theology. The Gifford Lectures, Edinburgh 1991*, Oxford: Oxford University Press 1993

—, 'Chronology 1. Israelite Chronology', in B. M. Metzger and M. D. Coogan, *Oxford Companion to the Bible*, New York: Oxford University Press 1993, 117–19

—, 'Scope and Problems in the Semantics of Classical Hebrew', *Zeitschrift für Althebräistik* 6/1, 1993, 3–14

—, Wilhelm Vischer and Allegory', in A. Graeme Auld (ed.), *Understanding Poets and Prophets. G.W.Anderson FS*, Sheffield: JSOT Press 1993, 38–60

—, 'The Synchronic, the Diachronic and the Historical: A Triangular Relationship', in J. C. de Moor (ed.), *Synchronic or Diachronic*, OTS 34, 1995, 1–14

—, 'Schriftbeweis', in *Evangelisches Kirchenlexikon*, Göttingen: Vandenhoeck & Ruprecht, Vol. 4, 1996, cols. 109–13

—, 'Allegory and Historicism', *JSOT* 69, 1996, 105–20

—, 'Ein Mann oder die Menschen? Zur Anthropologie von Genesis I', in H.-P. Mathys (ed.), *Ebenbild Gottes – Herrscher über die Welt*, Neukirchen: Neukirchener Verlag 1998, 75–93

—, 'Biblical Theology as Image World Description', forthcoming in *Ritschl FS*

—, 'Biblical Theology', forthcoming in *The International Encyclopedia of the Church*, Grand Rapids: Eerdmans

Barstad, Hans M., 'The Historical-Critical Method and the Problem of Old Testament Theology. A Few Marginal Remarks', *SEÅ* 45, 1980, 7–18

Barth, Christoph, 'Grundprobleme einer Theologie des Alten Testaments', *EvTh* 23, 1963, 342–72

—, *God With Us. A Theological Introduction to the Old Testament*, Grand Rapids: Eerdmans 1991

Barth, Karl, *The Epistle to the Romans*, Oxford: Oxford University Press 1933

—, *Church Dogmatics*, Edinburgh: T. & T.Clark 1936ff. ( = *CD*)

—, *Protestant Theology in the Nineteenth Century*, London: SCM Press 1979

Barthélemy, D., 'La Place de la Septante dans l'Église', in *Aux grands carrefours de la révélation et de l'exégèse de l'Ancien Testament*, Recherches Bibliques 8, Paris: Desclée de Brouwer 1967, 13–28 = D. Barthélemy, *Études d'histoire du texte de l'ancien Testament*, OBO 21, Fribourg 1978, 111–26

—, 'L'Ancien Testament a mûri à Alexandrie', *ThZ* 21, 1965, 358–70 = D. Barthélemy, *Études d'histoire du texte de l'ancien Testament*, OBO 21, Fribourg 1978, 127–37

Barton, John, 'Natural Law and Poetic Justice in the Old Testament', *JTS* 30, 1979, 1–14

—, *Amos' Oracles against the Nations*, Cambridge: Cambridge University Press 1980

—, 'Ethics in Isaiah of Jerusalem', *JTS* 32, 1981, 1–18

—, 'Old Testament Theology', in J. Rogerson (ed.), *Beginning Old Testament Study*, London: SPCK 1983, 90–112

—, *Reading the Old Testament. Method in Biblical Study*, London: Darton, Longman and Todd 1984

—, 'Classifying Biblical Criticism', *JSOT* 29, 1984, 19–35

—, 'Gerhard von Rad on the World-View of Early Israel', *JTS* 35, 1984, 301–23

—, '"The Law and the Prophets". Who are the Prophets?', *OTS* 23, 1984, 1–18

—, 'Begründungsversuche der prophetischen Unheilsankündigung im Alten Testament', *EvTh* 47, 1987, 427–35

—, *People of the Book?*, London: SPCK 1988

—, 'Should Old Testament Scholarship be More Theological?', *ExpT* 100, 1989, 443–8

—, 'Preparation in History for Christ', in R. Morgan (ed.), *The Religion of the Incarnation*, Bristol: Classical Press 1989, 60–73

—, *The Future of Old Testament Study*, Inaugural Lecture, Oxford: Clarendon Press 1993

—, 'Die Lehre von der rechten Zeit', in *Rechtfertigung und Erfahrung. G. Sauter FS*, Gütersloh: Gütersloher Verlagshaus 1995

—, 'Alttestamentliche Theologie nach Albertz?', *JBTh* 10, 1995, 25–34

—, 'The Basis of Ethics in the Hebrew Bible', in D. A. Knight (ed.), *Ethics and Politics in the Hebrew Bible*, Semeia 66, 1995, 11–22

—, *The Spirit and the Letter*, London: SPCK 1997

—, *Ethics and the Old Testament*, London: SCM Press 1998

—, 'What is a Book? Modern Exegesis and the Literary Conventions of Ancient Israel', in J. C. de Moor (ed.), *Intertextuality in Ugarit and Israel*, OTS 40, 1998, 1–14

—, (ed.), *The Cambridge Companion to Biblical Interpretation*, Cambridge: Cambridge University Press 1998

—, 'The Messiah and Old Testament Theology', in J. Day (ed.), *King and Messiah*, Sheffield (forthcoming)

Bartsch, H. W. (ed.), *Kerygma and Myth*, London: SPCK 1953

Batson, C. D., Beker, J. C., and Clark, W. M., *Commitment without Ideology. The Experience of Christian Growth*, Philadelphia: United Church Press and London: SCM Press 1973

Baxter, Christina A., 'Barth – a Truly Biblical Theologian?', *Tyndale Bulletin* 38, 1987, 3–27

—, 'Barth, Karl', in R. J. Coggins and J. L. Houlden, *A Dictionary of Biblical Interpretation*, London: SCM Press 1990, 77–9

Beker, J. Christiaan, 'Biblical Theology in a Time of Confusion', *Theology Today* 25, 1968–69, 185–94

—, 'Reflections on Biblical Theology', *Interpretation* 24, 1970, 303–20

—, see C. D. Batson, J. C. Beker and W. M. Clark, *Commitment without Ideology*, Philadelphia: United Church Press and London: SCM Press, 1973

—, *Paul the Apostle: The Triumph of God in Life and Thought*, Philadelphia: Fortress Press 1980

Berger, K., 'Zur Kritik der Theorie der impliziten Axiome', in W. Huber, E. Petzold and T. Sundermeier, *Implizite Axiome. Tiefstrukturen des Denkens und Handelns*, Munich: Christian Kaiser Verlag 1990, 229–45

Berkhof, Hendrikus, *Christian Faith*, Grand Rapids: Eerdmans 1979

Betz, H. D., *2 Corinthians 8 and 9*, Hermeneia, Philadelphia: Fortress Press 1985, 102–8

Beyerlin, W. (ed.), *Near Eastern Texts Relating to the Old Testament*, London: SCM Press 1978, ET of *Religionsgeschichtliches Textbuch zum Alten Testament*, Göttingen: Vandenhoeck & Ruprecht 1975

Bjerke, S., 'Ecology of Religion, Evolutionism and Comparative Religion', in L. Honko (ed.), *Science of Religion. Studies in Methodology*, The Hague, Paris and New York: Mouton 1979, 237–48

Bleeker, C. J., 'Comparing the Religio-Historical Method and the Theological Method', *Numen* 18, 1971, 9–29

Blenkinsopp, J., *A Sketchbook of Biblical Theology*, New York: Herder and Herder 1968

—, 'Old Testament Theology and the Jewish-Christian Connection', *JSOT* 28, 1984, 3–15

Bloom, Allan, *The Closing of the American Mind*, New York: Simon and Schuster 1987

Blum, W., Macholz, C., and Stegemann, E. W., *Die Hebräische Bibel und ihre zweifache Nachgeschichte. Rendtorff FS*, Neukirchen: Neukirchener Verlag 1990

Boers, H., *What is New Testament Theology?*, Philadelphia: Fortress Press 1979

Böhme, H. (ed.), *Evolution und Gottesglaube: ein Lese- und Arbeitsbuch zum Gespräch zwischen Naturwissenschaft und Theologie*, Göttingen: Vandenhoeck & Ruprecht 1988

Bono, Edward de, *I am Right – You are Wrong*, New York: Viking Books 1990

Borgen, P., Response to Lindars, 'The Place of the Old Testament in the Formation of New Testament Theology', *NTS* 23, 1976–7, 67–75

Bornkamm, G., 'Gesetz und Natur: Röm 2, 14–16', in *Studien zu Antike und Christentum* II, Munich: Christian Kaiser Verlag 1959

Bourke, Joseph, 'A Survey of Biblical Theology', in *Life of the Spirit* 18, 1963, 51–68

Braaten, Carl E., and Jenson, R. W. (eds.), *Reclaiming the Bible for the Church*, Grand Rapids: Eerdmans 1995

Branton, J. R., Burrows, M., Smart, J. D. and Brown, R. McA., symposium 'Our Present Situation in Biblical Theology', *Religion in Life* 26, 1956–7, 5–39

Braulik, G., Gross, W. and McEvenue, S. (eds.), *Biblische Theologie und gesellschaftlicher Wandel. Lohfink FS*, Freiburg: Herder 1993

Brennemann, J. E., *Canons in Conflict*, New York: Oxford University Press 1997

Brésard, L., Crouzel, H., and Borret, M. (eds), *Origène. Commentaire sur le Cantique des Cantiques*, Sources chrétiennes 375, Paris: Editions du Cerf 1991

Brett, M. G., *Biblical Criticism in Crisis? The Impact of the Canonical Approach on Old Testament Studies*, Cambridge: Cambridge University Press 1991

— (ed.), *Ethnicity and the Bible*, Leiden: Brill 1996

—, 'The Future of Old Testament Theology', forthcoming

Brettler, M. Z., 'Biblical History and Jewish Biblical Theology', *JR* 77, 1997, 563–83

Bright, John, *The Authority of the Old Testament*, Nashville: Abingdon Press and London: SCM Press 1967

Brooke, George J., 'The Qumran Scrolls and Old Testament Theology', in H.T.C.Sun and K. L. Eades, *Problems in Biblical Theology*, Grand Rapids: Eerdmans 1997, 59–75

Brooks, R., and Collins, J. J., *Hebrew Bible or Old Testament?*, Notre Dame, Indiana: University of Notre Dame Press 1990

Brown, David, *Tradition and Imagination*, Oxford: Clarendon Press forthcoming

Brown, R., 'The Sensus Plenior in the Last Ten Years', *CBQ* 25, 1963, 262–85

Bruce, F. F., and Rupp, E. G. (eds), *Holy Book and Holy Tradition*, Manchester: Manchester University Press 1968

Brueggemann, Walter, *In Man We Trust*, Richmond: John Knox Press 1972

—, *Old Testament Theology. Essays on Structure, Themes, and Text*, ed. Patrick D. Miller, Minneapolis: Fortress Press 1992

—, review of Childs, *Old Testament Theology in a Canonical Context*, in *Theology Today* 23, 1986, 284–7

—, 'Biblical Theology Appropriately Postmodern', *Biblical Theology Bulletin* 27, Spring 1997, no.1, 4–9

—, *Theology of the Old Testament*, Minneapolis: Fortress Press 1997

Brunner, E., *The Divine-Human Encounter*, London: SCM Press 1944

—, *Revelation and Reason*, Philadelphia: Westminster Press 1946

Buber, Martin, *I and Thou*, Edinburgh: T.& T.Clark 1937

Büchler, *Studies in Sin and Atonement in the Rabbinic Literature of the First Century*, London: Jews College Publications 11, 1928

Bultmann, R., 'Prophecy and Fulfilment', in C. Westermann ( ed.), *Essays on Old Testament Interpretation*, London: SCM Press 1963, 50–75

—, 'The Significance of the Old Testament for the Christian Faith', in B.W. Anderson (ed.), *The Old Testament and Christian Faith*, 8–35, ET of 'Die Bedeutung des Alten Testaments für den christlichen Glauben', in *Glauben und Verstehen* 1, 1933, 313–36

Buren, P. M. van, 'On Reading Someone Else's Mail: The Church and Israel's Scriptures', in W. Blum, C. Macholz and E. W. Stegemann, *Die Hebräische Bibel und ihre zweifache Nachgeschichte. Rendtorff FS*, Neukirchen 1990, 595–606

Burrows, Millar, *Outline of Biblical Theology*, Philadelphia: Westminster Press 1946

Caird, G. B., *New Testament Theology*, completed and edited by L. D. Hurst, Oxford: Clarendon Press 1993

Carson, D. A., and Williamson, H. G. M., *It is Written: Scripture Citing Scripture*, Cambridge: Cambridge University Press 1988

Chadwick, Owen, *From Bossuet to Newman*, Cambridge: Cambridge University Press [2]1987

Cheyne, A. C., 'Bible and Confession in Scotland: The Background to the Robertson Smith Case', in W. Johnstone (ed.), *William Robertson Smith. Essays in Reassessment*, Sheffield: JSOT Supplement Series 189, 1995, 24–40

Childs, B. S., *Myth and Reality in the Old Testament*, London: SCM Press 1960

—, *Memory and Tradition in Israel*, London: SCM Press 1962

—, 'Interpretation in Faith: The Theological Responsibility of an Old Testament Commentary', *Interpretation* 18, 1964, 432–49

—, *Biblical Theology in Crisis*, Philadelphia: Westminster Press 1970

—, 'The Old Testament as Scripture of the Church', *Concordia Theological Monthly* 43, 1972, 709–22

—, review of Sanders, *Torah and Canon*, in *Interpretation* 26, 1972, 20–9

—, *Exodus*, Old Testament Library, London: SCM Press and Philadelphia: Westminster Press 1974

—, 'Reflections on the Modern Study of the Psalms', in F. M. Cross et al. (eds), *Magnalia Dei*, Garden City: Doubleday 1976, 377–88

—, 'The Exegetical Significance of Canon', *VTS* 29, 1977, 66–88

—, *Introduction to the Old Testament as Scripture*, London, SCM Press 1979

—, 'A Response', *HBT* 2, 1980, 199–211

—, 'Response to Reviewers', *JSOT* 16, 1980, 52–60

—, 'Some Reflections on the Search for a Biblical Theology', *HBT* 4, 1982, 1–12

—, *The New Testament as Canon: An Introduction*, London: SCM Press 1984

—, Review of Barr, *Holy Scripture*, in *Interpretation* 38, 1984, 66–70

—, *Old Testament Theology in a Canonical Context*, London: SCM Press 1985 ( = *OTTCC*)

—, 'Gerhard von Rad in American Dress', in D. G. Miller (ed.), *The Hermeneutical Quest. J. L. Mays FS*, Allison Park: Pickwick Publications 1986, 77–86

—, 'Die Bedeutung des jüdischen Kanons in der alttestamentlichen Theologie', in M. Klopfenstein et al. (eds.), *Mitte der Schrift?*, Bern 1987, 269–81

—, 'Death and Dying in Old Testament Theology', in J. H. Marks and R. M. Good, *Love and Death in the Ancient Near East*, Guildford: Four Quarters 1987, 89–91

—, 'Karl Barth as Interpreter of Scripture', in D. L. Dickerman, *Karl Barth and the Future of Theology: A Memorial Colloquium*, New Haven: Yale Divinity School Association 1969

—, *Old Testament Theology in a Canonical Context*, London: SCM Press 1985 (= *OTTCC*)

—, 'Analysis of a Canonical Formula: "It shall be recorded for a future generation"', in W. Blum, C. Macholz and E. W. Stegemann, *Die Hebräische Bibel und ihre zweifache Nachgeschichte. Rendtorff FS*, Neukirchen 1990, 357–64

—, 'Critical Reflections on James Barr's Understanding of the Literal and the Allegorical', *JSOT* 46, 1990, 3–9

—, *Biblical Theology of the Old and New Testaments*, London: SCM Press 1992 (= *Biblical Theology*)

—, 'Die Bedeutung der hebräischen Bibel für die biblische Theologie', *TZ* 48, 1992, 382–90

—, 'Old Testament in Germany 1920–1940. The Search for a New Paradigm', in P. Mommer and W.Thiel, *Altes Testament. Forschung und Wirkung. Reventlow FS*, Frankfurt: Peter Lang 1994, 233–46

—, 'Old Testament Theology', in J. L. Mays, D. L. Petersen and K. H. Richards (eds), *Old Testament Interpretation: Past, Present and Future.Gene Tucker FS*, Nashville: Abingdon Press 1995, 293–301

Clavier, H., *Les Variétés de la pensée biblique et le problème de son unité*, Leiden: Brill 1976

Clements, R. E., *A Century of Old Testament Study*, Guildford and London: Lutterworth

Press 1976

—, *Old Testament Theology: A Fresh Approach*, London: Marshall, Morgan and Scott 1978

Clines, D. J. A., 'Holistic Interpretation', in R. J. Coggins and J. L. Houlden, *A Dictionary of Biblical Interpretation*, London: SCM Press 1990, 292ff.

—, review of J. Barr, *The Garden of Eden and the Hope of Immortality*, in *Theology* 96, November 1993, 502

Coakley, Sarah, *Christ without Absolutes. A Study of the Christology of Ernst Troeltsch*, Oxford: Clarendon Press 1988

—, and Pailin, David (eds), *The Making and Remaking of Christin Doctrine. Essays in Honour of Maurice Wiles*, Oxford: Oxford University Press 1993

Coats, G. W., 'Theology of the Hebrew Bible', in D. A. Knight and G. M. Tucker, *The Hebrew Bible and its Modern Interpreters*, Philadelphia: Fortress Press 1985, 239–62

—, *Rebellion in the Wilderness*, Nashville: Abingdon Press 1968

—, and Long, B. (eds), *Canon and Authority*, Philadelphia: Fortress Press 1977

Coggins, R. J., and Houlden, J. L., *A Dictionary of Biblical Interpretation*, London: SCM Press 1990 (= *DBI*)

Cohn-Sherbok, D., *The Jewish Heritage*, Oxford: Blackwell 1988

Collins, J. J., 'The "Historical Character" of the Old Testament in Recent Biblical Theology', *CBQ* 41, 1979, 199–204

—, 'Is a Critical Biblical Theology Possible?', in W. H. Propp, B. Halpern and D. N. Freedman, *The Hebrew Bible and its Interpreters*, Winona Lake: Eisenbrauns 1990, 1–17

Colpe, Carsten, *Die religionsgeschichtliche Schule*, Göttingen: Vandenhoeck & Ruprecht 1961

—, *Tradition, Ideologie, Religionswissenschaft*, Munich: Christian Kaiser 1980

Conzelmann, H., 'Fragen an Gerhard von Rad', *EvTh* 3, 1964, 113–25

Cordero, M. García, *Teología de la Biblia, Vol. 1, Antiguo Testamento*, Madrid: Editorial Católica 1970

Crenshaw, James L., 'Method in Determining Wisdom Influence upon "Historical" Literature', *JBL* 88, 1969, 129–42

—, 'The Eternal Gospel, Eccl. 3.11', in J. L. Crenshaw and J. T. Willis (eds.), *Essays in Old Testament Ethics, J.P. Hyatt in Memoriam*, New York 1974

— (ed.), *Studies in Ancient Israelite Wisdom*, New York: Ktav 1976

Creveld, M. van, *Supplying War*, Cambridge: Cambridge University Press 1977

Cross, F. L., and Livingstone, E. A. (eds), *The Oxford Dictionary of the Christian Church*, London: Oxford University Press ²1974

Crüsemann, F., 'Gerechtigkeit Jahwes ($s^e daqa/s\ddot{a}d\ddot{a}q$) im Alten Testament', *EvTh* 36, 1976, 427–50

—, 'Die Eigenständigkeit der Urgeschichte. Ein Beitrag zur Diskussion um den "Jahwisten"', in J. Jeremias and L. Perlitt (eds), *Die Botschaft und die Boten. Wolff FS*, Neukircher: Neukirchener Verlag 1981, 11–29

—, 'Religionsgeschichte oder Theologie? Elementare Überlegungen zu einer falschen Alternative', in *JBTh* 10, 1995, 69–78

—, *The Torah. Theology and Social History of Old Testament Law*, Edinburgh: T. & T. Clark 1997

Cullmann, O., *Christ and Time*, London: SCM Press 1951

—, *Immortality of the Soul or Resurrection of the Dead? The Witness of the New Testament*, London: Epworth Press 1958

—, *Salvation in History*, London: SCM Press 1967

Cwiekowski, F. J., 'Biblical Theology as Historical Theology', *CBQ* 24, 1962, 404–11

Danker, W. J., 'Non-Christian Religions and Franz Pieper's Christian Dogmatics. A Detective Case', in T. Sundermeier (ed.), *Fides pro mundi vita. Missionstheologie heute. H.-W. Gensichen FS*, Gütersloh 1980

David, A. Rosalie, *The Ancient Egyptians: Religious Beliefs and Practices*, London: Routledge 1982

Davies, Margaret, Review of B. S. Childs, *Old Testament Theology in a Canonical Context*, *JTS* 37, 1986, 442–5

Davies, Philip R., *Whose Bible is it Anyway?*, Sheffield: JSOT Supplement Series 204, 1995

Davies, W. D., 'Reflections about the Use of the Old Testament in the New in its Historical Context', *JQR* 74, 1983, 105–36

—, 'Canon and Christology', in L. D. Hurst and N. T. Wright, *The Glory of Christ in the New Testament. G. B. Caird volume*, Oxford: Clarendon Press 1987, 29–36

Dentan, R. C., *Preface to Old Testament Theology*, New Haven: Yale University Press 1950; revised ed., New York: Seabury Press 1963

Dever, W. G., 'The Contribution of Archaeology to the Study of Canaanite and Early Israelite Religion', in P. D. Miller, Jr., P. D. Hanson and S. Dean McBride (eds), *Ancient Israelite Religion*, Philadelphia: Fortress Press 1987, 209–47

De Vries, S. J., *The Achievements of Biblical Religion. A Prolegomenon to Old Testament Theology*, Lanham, Maryland: University Press of America 1983

—, review of Knierim, *The Task of Old Testament Theology*, in *RSR* 24, 1998, 37–41

Dirksen, Peter, 'Israelite Religion and Old Testament Theology', *SJOT* 4, 1990, 96–100

Dodd, C. H., *According to the Scriptures: The Sub-Structure of New Testament Theology*, London: Hodder and Stoughton 1952

Dohmen, C., and Oeming, W., *Biblischer Kanon: Warum und Wozu?*, Freiburg: Herder 1992

Donner, H., 'Gesichtspunkte zur Auflösung des klassischen Kanonbegriffes bei Johann Salomo Semler', in D. Rössler, G. Voigt and F. Wintzer, *Fides et Communicatio. M. Doerne FS*, Göttingen: Vandenhoeck & Ruprecht 1970, 56–68

Downing, F. G., *Has Christianity a Revelation?*, London: SCM Press 1964

Driver, S. R., *The Book of Genesis*, Westminster Commentaries, London: Methuen 1904

Dunn, J. D. G., *Unity and Diversity in the New Testament*, London: SCM Press 1977, [2]1990

—, 'The Authority of Scripture according to Scripture', *Churchman* 96, 1982, 104–22, 201–25

Ebeling, Gerhard, 'The Meaning of "Biblical Theology"', *JTS* 6, 1955, 210–25 = id., *Word and Faith*, London: SCM Press and Philadelphia: Fortress Press 1963, 79–97

—, 'The Significance of the Critical Historical Method for Church and Theology in Protestantism', in *Word and Faith*, 17–61; German *ZTK* 47, 1950, 1–46

—, 'Dogmatik und Exegese', *ZTK* 77, 1980, 269–86

Eichrodt, W., 'Hat die alttestamentliche Theologie noch selbständige Bedeutung innerhalb der alttestamentlichen Wissenschaft?', *ZAW* 47, 1929, 83–91

—, 'Zur Frage der theologischen Exegese des Alten Testamentes', *Theologische Blätter* 17, April 1938, cols. 73–87

Eichrodt, W., *Theology of the Old Testament* (2 vols), London: SCM Press and Philadelphia: Westminster Press 1961, 1967, ET of *Theologie des Alten Testaments* (2 vols), Stuttgart: Ehrenfried Klotz Verlag 1959, 1964

—, review of H. E. Fosdick, *A Guide to the Understanding of the Bible*, *JBL* 65, 1946, 205–17

—, *Man in the Old Testament*, London: SCM Press 1951

—, 'Les Rapports du Nouveau et de l'Ancien Testament', in J. Boisset (ed.), *Le Problème biblique dans le protestantisme*, Paris 1955, 105ff.

—, 'Religionsgeschichte Israels', in *Historia Mundi* 2, Bern and Munich: Francke 1953, 377–448

—, *Religionsgeschichte Israels*, Bern and Munich: Francke 1969

Eissfeldt, O., 'Israelitische-jüdische Religionsgeschichte und alttestamentliche Theologie', *ZAW* 44, 1926, 1–12

Elsas, C., and Kippenberg, H. G., *Loyalitätskonflikte in der Religionsgeschichte, Colpe FS*, Würzburg: Königshausen & Neumann 1990

Engnell, I., *Studies in Divine Kingship in the Ancient Near East*, Uppsala: Almquist and Wiksell 1943

Fishbane, M., *Judaism*, San Francisco, Harper and Row 1987

—, 'The Notion of a Sacred Text', in id., *The Garments of Torah: Essays in Biblical Hermeneutics*, Bloomington: Indiana University Press 1989, 121–33

Fleteren, F. van, 'Augustine's Exegesis of Wisdom 9.15', in E. A. Livingstone (ed.), *Studia Patristica XXVII*, Leuven 1993, 409–16

Fohrer, Georg, *Geschichte der israelitischen Religion*, Berlin: de Gruyter 1968

—, *Theologische Grundstrukturen des Alten Testaments*, Berlin: de Gruyter 1972

Ford, D., 'Barth's Interpretation of the Bible', in S. W. Sykes (ed.), *Karl Barth: Studies of his Theological Method*, Oxford: Clarendon Press 1979

Fosdick, H. E., *A Guide to Understanding the Bible. The Development of Ideas within the Old and New Testaments*, New York: Harper and Bros 1938

Fowler, J. D., *Theophoric Personal Names in Ancient Hebrew. A Comparative Study*, Sheffield: JSOT Supplement Series 49, 1988

Frankfort, H., *Ancient Egyptian Religion*, New York: Columbia University Press 1948

—, *Kingship and the Gods*, Chicago: University of Chicago Press 1948

—, et al., *The Intellectual Adventure of Early Man*, Chicago: University of Chicago Press 1946, revised as *Before Philosophy*, Harmondsworth: Penguin Books 1951

Fretheim, T. E., 'The Old Testament in Christian Proclamation', *Word and World* 3/3, 1983, 223–30

—, *The Suffering of God: An Old Testament Perspective*, Philadelphia: Fortress Press 1984

Fruchon, Pierre, 'Ressources et limites d'une herméneutique philosophique', *ArPh* 30, 1967, 411–38

—, 'Sur l'herméneutique de Gerhard von Rad', *RSPT* 55, 1971, 4–32

—, 'Herméneutique, langage et ontologie. Un discernement du platonisme chez H.-G. Gadamer', *ArPh* 36, 1973, 529–68; 37, 1974, 223–42, 353–75, 533–71

Fuller, R. H., 'New Testament Theology', in E. J. Epp and G. W. MacRae, *The New Testament and its Modern Interpreters*, Atlanta: Scholars Press 1989, 565–84

Gadamer, H. G., *Wahrheit und Methode*, Tübingen: J. C. B. Mohr 1960, ET *Truth and Method*, London: Sheed and Ward ²1989

Gammie, J. G., *Holiness in Israel*, Philadelphia: Fortress Press 1989

—, et al. (eds), *Israelite Wisdom: Theological and Literary Essays in Honor of Samuel Terrien*, New York: Scholars Press 1978

Gay, Peter, *The Enlightenment. An Interpretation. The Rise of Modern Paganism*, New York: Knopf 1966

Gerhardsson, B., *The Ethos of the Bible*, Philadelphia: Fortress Press 1981

Gerleman, G., *Studien zur alttestamentlichen Theologie*, Heidelberg: Lambert Schneider 1980

Gerstenberger, Erhard S., 'The Religion and Institutions of Ancient Israel: Toward a Contextual Theology of the Scriptures', in J. L. Mays, D. L. Petersen and K. H. Richards (eds.), *Old Testament Interpretation: Past, Present and Future. Gene Tucker FS*, Nashville: Abingdon Press 1995, 261–76

—, 'Der befreiende Gott: zum Standort lateinamerikanischer Theologie', in H. T. C. Sun and K. L. Eades, *Problems in Biblical Theology*, Grand Rapids: Eerdmans 1997, 145–66

Gese, Hartmut, 'Erwägungen zur Einheit der biblischen Theologie', *ZTK* 67, 1970, 417–36; in *Vom Sinai zum Zion*, Munich: Christian Kaiser 1974, 11–30

—, 'Das biblische Schriftverständnis', in *Zur biblischen Theologie*, Munich: Christian Kaiser 1977, 9–30

—, *Vom Sinai zum Zion. Alttestamentliche Beiträge zur biblischen Theologie*, Munich: Christian Kaiser 1974

—, *Zur biblischen Theologie*, Munich: Christian Kaiser 1977

—, 'Tradition and Biblical Theology', Ch. 13 in D. A. Knight (ed.), *Tradition and Theology in the Old Testament*, Philadelphia: Fortress Press 1977, 301–26

—, *Essays in Biblical Theology*, Minneapolis: Augsburg Publishing House 1981

—, section on ancient Syria in *Die Religionen Altsyriens, Altarabiens und der Mandäer*, Die Religionen der Menschheit, ed. C. A. Schröder, 10,2, Stuttgart: Kohlhammer 1970, 3–232

—, 'Die dreifache Gestaltwerdung des Alten Testaments', in M. Klopfenstein et al. (eds), *Die Mitte der Schrift*, 299–328

Gilkey, Langdon, 'Cosmology, Ontology, and the Travail of Biblical Language', *JR* 41, 1961, 194ff.

Goldingay, John, *Theological Diversity and the Authority of the Old Testament*, Grand Rapids: Eerdmans 1987

—, 'Theology (Old Testament)', in R. J. Coggins and J. L. Houlden, *A Dictionary of Biblical Interpretation*, London: SCM Press 1990, 691–4

Goldsworthy, Graeme L., 'Thus Says the Lord: The Dogmatic Basis of Biblical Theology', in *God Who is Rich in Mercy*, ed. Peter T. O'Brien and David G. Peterson, Grand Rapids: Baker Book House 1986

Goppelt, L., *Typos. Die typologische Deutung des Alten Testaments im Neuen*, Gütersloh: Bertelsmann 1939

Goppelt, L., *Theology of the New Testament* (2 vols), Grand Rapids: Eerdmans 1981, 1983

Gore, Charles (ed.), *Lux Mundi*, London: John Murray 1889

Goshen-Gottstein, M., 'Christianity, Judaism and Modern Bible Study', *VTS* 28, 1975, 69–88

—, '*hokmat yisra'el, heqer ha-miqra', wᵉte'ologiya miqra'it yᵉhudit*', in id. and U. Simon, *Studies in Bible and Exegesis. Arie Toeg in Memoriam*, Ramat Gan: Bar Ilan University Press 1980, 243–55

—, 'Jewish Biblical Theology and the Science of Biblical Religion', *Tarbiz* 50, 1980–81, 37–64 (+ English summary)

—, 'Modern Jewish Bible Research. Aspects of Integration', *Proceedings of the Eighth World Congress of Jewish Studies*, 1983, 1–18

—, 'Modern Jewish Bible-Exegesis and Biblical Theology', *Proceedings of the Tenth World Congress of Jewish Studies*, Division A, 1970, 39–50

—, 'From Tanakh to Modern Times: Aspects of Jewish Religion', in *From Ancient Israel to Modern Judaism. Martin Fox FS*, Atlanta: Scholars Press 1989, 55–60

—, 'Tanakh Theology: The Religion of the Old Testament and the Place of Jewish Biblical Theology', in Patrick D. Miller, Paul D. Hanson and S. Dean McBride, *Ancient Israelite Religion. F.M. Cross FS*, Philadelphia: Fortress Press 1987, 617–44

Gottwald, N., 'Biblical Theology or Biblical Sociology. On Affirming the "Uniqueness" of Israel', *Radical Religion* 2, 1975, 42–57

Graham, D. W., *Aristotle's Two Systems*, Oxford: Clarendon Press 1987

Grant, F. C. and Rowley, H. H., *Hastings' Dictionary of the Bible*, Edinburgh: T. & T. Clark 1963

Grässer, Erich, *Der Alte Bund im Neuen*, Tübingen: JCB Mohr 1985

Gray, G. Buchanan, *Studies in Hebrew Proper Names*, London: A. & C. Black 1896

Grelot, P., *Sens chrétien de l'Ancien Testament*, Paris: Desclée 1962

—, '"Theologie" des Alten Testaments oder "Biblische Theologie"?', in *Textgemäss. Würthwein FS*, Vandenhoeck & Ruprecht 1979, 39–46

Grosse, W., 'Lying Prophet and Disobedient Man of God in 1 Kings 13', Semeia 15, 1979, 97–135

Gunneweg, A. H. J., *Understanding the Old Testament*, London: SCM Press 1978, ET of *Vom Verstehen des Alten Testaments. Eine Hermeneutik*, Göttingen: Vandenhoeck & Ruprecht 1977

—, *Biblische Theologie des Alten Testaments. Eine Religionsgeschichte Israels in biblisch-theologischer Sicht*, Stuttgart: Kohlhammer 1993

Gyllenberg, R., 'Die Unmöglichkeit einer Theologie des Alten Testaments', in *In piam memoriam Alexander von Bulmerincq*, Riga: Abhandlungen der Herder-Gesellschaft und des Herder-Instituts zu Riga, Bd. 6, Nr. 3: Akt.-Ges. Ernst Plates, 1938, 64–8

Haas, Peter, 'Recent Theologies of Jewish-Christian Relations', *RSR* 16/4, October 1990, 316–20

Haenchen, E., *Die Bibel und Wir*, Tübingen: J. C. B. Mohr 1968

Halbe, J., *Das Privilegrecht Jahwes. Ex.34.10–26*, Göttingen: Vandenhoeck & Ruprecht 1975

—, '"Altorientalisches Weltordnungsdenken" und alttestamentliche Theologie. Zur Kritik eines Ideologems am Beispiel des israelitischen Rechts', *ZTK* 76, 1979, 381–418

Hanhart, R., 'Die Bedeutung der Septuaginta in neutestamentlicher Zeit', *ZThK* 81, 1984, 395–416

—, 'Die Übersetzung der Septuaginta im Licht ihr vorgegebener und auf ihr gründender Tradition', in Balentine, S. E., and Barton, J. (eds), *Language, Theology and the Bible. Barr FS*, Oxford: Clarendon Press 1994, 81–112

Hanson, Paul D., 'The Future of Biblical Theology', *HBT* 6, 1984, 13–24

Hardmeier, C., 'Systematische Elemente der Theologie in der Hebräischen Bibel. Das Loben Gottes – ein Kristallisationsmoment biblischer Theologie', *JBTh* 10, 1995, 111–28

Harrington, W., *The Path of Biblical Theology*, Dublin: Gill and Macmillan 1973

Hasel, G. F., *Old Testament Theology: Basic Issues in the Current Debate*, Grand Rapids: Eerdmans 1972, ⁴1991

—, 'A Decade of OT Theology: Retrospect and Prospect' [1969–78], *ZAW* 93, 1981, 165–83

—, 'The Problem of the Center in the OT Theology Debate', *ZAW* 86, 1974, 65–82

—, 'The Nature of Biblical Theology: Recent Trends and Issues', *AUSS* 32, 1994, 203–15

—, 'Recent Models of Biblical Theology: Three Major Perspectives', *AUSS* 33, 1995, 55–75

—, 'Proposals for a Canonical Biblical Theology', *AUSS* 34, 1996, 23–34

Hayes, John H., and Prussner, F., *Old Testament Theology. Its History and Development*, London: SCM Press and Atlanta: John Knox Press 1985

Heinisch, Paul, *Theology of the Old Testament*, Collegeville, Minnesota: Liturgical Press 1955

Hellbardt, H., 'Die Auslegung des Alten Testaments als theologische Disziplin', *Theologische Blätter*, July–Aug 1937, cols. 129–43

Hengel, M., 'Historische Methoden und theologische Auslegung des Neuen Testaments', *KuD* 19, 1973, 85–90

—, *Judaism and Hellenism* (2 vols), London: SCM Press and Philadelphia: Fortress Press 1974

Hengstenberg, E.W., *Christology of the Old Testament*, Grand Rapids: Kregel Publications 1956

Herberg, Will, *Judaism and Modern Man*, New York: Farrar, Straus and Young 1951

Herbert, A. S., 'Is There a Theology of the OT?', *ExpT* 12, 1950, 361–3

Herrmann, Siegfried, 'Die konstruktive Restauration. Das Deuteronomium als Mitte biblischer Theologie', in H. W. Wolff (ed.), *Probleme Biblischer Theologie. von Rad FS*, Munich: Christian Kaiser Verlag 1971, 155–70

—, 'Die Abwertung des Alten Testaments als Geschichtsquelle, Bemerkungen zu einem geistesgeschichtlichen Problem', in H. H. Schmid and J. Mehlhausen, *Sola Scriptura. Das reformatorische Schriftprinzip in einer säkularen Welt*, *Kongressband Dresden 1990*, Gütersloh 1991, 143–55

Hermisson, H.-J., 'Observations on the Creation Theology in Wisdom', in J. G. Gammie (ed.), *Israelite Wisdom. Terrien FS*, New York: Scholars Press 1978, 43–57

Heschel, A. J., *God in Search of Man*, New York: Farrar, Straus Cudahy 1955

Hesse, F., 'Kerygma oder geschichtliche Wirklichkeit? Kritische Fragen zu Gerhard von Rads "Theologie des Alten Testaments I. Teil"', *ZTK* 57, 1960, 17–26

—, 'Das Alte Testament in der gegenwärtigen Dogmatik', *NZSTh* 2, 1960, 1–44

—, 'Das Alte Testament als Kanon', *NZSTh* 3, 1961, 315–27

—, 'Wolfhart Pannenberg und das Alte Testament', *NZSTh* 7, 1965, 174–99

Hessen, J., *Griechische oder biblische Theologie?*, Munich: Reinhardt 1962

Hicks, R. Lansing, 'G. Ernest Wright and OT Theology', *Anglican Theological Review*, April 1976, 158–78

Hiebert, T., Review of Barr, *Biblical Faith and Natural Theology*, *Interpretation* 49, 1995, 298–300

Hinson, David F., *Theology of the Old Testament*, Theological Education Fund Study Guides 15, London: SPCK 1976

Höffken, P., 'Anmerkungen zum Thema Biblische Theologie', in M. Oeming and A. Graupner (eds.), *Altes Testament und christliche Verkündigung. Gunneweg FS*, Stuttgart: Kohlhammer 1987, 13–29

Høgenhaven, Jesper, *Problems and Prospects of Old Testament Theology*, Sheffield: JSOT Press 1988

Hodgson, Peter, *God in History*, Nashville: Abingdon Press 1989

Holtz, T., 'Neutestamentliche Theologie im Horizont der ganzen Schrift. Zu Peter Stuhlmachers Biblischer Theologie des Neuen Testaments', *JBTh* 10, 1995, 233–46

Honecker, M., 'Zum Verständnis der Geschichte in Gerhard von Rads Theologie des Alten Testaments', *EvTh* 23, 1963, 43–168

Honko, L. (ed.), *Science of Religion. Studies in Methodology*, The Hague, Paris and New York: Mouton 1979

Hooke, S. H. (ed.), *Myth and Ritual*, London: Oxford University Press 1933

– (ed.), *The Labyrinth*, London: SPCK 1935

Hooker, M. D., *Jesus and the Servant: The Influence of the Servant Concept of Deutero-Isaiah in the New Testament*, London: SPCK 1959

Hoskyns, E. C., and Davey, F.L., *The Fourth Gospel*, London: Faber [2]1947

Hubbard, R. L., Johnston, R. K., & Meye, R. P., *Studies in OT Theology*, Dallas: Word Books 1992

Huber, W., Petzold, E., and Sundermeier, T., *Implizite Axiome. Tiefstrukturen des Denkens und Handelns*, Munich: Christian Kaiser Verlag 1990

Hübner, H., *Biblische Theologie des Neuen Testaments* (2 vols.), Göttingen: Vandenhoeck & Ruprecht, 1990–

Hughes, J. R. M., *Secrets of the Times. Myth and History in Biblical Chronology*, Sheffield: JSOT Press 1990

Hunter, A. G., 'Canonical Criticism', *DBI*, 105–7

Hyatt, J. P., *The Bible in Modern Scholarship*, Nashville: Abingdon Press 1965


Imschoot, Paul van, *Théologie de l'Ancien Testament* (2 vols.), Tournai: Desclée, 1954, 1956; ET *Theology of the Old Testament* (1 vol.), New York: Desclée, 1965

Ingraffia, Brian D., *Postmodern Theory and Biblical Theology*, Cambridge: Cambridge University Press 1995

Inwood, M., *Hegel*, Oxford Readings in Philosophy, London: Oxford University Press 1985

Irwin, W. A., 'The Study of Israel's Religion', *VT* 7, 1957, 113–26

—, 'A still, small, Voice . . . said, What are you doing here?', *JBL* 78, 1959, 1–12


Jackson, B. S., 'Legalism', *JJS* 33, 1979, 1–22

Jacob, Edmond, *Theology of the Old Testament*, London: Hodder and Stoughton 1958 (French original 1955, later revised)

—, 'Possibilités et limites d'une théologie biblique', *RHPR 46*, 1966, 116–30

—, *Grundfragen alttestamentlicher Theologie* (Delitzsch Lectures 1965), Stuttgart: Kohlhammer 1970

—, 'Principe canonique et formation de l'Ancien Testament', *SVT Edinburgh Congress*, 1974, 101–22

—, 'L'Ancien Testament et la Théologie', Leçon publique faite à l'Université de Strasbourg 11 March 1980

—, *Bible, Culture et Foi*, Strasbourg: Association des Publications de la Faculté de Théologie Protestante 1998

Jacobs, Louis, 'Theology', in *Encyclopedia Judaica*, Jerusalem: Leter 1971, Vol. 15, 1103–10

—, *A Jewish Theology*, London: Darton, Longman & Todd 1973

James, E. O., *Christian Myth and Ritual*, London: John Murray 1933

Janowski, B., *Sühne als Heilsgeschehen*, WMANT 55, Neukirchen: Neukirchener Verlag 1982

—, *Gottes Gegenwart in Israel. Beiträge zur Theologie des Alten Testaments*, Neukirchen: Neukirchener Verlag 1993

Japhet, Sara, *The Ideology of the Book of Chronicles and its Place in Biblical Thought*, Frankfurt: Peter Lang 1989

Jenni, E., ' "Vom Herrn ist dies gewirkt": Ps 118.23', *ThZ* 35, 1979, 55–62

Jeppesen, K., 'The Study of the Israelite Religion and Old Testament. Where do we stand and where should we go?', *SJOT* 3, 1989, 140–5

—, 'Biblia Hebraica – et Septuaginta. A Response to Mogens Müller', *SJOT* 10, 1996, 271–81

Jepsen, A., 'The Scientific Study of the Old Testament', in C. Westermann (ed.), *Essays on Old Testament Interpretation*, London: SCM Press 1963, 246–84

Jodock, Darryl, 'Reciprocity between Scripture and Theology', *Interpretation* 44, 1990, 376

Johnstone, W. (ed.), *William Robertson Smith. Essays in Reassessment*, Sheffield: JSOT Supplement Series 189, 1995

Kaestli, J.-D., and Wermelinger, O., *Le Canon de l'Ancien Testament*, Geneva: Labor et Fides 1984

Kaiser, Otto, *Der Mensch unter dem Schicksal*, Berlin: de Gruyter 1985

—, 'The Law as Center of the Hebrew Bible', in M. Fishbane and M. Tov (eds), *Studies in the Bible, Qumran and the Ancient Near East. Talmon FS*, Winona Lake: Eisenbrauns 1992, 93–103

—, *Der Gott des Alten Testaments. Theologie des AT, 1: Grundlegung*, Göttingen: Vandenhoeck & Ruprecht 1993

Kaiser, Walter C., *Toward an Old Testament Theology*, Grand Rapids: Zondervan,1978

Kalimi, Isaac, 'Religionsgeschichte Israels oder Theologie des Alten Testaments? Das jüdische Interesse an der Biblischen Theologie', in *JBTh* 10, 1995, 45–68

—, 'History of Israelite Religion or Old Testament Theology? Jewish Interest in Biblical Theology', *SJOT* 11, 1997, 100–23

Käsemann, E., 'The Problem of a New Testament Theology', *NTS* 19, 1972/73, 235–45

—, *Das Neue Testament als Kanon*, Göttingen: Vandenhoeck & Ruprecht 1970

Keel, O., and Uehlinger, C., *Göttinnen, Götter und Gottessymbole*, Freiburg: Herder 1992, 474

Kelsey, D. H., *The Uses of Scripture in Recent Theology*, Philadelphia: Fortress Press and London: SCM Press 1975

Kermode, F., 'Canons', a review of J. Barr, *Holy Scripture: Canon, Authority, Criticism*, and of E. Leach and D. A. Aycock, *Structuralist Interpretation of Biblical Myth*, in *London Review of Books*, 2–15 February 1984, 3–4

Kinneavy, J. L., *Greek Rhetorical Origins of Christian Faith*, New York: Oxford University Press 1987

Klein, Günther, ' "Über das Weltregiment Gottes": Zum exegetischen Anhalt eines dogmatischen Lehrstücks', *ZTK* 90, 1993, 251–83

Klein, H., 'Leben – neues Leben. Möglichkeiten und Grenzen einer gesamtbiblischen Theologie des Alten und Neuen Testaments', *EvTh* 43, 1983, 91ff.

Klopfenstein, M., '1. Könige 13', in E. Busch, J. Fangmeier and M. Geiger (eds), *Parrhesia. Karl Barth FS*, Zurich: Theologischer Verlag 1966

Klopfenstein, M., Luz, U., Talmon, S. and Tov, E., *Mitte der Schrift? Ein jüdisch-christliches Gespräch. Texte des Berner Symposions vom 6.–12.Januar 1985*, Bern: Peter Lang 1987

Knierim, R. P., *The Task of Old Testament Theology*, Grand Rapids: Eerdmans 1995

Knight, D. A., 'Jeremiah and the Dimensions of the Moral Life', in J. L. Crenshaw and Samuel Sandmel (eds), *The Divine Helmsman. Studies on God's Control of Human Events, L.Silberman FS*, New York: Ktav 1979

—, *Rediscovering the Traditions of Israel*, SBL Dissertation Series 9, Missoula 1973

– (ed.), *Tradition and Theology in the Old Testament*, Philadelphia: Fortress Press 1977

– (ed.), *Ethics and Politics in the Hebrew Bible*, Semeia 66, Atlanta: Scholars Press 1995

Knight, G. A. F., *A Biblical Approach to the Doctrine of the Trinity*, Edinburgh: Oliver and Boyd 1953

—, *From Moses to Paul*, London: Lutterworth Press 1949

—, *A Christian Theology of the Old Testament*, London: SCM Press and Richmond: John Knox Press 1959

Koester, H., *Introduction to the New Testament, 2. History and Literature of Early Christianity*, Philadelphia: Fortress Press 1982

Koch, K., 'Rezeptionsgeschichte als notwendige Voraussetzung biblischer Theologie – oder: Protestantische Verlegenheit angesichts der Geschichtlichkeit des Kanons', in H. H. Schmid and J. Mehlhausen, *Sola Scriptura. Das reformatorische Schriftprinzip in einer säkularen Welt. Kongressband Dresden 1990*, Gütersloh 1991, 143–55

—, 'Gibt es ein hebräisches Denken?', *Pastoralblätter* 108, 1968, 258–76

Koester, H., *Introduction to the New Testament, 2. History and Literature of Early Christianity*, Philadelphia: Fortress Press 1982

Kohler, Kaufmann, *Jewish Theology, Systematically and Historically Considered*, New York: Ktav 1968 (reprint of 1918 original)

Köhler, L., 'Alttestamentliche Theologie', *ThR* 7, 1935, 255–76

—, *Old Testament Theology*, London: Lutterworth Press 1957 (German original 1935)

—, *Hebrew Man*, London: SCM Press 1956

Kottsieper, Ingo, et al., *'Wer ist wie du, Herr, unter den Göttern?' O. Kaiser FS*, Göttingen: Vandenhoeck & Ruprecht 1994

Kraftchick, S. J., Myers, C. D. J., and Ollenburger, Ben C. (eds.), *Biblical Theology: Problems and Perspectives*, Nashville: Abingdon Press 1995

Kruger, H. A. J., 'The Canon Critical Approach as a Means of Understanding the Old Testament', *OTE* (S Africa) 7, 1994, Special Edition 81–197

Kusche, U., *Die unterlegene Religion: das Judentum im Urteil deutscher Alttestamentler*, Studien zu Kirche und Israel 12, Berlin: Institut Kirche und Judentum 1991

Lampe, G., and Woollcombe, K., *Essays on Typology*, London: SCM Press 1957

Lauha, R., *Psychophysischer Sprachgebrauch im Alten Testament*, Helsinki: Annales Academiae Scientiarum Fennicae; Suomalainen tiedeakatemia 1983

Laurin, R. B., *Contemporary Old Testament Theologians*, Valley Forge: Judson Press 1970

Lawson, J., *The Biblical Theology of Saint Irenaeus*, London: Epworth Press 1948

Leeuw, G. van der, *Religion in Essence and Manifestation*, London: Allen and Unwin 1938, ET of *Phenomenologie der Religion*, Göttingen: Vandenhoeck & Ruprecht 1933

Lemche, N. P., 'Warum die Theologie des Alten Testaments einen Irrweg darstellt', *JBTh* 10, 1995, 79–92

Lemke, W. E., 'The Way of Obedience: I Kings 13 and the Structure of the Deuteronomistic History', in F. M. Cross, W. E. Lemke and P. D. Miller, Jr, *Magnalia Dei. The Mighty Acts of God. Essays on the Bible and Archaeology in Memory of G. Ernest Wright*, Garden City: Doubleday 1976, 301–26

—, 'Revelation through History in Recent Biblical Theology', *Interpretation* 36, 1982, 34–46

—, 'Is Old Testament Theology an Essentially Christian Theological Discipline?', *HBT* 11/1, 1989, 59–71

Levenson, J. D., *The Theology of the Program of Restoration of Ezekiel 40–48*, Missoula: Scholars Press 1976

—, 'Why Jews are not Interested in Biblical Theology', in J. Neusner, B. A. Levine and E. S. Frerichs, *Judaic Perspectives on Ancient Israel*, Philadelphia: Fortress Press 1987

—, *Creation and the Persistence of Evil: The Jewish Drama of Divine Omnipotence*, Princeton: Princeton University Press 1995

—, 'The Bible: Unexamined Commitments of Criticism', *First Things*, February 1993, 24–33

—, *The Hebrew Bible, The Old Testament, and Historical Criticism*, Louisville: Westminster Press 1993

—, 'The Universal Horizon of Biblical Particularism', in M. G. Brett (ed.), *Ethnicity and the Bible*, Leiden: Brill 1996

—, review of Knierim, *The Task of Old Testament Theology*, in *RSR* 24, 1998, 37–41

Lindars, B., 'The Place of the Old Testament in the Formation of New Testament Theology', *NTS* 23, 1976–7, 59–66

—, *New Testament Apologetic. The Doctrinal Significance of the Old Testament Quotations*, London: SCM Press 1961

Link, C., *Die Welt als Gleichnis*, Munich: Christian Kaiser Verlag 1976

Lohfink, Norbert, *Studien zur biblischen Theologie*, Stuttgart: Katholisches Bibelwerk 1993, and especially 'Kennt das Alte Testament einen Unterschied von "Gebot" und "Gesetz"? Zur bibeltheologischen Einstufung des Dekalogs', 206–38

—, *Theology of the Pentateuch*, Minneapolis: Fortress Press 1994

Long, Burke O., 'Ambitions of Dissent: Biblical Theology in a Postmodern Future', *JR* 76, 1996, 276–89

—, 'Letting Rival Gods be Rivals: Biblical Theology in a Postmodern Age', in H. T. C. Sun and K. L. Eades, *Problems in Biblical Theology*, Grand Rapids: Eerdmans 1997, 222–33

Louth, Andrew, *Discerning the Mystery. An Essay on the Nature of Theology*, London: Oxford University Press 1983

Luck, U., *Welterfahrung und Glaube als Grundproblem biblischer Theologie*, ThExH, Munich 1976

Lütgert, Wilhelm, *Schöpfung und Offenbarung*, Giessen and Basel: Brunnen Verlag 1984 (original publication 1934)

Marquardt, F. W., *Das christliche Bekenntnis zu Jesus, dem Juden. Eine Christologie* (2 vols), Munich: Christian Kaiser Verlag 1990–1991

Martin-Achard, Robert, 'Les Voies de la Théologie de l'Ancien Testament', *RThPh* 8, 1958, 217–26

—, 'A propos de la Théologie de l'Ancien Testament', *ThZ* 35, 1979, 63–71

Mathers, Donald, 'Biblical and Systematic Theology', *CJT* 5, 1959, 15–24

Matthews, I. G., *The Religious Pilgrimage of Israel*, New York: Harper 1947

Mattioli, A., *Dio e l'uomo nella Bibbia d'Israële. Theologia dell' Antico Testamento*, Casale Monferrato: Marietti 1981

Mauser, U., *Gottesbild und Menschwerdung*, Tübingen: J.C.B.Mohr 1971

—, 'Historical Criticism: Liberator or Foe of Biblical Theology', in John Reumann (ed.), *The Promise and Practice of Biblical Theology*, Minneapolis: Fortress Press 1991, 99–113

Mayo, S. M., *The Relevance of the Old Testament for the Christian Faith. Biblical Theology and Interpretative Methodology*, Washington: University Press of America 1982

Mays, J. L., Petersen, David L., and Richards, Kent H. (eds.), *Old Testament Interpretation: Past, Present and Future. Gene Tucker FS*, Nashville: Abingdon Press 1995

McGrath, A., *Historical Theology*, Oxford: Blackwell 1998

McKane, W., 'The Hermeneutical Method and OT Theology', in id., *A Late Harvest*, Edinburgh: T. & T. Clark 1995, ch.8

MacKenzie, R. A. F., 'The Concept of Biblical Theology', *CTSA Proceedings*, 1955, 48–73

McKenzie, J. L., 'The Task of Biblical Theology', *The Voice of St Mary's Seminary* 36, 1959, 7–9, 26–27

—, *A Theology of the Old Testament*, Garden City: Doubleday 1974

McKim, D. K. (ed.), *How Karl Barth changed my Mind*, Grand Rapids: Eerdmans 1986

McKnight, E. V., *Post-Modern Use of the Bible*, Nashville: Abingdon Press 1988

McLelland, J. C., 'La Signification théologique de l'election d'Israël', *ThZ* 16, 1960, 333–41

—, 'The Authority of the Canon', *CJT* 5, 1959, 35–43

Meeks, W., *The First Urban Christians. The Social World of the Apostle Paul*, New Haven: Yale University Press 1983

Mettinger, T. N. D., 'YHWH, El and Baal and the Distinctiveness of Israelite Faith', in W. Blum, C. Macholz and E. W. Stegemann, *Die Hebräische Bibel und ihre zweifache Nachgeschichte. Rendtorff FS*, Neukirchen: Neukirchener Verlag 1990, 393–417

Mildenberger, F., *Gottes Tat im Wort. Erwägungen zur alttestamentlichen Hermeneutik als Frage nach der Einheit der Testamente*, Gütersloh: Gerd Mohn 1964

—, *Die halbe Wahrheit oder die ganze Schrift. Zum Streit zwischen Bibelglauben und historischer Kritik*, Munich: Christian Kaiser Verlag 1967

—, *Gotteslehre. Eine dogmatische Untersuchung*, Tübingen: J. C. B. Mohr 1975

—, 'Gesetz und Heiligung in der protestantischen Tradition', in W. Huber, E. Petzold and T. Sundermeier, *Implizite Axiome. Tiefstrukturen des Denkens und Handelns*, Munich: Christian Kaiser Verlag 1990, 318–25

—, 'Biblische Theologie versus Dogmatik?', *JBTh* 6, 1991, 269–81

—, *Biblische Dogmatik. Eine Biblische Theologie in dogmatischer Perspektive* (3 vols.), Stuttgart: Kohlhammer Verlag 1991, 1992, 1993

Miller, P. D., Jr, 'Israelite Religion', in D. A. Knight and G. M. Tucker (eds.), *The Hebrew Bible and its Modern Interpreters*, Philadelphia: Fortress Press 1985, 201–37

—, Hanson, P. D., and McBride, S. Dean (eds.), *Ancient Israelite Religion*, Philadelphia: Fortress Press 1987

—, 'Biblical Theology', in D. W. Musser and J. L. Price (eds), *A New Handbook of Christian Theology*, Nashville: Abingdon Press 1992, 63–9

—, 'Creation and Covenant', in S. J. Kraftchick, C. D. Myers, Jr, and Ben C. Ollenburger (eds.), *Biblical Theology: Problems and Perspectives*, Nashville: Abingdon Press 1995, 155–68

—, review of O. Keel and C. Uehlinger, *Göttinnen, Götter und Gottessymbole* in *JBL* 113, 1994, 503–5

—, 'A Theocentric Theologian of Hope [Beker]', *PSB* 16, 1995, 22–35

Miskotte, K. H., *When the Gods are Silent*, New York: Harper and London: Collins 1967 (Dutch original 1956)

—, *Het Wezen der Joodse Religie*, Amsterdam: H.J.Paris 1932

Moberly, R. W. L., *The Old Testament of the Old Testament*, Philadelphia: Fortress Press 1991

—, *From Eden to Golgotha*, Atlanta: Scholars Press 1992

Mommer, P., and Thiel, W., *Altes Testament. Forschung und Wirkung. Reventlow FS*, Frankfurt: Peter Lang 1994

Moor, J. C. de, 'The Crisis of Polytheism in Late Bronze Ugarit', *OTS* 24, 1986, 1–20

—, *The Rise of Yahwism. The Roots of Israelite Yahwism*, Leuven: University Press 1990, ²1997

Morenz, S., *Ägyptische Religion*, Stuttgart: Kohlhammer Verlag 1960

Morgan, Robert, *The Nature of New Testament Theology*, London: SCM Press 1973
—, 'Theology (New Testament)', *DBI*, 689–91
—, 'Can the Critical Study of Scripture Provide a Doctrinal Norm?', *JR* 76, 1996, 206–32
—, 'The Bible and Christian Theology', in J.Barton (ed.), *The Cambridge Companion to Biblical Interpretation*, Cambridge: Cambridge University Press 1998
Muddiman, John, *The Bible: Fountain and Well of Truth*, Oxford: Blackwell 1983
Mueller, David L., 'Natural Theology', in Donald W. Musser and Joseph L. Price (eds), *A New Handbook of Christian Theology*, Nashville: Abingdon Press 1992, 328–31
Mulder, M. J. (ed.), *Mikra*, Philadelphia: Fortress Press 1988
Müller, H.-P., 'Bedarf die Alttestamentliche Theologie einer philosophischen Grundlegung?', in *Alttestamentlicher Glaube und biblische Theologie. FS Preuss*, Stuttgart: Kohlhammer 1994, 342–51
—, 'Fundamentalfragen jenseits der Alternative von Theologie und Religionsgeschichte', *JBTh* 10, 1995, 93–110
—, 'Alttestamentliche Theologie und Religionswissenschaft', in Ingo Kottsieper et al., '*Wer ist wie du, Herr, unter den Göttern?*' *O. Kaiser FS*, Göttingen: Vandenhoeck & Ruprecht 1994
Müller, Mogens, *The First Bible of the Church. A Plea for the Septuagint*, Sheffield: JSOT Supplement Series 206, 1996
—, 'The Septuagint as the Bible of the New Testament Church', *SJOT* 7, 1993, 194–207
Murphy, Roland E., 'The Relationship between the Testaments', *CBQ* 26, 1964, 349–59
—, 'Israel's Wisdom: A Biblical Model of Salvation', *Studia Missionalia* (Gregorian University) 30, 1981, 1–43
—, 'The Psalms and Worship', *Ex Auditu* 8, 1992, 23–31
Murphy, Roland E., 'Reflections on a Critical Biblical Theology', in Sun and Eades, *Problems in Biblical Theology*, Grand Rapids: Eerdmans 1997, 265–74
Musser, Donald W., and Price, Joseph (eds), *A New Handbook of Christian Theology*, Nashville: Abingdon Press 1992

Neill, Stephen T., *The Interpretation of the New Testament 1861–1961*, London: Oxford University Press 1966, second edition ed. N. T. Wright, *The Interpretation of the New Testament 1861–1986*, Oxford: Oxford University Press 1988
Neuser, W., 'Calvins Stellung zu den Apokryphen des Alten Testaments', in N. Brecht (ed.), *Text-Wort-Glaube. Aland FS*, Berlin and New York 1980, 298–323
Neusner, J., Levine, B. A. and Frerichs, E. S. (eds), *Judaic Perspectives on Ancient Israel*, Philadelphia: Fortress Press 1987
Newlands, George, 'The Old Testament and Christian Doctrine', *Modern Churchman*, April 1973, 238–44
Newman, John Henry, *Essay on the Development of Christian Doctrine* (1845), modern edition Hardmondsworth: Penguin Books 1973
Nicholson, E. W., with Baker, J., *The Commentary of Rabbi David Kimhi on Psalms CXX–CL*, Cambridge: Cambridge University Press 1973
—, *God and His People. Covenant and Theology in the Old Testament*, Oxford: Clarendon Press 1986
—, 'Story and History in the Old Testament', in S. E. Balentine and J. Barton, *Language, Theology and the Bible. Essays in Honour of James Barr*, Oxford: Clarendon Press 1994, 135–50
—, *The Pentateuch in the Twentieth Century. The Legacy of Julius Wellhausen*, Oxford:

Clarendon Press 1998

Noble, Paul R., *The Canonical Approach. A Critical Reconstruction of the Hermeneutics of Brevard S.Childs*, Leiden: Brill 1995

Noth, M., *A History of Pentateuchal Traditions*, Englewood Cliffs, NJ: Prentice-Hall 1972, reprinted Chico: Scholars Press 1981, ET of *Überlieferungsgeschichte des Pentateuchs* (1948)

Oeing-Hanhoff, L., *Anfang und Ende der Welt*, 1981

Oeming, M., 'Ist Genesis 15,6 ein Beleg für die Anrechnung des Glaubens zur Gerechtigkeit?', *ZAW* 95, 1983, 182–97

—, 'Bedeutung and Funktionen von "Fiktionen" in der alttestamentlichen Geschichtsschreibung', *EvTh* 44, 1984, 254–66

—, *Gesamtbiblische Theologien der Gegenwart*, Stuttgart: Kohlhammer 1985; [2]1987

—, and Graupner, A., *Altes Testament und christliche Verkündigung. Gunneweg FS*, Stuttgart: Kohlhammer 1987

Oesterley, W. O. E., and Robinson, T. H., *Hebrew Religion: Its Origin and Development*, London: SPCK 1930, [2]1937

Ogden, Schubert M., 'What Sense does it make to say "God acts in History"?', *JR* 43, 1963, 1–19; also in his *The Reality of God*, New York: Harper and Row and London: SCM Press 1963

Ollenburger, B., 'What Krister Stendahl "meant" – A Normative Critique of "Descriptive Biblical Theology"', *HBT* 6, 1966, 61–98

—, 'We Believe in God . . . Maker of Heaven and Earth', *HBT* 12, 1990, 64–96

—, Martens, E. A., and Hasel, G. F., *The Flowering of Old Testament Theology*, Winona Lake: Eisenbrauns 1992

—, 'Old Testament Theology', in S. J. Kraftchick, C. D. Myers, Jr, and B. C. Ollenburger (eds.), *Biblical Theology: Problems and Perspectives*, Nashville: Abingdon Press 1995, 81–103

Olyan, Saul M., 'Why an Altar of Unfinished Stones? Some Thoughts on Ex 20.25 and Dtn 27.6–5', *ZAW* 108, 1996, 161–71

Osswald, Eva, 'Theologie des ATs, eine bleibende Aufgabe', *TLZ* 99, 1974, cols. 641–58

Otto, E., 'Erwägungen zu den Prolegomena einer Theologie des Alten Testaments', *Kairos* 19, 1977, 53–72

—, 'Die Theologie des Buches Habakkuk', *VT* 35, 1985, 274–95

—, *Theologische Ethik des Alten Testaments*, Stuttgart: Kohlhammer Verlag 1994

Otzen, Benedikt, 'Das Problem der Apokryphen', *SJOT* 10, 1996, 254–70

Oyen, H. van, *Ethik des Alten Testaments*, Gütersloh: Gerd Mohn 1967

Pannenberg, W., 'Problems in a Theology of (Only) the Old Testament', in Sun and Eades, *Problems in Biblical Theology*, Grand Rapids: Eerdmans 1997, 275–80

Peacock, James L., 'Notes on a Theory of the Social Evolution of Ritual', in L. Honko (ed.), *Science of Religion. Studies in Methodology*, The Hague, Paris and New York: Mouton 1979, 390–401

Pedersen, J., *Israel. Its Life and Culture* (Danish original 1920; ET 1926, 2 vols), reprinted London: Oxford University Press 1954

Pedersen, S. (ed.), *New Directions in Biblical Theology*, Leiden: Brill 1992

Pelikan, Jaroslav, *Christianity and Classical Culture. The Metamorphosis of Natural Theology in the Christian Encounter with Hellenism*, New Haven: Yale University Press 1993

Perdue, Leo G., *The Collapse of History. Reconstructing Old Testament Theology*, Minneapolis: Fortress Press 1994

Perlitt, L., *Vatke und Wellhausen*, Berlin: Töpelmann 1965

—, 'Auslegung der Schrift – Auslegung der Welt', in T. Rendtorff (ed.), *Europäische Theologie*, Gütersloh: Gerd Mohn 1980

—, *Bundestheologie im Alten Testament?*, Neukirchen: Neukirchener Verlag 1969

Petersen, D.L., 'Israel and Monotheism: The Unfinished Agenda', in G. M. Tucker, D. L. Petersen and R. R.Wilson (eds), *Canon, Theology, and Old Testament Interpretation. Childs FS*, Philadelphia: Fortress Press 1988, 92–107

Petzke, G., 'Exegese und Praxis. Die Funktion der neutestamentlichen Exegese in einer christlichen oder nachchristlichen Gesellschaft', *ThPr* 10, 1975, 2–19

Pinnock, Clark, *The Scripture Principle*, New York: Harper and Row 1984

Piper, O., 'Biblical Theology and Systematic Theology', *JBR* 25, 1957, 106–11

Pokorny, P., 'Probleme biblischer Theologie', *ThLZ* 106, 1981, cols. 1ff.

Pons, J., *L'Oppression dans l'Ancien Testament*, Paris: Letouze & Ané 1981

Porteous, N. W., 'Old Testament Theology', in H. H. Rowley (ed.), *The Old Testament and Modern Study*, Oxford: Clarendon Press 1951, 311–45

—, 'The Necessity of the Old Testament', *Town and Gown Lectures*, Edinburgh, fifth series 1956–57, 3–13

—, 'A Question of Perspective', in H-J.Stoebe (ed.), *Wort – Gebot – Glaube. Eichrodt FS*, Zurich: Zwingli Verlag 1970, 117–31

Preuss, H. D., *Verspottung fremder Religionen im Alten Testament*, BWANT 12 (92), Stuttgart: Kohlhammer Verlag 1971

—, *Theologie des Alten Testaments* (2 vols), Stuttgart: Kohlhammer Verlag 1991 and 1992, ET *Old Testament Theology* (2 vols), Louisville, Ky: Westminster John Knox Press 1995, 1996

Procksch, Otto, *Theologie des Alten Testaments*, Gütersloh: Bertelsmann 1950

Provan, Iain, 'The Historical Books of the Old Testament', in J. Barton (ed.), *The Cambridge Companion to the Old Testament*, 198–211

Pury, A. de, 'Sagesse et Révélation dans l'Ancien Testament', *RThPh* 27, 1977, 1–50


Rad, G. von, 'Faith Reckoned as Righteousness', in G. von Rad, *The Problem of the Hexateuch and Other Essays*, Edinburgh: Oliver and Boyd 1966, reissued London: SCM Press 1984, ET of 'Die Anrechnung des Glaubens zur Gerechtigkeit', *TLZ* 76, 1951, 129–32 = *Gesammelte Studien*, Munich: Christian Kaiser Verlag 1958, 130–5

—, 'The Joseph Narrative and Ancient Wisdom', ibid., 292–300, ET of

—, 'Josephgeschichte und ältere Chokma', in *Biblische Studien*, Heft 5, Neukirchen: Neukirchener Verlag 1954

—, 'Die Josephgeschichte', ibid.

—, *Genesis*, London: SCM Press and Philadelphia: Westminster Press ²1972

—, *Old Testament Theology* (2 vols.), New York: Harper and Row and Edinburgh: Oliver and Boyd 1962 and 1965 reissued London: SCM Press 1975 (German originals 1957, 1960)

—, 'Offene Fragen im Umkreis einer Theologie des Alten Testaments', *TLZ* 88, 1963, cols. 401–16 = ThB 48, 289–312

—, *The Wisdom of Israel*, London: SCM Press and Nashville: Abingdon Press 1972

—, *Holy War in Ancient Israel* (German original 1951), Grand Rapids: Eerdmans 1991

Räisänen, H., 'Legalism and Salvation by the Law. Paul's Portrayal of the Jewish Religion as a Historical and Theological Problem', in S. Pedersen, *Die Paulinische Literatur und*

*Theologie*, Göttingen: Vandenhoeck & Ruprecht 1980, 63–83

—, *Das koranische Jesusbild*, Helsinki: Finnish Society for Missiology and Ecumenics 1971

—, 'The Portrait of Jesus in the Qur'an: Reflections of a Biblical Scholar', *The Muslim World* 70, 1980, 122–33

—, 'Joseph Smith und die Bibel', *TLZ* 109, 1984, 82–92

—, *Paul and the Law*, Philadelphia: Fortress Press 1986 (German original 1983)

—, *The Torah and Christ*, Publications of the Finnish Exegetical Society 45, Helsinki 1986, especially 'Zionstorah und biblische Theologie', 337–65

—, *Beyond New Testament Theology*, London: SCM Press 1990

—, *Marcion, Muhammad and the Mahatma*, London: SCM Press 1997

Reif, S. C., 'The Jewish Contribution to Biblical Interpretation', in J. Barton (ed.), *The Cambridge Companion to Biblical Interpretation*, Cambridge: Cambridge University Press 1998, 143–59

Reimer, David J., 'The Apocrypha and Biblical Theology: The Case of Interpersonal Forgiveness', in J. Barton and D. J. Reimer (eds.), *After the Exile. Rex Mason FS*, Macon, Ga: Mercer University Press 1996, 259–82

Rendtorff, Rolf, *Gesammelte Studien zum Alten Testament*, ThB 57, Munich: Christian Kaiser Verlag 1975

—, 'Die Entstehung der israelitischen Religion als religionsgeschichtliches und theologisches Problem', *TLZ* 88, 1963, cols. 735–46

—, 'Judenmission nach dem Holocaust', in T.Sundermeier (ed.), *Fides pro mundi vita. Missionstheologie heute. H.-W. Gensichen FS*, Gütersloh: Gerd Mohn 1980, 173–83

—, 'Must "Biblical Theology" be Christian Theology?', *Bible Review* 4, 1988, 40–3

—, *Canon and Theology*, Minneapolis: Fortress Press 1993

—, 'Die Hermeneutik einer kanonischen Theologie des Alten Testaments. Prolegomena', *JBTh* 10, 1995, 35–44

—, 'Approaches to Old Testament Theology', in H. T. C. Sun and K. L. Eades, *Problems in Biblical Theology*, Grand Rapids: Eerdmans 1997, 13–26

Rendtorff, Trutz (ed.), *Glaube und Toleranz. Das theologische Erbe der Aufklärung*, Gütersloh: Gerd Mohn 1982

Reumann, John (ed.), *The Promise and Practice of Biblical Theology*, Minneapolis: Fortress Press 1991

Revell, E. J., *The Designation of the Individual. Expressive Usage in Biblical Narrative*, Kampen: Kok Pharos 1996

Reventlow, H. Graf, 'Der Konflikt zwischen Exegese und Dogmatik. Wilhelm Vischers Ringen um den "Christus im AT"', in *Textgemäss. Würthwein FS*, Göttingen: Vandenhoeck & Ruprecht 1979, 110–22

—, *Problems of Old Testament Theology in the Twentieth Century*, London: SCM Press 1985

—, *Problems of Biblical Theology in the Twentieth Century*, London: SCM Press 1986

—, 'Zur Theologie des Alten Testaments', *ThR* 52, 1987, 221–67

—, 'Theologie und Hermeneutik des Alten Testaments', *ThR* 61, 1996, 48–102, 123–76

—, Sparn, W., and Woodbridge, John, *Historische Kritik und biblischer Kanon in der deutschen Aufklärung*, Wolfenbütteler Forschungen 41, Wiesbaden: Harrassowitz 1988

—, 'Mythos im Alten Testament – eine neue Wertung?', in G. Binder and B. Effe, *Mythos. Erzählende Weltdeutung im Spannungsfeld von Ritual, Geschichte und Rationalität*, Trier 1990

Richardson, A., 'Second Thoughts – III. Present Ideas in New Testament Theology', *ExpT* 75, 1964, 109–13

Richter, W., 'Beobachtungen zur theologischen Systembildung in der alttestamentlichen Literatur anhand des "kleinen geschichtlichen Credo"', in *Wahrheit und Verkündigung. M. Schmaus zum 70.Geburtstag*, Munich, Paderborn and Vienna: Schöningh 1967, 175–212

Ringgren, H., *Israelite Religion*, London: SPCK 1966

—, *Religions of the Ancient Near East*, London: SPCK 1973

Ritschl, D., *Memory and Hope. An Inquiry Concerning the Presence of Christ*, New York: Macmillan 1967

—, *The Logic of Theology*, London: SCM Press 1986, ET of *Zur Logik der Theologie*, Munich: Christian Kaiser Verlag 1984

—, '"Wahre", "reine" oder "neue" Biblische Theologie? Einige Anfragen zur neueren Diskussion um "Biblische Theologie"', *JBTh* 1,1986, 135–50

—, 'Biblizismus', *EKL* 1, 1986, 503f.

—, 'Anmerkungen zur Providentia-Lehre. Oder: Was heisst: "Gott behüte Dich"?', in W. Brändle and R. Stolina (eds)., *Geist und Kirche. Eckhardt Lessing FS*, Frankfurt: Peter Lang 1995, 1–18

—, 'Gottes Kritik an der Geschichte: Nachüberlegungen zu Jer. 31', forthcoming

Ritschl, D., and Jones, H. O., *'Story' als Rohmaterial der Theologie*, ThExH 192, Munich: Christian Kaiser Verlag 1976

Robinson, H. Wheeler, *Inspiration and Revelation in the Old Testament*, reprinted Oxford: Clarendon Press 1946

Robinson, J. M., *The New Quest of the Historical Jesus*, London: SCM Press 1959

—, 'The Future of New Testament Theology', *Drew Gateway* 45, 1974–5, 175–87

Rogerson, J. W., 'The Old Testament View of Nature: Some Preliminary Questions', in H. A. Brongers et al., *Instruction and Interpretation*, OTS 30, Leiden: Brill 1977, 67–84

Rowley, H. H., *The Faith of Israel*, London: SCM Press 1956

Ruether, R. R., 'Recent Theologies of Jewish-Christian Relations', *RSR* 16/4, October 1990, 320–3

Ruler, A. van, *The Christian Church and the Old Testament*, Grand Rapids: Eerdmans 1971 (Dutch original 1955)

Sæbø, M., 'Johann Philipp Gablers Bedeutung für die Biblische Theologie', *ZAW* 99, 1987, 1–16

—, *Hebrew Bible/Old Testament. The History of its Interpretation*, Göttingen: Vandenhoeck & Ruprecht 1996

Sahlins, M., and Service, E., *Evolution and Culture*, Ann Arbor: University of Michigan Press 1960

Sailhamer, John H., *Introduction to Old Testament Theology*, Grand Rapids: Zondervan 1995

Sakenfeld, K. D., '"Feminist" Theology and Biblical Interpretation', in S.J.Kraftchick, C.D.Myers, Jr and Ben C. Ollenburger (eds.), *Biblical Theology: Problems and Perspectives*, Nashville: Abingdon Press 1995, 247–59

Sander, R., *Furcht und Liebe im palästinischen Judentum*, BWANT 4th series, 16, Stuttgart: Kohlhammer 1935

Sanders, E. P., review of B. S. Childs, *The New Testament as Canon*, in *The Times Literary Supplement*,13 December 1985

Sanders, James A., *Torah and Canon*, Philadelphia: Fortress Press 1972

—, 'Adaptable for Life. The Nature and Function of Canon', in F. M. Cross (ed.), *Magnalia*

*Dei. The Mighty Acts of God. G. E. Wright Memorial Volume*, Garden City: Doubleday 1976, 531–60

—, 'Hermeneutics in True and False Prophecy', in G. W. Coats and B. Long (eds), *Canon and Authority*, Philadelphia: Fortress Press 1977, 21–41

—, 'Canonical Criticism: An Introduction', in J. D. Kaestli and O. Wermelinger, *Le Canon de l'Ancien Testament*, Geneva: Labor et Fides, 1984, 341–62

—, *From Sacred Story to Sacred Text. Canon as Paradigm*, and my review in *Critical Review of Books in Religion*, 1988, 137–41

—, 'Canon as Shape and Function' in John Reumann (ed.), *The Promise and Practice of Biblical Theology*, Minneapolis: Fortress Press 1991, 87–97

Sandys-Wunsch, J., and Eldredge, L., 'J. P. Gabler and the Distinction between Biblical and Dogmatic Theology: Translation, Commentary and Discussion of his Originality', *SJT* 33, 1980, 133–58

Sauter, G., *Zukunft und Verheissung. Das Problem der Zukunft in der gegenwärtigen theologischen und philosophischen Diskussion*, Zurich: Zwingli Verlag 1965

—, 'Jesus der Christus. Die Messianität Jesu als Frage an die gegenwärtige Christenheit', *EvTh* 42, 1982, 324–49

—, 'Jesus the Christ', *SJT* 37, 1984, 1–12

—, '"Exodus" and "Liberation" as Theological Metaphors: A Critical Case-study of the Use of Allegory and Misunderstood Analogies in Ethics', *SJT* 34, 1983, 481–507

—, 'Hermeneutisches und analytisches Denken in der Theologie', in J. Brantschen and P. Selvatico (eds), *Unterwegs zur Einheit. H. Stirnimann FS*, Freiburg: Universitätsverlag 1980, 486–99

Scalise, C. J., 'Canonical Hermeneutics: Childs and Barth', *SJT* 47, 1994, 61–88

Schechter, S., *Seminary Addresses and Other Papers*, Cincinnati: Ark 1915

Schlette, H. R., *Towards a Theology of Religions*, New York: Herder and Herder 1966

Schmid, H. H., *Gerechtigkeit als Weltordnung*, Tübingen: J. C. B. Mohr 1968

—, *Altorientalische Welt in der alttestamentlichen Theologie*, Zurich: Theologischer Verlag 1974

—, 'Was heisst "Biblische Theologie"?', in H. F. Geisser and W. Mostert (eds.), *Wirkungen hermeneutischer Theologie. Ebeling FS*, Zurich: Theologischer Verlag 1983, 35ff.

—, and Mehlhausen, J., *Sola Scriptura. Das reformatorische Schriftprinzip in der säkularen Welt*, Gütersloh: Gerd Mohn 1991

Schmid, J. H., *Biblische Theologie in der Sicht heutiger Alttestamentler*, Giessen: Brunnen Verlag 1986

Schmidt, W. H., '"Theologie des Alten Testaments" vor und nach Gerhard von Rad', *VuF* 17, 1972, 1–25

—, *The Faith of the Old Testament*, Oxford: Blackwell 1983 (German original 1968)

Schoberth, Ingrid, *Erinnerung als Praxis des Glaubens*, Munich: Christian Kaiser Verlag 1992

Schulte, H., *Der Begriff der Offenbarung im NT*, Munich: Christian Kaiser Verlag 1949

Schultz, S., *Die Mitte der Schrift*, Stuttgart: Kreuz Verlag 1976

Schweizer, E., *A Theological Introduction to the New Testament*, London: SPCK 1992

Seebass, H., 'Über den Beitrag des Alten Testaments zu einer theologischen Anthropologie', *KuD* 22, 1976, 41–63

—, *Der Gott der ganzen Bibel. Biblische Theologie zur Orientierung im Glauben*, Freiburg: Herder Verlag 1982

Segal, A. F., *Paul the Convert*, New Haven: Yale University Press 1990

Service, E., *Primitive Social Organization: An Evolutionary Perspective*, New York: Random House 1962

Sheppard, G. T., 'Barr on Canon and Childs: Can One Read the Bible as Scripture?', *TSF Bulletin* 7, November–December 1983, 2–4

Simon, Marcel, 'The Religionsgeschichtliche Schule, Fifty Years Later', *RS* 11, 1975, 135–44

Simon, Ulrich E., *A Theology of Salvation*, London: SPCK 1953

Smart, J. D., *The Interpretation of Scripture*, Philadelphia: Westminster Press and London: SCM Press 1961

—, *The Past, Present and Future of Biblical Theology*, Philadelphia: Westminster Press 1979

Smend, R., *Die Entstehung des Alten Testaments*, Stuttgart: Kohlhammer Verlag 1978

—, *Die Mitte des Alten Testaments*, Munich: Christian Kaiser Verlag 1986 (this includes [40–84] *Die Mitte des Alten Testaments*, Theologische Studien 101, Zurick: EVZ 1970)

—, 'Theologie im Alten Testament', in *Verificationen. Ebeling FS*, Mohr 1982 = *Die Mitte des Alten Testaments*, 104–17

—, 'Wellhausen und das Judentum', *ZTK* 79, 1982, 249–82

—, 'Ethik III: Altes Testament', *TRE* 10, 423–35

Smith, Mark, *The Early History of God*, San Francisco: Harper and Row 1990

Smith, Morton, 'Ps 151, David, Jesus and Orpheus', *ZAW* 93, 1981, 247–53

Smith, W. Robertson, *The Prophets of Israel*, Edinburgh: A. & C. Black 1882

Snaith, Norman, *The Distinctive Ideas of the Old Testament*, London: Epworth Press 1944

Sommer, B. D., 'The Scroll of Isaiah as Jewish Scripture, Or, Why Jews don't read Books', *SBL Seminar Paper, 132*nd *Annual Meeting*, Atlanta: Scholars Press 1986, 225–42

Spencer, B., and Gillen, F. J., *The Arunta: A Study of a Stone Age People*, London: Macmillan 1927

Spina, Frank, 'Canonical Criticism: Childs versus Sanders', in W. McCown and J. E. Massey ( eds.), *Interpreting God's Word for Today. An Inquiry into Hermeneutics from a Biblical Theological Perspective*, Wesleyan Theological Perspectives 2, Anderson, Indiana: Warner Press 1982, 165–94

Spriggs, D. G., *Two Old Testament Theologies*, London: SCM Press 1974

Steiert, F.-J., *Die Weisheit Israels – ein Fremdkörper im Alten Testament? Eine Untersuchung zum Buch der Sprüche auf dem Hintergrund der ägyptischen Weisheitslehren*, Freiburg: Herder Verlag 1990

Steiner, George, review of R. Alter and F. Kermode, *Literary Guide to the Bible*, in *The New Yorker*, 11 January 1988, 94–8

Steinmetz, D., 'The Superiority of Pre-Critical Exegesis', *Theology Today* 37, 1980, 27–38

Stendahl, K., *Immortality and Resurrection*, New York: Macmillan 1958

—, 'The Apostle Paul and the Introspective Conscience of the West', *HTR* 56, 1963, 199–215

—, 'Method in the Study of Biblical Theology', in J. P. Hyatt (ed.), *The Bible in Modern Scholarship*, Nashville: Abingdon Press 1965, 196–209

—, *The Bible and the Role of Women. A Case Study in Hermeneutics*, Philadelphia: Fortress Press 1966

—, 'Immortality is Too Much and Too Little', in K.Stendhal, *Meanings. The Bible as Document and Guide*, Philadelphia: Fortress Press 1984, 193–202

—, 'Biblical Theology, Contemporary', *IDB* 1, 418–32

Stietencron, H. von (ed.), *Theologen und Theologie in verschiedenen Kulturkreisen*, Düsseldorf: Patmos Verlag 1986, 46–69

Strecker, Georg, 'Das Problem der Theologie des Neuen Testaments', in *Wege der Forschung* 367, Darmstadt 1975, 1–31

—, ' "Biblische Theologie"?', in D. Lührmann and G. Strecker (eds), *Kirche. G. Bornkamm FS*, Tübingen: J. C. B. Mohr 1980, 425–45

—, 'The Law in the Sermon on the Mount, and the Sermon on the Mount as Law', in John Reumann (ed.), *The Promise and Practice of Biblical Theology*, Minneapolis: Fortress Press 1991, 35–49

Stroup, G. W., *The Promise of Narrative Theology*, London: SCM Press 1981

Stuhlmacher, P., 'Adolf Schlatter's Interpretation of Scripture', *NTS* 24, 1978, 433–66

—, *Historical Criticism and Theological Interpretation of Scripture*, London: SPCK 1979, with an introduction by James Barr (the American edition differs)

—, *Vom Verstehen des Neuen Testaments. Eine Hermeneutik*, Göttingen: Vandenhoeck & Ruprecht 1979

—, *Biblische Theologie des Neuen Testaments*, Vol. 1, Göttingen: Vandenhoeck & Ruprecht 1992

Sun, H. T. C., and Eades, K. L., with Robinson, J. M., and Moller, G. (eds), *Problems in Biblical Theology. Essays in Honor of Rolf Knierim*, Grand Rapids: Eerdmans 1997

Sundermeier, T (ed.), *Fides pro mundi vita. Missionstheologie heute. H.-W. Gensichen FS*, Gütersloh: Gerd Mohn 1980

—, 'Die "Stammesreligionen" als Thema der Religionsgeschichte. Thesen zu einer "Theologie der Religionsgeschichte"', in T.Sundermeier (ed.), *Fides pro mundi vita. Missionstheologie heute. H.-W. Gensichen FS*, Gütersloh: Gerd Mohn 1980, 159–67

—, 'Implizite Axiome in der Religionsgeschichte: Primäre und sekundäre Erfahrung', in W. Huber, E. Petzold and T. Sundermeier, *Implizite Axiome. Tiefstrukturen des Denkens und Handelns*, Munich: Christian Kaiser Verlag 1990, 79–92

—, 'Religionswissenschaft versus Theologie? Zur Verhältnisbestimmung von Religionswissenschaft und Theologie aus religionswissenschaftlicher Sicht', *JBTh* 10, 1995, 189–206

Sweeney, Marvin A., 'Tanak versus Old Testament: Concerning the Foundation for a Jewish Theology of the Bible', in H. T. C. Sun and K. L. Eades (eds), *Problems in Biblical Theology*, Grand Rapids: Eerdmans 1997, 353–72

Swinburne, R., *The Evolution of the Soul*, Oxford: Clarendon Press 1986

Terrien, Samuel, *Job*, Neuchâtel: Delachaux et Niestlé 1963

—, *The Elusive Presence: Towards a New Biblical Theology*, San Francisco: Harper and Row 1978

Theissen, G., *Biblical Faith. An Evolutionary Approach*, London: SCM Press 1984, ET of *Biblischer Glaube in evolutionärer Sicht*, Munich: Christian Kaiser 1984

—, 'Aporien im Umgang mit den Antijudaismen im Neuen Testament', in W. Blum, C. Macholz and E. W. Stegemann, *Die Hebräische Bibel und ihre zweifache Nachgeschichte. Rendtorff FS*, Neukirchen: Neukirchener Verlag 1990, 535–53

—, *Social Reality and the First Christians*, Minneapolis: Fortress Press 1992

Thomas, Keith, *Man and the Natural World*, New York: Pantheon Books 1983

Torrance, T. F., *Reality and Evangelical Theology*, Philadelphia: Westminster Press 1982

—, *The Trinitarian Faith*, Edinburgh: T. & T. Clark 1988

Torrey, C. C., *The Second Isaiah: A New Interpretation*, New York: Scribner 1928

Tov, E., 'Die Septuaginta in ihrem theologischen und traditionsgeschichtlichen Verhältnis zur hebräischen Bibel', in M. Klopfenstein (ed.), *Mitte der Schrift? Ein jüdisch-*

*christliches Gespräch*, Bern: Lang 1987, 237–268

Trible, Phyllis, *God and the Rhetoric of Sexuality*, Philadelphia: Fortress Press 1978, reissued London: SCM Press 1992

—, 'Five Loaves and Two Fishes: Feminist Hermeneutics and Biblical Theology', in John Reumann (ed.), *The Promise and Practice of Biblical Theology*, Minneapolis: Fortress Press 1991

—, 'Treasures Old and New: Biblical Theology and the Challenge of Feminism', in Francis Watson (ed.), *The Open Text: New Directions for Biblical Studies?*, London: SCM Press 1993, 32–56

Trillhaas, W,. *Dogmatics*, Berlin: de Gruyter ²1967

Tsevat, M., 'Theologie des Alten Testaments – eine jüdische Sicht', in M. Klopfenstein (ed.), *Mitte der Schrift? Ein jüdisch-christliches Gespräch*, Bern: Peter Lang 1987, 329–41

—, '*hᵃ-ra'uy kᵉ-patteaḥ te'ologiya yᵉhudit šel ha-miqra'?*', *Proceedings of the Ninth World Congress of Jewish Studies*, Jerusalem 1986, 101–7

—, 'Theology of the Old Testament – a Jewish View', *HBT* 8, 1986, 33–50, with response by B. W. Anderson

Tuckett, C., *Reading the New Testament. Methods of Interpretation*, London: SPCK 1987


Van Seters, J., *Abraham in History and Tradition*, New Haven: Yale University Press 1975

Vaux, R. de, 'A propos de la théologie biblique', *ZAW* 68, 1956, 225–7

—, 'Is it possible to write a "Theology of the Old Testament?"', in *The Bible and the Ancient Near East*, Garden City: Doubleday 1971, 49–62

Vicary, D. R., 'Liberalism, Biblical Criticism, and Biblical Theology', *ATR* 34, 1950, 114–21

Vriezen, T. C., 'Geloof, openbaring en geschiedenis in de nieuwste Oud-Testamentische Theologie', *Kerk en Theologie* 16, 1965, 97–113, 210–18

—, *An Outline of Old Testament Theology*, Oxford: Blackwell 1958, ²1970 (first Dutch edition 1949, much revised in ³1966)


Wacker, Marie-Theres, '"Religionsgeschichte Israels" oder "Theologie des Alten Testaments" – (k)eine Alternative? Anmerkungen aus feministisch-exegetischer Sicht', *JBTh* 10, 1995, 129–56

Wagner, Siegfried, 'Zur Frage nach dem Gegenstand einer Theologie des Alten Testaments', in *Fides et Communicatio. FS Doerne*, Göttingen: Vandenhoeck & Ruprecht 1970, 391–411

Wahl, H. M., '"Ich bin, der ich bin"', in Ingo Kottsieper et al., *'Wer ist wie du, Herr, unter den Göttern?' O. Kaiser FS*, Göttingen: Vandenhoeck & Ruprecht 1994, 32–48

Watson, Francis, *Paul, Judaism and the Gentiles*, Cambridge: Cambridge University Press 1986

– (ed.), *The Open Text. New Directions for Biblical Studies*, London: SCM Press 1993

—, *Text, Church and World*, Edinburgh: T. & T. Clark 1994

—, *Text and Truth. Redefining Biblical Theology*, Edinburgh: T. & T. Clark and Grand Rapids: Eerdmans 1997

Weber, O., *Grundlagen der Dogmatik* I, Neukirchen: Neukirchener Verlag 1955

Weir, D. A., *The Origins of the Federal Theology in Sixteenth-century Reformation Thought*, Oxford: Clarendon Press 1990

Weiser, Artur, 'Die theologische Aufgabe der alttestamentlichen Wissenschaft', in A. Weiser, *Glaube und Geschichte im Alten Testament*, Göttingen: Vandenhoeck & Ruprecht

1961, 182–200

—, 'Das theologische Gesamtverständnis des Alten Testaments', in A. Weiser, *Glaube und Geschichte im Alten Testament*, Göttingen: Vandenhoeck & Ruprecht 1961, 257–79

Wells, Paul, *James Barr and the Bible. Critique of a New Liberalism*, Phillipsburg, NJ: Presbyterian and Reformed Publishing Co. 1980

Wernberg-Müller, P., 'Is there an Old Testament Theology?' *Hibbert Journal*, 1960, 21–9

Westermann, Claus (ed.), *Essays on Old Testament Interpretation*, London: SCM Press 1963 = *Essays on Old Testament Hermeneutics*, Richmond: John Knox Press 1963, ET of *Probleme alttestamentlicher Hermeneutik*, Munich: Christian Kaiser Verlag 1960

—, *Der Schöpfungsbericht vom Anfang der Bibel*, Stuttgart: Calwer Verlag 1961

—, *Der Segen in der Bibel und im Handeln der Kirche*, 1968, ET *Blessing in the Bible and the Life of the Church*, Philadelphia: Fortress Press 1978

—, *Elements of Old Testament Theology*, Atlanta: John Knox Press 1982, ET of *Theologie des Alten Testaments in Grundzügen*, Göttingen:Vandenhoeck & Ruprecht 1978

—, 'Zu zwei Theologien des Alten Testaments' [on Fohrer and Zimmerli], *EvTh* 34, 1974, 96–112

—, 'Die Zukunft der Religionen', in T. Sundermeier (ed.), *Fides pro mundi vita. Missionstheologie heute. H.-W. Gensichen FS*, Gütersloh: Gerd Mohn 1980, 151–67

—, *Genesis 12–36*, Minneapolis: Augsburg Publishing House 1985

—, 'Karl Barths Nein. Eine Kontroverse um die theologia naturalis. Emil Brunner – Karl Barth (1934)', *EvTh* 47, 1987, 386–95

—, 'Schöpfung und Evolution', in H. Böhme (ed.), *Evolution und Gottesglaube: ein Lese- und Arbeitsbuch zum Gespräch zwischen Naturwissenschaft und Theologie*, Göttingen: Vandenhoeck & Ruprecht 1988, 240–50

—, 'Gottes Handeln und Gottes Reden im Alten Testament', in H. T. C. Sun and K. L. Eades, *Problems in Biblical Theology*, Grand Rapids: Eerdmans 1997, 389–403

Wharton, James A., 'Karl Barth as Exegete and his Influence on Biblical Interpretation', *USQR* 28, 1972, 5–13

—, 'The Occasion of the Word of God. An Unguarded Essay on the Character of the Old Testament as the Memory of God's Story with Israel', *Austin Seminary Bulletin Faculty Edition*, Austin, Texas, September 1968

Whybray, R. N., *Wisdom in Proverbs*, London: SCM Press 1965

—, *Introduction to the Pentateuch*, Grand Rapids: Eerdmans 1985

—, *The Making of the Pentateuch*, Sheffield:, JSOT Press 1987

—, 'Old Testament Theology – a Non-Existent Beast?', in Barry P. Thomson (ed.), *Scripture: Meaning and Method. A. T. Hanson Festschrift*, Hull: Hull University Press 1987, 168–80

Wilberforce, W., *Practical View of the Prevailing Religious System of Professed Christians*, 1797

Williams, Lukyn, *Adversus Judaeos: A Bird's Eye View of Christian Apologiae until the Renaissance*, Cambridge: Cambridge University Press 1935

Wimsatt, W. K., Jr, 'The Intentional Fallacy', *Sewanee Review* 54, 1946

—, *The Verbal Icon*, New York: Noonday 1954

Wolde, Ellen van, *Stories of the Beginning. Genesis 1–11 and the Creation Stories*, London: SCM Press 1996

Wolff, H. W,. 'The Hermeneutics of the Old Testament', in C.Westermann (ed.), *Essays in Old Testament Interpretation*, London: SCM Press 1960, 160–95, ET of *EvTh* 12, 1952, 6ff.

—, *Anthropology of the Old Testament*, London: SCM Press 1974

— (ed.), *Probleme Biblischer Theologie. von Rad FS*, Munich: Christian Kaiser Verlag 1971

—, Rendtorff, R., and Pannenberg, W., *Gerhard von Rad. Seine Bedeutung für die Theologie*, Munich: Christian Kaiser Verlag 1973

Wolterstorff, Nicholas, *Divine Discourse*, Cambridge: Cambridge University Press 1995

Wright, G. Ernest, *The Old Testament against its Environment*, London: SCM Press 1950

—, *God Who Acts*, London: SCM Press 1952

—, 'Reflections concerning Old Testament Theology', in *Studia Biblica et Semitica, Vriezen FS*, Wageningen: Veenman & Zonen 1966, 376–88

Wright, G. Ernest, *The Old Testament and Theology*, New York: Harper and Row 1969


Young, E. J., *The Study of Old Testament Theology Today*, Westwood, NJ: Revel, 1959

Young, Frances, 'The Non-Pauline Letters', in John Barton (ed.), *The Cambridge Companion to Biblical Interpretation*, Cambridge: Cambridge University Press 1998, 290–304

Zenger, Erich, *Das Erste Testament*, Düsseldorf: Patmos Verlag 1991

Zimmerli, W., Review of G. von Rad, *Theologie*, in *VT* 13, 1963, 100–11

—, *The Law and the Prophets. A Study of the Meaning of the Old Testament*, Oxford: Blackwell 1965

—, and Merk, O., 'Biblische Theologie I (AT)', *TRE* VI 3/4, 426–55

—, 'Alttestamentliche Traditionsgeschichte und Theologie', in *Probleme biblischer Theologie. von Rad FS*, Munich: Christian Kaiser 1971, 632–47 = ThB 51, 1974, 9–26

—, 'Erwägungen zur Gestalt einer alttestamentlichen Theologie', *TLZ* 98, 1973, cols 81–98 = ThB 51, 1974, 17–54

—, *Grundriss der alttestamentlichen Theologie*, Stuttgart: Kohlhammer 1972, ET *Old Testament Theology in Outline*, Edinburgh: T. & T. Clark 1978

—, 'Zum Problem der "Mitte des Alten Testamentes"', *EvTh* 35, 1975, 97–118

—, 'Die Seligpreisungen der Bergpredigt und das Alte Testament', in C.K. Barrett (ed.), *Donum Gentilicium (Daube FS)*, Oxford: Oxford University Press 1978, 8–26

—, 'The History of Israelite Religion', in G.W.Anderson (ed.), *Tradition and Interpretation*, Oxford: Clarendon Press 1979, 351–84

# Notes

## 1. Definitions: The Many Faces of Biblical Theology

1. In German, similarly, the authoritative encyclopaedic work *TRE* has one article 'Biblische Theologie' which is divided into two parts: I Old Testament (Zimmerli) and II New Testament (Merk).

2. Contrast Childs, *Biblical Theology*, 55, where he opens a crucial chapter with the assertion that 'Biblical theology is *by definition* theological reflection on both the Old Testament and New Testament' (my italics). I do not think that this 'definition' agrees with common usage in English.

3. Cf. the title of Oeming's important book *Gesamtbiblische Theologien der Gegenwart*, i.e. 'Pan-Biblical Theologies of the Present Day'; for specific discussion of this work see below, Ch. 28.

4. Thus, for example, John Reumann, *The Promise and Practice of Biblical Theology*, 8f., discusses the views of Georg Strecker as 'one who is critical of the concept of biblical theology'. However, as Reumann's exposé shows, Strecker's argument is primarily against a particular line of thinking that calls itself 'biblical theology' but in effect insists on being 'pan-biblical theology' of one limited kind. It does not automatically follow that he is arguing against biblical theology in the more general sense – as his article in the same volume, which looks very like 'biblical theology' in the latter sense, suggests, and as Reumann himself seems to agree (8f.).

5. J. J. Collins, 'Is a Critical Biblical Theology Possible?'. Cf. Paul Hanson's assessment in 1984: 'Most assessments [of the future of biblical theology] these days are marked by deep pessimism', *HBT* 6, 1984, 13. In the original 1949 edition, R. C. Dentan, *Preface to Old Testament Theology*, wrote: 'By the middle of the century it seemed clear that this long-neglected discipline had at last come into its own and was on the verge of entering a golden age' ($^2$1963, 71), but in a section added later, entitled 'A Golden Age', he concluded that 'the crest of the wave' was already past. Curiously, Brevard Childs, from a very different point of view, also speaks pessimistically. Summarizing the recent course of the subject, he concludes with this paragraph: 'In sum, it seems neither unfair nor an exaggeration to conclude [with a fine mixture of metaphors] that the field has run into a stalemate. In spite of the impressive legacy from the last generation for which one can only be grateful, the need is acute for a fresh proposal which can at least begin to point in a direction for overcoming the present impasse' (*OTTCC*, 5). Brueggemann also speaks of a 'stalemate' but gives a more optimistic assessment: 'it is possible that a striking convergence of categories indicates a break in the long-standing stalemate in Old Testament theology' (*Old Testament Theology*, 95).

6. In contrast with Collins and Hanson, the late G. F. Hasel, notable for his surveys of the subject, began his article 'The Nature of Biblical Theology: Recent Trends and Issues'

with the statement: 'There is today unprecedented interest in biblical theology.'

7. Since *all* articles in these two journals are relevant to our subject, I have refrained from citing them in my own bibliography, except where I have had special reason to mention them.

8. L. Perdue, *The Collapse of History*, 7.

9. In his article 'Biblical Theology', *DBI*, 86–9, Robert Morgan speaks of 'those religiously meaningful wanderings labelled "biblical theology"'; these, he thinks, 'appear in retrospect to have been in an intellectual wilderness' (88).

10. Admittedly, if one were to be absolutely strict, this would require a definition of what constitutes a 'biblical scholar'. I leave this aside, however, considering it sufficient for the present purpose if I say that I use the term in its normal and accepted present-day sense.

11. There are indeed some exceptions or partial exceptions. Perhaps the person who came closest to being both a biblical scholar and a doctrinal theologian was H.-J. Kraus, though mainly in the sense that he was first one and then the other. Some other doctrinal theologians have produced material that is close to biblical theology: I think of Miskotte with his *When the Gods are Silent*, which, however, most readers found totally unintelligible, and A. A. van Ruler with his *The Christian Church and the Old Testament*. On Miskotte cf. the remarks of Childs, *Biblical Theology*, 707. Another partial exception might be the work of F. Mildenberger, with its significant title *Biblische Dogmatik. Eine biblische Theologie in dogmatischer Perspektive* (3 vols), which will be discussed below, Ch. 29.

12. Thus J. Lawson, *The Biblical Theology of Saint Irenaeus*, is not itself a biblical Theology, but a book about the thinking of Irenaeus about the Bible. On the other hand, the work is written very much with the values of the then current biblical theology movement in view, and seeks to portray Irenaeus as very much in sympathy with these values, stressing his 'biblical' or 'Hebraic' thought, e.g. 115–18 and *passim*.

13. The approach taken here was already briefly adumbrated in my article 'Biblische Theologie' in *EKL* 1, 488–94, forthcoming in English in *The International Encyclopedia of the Church*.

14. I had already written this passage when I found the same allusion to Janus in S. J. Kraftchick's title 'Facing Janus: Reviewing the Biblical Theology Movement', in S. J. Kraftchick, C. D. Myers Jr and Ben C. Ollenburger (eds), *Biblical Theology: Problems and Perspectives*, 54–77.

15. I use the term 'doctrinal' because I do not think that theology in this sense is necessarily 'systematic'; and while it is concerned with *dogmas* I think it too narrow, and also invidious, to designate it simply as 'dogmatic'. Cf. the similar judgment of H. Berkhof, below, Ch. 15 n.15.

16. For an English text of this document, often mentioned but seldom read, see J. Sandys-Wunsch and L. Eldredge, 'J. P. Gabler and the Distinction between Biblical and Dogmatic Theology'. I have taken *fines* as 'limits' or 'boundaries' rather than 'aims' or 'objectives', as they translate it. As my wife Jane points out to me, *fines regere* is a standard legal term, used by Cicero and in Justinian's Codex, for 'to draw the boundaries, mark out the limits' (glossed thus by Lewis and Short, 1552). It seems clear that this is what Gabler meant.

17. On this see further below, Chs 2 and 3.

18. Collins, 'Is a Critical Biblical Theology Possible?', 1: 'The reasons for the decline of biblical theology are manifold, but one of the most deep-seated is the perennial tension between biblical theology and the historical critical method, with which its history has been closely intertwined.'

19. Particularly his voluminous *The Golden Bough* and *Comparative Folklore and the Old Testament*. On Frazer see the study by R. Ackerman, *J. G. Frazer. His Life and Work,* and my review in *JTS* 40, 1989, 692ff., where I point out that 'twentieth-century biblical theology, canonical criticism, and the like owe a little bit to Frazer'. Ironically so, for Frazer was a convinced atheist and, as Ackerman says, 'the implicit purpose of the work [*Folk-Lore in the Old Testament*] can be simply stated: to undermine the Bible and religion by insisting on the folkloric stratum, thereby associating it with savagery'. The work was 'an immediate publishing success', selling some thousands within the first year.

20. Barth, *CD* I/2, 302f.; Sundermeier, *JBTh* 10, 1995, 191.

21. On this see my *Biblical Faith and Natural Theology*, Ch. 6, 118ff.

22. Ibid., 118.

23. From the article 'Biblical Theology, Contemporary', in *IDB* 1. 'The past' here, as the reader will perceive, means in essence the non-Hellenic past.

24. See the comment by Childs, *Biblical Theology*,12, who calls this work 'unsuccessful' and connects this with the use of 'a more "liberal" dogmatic system'.

25. See my review in *JTS* 25, 1974, 182–6. Harrington's book is, in any case, more a survey of biblical theology, with a pan-biblical scope, than an attempt to write a pan-biblical theology itself.

26. See James A. Sanders, *From Sacred Story to Sacred Text. Canon as Paradigm*, and my review in *Critical Review of Books in Religion*, 1988, 137–41.

27. So Childs, *Biblical Theology in Crisis*, e.g. 93–6.

## 2. *The Origins of Modern Old Testament Theology*

1. Delitzsch, the son of the highly respected and conservative Old Testament scholar Franz Delitzsch, delivered his lectures before an august audience in Berlin including Kaiser Wilhelm himself, and the Kaiser, who took a real interest in these matters, responded with an article of his own. For a brief account see J. Barr, 'Delitzsch, Friedrich', in *Encyclopaedia of Religion* 4, 276–7.

2. A book that was particularly disliked for its advocacy of this approach was Samuel Angus, *The Mystery Religions and Christianity*.

3. Correspondingly, Stephen Neill used the phrase 'Re-enter Theology' for his chapter on the same move within New Testament studies: see his *The Interpretation of the New Testament 1861–1961*, second edition ed. N. T. Wright, *The Interpretation of the New Testament 1861–1986*.

4. I say 'in principle' because, at least on the Barthian side of dialectical theology, this acceptance was grudging and partial, and the advantages which it imparted to dialectical theology were largely thrown away by later developments.

5. On Vischer see especially H. Graf Reventlow, 'Der Konflikt zwischen Exegese und Dogmatik. Wilhelm Vischers Ringen um den "Christus im AT"'; R. Rendtorff, 'Christological Interpretation as a Way of "Salvaging" the Old Testament? Wilhelm Vischer and Gerhard von Rad', in R. Rendtorff, *Canon and Theology*, 76–91, and my article 'Wilhelm Vischer and Allegory'.

6. O. Eissfeldt, 'Israelitische-jüdische Religionsgeschichte', ET in Ollenburger, Martens and Hasel, *The Flowering of Old Testament Theology*, 20–9, with introduction by Ollenburger, 18f. On these discussions see Hayes and Prussner, 158ff.

7. Eichrodt's actual reply to Eissfeldt's article is in his 'Hat die alttestamentliche

Theologie noch selbstständige Bedeutung?' ; ET in Ollenburger *et al.*, *Flowering*, 30–9.

8. Quoted from Porteous, in H. H. Rowley (ed.), *The Old Testament and Modern Study*, 323.


## 3. A Typology of Old Testament Theologies

1. His name is sometimes spelt as Köhler, sometimes as Koehler; I do not know why.

2. For an example of Köhler's argumentation on a central biblical theme (Adam's 'Fall') see J. Barr, *The Garden of Eden and the Hope of Immortality*, 87–91.

3. Eichrodt I, 32f.

4. Eichrodt did alter the sequence of materials as against that followed by Procksch; see the comments of Rendtorff, *Canon and Theology*, 7.

5. Eichrodt I, 36ff.

6. For a good survey of the more recent discussion of this, see E. W. Nicholson, *God and His People. Covenant and Theology in the Old Testament*.

7. Thus even Childs, who might have been expected to share the covenantal emphasis, points out that within the New Testament it is 'a somewhat minor category' except for the Letter to the Hebrews: so his *Biblical Theology*, 438.

8. For Eichrodt's concise evaluations of some of the Theologies that followed soon after the first publication of his own work, see the note at I, 33f. of the English version of his Theology.

9. Vriezen, 146 (wording slightly different in the first edition, 120). What exactly Vriezen meant by 'phenomenological', and why there is something wrong with that, is not made clear. I fancy (in agreement with Clements, *Century*, 124, 139) that he had in mind something on the lines of his Dutch contemporary van der Leeuw's *Phenomenologie der Religion* (English title, *Religion in Essence and Manifestation*), which seeks to describe the various phenomena of religion on a world-wide scale, while avoiding theological value-judgments. For serious discussion by a doctrinal theologian, see Berkhof, *Christian Faith*, 12, 18, 45–50; he talks of 'the phenomenological approach we follow in this Introduction' (18), and says that he 'used the phenomenological-historical method, that is, we looked for the structures of Israel's relationship to God and their developments in history' (248). Though he is clear that phenomenology does not answer questions of truth, it is equally clear that it has a positive and useful place within theology. 'It is,' he later asserts, 'especially the influence of phenomenology that has freed theology from a sterile partnership with a static, indivi-dualistic conception of man, and has opened our eyes to the prime significance of relation in the Bible, in contrast to the preponderance of "being" in Greek thinking' (183). Cf. also 194f. Von Rad also uses 'phenomenological' (*Theology* 2,416), apparently in speaking of Eichrodt's work. So also Childs, e.g. *OTTCC*, 206, following von Rad and definitely calling Eichrodt's approach 'strictly phenomenological', but again with no explanation of what that means. Contrast the more recent work of Sundermeier, *JBTh* 10, 1995, 189–206, who asserts that 'in the academic study of religion phenomenology has always been the bridge over to understanding and to theology' (203), on which see further below, Ch. 8.

10. I think it surprising, in that Vriezen's general outlook and interests seem rather remote from Eissfeldt's. Eissfeldt, as already remarked, remained rather aloof from Old Testament theology, even if he produced a formula which was supposed to make room for its existence and acceptability. Vriezen was very definitely a biblical theologian himself. It is as if Vriezen took over the phrases and terms of the German scholar, but adapted them to

express a viewpoint that was very much his own.

11. Vriezen's reference is to Porteous's remarks in H. H. Rowley (ed.), *The Old Testament and Modern Study*, 321f.

12. Cf. Clements, *A Century of Old Testament Study*, 127: 'Vriezen has argued that the proper starting point for a theology of the Old Testament is to be found in an awareness that the true goal of the Old Testament lies in the New Testament. However, when it comes to a detailed study of Vriezen's presentation of the material it is hard to see how this overt Christian starting point has been incorporated into the material.' Cf. also Clements in Laurin, *Contemporary Old Testament Theologians*, 121–40, especially 134f., and the review of Vriezen by Childs in *JBL* 78, 1959, 258, quoted there.

13. Dentan is another who defines Old Testament theology expressly as a 'Christian theological discipline' (94, 122); but in a note to his Conclusion he rather backs away from this definition, saying: 'It should be emphasized that the adjective "Christian" is included here only because, as a matter of simple historical fact, Old Testament theology originated within the Christian theological curriculum. There is no theoretical reason why Jewish scholars should not also cultivate a biblical theology (although, for obvious reasons, it would not be called "Old Testament" theology).'

14. I begin by saying this, because this is how I myself viewed it when I wrote my review in *ExpT* 73, 1961–2, 142. I would now wish to withdraw some of this in favour of the more many-sided analysis presented by Oeming, for which see below, Ch. 28. What I have said here remains, however, as a suitable introductory comment.

15. He actually uses this term, *Theology*, 2, end.

16. *ExpT* 73, 1961–2, 142.

17. The approach is well exemplified in M. Noth, *A History of Pentateuchal Traditions*.

18. In both volumes, it should be noted, there is actually something of a mixture between what we can call 'canonical order' and historical order. Thus in Vol.1 the order is mainly that of the events as narrated, starting from creation, and this allows the Priestly Document to be slotted in with the story of Sinai. But if this were logically followed out, Chronicles could not be placed at the end, since some of its subject-matter goes back to David. And if Chronicles comes at the end, why should the P material of the primeval story not come there too? After all, Chronicles goes back to Adam. But one understands very well von Rad's need to make a compromise here: the order is basically that of the events narrated. In Vol. 2, however, the order is more determined by the common critical identification and sequencing of the various prophetic sources, as is seen especially in the placing of Deutero-Isaiah and Trito-Isaiah. The compromise works perfectly well, but its existence gives a premonition of the greater ambivalence about history itself which is to follow.

19. Von Rad, 1., v.

20. Von Rad, 2, 411.

21. Von Rad, 1, 114 n. For Eichrodt's reply to von Rad, see his note on p. 34, but much more his Excursus 'The Problem of Old Testament Theology', added to the later editions of his Vol. 1 and printed as pp. 512–20 of the English edition.

22. Von Rad, 2, vii.

23. Von Rad, I, vi

24. Ibid.

25. Ibid.

26. 'Biblical Theology Movement' is the designation of Childs for 'a particular way of doing theology in relation to biblical studies' which emerged in America after the Second World War. Though making much use of British and European writers, it had 'a specific

American stamp'. It 'underwent a period of slow dissolution beginning in the late fifties' and 'pressure from inside and outside the movement . . . brought it to a virtual end as a major force in American theology in the early sixties'. See Childs, *Biblical Theology in Crisis*, 31, 87, and generally. There is some controversy about the accuracy and appropriateness of Childs' account: see for instance the acrid disagreement of James D. Smart, *The Past, Present and Future of Biblical Theology*. Nevertheless for most purposes Childs' depiction provides an adequate and useful orientation.

27. There is a useful bibliography of Childs' works in Brett, *Biblical Criticism in Crisis?*, 229f.

28. Terrien, *The Elusive Presence*, 34; Hayes and Prussner, 247. Admittedly, Terrien's opinion was directed at this point at the nineteenth-century Theologies. However, 58 n.173 seems to make it clear that he includes in the same judgment the 'many essays on biblical theology' that 'are still written in the traditional framework of doctrinal ideas' and 'present a didactic pattern', and here he names Köhler, Heinisch, Gelin, van Imschoot and Procksch – though I am not sure how the last of these belongs with the others.

29. Köhler, 7.

30. *A Century of Old Testament Study*, 124. He credits phenomenology in the style of van der Leeuw with having made a new approach in this regard more acceptable, and this may indeed be right, though I myself was never aware of much influence of this Dutch scholar on biblical theology.

31. As the reader will have perceived, and if I have understood Clements correctly, *phenomenology* is here used in a favourable sense and not in the negative sense intended by those who criticized Eichrodt, as quoted above. Clements seems to mean that older theological approaches had always looked for 'ideas', while the phenomenological approach was interested in rites themselves, and that this latter is an improvement.

32. Brunner, *The Divine-Human Encounter*, 31.

33. Coats, 'Theology of the Hebrew Bible', 244.

34. Zimmerli, 48–58; Childs, *Biblical Theology*, 136f., 416–20. Berkhof, *Christian Faith*, emphasizes covenant throughout his treatment of the Old Testament, introducing God as 'the great covenant partner' (15) and asserting that 'through all of Israel's history runs the awareness that it was covenantly related to its God' (230).

35. Thus among Old Testament theologians especially Westermann, 34–7. Similarly, von Rad discusses covenants frequently, but seems to feel no compulsion to accord to them the governing role seen as obvious by Eichrodt. Note especially the differing reactions to the powerful work of L. Perlitt, *Bundestheologie im Alten Testament?*, which argued that covenant theology is a late phenomenon.

36. For a recent study cf. D. A. Weir, *The Origins of the Federal Theology in Sixteenth-century Reformation Thought*.

37. In fact, Vriezen's choice of *massa perditionis* as an example was hardly a happy one, for the expression does not belong to the New Testament at all and comes from fourth-century North Africa, with a possibility of some Manichaean influence behind it!

38. I am indebted to my Vanderbilt student Laura Newsome Pittman for pointing this aspect out to me.

39. He did indeed have difficulties in making this work for *everything*; see below, 173f. Nevertheless I think the principle was as I have stated.

40. This has been disputed, but seems to me unmistakable. I am pleased to see that Zimmerli made the same observation. He notes (*VT* 13, 1963, 104) the *kerygmatic* emphasis common to both, the idea of 'witness' which has to be 'heard', and the strikingly narrow

handling of the events of the *beginning*.

41. See von Rad, *Theology* 1, 172–3, 420, 454; also his 'Josephgeschichte und ältere Chokma' and 'Die Josephgeschichte'. For a decisive criticism of the classification of the Joseph story (and other narratives) as 'Wisdom' see J. L. Crenshaw, 'Method in Determining Wisdom Influence upon "Historical Literature"'.

42. Berkhof, *Christian Faith*, 230, noted Eichrodt's emphasis on the covenant and von Rad's on history, and thought that these could be combined by summarizing Israel's 'way' as 'covenant history', thus bringing together 'a wide spectrum of recent results of OT hermeneutics'. I questioned this in my 'Some Old Testament Aspects', 16.

43. B.S. Childs, 'Old Testament in Germany 1920–1940'.

44. Cf. the article, supportive of Childs' approach, by G. T. Sheppard, 'Barr on Canon and Childs: Can one Read the Bible as Scripture?'.

45. Cf. below, 408.

46. On this see already my review of Brett in *JTS* 43, 1992, 135–41.

## 4. A Wider Spectrum

1. Thus J. Høgenhaven, *Problems and Prospects of Old Testament Theology*, 94, discussing this same subject, writes: 'An obvious example of a work which fully deserves to be counted as biblical theology is the inquiry into OT covenant theology by Lothar Perlitt, which appeared in 1969.'

2. Cf. my review in *JTS* 38, 1987, 459.

3. B. S. Childs, *Myth and Reality in the Old Testament* and *Memory and Tradition in Israel*.

4. Westermann, *Der Segen in der Bibel und im Handeln der Kirche*.

5. J. Barr, *The Semantics of Biblical Language*; for further remarks on this, cf. below, Ch. 14.

6. On this see J. Barr, 'Scope and Problems in the Semantics of Classical Hebrew', on this point particularly p. 4, along with the response by U. Rütersworden, *Zeitschrift für Althebraistik* 6/1, 15–20.

7. This is correctly outlined by Childs, *Biblical Theology in Crisis*, 46.

8. See the good description by Hayes and Prussner, 224f.

9. See Harrington, *The Path of Biblical Theology*, 358ff.

10. J. Bright, *The Authority of the Old Testament*, 159f.; Harrington, *The Path of Biblical Theology*, 360.

11. See the comments by Childs, *Biblical Theology in Crisis?*, 54. Childs notes there 'the disappointing fact' that the Biblical Theology Movement 'did not result in producing commentaries of this quality'.

12. 'Devotional studies' is the expression used by Cross and Livingstone (eds.), *The Oxford Dictionary of the Christian Church*, ²1974, 1347.

13. U. E. Simon, *A Theology of Salvation*. After many years of acceptance of the common scholarly opinion that this body of prophetic text was addressed to the Jewish exiles in Babylonia around 540 BC, Simon came to be convinced by the arguments of C.C. Torrey that the text was much later, from about 400.

14. This has some degree of agreement with the position of Childs in *OTTCC*, 15, but differs in that the logic of his work seems to me to require the opposite, i.e. that the canon *would* provide the one right methodology. On this cf. further below, 395f., 422.

15. More on this in Ch. 14 below.

## *5. Difference from Doctrinal Theology*

1. On this see D. Ritschl, '"Wahre", "reine", oder "neue" Biblische Theologie?'.

2. Many other theologians of this century have done the same. Cf. for example the almost innumerable appeals to Collingwood's somewhat idealist philosophy of history, appeals intended to oppose a factual conception of history, deemed by many to be 'positivistic'.

3. E. Jacob, *Theology*, 31; see further below, 66f.

4. Thus Childs writes: 'it seems useful to focus first on the material from the perspective of biblical theology . . . before drawing some lines to the field of systematic theology. I do not consider it a serious problem if there is an occasional overlapping and blurring of disciplines' (*Biblical Theology*, 396f.).

5. Jacob, *Theology*, 31 (I have used 'basic material' where the published ET says 'raw material'). Jacob was exceptional for his time, as we shall see, in admitting natural theology, even if only for doctrinal theology.

6. '*Mais une théologie biblique devant être, selon le principe scripturaire, l'inspiratrice et la norme de l'ensemble de la théologie, nous voudrions aujourd'hui dans une tentative qui reste nécessairement fragmentaire et abusive montrer comment l'Ancien Testament peut inspirer la réflexion théologique dans son ensemble . . .*', E. Jacob, 'L'Ancien Testament et la théologie', 1f.

7. Wright, *God Who Acts*, 11.

8. See R. Bultmann, 'Prophecy and Fulfilment'; also his 'The Significance of the Old Testament for the Christian Faith'.

9. Cf. James A. Sanders, *From Sacred Story to Sacred Text*, and my review in *Critical Review of Books in Religion*, 1988, 137–41.

10. I stress 'some' of the 'liberal' churches, for some other traditions of 'liberal' Christianity have been very appreciative towards the Old Testament. Some Unitarianism, for instance, would be a good example. My own impression is that, whatever the 'liberal' theologians may have said or thought, the traditional emphasis on the Old Testament, with teaching of the narratives, preaching on Old Testament texts, appreciation of the prophets, and constant use of the Psalms, continued unchanged in the mainstream churches, at least in Europe, right through until after the liberal emphasis had waned.

11. One might think perhaps, of Friedrich Delitzsch as one who 'rejected' it, but he was in no sense a liberal, nor was his thinking accepted in liberal scholarship.

12. Cf. D. Ritschl, 'Biblizismus'.

13. Hence the sense of K. Stendahl that biblical theology, unless corrected, threatened to be 'imperialistic': 'Biblical Theology', *IDB*.

14. For some later studies of this interesting passage see M. Klopfenstein, '1. Könige 13'; W. E. Lemke, 'The Way of Obedience'; W. Grosse, 'Lying Prophet and Disobedient Man of God in 1 Kings 13'; and Childs, *OTTCC*, 142ff.

15. Cf my *Old and New in Interpretation*, 96 n.

16. Barth, *CD* I/2, 494.

17. Childs, *Biblical Theology*, 589, tells us with satisfaction that 'Barth's exegesis [of Romans 5] is an exercise in biblical theology'. Contrast R.Smend, whose first sentence in his article 'Post-critical Exegesis of Scripture' is: 'Dogmatics are not biblical theology, even for Karl Barth.' See his *Die Mitte des Alten Testaments*, 212.

18. For the really decisive statement in this regard, see below, Ch. 15.

19. The extreme rarity of any registration of 'biblical theology' in the indexes of his

*Church Dogmatics* is a good indication of this.

20. This argument is already set out in my *Biblical Faith and Natural Theology*, 201, and before that in my 'The Theological Case against Biblical Theology', though I do not actually mention Barth's name there. Childs, *Biblical Theology*, 370, refers to this article of mine, but appears not to perceive that it is built on a Barthian basis. He seems also to think that I am 'questioning the value of' biblical theology 'as lacking the integrity of a true discipline'. On the contrary, I think it is a true discipline, or rather a peculiar combination of some true disciplines: what I argued was that, even if a true discipline, it may not be *theology* in the strict or authentic sense of the term, and that, whatever its merits, as a pure matter of fact doctrinal theologians have been sceptical of its value.

21. 'The Theological Case', 9f.

22. E. Brunner, *The Divine-Human Encounter*, 30. For a similar, more recent, statement, cf. A. McGrath, *Historical Theology*, 5: 'The ultimate source of all Christian theology is the Bible.'

23. R. Morgan, 'The Bible and Christian Theology', in J. Barton (ed.), *The Cambridge Companion to Biblical Interpretation*, 117.

## 6. *Difference from Non-Theological Study*

1. Cf. Childs in *JSOT* 46, 1990, 8: 'the crucial problem of biblical theology . . . namely, the challenge of employing the common historical critical tools of our age in the study of the Bible while at the same time doing full justice to the unique theological subject matter of scripture as the self-revelation of God'.

2. For an earlier discussion of this 'purism', see my *Old and New in Interpretation*, 32, 40, 171–200. Back then, in 1966, I foresaw that purism in this sense would become a central fault in biblical theology.

3. Cf. above, 74.

4. I have argued this previously in various places: see for instance J. Barr, *Fundamentalism*, esp.230ff. For a more recent assessment see that of H. Räisänen, *Beyond New Testament Theology*, 59ff., on G. E. Ladd, D. Guthrie and L. Morris.

5. Cf. above, 31, and below, 126, 644 n.9

6. On Troeltsch see Sarah Coakley, *Christ without Absolutes*. Against common misconceptions of Troeltsch see especially 188–97 and the note on 189.

7. Cf. J. Barr, *Biblical Words for Time*.

8. J. Barr, *The Garden of Eden and the Hope of Immortality*.

9. The concluding remarks in his article 'The "Historical Character" of the Old Testament in Recent Biblical Theology' seem to be a more correct statement of the matter.

## 7. *Evolution and Anti-Evolutionism*

1. For another discussion see J. Goldingay, *Theological Diversity and the Authority of the Old Testament*, 101–4.

2. S. R. Driver, *The Book of Genesis*, 56.

3. Quotations from Hayes and Prussner, 174, taken from Fosdick, ix–xv. On Eichrodt's

careful, eloquent and moderate review of Fosdick's work, see below, 86ff.

4. So rightly Hayes and Prussner, 131, 168. For a good example of the reaction of biblical theologians to Oesterley and Robinson see J.D. Smart, *The Interpretation of Scripture*, 261–6. He says: 'One rises from the reading of the book with the idea that, if no more than this can be said, then, as far as Christians of today are concerned, the Old Testament may safely be ignored.' Whether this is fair or not, I think that it correctly represents the feeling at the time.

5. Of this work G. E. Wright complained that 'one fourth of this book is given over to the description of the animistic and magical background of Israel's religion', *The Old Testament against its Environment*, 12 n. 6.

6. For a serious recent discussion of this command, see Saul M. Olyan, 'Why an Altar of Unfinished Stones?'.

7. Thus W. E. Lemke, writing in 1989, strongly insists that in discussions of the relations between Old and New Testament, or between Judaism and Christianity, 'all notions which are of a unilaterally evolutionary nature must be resolutely rejected'; see *HBT* 11, 1989, 63.

8. Goldingay, *Theological Diversity*, 102; James D. Smart, *The Interpretation of Scripture*, 250. Smart actually applied this term to the 'belief in the inevitability of progress' (249), which is not quite the same thing, but he would doubtless have said the same of evolution also.

9. In *God Who Acts*, 31, he cites I. G. Matthews, *The Religious Pilgrimage of Israel*, which depicts Israel's history 'as evolving through some fourteen different religions or distinct religious formulations'. In such a viewpoint, he says, 'a biblical theology is completely impossible because the Bible has no unity'.

10. See for example 'the magic formula of "historical development"', Eichrodt I, 28; 'the magic word "development"', 30; 'the historical–developmental method . . . never allows the synthesis its rightful scope . . . the recalcitrant material is forced into a Procrustes' bed, because it has been made to fit a dogmatic arrangement foreign to the subject', 31.

11. W. Brueggemann, *Old Testament Theology*, 141; the article was originally published in *Theology Digest* 32, 1985, 303–25. In his 1997 *Theology of the Old Testament*, Brueggemann continues to rule out development, as a totally unacceptable idea.

12. Cf. Albright's statement, in his *History, Archaeology and Christian Humanism*, 141: 'The most reasonable philosophy of history, in my judgment, is evolutionary and organismic. Evolution is not unilateral progress . . .'

13. Albright, *Stone Age to Christianity*, 401.

14. *The Old Testament against its Environment*, 15 (my italics); cf. the same phrase again on p. 28. No one can doubt that the use of *mutation* was a positive use of evolutionary terminology.

15. In *The Old Testament against its Environment* Wright begins with a more nuanced approach (9ff.), accepting that there are both good and bad applications to the metaphor of growth or development. By p. 16, however, he is asserting that 'long before the history of Israel began, the ancient Near East had left any stage of animism or dynamism far behind'. There was an 'Israelite mutation' (15), which consisted in the fact that Israel's basis was 'history, not nature' (28), and thus Israel's religious literature was 'utterly different from that of its environment'.

16. Review of Fosdick, *JBL* 65, 1946, 209. The reader should note that this review, of a book published in 1938, came very late because it was delayed by wartime conditions – but opportunely for the rise of the Biblical Theology Movement. Albright, in his introductory abstract of the review, expressed it as Eichrodt's position that 'no trained scholar of today

would deny the great importance of the evolutionary principle in history', but that we have to be conscious 'of the danger of assuming unilinear evolution of institutions or ideas'; ibid., 205.

17. Eichrodt, I, 26.

18. Wright, *God who Acts*, 20.

19. Judges 11.

20. See Childs, *Old Testament Theology*, 168ff.

21. W. F. Albright, *Yahweh and the Gods of Canaan*, 1 and note.

22. See Goldingay, *Theological Diversity*, 103, though he leaves it uncertain what conclusions he draws from this. Brueggemann, *Theology of the Old Testament*, 665, writing about Wellhausen's view of the 'priestly model of presence' as a 'late, degenerate development', goes on to refer to it as an 'evolutionary construct'. This is evolution backwards!

23. For one example among many, cf. E. V. McKnight, *Post-Modern Use of the Bible*, 110 n.8: 'Biblical texts and meanings are to be understood in relationship but not in any relationship governed by evolutionary historical ideologies.'

24. S. Bjerke, 'Ecology of Religion, Evolutionism and Comparative Religion', 242. See also the full discussion of the theme, ibid., 221–98.

25. C. Westermann, 'Schöpfung und Evolution'.

26. Incidentally, some would make a sharp distinction between *evolution* and *development*; I think this is probably implied by Theissen's position as outlined above. But Westermann uses both terms, with no obvious discrimination between them. Where a distinction is made, some would see development as gradual change and evolution as taking place by sudden quantal leaps; evolution would then be an acceptable idea and development a bad one. Others would stress the biological connotations of evolution and use it in a derogatory sense, while development would be tolerable as a historical development of ideas and the like, even if not acceptable for use within the Bible itself. 'Development', one may remind the reader, has a respectable history within Christian theology in the phrase 'development of doctrine', which has been mainly a Catholic expression.

27. Quotation from L. Oeing-Hanhoff, *Anfang und Ende der Welt*, 1981, 22; cited by Westermann in 'Schöpfung und Evolution', 244.

28. As Westermann himself points out in n. 10 of his article, he has worked this out in detail in his great Genesis commentary, on ch. 27 of that book. The emphasis on the category of *blessing* is one of Westermann's great contributions to Old Testament theology; see below, Ch. 19.

29. Cf also Ellen van Wolde, *Stories of the Beginning*.

30. *CD* III/1, Preface: '*Die Naturwissenschaft hat freien Raum jenseits dessen, was die Theologie als das Werk des Schöpfers zu beschreiben hat.*'

31. Cf. the comments of Childs on this, *Biblical Theology*, 405: Barth 'was criticized for avoiding the problem of relating creation to natural science . . . but Barth was primarily concerned to recover for theology the full dimensions of the biblical witness in the light of his trinitarian starting-point without the distraction of apologetics', and further remarks there.

32. For one example, cf. Mildenberger, in Ch. 29 below, 525.

33. O. Chadwick, *From Bossuet to Newman*, 195.

34. J. Barton, 'Preparation in History for Christ'. See also his *People of the Book?*, Ch. 5.

35. Its being enclosed in a volume dedicated specifically to the commemoration of the historically important Anglican essays entitled *Lux Mundi* may have led some biblical scholars to neglect it.

## 8. *Difference from History of Religion*

1. Later republished, with some omissions, as *Before Philosophy,* 1951. For its effects on biblical theology see also Childs, *Biblical Theology in Crisis,* 49.

2. See in particular the brief Epilogue, 337–44, which emphatically dissociates the Hebrews from most of what has been said in detail in the rest of the book. 'The Hebrews, though in the Near East, were only partly of it' (338f.). 'The borrowed features in Hebrew culture, and those which have foreign analogies, are least significant" (339). 'In the light of Egyptian, and even Mesopotamian, kingship, that of the Hebrews lacks sanctity. The relation between the Hebrew monarch and his people was as nearly secular as is possible in a society wherein religion is a living force' (341). The emphatic, and indeed dogmatic, character of the assertions about Hebrew religion are incongruous in view of the brevity of the presentation and its lack of exegetical detail in comparison with the rest of the book. Note also, incidentally, the emphatic opposition to the 'patternism' of the 'Myth and Ritual school' as seen in S. H. Hooke, E. O. James and especially I. Engnell, 405 n. 1.

3. Albertz suggests that for much Old Testament scholarship the interest in the history of religion was too much concentrated on the question of influences from foreign cultures, as discussed above, and too little on the history of Israelite religion itself.

4. For an excellent recent presentation, see E. W. Nicholson, *The Pentateuch in the Twentieth Century,* 1ff.

5. For a recent discussion of this work see Albertz, I, 6f.

6. On this see the classic description by C. Colpe, *Die Religionsgeschichtliche Schule,* which, however, concentrates on the idea of a 'Gnostic saviour myth' based on Iranian evidence, and therefore has more relevance to New Testament studies, notably through Bultmann, on whom see 57ff. On the Iranian side the central figure was R. Reitzenstein. A good brief survey in English is Marcel Simon, 'The *Religionsgeschichtliche Schule,* Fifty Years Later', but this again is more interested in the New Testament area.

7. Gunkel's central contribution in the history of religion was his *Schöpfung und Chaos in Urzeit und Endzeit* (1895), which pursued the theme of a battle with chaotic powers from Babylonian times through to apocalyptic. But Gunkel contributed much in other areas – form criticism of the Psalms, for instance – and it may be too narrow to identify him with the *Religionsgeschichtliche Schule.*

8. See B. Spencer and F. J. Gillen, *The Arunta: A Study of a Stone Age People.*

9. For further exemplification of this position, see below, Ch. 18.

10. *CD*I/2, 303 (German *'der konzentrierte Ausdruck des menschlichen Unglaubens')*; Sundermeier, *JBTh* 10, 1995, 191.

11. Gerd Petzke, in his valuable article 'Exegesis und Praxis', 4ff., argues that the contrast between theology and religion has its roots in the Bible itself. There is a qualitative distinction between theology, which is always true (an insight I have heard, I think, from Philip Davies also) and religion; or, one can say, theology belongs to the one true religion, religion otherwise is false religion. The distinction is thus 'biblicistic' (the term is meant negatively): this means, I think, that it is a formal continuation of a biblical attitude, continued and elaborated after it has ceased to fit with reality. For the sociologist of religion, Petzke continues, Christian theology is a religious orientation system in just the same way as Judaism, Islam or Buddhism, or secular systems such as Marxism. Distinctions between theology, religion and world-view thus collapse.

12. It is not clear that, even as seen from Childs' own viewpoint, the history of religion could be said to have been so damaging: for it is arguable that it was the history-of-religion

approach of Johannes Weiss that did more than any other force to discredit the liberal picture of Jesus and the kingdom of God. Cf. also John Reumann's remarks in his introduction to Stendahl's *The Bible and the Role of Women*, x: 'Most noteworthy is Professor Stendahl's emphasis on how *Religionsgeschichte* proved to be a positive boon to Swedish biblical study by rescuing it from the liberal era and setting it upon new paths.' Likewise in the Old Testament area, where the 'evolution of ethical monotheism' had been seen as the central theme, Stendahl wrote: 'Here, again, it was the radicals of the *religionsgeschichtliche Schule* who caused the construction of this liberal interpretation to crumble' ('Biblical Theology', *IDB* 1, 423). For a brief review of this, see H. Räisänen, *Beyond New Testament Theology*, 22ff.

13. Childs, *Biblical Theology*, 211.

14. Childs, *OTTCC*, 90.

15. See J. Barr, 'The Synchronic, the Diachronic, and the Historical: A Triangular Relationship'.

16. Barr, *Biblical Faith and Natural Theology*, 132f.

17. This term is much used by Childs, sometimes with reference to the phenomenon here discussed, sometimes otherwise: for examples cf. his *Biblical Theology*, 23 (of C. Geertz), 80 (of recent 'biblical theological solutions', 85 (of the term *Sachkritik*), 173 (of John Barton, on which cf. below, 404).

18. Childs has a very brief passage touching on this, *Biblical Theology*, 351f. Contrast the fuller attention from Zimmerli, on which see below, 315.

19. Albertz, *History of Israelite Religion* I, 246 n.36, writes that 'the histories of religion written by Vriezen and Eichrodt are insignificant compared with their theologies'. Even if this is so, the fact that they wrote them at all means that they did not completely reject a history-of-religion approach.

20. See his 'The History of Israelite Religion', in G.W. Anderson (ed.), *Tradition and Interpretation*, 351–84.

21. Hayes and Prussner, 111.

22. Vriezen, *Religion*, 71.

23. Bruce in G. W. Anderson (ed.), *Tradition and Interpretation*, 388.

24. Quoted from Vriezen, *Religion*, 273.

25. It should be remembered, of course, that Davidson did not complete his Theology himself; it was prepared later on the basis of students' notes and other materials. But there is no reason to doubt the strength of his conviction on this question, in spite of the apparent inconsistency between his actual work, which clearly counts as theology, and this argument, which it contains. Cf. the comment of Professor A. C. Cheyne in his article 'Bible and Confession in Scotland: The Background to the Robertson Smith Case', in W. Johnstone (ed.), *William Robertson Smith. Essays in Reassessment*. He writes: 'A. B. Davidson towards the close of his long life (in 1891) wrote in *The Critical Review* that "Instead of an Old Testament Theology, the utmost that can be given is a historical view of the religion of Israel, or of the religion of Revelation during the Old Testament period. The truths can neither be exhibited nor understood apart from the history"' (36).

26. Albertz notes that 'there was never [in Sweden] the theological contempt for history-of-religions research that there was in Germany' (9).

27. Whom Ringgren mentions (1, n.2); on Vischer's strong emphasis on the human nature of the Bible see my article 'Wilhelm Vischer and Allegory'.

28. Albertz, however, criticizes Ringgren's work as still having too much in common with the tradition of Old Testament theology (I, 9, 11). The fact remains that

Ringgren was solidly and completely identified, in his own mind, with the history-of-religion approach.

29. *TLZ* 88, 1963, col. 737. In general, I wonder if his statement was not too sweeping, if we bear in mind the work of Gese and others, already coming to the fore at the time of his writing. But Albertz says: 'When I was a student in Heidelberg there were no longer any lectures on the history of Israelite religion' (243 n.1).

30. I refer to his section of the composite volume Gese, Höfner and Rudolph, *Die Religionen Altsyriens, Altarabiens und der Mandäer.*

31. Albertz, *History of Israelite Religion*, I, 2.

32. See for instance his article 'Return to Biblical Theology', reprinted in his *History, Archaeology and Christian Humanism*, 287–300.

33. Thus Jon D. Levenson, *The Hebrew Bible, The Old Testament, and Historical Criticism*, 35, with good reason includes Bright's *The Authority of the Old Testament* as an example of biblical theology, or at least as including it.

34. I am not sure that this is true of the general public, including even the church-going public, who now derive more of their ideas of religion from the media of press and television and not from theologians of any kind.

35. To give one example, in arguing against the common belief among biblical theologians that creation is an element secondary to redemption, Berkhof, *Christian Faith*, 152, couples history of religion and dogmatic arguments: 'From a religious-historical perspective it is highly improbable, and at the same time dogmatically very forced, to hold that the belief in creation was an extrapolation from the belief in redemption.'

36. Quotation from the Foreword to the ET by J. R. Porter, ix.

37. Albertz, *History of Israelite Religion*, 1,16; compare his longer discussion of this work (9f.). For a fuller statement of Albertz's point of view, see below, 118ff. On Schmidt's approach cf. Childs' comments, *Biblical Theology*, 102.

38. *JBTh* 10, 1995, 12. Cf. n. 42 on the same page, in which he invites the reader to decide 'whether Childs' *Biblical Theology* or my *History of Religion* catches more of the exciting theological disputes and decisions in ancient Israel'.

39. R. Albertz, *Persönliche Frömmigkeit und offizielle Religion.*

40. On the work of Jeannette Fowler, see my review in *JTS* 41, 1990, 137–9.

41. Albertz, *Persönliche Frömmigkeit*, 159.

42. Cf. Sundermeier in *JBTh* 200. Albertz, he writes, is too well schooled in hermeneutics to think that there is such a thing as a presuppositionless discipline. Presuppositions that he reveals include: the effect of Auschwitz and the need to move forward the dialogue with Judaism, which (he thinks) is retarded by theologies of the Old Testament; also, that he takes into account not only the external perspective of a religion but also its internal perspective; the observer becomes, at least sometimes, and occasionally passionately, a participant; again, an involvement in liberation theology.

43. Cf. below, Ch. 12, where I argue similarly.

44. Quotation from J. Barton, 'The Messiah and Old Testament Theology'.

45. Albertz, *JBTh* 10, 181f. n.1.

46. See also his articles 'Die Stammesreligionen'; 'Interreligiöser Dialog und die "Stammesreligionen"'. Critical comments by Mildenberger, *Biblische Dogmatik* II, 213f. n.47.

47. E. Gerstenberger, 'The Religion and Institutions of Ancient Israel', 274f., wording slightly modified by me. By 'contextual theology' he means theology related to the social context, somewhat like 'liberation theology'.

48. See P. R. Davies, *Whose Bible is it Anyway?*, 78. Commenting on 'Albertz's suggestion that history of Israelite religion should *replace* Old Testament theology', he goes on: 'The suggestion that one might replace the other implies some sort of common function and common space. In fact, Albertz seems to me to end up with a not dissimilar picture from that which some Old Testament theologians might develop. Studying a religion and studying bibles are different things completely, and to suggest that one should replace the other is curious. What should not be allowed . . . is that studying the Old Testament will of itself yield any insight into ancient Israelite religion, without the benefit of genuine historical research into ancient Palestine.'

49. For a relevant example, cf. John Rogerson's remarks, in criticism of von Rad: 'I am profoundly disturbed . . . by the way in which von Rad can speak of the perceptive apparatus of "Israel", without making it clear whether he means all Israelites, or a particular religious insight within Israel, though I fear that he intends the former.' See his 'The Old Testament View of Nature: Some Preliminary Questions', 78. He does not use the term 'elite'; however, he does say: 'these passages [like Ps 104] do not represent what the average Israelite felt; they are religious texts, containing a religious interpretation of the natural world, a religious interpretation that was certainly not "given" along with ordinary perception of the world . . .' (79).

50. See, e.g., W. G. Dever in his 'The Contribution of Archaeology to the Study of Canaanite and Early Israelite Religion', 220: 'A true phenomenology of religion will consider not only normative religion, or what the texts produced by the establishment insisted *should* have prevailed, but also popular or folk religion, what the majority of adherents actually practised. One of the difficulties with most histories of the religion of Israel is that they are based on texts that are both late and elitist.'

51. Von Rad, 2, 429; cf. above and below, 111.

52. For fuller discussion of this see below, Ch. 12. Cf. Childs, a serious critic of all claims of objectivity, who nevertheless begins his *Introduction* with the statement that he 'seeks to describe as objectively as possible' the canonical literature (16).

53. Cf. Jon Levenson, who seems to me, in his strong polemics against Old Testament theology, to idealize history of religion in a quite unrealistic way. Yehezqel Kaufmann's *History of Hebrew Religion*, which he quotes as an example, seems to me to be as full of ideological prejudices as any biblical theology ever written.

54. Cf. the comment on Levenson's arguments, below, Ch. 18.

55. C. J. Bleeker, 'Comparing the Religio-Historical Method and the Theological Method', quoted by Albertz, I, 247 n. 56.

56. Albertz, I, 247.

57. It is important to note that many Old Testament Theologies do *not* automatically accept as authoritative and right *everything* in the biblical corpus simply because it is there. The more usual tendency is to be theologically critical of some areas and details and of some portions considered marginal, while remaining stoutly affirmative of the rightness and authority of the whole. Indeed it is for its critical attitude to some portions – often, to tendencies in the latest texts – that Old Testament Theology has often come under considerable censure. On this see below, Ch. 17.

58. Hayes and Prussner, 267; Räisänen, *Beyond New Testament Theology*, 102 and 190 n. 37.

59. See above, 102 and below, 652 n.2.

60. Albertz, I, 87, aptly writes: 'To describe "Canaanite religion" sweepingly as a "fertility religion" when we still know so little of its details is largely a caricature created by

Protestant prudery.' A good illustration comes from W. Robertson Smith – certainly a leading critical scholar in other respects – who wrote: 'The exercises of Canaanite religion gave
the rein to the animal nature, and so took the form of Dionysiac orgies of the grossest type'
– so in his *The Prophets of Israel,* 87, cited by Robert Carroll in W. Johnstone (ed.), *William
Robertson Smith. Essays in Reassessment,* 156. In modern times Berkhof, *Christian Faith,*
describes Baalism as 'fertility religion' (17) and says that 'before the Babylonian exile the
struggle was against naturalism' (236); cf. his statement (161) that 'Israel's struggle with
Baalism was against the religious sacralization of the forces of nature' (161), and his account
of polytheism on 14–17.

61. For a thorough and recent study see J. C. de Moor, *The Rise of Yahwism.*
62. Cf. the thoughts of John Barton, above, 123ff.
63. Childs, *Biblical Theology,* 355.
64. For Albertz's discussion of this, see his I, 85ff.; among numerous other sources see
the articles of M. D. Coogan, P. Kyle McCarter, J. H. Tigay and others in Miller, Hanson
and McBride (eds.), *Ancient Israelite Religion.*
65. G. J. Brooke, 'The Qumran Scrolls and Old Testament Theology', 75.


## 9. *Difference in the Size of Complexes*

1. I take this phrase from Eichrodt, I, 28, but use it in a somewhat different sense.
Actually Eichrodt in using this expression did not mean what was usually thought by those
who complained about the divisive effects of the historical-critical approach. At this
point Eichrodt was actually talking about the attempt of older orthodoxy to combine *dicta
probantia* and an extensive typology, followed by the effect of rationalism, which showed that
it was impossible to make the manifold biblical world of thought into a compendium of
harmonious doctrine. As Eichrodt saw it, at least at this point, historical criticism in the
tradition of Herder, de Wette and Wellhausen *restored* a meaningfulness which had been
lost. This, he implies, was a major reason for the dominance which the historical approach
then attained. Modern writers have been less nuanced, and have tended to apply such terms
as 'meaninglessness of *disiecta membra*' to the *results* and *effects* of historical criticism. It is in
this sense that I have used it here.
2. Cf. above, Ch. 4.
3. B. C. Ollenburger, 'Old Testament Theology', in Kraftchick, Myers and C. Ollenburger (eds.), *Biblical Theology: Problems and Perspectives,* 93.
4. Ibid., 306 n.45; Preuss, *Theology,* Vol. I, 1.
5. Cf. Childs' recent statement (Mays *et al., Old Testament Interpretation,* 295): 'It is very
doubtful whether the way of the future lies in more attempts at such comprehensive
summaries of the Old Testament material. Because the older syntheses that emerged in
the 1950s and 1960s have largely come apart, scholars in the coming decades will probably
focus their energy on fresh, more limited analytical investigations in order to reconstitute
the field.' On the other hand, in the same article he seems to think that 'a larger synthesis'
is necessary in order to be able to 'reflect theologically'.

## 10. *Difference in the Way of Thinking: Philosophy and Natural Theology*

1. Among the few papers that even touch on the subject is that of H.-P. Müller, 'Bedarf die Alttestamentliche Theologie einer philosophischen Grundlegung?'. That Professor Müller should have written this paper is a sign of his high originality among biblical scholars. Cf. also the contribution of Oeming, below, Ch. 28.

2. Childs, *Biblical Theology in Crisis*, 17.

3. Bultmann in H. W. Bartsch (ed.), *Kerygma and Myth*, 25.

4. Wright, *God Who Acts*, 90; quotations from Brunner, 58f., 47f.

5. So still in recent years Preuss, Vol.I, 239: one should be careful about the use of later philosophical, theological categories of thought, such as *aseity*.

6. Hegelian biblical theologians can of course be found if one goes back into the nineteenth century: Vatke is the well-known case. See L. Perlitt, *Vatke und Wellhausen*. But twentieth-century biblical theologians generally regarded this aspect of Vatke's thought with horror. They seem to have implied that the mere mention of Hegel's name was sufficient to prove a position wrong. Cf. Albright's remarks, above, 91. For a contrary view, which seeks to demonstrate the positive value for Hegel's thought for modern theology and traces its influence in doctrinal theologians like Barth, see Peter Hodgson, *God in History*, and other works.

7. On this question see further below, Ch. 12.

8. See in general his Excursus 'The Theological Problem of Old Testament History', ibid., 196–206. Cf. the paragraph based on von Rad, 200.

9. Cf. Childs, *Biblical Theology*, 201: 'Beginning in the last quarter of the nineteenth century there emerged a fresh set of philosophical proposals which sought to lay a wholly new foundation for historiography . . . It is obviously impossible . . . to sketch even an outline of these various positions . . . My intention is rather to pick up certain important ideas, often shared by different writers, which have been appropriated by biblical scholars in an effort to reinterpret the problems of biblical history.'

10. Thus Childs, *Biblical Theology*, 41f., points out that few modern biblical scholars would follow St Thomas Aquinas in his appropriation of Aristotle. But then he goes on: 'Yet the basic hermeneutical issue at stake turns on the fact that no modern biblical theologian can function without some other conceptual framework. Much of the modern search for the recovery of only internal biblical categories has been extremely naive.'

11. A. Richardson, 'Second Thoughts – III. Present Issues in New Testament Theology'. Thus he writes: 'Bultmann is quite frank about his own identification of the assumptions of positivist philosophical theory with historical method as such' and goes on to credit Bultmann with 'the assumptions of the old positivistic *religionsgeschichtliche* School and of latter-day Ritschlianism' (!) (110). G. E. Wright seems to have thought that it was 'positivism' when scholars identified 'a remarkable series of religious geniuses' in the Bible, such as Moses, the prophets, Jesus, and Paul: according to him, it was 'positivist scholars' who explained things in this way. See *God Who Acts*, 35.

12. See his *Collapse of History*, 79.

13. J. Barton, 'The Basis of Ethics in the Hebrew Bible'.

14. See Childs' section on 'The Distinctive Biblical Mentality' in *Biblical Theology in Crisis*, 44–7.

15. K. Stendahl, 'Biblical Theology, Contemporary', in *IDB* I, 418; quoted already in Barr, *Biblical Faith and Natural Theology*, 120. It is interesting, incidentally, that it is *this* aspect of biblical theology, rather than others, that Stendahl concentrates on in his famous

article. Consider such phrases as 'a world of biblical thought which deserves the name "theology" just as much as do the thoughts of Augustine, Thomas, Calvin and Schleiermacher' (425), or 'the modes and patterns of thought in the Bible' (430).

16. Pedersen was a fully critical scholar, but in a distinctly moderate way. On the Pentateuch he wrote of 'the admirable researches carried on during the latter generations' and said that 'there is no reason to deny that the analysis of the documents is on the whole correct'. Nevertheless distinctions between J and E were doubtful, as were source divisions in the old narratives of Judges. More negatively, he wrote: 'Far too frequently modern logic, in these respects, has blinded the critics and prevented them from discerning the inner logic of the narratives . . . far too much importance has been attached to the problem of the time of composition' (I, 27). For Moses, on the other hand, 'we cannot make a direct use of our sources . . . All the laws . . . date from a far later period . . . We have no means of answering the question, what Moses was from an historical point of view' (I, 18). Of the concluding verses of Amos he wrote (II, 548): 'We have absolutely no guarantee that the general hopes for the future expressed at the end of the book of Amos have been formulated by him' – a distinctly moderate view. For the main content of his book, the presentation of the Israelite soul and mentality, Pedersen in practice worked as if the material formed one unitary block. Ironically, on the other hand, his great book *Israel* shows no interest in *theology* as such, and the word seems almost never to appear.

17. Brunner, 32; Childs, *Biblical Theology*, 45; Wright, *God Who Acts*, 90.

18. Brunner in B. W. Anderson (ed.), *Essays in Old Testament Interpretation*, 247ff. The essay was first published in 1930. Cf. Barr, *Old and New In Interpretation*, 45.

19. My own translation of the text as quoted by Oeming, 32. I cannot find the corresponding passage in the published ET, though some of the phrases are there. At the time of finalization I do not have access to the various relevant editions.

20. Cullmann, *Immortality*, 8; cf. Barr, *Old and New in Interpretation*, 46.

21. *CD* III/2, 283; cf. my *Old and New in Interpretation*, 45.

22. See now J. Pelikan, *Christianity and Classical Culture*.

23. G. A. F. Knight, *A Biblical Approach to the Doctrine of the Trinity*. Knight argues among other things that it was tragic that the Fathers read the Bible in the LXX rather than the Hebrew. 'The whole Greek world of thought represented by the LXX translation of the OT was inimical to the Hebraic approach, what we now call the biblical approach, to the claims of faith' (ibid., 3 ).

24. Childs, *Biblical Theology*, 482, quoting Torrance, *The Trinitarian Faith*, 123. For further remarks on this opinion, see above, 163, and below, 430.

25. On this matter in general see J. Barr, *The Garden of Eden and the Hope of Immortality*. Mentioning this book in his good recent article in Mays *et al.*, *Old Testament Interpretation*, Childs sees in it 'a conscious attempt to radically alter traditional theology on the subject of the soul and immortality'. This may be so, but I am not sure which traditional theology he has in mind. On one side, in arguing that in Genesis death is not the punishment for the sin of Adam (e.g. 8ff.), I am certainly differing from much traditional theology. In doing so, however, I think I have the agreement of much modern biblical theology, e.g. very expressly Westermann, *Elements*, 95f. In the matter of the immortality of the soul, on the other hand, the purpose of my argument was not to *advocate* such a view of the soul, but to point out that all traditional theology held such a view, and that most modern biblical theology, in saying the very opposite, was adopting a 'modernist' position quite contrary to the most revered older traditions.

26. Text in the English edition of J. T. McNeill and F. L. Battles, Library of Christian

Classics XX, Philadelphia: Westminster Press and London: SCM Press 1960, I, 183ff.: quotation 186. Note the connection of Calvin's phrase with the text of Wisdom 9.15, which will be discussed below, Ch. 31.

27. Thus Calvin, ibid., 192: 'It would be foolish to seek a definition of "soul" from the philosophers. Of them hardly one, except Plato, has rightly affirmed its immortal substance.'

28. Among Old Testament Theologies we note that some of the Roman Catholic works are closer to the older theological tradition in this respect. The Protestant Preuss, who himself maintains (*Theology*, II, 110) that the Old Testament has no idea of a split between body and soul or body, soul and spirit, notes in his admirably open way (ibid., 346 n.75) that a contrary view is taken by the very traditional Roman Catholic P. Heinisch, who roundly declares (*Theology of the Old Testament*, 171f.) that 'Israel at all times firmly believed that the soul, when separated from the body, does not cease to exist'. And Preuss in his note mentions the evidence of the Wisdom of Solomon. A more modern Roman Catholic treatment like that of P. van Imschoot (*Théologie*, II, 11ff.) is helpful in that it distinguishes between the thought of older Israel and that of the later books, naturally including Wisdom.

29. Rightly so Childs, *Biblical Theology*, 572.

30. Cf. above, 157f.

31. Cf. the remarks on the Humboldt philosophy of language, Ch. 28.

32. Cf. Childs in *Biblical Theology in Crisis*, 47.

33. For further discussion of the relations between semantics and biblical theology see below, 232ff.

34. If there is any area where these practices can be said to have revived, it is, regrettably, in feminist interpretation.

35. See below, Ch. 15.

36. *Biblical Theology*, 42.

37. See J. Barr, *Biblical Words for Time*, London: SCM Press 1966, 20–46.

38. On biblical chronology in general, see my 'Why the World was Created in 4004 BC: Archbishop Ussher and Biblical Chronology'; *Biblical Chronology: Legend or Science?*; 'Luther and Biblical Chronology'; more briefly, 'Chronology 1. Israelite Chronology', in Metzger and Coogan, *Oxford Companion to the Bible*.

39. Barr, *Biblical Faith and Natural Theology*, 17 and n.29.

40. See below, Ch. 19.

41. Barr, *Biblical Faith and Natural Theology*, 202.

42. Westermann, in an interesting 1987 article, 'Karl Barths Nein. Eine Kontroverse um die theologia naturalis', tells how Barth's 'No' was received among the younger theologians with great enthusiasm and almost 100% agreement. See further discussion of this article below, Ch. 27.

43. So also Westermann, ibid., 389, where he writes: 'Barth and Brunner alike assume this concept [i.e., natural theology]: neither of them asks from where the concept comes, what it means, or how it is to be judged on the basis of the Bible.' I do not understand why I did not quote Westermann's article in my *Biblical Faith and Natural Theology*, for I had read it and had a copy in my possession.

44. For a brief survey, see Barr, *Biblical Faith and Natural Theology*, 18.

45. Ibid., 13, 19.

46. See my short article with this title in Rom Harré and R. Lamb (eds.), *The Encyclopedic Dictionary of Psychology*.

47. Childs, *Exodus*, 72f.

*11. Connections with the New Testament*

1. McKenzie is an exception, see below.

2. Eichrodt cites John 4.22, 'Salvation is of the Jews', but only to confirm the position of the P document to the effect that Israel's 'privileged position' is firmly safeguarded (58). He says that there are two divergent lines of understanding of b^erit in the Old Testament and this is paralleled by a similar duality in the New Testament (66f., no details given). The actual effect of New Testament material in this passage is minimal.

3. Cf. Childs, *Biblical Theology*, who devotes a chapter (413–51) to the subject 'Covenant, Election, People of God', and notes, after a review of the evidence of Old and New Testaments, that 'up to this point within the New Testament, the term covenant, which was of such basic importance within the Old Testament, has emerged as a somewhat minor category' (438). He goes on to say that this is no longer the case in the Letter to the Hebrews. For this author the theology of covenant is a major concern; most likely 'he was consciously exploiting the double meaning of *diatheke* as both covenant and testament to illustrate the point that Christ died to ensure the validity of the promised eternal inheritance' (439). Childs is not very clear on this point, but appears to want to deny that Hebrews considers the old covenant to be abrogated through the new. On this cf. the section 'Diatheke im Hebräerbrief', in Erich Grässer, *Der Alte Bund im Neuen*, 95–115.

4. The only particular passage mentioned in the section is John 1. The footnote (79 n.2) lists six New Testament passages, but there is no discussion of them.

5. On this see von Rad in *ThLZ* 88, 1963, 407f., cited by Vriezen, 149 n.2.

6. Laurin on Jacob, in R. B. Laurin, *Contemporary Old Testament Theologians*, 167.

7. Ibid.

8. McKenzie, *Old Testament Theology*, 319.

9. Cf. his earlier *The Law and the Prophets. A Study of the Meaning of the Old Testament*, delivered as lectures in 1963, where the word 'meaning' of the title is very much focussed on the meaning for the New Testament and modern Christianity. It is not to be supposed that Zimmerli backed away from this interest in the course of time: he was passionately devoted to it throughout his life. Nevertheless, as I say, his actual Theology held back from expression of it. Already in *The Law and the Prophets* he was emphasizing the importance of brotherly dialogue with Israel and Judaism, cf. 3, 96.

10. Cf. Rendtorff, *Kanon und Theologie*, 91.

11. Zimmerli's roughly contemporary article 'Biblische Theologie I' , in *TRE*, appears also to give little or no attention to connections with the New Testament, though this may be a result of the organization of the volume, since the article is paired with O. Merk's 'Biblische Theologie II' on the New Testament.

12. Cf. likewise, more recently, Preuss's concluding section (II, 305ff.), similarly on 'The Openness of the Old Testament'. This phrase, he is careful to make clear, 'does not immediately mean, and does not only mean, its openness to the New Testament'. This latter, he goes on to say, is something that can be spoken of only by a 'Christian theologian whose approach is from the New Testament side and comes to the Old Testament in investigation and questioning'.

13. The English translation as published is somewhat misleading here, cf. German II, 304.

14. See above, 113ff.

15. Cf. the comments of Childs on Dodd and Lindars, *Biblical Theology*, 227f. There he says that 'Lindars prejudged the function of his material by assuming that the purpose of a

citation was primarily apologetic' and goes on to say that this 'initial construal' made the enterprise 'very subjective and far too speculative to be assured of its historical probability'. It does not seem to me that Lindars 'assumed' this: rather, he came to this conclusion in the course of his work. To Childs the term 'apologetic' might well seem offensive, as to the Barthian tradition in general. But Lindars did not mean the word in this sense: 'apologetic' here meant to him 'providing scriptural evidence of belief in Christ'. In any case in his Exodus commentary (22), Childs himself had earlier said that Lindars (and also Stendahl) was 'probably correct in emphasizing the apologetic element in Matthew's attempt to establish by means of proof texts the messianic claim of Jesus in terms of Bethlehem and Nazareth'.

16. As one small example, cf. my 'Paul and the LXX: A Note on Recent Work'.

17. Cf. H. D. Betz, *2 Corinthians 8 and 9*, 102–8.

18. Childs rightly, *Biblical Theology*, 94: 'There is an equal need to investigate those cases in which the New Testament made no use of the Old Testament, but stood at a great distance from its tradition history.'

19. See below, 417–22.

20. In B. W. Anderson, *The Old Testament and Christian Faith*, 8–35. Among many discussions cf. the recent one by Stuhlmacher, *Biblische Theologie des Neuen Testaments* I, 15–19, with special reference to the Old Testament on 17, 19.

21. See the short survey by Stuhlmacher, ibid., 20f.

22. Goppelt's dates were 1911–73; his New Testament Theology was edited posthumously by J. Roloff in 1975–76, *ET Theology of the New Testament* (2 vols).

23. L. Goppelt, *Typos. Die typologische Deutung des Alten Testaments im Neuen*.

24. See, however, the sympathetic assessment of Stuhlmacher, ibid. 27–9.

25. Spriggs, *Two Old Testament Theologies*, 69.

## 12. Evaluation, Commitment, Objectivity

1. Vol. 1, 1962, 32–48.

2. Also now Francis Watson; see 200ff. below.

3. See Smart, *The Past, Present and Future of Biblical Theology*, 41–3: quotation 43.

4. Childs, 'Interpretation in Faith: The Theological Responsibility of an Old Testament Commentary', quoted by Stendahl, 'Method in the Study of Biblical Theology', 203 n. 13. On Stendahl's views see further below.

5. Contrast Ben C. Ollenburger, who, in his 'What Krister Stendahl "meant" – a Normative Critique of "Descriptive Biblical Theology"', surely the best modern discussion of the matter, disagrees with Stendahl on this matter but examines the arguments in detail, entirely avoids any negative criticism of Stendahl, and writes that 'his contributions to biblical scholarship have been major and exemplary' (63).

6. In this, however, I should add that there has probably been a change between the time when Stendahl wrote – doubtless in the late 1950s, since his article was published in 1962, – and the present time of writing. With the rise of postmodernism, cynicism towards 'objectivity' has escalated enormously since that time.

7. Cf. perhaps the judgment of Childs, *Biblical Theology in Crisis*, 79, that 'Stendahl's article received such a ready response because he advocated what was, in fact, already happening. Certainly *The Interpreter's Bible* dramatically illustrated in its format the austere separation of descriptive exegesis and theology.' I very much doubt, however, whether

Stendahl considered the format of *The Interpreter's Bible* to represent what he intended.

8. W. Brueggemann, *Old Testament Theology*, 111. Note similarly the opinion of L.G. Perdue, *The Collapse of History*, 9, who notes 'an increasing number of biblical theologians rejecting the descriptive approach'.

9. Thus James Smart held up for derision, marked by his exclamation mark, the idea, supposed by him to follow from Stendahl's thinking, that 'All that is needed is an adequate historical methodology. The agnostic can tell us the meaning of what the first Christians testified concerning the cross and the resurrection of Jesus!' – so his *Past, Present and Future of Biblical Theology*, 42.

10. Childs, 'Interpretation in Faith: The Theological Responsibility of an Old Testament Commentary', 432–49. Cited already above, 189.

11. 'Method in the Study of Biblical Theology', 203 n. 13. Stendahl's note contains further useful arguments. On his views see further below.

12. For Kermode's discussion of Childs' proposal and of my criticisms of it see his 'Canons'.

13. In his recent article in Mays *et al.*, *Old Testament Interpretation*, 295, Childs says that Eichrodt made an 'appeal to objectivity', but I do not think that this is true. He went no farther than asserting the principles as I have stated above.

14. On this question see below, Chapter 15.

15. As set forth in his article 'Biblical Theology, Contemporary', *IDB* 1, 418–32.

16. On this see K. Stendahl, *The Bible and the Role of Women*.

17. See James Barr, *The Garden of Eden and the Hope of Immortality*, esp. 2, 52f., 94–9.

18. Ibid.

19. Note an interesting retort against Stendahl by P. Stuhlmacher, *Theologie des Neuen Testaments* I, 239ff., who takes Stendahl's ideas (and those of some others, e.g. A. F. Segal, E. P. Sanders, H. Räisänen, J. D. G. Dunn) as 'attacks' on justification by faith and seeks to vindicate what he himself calls the 'German' view of it. Cf. also Childs, *Biblical Theology*, 245, who classifies Stendahl's view, along with those of A. Schweitzer and E. P. Sanders, as 'a popular liberal construal of Paul'. I cannot see how Stendahl's view on this subject, whether right or wrong, can be correctly classified as 'liberal'; on the contrary, I have noticed the warm welcome it has received from many whose theological judgment would count as distinctly 'conservative'. Francis Watson mentions as part of this 'de-Lutheranization' of Paul such distinctly non-liberal scholars as Markus Barth, J. D. G. Dunn, and N. T. Wright: see his *Paul, Judaism and the Gentiles*, 18, and Chs. 1 and 10 in general.

20. Räisänen, *Beyond New Testament Theology*, 112. The example is germane, because Stendahl mentions Schweitzer quite a lot in his article on biblical theology, *IDB* 1, 418–19.

21. Thus Childs, *Biblical Theology in Crisis*, observes that: 'One often gained the impression that what distinguished Biblical Theology from the disciplined study of the Old and New Testaments was a homiletical topping' (93). This was, as he put it, 'one of the soft spots' of the movement. On the other hand, in the same pages he emphasizes the involvement in a present task. 'If Biblical studies are to remain vibrant for theology, they must benefit from active confrontation with the new questions of the age, and not be allowed to slip back into a state of scholarly antiquarianism' (ibid., 94f.). Biblical theology, Childs goes on to argue, must be revived and continued because 'Christian pastors' need it. They need to have a 'theological synthesis' of their own (95). But this does not answer the key question. It does not explain why their theological synthesis must consist of *biblical* theology: why should it not consist of dogmatic theology?

22. Cf. L. G. Perdue, *The Collapse of History*, 9, who writes: 'The descriptive approach

also does not attempt to engage present culture, leaving that task to those contemporary theologians (e.g., Paul Tillich) who see modern culture as an important consideration in theological discourse.' Stendahl's position is that there are two distinct *operations*, not that the second stage should or must be left to some other group of persons. He himself, as illustrated above, very much 'engaged present culture'.

23. Tsevat, 'Theologie des Alten Testaments', 333f. He describes Stendahl's formulation as short and clear, but then goes on to explain it in the terms as stated above, yet with the qualification that it does not appear so in Stendahl's version (*wiewohl anscheinend nicht in der Fassung Stendahls*). Tsevat goes on to plead that there should be no more exegesis of the Old Testament 'for our times' (335).

24. For further discussion of Mildenberger's general position see below, Ch. 29.

25. There is a further note to the same effect in his later *Text and Truth*, 28 n. 3.

26. See my article 'Allegory and Historicism'.

27. Cf the views of John Barton cited above, Ch. 8.

28. See my *Old and New in Interpretation*, 176f., 185–9.

29. For an earlier discussion of these examples see my *Holy Scripture: Canon, Authority, Criticism*, 151ff.

30. Francis Watson displays a ludicrous misunderstanding of Childs' thinking when he suggests that this usage on Childs' part is 'the standard critical appeal to the "time-conditioned" character of this or that feature of the New Testament texts as a way of excluding it from serious theological and hermeneutical consideration' (*Text and Truth*, 223 n. 41). The argument – though there may indeed be questions about its validity at this particular point – is repeatedly used as an anti-historical-critical one; and who will believe that Childs is seeking to exclude the texts from serious theological and hermeneutical consideration?

31. This is confirmed by the judgment of Gunneweg, see below, Ch. 26.

## *13. Historical Theology – A Possible Analogy*

1. One relevant study, exactly in line with our theme, is that of F. J. Cwiekowsky, 'Biblical Theology as Historical Theology'. It works, however, within a rather old-fashioned and scholastic framework.

2. This is implied, perhaps, though in the reverse direction, by the sharp critique of Jon D. Levenson, who wants (at least some of the time) to abolish *both* historical criticism and biblical theology; see below, Ch. 18.

3. J. Van Seters, *Abraham in History and Tradition*.

4. See below, Ch. 15.

5. In J. Barton (ed.), *Cambridge Companion*, 126.

6. J. Muddimann, *The Bible: Fountain and Well of Truth*, 7.

7. So J. J. Collins, cf. above, 83; M. Oeming, below, 505f., 512, and probably many others.

8. Quotation from my 'Some Old Testament Aspects', 14f.

## *14. Opposition to Biblical Theology*

1. Francis Watson, *Text and Truth*, should now apparently be added here.

2. W. A. Irwin, 'The Study of Israel's Religion', 124f.; also his 'A still, small Voice . . .

said, What are you doing here?', *JBL* 78, 1959, 1–12.

3. I do not know if he put this phrase in writing, but I heard him say it. The phrase is memorable: in certain respects, as my arguments may show, Irwin was fairly near the truth in this.

4. *JBL* 78, 1959, 12.

5. This is, for instance, the immediate response of James D. Smart to Irwin in his *The Interpretation of Scripture*, 26. This response by Smart is seen as 'devastating' by Childs, *Biblical Theology in Crisis*, 34.

6. Cf. for instance his theologically sensitive study *Wisdom in Proverbs*, London: SCM Press 1965.

7. See R.N. Whybray, 'Old Testament Theology – A Non-Existent Beast?', in Barry P. Thomson (ed.), *Scripture: Meaning and Method*, 172.

8. He pointed here to what he considered to be the lack of integration of Wisdom into the Theologies of Clements and Vriezen.

9. S. Morenz, *Ägyptische Religion*.

10. This is a somewhat surprising ending, and one that actually damages Whybray's argument quite a lot: for in fact Rowley's book itself was clearly conceived as belonging to the genus Old Testament theology. The lectures, said Rowley, 'fall within the field of Old Testament theology' (19f.), and his entire Introduction (13–22) makes this clear in detail. His book had an avowed limitation, in that it was impossible 'to present a complete biblical theology within the compass of seven lectures', so that only a selection of the aspects of such a theology could be treated (20). This work seems, surprisingly, not to be mentioned by Hayes and Prussner. See my review in *JSS* 2, 1957, 397–9. Behind the Bible, according to Rowley, there was a fundamental unity, and 'the inner unity within the revelation should be sought in a theological study'. It is difficult to see that this work of Rowley's supported Whybray's argument. Certainly Rowley, as he puts it, 'eschewed the singling out' of 'one key idea in terms of which to construct the whole, such as the covenant, or election, or salvation' and 'preferred to expound, one by one, "those elements of Israel's distinctive faith which, incipient at first, were developed in her history, and . . . those practices which, even though of older or alien origin, were accepted permanently into her faith and made its vehicle."' But these words of Rowley were surely intended to *support* the claim that his book was a work of Old Testament theology.

11. Whybray, 'Old Testament Theology – A Non-Existent Beast?', 169.

12. J. Christiaan Beker, 'Biblical Theology in a Time of Confusion'; 'Reflections on Biblical Theology'. The term 'imperialism' is highlighted on the first page of the *Theology Today* article, 185. Cf. the use of the same term by Stendahl, above, 200, and 666 n.32.

13. See C. D. Batson, J. C. Beker and W. M. Clark, *Commitment without Ideology. The Experience of Christian Growth*, see especially the portions written by Beker: 22–42, 52–182, and the general introduction, 11–20.

14. James D. Smart, *The Past, Present and Future of Biblical Theology*, 40f.

15. Cf. examples in Childs' argumentation, e.g. his *Biblical Theology*, 23 (referring to Kelsey and Ollenburger): 'In sum, I remain critical of any theological position in which ecclesiology takes precedence over christology.' The implication seems to be that these abstracts must be used and that there is a correct order or hierarchy within which one must use them. The average reader's feeling is surely: we don't know what you are talking about, all these terms and relationships are unreal.

16. *PSB* 16, 1995, 22. Cf. also Miller in Musser and Price, *A New Handbook of Christian Theology*, 63–9, with reference to Beker on 67.

17. See the group of essays in *PSB* 16, 1995, 1–35.

18. S. J. Kraftchick, C. D. Myers, Jr and Ben C. Ollenburger (eds.), *Biblical Theology: Problems and Perspectives*.

19. *PSB* 16, 1995, 23.

20. Here Gyllenberg refers to Vischer's *Christuszeugnis*, which he categorizes as an *Unding*, a non-thing or absurdity.

21. The reader should note the importance of this position in relation to the later suggestions of pan-biblical theology. These have tended to suggest that if all biblical theology in Old and New Testaments taken together were taken as one discipline, it would produce a unitary theology of the entire [Christian] Bible. As Gyllenberg saw it, the effect would be the opposite.

22. The works mainly addressed are: Francis Watson, *Text, Church and World* (see Davies, 17, 35–45), and Childs, *Introduction to the Old Testament as Scripture* (see Davies, 28–36, 44f., 79).

23. *Biblical Theology in Crisis*, 71f.; cf. also his review in *JBL* 80, 1961, 374–7.

24. Thus in *The Semantics of Biblical Language*, 273ff., I expressly explained that the sort of Old Testament theology represented by Eichrodt was not liable to most of the linguistic criticisms I had put forward. This may have been saying too much, but it was certainly what I thought at the time. In my article 'Biblical Theology' in the *IDB* supplement volume (1976), 107, I clearly stated that my attack on the use of Hebrew and Greek words 'was not an attack on biblical theology in itself'; I had maintained that 'biblical theology had encouraged the misuse of linguistic evidence, but not that it necessarily depended on such misuse'.

25. See *The Semantics of Biblical Language*, 108, 144–7. I nowhere suggested that these weaknesses were intrinsic to the general impression of Jacob's work, which I thought to have many creative and useful aspects. Contrast Hayes and Prussner, 226f., who incorporate these semantic criticisms in a basically very negative evaluation of Jacob's book.

26. Jacob died, much regretted, early in 1998; at the last moment in the preparation of this present work, by the kind courtesy of Professor Alfred Marx, I received a copy of his last publication, *Bible, Culture et Foi* (1998).

27. Thus my own review of von Rad's work, when it did appear complete, in *ExpT* 73, 1961–62, 142–6, was concerned much more with his emphasis on *history* as a theological category than on any linguistic or semantic defects. In fact von Rad very much adhered to the sort of linguistic philosophy that I opposed (on this see below, Ch. 28); but, as I saw it, his scholarship was so good that he did not allow it to affect his detailed exegetical statements too much. Something of the same sort, incidentally, is true of Bultmann.

28. J. Bourke, 'A Survey of Biblical Theology', 55f.

29. Or, to take a more recent example, Professor Clines in a generous review (in *Theology*, November 1993, 502) of my *The Garden of Eden and the Hope of Immortality*, writes: 'This is "biblical theology" at its best (though Barr would hate the term).' I quite understand that I may have caused that impression, but it is not my actual point of view and never was. I would hardly be writing this present volume if I simply hated biblical theology. I fully welcome Clines' understanding of that book as 'biblical theology'. My only qualification is that I myself would incline to think of it as a kind of mixture: some of it is indeed biblical theology, or a particular theme from biblical theology, while some of it is more like a survey of modern discussions and an argument with them, which last aspect may well be needed for biblical theology to have any effect, but which I would hardly class as being actual biblical theology. That element comes closer to (post-biblical) historical theology.

30. Torrance, I think, never thought that he had been wrong in these matters in the

slightest. See, for instance, his *Reality and Evangelical Theology*, 160 n. 18, where he writes: 'Barr's ill-judged attack on the lessons to be learned from etymology contrasts with Plato's wise judgment that we are often put on the right track of the objective semantic reference of a term by examining archaic forms (*Cratylus* 401C).' As I wrote in 'Exegesis as a Theological Discipline Reconsidered – and the Shadow of the Jesus of History', 45 n.31: 'All that Torrance proves by this argument is his inability to read Plato. The *Cratylus* is a satire in which it is shown how, from words, by "etymology", anything at all can be proved.' But there seems to have been an effect. For from just about this time Hebrew words and etymologies, and indeed the entire machinery of biblical theology, disappeared from Torrance's writings, which became abstract and more philosophical in type, using the character of modern science to prove his theology right, and thus moved closer to natural theology. Similarly, the appeal to Plato as a source of wisdom is itself a complete U-turn in comparison with older times. Cf. the reaction of Childs, *Biblical Theology*, 406; also Abraham, *Canon and Criterion in Christian Theology*, 386f. And on etymology in general see the remainder of my note quoted above. As I point out there, if etymologies and archaic meanings are to be so important, it is bad luck for theology, which has no resources to pronounce on such matters.

31. Barth, *CD* I/2, 821. See also the excellent article of John Barton, 'Should Old Testament Scholarship be More Theological?' .

32. Note here Stendahl's anxiety to ensure that scholarship should not use its linguistic abilities to impose arguments upon the church. This was what he meant by his allegation of 'imperialism' on the part of biblical theology.

33. McKenzie, *Theology*, 10.

34. Goshen-Gottstein, 'Tanakh Theology', 635 n. 5. The reference of both McKenzie and Goshen-Gottstein was probably to the concluding remarks of my review of von Rad in *ExpT* 73, 1961–62, 146. I was not against the writing of Theologies as such, but thought that, after von Rad, the next step was not the writing of further full-length works, but a series of smaller-scale investigations. This opinion, whether right or wrong, is in exact agreement with that of Childs, 'Old Testament Theology', 295, where he writes: 'it is doubtful whether the way of the future lies in more attempts at such comprehensive summaries of the Old Testament material . . . scholars in the coming decades will probably focus their energy on fresh, more limited analytical investigations . . .'

35. For example, I certainly do not 'stand in the solid tradition of modern historical criticism' (as I clearly explain, see *Holy Scripture. Canon, Authority, Criticism*, 130: as I say there, 'I was myself never much of a historical-critical scholar. I do not know that I ever detected a gloss, identified a source, proposed an emendation or assigned a date.' If people think this was a joke, they are much mistaken). Nor do I 'reject historical views of inspiration and biblical authority'; nor do I depend much on French structuralism or on Noam Chomsky; nor is Chomsky a French structuralist; nor is the emphasis of Dietrich Ritschl and myself primarily based on the Bible as literature; nor do I appeal much to Paul Ricoeur, much as I respect him; nor did the good Dr Paul Wells, with whom I was happy to work, 'suggest in his dissertation' that I am 'a representative of a well-defined neo-liberalism' – though he used it in his title, *James Barr and the Bible. Critique of a New Liberalism*, the actual argument of his dissertation advances no such case, and I doubt if the fatal word 'liberal' occurs within it, except with reference to *past* liberalism.

36. See for example Theissen, *Social Reality and the Early Christians*, and Meeks, *The First Urban Christians*.

37. Gottwald, 'Biblical Theology or Biblical Sociology?', 42.

38. Ibid., 52b.

39. Ibid., 56.

40. See Childs' main discussion of Gottwald in his *Biblical Theology*, 22f.

41. Cf. his *Biblical Theology*, 22–5, 666ff., 658–72, etc., also *OTTCC*, 24ff., 176f., 182, 186f. He does state that sociological work, like historical work, is entirely proper and useful (*Biblical Theology*, 136, etc.), but it is hard to see what sense this makes when in the rest of his book he invariably condemns all actual sociological approaches. See my comments in 'The Synchronic, the Diachronic and the Historical: a Triangular Relationship?'.

42. For a fair and balanced discussion see L.G. Perdue, *The Collapse of History*, 69–109. Being very much in sympathy with Perdue's analysis, I feel it unnecessary to go more deeply into the matter here.

43. On the significance of the 'New Criticism' see especially John Barton, *Reading the Old Testament. Method in Biblical Study*, especially Chapter 10, 140–57.

44. D. Ford, 'Barth's Interpretation of the Bible', 77; cf. J. Barr, *Biblical Faith and Natural Theology*, 129.

45. W. K. Wimsatt, Jr, 'The Intentional Fallacy'. Brief remarks by J. Barr, 'Reading the Bible as Literature', 21f. Note that Childs, *Biblical Theology*, 47, tells us that 'Calvin identified the literal sense with the author's intention'.

46. See Kermode, 'Canons'.


## *15. 'Real' Theology and Biblical Theology*

1. E. Brunner, *Revelation and Reason*, 290. See especially R. Smend, 'Theologie im Alten Testament'. Interestingly, R. Rendtorff has recently, in *JBTh* 10, 1995, 37, said precisely the opposite: 'A sentence like "the Old Testament has no theology" is in my eyes simply non-sense', but without reference to Brunner or anyone else who has uttered the remark.

2. On the central position of Brunner in the beginnings of the Biblical Theology Movement cf. Childs, *Biblical Theology in Crisis*, 17, who mentions this same book as one of his two most influential.

3. This is already indicated in a preliminary way above, 149.

4. Childs adds that as a result 'Biblical theologians were forced to do their own theology'.

5. J. Barr, 'The Theological Case against Biblical Theology', 5.

6. Cf. among others Reventlow in *ThR* 61, 1996, 123; Reumann, *Promise and Practice*, 9; Childs, *Biblical Theology*, 370, who appears to say that the article 'denigrates the value of biblical theology as lacking the integrity of a true discipline'. There is nothing in the article to this effect. So also Hasel in Ollenburger *et al.*, *Flowering*, 374, who quotes this article as evidence for the statement that: 'For Barr, biblical theology [and Old Testament theology] is descriptive, and clearly not normative or prescriptive' (11), But in the passage referred to I say '*let us suppose*' that this is so. I put this forward as one of 'two main extreme possibilities'. On the next page I say that this understanding is 'unrealistic'. These things are *suppositions* for discussion, not statements of my own opinion.

7. The one substantial exception that occurs to me is the powerful influence which the thought of von Rad exercised on the origins of the Pannenberg circle. But that group can hardly be said to have followed the guidance of von Rad; it seems rather to have felt itself forced to strike out in a new direction.

8. In this sense I think a theology that is more abstracted from biblical detail, like Tillich's (or indeed like some of the later writings of T. F. Torrance, on which cf. Childs,

*Biblical Theology*, 406), is *formally speaking* just as appropriate as a matrix for biblical interpretation as a theology full of pieces of exegesis, such as Barth's. This is relevant to the arguments of F. Watson, *Text and Truth*, 4.

9. In German: '*Man möchte nur wünschen, dass Eichrodt sich zu den verschiedenen Stufen in ihrer Unterschiedlichkeit des Kindlichen und des Vollendeten noch deutlicher bekennen würde und auch den letzten Rest der Meinung überwände, dass man damit irgend etwas am "Offenbarungsansehen" des Alten Testamentes abbreche.*'

10. From Barth's very limited references to biblical theology, and lack of discussion of it, I would surmise that he had in mind something like what Eichrodt was doing; or, if not this, then perhaps he thought of the older books from the beginning of the century, which often had titles like *Biblical Theology of the Old (or New) Testament*.

11. The good article of Christina Baxter, 'Barth – A Truly Biblical Theologian?', seems to show what is obvious, i.e. that Barth is a dogmatician who wanted 'to do theology in accordance with the Bible'. That he had a place for 'biblical theology' seems to me quite a different thing. See further below. Cf. also Baxter's article 'Biblical Theology' in *DBI*.

12. Barth *CD* 1/2, 483–4.

13. Wolterstorff, *Divine Discourse*, 68.

14. 'The study of the faith (Dutch *Geloofsleer*, cf. German *Glaubenslehre*; see translator's note, xv) is Berkhof's term for what I have called doctrinal theology; like me, he dislikes the traditional terms 'dogmatics' and 'systematic theology'.

15. G. Ebeling, 'The Meaning of Biblical Theology'.

16. The question raised here by Ebeling seems not to be discussed in Berkhof's *Christian Faith*.

17. *The Logic of Theology*, 68; wording of the English slightly altered by me. Ritschl may well have altered his view of these matters more recently – see his article in *JBTh* 1, 1986, 135–50 – but the view as stated by him in his *The Logic of Theology* remains suitable as a starting point for discussion.

18. 'The Meaning of Biblical Theology', 93f.

19. Smend, *Die Mitte des Alten Testaments*, 116.

20. Assmann, *Re und Amun*, 152ff., 174ff., 224f.

21. I repeat from above Childs' remark that 'Biblical theologians were forced to do their own theology'.

## 16. 'Christianizing' of the Old Testament?

1. See also Childs in *OTTCC*, 242, cited below, 259.

2. The idea of 'letting the Old Testament speak for itself' is sometimes decried on the grounds that it derives from the historical-critical approach and is contrary to principles of Christian theology, for which the Old Testament makes sense only when taken in combination with the New. That this interpretation is wrong is proved when we read a theological stalwart like H. Berkhof, who writes in his *Christian Faith*, 249: 'Already in paragraph 28 [on "Israel in the Christian Faith"] we pointed out that the Old Testament has been and often still is seriously neglected in the study of the faith. Christ is made the centre and starting-point, and from there one looks back on the Old Testament, with the result that it can no longer speak for itself and that the hermeneutical approach to it does not measure up to the requirements for a scientific study of the Bible. Therefore in paragraph 29 ["The Way of

Israel in the Old Testament"] *we tried to let the Old Testament speak for itself, without bringing in Christ.* The reader might expect that in paragraph 30 ["The Way of Israel in the New Testament"] we would now elucidate the Old Testament from the perspective of the New. But continuing the direction we took in paragraph 29, we want to do the opposite: elucidate the New Testament from the Old' (my italics).

3. Von Rad, German text, ³1960, 2, 11. He contrasts this approach with 'all this *Meistern und Dreinreden*' (on the part of Hesse, Hempel and Maag). Cf. my remarks in *ExpT* 73, 1962, 143ff.

4. See for example von Rad's discussion of the 'Immanuel Prophecy' of Isa. 7. 10–17: 2, 173f.

5. See especially C. Westermann (ed.), *Essays on Old Testament Interpretation*; G.Lampe and K. Woollcombe, *Essays on Typology*.

6. One exception is in Eichrodt, II, 80, who suggests that the relation of Spirit and Word in the Hebrew Bible is related to that of Word and Spirit in trinitarian doctrine. This is one of these purple passages at the end of a section where theologians have tended to break forth into Christian doctrinal conclusions, which as in this case were quite unnecessary and unrelated to the main material of the section which they ended. G. A. F. Knight's *A Biblical Approach to the Doctrine of the Trinity* might be the nearest approach to a real argument about this from within biblical, and especially Old Testament, theology. But this work is very eccentric, and the mere citation of it confirms my statement that Old Testament theology has seldom tried to bring the Old Testament material into direct contact with such doctrines as that of the Trinity. Cf., however, Childs, *Biblical Theology*, 83, who, while accepting that 'the Old Testament witness to creation does not ever sound the name of Jesus', goes on in the next sentence to say: 'At the same time, it is equally true that the Old Testament does not conceive of the creator God as a monad or monolithic block.' There is 'a dynamic activity within the Godhead', an eschatological relation between old and new, a diversity between transcendence and immanence. And this can well be argued. But Childs' *way* of utilizing it is distinctly by setting it within a *Christian* context, the 'profoundest dimension of the Christian Bible', expressed as 'reflecting on how this variety of witness to the God of Israel is to be understood in the light of the New Testament's witness'.

7. Childs, exceptionally, manages to bring this in: see his *Biblical Theology*, 482, but it is here in relation to the total Christian Bible and not to the theology of the Old Testament. On this see again below, 430.

8. Cf. above, Ch. 23.

9. Cf. Morna D. Hooker, *Jesus and the Servant*.

10. Westermann, 'Zu zwei Theologien', 110f.

11. Vriezen, 147, says that 'Von Rad derived the credal theory as a working hypothesis from the study of the New Testament (cf. his reply to Conzelmann in *EvTh*, 1964)'.

12. M. Oeming, 'Ist Genesis 15, 6 ein Beleg für die Anrechnung des Glaubens zur Gerechtigkeit?'.

13. G. von Rad, 'Die Anrechnung des Glaubens zur Gerechtigkeit'.

14. Another attack on von Rad's exegesis of this text, apparently independent of that of Oeming, is made by Jon D. Levenson, *The Hebrew Bible, the Old Testament, and Historical Criticism*, 56–61. He points out that although most of the rabbinic commentators understood the subject of the verb 'and he reckoned it' to be YHWH, Nachmanides 'argued that it was in fact Abraham who reckoned God as righteous'. He goes on: 'Luther's utter contempt for this interpretation originates in his Pauline theology, for on purely grammatical considerations either specification of the implied subject is defensible.' In the Hebrew Bible, he

maintains, 'righteousness could be imputed not only for faith, but also for observance'. For further discussion of Levenson's position in general, see below, Ch. 18.

15. Cf. also *OTTCC*, 219f.: 'Abraham's faith in God is declared to have established Abraham as righteous in God's sight. His righteousness is not the result of any accomplishment, whether of sacrifice or acts of obedience. Rather, it is stated programmatically that belief in God's promise alone has established Abraham's right relation to God. He has made the proper response through faith.'

16. Thus, for one recent example among many, Childs *(Reventlow FS*, 1994, 237f.) tells us that E. Hirsch 'took up Luther's contrast between law and gospel and distorted it into an aggressive attack against any authoritative role of the Jewish Scriptures for the Christian faith' and goes on to refer to it as a 'form of blatant Marcionism'. The use of the Marcionite bogey has been traditional and customary in many traditions of Old Testament theology in this century. For a critique of its validity, see my 'The Old Testament and the New Crisis of Biblical Authority'. Those who sought to secure the authority of the Old Testament by this means commonly knew nothing about Marcion and the other aspects of his thought: all they needed was the *name* of a heresy for use as a force in argument. The same tradition is continued and extended by F. Watson, *Text and Truth*, who finds Marcionism *everywhere* (even in Childs! – see his 269 n. 13).

17. A. van Ruler, *The Christian Church and the Old Testament*.

18. M.Goshen-Gottstein seems to have looked with some favour on van Ruler's thoughts; see his 'Tanakh Theology', 623 and 638 n.28.

19. Vriezen, 1–3, and 2 n.1.


## *17. Judaism after Biblical Times*

1. It is notable that Eichrodt here at least names the sources he has in mind, which he often fails to do (cf. below); but he still fails to provide any examples of the exact wording which might serve to justify his assertions.

2. *JBL* 65, 1946, 205–17. See discussion of this review in relation to evolution, above 85ff.

3. E.g. II, 339–40, with fairly ample notes, but only one mention of a Rabbinic source (340 n.3, one mention of Pirke Aboth).

4. Levenson, *The Hebrew Bible, the Old Testament, and Historical Criticism*, 40.

5. *JJS* 30, 1979, 1–22: quotation 2.

6. H. Berkhof, *Christian Faith*, 17, seems to agree with Eichrodt: 'After the exile, legalism became Israel's predominant religious outlook. All the emphasis was put on keeping a growing list of strict legal precepts of do's and don'ts. This development was at variance with the original faith perspective of Yahwism . . . Hence the course of the Old Testament makes such a strange impression on the reader: there seems to be no progress in it; it is anti-climactic, ending with the same problems with which it began.' He sees the covenant as having a 'crisis', already within the Hebrew Bible. And thus 'the crisis in which the covenant, according to the Old Testament itself, finds itself, and which according to Christian faith has been overcome by God himself, is of a permanent nature in Judaism' (22). Again, 'the way in which the Old Testament pictures the covenant and its crisis calls for a sequel. But if it is to be a genuine sequel, it has to add a new element by which the crisis either is overcome or made bearable' (23). 'Solutions' to this are offered in each of the three religions, Judaism, Christianity and Islam.

7. All this in his article 'The Hermeneutics of the Old Testament', in C. Westermann

(ed), *Essays in Old Testament Hermeneutics*, pages as indicated; original publication in German, *EvTh* 12, 1952, 6ff.

8. Cf. the long note, 121f. n.2, in which Vriezen seeks to answer the arguments of Jewish scholars who explain Christianity as the product of a syncretism with Hellenism, gnosticism, etc.

9. The reader would have to refer to Miskotte's *Het Wezen der Joodse Religie*, esp. 448ff., and other sources cited in the footnote.

10. On the idea of sin in Judaism see H. Berkhof, *Christian Faith*, 22.

11. Von Rad, 1, 91f. [published translation partly modified by me.]

12. Cf. the words of J. Blenkinsopp, 'This curious idea of a *Heilsgeschichte* which comes to an end at a certain point or (even more curious) which stops and starts again', in his 'Old Testament Theology and the Jewish-Christian Connection', 6; quoted in Levenson, *The Hebrew Bible, the Old Testament, and Historical Criticism*, 41.

13. This paper was read first at the Exegetical Days in Uppsala in 1966 and in various European universities thereafter. Forms of it were published in Swedish: 'Den teologiska värdering av den efterbibliska judendomen', *SEÅ* 32, 1967, 69–78, and in French: 'Le Judaïsme postbiblique et la théologie de l'Ancien Testament', *RThPh* 18, 1968, 209–17; but the English text was not previously published. Cf. also my Montefiore Lecture 'Judaism – Its Continuity with the Bible'. For references cf. Hayes and Prussner, 276ff.; Goshen-Gottstein, 'Modern Jewish Bible Research', 11 n. 37.

14. Review of Levenson in *JTS* 47, 1996, 557.

15. Räisänen, *Beyond New Testament Theology*, 120, 38; he cites G. Strecker, 'Das Problem der Theologie des Neuen Testaments'. Cf. also Räisänen's own works on *Paul and the Law*, etc.

16. The numerous works of E. P. Sanders are an obvious example, so also are those of Räisänen.

17. See Frances Young in J. Barton (ed.), *The Cambridge Companion to Biblical Interpretation*, 291, and 302 n. 6.

18. For the detailed references, see n.13 above.

## *18. Jewish Biblical Theology?*

1. There were indeed exceptions, at least in the later development of the subject: thus Vriezen in his *An Outline of Old Testament Theology* is in frequent conversation with Buber and (less often) with Klausner. He also mentions Flüsser, Seeligmann and Schoeps. There are some lengthy notes including these discussions (e.g. 12 n.1, 100 n. 4, 121 n.2, 400 n. 2). Moreover, much of this material was there in his first edition (Dutch original 1949), although it was amplified in the second.

2. In Miller, Hanson and McBride, *Ancient Israelite Religion*, 617f.

3. Cf. Gershom Scholem's saying 'not system but *commentary* is the legitimate form through which truth is approached'; cited by A. Graeme Auld, 'Can a Biblical Theology also be Academic or Ecumenical?',17.

4. Thus D. Cohn-Sherbok in his *The Jewish Heritage* mentions Franz Rosenzweig and Martin Buber as 'theologians' (176ff.), and under 'Jewish theologians in America' mentions Mordecai Kaplan, A.J. Heschel and Jacob Petuchowski (178ff.), followed by 'a number of Jewish theologians' (Ignaz Maybaum, Emile Fackenheim, Eliezer Berkovits, Richard Rubenstein) who 'have grappled with the question of whether it is possible to believe in

God' after the mass destruction of Jews in Europe (180ff.).

5. See, in addition to the article of Jacobs cited above, I. Kalimi, 'Religionsgeschichte Israels oder Theologie des Alten Testaments?', 56f. Kalimi's article reached me too late to receive full discussion here.

6. See Michael Fishbane, *Judaism*, 58.

7. See also Kalimi, 'Religionsgeschichte Israels', 62ff.

8. Tsevat, in Klopfenstein, *Mitte der Schrift?*, 329.

9. Ibid., 332.

10. In J. Neusner, B. A. Levine and E. S. Frerichs, *Judaic Perspectives on Ancient Israel*; now also reprinted in J.Levenson, *The Hebrew Bible, the Old Testament, and Historical Criticism*, 33–61, which contains other relevant articles. For some other reactions see R. E. Murphy in H. T. C. Sun and K. L. Eades, *Problems in Biblical Theology*, 271f.

11. Cf. for instance Räisänen, *Beyond New Testament Theology*, 192f. n. 73. The article was translated into German and appeared in *EvTh* 51, 1991, 402–30. See considerable citation of it in the articles of *JBTh* 10 and in Wahl's article in Kottsieper et al., *Kaiser FS*, 32–48.

12. I say 'he seems to favour' advisedly. In fact he speaks very strongly in favour of the history of religion. As I will indicate shortly, however, it is likely that a full commitment to this approach would create many difficulties for him which at this point he seems not to foresee.

13. Levenson, *The Hebrew Bible, the Old Testament, and Historical Criticism*, 36.

14. Wording as in the original publication as an article (284). Slightly altered in the book version (36).

15. Levenson, *The Hebrew Bible, the Old Testament, and Historical Criticism*, 37, quoting words of Goshen-Gottstein.

16. Quoted from Hasel, 173 (fourth edition, 198).

17. There is a similar incongruity in the emphatic opposition of Levenson to historical criticism, when his own work rather obviously accepts and affirms that same approach.

18. Levenson, *The Hebrew Bible, the Old Testament, and Historical Criticism*, 45.

19. Here again Levenson writes as if historical criticism was the actual *basis* of biblical theology, instead of the thing to which it sought to provide an alternative. This misconception may explain why he attacks them both as he does.

20. Cf. also the warmly welcoming article by Joseph Bourke OP, 'A Survey of Biblical Theology', along with the Editorial in *Life of the Spirit* 18, 50.

21. See *IDB Supplementary Volume*, 1976, 111.

22. Levenson, article, 287; book (diction slightly altered), 40. On this literature see Lukyn Williams, *Adversus Judaeos: A Bird's-Eye View of Christian Apologiae until the Renaissance*.

23. In S. Schechter, *Seminary Addresses and Other Papers*, 36–7.

24. See my *Fundamentalism*, 286 and 361 n.41. On these questions see now Ulrich Kusche, *Die unterlegene Religion*. Cf. other widespread discussions, e.g. the reviews by R. Ruether and P. Haas in *Religious Studies Review* 16/4, October 1990, 316–20, 320–3. It should be added that, so far as I can see, Schechter did not advance against contemporary criticism the objection that is now common and is discussed here, namely that it under-valued the late-biblical and post-biblical forms of the religion. His objection was a much simpler and cruder one: that it was anti-Semitism to suggest that Moses did not write the Pentateuch.

25. A scholar like James D. Smart is a good illustration. In the earlier days, while

accepting some moderate critical views, he was vehemently opposed to any idea that historical studies should have *leadership* in the field. Later, when he found that with Childs the critical results, or some of them, would be more or less expunged from the scholarly consciousness, he became equally vehement in opposing this. See his *The Past, Present and Future of Biblical Theology*.

26. In cases of this kind Barth prized the exegesis of the early church and looked with disapproval on the critical scholarship of Christians, whose product, he sometimes said, was similar to that of 'an unconverted Jew'.

27. Levenson, *The Hebrew Bible, the Old Testament, and Historical Criticism*, 123.

28. On this cf. the suggestions of Tsevat, above, 290f.

29. For another reaction to Levenson's book, this time by a Jewish scholar, see Kalimi, 'Religionsgeschichte Israels oder Theologie des Alten Testaments?', 55–61.

30. I must say that the vocalization Tenach or Tenakh is the one that is familiar to me and corresponds with the pronunciation I have heard over many years. I am pleased to see it used by Stefan Reif in his recent article 'The Jewish Contribution to Biblical Interpretation', in J. Barton (ed.), *The Cambridge Companion to Biblical Interpretation*, 150, 154.

31. Goshen-Gottstein, 'Tanakh Theology', 624f. For other comments see R. E. Murphy in H. T. C. Sun and K. L. Eades, *Problems in Biblical Theology*, 271.

32. Cf. his remark: 'We had better realize that it is only the belated entry of Jews into 20th-century Biblical scholarship that has prevented until now the development of a Jewish Biblical Theology', 'Christianity, Judaism and Modern Bible Study'.

33. 'Tanakh Theology', 623 and 638 n.26.

34. Ibid., 632f.

35. I do not use the term 'positivism' here in a derogatory way, as is common in theology: it was the term that Goshen-Gottstein himself used, and quite frequently, to state a major characteristic of Jewish and/or Israeli scholarship.

36. Ibid., 631, cf. 642 n.52.

37. Marvin A.Sweeney, 'Tanak versus Old Testament: Concerning the Foundation for a Jewish Theology of the Bible'.

38. Through the kindness of Professor John Barton I learn that Origen discussed the order of the books 'of Solomon', saying that Proverbs comes first because it imparts morality, Ecclesiastes second because it gives knowledge of the natural world, and Song of Songs third because it gives access to the vision of truth in God. This is indeed a theological interpretation of the order of books (but only of one group among them). Its basis, however, seems to lie in general philosophy, corresponding to Greek distinctions, and although the three books are compared to the three patriarchs Abraham, Isaac and Jacob, there is no hint of a tracing of the destiny of Israel by contrast with Christianity. It thus fails to confirm Professor Sweeney's view. For the source see L. Brésard, H. Crouzel and M. Borret (eds), *Origène. Commentaire sur le Cantique des Cantiques*, 6f., 128–43.

39. Thus, for instance, the location of Esther could plausibly fit in with a scheme like that of Josephus: for a sketch, see J. Barr, *Holy Scripture. Canon, Authority, Criticism*, 128f.

40. It is quite mistaken, in any case, to suppose that Eichrodt thought that Old Testament theology, as he conceived it, was not 'part of Christian theology'. Of course it was, to him, such a part, and its providing of a link with the New Testament was an essential element in his eyes. But he thought it was a descriptive part of Christian theology; the results of the description, however, were, I think, understood to be normative, though Eichrodt did not make this very plain.

41. *OTTCC*, 8.

42. In his *Biblical Theology*, 25f., Childs has a further short section on 'Jewish Biblical Theology' in which he observes how 'Jews continue to reflect theologically on the Bible in a variety of different and creative ways', and cites a number of distinguished examples. He appeals for 'an increased understanding between Jews and Christians'. Perhaps this section is intended to remove the impression that he *excluded* Jews from biblical theology, an impression created in the minds of many readers by his own remarks in *OTTCC*, 8. He then goes on to argue: 'whether this [Jewish] reflection should be called Biblical Theology is a secondary issue'. But this is not so. He uses the non-participation of Jews as part of his own definition of biblical theology as an essentially *Christian* enterprise. If Jews are participating in it, and if it is 'a secondary issue' whether it is biblical theology or not, then his own definition of biblical theology is simply *wrong* – or it is a 'secondary issue' whether it is right or wrong.

43. Thus Karl Barth in his *Church Dogmatics* quoted the Genesis commentary of Benno Jacob quite a lot, and often gave the impression of thinking that it was far better than those written by Christian scholars like Gunkel.

44. M. Z. Brettler, 'Biblical History and Jewish Biblical Theology'.

45. I. Kalimi, 'Religionsgeschichte Israels oder Theologie des Alten Testaments?'; id., 'History of Israelite Religion or Old Testament Theology? Jewish Interest in Biblical Theology'.


*19. Some Theologies of the 1970s*


1. Cf. Childs' recent judgment: 'In the period since the writing of these two classic theologies there have appeared a number of serious newer theological attempts . . . Yet in a real sense there have been no new major advances in these latter works.' So in Mays *et al.*, *Old Testament Interpretation*, 295.

2. His shorter work, *The Law and the Prophets*, has been mentioned above, Ch. 17. On the Theology, see my review in *BSOAS* 44, 1981, 358–9.

3. See W. Zimmerli, 'Alttestamentliche Traditionsgeschichte und Theologie'; also 'Erwägungen zur Gestalt einer alttestamentlichen Theologie'; and, most important perhaps, 'Biblische Theologie I (AT)'. This article, incidentally, contains a very thorough account of the earlier history of the subject.

4. Cf. especially his extensive review of von Rad in *VT* 13, 1963, 100–11.

5. Berkhof, *Christian Faith*, 233, wrote: 'The term "covenant" and what it stands for are rooted in Israel's early history and have, with interruptions, remained characteristic for Israel's faith through the centuries.' This was written against my own article 'Some Old Testament Aspects of Berkhof's *Christelijk Geloof*'. My article was a reaction to the original (Dutch) edition of his book and cited the misgivings of a variety of Old Testament scholars about the covenantal emphasis. I did not insist that these misgivings were *right*. I argued only: 'At least theologians have to give room in their minds to the possibility that this trend *might* be right. Perlitt's work in particular is likely to make a great impact.' On another aspect of Berkhof's remark as quoted above, see 219.

6. See Zimmerli, *Theology*, 24f., and his 'Erwägungen zur Gestalt einer alttestamentlichen Theologie'. Here he quite properly supports von Rad against my criticisms, but they still make a difference to his approach. Albrektson's *History and the Gods* is listed in the bibliographies of his *Theology*, 27. On the impact of the question cf. B. S. Childs, *Biblical*

*Theology in Crisis*, 65f., 77.

7. Zimmerli, *VT* 13, 1963, 105.

8. See especially his 'Zum Problem der "Mitte des Alten Testaments"'.

9. On this concluding passage see above, 177.

10. E.g. *TRE*, 450, where he mentions the avoidance of the name Yahweh by Qoheleth and other Wisdom books.

11. Cf. the criticisms of Goldingay, *Theological Diversity*, 213.

12. Published in *Tradition and Interpretation* (1979), so presumably written in the 1970s.

13. Zimmerli, 'Alttestamentliche Traditionsgeschichte und Theologie', 647 = ThB 51, 26.

14. This somewhat recalls the dislike of technical terms by Beker, mentioned above, 228.

15. Interestingly, Westermann remarks that the older exegetes did not raise the question what blessing, or an act of blessing, was, and gives the credit for opening the question to the history of religion, naming especially J. Pedersen's great book *Israel: Its Life and Culture* (1926). See C. Westermann, *Genesis 12–36*, 436.

16. We have seen above, Ch. 7, the connection between Westermann's emphasis on *blessing* and his thoughts about evolution.

17. For a discussion of this, see N. Lohfink, 'Kennt das Alte Testament einen Unterschied von "Gebot" und "Gesetz"?'.

18. Räisänen, *Beyond New Testament Theology*, 193 n. 73, writes that 'Westermann's *Elements* (1982) is still completely silent on Judaism!'.

19. The above points are, incidentally, closely related to positions which I have argued, see *Old and New in Interpretation* and *The Garden of Eden and the Hope of Immortality*.

20. See Knierim, *The Task of Old Testament Theology*, 183, and 185–98 in general.

21. Hayes and Prussner have only a brief passage on Fohrer's proposal about the 'centre' (253, 259), but otherwise nothing about the general characteristics of his Theology. Hasel's survey came out too late for the original appearance of Fohrer's Theology (in the same year, 1972), but he has adequate coverage of Fohrer in his fourth edition (see esp. 63–7). On Fohrer the best review is that by Westermann, 'Zu zwei Theologien des Alten Testaments'.

22. A. H. J. Gunneweg, *Biblische Theologie des Alten Testaments*, 34, acknowledges the adoption of the term from Fohrer and argues that 'God is not the object of an academic discipline but the object of faith. The object [of academic research] is rather the understanding of God, the understanding of self – with Fohrer the existential stance – of the Israelite-Jewish person.' For his many further uses of these terms within his book see the index.

23. For a perceptive analysis of some problems in Terrien's approach see Ben C. Ollenburger in *HBT* 8, 1986, 61–85, part of his discussion of Stendahl's contrast between 'what it meant' and 'what it means'.

24. See the good characterization of this aspect by Brueggemann, *Old Testament Theology*, 98–9; see also Hasel, 86–8, and Hayes and Prussner, 249–51.

25. Childs, *Biblical Theology*, 551–2, mentions Terrien only to say that, even if 'elusive presence' is an appropriate term for the Old Testament, it is 'clearly very misleading when it comes to grasping the nature of New Testament christology and cannot therefore be deemed successful' (so 551f.; also 15, where the same comment is made more briefly); Childs offers no *reason* why this is 'clearly' so. *OTTCC* lists Terrien in the index, but there is no substantive comment on his thought.

26. 'The real beginning of the Bible is not the first chapter of Genesis but the first chapter of Exodus', Westermann, *Der Schöpfungsbericht vom Anfang der Bibel*, 6; Barr, *Old*

*and New in Interpretation*, 74. Westermann's idea follows von Rad. See Childs, *OTTCC*, 32ff.

27. Goldingay helpfully compares R. Knierim's article 'Cosmos and History in Israel's Theology' (in *The Task of Old Testament Theology*, 171–224). Goldingay's summary is: '[Knierim] turns the whole emphasis on history on its head: the just and righteous order of Yahweh's creation is the fundamental salvation reality to which history belongs, from which it is separated, by which it is evaluated, and to which Israel's history of liberation witnesses' (215).

28. Cf. the comments of Childs, *Biblical Theology*, 490f. These comments are on Schmid's *Gerechtigkeit als Weltordnung* (1968), and he appears to make no reference to Schmid's general proposals for biblical theology. *OTTCC*, 32f., is only a passing comment. Hasel also has only brief comments, 160 and 169; on the latter, he says that Schmid 'goes too far in his claim that "creation" faith and theology is the "basic theme" of the OT as such' (n.6), but does not tell us why. For a better discussion see Reventlow, *Problems of Old Testament Theology*, 179–82, and *Problems of Biblical Theology*,148–78, especially 164–7.

29. On this see also my *Biblical Faith and Natural Theology*, 207–21. I regret that I failed there to cite Schmid's contributions in this respect.

30. This positive mention of the Enlightenment is again something of a fresh departure in the tradition of modern biblical theology, which has generally been strongly anti-Enlightenment. This anti-Enlightenment sentiment reaches a climax in the work of Childs, cf. also Brueggemann, *Old Testament Theology*, 64f., and also his *Theology of the Old Testament*, *passim*. These two giants appear to be competing over who can blacken the Enlightenment the most. For a theological view which sees the Enlightenment positively, as something in which some Christian aspects which Christianity had neglected were realized, the central person is surely Moltmann.

31. For comments on this aspect of Schmid's work, see Reventlow, *Problems of Biblical Theology*, 167.

32. F. Crüsemann, 'Gerechtigkeit Jahwes (*sedaqa/sädäq*) im Alten Testament'; J. Halbe, '"Altorientalisches Weltordnungsdenken" und alttestamentliche Theologie'.

33. The term forms the title of Halbe's central book, *Das Privilegrecht Jahwes*.

34. Reventlow, *Problems of Old Testament Theology*, 179ff.

35. See again below, Ch. 28.

36. J. L. Crenshaw, 'The Eternal Gospel, Eccl. 3.11', 32f. Cf. Reventlow, *Problems of Old Testament Theology*, 180.

37. Dedicated to Claus Westermann and published in English in his *The Task of Old Testament Theology*,1995, 171–224. There is a reference to Schmid in this respect on 183.

38. On this see Reventlow, *Problems of Biblical Theology*, 165–7.


## 20. *Overview of the Older Tradition*

1. Johannes Pedersen's *Israel* (1926) would be the most obvious alternative; cf. above, 233.

2. The mistake here, if there is one, may lie in supposing that this result comes from 'the unique quality of Israelite religion'. Maybe the same would be true of every religion?

3. Dentan, *Preface to Old Testament Theology*, 48 and 66; cited in Wright, *God Who Acts*, 36.

4. That '"The Old Testament" is a Christian entity' seems to me to be mistaken. 'The

Old Testament' is the Christian designation for a certain entity. If a different designation, such as 'The Hebrew Bible', is used, it would still be, or might be, the same theology.

5. 'System' was a standard expression. William Wilberforce's *Practical View of the Prevailing Religious System of Professed Christians* appeared in 1797; it was scarcely 'systematic theology', being rather 'a call to take seriously the duties of a Christian, especially those of repentance and hatred of sin' (wording of Cross and Livingstone, eds, *The Oxford Dictionary of the Christian Church*, 1479).

6. Doubtless memories of this were in the mind of G. E. Wright in his frequent complaints against 'system'.

7. Aristotle in fact had two systems, according to Daniel W. Graham, *Aristotle's Two Systems*: he first had one, later another, and in between he had some conflicts, if I understand it rightly. Jonathan Barnes, *Aristotle*, 36f., tells us that many have tried to show that Aristotle was not systematic: the 'anti-systematic interpretation of Aristotle's thought is now widely accepted', he writes. 'It has something to be said in its favour.' Barnes himself, however, does not share this view. He concludes: 'Aristotle was a systematic thinker; his surviving treatises present a partial and unfinished sketch of his system' (39). Whether Aristotle had a system or not does not concern us here; the point is that this question illustrates the existence of a widespread anti-systematic trend in modern culture, a trend which has had a large effect in biblical theology.

8. 'Even in speaking of the Hegelian system we must not think of a rigid, stable construction,' writes Barth, *Protestant Theology in the Nineteenth Century*, 39. M.Inwood, *Hegel*, reporting on the opinions of Robert C. Solomon, tells us that according to this view 'Hegel does not purport to present a closed system of eternal categories . . . Hegel's philosophical procedure is not rigidly systematic and necessitarian, but relatively free-wheeling' (7).

9. Cf. Berkhof, *Christian Faith*, 38: 'In the past it used to be said that this purpose was the construction of a system, a large, organic, conceptual unity, as a mirror of the unity of the divine thoughts as they are revealed to us. Nowadays one seldom hears this answer. We know too much of the limitations of our theological thinking. We regard the grasp for the system as a grasp in a vacuum, or at least as grasping for something which is beyond our ability.' Nevertheless, he continues: 'What do we aim at, if it is not a system? What alternative is there? We can discuss all kinds of subjects without relating them, but scientifically this means that we do only half the work.' Then he goes on: 'But the system is unattainable for us.' Again, however, 'This does not mean that the term "system" is meaningless for us.'

10. In common usage nowadays, indeed, 'system' is everywhere. While writing this I received in the post a package which, it said, contained 'Samples of Oil of Ulay's new Moisturizing Body Wash System'. The actual contents were two small packets of liquid and a 'puff' or sort of sponge. It is not to be thought that Eichrodt, a grave and serious man, would have contemplated this sort of system with equanimity.

11. Fishbane, *Judaism*, title of Ch. 2.

12. Preuss, II, 307.

13. See J. Barr, 'Biblical Language and Exegesis'.

14. In addition to the earlier quotations in *God Who Acts*, see the long and fulsome remarks in *The Old Testament and Theology*, 1969, 40ff.

15. In Knierim, *The Task of Old Testament Theology*, 9f. The reader should study, along with Knierim's article, the responses to it by W. Harrelson, W. Sibley Towner and R. E. Murphy, ibid., 21–32, and Knierim's response to them (33–56).

16. See J. R. M. Hughes, *Secrets of the Times: Myth and History in Biblical Chronology*.

17. W. Richter, 'Beobachtungen zur theologischen Systembildung'. Referred to by

R. Smend in his 'Theologie im Alten Testament', 25.

18. D. G. Spriggs, *Two Old Testament Theologies*, 70.

19. Vriezen, *Theology*, 160.

20. R. Smend, *Die Mitte des Alten Testaments*, 104–17.

21. On this see below, Ch. 26.

22. Cf. already above, Ch. 3, 37 and 47.

23. Wording of Hayes and Prussner, 239; cf. my review of von Rad, *ExpT*, 143–4.

24. The most extreme example of this direction in interpretation that I have seen is when W. C. Kaiser, *Toward an Old Testament Theology*, 5, tells us that with von Rad, in contrast to Eichrodt, 'Historicism had returned!' This is a staggering misreading of von Rad. More seriously, cf. Oeming, below, Ch. 28.

25. Cf. Zimmerli in *VT* 13, 1963, 105, who sees the same connection.

26. B. S. Childs, 'Old Testament in Germany 1920–1940', 245. See further discussion on 423 below.

## 21. Story and Biblical Theology

1. See J. Barr, *Old and New in Interpretation*; 'Story and History in Biblical Theology', also in *Explorations in Theology 7: The Scope and Authority of the Bible*, 1–17; 'Historical Reading and the Theological Interpretation of Scripture', ibid., 30–51. Cf. the comments by Childs, *Biblical Theology*, 18f., 205, etc.; contrast L. Perlitt, 'Auslegung der Schrift – Auslegung der Welt', 44f., 47.

2. See especially Dietrich Ritschl and Hugh O. Jones, *'Story' als Rohmaterial der Theologie*, and the fuller bibliography in Ingrid Schoberth, *Erinnerung als Praxis des Glaubens*.

3. Schoberth, *Erinnerung als Praxis des Glaubens*.

4. For a standard survey, cf. George W. Stroup, *The Promise of Narrative Theology*.

5. In the original of *Old and New in Interpretation* I gave 'the succession story of David' as the example here; in the light of more recent exegesis this seems to have been questionable.

6. From *Interpretation* 17, 1963, 197; quoted by Wolterstorff, *Divine Discourse*, 30.

7. It has sometimes been said that the sort of emphasis on history manifested in Wright's *God Who Acts* showed a dependence on 'facts' in a positivist sense. A glance at the work should be enough to show that this was not so. Wright, at least at this stage of his thinking, was interested in the contrast between two great *religious types*, one which had no relation with history and the other in which divine revelation was characteristically manifested in relation with history. The question of a basis in 'hard facts' did not enter in, at any rate at this stage.

8. D. H. Kelsey, *The Uses of Scripture in Recent Theology*, 33–8 and esp. 37.

9. Albrektson, *History and the Gods*, 114; cf. Barr, 'Story and History', 13.

10. Cf. the opinion of Wolterstorff, *Divine Discourse*, 71, about Karl Barth: 'There is thus in Barth's understanding of how God speaks a relentless *eventism*, as one might call it.'

11. See for example G. E. Wright's later restatement of his position in his *The Old Testament and Theology*, 44f.

12. Professor G.W.Anderson delivered a series of Speaker's Lectures in Oxford in the late 1970s, in which, noting how various existing Old Testament Theologies had been concentrated on a particular book or group of books (this was said, especially, of von Rad in relation to Deuteronomy), he proposed to develop a theology which would take *the Psalms*

as its centre and focus. The lectures have not as yet been published so far as I know.

13. Cf. above, Ch. 15, 243.

14. See D. Ritschl, 'Gottes Kritik an der Geschichte'; 'Anmerkungen zur Providentia-Lehre'.

15. Günther Klein, '"Über das Weltregiment Gottes"; Zum exegetischen Anhalt eines dogmatischen Lehrstücks', *ZThK* 90, 1993, 251–83.

16. Cf. below, 671 n.4.

17. 'Anmerkungen', 2.

18. Though this is the common view, there may well be exceptions. The clause 'He descended into hell' can hardly be said to constitute part of a summary of the essentials of the Gospels. To my inexpert eye it looks like a very primitive element, closely related to apocalyptic, which the more developed faith of the Gospels had left out. On the whole subject see recently W. J. Abraham, *Canon and Criterion*, 35f., and the reference to Pearson's discussion, ibid., 203.

19. S. E. Balentine and J. Barton, *Language, Theology and the Bible*, 385–97.

20. See, for example, the ample and carefully considered use of the term 'theology' by J. Assmann, *Re und Amun*, and in his other works.


## 22. Hartmut Gese and the Unity of Biblical Theology

1. In the field of *Religionsgeschichte* Gese wrote the large section on the religions of ancient Syria (mainly, in effect, of Ugarit) in the composite volume *Die Religionen Altsyriens, Altarabiens und der Mandäer*, 3–232.

2. For present purposes Gese's most important writings are conveniently contained in the two volumes of articles, *Vom Sinai zum Zion* and *Zur biblischen Theologie*, and within these the two articles 'Erwägungen zur Einheit der biblischen Theologie' and 'Das biblische Schriftverständnis' present the kernel of the material discussed here. Conveniently available in English are the article 'Tradition and Biblical Theology' and *Essays in Biblical Theology*.

3. Childs, *OTTCC*, 5, briefly mentions Gese's proposal and says that it 'has not resolved the problem', but does not say why. In his *Biblical Theology* he mentions it again on 76 as 'inaccurate' on the grounds that 'the New Testament is not a redactional layer on the Old Testament, and is not to be seen as an analogy to the Chronicler's editing of Kings' (did Gese ever think it was?). Some other references to Gese in Childs' works are more favourable (e.g. *Biblical Theology*, 455, 503), but these refer to other aspects of Gese's work. In general, Childs would agree with Gese in his opposition to any 'canon within the canon', but would very much disagree with his favouring the larger canon, including the 'apocryphal' books.

4. For an excellent account of this, see D. A. Knight, *Rediscovering the Traditions of Israel*, especially 92–176. I concentrate here on the German side of tradition history rather than the Scandinavian, since it is to the German side that Gese belongs.

5. See my article "The Authority of Scripture: the Book of Genesis and the Origin of Evil in Jewish and Christian Tradition'; also *The Garden of Eden and the Hope of Immortality* and *Biblical Faith and Natural Theology*; cf. also the similar opinion of Westermann, above, 318.

6. This thought runs parallel with those of Dietrich Ritschl in his '"Wahre", "reine" oder "neue" Biblische Theologie?'. My thinking owes much to his discussion. He says (145) that Gese (and so also Brevard Childs and P. Stuhlmacher) uses arguments of credal type at one point, but historical ones at others, a form of mixture that is acceptable only if it is

recognized for what it is.

7. On this see further below, Ch. 31.

8. Cf. Reventlow, *Problems of Biblical Theology in the Twentieth Century*, 153f.

9. '*Das Sein wird, und die Wahrheit ist geschichtlich geworden*' (*Erwägungen*, 30).

10. See J. Barr, *Old and New in Interpretation*, 156, etc; cf. D.Ritschl in Balentine and Barton (eds.), *Language, Theology and the Bible*, 388.

11. Cf. the remarks of Gunneweg, below, 460.

12. See the entire essay 'Das Gesetz', in Gese, *Zur biblischen Theologie*, 55–84, and especially 68–78. For a critical examination see especially H. Räisänen, 'Zionstora und biblische Theologie'; also Strecker, '"Biblische Theologie"?'. For Stuhlmacher's adoption of this approach see his *Biblische Theologie des Neuen Testaments* I, 257.

13. Gese, 'Das Gesetz', 78.

14. E.g. G. Strecker, 'Biblische Theologie?'; Reventlow, *Problems of Biblical Theology in the Twentieth Century*, 149–54, with full bibliography; see now Räisänen, *Beyond New Testament Theology*, 80f.

15. See his *Biblische Theologie*, particularly 1, 8, 10.

16. On this see especially his *Historical Criticism and Theological Interpretation of Scripture*, with an Introduction by me (this Introduction is not in the American edition); also his *Vom Verstehen des Neuen Testaments*.

## 23. *The Canonical Approach: First Stage*

1. Childs, *Biblical Theology in Crisis*, 102.

2. And sometimes these words were used in plenty. For example, in the representative and much-read volume edited in English by James L. Mays, Westermann's *Essays on Old Testament Interpretation*, the longish article by Alfred Jepsen, 'The Scientific Study of the Old Testament', 246–84, was in large part devoted to the canon and its importance. Some of this came close to what was later to be enunciated by 'canonical criticism', thus: 'A science of the Old Testament has to do with the canon of the church' (259), and: 'The theologian who works historically with the Old Testament may not remove it from its context, the context in which it now historically stands as canonical Scripture along with the New Testament' (278). On the other hand Jepsen in the same article gave strong positive emphasis to the tradition of historical criticism, the importance of which he traced back to Luther and the Reformation.

3. See the useful discussions in G. E. Wright, *The Old Testament and Theology*, 179–13; better, Goldingay, *Theological Diversity and the Authority of the Old Testament*, 122–7.

4. Wright, *God Who Acts*, 102–5.

5. Goldingay, *Theological Diversity and the Authority of the Old Testament*, 122 n. 91.

6. Wright, *God Who Acts*, 104.

7. All this in Wright, *God Who Acts*, 104.

8. Preuss is another who has found the Wisdom material theologically defective for Christianity, but I am not sure that he wanted it to be removed from the canon; Goldingay, *Theological Diversity and the Authority of the Old Testament*, 122 n. 91, speaks only of his 'inner canon'.

9. Thus J.A. Sanders, *Torah and Canon*, on a basis of wider experience than my own, wrote: 'Wright has been saying for years that biblical authority must be viewed from the

observation that there is in the Bible, in both testaments, a canon within the canon. He insists that the question of authority must be posed on that base . . .' (xv).

10. See Goldingay's clear and helpful discussion, *Theological Diversity and the Authority of the Old Testament*, 122–5.

11. Dunn, in *Churchman* 96, 216; cited from Goldingay, *Theological Diversity and the Authority of the Old Testament*, 125 and n. 107.

12. J. D. G. Dunn, *Unity and Diversity in the New Testament*, 374ff. Note that Dunn's position at this point is very close to that of G. E. Wright as outlined above.

13. For Kümmel, see particularly 92–7; for Käsemann, apart from his own article, his comments in the concluding survey: on Diem's article, 370f.; on Braun, 382–5 and finally 404f.

14. Sanders, *Torah and Canon*, xv.

15. Cf. my remarks about Zimmerli's preface to his Theology, below, 574.

16. Sanders, *Torah and Canon*, ix.

17. Notably James D. Smart, *Past, Present and Future*, 22–30, esp. 29–30.

18. Childs, *Crisis*, 87.

19. Ironically, Childs' own canonical approach ends up appealing to the 'fresh insights stemming from literary theory, analytical philosophy, the social sciences and other novel intellectual forces that count as post-critical or post-modern' (*JSOT* 46, 1990, 7; cf. Barr in *JSOT* 69, 1996, 113f., 119f.). What are these other than 'every shifting wind' that blows?

20. Again it is ironic to notice that by 1997, after the full development of the canonical approach, it also seems to have had very little to say about inspiration!

21. Childs, *Biblical Theology*, 525, with reference to D. Steinmetz, 'The Superiority of Pre-Critical Exegesis'. The passage is: 'Historical critical exegesis flounders at the crucial junction which must be crossed if one seeks to reflect theologically on what the Bible characterizes as the divine word. David Steinmetz is particularly cogent in focussing on the critical method's tendency endlessly to defer questions of truth.'

22. Cf. Alastair G. Hunter, 'Canonical Criticism', *DBI*, 107: 'Only [Childs'] *Exodus* gets down to the kind of detail which will enable canonical criticism to prove itself; and even there what is most effective is detail of a traditional historical critical kind.'

23. E.g. *Exodus*, 227: 'The biblical writer achieves this effect by skilfully splicing parts of the earlier sources into the Priestly narrative.' One does not doubt that they were indeed *spliced*; but that they were *skilfully* spliced has to be shown in detail, and would have required the citation of the complete texts in Hebrew.

24. M. G. Brett, *Biblical Criticism in Crisis?*, 38–57.

25. Cf. his piece in *Interpretation* 18, 1964, 432–49, referred to on his p. xvi. Scholars had said the same of the concluding paragraphs entitled *Ziel* or 'Aim' in the Biblischer Kommentar series.

26. See my review in *JSOT* 16, 1980, 12–23, and my *Holy Scripture: Canon, Authority, Criticism*. For other discussions see the remainder of *JSOT* 16, 1980, and *HBT* 2, 1980.

27. I have sometimes found myself blamed for taking the list of authoritative books as the proper meaning of 'canon', as if this was an idiosyncratic view. Since it is identical with Calvin's definition, I feel I am on safe ground in sticking to my view.

28. Cf. Alastair G. Hunter, 'Canonical Criticism', DBI, 107: 'Not so, however [i.e. in comparison with the Old Testament Introduction, which "as a whole was rather favourably received"], in the case of his application of the method to the New Testament. Here one senses a rather beleaguered defence of the earlier position with no new arguments and some improbable claims concerning the development of the New Testament, which prompted a

savage review by E. P. Sanders in the *Times Literary Supplement*, 13 December 1985, 1431.'

29. See the fine review of B.S. Childs, *The New Testament as Canon*, by E. P. Sanders in *The Times Literary Supplement*, 13 December 1985.

30. *The New Testament as Canon*, 548. The wording is: [the commentary] 'combines a cautious form-critical analysis with an older form of liberal, free church theology which, in my judgment, often badly obscures the biblical text'.

31. For another, and even more relevant, example, cf. Childs' handling of Käsemann, see below, Ch. 24, 404, 418f., etc. Cf. also his treatment (*Biblical Theology*, 357) of a proposal by Terence Fretheim: 'My initial response is to dismiss this paragraph as an egregious intrusion of modern American Process Theology!' That a scholar *is theological* does not help: on the contrary, it is a reason for immediate dismissal. Cf. further remarks about process theology on the same page.

32. It is not clear what Childs can mean by this. He seems to be pointing to a fault common to Eichrodt and von Rad, a fault that is overcome by his own canonical method. But what is the fault? Does it lie in the idea of a 'closed body of material'? But that sounds like just what Childs himself is advocating, i.e. an emphasis on the canon. Does it lie in the descriptive analysis? But, while this might be true of Eichrodt, it makes little sense for von Rad, who is no more a descriptive analyst than Childs himself. The reader is left with no idea what Childs can mean.

33. Cf. the remarks of Mark Brett as quoted above, 392; also my review in *JTS* 43, 1992, 135–41.

34. Contrast the excellent subject indexes in Eichrodt and to a less extent in Vriezen and von Rad.

## 24. *Childs' Theologies*

1. Albertz, *JBTh* 10, 182 n.14, says that it is 'a history of research and a history of dogma rather than a theology'.

2. Cf. works on presence like D. Ritschl, *Memory and Hope*. For a further comment on Childs' attitude to Terrien see below, 675 n.25.

3. E.g. M. G. Brett, *Biblical Criticism in Crisis?*, 8f., 156ff., 163f.: thus, 'It seems to me that Lindbeck represents the closest theological ally of the canonical approach' (164).

4. See above, Ch. 12.

5. H. Hübner, *Biblische Theologie des Neuen Testaments*, I, 70–5. Cf. also 182, 420.

6. Childs' article 'Die Bedeutung der hebräischen Bibel für die biblische Theologie' is almost entirely an attack on Hübner's ideas.

7. Moberly, reviewing Childs in *Anvil* 11, 1994, 272–4.

8. How could there be a 'canonical warrant' either for connecting Genesis with the Song of Songs or for not connecting them? Without our knowing the conditions for such a 'warrant', the statement is meaningless.

9. *JSOT* 16, 1980, 56.

10. See Barth, *CD* I/2, 597–603: 'It is only with human, not with divine, authority that a canon is handed down from previous stages of the church to later ones, and only with human, not with divine, authority that the Protestant church can protest against the differing Roman Catholic canon' (598). 'We can make a serious protest against the church's canon only . . . with the responsible intention of replacing, renewing the church's confession in

relation to the canon by a new one. This possibility is not excluded' (600).

11. Contrast W. J. Abraham's remark, *Canon and Criterion in Christian Theology*, 391: 'It is fascinating that the Barthian project was quickly challenged by the resurgence of lively forms of Liberal and Radical Protestantism.' Childs seems to want to treat liberalism as *dead*, so that any association with it is enough in itself to disprove a theological claim.

12. Cf. D. Ritschl in D. K. McKim (ed.), *How Karl Barth changed my Mind*, 89.

13. Cf. W. J. Abraham, *Canon and Criterion*, 383: 'He [Barth] was extremely pleased . . . that for the first time in history the Barmen Declaration made the rejection of natural theology a matter for official confession in the church. In short, his personal epistemic proposals were construed in his own eyes as nothing short of canonical.'

14. In my review of Brett, *JTS* 43, 1992, 141. Cf. Albertz in *JBTh* 10, 1995, 10 n.11, who points out that Childs depends on an extremely problematic and individualistic concept of theology and church. He goes on: 'For Karl Barth, to whom Childs likes to appeal, it is not the individual theologian, but the church community, that is the bearer of theology (*CD* IV/3, 879ff.).'

15. That Barth actually belonged in a certain sense to theological liberalism seems not to be considered by Childs. Contrast W.J. Abraham, *Canon and Criterion*, 409 n.32, who takes it as an obviously debatable question 'whether we locate the work of Karl Barth on canon within or outside the Liberal Protestant experiment.'

16. Cf above, 404.

17. 'Domestication' is a rather favourite term of Childs. It seems to suggest that the Bible is a savage beast, which human ingenuity has found means to tame, making it something like a toy poodle. The idea is that certain viewpoints, like those of Barthian theology and the canonical approach, prevent this from happening. But what if the production of the canon itself acted as a 'domesticating' force, smoothing out some of the rough edges of the older traditions?

18. On 'inclusive language' Childs seems to have changed his mind. In *OTTCC*, 40, he judges it 'quite appropriate' to 'make explicit the universal nature of God's invitation to salvation by the use of so-called "inclusive language"'. He wants, however, to make it clear that this is something quite different from 'liberating' the Bible from its 'time-conditioned flaws'. In *Biblical Theology*, 377f., on the other hand, 'within Christian theology it is very difficult to find a justification of the feminist insistence on the use of "inclusive language"'; popular forms of it 'often fail to comprehend the implicit attack on the church's doctrine of the Trinity'.

19. Barth, *CD* 1/2, 494; cf. Wolterstorff, *Divine Discourse*, 70. The 'last centuries', we may note, are roughly equivalent to 'the Enlightenment'.

20. On this see Wolterstorff, *Divine Discourse*, 70.

21. See for example Childs' late (1994) article 'Old Testament in Germany 1920–1940'. Looking back on this older period, it argues that 'the many serious attempts at a theological compromise which would build a confessional Old Testament theology directly on the foundation of historical critical methodology (Weiser, Eichrodt, von Rad, Zimmerli) have also failed' (245). According to Childs, von Rad in his dispute with Vischer 'launched his criticism from the perspective of historical criticism, not different in kind from that levelled by Köhler and Baumgartner. The only difference lay in his offering a new form of historical criticism based on the theories of Alt and Noth. Here he found a way opened by which to combine historical criticism and theological exegesis which was truly "*sachgemäss*".'

22. Barr, *Holy Scripture. Canon, Authority, Criticism*, 140ff.

23. The term 'canon' occurs only once in the *Institutes* (see Neuser, 'Calvins Stellung', 298f.).

24. Cf. the remarks of D. Ritschl in *JBTh* 1, 1986, 145, with reference to Childs, Gese, and Stuhlmacher. He writes: 'They make creed-like statements at this point, whereas at others their argument is historical. (There is no objection to this mixed form of argument provided that it is recognized to be such.)'

25. *CD* I/2, 483–4.

26. Stendahl, 'Method in the Study of Biblical Theology', 208.

27. See D. Ritschl, 'Biblizismus'.

28. Barth, *CD* I/2, 821.

29. In particular my article 'The Theological Case against Biblical Theology', which is rather roughly pushed aside by Childs himself, *Biblical Theology*, 370, as a 'denigration' of the value of biblical theology 'as lacking the integrity of a true discipline'. Perhaps he did not realize that I wrote with the weight of Barth's authority exactly in my mind, though I did not mention his name in this regard.

30. Contrast the usage of Mark Smith, who gives a list of scholars who 'vigorously defend the biblical witness to Israelite worship of Baal and Asherah', *The Early History of God*, xx.

31. Räisänen, *Beyond New Testament Theology*, 102, writes: '"Orthodoxy" and "Heresy" are, from the point of view of early Christian history, misleading categories which are to be dismissed. They can have a historical significance only: they tell us what was regarded as orthodox or heretical by some groups at some period of time.' This is correct, but Räisänen seems to apply it only to the history of religion, and not to a theology of Old or New Testament. In my opinion it applies equally to both the latter. Indeed, I would go farther, for it seems to me that *even in doctrinal theology* these concepts are historical in character. To say 'Pelagian' or 'Sabellian' is to talk about concepts that were applied, usefully or not, many centuries ago. Their applicability to any modern ideas is at the least questionable. Even 'ecclesial' organizations (Räisänen's own word) now find that they can no longer use 'heresy' except by a historical retro-projection.

32. Stendahl, 'Biblical Theology', 430a.

33. Cf. numerous references in Childs, e.g. 722, where he thinks that historical criticism assumes the right to 'filter the biblical literature according to its own criteria of "what really happened"'.

34. Here again, in spite of Childs' call for biblical scholars to 'be theological', when they *are* in his judgment theological this does not seem to have any favourable effect. Cf. my remark about Vincent Taylor, above, 394. Cf. likewise Childs' discussion of James A. Sanders' position in *OTTCC*, 136f.: 'Behind Sanders' interpretation of canonical hermeneutics lies *a strong theological concern*' (my italics). Moreover, 'no one should underestimate the great attraction which such a rendering of the Bible has for the contemporary generation'. All this, however, does Sanders no good. 'Needless to say, I am highly critical of this theological position for a variety of reasons.' Sanders' 'initial assumption . . . subverts the essential role of the canon'.

35. Did Käsemann actually say 'shattered'? I doubt it.

36. Cf. Philip Davies, *Whose Bible is it Anyway?*, 30: '[Childs'] claim that the "historical critics" have failed to take canon seriously involves him in making assertions about the Old Testament that are "historical" because they assert something about the past – but they are not "historical" assertions in the sense that they are arrived at by any historical methodology. They are simply dogmas.'

37. Cf. the statement: 'More crucial is the need to relate Paul's exegesis to his theology, that is, to his christology' (240).

38. Note the word 'descriptive', here used positively, in contradiction to Childs' many

negative evaluations.

39. Cf already above, 404.

40. See B. S. Childs, 'Old Testament in Germany 1920–1940', 245.

41. Cf. the same, in almost identical words, in Childs' essay in Braaten and Jenson, *Reclaiming the Bible for the Church*, 5, though there he expands the list of failures, the list now being: Eichrodt, von Rad, Zimmerli, Bultmann, Jeremias, Stuhlmacher and Küng. Childs' condemnations are erratic in two ways: first, in that at least some of the biblical theologians named certainly strove to avoid building their work 'on the foundation of a historical-critical method' – certainly Eichrodt, von Rad and above all Stuhlmacher; secondly, in that Childs himself built at least elements of his own theologies on the same foundation, as we have seen especially in his Exodus commentary.

42. 216, title of section.

43. See Kermode, 'Canons'.

44. J. Barr, *The Bible in the Modern World*, and 'Reading the Bible as Literature', both cited in Barton's book.

45. See my summing-up in *The Bible in the Modern World*, 73f.

46. See also J. Barr, 'The Synchronic, the Diachronic and the Historical', 1of.

47. Thus cf. recently Iain Provan in J. Barton (ed.), *The Cambridge Companion to Biblical Interpretation*, 209: 'What is striking about Childs is the way in which he characteristically takes historical-critical reality as a fairly obvious and self-evident starting point for his interpretation.'

48. On this cf. below, Chapter 28.

49. For a creative discussion of what 'scripture' (γραφή) meant in early Christianity, see John Barton, *The Spirit and the Letter*, e.g. 67f., 80, 102, etc.

50. This would seem to be the most important aspect in which he shows a substantial improvement as compared with his portrayal of the Biblical Theology Movement; cf. his *Biblical Theology in Crisis*, 44–7.

51. Not so, however, to so theological a scholar as C. Westermann, who several times repeats that the early wisdom of Israel was 'secular' (German *profan*): emphatically so in his *Elements of Old Testament Theology:* 'in its earlier stages wisdom is overwhelmingly secular', 11, so again 100, 123.

52. See Childs, *Biblical Theology*, 620 and 40–2. Some readers may well be surprised that Aquinas receives this favourable treatment from Childs. In early Barthianism, Roman Catholic theology was seen very negatively and the *analogia entis* was 'an invention of Antichrist'; but in later stages of the same movement Aquinas came to be regarded more positively and seen as one of the greatest theologians of all time.

53. On the relation of the Enlightenment to biblical studies and theology see my article 'Bibelkritik als theologische Aufklärung', in Trutz Rendtorff (ed.), *Glaube und Toleranz. Das theologische Erbe der Aufklärung*, 30–42, and also the whole range of other articles in the same volume.

54. K. Barth, *Protestant Theology in the Nineteenth Century*.

55. The tone reminds one of Peter Gay's title *The Enlightenment. An Interpretation. The Rise of Modern Paganism*.

56. Barth, *Protestant Theology in the Nineteenth Century*, 232.

57. Cf. for example Clark Pinnock, *The Scripture Principle*, xiii, 21, 130–3, and my review in *Virginia Seminary Journal*, September 1985. In order to use the Enlightenment as a bogey, one does not require to know anything about it. The average American conservative Christian who speaks with horror about the Enlightenment knows nothing about it: it

operates simply as a symbol of anti-religion. I do not for a moment suggest that Childs' own knowledge of it is inadequate: on the contrary, it is doubtless very complete and well-nourished. The fact remains that the symbol 'Enlightenment' operates as an unthinking and unknowing factor, and the way in which he uses it in his books encourages this. In fact, I suspect – though I have not gone into the question – that the idea of 'Enlightenment' as an object of horror is *modern* in conservative Protestantism and is more likely to be derived from conservative Barthianism and other similar trends, which were better informed in the history of ideas and such matters. The primeval American fundamentalist, I suspect, had no notion of an 'Enlightenment', even as a threat, in his mind.

58. Barth, *CD* I/2. 494. Cf. N. Wolterstorff, *Divine Discourse*, 70, also 73, where he speaks of 'honouring the legitimate results of biblical criticism'.

59. I am deeply indebted to Professor William Abraham for helpful discussion of this, though he is not responsible for the use I have made of the stimulus received from him.

60. W. Abraham, *Canon and Criterion in Christian Theology*, 384.

61. In *JSOT* 69, 1996, 107.

62. Incidentally, one has to admire Albright as one scholar who openly professed himself to be both positivist and historicist: see his *History, Archaeology and Christian Humanism*, where he says on p. 140 'I am a resolute "positivist"' and on p. 141 'I am . . . essentially a historicist' – though adding qualifications to these remarks. I am doubtful whether he tried to use these terms consistently. In the same book he uses them pejoratively, e.g. in talking of Robertson Smith (137), of 'English Old Testament scholarship', or 'German philosophical idealists' (279).

63. Cf. M. Oeming, *Gesamtbiblische Theologien der Gegenwart*, 208: 'Perhaps Childs' distaste for the alleged esoteric hermeneutics as also for the tradition-historical seeking for something *behind* the final form of the MT has its roots in a good American admiration for positivism. Only what one has in one's hands in black and white, the final text as it empirically lies before one, is of certain value.' Cf. also Hübner, *Biblische Theologie des Neuen Testaments*, 75 n. 201.

64. In *JTS* 37, 1986, 445.

65. Quotation from J. Barr, *Biblical Faith and Natural Theology*, 13.

66. So in *JSOT* 46, 1990, 4.

67. Gunneweg, *Biblische Theologie des Alten Testaments*, 1993, 33: 'Here Childs successfully avoids crude fundamentalism, but with the help of a new fundamentalism which is now canonical.' See his entire discussion, 32f.

68. On fundamentalism, incidentally, there is another instance of Childs' misinterpreting the views of others. Replying to my review of his *Introduction* in *JSOT* 16, 1980, 58, he says: 'If one has a fixation on Fundamentalism and considers it as the major threat to serious biblical scholarship . . .' – but of course I never said, and never for a moment thought, that fundamentalism is 'the major threat to serious biblical scholarship'. I do not think it is a serious threat to scholarship at all. I do think it is a serious menace to the church, which Childs wants us to care about, and that is why I addressed the question. It is certainly also a menace to the peace of the world.

## 25. *Other Canonical Possibilities*

1. Here, however, we must bear in mind the important objection of Benjamin D. Sommer, 'The Scroll of Isaiah as Jewish Scripture, Or, Why Jews don't read Books'.

According to Sommer, traditional Jewish reading is not interested in the 'whole' of a book like Isaiah. 'In Jewish scripturality, the literary unit of "book" is insignificant.' After the individual verse, the next unit that matters is the Bible as a whole. From this point of view, the attempt of [Christian] 'canonical' criticism to read a book 'as a whole' is insignificant. 'Classical Judaism regards Isaiah (like any prophetic book) as a collection of pericopes that relate to other parts of the Bible at least as much as they relate to each other' (231).

2. The best comparison of Sanders and Childs is the article of Frank Spina, 'Canonical Criticism: Childs versus Sanders'. However, this article was written at a somewhat early stage in the development of canonical criticism, and before Childs' own Theologies were published. The comparison is therefore more a comparison of *methods* than one of *theologies*, though Sanders's emphasis on 'monotheistic pluralism' is correctly mentioned (175).

3. Rendtorff, *Canon and Theology*, 126 n.3.

4. All this in *Bible Review* 24, IV/3, June 1988, 42f.

5. In his *Canon and Theology*, 46–56.

6. On this aspect see his article 'Revelation and History: Particularism and Universalism in Israel's View of Revelation', in *Canon and Theology*, Ch. 10, esp. 113–17 and 120ff.

7. *Canon and Theology*, 9f.

8. Rendtorff, in 'Approaches to Old Testament Theology', 22.

9. Rendtorff, *Canon and Theology*, 121.

10. Rendtorff, in 'Approaches to Old Testament Theology', 26. He here greets warmly the paper of Walter E. Lemke, 'Is Old Testament Theology an Essentially Christian Theological Discipline?'.

11. The neglect of post-biblical Hebrew on the part of Christian scholars has often been exaggerated in this discussion, notably by Levenson, *The Hebrew Bible, the Old Testament, and Historical Criticism*, 85 (here he followed Kugel, who wrote that 'among Semitic languages, there is one that has consistently been given the cold shoulder in Christian seminaries and secular universities: Mishnaic Hebrew'). As I wrote in my review (*JTS* 47, 1996, 557), this assertion is easily disproved: 'My predecessor H. Danby, Regius Professor of Hebrew in Oxford and Canon of Christ Church, was entirely a scholar of the Mishnah. In Edinburgh, one of my own teachers, Oliver Rankin, was at least as much a scholar of rabbinics and medieval Judaism as he was of the Bible.' S.R. Driver, known as the scholar who did most to make the new historical criticism acceptable in England, began his career with the publication of rabbinic texts. Consider likewise a central modern Old Testament scholar like E. W. Nicholson, who co-operated with Joshua Baker in editing *The Commentary of Rabbi David Kimhi on Psalms CXX–CL*.

12. For an excellent and up-to-date survey, see E. W. Nicholson, *The Pentateuch in the Twentieth Century. The Legacy of Julius Wellhausen*, especially Ch. 4, 95–131.

13. Ibid., 107, cf. 113, 116.

14. See ibid., 118f.

15. See J. Barton, 'Historical–critical Approaches', in J. Barton (ed.), *The Cambridge Companion to Biblical Interpretation*, 9–19; J. Barr, 'Bibelkritik als theologische Aufklärung'.

16. Luther, Prologue to Isaiah lectures of 1527; Fohrer, *Theologische Grundstrukturen*, 4f.

17. Luther, Prologue to Isaiah, 1528: quoted ibid.

18. See J. Barr, 'Luther and Biblical Chronology', in *BJRUL* 72, 1990, 51–67; abbreviated in *Luther Digest* 1, 1993, 1–3.

## 26. Some Recent Theologies

1. Notice in the *Book List* of the Society for Old Testament Studies, 1994, 109. For another useful discussion see H. M. Wahl, '"Ich bin, der ich bin"'.

2. See his richly learned notes to §7, also his thoughtful study of the death of Socrates and on Plato's Lysis, in O. Kaiser, *Der Mensch unter den Schicksal*, 196–205 and 206–31.

3. H.-P. Müller, 'Alttestamentliche Theologie und Religionswissenschaft', 31.

4. Brief review by J. Barr in *Theology 82*, May 1979, 211–13.

5. For a reference to this see above, 296, and J. Barr, review of Levenson, in *JTS* 47, 1996, 558,

6. This phrase, of course, may not have been written by the author himself.

7. This follows the argument of E. Grässer, *Der Alte Bund im Neuen*.

8. Thus it is striking, in view of the markedly *Christian* character of Gunneweg's thinking as a whole, that a Jewish scholar like Levenson greeted with delight his judgment that the Old Testament belongs to a religion quite different from Christianity. See Levenson, *The Hebrew Bible, the Old Testament, and Historical Criticism*, 29, and the review by J. Barr in *JTS* 47, 1996, 558; also above, 296.

9. It may be noted that Levenson's complaint, *The Hebrew Bible, the Old Testament, and Historical Criticism*, 54, that [Christian] Old Testament theology had neglected to consider *duties* as a central theme is disproved by Preuss's approach – the latter, incidentally, from a very Lutheran standpoint; see my review in *JTS* 47, 1996, 558.

10. I think this is the meaning: German '*dass seine wichtige Botschaft nicht zu kurz kommt*'. In Perdue's translation somewhat differently: 'that the important message of the Old Testament will not be treated in too cursory a fashion'.

11. To the other classic Theology of von Rad he gives a longer discussion than to any other (I, 12–15), but one that seems to emphasize the problems created by that work more than the possibility of continuing along that line.

12. Cf. the comments by Goldingay, *Theological Diversity and the Authority of the Old Testament*, 122 n.91, 210 and n. 38, 214 n. 49.

13. Cf. Oeming's view, above, 262, and Preuss II, 362 n.444.

14. Cf. Childs' opinion: 'Most recently, H.-D. Preuss has produced a very competent Old Testament theology that is remarkably comprehensive'; so in Mays *et al.*(eds.), *Old Testament Interpretation. Past, Present and Future*, 295.

## 27. Natural Theology within Biblical Theology

1. J. Barr, *Biblical Faith and Natural Theology*. For major reviews see Hiebert in *Interpretation*, July 1995, 298–300; J. Barton in *JTS* 45, 1995, 777–800; also references in W. J. Abraham, *Canon and Criterion in Christian Theology*, 50 n. 38. For a recent addition to the literature see A. Hilary Armstrong, 'Karl Barth, the Fathers of the Church, and "Natural Theology"'.

2. Barr, *Biblical Faith and Natural Theology*, 23–38.

3. See ibid., 85–9.

4. R. P. Knierim, 'On the Theology of Psalm 19', in his *The Task of Old Testament Theology*, 322–50: quotation 345. I regret that I did not know of this article until the last stages of preparation of the present book.

5. Note that J.D.Levenson writes: 'Quite apart from the specific self-disclosure of God

to Israel, the Bible assumes a natural knowledge of God available to all humanity'; this in his 'The Universal Horizon of Biblical Particularism'.

6. On these matters cf. J. Barr, *Biblical Faith and Natural Theology*, 148.

7. Westermann, *Schöpfungsbericht*, 6; cf. Barr, *Old and New in Interpretation*, 74. I think it is right to say this is 'in the tradition of von Rad', in spite of the arguments of Rendtorff, *Canon and Theology*, 94ff., and in H. T. C. Sun and K. L. Eades, *Problems in Biblical Theology*, 15f. Westermann, however, somewhat changed his position later on.

8. On this see Rendtorff in *Canon and Theology*, 92–113; also F. Crüsemann, 'Die Eigenständigkeit der Urgeschichte'.

9. On this section see Barr, *Old and New in Interpretation*, 95–101.

10. Ibid., 97.

11. Cf. Barr, *Biblical Faith and Natural Theology*, 94f.

12. See J. Barton, *Amos' Oracles against the Nations* and 'Natural Law and Poetic Justice in the Old Testament'.

13. One is not in principle against the idea that the deity spoke in Hebrew, audibly and with normal phonetics. Asking Adam 'Where art thou?' (Gen. 3.9) he will certainly have done so. But that he communicated the entire books of Amos, Isaiah or Jeremiah in this way seems a different matter. I already touch upon these questions in my section on verbal communication in *Old and New in Interpretation*, 77–81.

14. Cf. Barr, in *Biblical Faith and Natural Theology*, 90ff., but there I refrain from any extensive discussion of this theme, relying as I do on the excellent article of J. J. Collins, which I cite.

15. See ibid., 90–4.

16. Cf. above, 381.

17. Details in J. Barr, in *Biblical Faith and Natural Theology*, 91 n.13.

18. Steiert, *Die Weisheit Israels*, 6.

19. So S. Terrien, *Job*, 111.

20. Levenson, *The Hebrew Bible, the Old Testament, and Historical Criticism*, 36.

21. Barr, *Biblical Faith and Natural Theology*, 93f.

22. M. Hengel, *Judaism and Hellenism* I, 116.

23. Barr, *Biblical Faith and Natural Theology*, 192.

24. Cf. for instance Childs, *Biblical Theology*, 286 and 367, which give no hint of the natural-theology possibility. Especially on 367 he connects λόγος with Hebrew *dabar*, 'word'.

25. In the LXX, over the books of the Hebrew canon, λόγος appears as the rendering of *dabar* in a relation of about 2:1 to the other most common rendering, ῥῆμα (Gerleman, in *THAT* I, 442). Much then depends on the books at which one looks. In the Torah up to the end of Numbers λόγος is relatively rare and ῥῆμα is much preponderant. In Deuteronomy the proportion of λόγος increases. In the prophetic books ῥῆμα becomes much less common.

26. See above, 182f.

27. Link, *Die Welt als Gleichnis*, 89, quoting G. Bornkamm, 'Gesetz und Natur: Röm 2, 14–16', 111, 117. See also my general comments in *Biblical Faith and Natural Theology*, 56f.

28. Cf. Childs, *Biblical Theology*, 595–612.

29. D. M. Baillie, *Faith in God and its Christian Consummation*, 5; quoted by Kinneavy, *Greek Rhetorical Origins*, 5.

30. Berkhof, *Christian Faith*, however, writes: 'The word *faith* is used very often in the New Testament; it is derived from the Old Testament where it is still sparsely used, though

in some passages it becomes a very important word' (16); he regards 'Old Testament faith' as the infrastructure which 'remains determinatively present in Christian faith' (19, 21). Old Testament religion is thus a 'faith-religion': the 'faith-religion of Abraham and Moses' was too much for the majority of the people (17).

31. Published in *EvTh* 47, 1987, 386–95. I much regret that I had not come across this article when I wrote my *Biblical Faith and Natural Theology*.

32. So Berkhof, *Christian Faith*, 102: 'It has been noted more often that the OT does not have a central term for "reveal".'

33. In F. C. Grant and H. H. Rowley (eds.), *Hastings' Dictionary of the Bible*, 847–9.

34. *The Logic of Theology*, 104; Ritschl here compares his *Memory and Hope*, Ch. 1.

35. Note that the 'forceful attacks' by Downing and myself are noted with respect by H. Berkhof, *Christian Faith*, 45, 103. He writes: 'The danger existed that the revelation concept was too easily used as a Prolegomenon, without sufficiently investigating the correctness of the choice and reckoning with the problematics that it entails' (45). He notes with interest doubt about the rightness of this choice by Trillhaas, *Dogmatik*, 44, and O. Weber, *Grundlagen der Dogmatik* I, 187f. Also H. Schulte had asked, *Der Begriff der Offenbarung im NT*, 'Does the New Testament really know of a concept of revelation?' (9), and concluded that: 'It [the NT] is not concerned with an independent theme which it has to take notice of, safeguard, delineate and elaborate' (87).

36. Berkhof, *Christian Faith*, 103–4, points out that several 'lines of thought are being developed in Protestant theology which more than ever before emphasize the provisional nature of revelation', involving 'a historicistic or futuristic view of existence'. He cites Pannenberg, Moltmann, and G. Sauter, *Zukunft und Verheissung*.

37. Berkhof, *Christian Faith*, 64f. I found it a great honour to be coupled in the same sentence with Pannenberg! In his remark about salvation history Berkhof probably has in mind the position of O. Cullmann in his *Salvation in History*, of which Berkhof in the previous paragraph wrote: 'The categories which he [Cullmann] developed for it . . . were, however, still insufficiently worked out, both to do justice to the complexity of the relations in the Old Testament and to meet the systematic problems involved in the concept of revelation' (64). For a different evaluation of *Old and New in Interpretation* see F. Watson, *Text and Truth*, 223 n. 37, who perceives in it a 'generally negative tenor'.

38. Ritschl, *Memory and Hope*, 17.

39. Cf. ibid., 18 nn.1–3. In n. 3 he points out that the 'no revelation after Ezra' principle was not applied by the post-apostolic church.

40. Cf. F. Watson, *Text and Truth*, *passim*.

41. *Canon and Criterion in Christian Theology*, 385.

42. Berkhof, *Christian Faith*, 47.

43. See further Berkhof's description of discussion during this century, ibid., 49f.

44. See my article 'Man and Nature: the Ecological Controversy and the Old Testament'. Looking back on this, I have a certain bad conscience, feeling that I strove rather too much to reduce the suggestion of human domination and exploitation in Gen. 1, and that other scholars have done the same. It is hoped that the new presentation given here may help to correct this somewhat.

45. Keith Thomas, *Man and the Natural World*, 23f., points out: 'In modern times the Japanese worship of nature has not prevented the industrial pollution of Japan.'

46. See J. Pelikan, *Christianity and Classical Culture*.

47. See my *Biblical Faith and Natural Theology*, 106.

48. Ibid., 180.

49. Cf. above, 469f.
50. *Biblical Faith and Natural Theology*, 219f.
51. O. Keel and C. Uehlinger, *Göttinnen, Götter und Gottessymbole*, 474.
52. From David L. Mueller, 'Natural Theology', 330f.

## *28. Oeming*

1. This aspect was criticized already by Zimmerli, *VT* 13, 1963, 109f.
2. I have here collapsed into three a list which in Oeming's original comprises six.
3. On these terms, cf. the remarks of R. Knierim, *The Task of Old Testament Theology*, 217: 'Inasmuch as it is a factor of the historical process itself, the reference to the "charismatic-eclectic interpretation" is insufficient, unless we assume that every "charismatic-eclectic interpretation" is true and valid by virtue of being charismatic-eclectic. The biblical tradition in both the Old and the New Testament gives us every reason not to subscribe to this assumption.'
4. P. Fruchon, on this subject primarily 'Sur l'herméneutique de Gerhard von Rad', and, more generally, 'Ressources et limites d'une herméneutique philosophique'; 'Herméneutique, langage et ontologie. Un discernement du platonisme chez H.-G. Gadamer'.
5. For more about this paragraph, see below, 510.
6. In my review of Brett in *JTS* 43, 1992, 137f.
7. J. M. Robinson, *A New Quest of the Historical Jesus;* Andrew Louth, *Discerning the Mystery*; M.G. Brett, *Biblical Criticism in Crisis?*; cf. my review of Brett in *JTS*, 43, 1992, 137f.
8. D. L. Baker, *Two Testaments – One Bible*, 239; Oeming, 92 and n. 38.
9. Here one should now add F. Watson, *Text and Truth*,1997, especially 197–209.
10. Oeming, 98.
11. See above, Ch. 19.
12. Texts in Oeming, 149.
13. The metaphor comes, so far as I know, from military history: armies in older times, troubled above all by problems of supply, were forced to 'advance', not positively in order to conquer territory but in order to gain resources which were not available if they stayed where they were. So e.g. in M. van Creveld, *Supplying War*, e.g. 13–17, on the campaigns of Gustavus Adolphus. In any case, the metaphor is an excellent one for application to 'post-critical' and 'post-modern' notions in exegesis, and Oeming is to be congratulated on the introduction of it.
14. This portion abbreviated from Oeming, 229–30.
15. I found this difficult to understand in itself. Oeming, however, refers to the work of Clavier, 132–5.
16. Cf. above, 111, 427.
17. Cf. above, 292.
18. Oeming, 78.
19. Not in the English translation. Quoted in full by Oeming, 44.

### 29. Mildenberger

1. I wish to thank my colleagues Eugene TeSelle and Paul DeHart, who have read drafts of this chapter and discussed its contents with me. They are not, of course, responsible for the final form of it.

2. F. Mildenberger, *Gottes Tat im Wort.*

3. F. Mildenberger, *Die halbe Wahrheit oder die ganze Schrift.*

4. F. Mildenberger, *Gotteslehre. Eine dogmatische Untersuchung.*

5. He agrees with Westermann about Job (II, 280 n. 157); he disagrees with him again about Jacob and the meeting at the Jabbok, etc. (II, 312–15; note especially II, 315 n. 58; cf. again II, 422 n. 63). Other disagreements: III, 241 n.8; III, 304 n. 108 .

6. Other mentions of von Rad include: exegesis of Ps 73, II, 77; Noah's sacrifice and oikonomia, 108n.; meaning of prophetic 'openness', II, 157 n.201; his view of Chronicles, II, 252 n.26, again 256 n.42; on wisdom, III, 303 n. 108, 315 n.176, 416; on Ps.90, 325ff.; on *Uroffenbarung*, III, 440 n.58.

7. On *Heilsgeschichte* see particularly the critical discussion, I, 163ff., with special reference to Cullmann.

8. Exceptions are very marginal: I, 11n., 15n.; II, 130n. (*Lichterlehre* III, 447 n. 92).

9. I am grateful to my neighbours Dr and Mrs Robin Harrison for their help with this expression.

10. On scripture as means of grace, as contrasted with scripture seen as an epistemological authority, see W.J. Abraham, *Canon and Criterion.*

11. The references are: Childs, *Introduction*, 452ff.; Otto, 'Die Theologie des Buches Habakkuk'. Mildenberger gives a good summary of the arguments and indicates a mediating position, adding (doubtless rightly) that neither of the parties are likely to accept any such solution.

12. The reference is to F. W. Marquardt, *Das christliche Bekenntnis zu Jesus, dem Juden. Eine Christologie.*

13. On this cf. the title of W. Pannenberg's contribution to H. T. C. Sun and K. L. Eades, *Problems in Biblical Theology*, 'Problems in a Theology of (Only) the Old Testament'.

14. I had just this in mind in entitling my own earlier book *Old and New in Interpretation. A Study of the Two Testaments.* I thought of relations between the old and the new which included, but were not to be identified with, the relations between the two corpuses of text. On the use of the term 'dispensations', this reminds one of the thoughts of Moberly, *The Old Testament of the Old Testament.*

15. Cf. the earlier reference to Strecker, above, Ch. 1 n.4.

16. In volumes II and III, however, references to Tillich become much less frequent than references to Schleiermacher and to Barth.

17. For a fuller statement of the discussion summarized here, see I, 236–43.

18. I think that the doctrine of the threefold form of the Word of God has worked *effectively* over several decades and has thus been *useful* as a barrier against both liberalism and fundamentalism (as it was surely intended to be); but already in *Old and New in Interpretation* (1966) I was indicating dissatisfaction with it. I wrote: 'Jesus Christ in turn cannot be aligned as the Revealed Word in a threefold scheme in which the Bible is the second term; Christ and Bible are not commensurable in that way, even under the guidance of revelation' (101). This very primitive reaction can be extended considerably.

## 30. Räisänen

1. See H.Räisänen, *Das koranische Jesusbild;* 'The Portrait of Jesus in the Qur'an: Reflections of a Biblical Scholar'; 'Joseph Smith und die Bibel'; *Marcion, Muhammad and the Mahatma*. In this last work the sections on Marcion, especially Ch. 5, 'Attacking the Book, not the People: Marcion and the Jewish Roots of Christianity' (64–80), are particularly relevant to our present study. See also the important study by J. Barton, *The Spirit and the Letter*.

2. *Paul and the Law*; *The Torah and Christ*.

3. *The Torah and Christ*, 3.

4. Ibid., 23.

5. For the text of Wrede's essay and relevant discussion see R. Morgan, *The Nature of New Testament Theology*; Wrede's text is on 68–116.

6. I take this phrase from Räisänen, *Beyond New Testament Theology*, 93, where, however, it refers to New Testament theology.

7. On this see P. Stuhlmacher, *Historical Criticism and Theological Interpretation of Scripture*; *Vom Verstehen des Neuen Testaments. Eine Hermeneutik*; *Biblische Theologie des Neuen Testaments*, Vol.1.

8. A lively review by Walter Brueggemann described this book as a 'dreary disappointment': *Theology Today* 53, 1996–7, 236. He wrote: 'They make no serious arguments . . . The book has the feel of all "the guys" in the club going into the woods to recite the mantra.'

9. P.R. Davies, *Whose Bible is it Anyway?*, 17.

10. But similar expressions are common in his writings, e.g. (at random) *Text and Truth*, 205f., 'an Old Testament scholarship which pursues its various historical and exegetical projects in isolation from the New Testament and Christian theology'.

11. G. Petzke, 'Exegese und Praxis'. For a short summary of this interesting article see Räisänen, *Beyond New Testament Theology*, 85.

12. Cf. above, 3.

13. Cf. Wrede in Morgan, *The Nature of New Testament Theology*, 74ff.

14. Bultmann was less influential because of the limited role he accorded to the Old Testament; on the other hand, his general hermeneutical ideas remained influential.

15. Carl E. Braaten and Robert W. Jenson (eds), *Reclaiming the Bible for the Church*.

16. Räisänen, *Beyond New Testament Theology*, 111f.


## 31. Brueggemann

1. This passage is a slightly rewritten version of what I wrote in my article 'Divine Action and Hebrew Wisdom', in S. Coakley and D. Pailin (eds), *The Making and Remaking of Christian Doctrine. Essays in Honour of Maurice Wiles*, 1–12.

2. W.Brueggemann, *In Man We Trust*, 118.

3. Ibid., pp. 120f.

4. For a useful short survey of Brueggemann's approaches to a 'theology of the imagination' from the 1980s on, emphasizing his commentary on Jeremiah, see Perdue, *Collapse of History*, 285–98. For another valuable discussion of the full Theology see M. Brett, 'The Future of Old Testament Theology'.

5. Cf. Oeming's remark, Ch. 28 above, that for Gadamer language is more real than

reality.

6. Perdue, *The Collapse of History*, 298; cf. also 296f.

7. See above, 693 n.8.

8. E.g. Childs, *OTTCC*, 80: David's actions 'should have evoked the punishment by death in Israel had not an exception been made because of David's repentance'.

9. Cf. above, 686 n.68.

10. Moberly, *The Old Testament of the Old Testament*, 162, complains of those who 'leave "supersessionism" as an unanalysed bogey word'. That is certainly how it works in my experience.

11. Note the similarity here to my own position as stated above, 186.

12. At this point there is a certain discordance in the parallel cited: the basic contrast is not between the waiting of Jews for the Messiah and the waiting of Christians for the 'second coming', but between the waiting of Jews for the Messiah and the conviction of Christians that he *has already come*. This makes the two positions less similar in structure.

13. Brueggemann loves to make the association, e.g. 27,159, 264f. I have nothing against it in principle but is it factually true? Eichrodt must have basically thought out his Theology well before Nazism was perceived as a major phenomenon (the Preface to the first edition is dated July 1933, and the fundamental article was published in 1929). On the other side, von Rad's Theology did not begin to appear until 1957, well after the war was over. His essay on the theological place of creation, published in 1936, is emphasized by Brueggemann (159), but it seems to me to derive from his *critical* method and from the *theological* debate between creation and redemption, and to give no explicit indication of a political interest or motivation at all. The only person he mentions with some degree of critique is Wilhelm Lütgert, who thought that the 'prophetic word' would not have been credible without the previous self-testimony of creation. This is a perfectly reasonable argument. According to the biographical note, Lütgert was fully opposed to the German Christians, though in a mode quite different from Barth's, and in due course was deposed by the government and had some of his writings seized by the Gestapo. See the Preface by W. Neuser to the second edition of his *Schöpfung und Offenbarung*. In any case, I do not see *why* modern Americans feel it so important to connect their subject-matter with events in Germany in the 1930s.

14. On this see my article 'Allegory and Historicism', especially 113f.

15. For a brief statement, parallel to his large book, see W. Brueggemann, 'Biblical Theology Appropriately Postmodern'.

16. Brueggemann, *Old Testament Theology*, 65.

17. As already indicated in the quotation from Stendahl, above, 157f.

18. See above, Ch. 24, 404.

## 32. *Apocryphal and Other Non-canonical Books*

1. This is a rough statement rather than an absolutely accurate one: some of the books could have been composed after the first beginnings of Christianity.

2. This requires a small qualification, since there may be non-Jewish – most obviously, Christian – interpolations here and there, and indeed at times there have been theories that some books might be largely Christian in origin, notably the Testaments of the Twelve Patriarchs. Nevertheless basic Jewish origin remains accepted for the vast majority.

3. Quoted from the introduction to the book in the Revised Standard Verson, *New Oxford Annotated Bible*, London: Oxford University Press 1977.

4. Cf. the comments of D. Dimant on the use of this term in Mulder (ed.), *Mikra*, 402; she herself introduces the useful distinction between the *compositional* and the *expositional* use of biblical elements (382f.). Here I am drawing attention to the compositional usages.

5. It also has the chapters in a markedly different order, but this may be by-passed for our present purpose.

6. Wording of Cross and Livingstone (eds.), *The Oxford Dictionary of the Christian Church*, 71.

7. See the important article of W. Neuser, 'Calvins Stellung zu den Apokryphen des Alten Testaments'.

8. On this see ibid., especially 300f.

9. On this see ibid., 308.

10. For a valuable account of this see S. Amsler, 'La politique d'édition des Sociétés bibliques au XIX^e siècle'.

11. E.g. the 'as *Hierome* saith' of the Thirty-Nine Articles, as quoted above.

12. Otzen agrees with Gese in this, explaining the decision of the Reformers as 'unter dem Einfluss des Bibelhumanismus': so his article 'Das Problem der Apokryphen', 269. Childs, *Biblical Theology*, 66, maintains that 'the great strength' of the Reformers' returning to the Hebrew canon 'lay in their concern to establish the truth of the biblical witness according to its most pristine and purest form'. But this again looks like a humanistic principle, and the opposite of a canonical one: the search for 'pristine' forms of text is one of the things most frequently condemned in the canonical approach. However, Childs goes on to write, surprisingly, of 'the weakness of the Reformers' use of a critical norm and its insufficiency in practice'.

13. Childs, *Biblical Theology*, 62, writes: 'It is a striking fact that the New Testament does not *cite as scripture* any book of the Apocrypha or Pseudepigrapha. (The reference to Enoch in Jude 14–15 is not an exception.)' But it *is* an exception. Childs' argument rests on the fiction that citing as an authoritative prophetic document did not count as citing as scripture, in other words that the meaning of 'scripture' in the New Testament is the same as its meaning in later doctrines about the canon.

14. See F. van Fleteren, 'Augustine's Exegesis of Wisdom 9.15'.

15. H. Berkhof, in his *Christian Faith*, 65, ending his section on 'Revelation as History', writes: 'A consequence of what was said above is that we should begin to think about the revelational function of the inter-testamentary period. If revelational history is a cumulative process and we thus reject Cullmann's idea "that it is essential to biblical salvation history that it shows *gaps* which are quite remarkable from an historical standpoint, and which unfold entirely by leaps" [Cullmann, *Salvation in History*, 153f.], then the inter-testamentary period also fills a connecting role in this process.' He returns to the topic: 'Hence in the New Testament an apocryphal writing is more than once authoritatively quoted as "the Scripture" (Luke 11.49; John 7.38; I Cor.2.9; James 4.5; Jude 14ff.). The manner in which the interpretations of the interim period are connected with the revelation in the New Testament has made them a part of the history of revelation' (81). And he repeats: 'Owing to its bridge-function between Old and New Testaments, a theological evaluation of the so-called interim period is urgently required' (240).

16. Quoted by Augustine, *de Doctr. Christ*. III, 14, 22.

17. David J. Reimer, 'The Apocrypha and Biblical Theology: The Case of Interpersonal Forgiveness', 271, 272 and 277.

18. Another, and a less likely, path is taken by the Lausanne Reformer Pierre Viret, who thinks of the possibility that the passage was a gloss put in the margin by a reader, a gloss

which later accidentally slipped into the text. See Bavaud, in Kaestli and Wermelinger, *Le Canon de l'ancien Testament*, 247. Viret, though a fiercely Protestant spirit, was unwilling to be excessively deprecatory towards II Maccabees.

19. On the 'canon within the canon' cf. above, Ch. 23.

20. Published as *Holy Scripture: Canon, Authority, Criticism*.

21. In later editions (I have consulted the fourth German edition, 1982), Zimmerli modified this statement by adding further explanation.

22. Cf. Childs, *Introduction*, 664ff. Here he insists that it is 'crucial' that Christians have the same scriptural canon as Jews. He also expresses respect for Christians who follow St Augustine in supporting a larger canon. 'I would not disparage the claims of those Christians who follow Augustine in supporting a larger canon' (666). But what use is this respect if it is 'crucial' to follow the Jewish canon? Cf. my remarks in my review, *JSOT* 16, 1980, 12–23, where I argue that the presence of the *New Testament* in the Christian Bible is so great an obstacle for Jewish perception that by comparison the question of the 'Apocrypha' must be a rather minor and marginal one. One should also remark that the reason Childs gives for Christian adoption of the Jewish canon, namely that it is essential for the relationship with Judaism that the church should have the same canon, is, so far as I know, a quite modern and innovative reason, one that was unknown to the early church or the Reformers.

23. Childs, *Introduction*, 665.

24. H. Berkhof, *Christian Faith*, 82, in his section on 'Fixation and Transmission', writes: 'Our conclusion, therefore, is that as such there is no reason why the Protestant churches should not return to the earlier, wider canon.' Cf. the thoughts of Gese, above, Ch. 22.

25. Among important discussions of the theological issues involved, see especially R. Hanhart, 'Die Bedeutung der Septuaginta in neutestamentlicher Zeit'; also, more recently, his 'Die Übersetzung der Septuaginta im Licht ihr vorgegebener und auf ihr gründender Tradition'.

26. D. Barthélemy, 'La Place de la Septante dans l'Église' = *Études d'histoire du texte de l'ancien Testament*, OBO 21, 111–26; id., 'L'Ancien Testament a mûri à Alexandrie', = ibid., 127–39. I cite them by the pagination of the OBO edition.

27. Incidentally, Barthélemy is sceptical about the qualities of Jerome, whom he calls a '*nouveau riche de la culture hébraïque frotté de vernis rabbinique*', a *nouveau riche* of Hebrew culture, rubbed with Rabbinic varnish, OBO, 139. He also gives a short historical account which suggests that the success of Jerome's Vulgate in the Latin church was the result of historical accident: the flood of barbarian invasions submerged the church, which was still using the pre-Jerome Old Latin, and when things settled down the leadership lay with persons who thought of Jerome's work as the *dernier cri de la science biblique* (OBO,115).

28. *Canon and Theology*, 55.

29. On this see George J. Brooke, 'The Qumran Scrolls and Old Testament Theology'.

30. See above, 285.

## 33. *The Distribution of Resources and Pan-Biblical Theology*

1. This is what I called it in the paper I read to the section on 'Theology of Hebrew Scriptures' of the Society of Biblical Literature at Anaheim, California on 18 November, 1989.

2. See above, 301.

3. He seems to have thought that this concept was beyond the understanding of

historical critics.

4. I am grateful to Dr Reimer for the sentence but regret that I seem to have lost the source.

5. So F. Watson, *Text and Truth*, who sees Marcionism everywhere, even in Childs (!, cf. his 269 n. 13).

6. The final chapter of his *Text and Truth* is based on Justin's *Dialogue with Trypho*, which, he maintains, is based on 'the Jewishness of Christianity' (313).

## *34. David Brown*

1. It should be noted that this is the first of a pair of two volumes, the second of which, *Disciplineship and Imagination*, I have not seen. Unfortunately page numbers for the quotations from the book were not available for inclusion here.

2. On Descartes, see the quotation from W. J. Abraham, cited above, Ch. 24. On Rousseau, cf. Barth's remark, quoted above, Ch. 24.

3. On the importance of *relative* objectivity see already my remarks in *Old and New in Interpretation*, and Räisänen, Ch. 30 above, as against the common tendency to attack 'absolute' objectivity and then suppose that the impossibility of absolute objectivity means that no effort towards objectivity should be made at all.

4. Cf my own argument, above, Ch. 17.

5. He here notes with approval that 'a number of Christian scholars also now follow this interpretation', and refers particularly to the discussion by R. W. L. Moberly, *From Eden to Golgotha*, 30–54, see also 138 n.23. Cf. my own mention of Oeming's discussion, above, 262.

6. *Tradition and Imagination*, 193 n.119. Cf. above, Ch. 30. Brown here draws attention to 'the implications of this for inter-faith dialogue', referring to the later discussion in his Chapter 5.

7. 'The notion that revelation lacks any classical parallel only holds for so long as we insist that it must be thought of in narrowly propositional terms'.

8. Cf. Berkhof, *Christian Faith*, 49, who tells us how Zwingli 'expressed the conviction, much to the indignation of Luther, that in eternal life he also expected to meet people like Socrates, Aristides, the Catos, the Scipios, Seneca, and many other Greeks and Romans'. Berkhof connects this viewpoint back to that of Justin.

9. There is a certain similarity between this argument and that of H. Braun about the canon within the canon, cited above, Ch. 23. But H. Braun's conception is of an interior correction of the totality of the canon; Brown's is of a correction of the [entire] biblical canon by the [post-biblical] realization of the incarnation which is the focus of it all.

10. Cf. above, Ch. 32.

11. RSV has for the relevant phrase 'in the midst of the years renew it'. The Hebrew *šnym*, in the unpointed text of ancient times, was read by MT as *sanim*, 'years', but by LXX as a form of *šᵉnayim* 'two', and similarly the form read by MT as the imperative verb 'revive it!' was read by LXX as belonging to the noun for 'wild beast'. Brown points out in a foot-note that 'the continuing influence of Pseudo-Matthew is all the more surprising in view of the fact that the Vulgate has "in the midst of the years": *in medio annorum*' [i.e. following the MT – J.B.]. See Isa. 1.3; Hab.3.2.

12. The term ἀγάπητος occurs three times in the narrative, vv. 2, 12, 16, as Brown notes. This example is not so much a creative mistranslation; rather it was a correct translation that was, probably unwittingly, taken in a different sense from that which the

translators had had in mind. The term was used from ancient times in a sense based on the verb, 'that with which one must be content, acquiesce'. If one has only one child, one must accept that as sufficient (LSJ). This is what the LXX meant. It was very easy, and natural, however, to understand it as 'beloved'. I have explained this in my 'Words for Love in Biblical Greek', 15f. The process is the same as that with the most famous of all LXX renderings, that of παρθένος at Isa. 7.14. This has often been explained as a mistake or a deliberate falsification. Not at all: the translator used it in the sense 'girl, young woman', quite correctly. But it was easy and natural to understand it in the more specific sense of the same word as 'virgin'.

13. Thus I wrote (*Holy Scripture: Canon, Authority, Criticism*, 30): 'But for biblical criticism Protestantism would never have come to acknowledge the positive importance of tradition as it has come to do.'

14. On this see above, 197.

15. On Gadamer cf. above, 501f., 510ff., 553.

16. Cf. Brown's complaint that 'the christology of certainty and infused knowledge has dominated the history of Christianity', which (in the example under discussion here) has affected the understanding of Christ's temptations and, through that, the understanding of the story of Joseph.

## 35. Conclusion

1. J.Barton , *Reading the Old Testament*, 100.

2. See J. Barr, 'Ein Mann oder die Menschen? Zur Anthropologie von Genesis 1'; more briefly, J.Barr, 'Adam: Single Man, or All Humanity?'.

3. Cf. the remarks of Crüsemann, reported above, Ch. 8.

# Index of Names

*Entries in **bold** indicate the discussion of a major work*

Cullmann, O., 52, 54, 171, 658 n.20, 690
  n.37, 692 n.7, 695 n.15
Cwiekowski, F. J., 663 n.1

Dahl, N. A., 403
Danby, H., 687 n.11
Davidson, A. B., 112, 653 n.25
Davies, M., 435
Davies, P. R., 127–8, 231f., 332, 342, 344,
  532, 652 n.11, 655 n.48, 665 n.22, 684
  n.36, 693 n.9
DeHart, P., 692 n.1
Delitzsch, Franz, 71
Delitzsch, Friedrich, 19, 643 n.1, 648 n.11
Dentan, R. C., 38, 29, 39, 40, 292, 293,
  295, 332, 641 n.5, 645 n.13, 676 n.3
Derrida, J., 556
Dever, W. G., 655 n.50
Dhorme, E., 56
Diem, H., 681 n.13
Dillmann, A., 331
Dilthey, W., 181
Dimant, D., 695 n.4
Dodd, C. H., 182, 660f. n.15
Dohmen, C., 606
Donner, H., 117
Downing, F. G., 485, 690 n.35
Driver, S. R., 85, 649 n.2, 687 n.11
Dulles, A., 413
Dunn, J. D. G., 382, 385, 386, 420, 662
  n.19, 681 nn.11, 12

Ebeling, G., 246, 247, 250, 251, 430, 513,
  668 nn.15, 16
Eichrodt, W., 6, 24, 25, 26, 27, 28, **29–31**,
  32, 33, 34, 35, 37, 39, **41–2**, 44, 45, 47,
  48, 51, 54, 59, 62, 63–5, 66, 67–72, 78,
  82, 86, 87, 88, 89, 90, 90, 91, 92, 109,
  110, 111, 116, 123, 129, 143, 156, 172,
  173–4, 185, 186, 193f., 223, 225, 230,
  233, 234, 243, 244, 245, 254, 259,
  **266–73**, 274, 276, 278, 285, 292, 295f.,
  297, 298, 303, 304, 305, 307, 309, 312,
  313, 314, 315, 317, 319, 331–7, 338–42,
  344, 350, 395, 423, 426f., 460, 464, 466,
  467, 497, 519, 542, 546, 606, 643f. n.7,
  644f. n.10, 645 n.21, 646 nn.31, 35, 647
  n.42, 649 n.3, 650 nn.10, 16, 651 n.17,

656 n.1, 660 n.2, 662 n.13, 665 n.24,
  668 nn.9, 10, 669 n.6, 670 nn.1, 6, 673
  n.40, 677 n.10, 678 n.24, 682 nn.32, 34,
  683 n.21, 685 n.41, 694 n.13
Eissfeldt, O., 24, 31, 32, 63, 132
Eldredge, L., 642 n.16
Elert, M., 522
Engnell, I., 256, 652 n.2
Eskhult, M., 557

Fabry, H. -J., 54, 298
Fackenheim, E., 671 n.4
Fishbane, M., 287, 311, 672 n.6, 677 n.11
Fleteren, F. van , 695 n.14
Flüsser, D., 671 n.1
Fohrer, G., 111, 219, 257, **319–23**, 336,
  338, 426, 450, 457, 461, 467, 503, 518,
  675 nn.21, 22, 687 n.16
Ford, D., 238, 667 n.44
Fosdick, H. E., 83–7, 88, 89, 92, 269, 649f.
  n.3, 650 n.16
Foucault, M., 556
Fowler, J. D., 654 n.40
Frankfort, H., 102
Frazer, J. G., 87, 643 n.19
Freedman, D. N., 392
Frei, H., 238, 242, 405, 587, 600
Frerichs, E. S., 672 n.10
Fretheim, T. E., 682 n.31
Friedrich, G., 36
Fruchon, P., 501, 691 n.4
Frymer-Kensky, T., 311

Gabler, J. P., 6, 7, 62, 64, 66, 74, 77, 123,
  292, 642 n.16
Gadamer, H. -G., 497f., 501f., 510f., 512,
  553, 599, 699 n.5
Gammie, J., 54, 541
Gardner, H., 238
Gay, P., 685 n.559
Geertz, C., 653 n.17
Gelin, A., 646 n.28
Georgi, D., 575
Gerleman, G., 689 n.25
Gerstenberger, E. S., 127, 654 n.47
Gese, H., xv, 91, 117, 180, 182, 187,
  **362–77**, 417, 461, 504, 518, 521, 523,
  563, 568, 579f., 584, 585, 654 nn.29, 30,

Snaith, N., 55
Solomon, R. C., 677 n.8
Sommer, D. F., 686f. n.1
Sparks, H. F. D., 368
Spencer, B., 652 n.8
Spina, F., 687 n.2
Spriggs, D. G., 173, 338, 661 n.25, 678
    n.18
Steck, H., 328
Steiert, F. -J., 476, 689 n.18
Steinmetz, D., 390, 681 n.21
Stendahl, K., 3, 12, 157, 189–91, 192–3,
    **195–205**, 207, 397f., 404, 412, 414, 416,
    519, 598, 648 n.13, 652f. n.12, 657 n.15,
    661, 662, 663 nn.22, 23, 666 n.32, 675
    n.23, 679 n.6, 684 n.26, 694 n.17
Strecker, G., 523f., 641 n.4, 671 n.15, 680
    n.13
Stroup, G., 354, 678 n.4
Stuhlmacher, P., 180, 354, 374, 377, 417,
    661, 662 n.19, 680 n.12, 684 n.24, 685
    n.41, 693 n.7
Sundermeier, T., 126–7, 525, 643 n.20,
    644 n.9, 652 n.10, 654 n.42
Sweeney, M. A., **307–9**, 673 nn.37, 38
Swinburne, R., 97

Taylor, V., 394
Temple, W., 56
Terrien, S., 40, 56, 180, **323–5**, 338, 402,
    646 n.28, 675 nn.23, 25, 682 n.2, 689
    n.190
TeSelle, E., 692 n.1
Theissen, G., **92–4**, 95, 98, 99, 236, 651
    n.26, 651 n.26, 666 n.36
Thomas, K., 690 n.45
Tigay, J. H., 656 n.64
Tillich, P., 504, 515, 516, 527, 663 n.22,
    667 n.8, 682 n.16
Torrance, T. F., 163, 234, 405, 430, 658
    n.24, 665 n.30, 667 n.8
Torrey, C. C., 647 n.13
Towner, W. S., 677 n.15
Trible, P., 541, 542
Trillhaas, W., 690 n.35
Troeltsch, E., 82, 206, 302, 649 n.6
Tsevat, M., 200, **289–91**, 292, 300, 581,
    585, 663 n.23, 672 n.8

Tur-Sinai, N. H., 56

Uehlinger, C., 493, 691 n.51

Vermes, G., 564
Vielhauer, P., 503
Viret, P., 695f. n.18
Vischer, W., 23, 114, 256, 653 n.27, 665f.
    n.20, 683 n.21
Vriezen, T. C., 27, **31–2**, 33, 35, 39, **43–5**,
    82, 111f., 114, 172, 173, 174–5, 192,
    193, 225, 233, 245, 264, 274, 276, 278,
    309, 332, 338, 373, 420, 426f., 459, 467,
    519, 643 n.5, 644 nn.9, 10, 645 nn.11,
    12, 646 n.36, 653, 660 n.5, 664 n.86, 669
    n.11, 670 n.19, 671 n.8, 682 n.34

Wagner, S., 525
Wahl, H. M., 672 n.11, 688 n.1
Watson, F., 2, 200–2, 231, 236, 532, 584,
    661 n.2, 662 n.19, 663nn.30, 1, 665
    n.22, 667f. n.8, 670 n.16, 690 n.37, 691
    n.9, 697 n.4, 697 n.6
Weber, M., 507, 512
Weber, O., 690 n.35
Weingreen, J., 310
Weippert, H., 117, 524
Weir, D. A., 646 n.36
Weiser, A., 344, 423, 683 n.21
Weiss, J., 198, 532, 652f. n.12
Wellhausen, J., 25, 91, 104, 105, 296,
    298f., 338, 651 n.22, 656 n.1
Wells, P., 666 n.35
Wermelinger, O., 696 n.18
Westermann, C., 37, 54, 95–6, 97, 98, 127,
    143, 178, **179f.**, 257, 312, **316–19**, 328,
    461, 473, **481–4**, 490, 503, 518, 521,
    522, 606, 646 n.35, 647 n.4, 651 n.658
    n.25, 659 nn.42, 43, 669 nn.5, 10, 675,
    676 nn.26, 36, 679 n.5, 685 n.51, 689
    n.7, 692 n.5
Wharton, J. A., 345
Whybray, R. N., 226f., 664
Williams, L., 672 n.22
Williamson, H. G. M., 182
Wimsatt, W. K., Jr, 238, 667 n.45
Wolde, E. van, 651 n.29

Wolff, H. W., 55, 272
Wolterstorff, N., 245, 668 n.13, 678 nn.6,
 10, 683 nn.19, 20, 686 n.58
Woollcombe, K. J., 669 n.5
Wrede, W., 531, 535, 691 nn.5, 13
Wright, G. E., 29, 55, 67, 86, 88, 89, 90,
 92, 93, 102, 134, 136, 149, 324, 332,
 336, 348f., 380–2, 384–6, 476, 536, 559,
 575, 648 n.7, 650 nn.5, 15, 651 n.18,
 657 nn.4, 11, 676 n.3, 677 n.6, 678 nn.7,
 11, 580, 681 n.12

Wright, N. T., 643 n.3, 662 n.19

Young, F., 671 n.17

Zimmerli, W., 42, 48, 111, 177, 245, 257,
 277, **312–16**, 318, 319, 338, 340, 344,
 373, 423, 426f., 461, 505, 518, 574, 578,
 641 n.1, 646 nn.34, 40, 653 n.18, 660
 nn.9, 22, 674 nn.3, 6, 678 n.25, 681
 n.15, 683 n.21, 685 n.41, 691 n.1, 696
 n.21

# Index of Concepts

# Index of Scriptural Passages Cited